D1246908

The Laws of Human Nature

Also by Robert Greene

Mastery

The 50th Law (with 50 Cent)

The 33 Strategies of War (a Joost Elffers Production)

The Art of Seduction (a Joost Elffers Production)

The 48 Laws of Power (a Joost Elffers Production)

The Laws

of Human Nature

◇

Robert Greene

VIKING

VIKING

An imprint of Penguin Random House LLC
375 Hudson Street
New York, New York 10014
penguinrandomhouse.com

ISBN 9780525428145 (hardcover)
ISBN 9780698184541 (ebook)
ISBN 9780525561804 (international edition)

Printed in the United States of America
3   5   7   9   10   8   6   4

Set in Bembo Book MT Std
Designed by Cassandra Garruzzo

To my mother

Contents

The Laws of Human Nature

Introduction

If you come across any special trait of meanness or stupidity . . . you must be careful not to let it annoy or distress you, but to look upon it merely as an addition to your knowledge—a new fact to be considered in studying the character of humanity. Your attitude towards it will be that of the mineralogist who stumbles upon a very characteristic specimen of a mineral.

—*Arthur Schopenhauer*

Throughout the course of our lives, we inevitably have to deal with a variety of individuals who stir up trouble and make our lives difficult and unpleasant. Some of these individuals are leaders or bosses, some are colleagues, and some are friends. They can be aggressive or passive-aggressive, but they are generally masters at playing on our emotions. They often appear charming and refreshingly confident, brimming with ideas and enthusiasm, and we fall under their spell. Only when it is too late do we discover that their confidence is irrational and their ideas ill-conceived. Among colleagues, they can be those who sabotage our work or careers out of secret envy, excited to bring us down. Or they could be colleagues or hires who reveal, to our dismay, that they are completely out for themselves, using us as stepping-stones.

What inevitably happens in these situations is that we are caught off guard, not expecting such behavior. Often these types will hit us with elaborate cover stories to justify their actions, or blame handy scapegoats. They know how to confuse us and draw us into a drama they control. We might protest or become angry, but in the end we feel rather helpless—the damage is done. Then another such type enters our life, and the same story repeats itself.

We often notice a similar sensation of confusion and helplessness when it comes to ourselves and our own behavior. For instance, we suddenly say something that offends our boss or colleague or friend—we are not quite sure where it came from, but we are frustrated to find that some anger and tension from within has leaked out in a way that we regret. Or perhaps we enthusiastically throw our weight into some project or scheme, only to realize it was quite foolish and a terrible waste of time. Or perhaps we fall in love with a person who is precisely the wrong type for us and we know it, but we cannot help ourselves. What has come over us, we wonder?

In these situations, we catch ourselves falling into self-destructive patterns of behavior that we cannot seem to control. It is as if we harbor a stranger within us, a little demon who operates independently of our willpower and pushes us into doing the wrong things. And this stranger within us is rather weird, or at least weirder than how we imagine ourselves.

What we can say about these two things—people's ugly actions and our own occasionally surprising behavior—is that we usually have no clue as to what causes them. We might latch onto some simple explanations: "That person is evil, a sociopath" or "Something came over me; I wasn't myself." But such pat descriptions do not lead to any understanding or prevent the same patterns from recurring. The truth is that we humans live on the surface, reacting emotionally to what people say and do. We form opinions of others and ourselves that are rather simplified. We settle for the easiest and most convenient story to tell ourselves.

What if, however, we could dive below the surface and see deep within, getting closer to the actual roots of what causes human behavior? What if we could understand why some people turn envious and try to sabotage our work, or why their misplaced confidence causes them to imagine themselves as godlike and infallible? What if we could truly fathom why people suddenly behave irrationally and reveal a much darker side to their character, or why they are always ready to provide a rationalization for their behavior, or why we continually turn to leaders who appeal to the worst in us? What if we could look deep inside and judge people's character, avoiding the bad hires and personal relationships that cause us so much emotional damage?

If we really understood the roots of human behavior, it would be much harder for the more destructive types to continually get away with their actions. We would not be so easily charmed and misled. We would be able to anticipate their nasty and manipulative maneuvers and see through their cover stories. We would not allow ourselves to get dragged into their dramas, knowing in advance that our interest is what they depend on for their control. We would finally rob them of their power through our ability to look into the depths of their character.

Similarly, with ourselves, what if we could look within and see the source of our more troubling emotions and why they drive our behavior, often against our own wishes? What if we could understand why we are so compelled to desire what other people have, or to identify so strongly with a group that we feel contempt for those who are on the outside? What if we could find out what causes us to lie about who we are, or to inadvertently push people away?

Being able to understand more clearly that stranger within us would help us to realize that it is not a stranger at all but very much a part of ourselves, and that we are far more mysterious, complex, and interesting than we had imagined. And with that awareness we would be able to break the negative patterns in our lives, stop making excuses for ourselves, and gain better control of what we do and what happens to us.

Having such clarity about ourselves and others could change the course of our lives in so many ways, but first we must clear up a common misconception: we tend to think of our behavior as largely conscious and willed. To imagine that we are not always in control of what we do is a frightening thought, *but in fact it is the reality*. We are subject to forces from deep within us that drive our behavior and that operate below the level of our awareness. We see the results—our thoughts, moods, and actions—but have little conscious access to what actually moves our emotions and compels us to behave in certain ways.

Look at our anger, for instance. We usually identify an individual or a group as the cause of this emotion. But if we were honest and dug down deeper, we would see that what often triggers our anger or frustration has deeper roots. It could be something in our childhood or some particular set of circumstances that triggers the emotion. We can discern distinct patterns if we look—when this or that happens, we get angry. But in the moment that we feel anger, we are not reflective or rational—we merely ride the emotion and point fingers. We could say something similar about a whole slew of emotions that we feel—specific types of events trigger sudden confidence, or insecurity, or anxiety, or attraction to a particular person, or hunger for attention.

Let us call the collection of these forces that push and pull at us from deep within *human nature*. Human nature stems from the particular wiring of our brains, the configuration of our nervous system, and the way we humans process emotions, all of which developed and emerged over the course of the five million years or so of our evolution as a species. We can ascribe many of the details of our nature to the distinct way we evolved as a social animal to ensure our survival—learning to cooperate with others, coordinating our actions with the group on a high level, creating novel forms of communication and ways of maintaining group discipline. This early development lives on within us and continues to determine our behavior, even in the modern, sophisticated world we live in.

To take one example, look at the evolution of human emotion. The survival of our earliest ancestors depended on their ability to communicate with one another well before the invention of language. They evolved new and complex emotions—joy, shame, gratitude, jealousy, resentment, et cetera. The signs of these emotions could be read immediately on their faces, communicating their moods quickly and effectively. They became extremely permeable to the emotions of others as a way to bind the group more tightly together—to feel joy or grief as one—or to remain united in the face of danger.

To this day, we humans remain highly susceptible to the moods and emotions of those around us, compelling all kinds of behavior on our part—unconsciously imitating others, wanting what they have, getting swept up in viral feelings of anger or outrage. We imagine we're acting of our own free will, unaware of how deeply our susceptibility to the emotions of others in the group is affecting what we do and how we respond.

We can point to other such forces that emerged from this deep past and that similarly mold our everyday behavior—for instance, our need to continually rank ourselves and measure our self-worth through our status is a trait that is noticeable among all hunter-gatherer cultures, and even among chimpanzees, as are our tribal instincts, which cause us to divide people into insiders or outsiders. We can add to these primitive qualities our need to wear masks to disguise any behavior that is frowned upon by the tribe, leading to the formation of a shadow personality from all the dark desires we have repressed. Our ancestors understood this shadow and its dangerousness, imagining it originated from spirits and demons that needed to be exorcised. We rely on a different myth—"something came over me."

Once this primal current or force within us reaches the level of consciousness, we have to react to it, and we do so depending on our individual spirit and circumstances, usually explaining it away superficially without really understanding it. Because of the precise way in which we evolved, there are a limited number of these forces of human nature, and they lead to the behavior mentioned above—envy, grandiosity, irrationality, shortsightedness, conformity, aggression, and passive aggression, to name a few. They also lead to empathy and other positive forms of human behavior.

For thousands of years, it has been our fate to largely grope in the shadows when it comes to understanding ourselves and our own nature. We have labored under so many illusions about the human animal—imagining we descended magically from a divine source, from angels instead of primates. We have found any signs of our primitive nature and our animal roots deeply distressing, something to deny and repress. We have covered up our darker impulses with all kinds of excuses and rationalizations, making it easier for some people to get away with the most unpleasant behavior. But finally we're at a point where we can overcome our resistance to the truth about who we are through the sheer weight of knowledge we have now accumulated about human nature.

We can exploit the vast literature in psychology amassed over the last one hundred years, including detailed studies of childhood and the impact of our early development (Melanie Klein, John Bowlby, Donald Winnicott), as well as works on the roots of narcissism (Heinz Kohut), the shadow sides of our personality (Carl Jung), the roots of our empathy (Simon Baron-Cohen), and the configuration of our emotions (Paul Ekman). We can now cull the many advances in the sciences that can aid us in our self-understanding—studies of the brain (Antonio Damasio, Joseph E. LeDoux), of our unique biological makeup (Edward O. Wilson), of the relationship between the body and the mind (V. S. Ramachandran), of primates (Frans de Waal) and hunter-gatherers (Jared Diamond), of our economic behavior (Daniel Kahneman), and of how we operate in groups (Wilfred Bion, Elliot Aronson).

We can also include in this the works of certain philosophers (Arthur Schopenhauer, Friedrich Nietzsche, José Ortega y Gasset) who have illuminated so many aspects of human nature, as well as the insights of many novelists (George Eliot, Henry James, Ralph Ellison), who are often the most sensitive to the unseen parts of our behavior. And finally, we can include the rapidly expanding library of biographies now available, revealing human nature in depth and in action.

This book is an attempt to gather together this immense storehouse of knowledge and ideas from different branches (see the bibliography for the key sources), to piece together an accurate and instructive guide to human nature, basing itself on the evidence, not on particular viewpoints or moral judgments. It is a brutally realistic appraisal of our species, dissecting who we are so we can operate with more awareness.

Consider *The Laws of Human Nature* a kind of codebook for deciphering people's behavior—ordinary, strange, destructive, the full gamut. Each chapter deals with a particular aspect or law of human nature. We can call them laws in that under the influence of these elemental forces, we humans tend to react in relatively predictable ways. Each chapter has the story of some iconic individual or individuals who illustrate the law (negatively or positively), along with ideas and strategies on how to deal with yourself and others under the influence of this law. Each chapter ends with a section on how to transform this basic human force into something more positive and productive, so that we are no longer passive slaves to human nature but actively transforming it.

You might be tempted to imagine that this knowledge is a bit old-fashioned. After all, you might argue, we are now so sophisticated and technologically advanced, so progressive and enlightened; we have moved well beyond our primitive roots; we are in the process of rewriting our nature. But the truth is in fact the opposite—we have never been more in the thrall of human nature and its destructive potential than now. And by ignoring this fact, we are playing with fire.

Look at how the permeability of our emotions has only been heightened through social media, where viral effects are continually sweeping through us and where the most manipulative leaders are able to exploit and control us. Look at the aggression that is now openly displayed in the virtual world, where it is so much easier to play out our shadow sides without repercussions. Notice how our propensities to compare ourselves with others, to feel envy, and to seek status through attention have only become intensified with our ability to communicate so quickly with so many people. And finally, look at our tribal tendencies and how they have now found the perfect medium to operate in—we can find a group to identify with, reinforce our tribal opinions in a virtual echo chamber, and demonize any outsiders, leading to mob intimidation. The potential for mayhem stemming from the primitive side of our nature has only increased.

It is simple: Human nature is stronger than any individual, than any institution or technological invention. It ends up shaping what we create to reflect itself and its primitive roots. It moves us around like pawns.

Ignore the laws at your own peril. Refusing to come to terms with human nature simply means that you are dooming yourself to patterns beyond your control and to feelings of confusion and helplessness.

THE LAWS OF HUMAN NATURE IS DESIGNED TO IMMERSE YOU IN ALL ASPECTS OF human behavior and illuminate its root causes. If you let it guide you, it will radically alter how you perceive people and your entire approach to dealing with them. It will also radically change how you see yourself. It will accomplish these shifts in perspective in the following ways:

First, the Laws will work to transform you into a calmer and more strategic observer of people, helping to free you from all the emotional drama that needlessly drains you.

Being around people stirs up our anxieties and insecurities as to how others perceive us. Once we feel such emotions, it becomes very hard to observe people as we are drawn into our own feelings, evaluating what people say and do in *personal* terms—do they like me or dislike me? The Laws will help you avoid falling into this trap by revealing that people are generally dealing with emotions and issues that have deep roots. They're experiencing some desires and disappointments that predate you by years and decades. You cross their path at a particular moment and become the convenient target of their anger or frustration. They're projecting onto you certain qualities they want to see. In most cases, they're not relating to you as an individual.

This should not upset you but liberate you. The book will teach you to stop taking personally their insinuating comments, shows of coldness, or moments of irritation. The more you grasp this, the easier it will be to react not with your emotions but rather with the desire to understand where their behavior might come from. You will feel much calmer in the process. And as this takes root in you, you will be less prone to moralize and judge people; instead you will accept them and their flaws as part of human nature. People will like you all the more as they sense this tolerant attitude in you.

Second, the Laws will make you a master interpreter of the cues that people continually emit, giving you a much greater ability to judge their character.

Normally, if we pay attention to people's behavior, we are in a rush to fit their actions into categories and to hurry to conclusions, so we settle for the judgment that suits our own preconceptions. Or we accept their self-serving explanations. The Laws will rid you of this habit by making it clear how easy it is to misread people and how deceptive first impressions can be. You will slow yourself down, mistrust your initial judgment, and instead train yourself to *analyze* what you see.

You will think in terms of opposites—when people overtly display some trait, such as confidence or hypermasculinity, they are most often concealing the contrary reality. You will realize that people are continually playing to the public, making a show of being progressive and saintly only to better disguise their shadow. You will see the signs of this shadow leaking out in everyday life.

If people take an action that seems out of character, you will take note: what often appears out of character is actually more of their true character. If people are essentially lazy or foolish, they leave clues to this in the smallest of details that you can pick up well before their behavior harms you. The ability to gauge people's true worth, their degree of loyalty and conscientiousness, is one of the most important skills you can possess, helping you avoid the bad hires, partnerships, and relationships that can make your life miserable.

Third, the Laws will empower you to take on and outthink the toxic types who inevitably cross your path and who tend to cause long-term emotional damage.

Aggressive, envious, and manipulative people don't usually announce themselves as such. They have learned to appear charming in initial encounters, to use flattery and other means of disarming us. When they surprise us with their ugly behavior, we feel betrayed, angry, and helpless. They create constant pressure, knowing that in doing so they overwhelm our minds with their presence, making it doubly hard to think straight or strategize.

The Laws will teach you how to identify these types in advance, which is your greatest defense against them. Either you will steer clear of them or, foreseeing their manipulative actions, you will not be blindsided and thus will be better able to maintain your emotional balance. You will learn to mentally cut them down to size and focus on the glaring weaknesses and insecurities behind all of their bluster. You will not fall for their myth, and this will neutralize the intimidation they depend on. You will scoff at their cover stories and elaborate explanations for their selfish behavior. Your ability to stay calm will infuriate them and often push them into overreaching or making a mistake.

Instead of being weighed down by these encounters, you might even come to appreciate them as a chance to hone your skills of self-mastery and toughen yourself up. Outsmarting just one of these types will give you a great deal of confidence that you can handle the worst in human nature.

Fourth, the Laws will teach you the true levers for motivating and influencing people, making your path in life that much easier.

Normally, when we meet resistance to our ideas or plans, we cannot help trying to directly change people's minds by arguing, lecturing, or cajoling them, all of which makes them more defensive. The Laws will teach you that people are naturally stubborn and resistant to influence. You must begin any attempt by lowering their resistance and never inadvertently feeding their defensive tendencies. You will train yourself to discern their insecurities and never inadvertently stir them up. You will think in terms of *their* self-interest and the self-opinion they need validated.

Understanding the permeability of emotions, you will learn that the most effective means of influence is to alter your moods and attitude. People are responding to your energy and demeanor even more than to your words. You will get rid of any defensiveness on your part. Instead, feeling relaxed and genuinely interested in the other person will have a positive and hypnotic effect. You will learn that as a leader your best means of moving people in your direction lies in setting the right tone through your attitude, empathy, and work ethic.

Fifth, the Laws will make you realize how deeply the forces of human nature operate within you, giving you the power to alter your own negative patterns.

Our natural response to reading or hearing about the darker qualities in human nature is to exclude ourselves. It is always the other person who is narcissistic, irrational, envious, grandiose, aggressive, or passive-aggressive. We almost always see ourselves as having the best intentions. If we go astray, it is the fault of circumstances or people forcing us to react negatively. The Laws will make you stop once and for all this self-deluding process. We are all cut from the same cloth, and we all share the same tendencies. The sooner you realize this, the greater your power will be in overcoming these potential negative traits within you. You will examine your own motives, look at your own shadow, and become aware of your own passive-aggressive tendencies. This will make it that much easier to spot such traits in others.

You will also become humbler, realizing you're not superior to others in the way you had imagined. This will not make you feel guilty or weighed down by your self-awareness, but quite the opposite. You will accept yourself as a complete individual, embracing both the good and the bad, dropping your falsified self-image as a saint. You will feel relieved of your hypocrisies and free to be more yourself. People will be drawn to this quality in you.

Sixth, the Laws will transform you into a more empathetic individual, creating deeper and more satisfying bonds with the people around you.

We humans are born with a tremendous potential for understanding people on a level that is not merely intellectual. It is a power developed by our earliest ancestors, in which they learned how to intuit the moods and feelings of others by placing themselves in their perspective.

The Laws will instruct you in how to bring out this latent power to the highest degree possible. You will learn to slowly cut off your incessant interior monologue and listen more closely. You will train yourself to assume the other's viewpoint as best you can. You will use your imagination and experiences to help you feel how they might feel. If they are describing something painful, you have your own painful moments to draw upon as analogues. You will not be simply intuitive, but rather you will analyze the information you glean in this empathic fashion, gaining insights. You will continually cycle between empathy and analysis, always updating what you observe and increasing your ability to see the world through their eyes. You will notice a physical sensation of connection between you and the other that will emerge from this practice.

You will need a degree of humility in this process. You can never know exactly what people are thinking and can easily make mistakes, and so you must not rush to judgments but keep yourself open to learning more. People are more complex than you imagine. Your goal is to simply see their point of view better. As you go through this process, it becomes like a muscle that gets stronger the more you exercise it.

Cultivating such empathy will have innumerable benefits. We are all self-absorbed, locked in our own worlds. It is a therapeutic and liberating experience to be drawn outside ourselves and into the world of another. It is what attracts us to film and any form of fiction, entering the minds and perspectives of people so different from ourselves. Through this practice your whole way of thinking will shift. You are training yourself to let go of preconceptions, to be alive in the moment, and to continually adapt your ideas about people. You will find such fluidity affecting how you attack problems in general—you will find yourself entertaining other possibilities, taking alternative perspectives. This is the essence of creative thinking.

Finally, the Laws will alter how you see your own potential, making you aware of a higher, ideal self within you that you will want to bring out.

We can say that we humans have two contrary selves within us—a lower and a higher. The lower tends to be stronger. Its impulses pull us down into emotional reactions and defensive postures, making us feel self-righteous and superior to others. It makes us grab for immediate pleasures and distractions, always taking the path of least resistance. It induces us to adopt what other people are thinking, losing ourselves in the group.

We feel the impulses of the higher self when we are drawn out of ourselves, wanting to connect more deeply with others, to absorb our minds in our work, to think instead of react, to follow our own path in life, and to discover what makes us unique. The lower is the more animal and reactive side of our nature, and one that we easily slip into. The higher is the more truly human side of our nature, the side that makes us thoughtful and self-aware. Because the higher impulse is weaker, connecting to it requires effort and insight.

Bringing out this ideal self within us is what we all really want, because it is only in developing this side of ourselves that we humans feel truly fulfilled. The book will help you accomplish this by making you aware of the potentially positive and active elements contained within each law.

Knowing our propensity for irrationality, you will learn to become aware of how your emotions color your thinking (chapter 1), giving you the ability to subtract them and become truly rational. Knowing how our attitude in life effects what happens to us, and how naturally our minds tend to close up out of fear (chapter 8), you will learn how to forge an attitude that is expansive and fearless. Knowing you have the propensity to compare yourself with others (chapter 10), you will use this as a spur to excel in society through your superior work, to admire those who achieve great things, and to be inspired by their example to emulate them. You will work this magic on each of the primal qualities, using your expanded knowledge of human nature to resist the strong downward pull of your lower nature.

Think of the book in the following way: you are about to become an apprentice in human nature. You will be developing some skills—how to observe and measure the character of your fellow humans and see into your own depths. You will work on bringing out your higher self. And through practice you will emerge a master of the art, able to thwart the worst that other people can throw at you and to mold yourself into a more rational, self-aware, and productive individual.

> Man will only become better when you make him see what he is like.
>
> —*Anton Chekhov*

1

Master Your Emotional Self

———————— ◇ ————————

The Law of Irrationality

Y*ou like to imagine yourself in control of your fate, consciously planning the course of your life as best you can. But you are largely unaware of how deeply your emotions dominate you. They make you veer toward ideas that soothe your ego. They make you look for evidence that confirms what you already want to believe. They make you see what you want to see, depending on your mood, and this disconnect from reality is the source of the bad decisions and negative patterns that haunt your life. Rationality is the ability to counteract these emotional effects, to think instead of react, to open your mind to what is really happening, as opposed to what you are feeling. It does not come naturally; it is a power we must cultivate, but in doing so we realize our greatest potential.*

The Inner Athena

One day toward the end of the year 432 BC, the citizens of Athens received some very disturbing news: representatives from the city-state of Sparta had arrived in town and presented to the Athenian governing council new terms of peace. If Athens did not agree to these terms, then Sparta would declare war. Sparta was Athens's archenemy and in many ways its polar opposite. Athens led a league of democratic states in the region, while Sparta led a confederation of oligarchies, known as the Peloponnesians. Athens depended on its navy and on its wealth—it was the preeminent commercial power in the Mediterranean. Sparta depended on its army. It was a total military state. Up until then, the two powers had largely avoided a direct war because the consequences could be devastating—not only could the defeated side lose its influence in the region, but its whole way of life could be put in jeopardy—certainly for Athens its democracy and its wealth. Now, however, war seemed inevitable and a sense of impending doom quickly settled on the city.

A few days later, the Athenian Assembly met on the Pnyx Hill overlooking the Acropolis to debate the Spartan ultimatum and decide what to do. The Assembly was open to all male citizens, and on that day close to ten thousand of them crowded on the hill to participate in the debate. The hawks among them were in a state of great agitation—Athens should seize the initiative and attack Sparta first, they said. Others reminded them that in a land battle the Spartan forces were nearly unbeatable. Attacking Sparta in this way would play straight into their hands. The doves were all in favor of accepting the peace terms, but as many pointed out, that would only show fear and embolden the Spartans. It would only give them more time to enlarge their army. Back and forth went the debate, with emotions getting heated, people shouting, and no satisfactory solution in sight.

Then toward the end of the afternoon, the crowd suddenly grew quiet as a familiar figure stepped forward to address the Assembly. This was Pericles, the elder statesman of Athenian politics, now over sixty years old. Pericles was beloved, and his opinion would matter more than anyone's, but despite the Athenians' respect for him, they found him a very peculiar leader—more of a philosopher than a politician. To those old enough to remember the start of his career, it was truly surprising how powerful and successful he had become. He did nothing the usual way.

In the earliest years of their democracy, before Pericles had appeared on the scene, the Athenians had preferred a certain personality type in their leaders—men who could give an inspiring, persuasive speech and had a flair for drama. On the battlefield these men were risk takers; they often pushed for military campaigns that they could lead, giving them a chance to gain glory and attention. They advanced their careers by representing some faction in the Assembly—landowners, soldiers, aristocrats—and doing everything they could to further its interests. This led to highly divisive politics. Leaders would rise and fall in cycles of a few years, but the Athenians were fine with this; they mistrusted anyone who lasted long in power.

Then Pericles entered public life around 463 BC, and Athenian politics would never be the same. His first move was the most unusual of all. Although he came from an illustrious aristocratic family, he allied himself with the growing lower and middle classes of the city—farmers, oarsmen in the navy, the craftsmen who were the pride of Athens. He worked to increase their voice in the Assembly and give them greater power in the democracy. This was not some small faction he now led but the majority of Athenian citizens. It would seem impossible to control such a large, unruly mob of men, with their varied interests, but he was so fervent in increasing their power that he slowly gained their trust and backing.

As his influence grew, he started to assert himself in the Assembly and alter its policies. He argued against expanding Athens's democratic empire. He feared the Athenians would overreach and lose control. He worked to consolidate the empire and strengthen existing alliances. When it came to war and to serving as a general, he strove to limit campaigns and to win through maneuvers, with minimal loss of lives. To many this seemed unheroic, but as these policies took effect, the city entered a period of unprecedented prosperity. There were no more needless wars to drain the coffers, and the empire was functioning more smoothly than ever.

What Pericles did with the growing surplus of money startled and amazed the citizenry: instead of using it to buy political favors, he initiated a massive public building project in Athens. He commissioned temples, theaters, and concert halls, putting all of the Athenian craftsmen to work. Everywhere one looked, the city was becoming more sublimely beautiful. He favored a form of architecture that reflected his personal aesthetics—ordered, highly geometric, monumental yet soothing to the eye. His greatest commission was that of the Parthenon, with its enormous forty-foot statue of Athena. Athena was the guiding spirit of Athens, the goddess of wisdom and practical intelligence. She represented all of the values Pericles wanted to promote. Singlehandedly Pericles had transformed the look and spirit of Athens, and it entered a golden age in all of the arts and sciences.

What was perhaps the strangest quality of Pericles was his speaking style— restrained and dignified. He did not go in for the usual flights of rhetoric. Instead, he worked to convince an audience through airtight arguments. This would make people listen closely, as they followed the interesting course of his logic. The style was compelling and calming.

Unlike any of the other leaders, Pericles remained in power year after year, decade after decade, putting his total stamp on the city in his quiet, unobtrusive way. He had his enemies. This was inevitable. He had stayed in power so long that many accused him of being a secret dictator. He was suspected of being an atheist, a man who scoffed at all traditions. That would explain why he was so peculiar. But nobody could argue against the results of his leadership.

And so now, as he began to address the Assembly that afternoon, his opinion on war with Sparta would carry the most weight, and a hush came over the crowd as they anxiously waited to hear his argument.

"Athenians," he began, "my views are the same as ever: I am against making any concessions to the Peloponnesians, even though I am aware that the enthusiastic state of mind in which people are persuaded to enter upon a war is not retained when it comes to action, and that people's minds are altered by the course of events." Differences between Athens and Sparta were supposed to be settled through neutral arbitrators, he reminded them. It would set a dangerous precedent if they gave in to the Spartans' unilateral demands. Where would it end? Yes, a direct land battle with Sparta would be suicide. What he proposed instead was a completely novel form of warfare—limited and defensive.

He would bring within the walls of Athens all those living in the area. Let the Spartans come and try to lure us into fighting, he said; let them lay waste to our lands. We will not take the bait; we will not fight them on land. With our access to the sea we will keep the city supplied. We will use our navy to raid their coastal towns. As time goes on, they will grow frustrated by the lack of battle. Having to feed and supply their standing army, they will run out of money. Their allies will bicker among themselves. The war party within Sparta will be discredited and a real lasting peace will be agreed upon, all with minimal expenditure of lives and money on our part.

"I could give you many other reasons," he concluded, "why you should feel confident in ultimate victory, if only you will make up your minds not to add to the empire while the war is in progress, and not to go out of your way to involve yourselves in new perils. What I fear is not the enemy's strategy but our own mistakes." The novelty of what he was proposing aroused great debate. Neither hawks nor doves were satisfied with his plan, but in the end, his reputation for wisdom carried the day and his strategy was approved. Several months later the fateful war began.

In the beginning, all did not proceed as Pericles had envisioned. The Spartans and their allies did not grow frustrated as the war dragged on, but only bolder. The Athenians were the ones to become discouraged, seeing their lands destroyed without retaliation. But Pericles believed his plan could not fail as long as the Athenians remained patient. Then, in the second year of the war, an unexpected disaster upended everything: a powerful plague entered the city;

with so many people packed within the walls it spread quickly, killing over one third of the citizenry and decimating the ranks of the army. Pericles himself caught the disease, and as he lay dying he witnessed the ultimate nightmare: all that he had done for Athens over so many decades seemed to unravel at once, the people descending into group delirium until it was every man for himself. If he had survived, he almost certainly would have found a way to calm the Athenians down and broker an acceptable peace with Sparta, or adjust his defensive strategy, but now it was too late.

Strangely enough, the Athenians did not mourn for their leader. They blamed him for the plague and railed at the ineffectiveness of his strategy. They were not in a mood anymore for patience or restraint. He had outlived his time, and his ideas were now seen as the tired reactions of an old man. Their love of Pericles had turned to hate. With him no longer there, the factions returned with a vengeance. The war party became popular. The party fed off the people's growing bitterness toward the Spartans, who had used the plague to advance their positions. The hawks promised they would regain the initiative and crush the Spartans with an offensive strategy. For many Athenians, such words came as a great relief, a release of pent-up emotions.

As the city slowly recovered from the plague, the Athenians managed to gain the upper hand, and the Spartans sued for peace. Wanting to completely defeat their enemy, the Athenians pressed their advantage, only to find the Spartans recover and turn the tables. Back and forth it went, year after year. The violence and bitterness on both sides increased. At one point Athens attacked the island of Melos, a Spartan ally, and when the Melians surrendered, the Athenians voted to kill all of their men and sell the women and children into slavery. Nothing remotely like this had ever happened under Pericles.

Then, after so many years of a war without end, in 415 BC several Athenian leaders had an interesting idea about how to deliver the fatal blow. The city-state of Syracuse was the rising power on the island of Sicily. Syracuse was a critical ally of the Spartans, supplying them with much-needed resources. If the Athenians, with their great navy, could launch an expedition and take control of Syracuse, they would gain two advantages: it would add to their empire, and it would deprive Sparta of the resources it needed to continue the war. The Assembly voted to send sixty ships with an appropriate-sized army on board to accomplish this goal.

One of the commanders assigned to this expedition, Nicias, had great doubts as to the wisdom of this plan. He feared the Athenians were underestimating the strength of Syracuse. He laid out all of the possible negative scenarios; only a much larger expedition could ensure victory. He wanted to squelch the plan, but his argument had the opposite effect. If a larger expedition was necessary, then that was what they would send—one hundred ships and double the number of soldiers. The Athenians smelled victory in this strategy and nothing would deter them.

In the ensuing days, Athenians of all ages could be seen in the streets drawing maps of Sicily, dreaming of the riches that would pour into Athens and the final humiliation of the Spartans. The day of the launching of the ships turned into a great holiday and the most awe-inspiring spectacle they had ever seen—an enormous armada filling the harbor as far as the eye could see, the ships beautifully decorated, the soldiers, glistening in their armor, crowding the decks. It was a dazzling display of the wealth and power of Athens.

As the months went by, the Athenians desperately sought news of the expedition. At one point, through the sheer size of the force, it seemed that Athens had gained the advantage and had laid siege to Syracuse. But at the last moment, reinforcements arrived from Sparta, and now the Athenians were on the defensive. Nicias sent off a letter to the Assembly describing this negative turn of events. He recommended either giving up and returning to Athens, or the sending of reinforcements right away. Unwilling to believe in the possibility of defeat, the Athenians voted to send reinforcements—a second armada of ships almost as large as the first. In the months after this, the Athenians' anxiety reached new heights—for now the stakes had been doubled and Athens could not afford to lose.

One day a barber in Athens's port town of Piraeus heard a rumor from a customer that the Athenian expedition, every ship and almost every man, had been wiped out in battle. The rumor quickly spread to Athens. It was hard to believe, but slowly panic set in. A week later the rumor was confirmed and Athens seemed doomed, drained of money, ships, and men.

Miraculously, the Athenians managed to hold on. But over the next few years, severely imbalanced by the losses in Sicily, they staggered from one reeling blow to another, until finally in 405 BC Athens suffered its final loss and was forced to agree to the harsh terms of peace imposed by Sparta. Their years of glory, their great democratic empire, the Periclean golden age were now and forever over. The man who had curbed their most dangerous emotions—aggression, greed, hubris, selfishness—had been gone from the scene for too long, his wisdom long forgotten.

Interpretation: As Pericles surveyed the political scene early in his career, he noticed the following phenomenon: Every Athenian political figure believed he was rational, had realistic goals, and plans on how to get there. They all worked hard for their political factions and tried to increase their power. They led Athenian armies into battle and often came out ahead. They strove to expand the empire and bring in more money. And when their political maneuvering suddenly backfired, or the wars turned out badly, they had excellent reasons for why this had happened. They could always blame the opposition or, if need be, the gods. And yet, if all these men were so rational, why did their policies add up to so much chaos and self-destructiveness? Why was Athens such a mess and the democracy itself so fragile? Why was there so much corruption and turbulence? The answer was simple: his fellow Athenians were not rational at all, merely selfish and shrewd. What guided their decisions was their base emotions—hunger for power, attention, and money. And for those purposes they could be very tactical and clever, but none of their maneuvers led to anything that lasted or served the overall interests of the democracy.

What consumed Pericles as a thinker and a public figure was how to get out of this trap, how to be truly rational in an arena dominated by emotions. The solution he came up with is unique in history and devastatingly powerful in its results. It should serve as our ideal. In his conception, the human mind has to worship something, has to have its attention directed to something it values above all else. For most people, it is their ego; for some it is their family, their clan, their god, or their nation. For Pericles it would be *nous*, the ancient Greek word for "mind" or "intelligence." *Nous* is a force that permeates the universe, creating meaning and order. The human mind is naturally attracted to this order; this is the source of our intelligence. For Pericles, the *nous* that he worshipped was embodied in the figure of the goddess Athena.

Athena was literally born from the head of Zeus, her name itself reflecting this—a combination of "god" (*theos*) and "mind" (*nous*). But Athena came to represent a very particular form of *nous*—eminently practical, feminine, and earthy. She is the voice that comes to heroes in times of need, instilling in them a calm spirit, orienting their minds toward the perfect idea for victory and success, then giving them the energy to achieve this. To be visited by Athena was the highest blessing of them all, and it was her spirit that guided great generals and the best artists, inventors, and tradesmen. Under her influence, a man or woman could see the world with perfect clarity and hit upon the action that was just right for the moment. For Athens, her spirit was invoked to unify the city, make it prosperous and productive. In essence, Athena stood for rationality, the greatest gift of the gods to mortals, for it alone could make a human act with divine wisdom.

To cultivate his inner Athena, Pericles first had to find a way to master his emotions. Emotions turn us inward, away from *nous*, away from reality. We dwell on our anger or our insecurities. If we look out at the world and try to solve problems, we see things through the lens of these emotions; they cloud our vision. Pericles trained himself to never react in the moment, to never make a decision while under the influence of a strong emotion. Instead, he analyzed his feelings. Usually when he looked closely at his insecurities or his anger, he saw that they were not really justified, and they lost their significance under scrutiny. Sometimes he had to physically get away from the heated Assembly and retire to his house, where he remained alone for days on end, calming himself down. Slowly, the voice of Athena would come to him.

He decided to base all of his political decisions on one thing—what actually served the greater good of Athens. His goal was to unify the citizenry through genuine love of democracy and belief in the superiority of the Athenian way. Having such a standard helped him avoid the ego trap. It impelled him to work to increase the participation and power of the lower and middle classes, even though such a strategy could easily turn against him. It inspired him to limit wars, even though this meant less personal glory for him. And finally it led to his greatest decision of all—the public works project that transformed Athens.

To help himself in this deliberative process, he opened his mind to as many ideas and options as possible, even to those of his opponents. He imagined all of the possible consequences of a strategy before committing to it. With a calm spirit and an open mind, he hit upon policies that sparked one of the true golden ages in history. One man was able to infect an entire city with his rational spirit. What happened to Athens after he departed from the scene speaks for itself. The Sicilian expedition represented everything he had always opposed— a decision secretly motivated by the desire to grab more land, blinded to its potential consequences.

Understand: Like everyone, you think you are rational, but you are not. Rationality is not a power you are born with but one you acquire through training and practice. The voice of Athena simply stands for a higher power that exists within you right now, a potential you have perhaps felt in moments of calmness and focus, the perfect idea coming to you after much thinking. You are not connected to this higher power in the present because your mind is weighed down with emotions. Like Pericles in the Assembly, you are infected by all of the drama that others churn up; you are continually reacting to what people give you, experiencing waves of excitement, insecurity, and anxiety that make it hard to focus. Your attention is pulled this way and that, and without the rational standard to guide your decisions, you never quite reach the goals that you set. At any moment this can change with a simple decision—to cultivate your inner Athena. Rationality is then what you will value the most and that which will serve as your guide.

Your first task is to look at those emotions that are continually infecting your ideas and decisions. Learn to question yourself: Why this anger or resentment? Where does this incessant need for attention come from? Under such scrutiny, your emotions will lose their hold on you. You will begin to think for yourself instead of reacting to what others give you. Emotions tend to narrow the mind, making us focus on one or two ideas that satisfy our immediate desire for power or attention, ideas that usually backfire. Now, with a calm spirit, you can entertain a wide range of options and solutions. You will deliberate longer before acting and reassess your strategies. The voice will become clearer and clearer. When people besiege you with their endless dramas and petty emotions, you will resent the distraction and apply your rationality to think past them. Like an athlete continually getting stronger through training, your mind will become more flexible and resilient. Clear and calm, you will see answers and creative solutions that no one else can envision.

It's just as though one's second self were standing beside one; one is sensible and rational oneself, but the other self is impelled to do something perfectly senseless, and sometimes very funny; and suddenly you notice that you are longing to do that amusing thing, goodness knows why; that is, you want to, as it were, against your will; though you fight against it with all of your might, you want to.

—Fyodor Dostoyevsky, *A Raw Youth*

Keys to Human Nature

Whenever anything goes wrong in our life, we naturally seek an explanation. To not find some cause for why our plans went awry, or why we faced sudden resistance to our ideas, would be deeply disturbing to us and intensify our pain. But in looking for a cause, our minds tend to revolve around the same types of explanations: someone or some group sabotaged me, perhaps out of dislike; large antagonistic forces out there, such as the government or social conventions, hindered me; I received bad advice, or information was kept from me. Finally—if worse comes to worst—it was all bad luck and unfortunate circumstances.

These explanations generally emphasize our helplessness. "What could I have done differently? How could I have possibly foreseen the nasty actions of X against me?" They are also somewhat vague. We usually can't point to specific malicious actions of others. We can only suspect or imagine. These explanations tend to intensify our emotions—anger, frustration, depression—which we can then wallow in and feel bad for ourselves. Most significantly, our first reaction is to look outward for the cause. Yes, we might be responsible for some of what happened, but for the most part, other people and antagonistic forces tripped us up. This reaction is deeply ingrained in the human animal. In ancient times, it might have been the gods or evil spirits who were to blame. We of the present choose to call them other names.

The truth, however, is very different from this. Certainly there are individuals and larger forces out there that continually have an effect on us, and there is much we cannot control in the world. But generally what causes us to go astray in the first place, what leads to bad decisions and miscalculations, is our deep-rooted irrationality, the extent to which our minds are governed by emotion. We cannot see this. It is our blind spot, and as exhibit A of this blind spot, let's look at the crash of 2008, which can serve as a compendium of all varieties of human irrationality.

In the aftermath of the crash, the following were the most common explanations in the media for what had happened: trade imbalances and other factors led to cheap credit in the early 2000s, which led to excess leverage; it was impossible to place accurate value on the highly complex derivatives that were being traded, so no one really could gauge profits and losses; there existed a shrewd and corrupt cabal of insiders who had incentives to manipulate the system for quick profits; greedy lenders pushed subprime mortgages on unsuspecting homeowners; there was too much government regulation; there was not enough government oversight; computer models and trading systems ran amok.

These explanations reveal a remarkable denial of a basic reality. Leading up to the crash of 2008, millions of people made daily decisions on whether to invest or not invest. At each point of these transactions, buyers and sellers could have pulled back from the riskiest forms of investment but decided not to. There were plenty of people out there warning of a bubble. Only a few years before, the crash of the giant hedge fund Long-Term Capital Management showed exactly how a larger crash could and would occur. If people had longer memories, they could think back to the bubble of 1987; if they read history, the stock market bubble and crash of 1929. Almost any potential homeowner can understand the risks of no-money-down mortgages and lending terms with fast-rising interest rates.

What all of the analysis ignores is the basic irrationality that drove these millions of buyers and sellers up and down the line. They became infected with the lure of easy money. This made even the most educated investor emotional. Studies and experts were pulled in to bolster ideas that people were already disposed to believe in—such as the proverbial "this time it's different" and "housing prices never go down." A wave of unbridled optimism swept through masses of people. Then came the panic and crash and the ugly confrontation with reality. Instead of coming to terms with the orgy of speculation that had overwhelmed one and all, making smart people look like idiots, fingers were pointed at outside forces, anything to deflect the real source of the madness. This is not something peculiar to the crash of 2008. The same types of explanations were trotted out after the crashes of 1987 and 1929, the railway mania in the 1840s in England, and the South Sea bubble of the 1720s, also in England. People spoke of reforming the system; laws were passed to limit speculation. And none of this worked.

Bubbles occur because of the intense emotional pull they have on people, which overwhelms any reasoning powers an individual mind might possess. They stimulate our natural tendencies toward greed, easy money, and quick results. It is hard to see other people making money and not join in. There is no regulatory force on the planet that can control human nature. And because we do not confront the real source of the problem, bubbles and crashes keep repeating, and will keep repeating as long as there are suckers and people who do not read history. The recurrence of this mirrors the recurrence in our own lives of the same problems and mistakes, forming negative patterns. It is hard to learn from experience when we are not looking inward, at the true causes.

Understand: The first step toward becoming rational is to understand our *fundamental irrationality*. There are two factors that should render this more palatable to our egos: nobody is exempt from the irresistible effect of emotions on the mind, not even the wisest among us; and to some extent irrationality is a function of the structure of our brains and is wired into our very nature by the way we process emotions. Being irrational is almost beyond our control. To understand this, we must look at the evolution of emotions themselves.

For millions of years, living organisms depended on finely tuned instincts for survival. In a split second, a reptile could sense danger in the environment and respond with an instantaneous flight from the scene. There was no separation between impulse and action. Then, slowly, for some animals this sensation evolved into something larger and longer—a feeling of fear. In the beginning this fear merely consisted of a high level of arousal with the release of certain chemicals, alerting the animal to a possible danger. With this arousal and the attention that came with it, the animal could respond in several ways instead of just one. It could become more sensitive to the environment and learn. It stood a better chance of survival because its options were widened. This sensation of fear would last only a few seconds or even less, for speed was of the essence.

For social animals, these arousals and feelings took on a deeper and more important role: they became a critical form of communication. Vicious sounds or hair standing on end could display anger, warding off an enemy or signaling a danger; certain postures or smells revealed sexual desire and readiness; postures and gestures signaled the desire to play; certain calls from the young revealed deep anxiety and the need for the mother to return. With primates, this became ever more elaborate and complex. It has been shown that chimpanzees can feel envy and the desire for vengeance, among other emotions. This evolution took place over the course of hundreds of millions of years. Much more recently, cognitive powers developed in animals and humans, culminating in the invention of language and abstract thinking.

As many neuroscientists have affirmed, this evolution has led to the higher mammalian brain being composed of three parts. The oldest is the reptilian part of the brain, which controls all automatic responses that regulate the body. This is the instinctive part. Above that is the old mammalian or limbic brain, governing feeling and emotion. And on top of that has evolved the neocortex, the part that controls cognition and, for humans, language.

Emotions originate as physical arousal designed to capture our attention and cause us to take notice of something around us. They begin as chemical reactions and sensations that we must then translate into words to try to understand. But because they are processed in a different part of the brain from language and thinking, this translation is often slippery and inaccurate. For instance, we feel anger at person X, whereas in fact the true source of this may be envy; below the level of conscious awareness we feel inferior in relation to X and want something he or she has. But envy is not a feeling that we are ever comfortable with, and so often we translate it as something more palatable— anger, dislike, resentment. Or let us say one day we are feeling a mood of frustration and impatience; person Y crosses our path at the wrong moment and we lash out, unaware that this anger is prompted by a different mood and out of proportion to Y's actions. Or let us say that we are truly angry at person Z. But the anger is sitting inside of us, caused by someone in our past who hurt us deeply, perhaps a parent. We direct the anger at Z because they remind us of this other person.

In other words, we do not have conscious access to the origins of our emotions and the moods they generate. Once we feel them, all we can do is try to interpret the emotion, translate it into language. But more often than not we get this wrong. We latch onto interpretations that are simple and that suit us. Or we remain baffled. We don't know why we feel depressed, for example. This unconscious aspect of emotions also means that it is very hard for us to learn from them, to stop or prevent compulsive behavior. Children who felt abandoned by their parents will tend to create patterns of abandonment in later life, without seeing the reason. (See *Trigger Points from Early Childhood*, on page 32.)

The communicating function of emotions, a critical factor for social animals, also becomes somewhat tricky for us. We communicate anger when it is something else we are feeling, or about someone else, but the other person cannot see this and so they react as if personally attacked, which can create cascading misinterpretations.

Emotions evolved for a different reason than cognition. These two forms of relating to the world are not connected seamlessly in our brains. For animals, unburdened by the need to translate physical sensations into abstract language, emotions function smoothly, as they were meant to. For us, the split between our emotions and our cognition is a source of constant internal friction, comprising a second Emotional Self within us that operates beyond our will. Animals feel fear for a brief time, then it is gone. We dwell on our fears, intensifying them and making them last well past the moment of danger, even to the point of feeling constant anxiety.

Many might be tempted to imagine that we have somehow tamed this Emotional Self through all of our intellectual and technological progress. After all, we don't appear as violent or passionate or superstitious as our ancestors; but this is an illusion. Progress and technology have not rewired us; they have merely altered the forms of our emotions and the type of irrationality that comes with them. For instance, new forms of media have enhanced the age-old ability of politicians and others to play on our emotions, in ever subtler and more sophisticated ways. Advertisers bombard us with highly effective subliminal messages. Our continual connection to social media makes us prone to new forms of viral emotional effects. These are not media designed for calm reflection. With their constant presence, we have less and less mental space to step back and think. We are as besieged with emotions and needless drama as the Athenians in the Assembly, because human nature has not changed.

Clearly the words *rational* and *irrational* can be quite loaded. People are always labeling those who disagree with them "irrational." What we need is a simple definition that can be applied as a way of judging, as accurately as possible, the difference between the two. The following shall serve as our barometer: We constantly feel emotions, and they continually infect our thinking, making us veer toward thoughts that please us and soothe our egos. It is impossible to not have our inclinations and feelings somehow involved in what we think. Rational people are aware of this and through introspection and effort are able, to some extent, to subtract emotions from their thinking and counteract their effect. Irrational people have no such awareness. They rush into action without carefully considering the ramifications and consequences.

We can see the difference in the decisions and actions that people take and the results that ensue. Rational people demonstrate over time that they are able to finish a project, to realize their goals, to work effectively with a team, and to create something that lasts. Irrational people reveal in their lives negative patterns—mistakes that keep repeating, unnecessary conflicts that follow them wherever they go, dreams and projects that are never realized, anger and desires for change that are never translated into concrete action. They are emotional and reactive and unaware of this. Everyone is capable of irrational decisions, some of which are caused by circumstances beyond our control. And even the most emotional types can hit upon great ideas or succeed momentarily through boldness. So it is important to judge over time whether a person is rational or irrational. Can they sustain success and hit upon several good strategies? Can they adjust and learn from failures?

We can also see the difference between a rational and irrational person in particular situations, when it comes to calculating long-term effects and seeing what truly matters. For instance: In a divorce proceeding with child custody issues, rational people will manage to let go of their bitterness and prejudice and reason what is in the best overall long-term interests of the child. Irrational people will become consumed with a power struggle against the spouse, will let resentments and desires for vengeance secretly guide their decisions. This will lead to a protracted battle and a damaged child.

When it comes to hiring an assistant or partner, rational people will use competence as their barometer—can this person do the job? An irrational person will easily fall under the spell of those who are charming, who know how to feed their insecurities, or who pose little challenge or threat, and will hire them without realizing the reasons. This will lead to mistakes and inefficiencies, for which the irrational person will blame others. When it comes to career decisions, rational people will look for positions that fit their long-term goals. Irrational types will decide based on how much money they can immediately make, what they feel they deserve in life (sometimes very little), how much they can slack off on the job, or how much attention the position might bring them. This will lead to career dead ends.

In all cases, the degree of awareness represents the difference. Rational people can readily admit their own irrational tendencies and the need to be vigilant. On the other hand, irrational people become highly emotional when challenged about the emotional roots of their decisions. They are incapable of introspection and learning. Their mistakes make them increasingly defensive.

It is important to understand that rationality is not some means of transcending emotion. Pericles himself valued bold and adventurous action. He *loved* the spirit of Athena and the inspiration she brought. He wanted Athenians to feel love for their city and empathy for their fellow citizens. What he envisioned was a state of balance—a clear understanding of why we feel the way we do, conscious of our impulses so that we can think without being secretly compelled by our emotions. Pericles wanted the energy that comes from impulses and emotions to serve our thinking self. That was his vision of rationality, and our ideal.

Fortunately, to acquire rationality is not complicated. It simply requires knowing and working through a three-step process. First, we must become aware of what we shall call *low-grade irrationality*. This is a function of the continual moods and feelings that we experience in life, below the level of consciousness. When we plan or make decisions, we are not aware of how deeply these moods and feelings skew the thinking process. They create in our thinking pronounced biases that are so deeply ingrained in us that we see evidence of them in all cultures and all periods of history. These biases, by distorting reality, lead to the mistakes and ineffective decisions that plague our lives. Being aware of them, we can begin to counterbalance their effects.

Second, we must understand the nature of what we shall call *high-grade irrationality*. This occurs when our emotions become inflamed, generally because of certain pressures. As we think about our anger, excitement, resentment, or suspicion, it intensifies into a reactive state—everything we see or hear is interpreted through the lens of this emotion. We become more sensitive and more prone to other emotional reactions. Impatience and resentment can bleed into anger and deep distrust. These reactive states are what lead people to violence, to manic obsessions, to uncontrollable greed, or to desires to control another person. This form of irrationality is the source of more acute problems—crises, conflicts, and disastrous decisions. Understanding how this type of irrationality operates can allow us to recognize the reactive state as it is happening and pull back before we do something we regret.

Third, we need to enact certain strategies and exercises that will strengthen the thinking part of the brain and give it more power in the eternal struggle with our emotions.

The following three steps will help you begin on the path toward rationality. It would be wise to incorporate all three into your study and practice in human nature.

Step One: Recognize the Biases

Emotions are continually affecting our thought processes and decisions, below the level of our awareness. And the most common emotion of them all is the desire for pleasure and the avoidance of pain. Our thoughts almost inevitably revolve around this desire; we simply recoil from entertaining ideas that are unpleasant or painful to us. We imagine we are looking for the truth, or being realistic, when in fact we are holding on to ideas that bring a release from tension and soothe our egos, make us feel superior. This *pleasure principle in thinking* is the source of all of our mental biases. If you believe that you are somehow immune to any of the following biases, it is simply an example of the pleasure principle in action. Instead, it is best to search and see how they continually operate inside you, as well as learn how to identify such irrationality in others.

Confirmation Bias

I look at the evidence and arrive at my decisions through more or less rational processes.

To hold an idea and convince ourselves we arrived at it rationally, we go in search of evidence to support our view. What could be more objective or scientific? But because of the pleasure principle and its unconscious influence, we manage to find the evidence that confirms what we *want* to believe. This is known as *confirmation bias*.

We can see this at work in people's plans, particularly those with high stakes. A plan is designed to lead to a positive, desired objective. If people considered the possible negative and positive consequences equally, they might find it hard to take any action. Inevitably they veer toward information that confirms the desired positive result, the rosy scenario, without realizing it. We also see this at work when people are supposedly asking for advice. This is the bane of most consultants. In the end, people want to hear their own ideas and preferences confirmed by an expert opinion. They will interpret what you say in light of what they want to hear; and if your advice runs counter to their desires, they will find some way to dismiss your opinion, your so-called expertise. The more powerful the person, the more they are subject to this form of the confirmation bias.

When investigating confirmation bias in the world, take a look at theories that seem a little too good to be true. Statistics and studies are trotted out to prove them; these are not very difficult to find, once you are convinced of the rightness of your argument. On the internet, it is easy to find studies that support both sides of an argument. In general, you should never accept the validity of people's ideas because they have supplied "evidence." Instead, examine the evidence yourself in the cold light of day, with as much skepticism as you can muster. Your first impulse should always be to find the evidence that disconfirms your most cherished beliefs and those of others. That is true science.

Conviction Bias

I believe in this idea so strongly. It must be true.

We hold on to an idea that is secretly pleasing to us, but deep inside we might have some doubts as to its truth, and so we go an extra mile to convince ourselves—to believe in it with great vehemence and to loudly contradict anyone who challenges us. How can our idea not be true if it brings out in us such energy to defend it, we tell ourselves? This bias is revealed even more clearly in our relationship to leaders—if they express an opinion with heated words and gestures, colorful metaphors and entertaining anecdotes, and a deep well of conviction, it must mean they have examined the idea carefully to express it with such certainty. Those, on the other hand, who express nuances, whose tone is more hesitant, reveal weakness and self-doubt. They are probably lying, or so we think. This bias makes us susceptible to salesmen and demagogues who display conviction as a way to convince and deceive. They know that people are hungry for entertainment, so they cloak their half-truths with dramatic effects.

Appearance Bias

I understand the people I deal with; I see them just as they are.

We see people not as they are, but as they appear to us. And these appearances are usually misleading. First, people have trained themselves in social situations to present the front that is appropriate and that will be judged positively. They seem to be in favor of the noblest causes, always presenting themselves as hardworking and conscientious. We take these masks for reality. Second, we are prone to fall for the *halo effect*—when we see certain negative or positive qualities in a person (social awkwardness, intelligence), other positive or negative qualities are implied that fit with this. People who are good-looking generally seem more trustworthy, particularly politicians. If a person is successful, we imagine they are probably also ethical, conscientious, and deserving of their good fortune. This obscures the fact that many people who have gotten ahead have done so through less-than-moral actions, which they cleverly disguise from view.

The Group Bias

My ideas are my own. I do not listen to the group. I am not a conformist.

We are social animals by nature. The feeling of isolation, of difference from the group, is depressing and terrifying. We experience tremendous relief when we find others who think the same way we do. In fact, we are motivated to take up ideas and opinions *because* they bring us this relief. We are unaware of this pull and so imagine we have come to certain ideas completely on our own. Look at people who support one party or the other, one ideology—a noticeable orthodoxy or correctness prevails, without anyone saying anything or applying overt pressure. If someone is on the right or the left, their opinions will almost always follow the same direction on dozens of issues, as if by magic, and yet few would ever admit this influence on their thought patterns.

The Blame Bias

I learn from my experience and mistakes.

Mistakes and failures elicit the need to explain. We want to learn the lesson and not repeat the experience. But in truth, we do not like to look too closely at what we did; our introspection is limited. Our natural response is to blame others, circumstances, or a momentary lapse of judgment. The reason for this bias is that it is often too painful to look at our mistakes. It calls into question our feelings of superiority. It pokes at our ego. We go through the motions, pretending to reflect on what we did. But with the passage of time, the pleasure principle rises and we forget what small part in the mistake we ascribed to ourselves. Desire and emotion will blind us yet again, and we will repeat exactly the same mistake and go through the same mild recriminating process, followed by forgetfulness, until we die. If people truly learned from their experience, we would find few mistakes in the world and career paths that ascend ever upward.

Superiority Bias

I'm different. I'm more rational than others, more ethical as well.

Few would say this to people in conversation. It sounds arrogant. But in numerous opinion polls and studies, when asked to compare themselves with others, people generally express a variation of this. It's the equivalent of an optical illusion—we cannot seem to see our faults and irrationalities, only those of others. So, for instance, we'll easily believe that those in the other political party do not come to their opinions based on rational principles, but those on our side have done so. On the ethical front, few of us will ever admit that we have resorted to deception or manipulation in our work or have been clever and strategic in our career advancement. Everything we've got, or so we think, comes from natural talent and hard work. But with other people, we are quick to ascribe to them all kinds of Machiavellian tactics. This allows us to justify whatever we do, no matter the results.

We feel a tremendous pull to imagine ourselves as rational, decent, and ethical. These are qualities highly promoted in the culture. To show signs otherwise is to risk great disapproval. If all of this were true—if people were rational and morally superior—the world would be suffused with goodness and peace.

We know, however, the reality, and so some people, perhaps all of us, are merely deceiving ourselves. Rationality and ethical qualities must be achieved through awareness and effort. They do not come naturally. They come through a maturation process.

Step Two: Beware the Inflaming Factors

Low-grade emotions continually affect our thinking, and they originate from our own impulses—for instance, the desire for pleasing and comforting thoughts. High-grade emotion, however, comes at certain moments, reaches an explosive pitch, and is generally sparked by something external—a person who gets under our skin, or particular circumstances. The level of arousal is higher and our attention is captured completely. The more we think about the emotion, the stronger it gets, which makes us focus even more on it, and so on and so forth. Our minds tunnel into the emotion, and everything reminds us of our anger or excitement. We become reactive. Because we are unable to bear the tension this brings, high-grade emotion usually culminates in some rash action with disastrous consequences. In the middle of such an attack we feel possessed, as if a second, limbic self has taken over.

It is best to be aware of these factors so that you can stop the mind from tunneling and prevent the releasing action that you will always come to regret. You should also be aware of high-grade irrationality in others, to either get out of their way or help bring them back to reality.

Trigger Points from Early Childhood

In early childhood we were at our most sensitive and vulnerable. Our relationship to our parents had a much greater impact on us the further back in time we go. The same could be said for any early powerful experience. These vulnerabilities and wounds remain buried deep within our minds. Sometimes we try to repress the memory of these influences, if they happen to be negative—great fears or humiliations. Sometimes, however, they are associated with positive emotions, experiences of love and attention that we continually want to relive. Later in life, a person or event will trigger a memory of this positive or negative experience, and with it a release of powerful chemicals or hormones associated with the memory.

Take, for example, a young man who had a distant, narcissistic mother. As an infant or child, he experienced her coldness as abandonment, and to be abandoned must mean he was somehow unworthy of her love. Or similarly, a new sibling on the scene caused his mother to give him much less attention, which he equally experienced as abandonment. Later in life, in a relationship, a woman might hint at disapproval of some trait or action of his, all of which is part of a healthy relationship. This will hit a trigger point—she is noticing his flaws, which, he imagines, precedes her abandonment of him. He feels a powerful rush of emotion, a sense of imminent betrayal. He does not see the source of this; it is beyond his control. He overreacts, accuses, withdraws, all of which leads to the very thing he feared—abandonment. His reaction was to some reflection in his mind, not to the reality. This is the height of irrationality.

The way to recognize this in yourself and in others is by noticing behavior that is suddenly childish in its intensity and seemingly out of character. This could center on any key emotion. It could be fear—of losing control, of failure. In this case, we react by withdrawing from the situation and the presence of others, like a child curling up into a ball. A sudden illness, brought on by the intense fear, will conveniently cause us to have to leave the scene. It could be love—desperately searching to re-create a close parental or sibling relationship in the present, triggered by someone who vaguely reminds us of the lost paradise. It could be extreme mistrust, originating from an authority figure in early childhood who disappointed or betrayed us, generally the father. This often triggers a sudden rebellious attitude.

The great danger here is that in misreading the present and reacting to something in the past, we create conflict, disappointments, and mistrust that only strengthen the wound. In some ways, we are programmed to repeat the early experience in the present. Our only defense is awareness as it is happening. We can recognize a trigger point by the experience of emotions that are unusually primal, more uncontrollable than normal. They trigger tears, deep depression, or excessive hope. People under the spell of these emotions will often have a very different tone of voice and body language, as if they were physically reliving a moment from early life.

In the midst of such an attack, we must struggle to detach ourselves and contemplate the possible source—the wound in early childhood—and the patterns it has locked us into. This deep understanding of ourselves and our vulnerabilities is a key step toward becoming rational.

Sudden Gains or Losses

Sudden success or winnings can be very dangerous. Neurologically, chemicals are released in the brain that give a powerful jolt of arousal and energy, leading to the desire to repeat this experience. It can be the start of any kind of addiction and manic behavior. Also, when gains come quickly we tend to lose sight of the basic wisdom that true success, to really last, must come through hard work. We do not take into account the role that luck plays in such sudden gains. We try again and again to recapture that high from winning so much money or attention. We acquire feelings of grandiosity. We become especially resistant to anyone who tries to warn us—they don't understand, we tell ourselves. Because this cannot be sustained, we experience an inevitable fall, which is all the more painful, leading to the depression part of the cycle. Although gamblers are the most prone to this, it equally applies to businesspeople during bubbles and to people who gain sudden attention from the public.

Unexpected losses or a string of losses equally create irrational reactions. We imagine we are cursed with bad luck and that this will go on indefinitely. We become fearful and hesitant, which will often lead to more mistakes or failures. In sports, this can induce what is known as choking, as previous losses and misses weigh on the mind and tighten it up.

The solution here is simple: whenever you experience unusual gains or losses, that is precisely the time to step back and counterbalance them with some necessary pessimism or optimism. Be extra wary of sudden success and attention—they are not built on anything that lasts and they have an addictive pull. And the fall is always painful.

Rising Pressure

The people around you generally appear sane and in control of their lives. But put any of them in stressful circumstances, with the pressure rising, and you will see a different reality. The cool mask of self-control comes off. They suddenly lash out in anger, reveal a paranoid streak, and become hypersensitive and often petty. Under stress or any threat, the most primitive parts of the brain are aroused and engaged, overwhelming people's reasoning powers. In fact, stress or tension can reveal flaws in people that they have carefully concealed from view. It is often wise to observe people in such moments, precisely as a way to judge their true character.

Whenever you notice rising pressure and stress levels in your life, you must watch yourself carefully. Monitor any signs of unusual brittleness or sensitivity, sudden suspicions, fears disproportionate to the circumstances. Observe with as much detachment as possible, finding time and space to be alone. You need perspective. Never imagine that you are someone who can withstand rising stress without emotional leakage. It is not possible. But through self-awareness and reflection you can prevent yourself from making decisions you will come to regret.

Inflaming Individuals

There are people in the world who by their nature tend to trigger powerful emotions in almost everyone they encounter. These emotions range among the extremes of love, hatred, confidence, and mistrust. Some examples in history would include King David in the Bible, Alcibiades in ancient Athens, Julius Caesar in ancient Rome, Georges Danton during the French Revolution, and Bill Clinton. These types have a degree of charisma—they have the ability to express eloquently emotions they are feeling, which inevitably stirs parallel emotions in others. But some of them can also be quite narcissistic; they project their internal drama and troubles outward, catching other people up in the turmoil they create. This leads to profound feelings of attraction in some and repulsion in others.

It is best to recognize these inflamers by how they affect others, not just yourself. No one can remain indifferent to them. People find themselves incapable of reasoning or maintaining any distance in their presence. They make you think of them continually when not in their presence. They have an obsessive quality, and they can lead you to extreme actions as a devoted follower or as an inveterate enemy. On either end of the spectrum—attraction or repulsion—you will tend to be irrational and you will desperately need to distance yourself. A good strategy to utilize is to see through the front they project. They inevitably try to cast a larger-than-life image, a mythic, intimidating quality; but in fact they are all too human, full of the same insecurities and weaknesses we all possess. Try to recognize these very human traits and demythologize them.

The Group Effect

This is the high-grade variety of the *group bias*. When we are in a group of a large enough size, we become different. Notice yourself and others at a sporting event, a concert, a religious or political gathering. It is impossible to not feel yourself caught up in the collective emotions. Your heart beats faster. Tears of joy or sadness come more readily. Being in a group does not stimulate independent reasoning but rather the intense desire to belong. This can happen equally in a work environment, particularly if the leader plays on people's emotions to spur competitive, aggressive desires, or creates an us-versus-them dynamic. The group effect does not necessarily require the presence of others. It can occur virally, as some opinion spreads over social media and infects us with the desire to share the opinion—generally of a strong variety, such as outrage.

There is an exhilarating, positive aspect to the stimulation of group emotions. It is how we can be rallied to do something for the collective good. But if you notice the appeal is to more diabolical emotions, such as hatred of the other, rabid patriotism, aggression, or sweeping worldviews, you need to inoculate yourself and see through the powerful pull as it works on you. It is often best to avoid the group setting if possible in order to maintain your reasoning powers, or to enter such moments with maximum skepticism.

Be aware of demagogues who exploit the group effect and stimulate outbreaks of irrationality. They inevitably resort to certain devices. In a group setting, they begin by warming up the crowd, talking about ideas and values that everyone shares, creating a pleasant feeling of agreement. They rely on vague but loaded words full of emotive quality such as *justice* or *truth* or *patriotism*. They talk of abstract, noble goals rather than the solving of specific problems with concrete action.

Demagogues in politics or the media try to stir a continual sense of panic, urgency, and outrage. They must keep the emotional levels high. Your defense is simple: Consider your reasoning powers, your ability to think for yourself, your most precious possession. Resent any kind of intrusion upon your independent mind by others. When you feel you are in the presence of a demagogue, become doubly wary and analytical.

A FINAL WORD ON THE IRRATIONAL IN HUMAN NATURE: DO NOT IMAGINE THAT THE more extreme types of irrationality have somehow been overcome through progress and enlightenment. Throughout history we witness continual cycles of rising and falling levels of the irrational. The great golden age of Pericles, with its philosophers and its first stirrings of the scientific spirit, was followed by an age of superstition, cults, and intolerance. This same phenomenon happened after the Italian Renaissance. That this cycle is bound to recur again and again is part of human nature.

The irrational simply changes its look and its fashions. We may no longer have literal witch hunts, but in the twentieth century, not so very long ago, we witnessed the show trials of Stalin, the McCarthy hearings in the U.S. Senate, and the mass persecutions during the Chinese Cultural Revolution. Various cults are continually being generated, including cults of personality and the fetishizing of celebrities. Technology now inspires religious fervor. People have a desperate need to believe in something and they will find it anywhere. Polls have revealed that increasing numbers of people believe in ghosts, spirits, and angels, in the twenty-first century.

As long as there are humans, the irrational will find its voices and means of spreading. Rationality is something to be acquired by individuals, not by mass movements or technological progress. Feeling superior and beyond it is a sure sign that the irrational is at work.

Step Three: Strategies Toward Bringing Out the Rational Self

Despite our pronounced irrational tendencies, two factors should give us all hope. First and foremost is the existence throughout history and in all cultures of people of high rationality, the types who have made progress possible. They serve as ideals for all of us to aim for. These include Pericles, the ruler Aśoka of ancient India, Marcus Aurelius of ancient Rome, Marguerite de Valois in medieval France, Leonardo da Vinci, Charles Darwin, Abraham Lincoln, the writer Anton Chekhov, the anthropologist Margaret Mead, and the businessman Warren Buffett, to name but a few. All of these types share certain qualities—a realistic appraisal of themselves and their weaknesses; a devotion to truth and reality; a tolerant attitude toward people; and the ability to reach goals that they have set.

The second factor is that almost all of us at some point in our lives have experienced moments of greater rationality. This often comes with what we shall call the *maker's mind-set*. We have a project to get done, perhaps with a deadline. The only emotion we can afford is excitement and energy. Other emotions simply make it impossible to concentrate. Because we have to get results, we become exceptionally practical. We focus on the work—our mind calm, our ego not intruding. If people try to interrupt or infect us with emotions, we resent it. These moments—as fleeting as a few weeks or hours—reveal the rational self that is waiting to come out. It just requires some awareness and some practice.

The following strategies are designed to help you bring out that inner Pericles or Athena:

Know yourself thoroughly. The Emotional Self thrives on ignorance. The moment you are aware of how it operates and dominates you is the moment it loses its hold on you and can be tamed. Therefore, your first step toward the rational is always inward. You want to catch that Emotional Self in action. For this purpose, you must reflect on how you operate under stress. What particular weaknesses come out in such moments—the desire to please, to bully or control, deep levels of mistrust? Look at your decisions, especially those that have been ineffective—can you see a pattern, an underlying insecurity that impels them? Examine your strengths, what makes you different from other people. This will help you decide upon goals that mesh with your long-term interests and that are aligned with your skills. By knowing and valuing what marks you as different, you will also be able to resist the pull of the group bias and effect.

Examine your emotions to their roots. You are angry. Let the feeling settle from within, and think about it. Was it triggered by something seemingly trivial or petty? That is a sure sign that something or someone else is behind it. Perhaps a more uncomfortable emotion is at the source—such as envy or paranoia. You need to look at this square in the eye. Dig below any trigger points to see where they started. For these purposes, it might be wise to use a journal in which you record your self-assessments with ruthless objectivity. Your greatest danger here is your ego and how it makes you unconsciously maintain illusions about yourself. These may be comforting in the moment, but in the long run they make you defensive and unable to learn or progress. Find a neutral position from which you can observe your actions, with a bit of detachment and even humor. Soon all of this will become second nature, and when the Emotional Self suddenly rears its head in some situation, you will see it as it happens and be able to step back and find that neutral position.

Increase your reaction time. This power comes through practice and repetition. When some event or interaction requires a response, you must train yourself to step back. This could mean physically removing yourself to a place where you can be alone and not feel any pressure to respond. Or it could mean writing that angry email but not sending it. You sleep on it for a day or two.

You do not make phone calls or communicate while feeling some sudden emotion, particularly resentment. If you find yourself rushing to commit to people, to hire or be hired by them, step back and give it a day. Cool the emotions down. The longer you can take the better, because perspective comes with time. Consider this like resistance training—the longer you can resist reacting, the more mental space you have for actual reflection, and the stronger your mind will become.

Accept people as facts. Interactions with people are the major source of emotional turmoil, but it doesn't have to be that way. The problem is that we are continually judging people, wishing they were something that they are not. We want to change them. We want them to think and act a certain way, most often the way we think and act. And because this is not possible, because everyone is different, we are continually frustrated and upset. Instead, see other people as phenomena, as neutral as comets or plants. They simply exist. They come in all varieties, making life rich and interesting. Work with what they give you, instead of resisting and trying to change them. Make understanding people a fun game, the solving of puzzles. It is all part of the human comedy. Yes, people are irrational, but so are you. Make your acceptance of human nature as radical as possible. This will calm you down and help you observe people more dispassionately, understanding them on a deeper level. You will stop projecting your own emotions on to them. All of this will give you more balance and calmness, more mental space for thinking.

It is certainly difficult to do this with the nightmare types who cross our path—the raging narcissists, the passive aggressors, and other inflamers. They remain a continual test to our rationality. Look at the Russian writer Anton Chekhov, one of the most fiercely rational people who ever lived, as the model for this. His family was large and poor, and his father, an alcoholic, mercilessly beat all of the children, including young Chekhov. Chekhov became a doctor and took up writing as a side career. He applied his training as a doctor to the human animal, his goal to understand what makes us so irrational, so unhappy, and so dangerous. In his stories and plays, he found it immensely therapeutic to get inside his characters and make sense of even the worst types. In this way, he could forgive anybody, even his father. His approach in these cases was to imagine that each person, no matter how twisted, has a reason for what they've become, a logic that makes sense to them. In their own way, they are striving for fulfillment, but irrationally. By stepping back and imagining their story from the inside, Chekhov demythologized the brutes and aggressors; he cut them down to human size. They no longer elicited hatred but rather pity. You must think more like a writer in approaching the people you deal with, even the worst sorts.

Find the optimal balance of thinking and emotion. We cannot divorce emotions from thinking. The two are completely intertwined. But there is inevitably a dominant factor, some people more clearly governed by emotions than others. What we are looking for is the proper ratio and balance, the one that leads to the most effective action. The ancient Greeks had an appropriate metaphor for this: the rider and the horse.

The horse is our emotional nature continually impelling us to move. This horse has tremendous energy and power, but without a rider it cannot be guided; it is wild, subject to predators, and continually heading into trouble. The rider is our thinking self. Through training and practice, it holds the reins and guides the horse, transforming this powerful animal energy into something productive. The one without the other is useless. Without the rider, no directed movement or purpose. Without the horse, no energy, no power. In most people the horse dominates, and the rider is weak. In some people the rider is too strong, holds the reins too tightly, and is afraid to occasionally let the animal go into a gallop. The horse and rider must work together. This means we consider our actions beforehand; we bring as much thinking as possible to a situation before we make a decision. But once we decide what to do, we loosen the reins and enter action with boldness and a spirit of adventure. Instead of being slaves to this energy, we channel it. That is the essence of rationality.

As an example of this ideal in action, try to maintain a perfect balance between skepticism (rider) and curiosity (horse). In this mode you are skeptical about your own enthusiasms and those of others. You do not accept at face value people's explanations and their application of "evidence." You look at the results of their actions, not what they say about their motivations. But if you take this too far, your mind will close itself off from wild ideas, from exciting speculations, from curiosity itself. You want to retain the elasticity of spirit you had as a child, interested in everything, while retaining the hard-nosed need to verify and scrutinize for yourself all ideas and beliefs. The two can coexist. It is a balance that all geniuses possess.

Love the rational. It is important to not see the path to rationality as something painful and ascetic. In fact, it brings powers that are immensely satisfying and pleasurable, much deeper than the more manic pleasures the world tends to offer us. You have felt this in your own life when absorbed in a project, time flowing by, and experiencing occasional bursts of excitement as you make discoveries or progress in your work. There are other pleasures as well. Being able to tame the Emotional Self leads to an overall calmness and clarity. In this state of mind you are less consumed by petty conflicts and considerations. Your actions are more effective, which also leads to less turmoil. You have the immense satisfaction of mastering yourself in a deep way. You have more mental space to be creative. You feel more in control.

Knowing all of this, it will become easier to motivate yourself to develop this power. In this sense, you are following the path of Pericles himself. He envisioned the goddess Athena embodying all of the practical powers of rationality. He worshipped and loved this goddess above all others. We may no longer venerate the goddess as a deity, but we can appreciate on a deep level all of those who promote rationality in our own world, and we can seek to internalize their power as much as we can.

"Trust your feelings!"—But feelings are nothing final or original; behind feelings there stand judgments and evaluations which we inherit in the form of . . . inclinations, aversions. . . . The inspiration born of a feeling is the grandchild of a judgment—and often of a false judgment!—and in any event not a child of your own! To trust one's feelings—means to give more obedience to one's grandfather and grandmother and their grandparents than to the gods which are in us: our reason and our experience.

—Friedrich Nietzsche

2

Transform Self-love into Empathy

◇

The Law of Narcissism

*W*e all naturally possess the most remarkable tool for connecting to people and attaining social power—empathy. When cultivated and properly used, it can allow us to see into the moods and minds of others, giving us the power to anticipate people's actions and gently lower their resistance. This instrument, however, is blunted by our habitual self-absorption. We are all narcissists, some deeper on the spectrum than others. Our mission in life is to come to terms with this self-love and learn how to turn our sensitivity outward, toward others, instead of inward. We must recognize at the same time the toxic narcissists among us before getting enmeshed in their dramas and poisoned by their envy.

The Narcissistic Spectrum

From the moment we are born, we humans feel a never-ending need for attention. We are social animals to the core. Our survival and happiness depend on the bonds we form with others. If people do not pay attention to us, we cannot connect to them on any level. Some of this is purely physical—we must have people looking at us to feel alive. As those who have gone through long periods of isolation can attest, without eye contact we begin to doubt our existence and to descend into a deep depression. But this need is also deeply psychological: through the quality of attention we receive from others, we feel recognized and appreciated for who we are. Our sense of self-worth depends on this. Because this is so important to the human animal, people will do almost anything to get attention, including committing a crime or attempting suicide. Look behind almost any action, and you will see this need as a primary motivation.

In trying to satisfy our hunger for attention, however, we face an inevitable problem: there is only so much of it to go around. In the family, we have to compete with our siblings; at school, with classmates; at work, with colleagues. The moments in which we feel recognized and appreciated are fleeting. People can largely be indifferent to our fate, as they must deal with their own problems. There are even some who are downright hostile and disrespectful to us. How do we handle those moments when we feel psychologically alone, or even abandoned? We can double our efforts to get attention and notice, but this can exhaust our energy and it can often have the opposite effect—people who try too hard seem desperate and repulse the attention they want. We simply cannot rely on others to give us constant validation, and yet we crave it.

Facing this dilemma from early childhood on, most of us come up with a solution that works quite well: we create a self, an image of ourselves that comforts us and makes us feel validated *from within*. This self is composed of our tastes, our opinions, how we look at the world, what we value. In building this self-image, we tend to accentuate our positive qualities and explain away our flaws. We cannot go too far in this, for if our self-image is too divorced from reality, other people will make us aware of the discrepancy, and we will doubt ourselves. But if it is done properly, in the end we have a self that we can love and cherish. Our energy turns inward. *We* become the center of our attention. When we experience those inevitable moments when we are alone or not feeling appreciated, we can retreat to this self and soothe ourselves. If we have moments of doubt and depression, our self-love raises us up, makes us feel worthy and even superior to others. This self-image operates as a thermostat, helping us to regulate our doubts and insecurities. We are no longer completely dependent on others for attention and recognition. We have *self-esteem*.

This idea might seem strange. We generally take this self-image completely for granted, like the air we breathe. It operates on a largely unconscious basis. We don't feel or see the thermostat as it operates. The best way to literally visualize this dynamic is to look at those who lack a coherent sense of self—people we shall call *deep narcissists*.

In constructing a self that we can hold on to and love, the key moment in its development occurs between the ages of two and five years old. As we slowly separate from our mother, we face a world in which we cannot get instant gratification. We also become aware that we are alone and yet dependent on our parents for survival. Our answer is to identify with the best qualities of our parents—their strength, their ability to soothe us—and incorporate these qualities into ourselves. If our parents encourage us in our first efforts at independence, if they validate our need to feel strong and recognize our unique qualities, then our self-image takes root, and we can slowly build upon it. Deep narcissists have a sharp break in this early development, and so they never quite construct a consistent and realistic feeling of a self.

Their mothers (or fathers) might be deep narcissists themselves, too self-absorbed to acknowledge the child, to encourage its early efforts at independence. Or alternatively the parents could be enmeshers—overinvolved in the child's life, suffocating it with attention, isolating it from others, and living through its advancement as a means to validate their own self-worth. They give the child no room to establish a self. In the backgrounds of almost all deep narcissists we find either abandonment or enmeshment. The result is that they have no self to retreat to, no foundation for self-esteem, and are completely dependent on the attention they can get from others to make them feel alive and worthy.

In childhood, if such narcissists are extroverts, they can function reasonably well, and even thrive. They become masters at attracting notice and monopolizing attention. They can appear vivacious and exciting. In a child, such qualities can seem a sign of future social success. But underneath the surface, they are becoming dangerously addicted to the hits of attention they stimulate to make them feel whole and worthy. If they are introverts, they will retreat to a fantasy life, imagining a self that is quite superior to others. Since they will not get validation of this self-image from others because it is so unrealistic, they will also have moments of great doubt and even self-loathing. They are either a god or a worm. Lacking a coherent core, they could imagine themselves to be anyone, and so their fantasies will keep shifting as they try on new personalities.

The nightmare for deep narcissists generally arrives in their twenties and thirties. They have failed to develop that inner thermostat, a cohesive sense of self to love and depend upon. The extroverts must constantly attract attention to feel alive and appreciated. They become more dramatic, more exhibitionistic and grandiose. This can become tiresome and even pathetic. They have to change friends and scenes so that they can have a fresh audience. Introverts fall deeper into a fantasy self. Being socially awkward yet radiating superiority, they tend to alienate people, increasing their dangerous isolation. In both cases, drugs or alcohol or any other form of addiction can become a necessary crutch to soothe them in the inevitable moments of doubt and depression.

You can recognize deep narcissists by the following behavior patterns: If they are ever insulted or challenged, they have no defense, nothing internal to soothe them or validate their worth. They generally react with great rage, thirsting for vengeance, full of a sense of righteousness. This is the only way they know how to assuage their insecurities. In such battles, they will position themselves as the wounded victim, confusing others and even drawing sympathy. They are prickly and oversensitive. Almost everything is taken personally. They can become quite paranoid and have enemies in all directions to point to. You can see an impatient or distant look on their face whenever you talk about something that does not directly involve them in some way. They immediately turn the conversation back to themselves, with some story or anecdote to distract from the insecurity behind it. They can be prone to vicious bouts of envy if they see others getting the attention they feel they deserve. They frequently display extreme self-confidence. This always helps to gain attention, and it neatly covers up their gaping inner emptiness and their fragmented sense of self. But beware if this confidence is ever truly put to the test.

When it comes to other people in their lives, deep narcissists have an unusual relationship that is hard for us to understand. They tend to see others as extensions of themselves, what is known as *self-objects*. People exist as instruments for attention and validation. Their desire is to control them like they control their own arm or leg. In a relationship, they will slowly make the partner cut off contact with friends—there must be no competition for attention.

Some highly talented deep narcissists (see stories starting on page 54 for examples) manage to find some redemption through their work, channeling their energies and getting the attention they crave through their accomplishments, although they tend to remain quite erratic and volatile. For most deep narcissists, however, it can be difficult to concentrate on their work. Lacking the self-esteem thermostat, they are prone to continually worrying about what others think of them. This makes it hard to actually focus attention outward for long periods of time, and to deal with the impatience and anxiety that comes with work. Such types tend to change jobs and careers quite frequently. This becomes the nail in their coffin—unable to attract genuine recognition through their accomplishments, they are forever thrown back on the need to artificially stimulate attention.

Deep narcissists can be annoying and frustrating to deal with; they can also become quite harmful if we get too close to them. They entangle us in their never-ending dramas and make us feel guilty if we are not continually paying them attention. Relationships with them are most unsatisfying, and having one as a partner or spouse can be deadly. In the end, everything must revolve around them. The best solution in such cases is to get out of their way, once we identify them as a deep narcissist.

There is one variety of this type, however, that is more dangerous and toxic, because of the levels of power he or she can attain—namely the *narcissistic leader*. (This type has been around for a long time. In the Bible, Absalom was perhaps the first recorded example, but we find frequent references in ancient literature to others—Alcibiades, Cicero, and Emperor Nero, to name a few.) Almost all dictator types and tyrannical CEOs fall into this category. They generally have more ambition than the average deep narcissist and for a while can funnel this energy into work. Full of narcissistic self-confidence, they attract attention and followers. They say and do things that other people don't dare say or do, which seems admirable and authentic. They might have a vision for some innovative product, and because they radiate such confidence, they can find others to help them realize their vision. They are experts at using people.

If they have success, a terrible momentum is set in place—more people are attracted to their leadership, which only inflates their grandiose tendencies. If anyone dares to challenge them, they are more prone than others to go into that deep narcissistic rage. They are hypersensitive. They also like to stir up constant drama as a means to justify their power—they are the only ones who can solve the problems they create. This also gives them more opportunities to be the center of attention. The workplace is never stable under their direction.

Sometimes they can become entrepreneurs, people who found a company because of their charisma and ability to attract followers. They can have creative flair as well. But for many of these leader types, eventually their own inner instability and chaos will come to be mirrored in the company or group they lead. They cannot forge a coherent structure or organization. Everything must flow through them. They have to control everything and everyone, their self-objects. They will proclaim this as a virtue—as being authentic and spontaneous—when really they lack the ability to focus and create something solid. They tend to burn and destroy whatever they create.

Let us imagine narcissism as a way of gauging the level of our self-absorption, as if it existed on a measurable scale from high to low. At a certain depth, let us say below the halfway mark on the scale, people enter the realm of deep narcissism. Once they reach this depth, it is very difficult for them to raise themselves back up, because they lack the self-esteem device. The deep narcissist becomes completely self-absorbed, almost always below the mark. If for a moment they manage to engage with others, some comment or action will trigger their inse-curities and they will go plummeting down. But mostly they tend to sink deeper into themselves over time. Other people are instruments. Reality is just a reflection of their needs. Constant attention is their only way of survival.

Above that halfway mark is what we shall call the *functional narcissist*, where most of us reside. We also are self-absorbed, but what prevents us from falling deep into ourselves is a coherent sense of self that we can rely upon and love. (It is ironic that the word *narcissism* has come to mean self-love, when it is in fact the case that the worst narcissists have no cohesive self to love, which is the source of their problem.) This creates some inner resiliency. We may have deeper narcissistic moments, fluctuating below the mark, particularly when depressed or challenged in life, but inevitably we elevate ourselves. Not feeling continually insecure or wounded, not always needing to fish for attention, functional narcissists can turn their attention outward, into their work and into building relationships with people.

Our task, as students of human nature, is threefold. First, we must fully understand the phenomenon of the deep narcissist. Although they are in the minority, some of them can inflict an unusual amount of harm in the world. We must be able to distinguish the toxic types that stir up drama and try to turn us into objects they can use for their purposes. They can draw us in with their unusual energy, but if we become enmeshed, it can be a nightmare to dis-engage. They are masters at turning the tables and making others feel guilty. Narcissistic leaders are the most dangerous of all, and we must resist their pull and see through the façade of their apparent creativity. Knowing how to han-dle the deep narcissists in our lives is an important art for all of us.

Second, we must be honest about our own nature and not deny it. We are all narcissists. In a conversation we are all champing at the bit to talk, to tell our story, to give our opinion. We like people who share our ideas—they reflect back to us our good taste. If we happen to be assertive, we see assertiveness as a positive quality because it is ours, whereas others, more timid, will rate it as obnoxious and value introspective qualities. We are all prone to flattery be-cause of our self-love. Moralizers who try to separate themselves and denounce the narcissists in the world today are often the biggest narcissists of them all— they love the sound of their voice as they point fingers and preach. *We are all on the spectrum of self-absorption.* Creating a self that we can love is a healthy de-velopment, and there should be no stigma attached to it. Without self-esteem from within, we would fall into deep narcissism. But to move beyond functional narcissism, which should be our goal, we must first be honest with ourselves. Trying to deny our self-absorbed nature, trying to pretend we are somehow more altruistic than others, makes it impossible for us to transform ourselves.

Third and most important, we must begin to make the transformation into the *healthy narcissist*. Healthy narcissists have a stronger, even more resilient sense of self. They tend to hover closer to the top of the scale. They recover more quickly from any wounds or insults. They do not need as much validation from others. They realize at some point in life that they have limits and flaws. They can laugh at these flaws and not take slights so personally. In many ways, by embracing the full picture of themselves, their self-love is more real and complete. From this stronger inner position, they can turn their attention outward more often and more easily. This attention goes in one of two directions, and sometimes both. First, they are able to direct their focus and their love into their work, becoming great artists, creators, and inventors. Because their outward focus on the work is more intense, they tend to be successful in their ventures, which gives them the necessary attention and validation. They can have moments of doubt and insecurity, and artists can be notoriously brittle, but work stands as a continual release from too much self-absorption.

The other direction healthy narcissists take is toward people, developing empathic powers. Imagine empathy as the realm lying at the very top of the scale and beyond—complete absorption in others. By our very nature, we humans have tremendous abilities to understand people from the inside out. In our earliest years, we felt completely bonded with our mother, and we could sense her every mood and read her every emotion in a preverbal way. Unlike any other animal or primate, we also had the ability to extend this beyond the mother to other caregivers and people in our vicinity.

This is the physical form of empathy that we feel even to this day with our closest friends, spouses, or partners. We also have a natural ability to take the perspective of others, to think our way inside their minds. These powers largely lie dormant because of our self-absorption. But in our twenties and beyond, feeling more confident about ourselves, we can begin to focus outward, on people, and rediscover these powers. Those who practice this empathy often become superior social observers in the arts or sciences, therapists, and leaders of the highest order.

The need to develop this empathy is greater than ever. Various studies have indicated a gradual increase in levels of self-absorption and narcissism in young people since the late 1970s, with a much higher spike since 2000. Much of this can be attributed to technology and the internet. People simply spend less time in social interactions and more time socializing online, which makes it increasingly difficult to develop empathy and sharpen social skills. Like any skill, empathy comes through the quality of attention. If your attention is continually interrupted by the need to look at your smartphone, you are never really gaining a foothold in the feelings or perspectives of other people. You are continually drawn back to yourself, flitting about the surface of social interactions, never really engaging. Even in a crowd, you remain essentially alone. People come to serve a function—not to bond with but to placate your insecurities.

Our brains were built for continual social interaction; the complexity of this interaction is one of the main factors that drastically increased our intelligence as a species. At a certain point, involving ourselves less with others has a net negative effect on the brain itself and atrophies our social muscle. To make matters worse, our culture tends to emphasize the supreme value of the individual and individual rights, encouraging greater self-involvement. We find more and more people who cannot imagine that others have a different perspective, that we are all not exactly the same in what we desire or think.

You must try to run counter to these developments and create empathic energy. Each side of the spectrum has its peculiar momentum. Deep narcissism tends to sink you deeper, as your connection to reality lessens and you are unable to really develop your work or your relationships. Empathy does the opposite. As you increasingly turn your attention outward, you get constant positive feedback. People want to be around you more. You develop your empathic muscle; your work improves; without trying, you gain the attention that all humans thrive on. Empathy creates its own upward, positive momentum.

The following are the four components that go into the empathic skill set.

The empathic attitude: Empathy is more than anything a state of mind, a different way of relating to others. The greatest danger you face is your general assumption that you really understand people and that you can quickly judge and categorize them. Instead, you must begin with the assumption that you are ignorant and that you have natural biases that will make you judge people incorrectly. The people around you present a mask that suits their purposes. You mistake the mask for reality. Let go of your tendency to make snap judgments. Open your mind to seeing people in a new light. Do not assume that you are similar or that they share your values. Each person you meet is like an undiscovered country, with a very particular psychological chemistry that you will carefully explore. You are more than ready to be surprised by what you uncover. This flexible, open spirit is similar to creative energy—a willingness to consider more possibilities and options. In fact, developing your empathy will also improve your creative powers.

The best place to begin this transformation in your attitude is in your numerous daily conversations. Try reversing your normal impulse to talk and give your opinion, desiring instead to hear the other person's point of view. You have tremendous curiosity in this direction. Cut off your incessant interior monologue as best you can. Give full attention to the other. What matters here is the quality of your listening, so that in the course of the conversation you can mirror back to the other person things they said, or things that were left unsaid but that you sensed. This will have a tremendous seductive effect.

As part of this attitude, you are giving people the same level of indulgence that you give yourself. For instance, we all have a tendency to do the following: When we make a mistake, we attribute it to circumstances that pushed us into doing it. But when others make a mistake, we tend to see it as a character flaw, as something that flowed from their imperfect personality. This is known as the *attribution bias*. You must work against this. With an empathic attitude, you consider first the circumstances that might have made a person do what they did, giving them the same benefit of the doubt as you give yourself.

Finally, adopting this attitude depends on the quality of your self-love. If you feel terribly superior to others, or gripped by insecurities, your moments of empathy and absorption in people will be shallow. What you need is a complete acceptance of your character, including your flaws, which you can see clearly but even appreciate and love. You are not perfect. You are not an angel. You have the same nature as others. With this attitude, you can laugh at yourself and let slights wash over you. From a position of genuine inner strength and resilience, you can more easily direct your attention outward.

Visceral empathy: Empathy is an instrument of emotional attunement. It is hard for us to read or figure out the thoughts of another person, but feelings and moods are much easier for us to pick up. We are all prone to catching the emotions of another person. The physical boundaries between us and other people are much more permeable than we realize. People are continually affecting our moods. What you are doing here is turning this physiological response into knowledge. Pay deep attention to the moods of people, as indicated by their body language and tone of voice. When they talk, they have a feeling tone that is either in sync or not in sync with what they are saying. This tone can be one of confidence, insecurity, defensiveness, arrogance, frustration, elation. This tone manifests itself physically in their voice, their gestures, and their posture. In each encounter, you must try to detect this before even paying attention to what they are saying. This will register to you viscerally, in your own physical response to them. A defensive tone on their part will tend to create a like feeling in you.

A key element you are trying to figure out is people's intentions. There is almost always an emotion behind any intention, and beyond their words, you are attuning yourself to what they want, their goals, which will also register physically in you if you pay attention. For instance, someone you know suddenly shows unusual interest in your life, gives you the kind of attention you've never had before. Is it a real attempt to connect or a distraction, a means of softening you up so they can use you for their own purposes? Instead of focusing on their words, which show interest and excitement, focus on the overall feeling tone that you pick up. How deeply are they listening? Are they making consistent eye contact? Does it feel like even though they are listening to you, they are absorbed in themselves? If you are the object of sudden attention but it seems unreliable, they are probably intending to ask something of you, to use and manipulate you in some way.

This kind of empathy depends largely on mirror neurons—those neurons that fire in our brain when we watch someone do something, such as picking up an object, just as if we were doing it ourselves. This allows us to put ourselves in the shoes of others and to feel what it must be like. Studies have revealed that people who score high on tests of empathy are generally excellent mimics. When someone smiles or winces in pain, they tend to unconsciously imitate the expression, giving them a feel for what others are feeling. When we see someone smiling and in a good mood, it tends to have a contagious effect on us. You can consciously use this power in trying to get into the emotions of others, either by literally mimicking their facial gestures or by conjuring up memories of similar experiences that stirred such emotions. Before Alex Haley began writing *Roots*, he spent some time in the dark interior of a ship, trying to re-create the claustrophobic horror slaves must have experienced. A visceral connection to their feelings allowed him to write himself into their world.

As an adjunct to this, mirroring people on any level will draw out an empathic response from them. This can be physical, and is known as the *chameleon effect*. People who are connecting physically and emotionally in a conversation will tend to mimic each other's gestures and posture, both crossing their legs, for instance. To a degree, you can do this consciously to induce a connection by deliberately mimicking someone. Similarly, nodding your head as they talk and smiling will deepen the connection. Even better, you can enter the spirit of the other person. You absorb their mood deeply and reflect it back to them. You create a feeling of rapport. People secretly crave this emotional rapport in their daily lives, because they get it so rarely. It has a hypnotic effect and appeals to people's narcissism as you become their mirror.

In practicing this type of empathy, keep in mind that you must maintain a degree of distance. You are not becoming completely enmeshed in the emotions of another. This will make it hard for you to analyze what you are picking up and can lead to a loss of control that is not healthy. Also, doing this too strongly and obviously can create a creepy effect. The nodding, smiling, and mirroring at selected moments should be subtle, almost impossible to detect.

Analytic empathy: The reason you are able to understand your friends or partner so deeply is that you have a lot of information about their tastes, values, and family background. We have all had the experience of thinking we know someone but over time having to adjust our original impression once we get more information. So while physical empathy is extremely powerful, it must be supplemented by analytic empathy. This can prove particularly helpful with people toward whom we feel resistant and whom we have a hard time identifying with—either because they are very different from us or because there is something about them that repels us. In such cases we naturally resort to judging and putting them into categories. There are people out there who are not worth the effort—supreme fools or true psychopaths. But for most others who seem hard to figure out, we should see it as an excellent challenge and a way to improve our skills. As Abraham Lincoln said, "I don't like that man. I must get to know him better."

Analytic empathy comes mostly through conversation and gathering information that will allow you to get inside the spirit of others. Some pieces of information are more valuable than others. For instance, you want to get a read on people's values, which are mostly established in their earliest years. People develop concepts of what they consider strong, sensitive, generous, and weak often based on their parents and their relationship to them. One woman will see a man crying as a sign of sensitivity and be attracted to it, while another will see it as weak and repulsive. By not understanding people's values on this level, or by projecting your own, you will misread their reactions and create unnecessary conflicts.

Your goal, then, is to gather as much as you can about the early years of the people you are studying and their relationship to their parents and siblings. Keep in mind that their current relationship to family will also speak volumes about the past. Try to get a read on their reactions to authority figures. This will help you see to what extent they have a rebellious or submissive streak. Their taste in partners will also say a lot.

If people seem reluctant to talk, try asking open-ended questions, or begin with a sincere admission of your own to establish trust. In general people love to talk about themselves and their past, and it is usually quite easy to get them to open up. Look for trigger points (see chapter 1) that indicate points of extreme sensitivity. If they come from another culture, it is all the more important to understand this culture from within their experience. Your goal in general is to find out what makes them unique. You are looking precisely for what is different from yourself and the other people you know.

The empathic skill: Becoming empathetic involves a process, like anything. In order to make sure that you are really making progress and improving your ability to understand people on a deeper level, you need feedback. This can come in one of two forms: direct and indirect. In the direct form, you ask people about their thoughts and feelings to get a sense of whether you have guessed correctly. This must be discreet and based on a level of trust, but it can be a very accurate gauge of your skill. Then there is the indirect form—you sense a greater rapport and how certain techniques have worked for you.

To work on this skill, keep several things in mind: The more people you interact with in the flesh, the better you will get at this. And the greater the variety of people you meet, the more versatile your skill will become. Also, keep a sense of flow. Your ideas about people never quite settle into a judgment. In an encounter, keep your attention active to see how the other person changes over the course of a conversation and the effect you are having on them. Be alive to the moment. Try to see people as they interact with others besides you—people are often very different depending on the person they are involved with. Try to focus not on categories but on the feeling tone and mood that people evoke in you, which is continually shifting. As you get better at this, you will discover more and more cues that people give as to their psychology. You will notice more. Continually mix the visceral with the analytic.

Seeing improvement in your skill level will excite you greatly and motivate you to go deeper. In general you will notice a smoother ride through life, as you avoid unnecessary conflicts and misunderstandings.

> The deepest principle of Human Nature is the craving to be appreciated.
>
> —*William James*

Four Examples of Narcissistic Types

1. The Complete Control Narcissist. When most people first met Joseph Stalin (1879–1953) in the early part of his reign as premier of the Soviet Union, they found him surprisingly charming. Although older than most of his lieutenants, he encouraged them all to address him with the familiar "you" form in Russian. He made himself completely accessible even to junior officials. When he listened to you, it was with such intensity and interest, his eyes boring into you. He seemed to pick up your deepest thoughts and doubts. But his greatest trait was to make you feel important and part of the inner circle of revolutionaries. He would put his arm around you as he accompanied you out of his office, always ending the meeting on an intimate note. As one young man later wrote, people who saw him were "anxious to see him again," because "he created a sense that there was now a bond that linked them forever." Sometimes he would turn slightly aloof, and it would drive his courtiers crazy. Then the mood would pass, and they would bask again in his affection.

Part of his charm lay in the fact that he epitomized the revolution. He was a man of the people, rough and a bit rude but someone an average Russian could identify with. And more than anything, Joseph Stalin could be quite entertaining. He loved to sing and to tell earthy jokes. With these qualities it was no wonder that he slowly amassed power and assumed complete control of the Soviet machinery. But as the years wore on and his power grew, another side to his character slowly leaked out. The apparent friendliness was not as simple as it had seemed. Perhaps the first significant sign of this among his inner circle was the fate of Sergey Kirov, a powerful member of the Politburo and, since the suicide of Stalin's wife in 1932, his closest friend and confidant.

Kirov was an enthusiastic, somewhat simple man who made friends easily and had a way of comforting Stalin. But Kirov was starting to become a little too popular. In 1934, several regional leaders approached him with an offer: they were tired of Stalin's brutal treatment of the peasantry; they were going to instigate a coup and wanted to make Kirov the new premier. Kirov remained loyal—he revealed the plot to Stalin, who thanked him profusely. But something changed in his manner toward Kirov from then on, a coldness that had never been there before.

Kirov understood the predicament he had created—he had revealed to Stalin that he was not as popular as he had thought, and that one person in particular was more liked than him. He felt the danger he was now in. He tried everything he could to assuage Stalin's insecurities. In public appearances he mentioned Stalin's name more than ever; his expressions of praise became more fulsome. This only seemed to make Stalin even more suspicious, as if Kirov were trying too hard to cover up the truth. Now Kirov remembered the many rough jokes he had made at Stalin's expense. At the time, it had been an expression of their closeness that Kirov dared to laugh at him, but now Stalin would certainly see these jokes in a different light. Kirov felt trapped and helpless.

In December 1934, a lone gunman assassinated Kirov outside his office. Although no one could directly implicate Stalin, it seemed almost certain that the killing had his tacit approval. In the years after the assassination, one close friend of Stalin after another was arrested, all of this leading to the great purge within the party during the late 1930s, in which hundreds of thousands lost their lives. Almost all of his top lieutenants caught up in the purge were tortured for a confession, and afterward Stalin would listen eagerly as those who had conducted the torture would tell him of the desperate behavior of his once-brave friends. He laughed at the accounts of how some got down on their knees and, weeping, begged for an audience with Stalin to ask for forgiveness of their sins and to be allowed to live. He seemed to relish their humiliation.

What had happened to him? What had changed this once so congenial man? With his closest friends he could still show unadulterated affection, but in an instant he could turn against them and send them to their deaths. Other odd traits became apparent. Outwardly Stalin was extremely modest. He was the proletariat incarnate. If someone suggested that he be paid some public tribute, he would react angrily—one man should not be the center of so much attention, he would proclaim. But slowly his name and image began to appear everywhere. The newspaper *Pravda* ran stories on his every move, almost deifying him. At a military parade, planes would fly overhead in a formation spelling the name *Stalin*. He denied having any involvement in this growing cult around him, but he did nothing to stop it.

He increasingly spoke of himself in the third person, as if he had become an impersonal revolutionary force, and as such he was infallible. If he happened to mispronounce a word in a speech, every subsequent speaker from then on would have to pronounce it that way. "If I'd said it right," confessed one of his top lieutenants, "Stalin would have felt I was correcting him." And that could prove suicidal.

As it seemed certain that Hitler was preparing to invade the Soviet Union, Stalin began to oversee every detail of the war effort. He continually berated his lieutenants for slackening their efforts: "I am the *only* one dealing with all these problems. . . . I am out there by *myself*," he once complained. Soon many of his generals felt like they were in a double bind: if they spoke their mind he could be terribly insulted, but if they deferred to his opinion he would fly into a rage. "What's the point of talking to you?" he once shouted to a group of generals. "Whatever I say, you reply, 'Yes Comrade Stalin; of course, Comrade Stalin . . . wise decision, Comrade Stalin.'" In his fury at feeling alone in the war effort, he fired his most competent and experienced generals. He now oversaw every detail of the war effort, down to the size and shape of bayonets.

It soon became a matter of life or death for his lieutenants to accurately read his moods and whims. It was critical to never make him anxious, which made him dangerously unpredictable. You had to look him in the eye so that it did not seem like you were hiding something, but if you looked for too long, he became nervous and self-conscious, a very risky blend. You were supposed to take notes when he talked but not write down everything, or you would seem suspicious. Some who were blunt with him did well, while others ended up in prison. Perhaps the answer was to know when to mix in a touch of bluntness but to largely defer. Figuring him out became an arcane science that they would discuss with one another.

The worst fate of all was to be invited to dinner and a late-night movie at his house. It was impossible to refuse such an invitation, and they became more and more frequent after the war. Outwardly it was just like before—a warm, intimate fraternity of revolutionaries. But inwardly it was sheer terror. Here, during all-night drinking bouts (his own drinks were heavily diluted), he would keep a watchful eye on all of his top lieutenants. He forced them to drink more and more so they would lose their self-control. He secretly delighted in their struggles to not say or do anything that would incriminate them.

The worst was toward the end of the evening, when he would pull out the gramophone, play some music, and order the men to dance. He would make Nikita Khrushchev, the future premier, do the *gopak*, a highly strenuous dance that included much squatting and kicking. It would often make Khrushchev sick to his stomach. The others he would have slow dance together while he smiled and laughed uproariously at the sight of grown men dancing as a couple. It was the ultimate form of control: the puppet master choreographing their every move.

Interpretation: The great riddle that Joseph Stalin and his type present is how people who are so deeply narcissistic can also be so charming and, through their charm, gain influence. How can they possibly connect with others when they are so clearly self-obsessed? How are they able to mesmerize? The answer lies in the early part of their careers, before they turn paranoid and vicious.

These types generally have more ambition and energy than the average deep narcissist. They also tend to have even greater insecurities. The only way they can mollify these insecurities and satisfy their ambition is by gaining from others more than the usual share of attention and validation, which can really only come through securing social power in either politics or business. Early on in life, these types stumble upon the best means for doing so. As with most deep narcissists, they are hypersensitive to any perceived slight. They have fine antennae attuned to people to probe their feelings and thoughts—to suss out if there is any hint of disrespect. But what they discover at some point is that this sensitivity can be tuned to others to probe *their* desires and insecurities. Being so sensitive, they can listen to people with deep attention. They can mimic empathy. The difference is that from within, they are impelled not by the need to connect but by the need to control people and manipulate them. They listen and probe you in order to discover weaknesses to play on.

Their attention is not all faked or it would have no effect. In the moment, they can feel camaraderie as they put their arm around your shoulder, but afterward they control and stifle its blossoming into anything real or deeper. If

they did not do so, they would risk losing control of their emotions and opening themselves up to being hurt. They pull you in with a display of attention
and affection, then lure you in deeper with the inevitable coldness that follows.
Did you do or say something wrong? How can you regain their favor? It can be
subtle—it can register in a glance that lasts a second or two—but it has its effect. It is the classic push and pull of the coquette that makes you want to reexperience the warmth you once felt. Combined with the unusually high levels of
confidence displayed by this type, this can have a devastatingly seductive effect
on people and attract followers. Complete control narcissists stimulate your
desire to get closer to them but keep you at arm's distance.

All of this is about control. They control their emotions, and they control
your reactions. At some point, as they get more secure in their power, they will
resent the fact that they had to play the charm game. Why should they have to
pay attention to others when it should be the other way around? So they will
inevitably turn against former friends, revealing the envy and hatred that was
always just below the surface. They control who is in and who is out, who lives
and who dies. By creating double binds in which nothing you say or do will
please them, or by making it seem arbitrary, they terrorize you with this insecurity. They now control *your* emotions.

At some point, they will become total micromanagers—whom can they trust
anymore? People have turned into automatons, incapable of making decisions, so
they must oversee everything. If they reach such extremes, these types will end
up destroying themselves, because it is actually impossible to rid the human animal of free will. People rebel, even the most cowed. In Stalin's last days he suffered a stroke, but none of his lieutenants dared to help him or call for a doctor.
He died from their neglect, as they had come to both fear and loathe him.

You will almost inevitably encounter this type in your life, because through
their ambition they tend to become bosses and CEOs, political figures, cult
leaders. The danger they represent to you is in the beginning, when they first
apply their charm. You can see through them by employing your visceral empathy. Their show of interest in you is never deep, never lasts too long, and is
inevitably followed by a coquettish pullback. If you stop being distracted by
the outward attempt at charm, you can sense this coldness and the degree to
which the attention inevitably flows to them.

Look at their past. You will notice that they do not have one single deep and
intimate relationship in which they exposed any vulnerability. Look for signs

of a troubled childhood. Stalin himself had a father who beat him mercilessly and a rather cold and unloving mother. Listen to people who have seen their true nature and have tried to warn others. Indeed, Stalin's predecessor, Vladimir Lenin, had understood his lethal nature, and on his deathbed he tried to signal this to others, but his warnings went unheeded. Notice the terrified expressions of those who serve such types on a daily basis. If you suspect you are dealing with this type, you must keep your distance. They are like tigers—once you are too close, you cannot get away, and they will devour you.

2. The Theatrical Narcissist. In 1627, the prioress of the Ursuline nuns in Loudun, France, welcomed into the house a new sister, Jeanne de Belciel (1602–1665). Jeanne was a strange creature. Rather dwarfish in size, she had a pretty, angelic face but a malicious glint in her eye. In her previous house she had made a lot of enemies with her continual sarcasm. But to the prioress's surprise, transferred to this new house, Jeanne seemed to undergo a transformation. She now acted like a complete angel, offering to help the prioress in all of her daily tasks. Moreover, given some books to read on Saint Teresa and mysticism, Jeanne became engrossed in the subject. She spent long hours discussing spiritual questions with the prioress. Within months she had become the house expert on mystical theology. She could be seen meditating and praying for hours, more than any other sister. Later that same year the prioress was transferred to another house. Deeply impressed by Jeanne's behavior and ignoring the advice of others who did not think so highly of her, the prioress recommended Jeanne as her replacement. Suddenly, at the very young age of twenty-five, Jeanne now found herself the head of the Ursuline nuns in Loudun.

Several months later, the sisters at Loudun began to hear some very strange stories from Jeanne. She had had a series of dreams, in which a local parish priest, Urbain Grandier, had visited and physically assaulted her. The dreams became increasingly erotic and violent. What was strange was that before these dreams, Jeanne had invited Grandier to become the director of the Ursuline house, but he had politely declined. In Loudun, locals considered Grandier a gallant seducer of young ladies. Was Jeanne merely indulging in her own fantasies? She was so pious that it was hard to believe she was making it all up, and the dreams seemed very real and unusually graphic. Soon after she began telling them to others, several sisters reported having similar dreams. One day the house confessor, Canon Mignon, heard a sister recount such a dream. Mignon, like many others, had long despised Grandier, and he saw in these dreams an opportunity to finally do him in. He called in some exorcists to work on the nuns, and soon almost all of the sisters were reporting nightly visits from Grandier. To the exorcists it was clear—these nuns were possessed by devils under the control of Grandier.

For the edification of the citizenry, Mignon and his allies opened the exorcisms up to the public, who now flocked from far and wide to witness a most entertaining scene. The nuns would roll on the ground, writhing, showing their legs, screaming endless obscenities. And of all the sisters, Jeanne seemed the most possessed. Her contortions were more violent, and the demons that spoke through her were more strident in their satanic oaths. It was one of the strongest possessions they had ever seen, and the public clamored to witness her exorcisms above all the others. It now seemed apparent to the exorcists that Grandier, despite never having set foot in the house or having met Jeanne, had somehow bewitched and debauched the good sisters of Loudun. He was soon arrested and charged with sorcery.

Based on the evidence, Grandier was condemned to death. After much torture, he was burned at the stake on August 18, 1634, before an enormous crowd. Soon the whole business quieted down. The nuns were suddenly cleared of demons—all except Jeanne. The demons were not only refusing to leave her but were gaining a stronger hold on her. The Jesuits, hearing of this notorious possession, decided to take charge of the affair and sent father Jean-Joseph Surin to exorcise her once and for all. Surin found her a fascinating subject. She was completely versed in matters concerning demonology and was clearly despondent at her fate. And yet she did not seem to resist strongly enough the demons who inhabited her. Perhaps she had succumbed to their influence.

One thing was certain: she had taken an unusual liking to Surin and kept him in the house for hours for spiritual discussions. She started to pray and meditate with more energy. She got rid of all possible luxuries: she slept on the hard floor and had vomit-inducing potions of wormwood poured over her food. She reported to Surin her progress and confessed to him "that she had come so near to God that she had received . . . a kiss from his mouth."

With Surin's help, one demon after another fled her body. And then came her first miracle: the name *Joseph* could be read quite clearly in the palm of her left hand. When this faded away after several days, it was replaced by the name of Jesus, and then Mary, and then other names. It was a stigmata, a sign of true grace from God. After this Jeanne fell deeply ill and seemed close to death. She reported being visited by a beautiful young angel with long, flowing blond hair. Then Saint Joseph himself came to her and touched her side, where she felt the greatest pain, and anointed her with a fragrant oil. She recovered, and the oil left a mark on her chemise in the form of five clear drops. The demons were now gone, to Surin's enormous relief. The story was over, but Jeanne surprised him with a strange request: she wanted to go on a tour of Europe, displaying these miracles to one and all. She felt it was her duty to do so. It seemed oddly contradictory to her modest character and ever so slightly worldly, but Surin agreed to accompany her.

In Paris, enormous crowds filled the streets outside her hotel, wanting to catch a glimpse of her. She met Cardinal Richelieu, who seemed quite moved and kissed the fragrant chemise, now a saintly relic. She showed her stigmata to the King and Queen of France. The tour moved on. She met the greatest aristocrats and luminaries of her era. In one town, every day crowds of seven thousand people would enter the convent where she was staying. The demand to hear her story was so intense that she decided to issue a printed booklet in which she described in great detail her possession, her most intimate thoughts, and the miracle that had occurred.

At her death in 1665, the head of Jeanne des Anges, as she was now known, was decapitated, mummified, and placed in a silver-gilt box with crystal windows. It was displayed next to the anointed chemise for those who wanted to see it, at the Ursuline house in Loudun, until its disappearance during the French Revolution.

Interpretation: In her earliest years, Jeanne de Belciel displayed an insatiable appetite for attention. She wearied her parents, who finally got rid of her by sending her to a convent in Poitiers. There she proceeded to drive the nuns insane with her sarcasm and incredible air of superiority. Sent off to Loudun, it seemed she decided to try a different approach to gaining the recognition she so desperately needed. Given books on spirituality, she determined she would excel all others in her knowledge and pious behavior. She made a complete show of both and gained the good favor of the prioress. But as head of the house, she felt bored, and the attention she now received inadequate. Her dreams of Grandier were a mix of fabrication and autosuggestion. Soon after the exorcists arrived, she was given a book on demonology, which she devoured, and knowing the various ins and outs of devil inhabitation, she proceeded to give herself all of the most dramatic traits, which would be picked up by the exorcists as sure signs of possession. She became the star of the public spectacle. While possessed, she went further than all others in her degradation and lewd behavior.

After Grandier's gruesome execution, which profoundly affected the other nuns, who certainly felt guilt at the part they had played in the death of an innocent man, Jeanne alone felt the sudden lack of attention as unbearable and so she upped the ante by refusing to let go of the demons. She had become a master at sensing the weaknesses and hidden desires of those around her—first the prioress, and then the exorcists, and now Father Surin. He wanted so badly to be the one to redeem her that he would fall for the simplest of miracles. As for the stigmata, some later speculated that she had etched these names with acid, or traced them through colored starch. It seemed odd that they appeared only on her left hand, where it would be easy for her to write them out. It is known that in extreme hysteria the skin becomes particularly sensitive, and a fingernail can do the trick. As someone who had long experimented in concocting herbal remedies, it was easy for her to apply fragrant drops. Once people believed in the stigmata, it would be hard for them to doubt the anointment.

Even Surin found the need for a tour dubious. At this point, she could no longer disguise her true appetite for attention. Years later, Jeanne wrote an autobiography in which she admitted to a completely theatrical side to her personality. She was continually playing a part, although she maintained that the final miracle was sincere and real. Many of the sisters who dealt with her on a daily basis saw through the façade and described her as a consummate actress addicted to attention and fame.

One of the strange paradoxes about deep narcissism is that it often goes unnoticed by others, until the behavior becomes too extreme to ignore. The reason for this is simple: deep narcissists can be masters of disguise. They sense early on that if they revealed their true selves to others—their need for constant attention and to feel superior—they would repel people. They use their lack of a coherent self as an advantage. They can play many parts. They can disguise their need for attention through various dramatic devices. They can go further than anyone in seeming moral and altruistic. They never just give or support the right cause— *they make a show of it.* Who wants to doubt the sincerity of this display of morality? Or they go in the opposite direction, reveling in their status as a victim, as someone suffering at the hands of others or neglected by the world. It is easy to get caught up in the drama of the moment, only to suffer later as they consume you with their needs or use you for their purposes. They play on *your* empathy.

Your only solution is to see through the trick. Recognize this type by the fact that the focus always seems to be on them. Notice how they are always superior in supposed goodness or suffering or squalor. See the continual drama and the theatrical quality of their gestures. Everything they do or say is for public consumption. Do not let yourself become collateral damage in their drama.

3. **The Narcissistic Couple.** In 1862, several days before thirty-two-year-old Leo Tolstoy was to wed Sonya Behrs, only eighteen years old at the time, he suddenly decided that there should be no secrets between them. As part of that, he brought her his diaries, and to his surprise, what she read made her weep and get quite angry as well. In these pages he had written about his many previous love affairs, including his ongoing infatuation with a nearby peasant woman with whom he had had a child. He also wrote about the brothels he frequented, the gonorrhea he had caught, and his endless gambling. She felt intense jealousy and disgust at the same time. Why make her read this? She accused him of having second thoughts, of not really loving her. Taken aback by this reaction, he accused her of the same. He wanted to share with her his old ways, so that she would understand he was happily forsaking them for a new life, with her. Why should she rebuke his attempt at honesty? She clearly did not love him as much as he had thought. Why was it so painful for her to say good-bye to her family before the wedding? Did she love them more than him? They managed to reconcile and the wedding took place, but a pattern was set that would continue for forty-eight years.

For Sonya, despite their frequent arguments, the marriage eventually settled into a relatively comfortable rhythm. She had become his most trusted assistant. Besides bearing eight children in twelve years, five of whom survived, she carefully copied out his books for him, including *War and Peace* and *Anna Karenina*, and managed much of the business side of publishing his books. Everything seemed to be going along well enough—he was a rich man, from both the family estates he had inherited and the sales of his books. He had a large family who doted on him. He was famous. But suddenly, at the age of fifty, he felt immensely unhappy and ashamed of the books he had written. He no longer knew who he was. He was undergoing a deep spiritual crisis, and he found the Orthodox Church too strict and dogmatic to help him. His life had to change. He would write no more novels, and henceforth he would live like a common peasant. He would give up his property and renounce all copyrights on his books. And he asked his family to join him in this new life devoted to helping others and to spiritual matters.

To his dismay the family, Sonya leading the way, reacted angrily. He was asking them to give up their style of living, their comforts, and the children's future inheritance. Sonya did not feel the need for any drastic change in their lifestyle, and she resented his accusations that she was somehow evil and materialistic for resisting. They fought and fought, and neither budged. Now when Tolstoy looked at his wife, all he could see was someone who was using him for his fame and his money. That was clearly why she had married him. And when she looked at him, all she could see was a rank hypocrite. Although he had given up his property rights, he continued living like a lord and asking her for money for his habits. He dressed like a peasant, but if he fell ill he would travel to the South in a luxury private railway coach to a villa in which he could convalesce. And despite his new vow of celibacy, he kept making her pregnant.

Tolstoy craved a simple, spiritual life, and she was now the main stumbling block to this. He found her presence in the house oppressive. He wrote her a letter in which he finished by saying, "You attribute what has happened to everything except the one thing, that you are the unwitting, unintentional cause of my sufferings. A struggle to the death is going on between us." Out of his increasing bitterness at her materialistic ways, he wrote the novella *The Kreutzer Sonata*, clearly based on their marriage and painting her in the worst light. For Sonya, the effect of all this was that she felt like she was losing her mind. Finally, in 1894, she snapped. Imitating one of the characters in a Tolstoy story, she decided to commit suicide by walking out into the snow and freezing herself to death. A family member caught up with her and dragged her back to the house. She repeated the attempt twice more, with no better effect.

Now the pattern became sharper and more violent. Tolstoy would push her buttons; she would do something desperate; Tolstoy would feel remorse for his coldness and beg for her forgiveness. He would give in to her on some issues, for instance, allowing the family to retain the copyrights on his earlier books. Then some new behavior on her part would make him regret this. She constantly tried to pit the children against him. She had to read everything he wrote in his diaries, and if he hid them, she would somehow find them and read them on the sly. She watched his every move. He would berate her wildly for her meddling, sometimes falling ill in the process, which made her regret her actions. What was holding them together? Each one craved the acceptance and love of the other, but it seemed impossible to expect that anymore.

After years of suffering through this, in late October of 1910, Tolstoy finally had had enough: in the middle of the night he stole away from the house with a doctor friend accompanying him, determined to finally leave Sonya. He was trembling all the way, in terror of being surprised and overtaken by his wife, but finally he boarded a train and got away from her. When she got the news, Sonya attempted suicide yet again, throwing herself in the nearby pond, only to be rescued just in time. She wrote Tolstoy a letter, begging him to come back. Yes, she would change her ways. She would renounce all luxuries. She would become spiritual. She would love him unconditionally. She could not live without him.

For Tolstoy, his taste of freedom was short-lived. The newspapers were now full of accounts of his running away from his wife. Everywhere the train stopped, reporters, devoted fans, and the curious mobbed him. He could not take anymore the packed and freezing conditions on the train. Soon he fell deathly ill and had to be carried to a stationmaster's cottage near the railway tracks in some out-of-the-way village. In bed, it was clear now he was dying. He heard that Sonya had arrived in town but could not bear the thought of seeing her now. The family kept her outside, where she continued to peer through the window at him as he lay dying. Finally, when he was unconscious, she was allowed in. She knelt beside him, kissed him continually on the forehead, and whispered into his ear, "Forgive me. Please forgive me." He died shortly thereafter. A month later, a visitor to the Tolstoy house reported the following words from Sonya: "What happened to me? What came over me? How could I have done it? . . . You know I killed him."

Interpretation: Leo Tolstoy displayed all of the signs of the deep narcissist. His mother had died when he was two and left a giant hole in him that he could never fill, although he tried to do so with his numerous affairs. He behaved recklessly in his youth, as if this could somehow make him feel alive and whole. He felt continually disgusted with himself and could not figure out who exactly he was. He poured this uncertainty into his novels, assuming different roles in the characters he created. And by the age of fifty, he finally fell into a deep crisis over his fragmented self. Sonya herself rated high on the self-absorption scale. But in looking at people we tend to overemphasize their individual traits and not look at the more complex picture of how each side in a relationship continually shapes the other. A relationship has a life and personality all its own. And a relationship can also be deeply narcissistic, accentuating or even bringing out the narcissistic tendencies of both sides.

What generally makes a relationship narcissistic is the lack of empathy that makes the partners retreat deeper and deeper into their own defensive positions. In the case of the Tolstoys this started right away, with the reading of his diary. Each side had their divergent values through which they viewed the other. To Sonya, raised in a conventional household, this was the act of a man who clearly regretted his marriage proposal; to Tolstoy, the iconoclastic artist, her reaction meant she was incapable of seeing into his soul, of trying to understand his desire for a new married life. They each misunderstood the other and fell into hardened positions that lasted for forty-eight years.

Tolstoy's spiritual crisis epitomized this narcissistic dynamic. If only in that moment they each could have attempted to see this action through the eyes of the other. Tolstoy could have clearly foreseen her reaction. She had lived her whole life in relative comfort, which had helped her manage the frequent pregnancies and upbringing of so many children. She had never been deeply spiritual. Their connection had always been more physical. Why should he expect her to suddenly change? His demands were almost sadistic. He could have simply explained his own side without demanding that she follow him, even expressing his understanding of her own position and needs. That would have revealed true spirituality on his part. And she, instead of focusing only on his hypocrisy, could have seen a man who was clearly unhappy with himself, someone who had never felt loved enough since early childhood and who was undergoing a very real personal crisis. She could have offered her love and support for his new life while gently declining to follow him all the way.

Such use of empathy has the opposite effect of mutual narcissism. Coming from one side, it tends to soften the other one up and invite his or her empathy as well. It is hard to stay in one's defensive position when the other person is seeing and expressing your side and entering your spirit. It beckons you to do the same. Secretly people yearn to let go of their resistance. It is exhausting to continually be so defensive and suspicious.

The key to employing empathy within a relationship is to understand the value system of the other person, which inevitably is different from yours. What they interpret as signs of love or attention or generosity tends to diverge from your way of thinking. These value systems are largely formed in early childhood and are not consciously created by people. Keeping in mind their value system will allow you to enter their spirit and perspective precisely in the moment you would normally turn defensive. Even deep narcissists can be pulled out of their shell in this way, because such attention is so rare. Measure all of your relationships on the narcissism spectrum. It is not one person or the other but the dynamic itself that must be altered.

4. The Healthy Narcissist—the Mood Reader. In October of 1915, the great English explorer Sir Ernest Henry Shackleton (1874–1922) ordered the abandonment of the ship *Endurance*, which had been trapped in an ice floe in Antarctica for over eight months and was beginning to take on water. For Shackleton this meant he essentially had to give up on his great dream of leading his men on the first land crossing of the Antarctic continent. This was to have been the culmination of his illustrious career as an explorer, but now a much greater responsibility weighed on his mind—to somehow get the twenty-seven men of his crew safely back home. Their lives would depend on his daily decisions.

To realize this goal, he faced many obstacles: the harsh winter weather about to hit them, the drifting currents that could pull the ice floe they were to camp on in any direction, the coming days without any light, the dwindling food supplies, the lack of any radio contact or ship to transport them. But the greatest danger of all, the one that filled him with the most dread, was the morale of the men. All it would take was a few malcontents to spread resentment and negativity; soon the men would not work as hard; they would tune him out and lose faith in his leadership. Once that happened, it could be every man for himself, and in this climate that could easily spell disaster and death. He would have to monitor their group spirit even more closely than the changing weather.

The first thing he had to do was get out ahead of the problem and infect the crew with the proper spirit. It all started from the leader. He would have to hide all of his own doubts and fears. The first morning on the ice floe, he got up earlier than anyone and prepared an extra-large helping of hot tea. As he personally served it to the men, he sensed they were looking to him for cues on how to feel about their plight, so he kept the mood light, mixing in some humor about their new home and the coming darkness. It was not the right time to discuss his ideas for getting out of this mess. That would make them too anxious. He would not verbalize his optimism about their chances but would let the men feel it in his manner and body language, even if he had to fake it.

They all knew they were trapped there for the coming winter. What they needed was distractions, something to occupy their minds and keep their spirits up. For that purpose, every day he drew up a duty roster outlining who would be doing what. He tried to mix it up as much as possible, shifting the men around in various groups and making sure they never did the same task too often. For each day there was a simple goal to accomplish—some penguins or seals to hunt, some more stores from the ship to bring to the tents, the construction of a better campground. At the end of the day, they could sit around the campfire feeling they had done something to make their lives a little easier.

As the days wore on, he developed an increasingly sharp attunement to the men's shifting moods. Around the campfire, he would walk up to each man and engage him in a conversation. With the scientists he talked science; with the more aesthetic types he talked of his favorite poets and composers. He got into their particular spirit and was especially attentive to any problems they were experiencing. The cook seemed particularly aggrieved that he would have to kill his pet cat; they were out of food to feed it. Shackleton volunteered to do it for him. It was clear that the physicist on board was having a difficult time with the hard labor; at night he ate slowly and sighed wearily. When Shackleton talked to him, he could feel that his spirit was lowering by the day. Without making him feel like he was shirking, Shackleton changed the roster around to give him lighter but equally important tasks.

He quickly recognized a few weak links in the group. First there was Frank Hurley, the ship's photographer. He was good at his job and never complained about doing other chores, but he was a man who needed to feel important. He had a snobbish bent. So on those first days on the ice, Shackleton made a point of asking Hurley for his opinion on all significant matters, such as food stores, and complimenting him on his ideas. Furthermore he assigned Hurley to his own tent, which both made Hurley feel more important than the others and made it easier for Shackleton to keep an eye on him. The navigator, Huberht Hudson, revealed himself to be very self-centered and a terrible listener. He needed constant attention. Shackleton talked with him more than with any of the others and also brought him into his tent. If there were other men he suspected of being latent malcontents, he spread them around in different tents, diluting their possible influence.

As the winter wore on, he doubled his attentiveness. At certain moments, he could feel the boredom of the men in how they carried themselves, in how they talked less and less to one another. To combat this, he organized sporting events on the ice during the sunless days and entertainments at night—music, practical jokes, storytelling. Every holiday was carefully observed, with a large feast set out for the men. The endless days of drifting somehow were filled with highlights, and soon he began to notice something remarkable: the men were decidedly cheery and even seemed to be enjoying the challenges of life on a drifting ice floe.

At one point the floe they were on had become dangerously small, and so he ordered the men into the three small lifeboats they had salvaged from the *Endurance*. They needed to head for land. He kept the boats together and, braving the rough waters, they managed to land on the nearby Elephant Island, on a narrow patch of beach. As he surveyed the island that day, it was clear the conditions on it were in some ways worse than the ice floe. Time was against them. That same day, Shackleton ordered one boat to be prepared for an extremely risky attempt to reach the most accessible and inhabited patch of land in the area—South Georgia Island, some eight hundred miles to the northeast. The chances of making it were slim, but the men could not survive long on Elephant Island, with its exposure to the sea and the paucity of animals to kill.

Shackleton had to choose carefully the five other men, besides himself, for this voyage. One man he selected, Harry McNeish, was a very odd choice. He was the ship's carpenter and the oldest member of the crew at fifty-seven. He could be grumpy and did not take well to hard labor. Even though it would be an extremely rough journey in their small boat, Shackleton was too afraid to leave him behind. He put him in charge of fitting out the boat for the trip. With this task, he would feel personally responsible for the boat's safety, and on the journey his mind would be continually occupied with keeping track of the boat's seaworthiness.

At one point during the voyage, he noticed McNeish's spirits sinking, and suddenly the man stopped rowing. Shackleton sensed the danger here—if he yelled at McNeish or ordered him to row, he would probably become even more rebellious, and with so few men crowded together for so many weeks with so little food, this could turn ugly. Improvising in the moment, he stopped the boat and ordered the boiling of hot milk for everyone. He said they were all getting tired, including himself, and they needed their spirits lifted. McNeish was spared the embarrassment of being singled out, and for the rest of journey, Shackleton repeated this ploy as often as necessary.

A few miles from their destination, a sudden storm pushed them back. As they desperately looked for a new approach to the island, a small bird kept hovering over them, trying to land on their boat. Shackleton struggled to maintain his usual composure, but suddenly he lost it, standing and swinging wildly at the bird while swearing. Almost immediately he felt embarrassed and sat back down. For fifteen months he had kept all of his frustrations in check for the sake of the men and to maintain morale. He had set the tone. Now was not the time to go back on this. Minutes later, he made a joke at his own expense and vowed to himself never to repeat such a display, no matter the pressure.

After a journey over some of the worst ocean conditions in the world, the tiny boat finally managed to land at South Georgia Island, and several months later, with the help of the whalers who worked there, all of the remaining men on Elephant Island were rescued. Considering the odds against them, the climate, the impossible terrain, the tiny boats, and their meager resources, it was one of the most remarkable survival stories in history. Slowly word spread of the role that Shackleton's leadership had played in this. As the explorer Sir Edmund Hillary later summed it up: "For scientific leadership give me Scott; for swift, efficient travel, Amundsen; but when you are in a hopeless situation, when there seems no way out, get down on your knees and pray for Shackleton."

Interpretation: When Shackleton found himself responsible for the lives of so many men in such desperate circumstances, he understood what would spell the difference between life or death: the men's attitude. This is not something visible. It is rarely discussed or analyzed in books. There are no training manuals on the subject. And yet it was the most important factor of all. A slight dip in their spirit, some cracks in their unity, and it would become too difficult to make the right decisions under such duress. One attempt at getting free of the floe, taken out of the impatience and pressure from a few, would certainly lead to death. In essence, Shackleton was thrown back into the most elemental and primal condition of the human animal—a group in danger, dependent on one another for survival. It was in just such circumstances that our most distant ancestors evolved superior social skills, the uncanny human ability to read the moods and minds of others, and to cooperate. And in the sunless months on the ice floe, Shackleton himself would rediscover these ancient empathic skills that lie dormant in us all, because he had to.

How Shackleton went about this task should serve as the model for all of us. First, he understood the primary role that his own attitude would play in this. The leader infects the group with his mind-set. Much of this occurs on the nonverbal level, as people pick up on the leader's body language and tone of voice. Shackleton imbued himself with an air of complete confidence and optimism and watched how this infected the men's spirit.

Second, he had to divide his attention almost equally between individuals and the group. With the group he monitored levels of chattiness at mealtimes, the amount of swearing he heard during work, how quickly the mood elevated when some entertainment had begun. With individuals he read their emotional states in their tone of voice, how quickly they ate their food, how slowly they rose out of bed. If he noticed a particular mood of theirs that day, he would try to anticipate what they might do by putting himself in a similar mood. He looked for any signs of frustration or insecurity in their words and gestures. He had to treat each person differently, depending on his particular psychology. He also had to constantly adjust his readings, as people's moods shifted quickly.

Third, in detecting any dips in spirit or negativity, he had to be gentle. Scolding would only make people feel ashamed and singled out, which would lead to contagious effects down the road. Better to engage them in talk, to enter their spirit, and to find indirect ways to either elevate their mood or isolate them without making them realize what he was doing. As Shackleton practiced this, he noticed how much better he became at it. In one quick glance in the morning, he could almost anticipate how the men would act during the entire day. Some fellow crew members thought he was psychic.

Understand: What makes us develop these empathic powers is necessity. If we feel our survival depends on how well we gauge the moods and minds of others, then we will find the requisite focus and tap into the powers. Normally we do not feel the need for this. We imagine that we understand quite well the people we deal with. Life can be harsh and we have too many other tasks to attend to. We are lazy and prefer to rely upon predigested judgments. But in fact it *is* a matter of life and death and our success *does* depend on the development of these skills. We simply are not aware of this because we do not see the connection between problems in our lives and our constant misreading of people's moods and intentions and the endless missed opportunities that accrue from this.

The first step, then, is the most important: to realize you have a remarkable social tool that you are not cultivating. The best way to see this is to try it out. Stop your incessant interior monologue and pay deeper attention to people. Attune yourself to the shifting moods of individuals and the group. Get a read on each person's particular psychology and what motivates them. Try to take their perspective, enter their world and value system. You will suddenly become aware of an entire world of nonverbal behavior you never knew existed, as if your eyes could now suddenly see ultraviolet light. Once you sense this power, you will *feel* its importance and awaken to new social possibilities.

I do not ask the wounded person how he feels. . . . I myself become the wounded person.

—Walt Whitman

3

See Through People's Masks

◇

The Law of Role-playing

*P*eople tend to wear the mask that shows them off in the best possible light—humble, confident, diligent. They say the right things, smile, and seem interested in our ideas. They learn to conceal their insecurities and envy. If we take this appearance for reality, we never really know their true feelings, and on occasion we are blindsided by their sudden resistance, hostility, and manipulative actions. Fortunately, the mask has cracks in it. People continually leak out their true feelings and unconscious desires in the nonverbal cues they cannot completely control—facial expressions, vocal inflections, tension in the body, and nervous gestures. You must master this language by transforming yourself into a superior reader of men and women. Armed with this knowledge, you can take the proper defensive measures. On the other hand, since appearances are what people judge you by, you must learn how to present the best front and play your role to maximum effect.

The Second Language

One morning in August 1919 seventeen-year-old Milton Erickson, future pioneer in hypnotherapy and one of the most influential psychologists of the twentieth century, awoke to discover parts of his body suddenly paralyzed. Over the next few days the paralysis spread. He was soon diagnosed with polio, a near epidemic at the time. As he lay in bed, he heard his mother in another room discussing his case with two specialists the family had called in. Assuming Erickson was asleep, one of the doctors told her, "The boy will be dead by morning." His mother came into his room, clearly trying to disguise her grief, unaware that her son had overhead the conversation. Erickson kept asking her to move the chest of drawers near his bed over here, over there. She thought he was delusional, but he had his reasons: he wanted to distract her from her anguish, and he wanted the mirror on the chest positioned just right. If he began to lose consciousness, he could focus on the sunset in the reflected mirror, holding on to this image as long as he could. The sun always returned; maybe he would as well, proving the doctors wrong. Within hours he fell into a coma.

Erickson regained consciousness three days later. Somehow he had cheated death, but now the paralysis had spread to his entire body. Even his lips were paralyzed. He could not move or gesture, nor communicate to others in any way. The only body parts he could move were his eyeballs, allowing him to scan the narrow space of his room. Quarantined in the house on the farm in rural Wisconsin where he grew up, his only company was his seven sisters, his one brother, his parents, and a private nurse. For someone with such an active mind, the boredom was excruciating. But one day as he listened to his sisters talking among themselves, he became aware of something he had never noticed before. As they talked, their faces made all kinds of movements, and the tone of their voices seemed to have a life of its own. One sister said to another, "Yes, that's a good idea," but she said this in a monotone and with a noticeable smirk, all of which seemed to say, "I actually don't think it's a good idea at all." Somehow a *yes* could really mean no.

Now he paid attention to this. It was a stimulating game. In the course of the next day he counted sixteen different forms of *no* that he heard, indicating various degrees of hardness, all accompanied by different facial expressions. At one point he noticed one sister saying yes to something while actually shaking her head no. It was very subtle, but he saw it. If people said yes but really felt no, it appeared to show up in their grimaces and body language. On another occasion he watched closely from the corner of his eye as one sister offered another an apple, but the tension in her face and tightness in her arms indicated she was just being polite and clearly wanted to keep it for herself. This signal was not picked up, and yet it seemed so clear to him.

Unable to participate in conversations, he found his mind completely absorbed in observing people's hand gestures, their raised eyebrows, the pitch of their voices, and the sudden folding of their arms. He noticed, for instance, how often the veins in his sisters' necks would begin to pulsate when they stood over him, indicating the nervousness they felt in his presence. Their breathing patterns as they spoke fascinated him, and he discovered that certain rhythms indicated boredom and were generally followed by a yawn. Hair seemed to play an important role with his sisters. A very deliberate brushing back of strands of hair would indicate impatience—"I've heard enough; now please shut up." But a quicker, more unconscious stroke could indicate rapt attention.

Trapped in bed, his hearing became more acute. He could now pick up conversations in the other room, where people were not trying to put on a pleasant show in front of him. And soon he noticed a peculiar pattern—in a conversation people were rarely direct. A sister could spend minutes beating around the bush, leaving hints to others about what she really wanted—such as to borrow an article of clothing or hear an apology from someone. Her hidden desire was clearly indicated by her tone of voice, which gave emphasis to certain words. Her hope was that the others would pick this up and offer what she desired, but often the hints were ignored and she would be forced to come out and say what she wanted. Conversation after conversation fell into this recurring pattern. Soon it became a game for him to guess within as few seconds as possible what the sister was hinting at.

It was as if in his paralysis he had suddenly become aware of a second channel of human communication, a second language in which people expressed something from deep within themselves, sometimes without being aware of it. What would happen if he could somehow master the intricacies of this language? How would it alter his perception of people? Could he extend his reading powers to the nearly invisible gestures people made with their lips, their breath, the level of tension in their hands?

One day several months later, as he sat near a window in a special reclining chair his family had designed for him, he listened to his brother and sisters playing outside. (He had regained movement in his lips and could speak, but his body remained paralyzed.) He wanted so desperately to join them. As if momentarily forgetting his paralysis, in his mind he began to stand up, and for a brief second he experienced the twitching of a muscle in his leg, the first time he had felt any movement in his body at all. The doctors had told his mother he would never walk again, but they had been wrong before. Based on this simple twitch, he decided to try an experiment. He would focus deeply on a particular muscle in his leg, remembering the sensation he had before his paralysis, wanting badly to move it, and imagining it functioning again. His nurse would massage that area, and slowly, with intermittent success, he would feel a twitch and then the slightest bit of movement returning to the muscle. Through this excruciatingly slow process he taught himself to stand, then take a few steps, then walk around his room, then walk outside, increasing the distances.

Somehow, by drawing upon his willpower and imagination, he was able to

alter his physical condition and regain complete movement. Clearly, he realized, the mind and the body operate together, in ways we are hardly aware of.
Wanting to explore this further, he decided to pursue a career in medicine and
psychology, and in the late 1920s he began to practice psychiatry in various
hospitals. Quickly he developed a method that was completely his own and
diametrically opposed to others trained in the field. Almost all practicing psychiatrists focused largely on words. They would get patients to talk, particularly going over their early childhood. In this way they hoped to gain access to
their patients' unconscious. Erickson instead focused mostly on people's physical presence as an entrée into their mental life and unconscious. Words are often
used as a cover-up, a way to conceal what is really going on. Making his patients completely comfortable, he would detect signs of hidden tension and
unmet desires that came through in their face, voice, and posture. As he did
this, he explored in greater depth the world of nonverbal communication.

His motto was "observe, observe, observe." For this purpose he kept a notebook, writing down all of his observations. One element that particularly fascinated him was the walking styles of people, perhaps a reflection of his own
difficulties in relearning how to use his legs. He would watch people walking in
every part of the city. He paid attention to the heaviness of the step—there was
the emphatic walk of those who were persistent and full of resolve;
the light step of those who seemed more indecisive; the loping, fluid walk
of those who seemed rather lazy; the meandering walk of the person lost in
thought. He observed closely the extra swaying of the hips or the strut that
seemed to elevate the head, indicating high levels of confidence in a person. There
was the walk that people put on to cover up some weakness or insecurity—the
exaggerated masculine stride, the nonchalant shuffle of the rebellious teenager.
He took note of the sudden changes in people's walk as they became excited or
nervous. All of this supplied him endless information about people's moods and
self-confidence.

In his office, he placed his desk at the far end of the room, making his patients walk toward him. He would notice changes in the walk from before to
after the session. He would scrutinize their way of sitting down, the level of
tension in their hands as they grasped the arms of the chair, the degree to which
they would face him as they talked, and in a matter of a few seconds, without
words being exchanged, he had a profound read on their insecurities and rigidi-
ties, as mapped clearly in their body language.

At one point in his career, Erickson worked in a ward for the mentally disturbed. In one instance the psychologists there were perplexed by the case of a particular patient—a former businessman who had made a fortune and then lost everything because of the Depression. All the man could do was cry and continually move his hands back and forth, straight out from his chest. Nobody could figure out the source of this tic or how to help him. Getting him to talk was not easy and it led nowhere. To Erickson, however, the moment he saw the man he understood the nature of the problem—through this gesture he was literally expressing the futile efforts in his life to get ahead and the despair this had brought him. Erickson went up to him and said, "Your life has had many ups and downs," and as he did so, he shifted the motion of the arms to up and down. The man seemed interested in this new motion and it now became his tic.

Working with an occupational therapist on site, Erickson placed blocks of sandpaper in each of the man's hands and put a rough piece of lumber in front of him. Soon the man became enthralled with the sanding of the wood and the smell of it as he polished it. He stopped crying and took woodworking classes, carving elaborate chess sets and selling them. By focusing exclusively on his body language and altering his physical motion, Erickson could alter the locked position of his mind and cure him.

One category that fascinated him was the difference in nonverbal communication between men and women and how this reflected a different way of thinking. He was particularly sensitive to the mannerisms of women, perhaps a reflection of the months he had spent closely observing his sisters. He could dissect every nuance of their body language. One time, a beautiful young woman came to see him, saying she had seen various psychiatrists but none of them were quite right. Could Erickson possibly be the right one? As she talked some more, never discussing the nature of her problem, Erickson watched her pick some lint off her sleeve. He listened and nodded, then posed some rather uninteresting questions.

Suddenly, out of the blue, he said in a very confident tone that he was the right, in fact the only psychiatrist for her. Taken aback by his conceited attitude, she asked him why he felt that way. He said he needed to ask her one more question in order to prove it.

"How long," he asked, "have you been wearing women's clothes?"

"How did you know?" the man asked in astonishment. Erickson explained that he had noticed the way he had picked off the lint, without making a naturally wide detour around the breast area. He had seen that motion too many times to be fooled by anything else. In addition, his assertive way of discussing his need to test Erickson first, all expressed in a very staccato vocal rhythm, was decidedly masculine. All of the other psychiatrists had been taken in by the young man's extremely feminine appearance and the voice he had worked on so carefully, but the body does not lie.

On another occasion Erickson entered his office to see a new female patient waiting for him. She explained that she had sought him out because she had a phobia of flying. Erickson interrupted her. Without explaining why, he asked her to leave the office and reenter. She seemed annoyed but complied, and he studied her walk closely, as well as her posture as she settled into the chair. He then asked her to explain her problem.

"My husband is taking me a-broad in September and I have a deathly fear of being on an airplane."

"Madam," Erickson said, "when a patient comes to a psychiatrist there can be no withholding of information. I know something about you. I am going to ask you an unpleasant question. . . . Does your husband know about your love affair?"

"No," she said with astonishment, "but how did you?"

"Your body language told me." He explained how her legs were crossed in a very tight position, with one foot completely tucked around the ankle. In his experience, every married woman having an affair locks her body up in a similar way. And she had clearly said "a-broad" instead of "abroad," in a hesitant tone, as if she were ashamed of herself. And her walk indicated a woman who felt trapped in complicated relationships. In subsequent sessions she brought in her lover, who was also married. Erickson asked to see the wife of the lover, and when she came, she sat in the exact same locked position, with the foot under the ankle.

"So you're having an affair," he told her.

"Yes, did my husband tell you?"

"No, I got it from your body language. Now I know why your husband suffers from chronic headaches." Soon he was treating them all and helping them out of their locked and painful positions.

Over the years, his observation powers extended to elements of nonverbal communication that were nearly imperceptible. He could determine people's states of mind by their breathing patterns, and by mirroring these patterns himself he could lead the patient into a hypnotic trance and create a feeling of deep rapport. He could read subliminal and subvocal speech as people would mouth a word or name in a barely visible manner. This was how fortune-tellers, psychics, and some magicians would make a living. He could tell when his secretary was menstruating by the heaviness of her typing. He could guess the career backgrounds of people by the quality of their hands, the heaviness of their step, the way they tilted their heads, and their vocal inflections. To patients and friends it seemed as if Erickson possessed psychic powers, but they were simply unaware of how long and hard he had studied this, gaining mastery of the second language.

Interpretation: For Milton Erickson, his sudden paralysis opened his eyes to not only a different form of communication but also a completely different way of relating to people. When he listened to his sisters and picked up new information from their faces and voices, he not only registered this with his senses but also felt himself experiencing some of what was going on in their minds. He had to imagine why they said yes but really meant no, and in doing so he had to momentarily feel some of their contrary desires. He had to see the tension in their necks and register it physically as tension within himself to understand why they were suddenly uncomfortable in his presence. What he discovered is that nonverbal communication cannot be experienced simply through thinking and translating thoughts into words but must be felt physically as one engages with the facial expressions or locked positions of other people. It is a different form of knowledge, one that connects with the animal part of our nature and involves our mirror neurons.

To master this language, he had to relax and control the continual need to interpret with words or categorize what he was seeing. He had to tamp down his ego—thinking less of what he wanted to say and instead directing his attention outward into the other person, attuning himself to their changing moods as reflected in their body language. As he discovered, such attention changed him. It made him more alive to the signs people continually emit and transformed him into a superior social actor, capable of connecting to others' inner lives and developing greater rapport.

As Erickson progressed in this self-transformation, he noticed that most people go in the opposite direction—becoming more self-absorbed and unobservant with each passing year. He liked to accumulate anecdotes from his work that demonstrated this. For instance, he once asked a group of interns in the hospital where he worked to silently observe an elderly woman lying under the covers in a hospital bed until they saw something that would indicate a possible diagnosis for her bedridden condition. They watched her for three hours to no avail, none of them taking notice of the obvious fact that both her legs had been amputated. Or there were the people who attended his public lectures; many of them would ask why he never used that strange-looking pointer he carried in his hand as part of his presentation. They had failed to observe his rather noticeable limp and need for a cane. As Erickson saw it, the harshness of life makes most people turn inward. They have no mental space left over for simple observations, and the second language largely passes them by.

Understand: We are the preeminent social animal on the planet, depending on our ability to communicate with others for our survival and success. It is estimated that over 65 percent of all human communication is nonverbal but that people pick up and internalize only about 5 percent of this information. Instead, almost all of our social attention is absorbed by what people say, which more often than not actually serves to conceal what they are really thinking and feeling. Nonverbal cues tell us what people are trying to emphasize with their words and the subtext of their message, the nuances of communication. These cues tell us what they are actively hiding, their real desires. They reflect in an immediate way people's emotions and moods. To miss this information is to operate blindly, to invite misunderstanding, and to lose endless opportunities to influence people by not noticing the signs of what they really want or need.

Your task is simple: First you must recognize your state of self-absorption and how little you actually observe. With this understanding you will be motivated to develop observation skills. Second you must understand, as Erickson did, the different nature of this form of communication. It requires opening up your senses and relating to people more on the physical level, absorbing their physical energy and not just their words. You do not simply observe their facial expression, but you register it from within, so that the impression stays with you and communicates. As you gain greater vocabulary in this language, you will be able to correlate a gesture with a possible emotion. As your sensitivity increases, you will begin to notice more and more of what you have been missing. And equally important, you will discover a new and deeper way of relating to people, with the increased social powers this will bring you.

You will always be the prey or the plaything of the devils and fools in this world, if you expect to see them going about with horns or jangling their bells. And it should be borne in mind that, in their

> intercourse with others, people are like the moon: they show you
> only one of their sides. Every man has an innate talent for . . .
> making a mask out of his physiognomy, so that he can always look
> as if he really were what he pretends to be . . . and its effect is
> extremely deceptive. He dons his mask whenever his object is to
> flatter himself into some one's good opinion; and you may pay just
> as much attention to it as if it were made of wax or cardboard.

—Arthur Schopenhauer

Keys to Human Nature

We humans are consummate actors. We learn at an early age how to get what
we want from our parents by putting on certain looks that will elicit sympathy
or affection. We learn how to conceal from our parents or siblings exactly what
we're thinking or feeling, to protect ourselves in vulnerable moments. We become good at flattering those whom it is important to win over—popular
peers or teachers. We learn how to fit into the group by wearing the same
clothes and speaking the same language. As we get older and strive to carve out
a career, we learn how to create the proper front in order to be hired and to fit
into a group culture. If we become an executive or a professor or a bartender,
we must act the part.

Imagine a person who never develops these acting skills, whose face instantly grimaces when he dislikes what you say or cannot suppress a yawn
when you fail to entertain him, who always speaks his mind, who completely
goes his own way in his ideas and style, who acts the same whether he's talking
to his boss or to a child, and you have imagined a person who would be shunned,
ridiculed, and despised.

We are all such good actors that we're not even aware of this as it happens.
We imagine we are almost always being sincere in our social encounters, which
any good actor will tell you is the secret behind really believable acting. We
take these skills for granted, but to see them in action, try to look at yourself as
you interact with different members of your family and with your boss and
colleagues at work. You will see yourself subtly changing what you say, your
tone of voice, your mannerisms, your whole body language, to suit each

individual and situation. For people you are trying to impress, you wear a much different face than with those with whom you are familiar and can let down your guard. You do this almost without thinking.

Over the centuries various writers and thinkers, looking at humans from an outside perspective, have been struck by the theatrical quality of social life. The most famous quote expressing this comes from Shakespeare: "All the world's a stage, / And all the men and women merely players; / They have their exits and their entrances, / And one man in his time plays many parts." If the theater and actors were traditionally represented by the image of masks, writers such as Shakespeare are implying that all of us are constantly wearing masks. Some people are better actors than others. Villainous types such as Iago in the play *Othello* are able to conceal their hostile intentions behind a friendly, benign smile. Others are able to act with more confidence and bravado—they often become leaders. People with consummate acting skills can better navigate our complex social environments and get ahead.

Although we are all expert actors, at the same time we secretly experience this need to act and play a part as a burden. We are the most successful social animal on the planet. For hundreds of thousands of years our hunter-gatherer ancestors could survive only by constantly communicating with one another through nonverbal cues. Developed over so much time, before the invention of language, that is how the human face became so expressive, and gestures so elaborate. This is bred deep within us. We have a continual desire to communicate our feelings and yet at the same time the need to conceal them for proper social functioning. With these counterforces battling inside us, we cannot completely control what we communicate. Our real feelings continually leak out in the form of gestures, tones of voice, facial expressions, and posture. We are not trained, however, to pay attention to people's nonverbal cues. By sheer habit, we fixate on the words people say, while also thinking about what we'll say next. What this means is that we are using only a small percentage of the potential social skills we all possess.

Imagine, for instance, conversations with people you've recently met. By paying extra-close attention to the nonverbal cues they emit, you can pick up their moods and mirror these moods back to them, getting them to unconsciously relax in your presence. As the conversation progresses, you can pick up signs that they are responding to your gestures and mirroring, which gives you license to go further and deepen the spell. In this way, you can build up rapport and win over a valuable ally. Conversely, imagine people who almost immediately reveal signs of hostility toward you. You are able to see through their fake, tight smiles, to pick up the flashes of irritation that cross their face and the signs of subtle discomfort in your presence. Registering all this as it happens, you can then politely disengage from the interaction and remain wary of them, looking for further signs of hostile intentions. You have probably saved yourself from an unnecessary battle or an ugly act of sabotage.

Your task as a student of human nature is twofold: First, you must understand and accept the theatrical quality of life. You do not moralize and rail against the role-playing and the wearing of masks so essential to smooth social functioning. In fact, your goal is to play your part on the stage of life with consummate skill, attracting attention, dominating the limelight, and making yourself into a sympathetic hero or heroine. Second, you must not be naive and mistake people's appearances for reality. You are not blinded by people's acting skills. You transform yourself into a master decoder of their true feelings, working on your observation skills and practicing them as much as you can in daily life.

And so, for these purposes, there are three aspects to this particular law: understanding *how* to observe people; learning some basic keys for decoding nonverbal communication; and mastering the art of what is known as *impression management*, playing your role to maximum effect.

Observational Skills

When we were children, we were almost all great observers of people. Because we were small and weak, our survival depended on decoding people's smiles and tones of voice. We were often struck by the peculiar walking styles of adults, their exaggerated smiles and affected mannerisms. We would imitate them for fun. We could sense that an individual was threatening from something in his or her body language. This is why children are the bane of inveterate liars, con artists, magicians, and people who pretend to be something they are not. Children quickly see through their front. Slowly, from the age of five onward, this sensitivity is lost as we start to turn inward and become more concerned with how others see us.

You must realize that it is not a matter of acquiring skills you do not possess but rather of rediscovering those you once had in your earliest years. This means slowly reversing the process of self-absorption and regaining that outward-directed view and curiosity you had as a child.

As with any skill, this will require patience. What you are doing is slowly rewiring your brain through practice, mapping new neuronal connections. You do not want to overload yourself in the beginning with too much information. You need to take baby steps, to see small but daily progress. In a casual conversation with someone, give yourself the goal of observing one or two facial expressions that seem to go against what the person is saying or indicate some additional information. Be attentive to microexpressions, quick flashes on the face of tension, or forced smiles (see the next section for more on this). Once you succeed in this simple exercise with one person, try it with someone else, always focusing on the face. Once you find it easier to notice cues from the face, attempt to make a similar observation about an individual's voice, noting any changes in pitch or the pace of talking. The voice says a lot about people's level of confidence and their contentment. Later on graduate to elements of body language—such as posture, hand gestures, positioning of legs. Keep these exercises simple, having simple goals. Write down any observations, particularly any patterns you notice.

As you practice these exercises, you must be relaxed and open to what you see, not champing at the bit to interpret your observations with words. You must be engaged in the conversation while talking less and trying to get them to talk more. Try to mirror them, making comments that play off something they have said and reveal you are listening to them. This will have the effect of making them relax and want to talk more, which will make them leak out more nonverbal cues. But your observing of people must never be obvious. Feeling scrutinized, people will freeze up and try to control their expressions. Too much direct eye contact will betray you. You must appear natural and attentive, using only quick peripheral glances to notice any changes in the face, voice, or body.

In observing any particular individual over time, you need to establish their baseline expression and mood. Some people are naturally quiet and reserved, their facial expression revealing this. Some are more animated and energetic, while still others continually wear an anxious look. Aware of a person's usual demeanor, you can pay greater attention to any deviations—for instance, sudden animation in someone who is generally reserved, or a relaxed look from the habitually nervous. Once you know a person's baseline, it will be much easier to see signs of dissimulation or distress in them. The ancient Roman Mark Antony was naturally a jovial person, always smiling, laughing, and poking fun at people. It was when he suddenly turned silent and sullen in their meetings after the assassination of Julius Caesar that Antony's rival Octavius (later Augustus) understood that Antony was up to something and had hostile intentions.

Related to the baseline expression, try to observe the same person in different settings, noticing how their nonverbal cues change if they are talking to a spouse, a boss, an employee.

For another exercise, observe people who are about to do something exciting—a trip to some alluring place, a date with someone they've been pursuing, or any event for which they have high expectations. Note the looks of anticipation, how the eyes open wider and stay there, the face flushed and generally animated, a slight smile on the lips as they think of what's about to come. Contrast this with the tension exhibited by a person about to take a test or go on a job interview. You are increasing your vocabulary when it comes to correlating emotions and facial expressions.

Pay great attention to any mixed signals you pick up: a person professes to love your idea, but their face shows tension and their tone of voice is strained; or they congratulate you on your promotion, but the smile is forced and the expression seems sad. Such mixed signals are very common. They can also involve different parts of the body. In the novel *The Ambassadors* by Henry James, the narrator notices that a woman who has visited him smiles at him during most of the conversation but holds her parasol with a great deal of tension. Only by noticing this can he sense her real mood—discomfort. With mixed signals, you need to be aware that a greater part of nonverbal communication involves the leakage of negative emotions, and you need to give greater weight to the negative cue as indicative of the person's true feelings. At some point, you can then ask yourself why they might feel sadness or antipathy.

To take your practice further, try a different exercise. Sit in a café or some public space, and without the burden of having to be involved in a conversation, observe the people around you. Listen in on their conversations for vocal cues. Take note of walking styles and overall body language. If possible, take notes. As you get better at this, you can try to guess people's profession by the cues you pick up, or something about their personality from their body language. It should be a pleasurable game.

As you progress, you will be able to split your attention more easily—listening attentively to what people have to say, but also taking careful note of nonverbal cues. You will also become aware of signals you had not noticed before, continually expanding your vocabulary. Remember that everything people do is a sign of some sort; there is no such thing as a gesture that does not communicate. You will pay attention to people's silences, the clothes they wear, the arrangement of objects on their desk, their breathing patterns, the tension in certain muscles (particularly in the neck), the subtext in their conversations—what is not said or what is implied. All of these discoveries should excite and impel you to go further.

In practicing this skill you must be aware of some common errors you can fall into. Words express direct information. We can argue about what people mean when they say something, but the interpretations are fairly limited. Non-verbal cues are much more ambiguous and indirect. There is no dictionary to tell you what this or that means. It depends on the individual and the context. If you are not careful, you will glean signs but quickly interpret them to fit your own emotional biases about people, which will make your observations not only useless but also dangerous. If you are observing someone you naturally dislike, or who reminds you of someone unpleasant in your past, you will tend to see almost any cue as unfriendly or hostile. You will do the opposite for people you like. In these exercises you must strive to subtract your personal preferences and prejudices about people.

Related to this is what is known as *Othello's error.* In the play *Othello* by Shakespeare, the main character, Othello, assumes that his wife, Desdemona, is guilty of adultery based on her nervous response when questioned about some evidence. In truth Desdemona is innocent, but the aggressive, paranoid nature of Othello and his intimidating questions make her nervous, which he interprets as a sign of guilt. What happens in such cases is that we pick up certain emotional cues from the other person—nervousness, for instance—and we assume they come from a certain source. We rush to the first explanation that fits what we want to see. But the nervousness could have several explanations, could be a temporary reaction to our questioning or the overall circumstances. The error is not in the observing but in the decoding.

In 1894 Alfred Dreyfus, a French military officer, was wrongly arrested for passing along secrets to the Germans. Dreyfus was a Jew, and many French at the time had anti-Semitic feelings. When first appearing before the public for questioning, Dreyfus answered in a calm, efficient tone that was part of his training as a bureaucrat and was also a result of his trying to contain his nervousness. Most of the public assumed that an innocent man would protest loudly. His demeanor was seen as a sign of his guilt.

Keep in mind that people from different cultures will consider different forms of behavior acceptable. These are known as *display rules*. In some cultures people are conditioned to smile less or touch more. Or their language involves greater emphasis on vocal pitch. Always consider the cultural background of people, and interpret their cues accordingly.

As part of your practice, try to observe yourself as well. Notice how often and when you tend to put on a fake smile, or how your body registers nervousness—in your voice, the drumming of your fingers, the twiddling with your hair, the quivering of your lips, and so on. Becoming acutely aware of your own nonverbal behavior will make you more sensitive and alert to the signals of others. You will be better able to imagine the emotions that go with the cue. And you will also gain greater control of your nonverbal behavior, something very valuable for playing the right social role (see the last section of this chapter).

Finally, in developing these observational skills you will notice a physical change in yourself and in your relation to people. You will become increasingly sensitive to people's shifting moods and even anticipate them as you feel inside something of what they're feeling. Taken far enough, such powers can make you seem almost psychic, as they did with Milton Erickson.

Decoding Keys

Remember that people are generally trying to present the best possible front to the world. This means concealing their possible antagonistic feelings, their desires for power or superiority, their attempts at ingratiation, and their insecurities. They will use words to hide their feelings and distract you from the reality, playing on people's verbal fixation. They will also use certain facial expressions that are easy to put on and that people assume mean friendliness. Your task is to look past the distractions and become aware of those signs that leak out automatically, revealing something of the true emotion beneath the mask. The three categories of the most important cues to observe and identify are *dislike/ like*, *dominance/submission*, and *deception*.

Dislike/like cues: Imagine the following scenario: Someone in a group dislikes you, whether out of envy or mistrust, but in the group environment they cannot express this overtly or they will look bad—not a team player. And so they smile at you, engage you in conversation, and even seem to support your ideas. At times you might feel something is not quite right, but the signs are subtle and you forget them as you pay attention to the front they present. Then suddenly, as if out of the blue, they obstruct you or display an ugly attitude. The mask has come off. The price you pay is not only difficulties in your work or personal life, but also the emotional toll, which can have a lingering effect.

Understand: People's hostile or resistant actions never come out of the blue. There are always signs before they take any action. It is too much of a strain for them to completely suppress such strong emotions. The problem is not only that we are not paying attention but also that we inherently do not like the thought of conflict or disagreement. We prefer to avoid thinking about it and to assume that people are on our side, or at least neutral. Most often, we *feel* something is not quite right with the other person but ignore the feeling. We must learn to trust such intuitive responses and to look for those signs that should trigger a closer examination of the evidence.

People give out clear indications in their body language of active dislike or hostility. These include the sudden squinting of the eyes at something you have said, the glare, the pursing of the lips until they nearly disappear, the stiff neck, the torso or feet that turn away from you while you are still engaged in a conversation, the folding of the arms as you try to make a point, and an overall tenseness in the body. The problem is that you will not usually see such signs unless a person's displeasure has become too strong to conceal at all. Instead, you must train yourself to look for the microexpressions and the other more subtle signs that people give out.

The microexpression is a recent discovery among psychologists who have been able to document its existence through film. It lasts less than a second. There are two varieties of this: The first comes when people are aware of a negative feeling and try to suppress it, but it leaks out in a fraction of a second. The other comes when we are unaware of their hostility and yet it shows itself in quick flashes on the face or in the body. These expressions will be a momentary glare, tensing of the facial muscles, pursing of the lips, the beginnings of a frown or sneer or look of contempt, with the eyes looking down. Aware of this phenomenon, we can look for these expressions. You will be surprised at how often they occur, because it is nearly impossible to completely control the facial muscles and repress the signs in time. You must be relaxed and attentive, not obviously looking for them but catching them out of the corner of your eye. Once you begin to notice such expressions, you will find it easier to catch them.

Equally eloquent are those signs that are subtle but can last for several seconds, revealing tension and coldness. For instance, when you first approach someone who harbors negative thoughts toward you, if you surprise them by coming up on them from an angle, you will clearly see signs of displeasure at your approach before they have had time to fit on their affable mask. They are not so happy to see you and it shows for a second or two. Or you are expressing a strong opinion and their eyes begin to roll, which they try to quickly cover up with a smile.

Sudden silence can say a lot. You have said something that triggers a twinge of envy or dislike, and they cannot help but lapse into silence and brood. They may try to hide this with a smile as they inwardly fume. As opposed to simple shyness or having nothing to say, you will detect definite signs of irritation. In this case, it is best to notice this a few times before coming to any conclusions.

People will often give themselves away with the mixed signal—a positive comment to distract you but some clearly negative body language. This offers them relief from the tension of always having to be pleasant. They are betting on the fact that you will tend to focus on the words and gloss over the grimace or lopsided smile. Pay attention as well to the opposite configuration—someone says something sarcastic and pointed, directed at you, but they do this with a smile and a jokey tone of voice, as if to signal it is all in good humor. It would be impolite to not take it in this vein. But in fact, particularly if this occurs a few times, you should pay attention to the words and not the body language. It is their repressed way of expressing their hostility. Take notice of people who praise or flatter you without their eyes lighting up. This could be a sign of hidden envy.

In the novel *The Charterhouse of Parma* by Stendhal, Count Mosca receives an anonymous letter designed to stir up jealous feelings about his mistress, whom he is desperately in love with. In thinking over who could have sent it, he recalls a conversation earlier that day with the Prince of Parma. The prince was talking about how the pleasures of power pale in comparison with the pleasures afforded by love, and as he said this, the count detected a particularly malicious glint in his eye, accompanied by an ambiguous smile. The words were about love in general but the look was directed at him. From that he correctly deduces that the prince had sent the letter; he could not completely contain his venomous glee at what he had done, and it had leaked out. This is a variation on the mixed signal. People say something relatively strong about a general topic, but with subtle looks they point at you.

An excellent gauge for decoding antagonism is to compare people's body language toward you and toward others. You might detect that they are noticeably friendlier and warmer toward other people and then put on a polite mask with you. In a conversation they cannot help showing brief flashes of impatience and irritation in their eyes, but only when you talk. Also keep in mind that people will tend to leak out more of their true feelings, and certainly hostile ones, when they are drunk, sleepy, frustrated, angry, or under stress. They will later tend to excuse this, as if they weren't themselves for the moment, but in fact they were actually being more themselves than ever.

In looking for these signs, one of the best methods is to set up tests, even traps for people. King Louis XIV was a master of this. He stood at the top of a court in Versailles filled with members of the nobility seething with hostility and resentment toward him and the absolute authority he was trying to impose. But in the civilized realm of Versailles they all had to be consummate actors and hide their feelings, particularly toward the king. Louis had his ways, however, of testing them. He would suddenly appear in their presence, without warning, and look for the immediate expressions on their faces. He would request a nobleman to move himself and his family to the palace of Versailles, knowing that this was costly and unpleasant. He carefully observed any signs of annoyance in the face or voice. He would say something negative about another courtier, an ally of theirs, and notice their immediate reaction. Enough signs of discomfort indicated secret hostility.

If you suspect someone of feeling envy, talk about the latest good news for you without appearing to brag. Look for microexpressions of disappointment on their face. Use similar tests to probe for hidden anger and resentments, eliciting the responses that people cannot suppress so quickly. In general, people will want to see more of you, want to see less of you, or be rather indifferent. They may fluctuate among the three states, but they will tend to veer toward one. They will reveal this in how quickly they respond to your emails or texts, their body language on first seeing you, and the overall tone they take in your presence.

The value in detecting possible hostility or negative feelings early on is that it increases your strategic options and room to maneuver. You can lay a trap for people, intentionally stirring their hostility and goading them into some aggressive action that will embarrass them in the long run. Or you can work doubly hard to neutralize their dislike of you and even win them over through a charm offensive. Or you can simply create distance—not hiring them, firing them, refusing to interact with them. In the end, you will make your path much smoother by avoiding surprise battles and acts of sabotage.

On the other side of the coin, we generally have less of a need to hide positive emotions from others, but nonetheless we often do not like to emit obvious signs of joy and attraction, especially in work situations, or even in courtship. People often prefer to display a cool social front. So there is great value in being able to detect the signs that people are falling under your spell.

According to research studies on facial cues by psychologists such as Paul Ekman, E. H. Hess, and others, people who feel positive emotions for you will display noticeable signs of relaxation in the facial muscles, particularly in the lines of the forehead and the area around the mouth; their lips will appear more fully exposed and the whole area around their eyes will widen. These are all involuntary expressions of comfort and openness. If the feelings are more intense, such as falling in love, blood rushes to the face, animating all of the features. As part of this excited state the pupils will dilate, an automatic response in which the eyes let in more light. It is a sure sign that a person is comfortable and likes what they are seeing. Along with the dilation the eyebrows will rise, making the eyes look even bigger. We do not usually pay attention to eye pupils because looking intently into another's eyes has an overtly sexual connotation. We must train ourselves to glance quickly at the pupils when we notice any widening of the eyes.

In developing your skills in this arena, you must learn to distinguish between the fake and the genuine smile. In trying to hide our negative feelings, we most often resort to the fake smile, because it is easy and people generally do not pay attention to the subtleties of smiles. Because the genuine variety is less common, you must know how to recognize it. The genuine smile will affect the muscles around the eyes and widen them, often revealing crow's-feet on the sides of the eyes. It will also tend to pull the cheeks upward. There is no genuine smile without a definite change in the eyes and cheeks. Some people will try to create the impression of the genuine variety by putting on a very broad smile, which will partially alter the eyes as well. So in addition to the physical signs, you must look at the context. The genuine smile usually comes from some action or words that suddenly elicit the response; it is spontaneous. Is the smile in this case somewhat unrelated to the circumstances, not warranted by what was said? Is it a situation in which a person is straining to impress or has strategic goals in mind? Is the timing of the smile slightly off?

Perhaps the most telling indication of positive emotions comes from the voice. It is much easier for us to control the face; we can look in a mirror for such purposes. But unless we are professional actors, the voice is very difficult to consciously modulate. When people are engaged and excited to talk to you, the pitch of their voice rises, indicating emotional arousal. Even if people are nervous, the tone of the voice will be warm and natural, as opposed to the simulated warmth of a salesman. You can detect an almost purring quality to the voice, which some have likened to a vocal smile. You will notice also an absence of tension and hesitation. In the course of a conversation there is an equal level of banter, with the pace quickening, indicating increasing rapport. A voice that is animated and happy tends to infect us with the mood and elicit a similar response. We know it when we feel it, but often we ignore these feelings and instead concentrate on the friendly words or sales pitch.

Finally, monitoring nonverbal cues is essential in your attempts at influencing and seducing people. It is the best way to gauge the degree to which a person is falling under your spell. When people start to feel comfortable in your presence, they will stand closer to you or lean in, their arms not folded or revealing any tension. If you are giving a talk or telling a story, frequent head nods, attentive gazes, and genuine smiles will indicate that people agree with what you are saying and are losing their resistance. They exchange more looks. Perhaps the best and most exciting sign of all is synchrony, the other person unconsciously mirroring you. Their legs cross in the same direction, the head tilts in a similar manner, one smile inducing another. At the deepest level of synchrony, as Milton Erickson discovered, you will find breathing patterns falling into the same rhythm, which can sometimes end in the complete synchrony of a kiss.

You can also train yourself to not only monitor these changes that show your influence but induce them as well by displaying positive cues yourself. You begin to slowly stand or lean closer, revealing subtle signs of openness. You nod and smile as others talk. You mirror their behavior and their breathing patterns. As you do so, you watch for signs of emotional infection, going further only when you detect the slow crumbling of resistance.

With expert seducers who use all of the positive cues to mimic the appearance that they are falling in love only to bring you more deeply under their control, keep in mind that very few people naturally reveal so much emotion so early on. If your supposed effect on them seems a bit too rushed and perhaps contrived, tell them to slow down and monitor their face for microexpressions of frustration.

Dominance/submission cues: As the most complex social animal on the planet, we humans form elaborate hierarchies based on position, money, and power. We are aware of these hierarchies, but we do not like talking explicitly about relative power positions, and we are generally uncomfortable when others talk about their superior rank. Instead, signs of dominance or weakness are more often expressed in nonverbal communication. We have inherited this communication style from other primates, notably chimpanzees, who have elaborate signals to denote an individual chimp's place in the social rank. Keep in mind that the feeling of being in a superior social position gives people a confidence that will radiate outward in their body language. Some feel this confidence before they attain a position of power, and it becomes a self-fulfilling prophecy as others are drawn to them. Some who are ambitious might try to simulate these cues, but it has to be done well. Fake confidence can be quite off-putting.

Confidence usually comes with a greater feeling of relaxation that is clearly reflected in the face, and with a greater freedom of movement. Those who are powerful will feel allowed to look around more at others, choosing to make eye contact with whomever they please. Their eyelids are more closed, a sign of seriousness and competence. If they feel bored or annoyed, they show it more freely and openly. They often smile less, frequent smiling being a sign of overall insecurity. They feel more entitled to touch people, such as with friendly pats on the back or on the arm. In a meeting, they will tend to take up more space and create more distance around themselves. They stand taller, and their gestures are relaxed and comfortable. Most important, others feel compelled to imitate their style and mannerisms. The leader will tend to impose a form of nonverbal communication on the group in very subtle ways. You will notice people mimicking not only their ideas but also their calm or more frenetic energy.

Alpha males like to signal their superior position in the rank in several ways: They speak faster than others and feel entitled to interrupt and control the flow of the conversation. Their handshake is extra vigorous, almost crushing. When they walk in the office, you will see them assume a taller stance and a purposeful stride, generally making inferiors walk behind them. Watch chimpanzees in a zoo and you will notice similar behavior on the part of the alpha chimp.

For women in leadership positions, what often works best is a calm, confident expression, warm yet businesslike. Perhaps the best example of this would be current German chancellor Angela Merkel. Her smiles are even less frequent than the average male politician, but when they occur they are especially meaningful. They never seem fake. She listens to others with looks of complete absorption, her face remarkably still. She has a way of getting others to do most of the talking while always seeming to be in control of the course of the conversation. She does not need to interrupt to assert herself. When she wants to attack someone, it is with looks of boredom, iciness, or contempt, never with blustery words. When Russian president Vladimir Putin tried to intimidate her by bringing his pet dog into a meeting, knowing Merkel had once been bitten and had a fear of dogs, she visibly tensed, then quickly composed herself and looked him calmly in the eye. She put herself in the one-up position in relation to Putin by not making anything of his ploy. He seemed rather childish and petty in comparison. Her style does not include all of the alpha male body posturing. It is quieter and yet extremely powerful in its own way.

As women come to attain more leadership positions, this less obtrusive style of authority might begin to alter our perception of some of the dominance cues so long associated with power.

It is worth observing those in positions of power in your group for signs of dominance cues and for their absence. Leaders who display tension and hesitation in their nonverbal cues are generally insecure in their power and feel it threatened. Signs of such anxiety and insecurity are generally easy to spot. They will talk in a more halting manner, with long pauses. Their voice will rise in pitch and stay there. They will tend to avert their gaze and control their eye movements, although they will often blink more. They will put on more forced smiles and emit nervous laughs. As opposed to feeling entitled to touch others, they will tend to touch themselves in what is known as pacifying behavior. They will touch their hair, their neck, their forehead, all in an attempt to soothe their nerves. People trying to hide their insecurities will assert themselves a little too loudly in a conversation, their voices rising. As they do this, they look around nervously, eyes wide open. Or as they talk in an animated way, their hands and bodies are unusually still, always a sign of anxiety. They will inevitably give off mixed signals, and you must pay greater attention to those that signal underlying insecurity.

Nicolas Sarkozy, president of France (2007–2012), was someone who liked to assert his presence through body language. He would pat people on the back, be the one to direct them where to stand, fix them with his stare, interrupt what they were saying, and generally try to dominate the room. During one meeting with him in the midst of the euro crisis, Chancellor Merkel saw his usual domineering act but could not help but notice his foot nervously jiggling the entire time. The extra assertive style was perhaps his way of distracting others from his insecurities. This was valuable information Merkel could put to use.

People's actions will often contain dominance and submission cues. For instance, people will often show up late to indicate their superiority, real or imagined. They are not obligated to be on time. Also, conversation patterns reveal the relative position people feel they occupy. For instance, those who feel dominant will tend to talk more and interrupt frequently, as a means of asserting themselves. When there's an argument that turns personal, they will resort to what is known as punctuation—they will find an action on the other side that started it all, even though clearly it is part of the relationship pattern. They assert their interpretation of who is to blame through their tone of voice and piercing looks. If you observe a couple from the outside, you will frequently notice one person who is in the dominant position. If you converse with them, the dominant one will make eye contact with you but not with his or her partner, and will appear to only half listen to what the partner says. Smiles can also be a subtle cue for indicating superiority, especially through what we shall call the tight smile. This usually comes in response to something someone said, and it is a smile that tightens the facial muscles and indicates irony and contempt for the person they see as inferior but gives them the cover of appearing friendly.

One final but very subtle nonverbal means of asserting dominance in a relationship comes through the *symptom*. One partner suddenly develops headaches or some other illness, or starts drinking, or generally falls into a negative pattern of behavior. This forces the other side to play by their rules, to tend to their weaknesses. It is the willful use of sympathy to gain power and it is extremely effective.

Finally, use the knowledge you glean from these cues as a valuable means of gauging the levels of confidence in people and acting appropriately. With leaders who are riddled with insecurities that poke through nonverbally, you can play to their insecurities and gain power through this, but often it is best to avoid attaching yourself too closely to such types, as they tend to do poorly over time and can drag you down with them. With those who are not leaders but are trying to assert themselves as if they were, your response should depend on their personality type. If they are rising stars, full of self-belief and a sense of destiny, it might be wise to try to rise with them. You will notice such types by the positive energy that surrounds them. On the other hand, if they are simply arrogant and petty despots, these are precisely the types you should always strive to avoid, as they are masters at making others pay lip service to them without giving anything in return.

Deception cues: We humans are by nature quite gullible. We *want* to believe in certain things—that we can get something for nothing; that we can easily regain or rejuvenate our health thanks to some new trick, perhaps even cheat death; that most people are essentially good and can be trusted. This propensity is what deceivers and manipulators thrive on. It would be immensely beneficial for the future of our species if we were all less gullible, but we cannot change human nature. Instead, the best we can do is to learn to recognize certain telltale signs of an attempt at deception and maintain our skepticism as we examine the evidence further.

The most clear and common sign comes when people assume an extra-animated front. When they smile a lot, seem more than friendly, and even are quite entertaining, it is hard for us to not be drawn in and lower ever so slightly our resistance to their influence. When Lyndon Johnson was trying to pull the wool over the eyes of a fellow senator, he would go an extra mile with his physical presence, cornering them in the cloakroom, telling some off-color jokes, touching them on the arm, looking extra sincere, and cracking the biggest smiles he could muster. Similarly, if people are trying to cover something up, they tend to become extra vehement, righteous, and chatty. They are playing on the conviction bias (see chapter 1)—if I deny or say something with so much gusto, with an air of being a victim, it is hard to doubt me. We tend to take extra conviction for truth. In fact, when people try to explain their ideas with so much exaggerated energy, or defend themselves with an intense level of denial, that is precisely when you should raise your antennae.

In both cases—the cover-up and the soft sell—the deceiver is striving to distract you from the truth. Although an animated face and gestures might come from sheer exuberance and genuine friendliness, when they come from someone you don't know well, or from someone who just might have something to hide, you must be on your guard. Now you are looking for nonverbal signs to confirm your suspicions.

With such deceivers you will often notice that one part of the face or the body is more expressive to attract your attention. This will often be the area around the mouth, with large smiles and changing expressions. This is the easiest area of the body for people to manipulate and create an animated effect. But it could also be exaggerated gestures with the hands and arms. The key is that you will detect tension and anxiety in other parts of the body, because it is impossible for them to control all of the muscles. When they flash a big smile, the eyes are tense with little movement or the rest of the body is unusually still, or if the eyes are trying to fool you with looks to garner your sympathy, the mouth quivers slightly. These are signs of contrived behavior, of trying too hard to control one part of the body.

Sometimes really clever deceivers will attempt to create the opposite impression. If they are covering up a misdeed, they will hide their guilt behind an extremely serious and competent exterior, the face becoming unusually still. Instead of loud denials, they will offer a highly plausible explanation of the chain of events, even going through the "evidence" that confirms this. Their picture of reality is nearly seamless. If they are trying to gain your money or support, they will pose as the highly competent professional, to the point of being somewhat boring, even hitting you with a lot of numbers and statistics. Con artists often employ this front. The great con artist Victor Lustig would lull his victims to sleep with a professional patter, making himself come off as a bureaucrat or the dull expert in bonds and securities. Bernie Madoff seemed so bland nobody could possibly suspect him of such an audacious con game as the one he pulled off.

This form of deception is harder to see through because there is less to notice. But once again you are looking for contrived impressions. Reality is never so pat and seamless. Real events involve sudden random intrusions and accidents. Reality is messy and the pieces rarely fit so perfectly. That was what was wrong with the Watergate cover-up and raised suspicions. When the explanation or the come-on is just a little too slick or professional, that is what should trigger your skepticism. Looking at this from the other side, as a character in Dostoyevsky's novel *The Idiot* advised, "When you are lying, if you skillfully put in something not quite ordinary, something eccentric, something, you know, that never has happened, or very rarely, it makes the lie sound much more probable."

In general, the best thing to do when you suspect people of trying to distract you from the truth is not to actively confront them in the beginning, but in fact to encourage them to continue by showing interest in what they are saying or doing. You want them to talk more, to reveal more signs of tension and contrivance. At the right moment you must surprise them with a question or remark that is designed to make them uncomfortable, revealing you are onto them. Pay attention to the microexpressions and body language they emit at such moments. If they are really deceiving, they will often have a freeze response as they take this in, and then quickly try to mask the underlying anxiety. This was the favorite strategy of detective Columbo in the television series of the same name—facing criminals who had tried to reverse engineer the evidence to make it look like someone else had done it, Columbo would pretend to be perfectly friendly and harmless but then would suddenly ask an uncomfortable question and then pay extra attention to the face and body.

Even with the most practiced deceivers, one of the best ways to unmask them is to notice how they give emphasis to their words through nonverbal cues. It is very difficult for humans to fake this. Emphasis comes through raised vocal pitch and assertive tone, forceful hand gestures, the raising of eyebrows and the widening of eyes. We might also lean forward or rise up on the balls of our feet. We engage in such behavior when we are filled with emotion and trying to add an exclamation point to what we are saying. It is hard for deceivers to mimic this. The emphasis they place with their voice or body is not exactly correlated to what they are saying, does not quite fit the context of the moment, or comes a little too late. When they pound the table with their fist, it is not at the moment they should be feeling the emotion, but a little earlier, as if on cue, as if to create an effect. These are all cracks in the veneer of the realness they are trying to project.

Finally, with deception keep in mind that there is always a scale involved. At the bottom of the scale we find the most harmless varieties, little white lies. These could include all forms of flattery in daily life: "You look great today"; "I loved your screenplay." They could include not revealing to people exactly what you did that day or withholding bits of information because it is annoying to be completely transparent and have no privacy. These small forms of deception can be detected if we pay attention, such as by noticing the genuineness of a smile. But in fact it is best to simply ignore this lower end. Polite, civilized society depends on the ability to say things that are not always sincere. It would be too damaging socially to become constantly aware of this subrealm of deception. Save your alertness for those situations in which the stakes are higher and people might be angling to get something valuable out of you.

The Art of Impression Management

In general the word *role-playing* has negative connotations. We contrast it with authenticity. A person who is truly authentic doesn't need to play a role in life, we think, but can simply be him- or herself. This concept has value in friendships and in our intimate relationships, where, hopefully, we can drop the masks we wear and feel comfortable in displaying our unique qualities. But in our professional life it is much more complicated. When it comes to a specific job or role to play in society, we have expectations about what is professional. We would be made to feel uncomfortable if our airplane pilot suddenly started to act like a car salesman, or a mechanic like a therapist, or a professor like a rock musician. If such people acted completely like themselves, dropping their masks and refusing to play their roles, we would question their competence.

A politician or public figure whom we see as more authentic than others is generally better at projecting such a quality. They know that appearing humble, or discussing their private life, or telling an anecdote that reveals some vulnerability will have the "authentic" effect. We are not seeing them as they are in the privacy of their home. Life in the public sphere means wearing a mask, and sometimes some people wear the mask of "authenticity." Even the hipster or the rebel is playing a role, with prescribed poses and tattoos. They do not have the freedom to suddenly wear a business suit, because others in their circle would begin to question their sincerity, which depends on displaying the right appearance. People have more freedom to bring more of their personal qualities into the role they play once they have established themselves and their competence is no longer in question. But this is always within limits.

Consciously or unconsciously most of us adhere to what is expected of our role because we realize our social success depends on this. Some may refuse to play this game, but in the end they are marginalized and forced to play the outsider role, with limited options and decreasing freedom as they get older. In general, it is best to simply accept this dynamic and derive some pleasure from it. You are not only aware of the proper appearances you must present but know how to shape them for maximum effect. You can then transform yourself into a superior actor on the stage of life and enjoy your moment in the limelight.

The following are some basics in the art of impression management.

Master the nonverbal cues. In certain settings, when people want to get a fix on who we are, they pay greater attention to the nonverbal cues we emit. This could be in a job interview, a group meeting, or a public appearance. Aware of this, smart social performers will know how to control these cues to some degree and consciously emit the signs that are suitable and positive. They know how to seem likable, flash genuine smiles, use welcoming body language, and mirror the people they deal with. They know the dominance cues and how to radiate confidence. They know that certain looks are more expressive than words in conveying disdain or attraction. In general, you want to be aware of your nonverbal style so you can consciously alter certain aspects for better effect.

Be a method actor. In method acting you train yourself to be able to display the proper emotions on command. You feel sad when your part calls for it by recalling your own experiences that caused such emotions, or if necessary by simply imagining such experiences. The point is that you have control. In real life it is not possible to train ourselves to such a degree, but if you have no control, if you are continually emoting whatever comes to you in the moment, you will subtly signal weakness and an overall lack of self-mastery. Learn how to consciously put yourself in the right emotional mood by imagining how and why you should feel the emotion suitable to the occasion or performance you are about to give. Surrender to the feeling for the moment so that the face and body are naturally animated. Sometimes by actually making yourself smile or frown, you will experience some of the emotions that go with these expressions. Just as important, train yourself to return to a more neutral expression at a natural moment, careful to not go too far with your emoting.

Adapt to your audience. Although you conform to certain parameters set by the role you play, you must be flexible. A master performer like Bill Clinton never lost sight of the fact that as president he had to project confidence and power, but if he was speaking to a group of autoworkers he would adjust his accent and his words to fit the audience, and he would do the same for a group of executives. Know your audience and shape your nonverbal cues to their style and taste.

Create the proper first impression. It has been demonstrated how much people tend to judge based on first impressions and the difficulties they have in reassessing these judgments. Knowing this, you must give extra attention to your first appearance before an individual or group. In general it is best to tone down your nonverbal cues and present a more neutral front. Too much excitement will signal insecurity and might make people suspicious. A relaxed smile, however, and looking people in the eye in these first encounters can do wonders for lowering their natural resistance.

Use dramatic effects. This mostly involves mastering the art of presence/absence. If you are too present, if people see you too often or can predict exactly what you will do next, they will quickly grow bored with you. You must know how to selectively absent yourself, to regulate how often and when you appear before others, making them want to see more of you, not less. Cloak yourself in some mystery, displaying some subtly contradictory qualities. People don't need to know everything about you. Learn to withhold information. In general, make your appearances and your behavior less predictable.

Project saintly qualities. No matter what historical period we are living through, there are certain traits that are always seen as positive and that you must know how to display. For instance, the appearance of saintliness never goes out of fashion. Appearing saintly today is certainly different in content from the sixteenth century, but the essence is the same—you embody what is considered good and above reproach. In the modern world, this means showing yourself as progressive, supremely tolerant, and open-minded. You will want to be seen giving generously to certain causes and supporting them on social media. Projecting sincerity and honesty always plays well. A few public confessions of your weaknesses and vulnerabilities will do the trick. For some reason people see signs of humility as authentic, even though people might very well be simulating them. Learn how to occasionally lower your head and appear humble. If dirty work must be done, get others to do it. Your hands are clean. Never overtly play the Machiavellian leader—that only works well on television. Use the appropriate dominance cues to make people think you are powerful, even before you reach the heights. You want to seem like you were *destined* for success, a mystical effect that always works.

The master of this game has to be Emperor Augustus (63 BC–AD 14) of ancient Rome. Augustus understood the value of having a good enemy, a villain with whom he could contrast himself. For this purpose he used Mark Antony, his early rival for power, as the perfect foil. Augustus personally allied himself with everything traditional in Roman society, even placing his home near the spot where the city had supposedly been founded. While Antony was off in Egypt, dallying with Queen Cleopatra and giving in to a life of luxury, Augustus could continually point to their differences, showing himself off as the embodiment of Roman values, which Antony had betrayed. Once he became the supreme leader of Rome, Augustus made a public show of humility, of giving back powers to the Senate and to the people. He spoke a more vernacular Latin and lived simply, like a man of the people. And for all this he was revered. It was, of course, all a show. In fact he spent most of his time in a luxurious villa outside Rome. He had many mistresses, who came from places as exotic as Egypt. And while seeming to give away power, he held on tightly to the real reins of control, the military. Obsessed with the theater, Augustus was a master showman and wearer of masks. He must have realized this, for these were the last words he spoke on his deathbed: "Have I played my part in the farce of life well enough?"

Realize the following: The word *personality* comes from the Latin *persona*, which means "mask." In the public we all wear masks, and this has a positive function. If we displayed exactly who we are and spoke our minds truthfully, we would offend almost everyone and reveal qualities that are best concealed. Having a persona, playing a role well, actually protects us from people looking too closely at us, with all of the insecurities that would churn up. In fact, the better you play your role, the more power you will accrue, and with power you will have the freedom to express more of your peculiarities. If you take this far enough, the persona you present will match many of your unique characteristics, but always heightened for effect.

> "You appeared to read a good deal upon her which was quite invisible to me." "Not invisible but unnoticed, Watson. You did not know where to look, and so you missed all that was important. I can never bring you to realize the importance of sleeves, the suggestiveness of thumbnails, or the great issues that may hang from a boot-lace."
>
> —*Sir Arthur Conan Doyle, "A Case of Identity"*

4

Determine the Strength of People's Character

---◇---

The Law of Compulsive Behavior

*W*hen choosing people to work and associate with, do not be mesmerized by their reputation or taken in by the surface image they try to project. Instead, train yourself to look deep within them and see their character. People's character is formed in their earliest years and by their daily habits. It is what compels them to repeat certain actions in their lives and fall into negative patterns. Look closely at such patterns and remember that people never do something just once. They will inevitably repeat their behavior. Gauge the relative strength of their character by how well they handle adversity, their ability to adapt and work with other people, their patience and ability to learn. Always gravitate toward those who display signs of strength, and avoid the many toxic types out there. Know thoroughly your own character so you can break your compulsive patterns and take control of your destiny.

The Pattern

To his aunts, uncles, and grandparents who watched him grow up in Houston, Texas, Howard Hughes Jr. (1905–1976) was a rather shy and awkward boy. His mother had nearly died giving birth to him and consequently could not have other children, so she completely doted on her son. Continually anxious that he might catch some illness, she watched his every move and did all she could to protect him. The boy seemed in awe of his father, Howard Sr., who in 1909 had started the Sharp-Hughes Tool Company, which would soon make the family a fortune. His father was not home much, always traveling for business, so

Howard spent a great deal of time with his mother. To the relatives he could seem nervous and hypersensitive, but as he got older he became a remarkably polite, soft-spoken young man, completely devoted to his parents.

Then in 1922 his mother, at the age of thirty-nine, suddenly died. His father never quite recovered from her early death and passed away two years later. Now, at the age of nineteen, young Howard was alone in the world, having lost the two people who had been his closest companions and who had directed every phase of his life. His relatives decided they would have to fill the void and give the young man the guidance he needed. But in the months after the death of his father, they suddenly had to confront a Howard Hughes Jr. they had never seen before or suspected. The soft-spoken young man suddenly became rather abusive. The obedient boy was now the complete rebel. He would not continue college as they advised. He would not follow any of their recommendations. The more they insisted, the more belligerent he became.

Inheriting the family wealth, young Howard could now become completely independent, and he meant to take this as far as he could. He immediately went to work to buy out all of the shares in the Sharp-Hughes Tool Company that his relatives possessed and to gain complete control of the highly lucrative business. Under Texas law he could petition the courts to declare him an adult, if he could prove himself competent enough to assume the role. Hughes befriended a local judge and soon got the declaration he wanted. Now he could run his own life and the tool company with no interference. His relatives were shocked by all of this, and soon both sides would cut off almost all contact with each other for the rest of their lives. What had changed the sweet boy they had known into this hyperaggressive, rebellious young man? It was a mystery they would never solve.

Shortly after declaring his independence, Howard settled in Los Angeles, where he was determined to follow his two newest passions—filmmaking and piloting airplanes. He had the money to indulge himself in both of these interests, and in 1927 he decided to combine them, producing an epic, high-budget film about airmen during World War I, to be called *Hell's Angels*. He hired a director and a team of writers to come up with the script, but he had a falling-out with the director and fired him. He then hired another director, Luther Reed, a man who was also an aviation buff and could relate better to the project, but soon he quit, tired of Hughes's constant interfering in the project. His last words to Hughes were "If you know so much, why don't you direct it yourself?" Hughes followed his advice and named himself the director.

The budget began to soar as he strove for the utmost in realism. Month after month, year after year went by as Hughes ran through hundreds of crewmembers and stunt pilots, three of whom died in fiery accidents. After endless battles, he ended up firing almost every head of a department and running things himself. He fussed over every shot, every angle, every storyboard. Finally *Hell's Angels* premiered in 1930 and it was a smash hit. The story was a mess, but the flying and action sequences thrilled audiences. Now the legend of Howard Hughes was born. He was the dashing young maverick who had bucked the system and created a hit. He was the rugged individualist who did everything himself.

The film had cost a whopping $3.8 million to make and had lost close to $2 million, but nobody paid attention to this. Hughes himself was humble and claimed to have learned his lesson on the production: "Making *Hell's Angels* by myself was my biggest mistake. . . . Trying to do the work of twelve men was just dumbness on my part. I learned by bitter experience that no one man can know everything."

During the 1930s the Hughes legend only seemed to grow as he piloted planes to several world records in speed, courting death on several occasions. Hughes had spun off from his father's company a new business venture called Hughes Aircraft, which he hoped to transform into the biggest manufacturer of airplanes in the world. At the time, this required procuring large military contracts for planes, and as the U.S. entered World War II Hughes made a big play for such a contract.

In 1942 various officials in the Defense Department, impressed by his aviation feats, the meticulous attention to detail he revealed in his interviews, and his tireless lobbying efforts, decided to award Hughes Aircraft an $18 million grant to produce three enormous transport planes, called the Hercules, which would be used to ferry soldiers and supplies to various fronts in the war. The planes were called flying boats and were to have wingspans longer than a football field and stand over three stories high at the hull. If the company did a good job on this, bringing the planes in on time and on budget, they would order many more and Hughes could corner the market in transport planes.

Less than a year later, there was more good news. Impressed with the beautiful and sleek design of his smaller D-2 plane, the air force put in an order for one hundred photo-reconnaissance planes for $43 million, to be reconfigured along the lines of the D-2. But soon word began to spread of trouble at Hughes Aircraft. The company had started as a sort of hobby for Hughes. He had placed various Hollywood friends and aviation buddies in high-level positions. As the company grew, so did the number of departments, but there was little communication among them. Everything had to flow through Hughes himself. He had to be consulted on the smallest decision. Frustrated by all of his interference in their work, several top-notch engineers had already quit.

Hughes saw the problem and hired a general manager to help with the Hercules project and straighten the company out, but the general manager quit after two months. Hughes had promised him carte blanche in restructuring the company, but only several days into the job he began vetoing his decisions and undermining his authority. By the late summer of 1943, $6 million of the $9 million set aside for the production of the first Hercules plane had already been spent, but the plane was nowhere near completion. Those in the Defense Department who had endorsed Hughes for the job began to panic. The photo-reconnaissance order was a critical one for the war effort. Did the internal chaos and delays with the Hercules bode problems with the more important reconnaissance order? Had Hughes duped them with his charm and his publicity campaign?

By early 1944, the order for the reconnaissance planes had fallen hopelessly behind schedule. The military now insisted he hire a new general manager to salvage something from the order. Fortunately one of the best men for the job was available at the time: Charles Perelle, the "boy wonder" of aircraft production. Perelle did not want the job. He knew, like everyone in the business, of the chaos within Hughes Aircraft. Now Hughes himself, feeling desperate, went on a charm offensive. He insisted he had realized the error of his ways. He needed Perelle's expertise. He was not what Perelle had expected—he was completely humble and made it seem as if he were the victim of unscrupulous executives within the company. He knew all the technical details of producing a plane, which impressed Perelle. He promised to give Perelle the authority he needed. Against his better judgment, Perelle took the job.

After only a few weeks, however, Perelle regretted his decision. The planes were further behind schedule than he had been led to believe. Everything he saw reeked of a lack of professionalism, down to the shoddy drawings of the planes. He went to work, cutting wasteful spending and streamlining departments, but nobody respected his authority. Everybody knew who really ran the company, as Hughes kept undermining Perelle's reforms. As the order fell further behind and the pressure mounted, Hughes disappeared from the scene, apparently having a nervous breakdown. By the end of the war, not a single reconnaissance plane had been produced, and the air force canceled the contract. Perelle himself, broken by the experience, quit his job in December of that year.

Hughes, trying to salvage something from the war years, could point to the completion of one of the flying boats, later known as the Spruce Goose. It was a marvel, he claimed, a brilliant piece of engineering on a massive scale. To prove the doubters wrong, he decided to test-fly the plane himself. As he flew over the ocean, however, it became painfully clear that the plane did not have nearly enough power for its enormous weight, and after a mile he gently set it down on the water and had it towed back. The plane would never fly again and would be dry-docked in a hangar at a cost of $1 million per year, Hughes refusing to take it apart for scrap.

By 1948 the owner of RKO Pictures, Floyd Odlum, was looking to sell. RKO was one of Hollywood's most profitable and prestigious studios, and Hughes was itching to get back in the limelight by establishing himself in the film business. He bought Odlum's shares and gained a controlling interest. Within RKO there was panic. Executives there knew of his reputation for meddling. The company had just brought in a new regime, headed by Dore Schary, that was going to transform RKO into the hottest studio for young directors. Schary decided to quit before being humiliated, but he agreed to first meet Hughes, mostly out of curiosity.

Hughes was all charm. He took hold of Schary's hand, looked him straight in the eye, and said, "I want no part of running the studio. You'll be left alone." Schary, surprised by his sincerity and agreement with Schary's proposed transformation of the studio, relented, and for the first few weeks all was as Hughes had promised. But then the phone calls began. Hughes wanted Schary to replace an actress on the latest film in production. Realizing his mistake, Schary immediately resigned, taking with him many of his own staff.

Hughes began filling positions with men who followed his orders, hiring exactly the actors and actresses that he himself liked. He bought a screenplay called *Jet Pilot* and planned on making it the 1949 version of *Hell's Angels*. It was to star John Wayne, and the great Josef von Sternberg was to direct. After a few weeks Sternberg could not endure one more phone call and quit. Hughes took over. In a complete repeat of the production of *Hell's Angels*, it took nearly three years to finish, mostly because of the aerial photography, and the budget soared to $4 million. Hughes had shot so much footage he could not decide how to cut it down. It took six years before it was ready, and by then the jet scenes were completely out of date and Wayne looked considerably older. The film subsequently fell into complete obscurity. Soon the once-bustling studio was losing substantial sums, and in 1955, with stockholders furious at his mismanagement, Hughes sold RKO to the General Tire Company.

In the 1950s and early '60s, the U.S. military decided to adapt some of its fighting philosophy to the times. To wage war in places like Vietnam it needed helicopters, including a light observation helicopter to help in reconnaissance. The army searched out potential manufacturers and in 1961 selected two of them that had submitted the best proposals, rejecting the design of Hughes's second aircraft company, which he had spun off from Hughes Tool (the original version of Hughes Aircraft was now run completely independently from Hughes himself). Hughes refused to accept this setback. His publicity team went on a massive lobbying campaign, wining and dining army brass, much as they had done some twenty years earlier with the photo-reconnaissance planes, spending money lavishly. The campaign was a success and the Hughes entry was now in the running along with the other two. The army decided that the company that came in with the best price would win.

The price Hughes submitted surprised the military—it was so low it seemed impossible for the company to make any money on the manufacture of the helicopters. It seemed clear that his strategy was to lose money on the initial production in order to win the auction, get the contract, and then raise the price on subsequent orders. In 1965 the army finally awarded the contract to Hughes, an incredible coup for a company that had had so little success in airplane production. If they were made well and on time, the army could potentially order thousands of helicopters, and Hughes could use this as a springboard into the production of commercial helicopters, an expanding business.

As the Vietnam War heated up, the army was certain to increase its order and Hughes would reap the bonanza, but as they waited for the delivery of the first helicopters, those who had awarded the contract to Hughes began to panic: the company was falling way behind the schedule they had agreed upon, and so they launched an investigation to find out what was going on. To their horror, there seemed to be no organized production line. The plant was too small to handle such an order. The details were all wrong—the drawings were unprofessional, the tools inadequate, and there were too few skilled workers on site. It was as if the company had no experience in designing planes and was trying to figure it out as it went. It was the exact same predicament as with the photo-reconnaissance planes, which only a few in the military could remember. It was clear that Hughes had not learned a single lesson from the earlier fiasco.

As they now could predict, the helicopters only trickled in. Feeling desperate, army brass decided to conduct a new auction for the much larger order of the 2,200 helicopters they now needed, hoping a more experienced company would come in with a lower price and force out Hughes. Hughes went into panic mode. To lose this follow-on bid would spell ruin. The company was counting on raising its price for this new order to recoup the enormous losses it had incurred with the initial production. That was the bet Hughes had placed. If he tried to come in with a low price for the additional helicopters, he could not return a profit, and yet if his bid was not low enough, he would be underbid, which was what eventually happened. The loss to Hughes in the end for the helicopters he produced was an astronomical $90 million and had a devastating effect on the company.

In 1976 Howard Hughes died in an airplane en route from Acapulco to Houston, and as the autopsy was performed on his body, the public finally became aware of what had happened to him in the last decade of his life. For years he had been addicted to pain pills and narcotics. He had lived in tightly sealed hotel rooms, deathly afraid of the slightest possible contamination by germs. At the time of his death he weighed a mere ninety-three pounds. He had lived in near-total isolation, attended to by a few assistants, desperately trying to keep all of this out of the public eye. It was the ultimate irony that the man who feared more than anything the slightest loss of control had ended up in his last years at the complete mercy of a handful of assistants and executives, who oversaw his slow death by drugs and wrested essential control of the company from him.

Interpretation: The pattern of Howard Hughes's life was set from very early on. His mother had an anxious nature, and after learning she could have no more children, she directed a great deal of her anxiety toward her only son. She smothered him with constant attention; she became his closest companion, almost never letting him out of sight. The father placed tremendous expectations on his son to carry on the family name. His parents determined everything he did—what he wore, what he ate, and who his friends were (although they were few). They shuttled him from school to school looking for the perfect environment for their son, who had shown himself to be hypersensitive and not easy to get along with. He was completely dependent on them for everything, and out of a tremendous fear of disappointing them, he became supremely polite and obedient.

The truth, however, was that he bitterly resented his total dependence. Once his parents died, his true character could finally emerge from beneath the smiles and obedience. He felt no love toward his relatives. He would rather face the future alone than have the slightest bit of authority above him. He had to have complete control, even at the age of nineteen, over his fate; anything less would stir up the old anxieties from childhood. And with the money he inherited, he had the power to realize his dream of total independence. His love of flying reflected this character trait. Only in the air, alone and at the helm, could he really experience the exhilaration of control and release from his anxieties. He could soar high above the masses, whom he secretly despised. He could brave death, which he did many times, because it would be a death under his own power.

His character came out even more clearly in the leadership style that he evolved in Hollywood and his other business ventures. If writers, directors, or executives came forward with their own ideas, he could only see this as a personal challenge to his authority. This would stir up his old anxieties about being helpless and dependent on others. To combat this anxiety he would have to keep control of all aspects of the business, overseeing even the spelling and grammar of the smallest publicity notice. He would have to create a very loose structure within his companies, making all of the executives fight among themselves for his attention. Better to have some internal chaos as long as everything flowed through him.

The paradox of this was that by trying to gain such total control he tended to lose it; one man could not possibly keep on top of everything, and so all kinds of unforeseen problems would arise. And when projects fell apart and the heat became intense, he would disappear from the scene or conveniently fall ill. His need to control everything around him even extended to the women he dated—he scrutinized their every action, had them followed by private investigators.

The problem that Howard Hughes presented to all those who chose to work with him in some capacity was that he carefully constructed a public image that concealed the glaring weaknesses in his character. Instead of the irrational micromanager, he could present himself as the rugged individualist and the consummate American maverick. Most damaging of all was his ability to portray himself as a successful businessman leading a billion-dollar empire. In truth, he had inherited a highly profitable tool business from his father. Over the years, the only parts of his empire that ran substantial profits were the tool company and an earlier version of Hughes Aircraft that he had spun out of the tool company. For various reasons, both of these businesses were run completely independently of Hughes; he had no input on their operations. The many other businesses he personally ran—his later aircraft division, his film ventures, his hotels and real estate in Las Vegas—all lost substantial amounts that were fortunately covered by the other two.

In fact, Hughes was a terrible businessman, and the pattern of failures that revealed this was plain for everyone to see. But this is the blind spot in human nature: we are poorly equipped to gauge the character of the people we deal with. Their public image, the reputation that precedes them, easily mesmerizes us. We are captivated by appearances. If they surround themselves with some alluring myth, as Hughes did, we *want* to believe in it. Instead of determining people's character—their ability to work with others, to keep to their promises, to remain strong in adverse circumstances—we choose to work with or hire people based on their glittering résumé, their intelligence, and their charm. But even a positive trait such as intelligence is worthless if the person also happens to be of weak or dubious character. And so, because of our blind spot, we suffer under the irresolute leader, the micromanaging boss, the conniving partner. This is the source of endless tragedies in history, our pattern as a species.

At all costs, you must alter your perspective. Train yourself to ignore the front that people display, the myth that surrounds them, and instead plumb their depths for signs of their character. This can be seen in the patterns they reveal from their past, the quality of their decisions, how they have chosen to solve problems, how they delegate authority and work with others, and countless other signs. A person of strong character is like gold—rare but invaluable. They can adapt, learn, and improve themselves. Since your success depends on the people you work with and for, make their character the primary object of your attention. You will spare yourself the misery of discovering their character when it is too late.

Character is destiny.

—Heraclitus

Keys to Human Nature

For thousands of years, we humans believed in fate: some kind of force—spirits, gods, or God—compelled us to act in a certain way. At birth our entire lives were laid out in advance; we were fated to succeed or fail. We see the world much differently now. We believe that we are largely in control of what happens to us, that we create our own destiny. Upon occasion, however, we might have a fleeting sensation that approximates what our ancestors must have felt. Perhaps a personal relationship goes bad or our career path hits a snag, and these difficulties are uncannily similar to something that happened to us in the past. Or we realize that our way of working on a project needs some improvement; we could do things better. We try to alter our methods, only to find ourselves doing things in exactly the same way, with nearly the same results. We might feel for a moment that some kind of malignant force in the world, some curse, compels us to relive the same situations.

We can often notice this phenomenon more clearly in the actions of others, particularly those closest to us. For instance, we see friends continually fall for exactly the wrong person or unconsciously push away the right person. We cringe at some foolish behavior of theirs, such as an ill-considered investment or career choice, only to see them repeat the foolishness a few years later, once they have forgotten the lesson. Or we know someone who always manages to offend the wrong person at the wrong time, creating hostility wherever he or she goes. Or they crumble under pressure, always in the same way, but blaming others or bad luck for what happens. And of course we know the addicts who get out of their addiction, only to fall back in or find some other form of addiction. We see these patterns and they don't, because nobody likes to believe that they are operating under some kind of compulsion beyond their control. It is too disturbing a thought.

If we are honest with ourselves, we must admit there is some truth to the concept of fate. We are prone to repeat the same decisions and methods of dealing with problems. There is a pattern to our life, particularly visible in our mistakes and failures. But there is a different way of looking at this concept: it is not spirits or gods that control us but rather our *character*. The etymology of the word *character*, from the ancient Greek, refers to an engraving or stamping instrument. Character, then, is something that is so deeply ingrained or stamped within us that it compels us to act in certain ways, beyond our awareness and control. We can conceive of this character as having three essential components, each layered on top of the other, giving this character depth.

The earliest and deepest layer comes from genetics, from the particular way our brains are wired, which predisposes us toward certain moods and preferences. This genetic component can make some people prone to depression, for instance. It makes some people introverts and others extroverts. It might even incline some toward becoming especially greedy—for attention or privilege or possessions. The psychoanalyst Melanie Klein, who studied infants, believed that the greedy and grasping type of child came into the world predisposed toward this character trait. There might be other genetic factors as well that predispose us toward hostility or anxiety or openness.

The second layer, which forms above this, comes from our earliest years and from the particular type of attachments we formed with our mother and caregivers. In these first three or four years our brains are especially malleable. We experience emotions much more intensely, creating memory traces that are much deeper than anything that will follow. In this period of life we are at our most susceptible to the influence of others, and the stamp from these years is profound.

John Bowlby, an anthropologist and psychoanalyst, studied patterns of attachment between mothers and children and came up with four basic schemas: *free/autonomous, dismissing, enmeshed-ambivalent,* and *disorganized.* The free/autonomous stamp comes from mothers who give their children freedom to discover themselves and are continually sensitive to their needs but also protect them. Dismissing mothers are often distant, even sometimes hostile and rejecting. Such children are stamped with a feeling of abandonment and the idea that they must continually fend for themselves. The enmeshed-ambivalent mothers are not consistent with their attention—sometimes suffocating and overinvolved, other times retreating because of their own problems or anxieties. They can make their children feel as if they have to take care of the person who should be taking care of them. Disorganized mothers send highly conflicting signals to their children, reflecting their own inner chaos and perhaps early emotional traumas. Nothing their children do is right, and such children can develop powerful emotional problems.

There are, of course, many gradations within each type and combinations of them, but in every case the quality of attachment that we had in our earliest years will create deep tendencies within us, in particular the way we use relationships to handle or modulate our stress. For instance, children of the dismissing parent will tend to avoid any kind of negative emotional situation and to wall themselves off from feelings of dependency. They might find it harder to commit to a relationship or will unconsciously push people away. The children of the enmeshed variety will experience a great deal of anxiety in relationships and will feel many conflicting emotions. They will always be ambivalent toward people, and this will set noticeable patterns in their life in which they pursue people and then unconsciously retreat.

In general, from these earliest years people will display a particular tone to their character—hostile and aggressive, secure and confident, anxious and avoidant, needy and enmeshing. These two layers are so deep that we have no real conscious awareness of them and the behavior they compel, unless we expend great effort in examining ourselves.

Above this a third layer will form from our habits and experiences as we get older. Based on the first two layers, we will tend to rely on certain strategies for dealing with stress, looking for pleasure, or handling people. These strategies now become habits that are set in our youth. There will be modifications to the particular nature of our character depending on the people we deal with—friends, teachers, romantic partners—and how they respond to us. But in general these three layers will establish certain noticeable patterns. We will make a particular decision. This is engraved in our brains neurologically. We are compelled to repeat this because the path is already laid. It becomes a habit, and our character is formed out of these thousands of habits, the earliest ones set well before we could be conscious of them.

There is a fourth layer as well. It often is developed in late childhood and adolescence as people become aware of their character flaws. They do what they can to cover them up. If they sense that deep inside they are an anxious, timid type of person, they come to realize that this is not a socially acceptable trait. They learn to disguise it with a front. They compensate by trying to appear outgoing or carefree or even domineering. This makes it all the more difficult for us to determine the nature of their character.

Some character traits can be positive and reflect inner strength. For instance, some people have a propensity toward being generous and open, empathetic, and resilient under pressure. But these stronger, more flexible qualities often require awareness and practice to truly become habits that can be relied upon. As we get older, life tends to weaken us. Our empathy is harder to hold on to (see chapter 2). If we are reflexively generous and open to everyone we meet, we can end up in a lot of trouble. Confidence without self-awareness and control can become grandiosity. Without conscious effort, these strengths will tend to wear down or turn into weaknesses. What this means is that the weakest parts of our character are the ones that create habits and compulsive behavior, because they do not require effort or practice to maintain.

Finally, we can develop conflicting character traits, perhaps stemming from a difference between our genetic predispositions and our earliest influences, or from parents who stamp in us different values. We might feel both idealistic and materialistic, the two parts fighting within us. The law remains the same. The conflicted character, which is developed in the earliest years, will merely reveal a different kind of pattern, with decisions that tend to reflect a person's ambivalence, or that swing back and forth.

As a student of human nature your task is twofold: First you must come to understand your own character, examining as best you can the elements in your past that have gone into forming it, and the patterns, mostly negative, that you can see recurring in your life. It is impossible to get rid of this stamp that constitutes your character. It is too deep. But through awareness, you can learn to mitigate or stop certain negative patterns. You can work to transform the negative and weak aspects of your character into actual strengths. You can try to create new habits and patterns that go with them through practice, actively shaping your character and the destiny that goes with it. (For more on this, see the last section of this chapter.)

Second, you must develop your skill in reading the character of the people you deal with. To do so, you must consider character as a primary value when it comes to choosing a person to work for or with or an intimate partner. This means giving it more value than their charm, intelligence, or reputation. The ability to observe people's character—as seen in their actions and patterns—is an absolutely critical social skill. It can help you avoid precisely those kinds of decisions that can spell years of misery—choosing an incompetent leader, a shady partner, a scheming assistant, or the kind of incompatible spouse who can poison your life. But it is a skill you must consciously develop, because we humans are generally inept when it comes to such assessments.

The general source of our ineptness is that we tend to base our judgments of people on what is most apparent. But as stated earlier, people often try to cover up their weaknesses by presenting them as something positive. We see them brimming with self-confidence, only to later discover that they are actually arrogant and incapable of listening. They seem frank and sincere, but over time we realize that they are actually boorish and unable to consider the feelings of others. Or they seem prudent and thoughtful, but eventually we see that they are in fact timid at their core and afraid of the slightest criticism. People can be quite adept at creating these optical illusions, and we fall for them. Similarly, people will charm and flatter us and, blinded by our desire to like them, we fail to look deeper and see the character flaws.

Related to this, when we look at people we often are really seeing only their reputation, the myth that surrounds them, the position they occupy, and not the individual. We come to believe that a person who has success must by nature be generous, intelligent, and good, and that they deserve everything they have gotten. But successful people come in all shapes. Some are good at using others to get where they have gotten, masking their own incompetence. Some are completely manipulative. Successful people have just as many character flaws as anyone else. Also, we tend to believe that someone who adheres to a particular religion or political belief system or moral code must have the character to go with this. But people bring the character they have to the position they occupy or to the religion they practice. A person can be a progressive liberal or a loving Christian and still be an intolerant tyrant at heart.

The first step, then, in studying character is to be aware of these illusions and façades and to train ourselves to look through them. We must scrutinize everybody for signs of their character, no matter the appearance they present or the position they occupy. With this firmly in mind, we can then work on several key components to the skill: recognizing certain signs that people emit in certain situations and that clearly reveal their character; understanding some general categories that people fit into (strong versus weak character, for instance), and finally being aware of certain types of characters that often are the most toxic and should be avoided if possible.

Character Signs

The most significant indicator of people's character comes through their actions over time. Despite what people say about the lessons they have learned (see Howard Hughes), and how they have changed over the years, you will inevitably notice the same actions and decisions repeating in the course of their life. In these decisions they reveal their character. You must take notice of any salient forms of

behavior—disappearing when there is too much stress, not completing an important piece of work, turning suddenly belligerent when challenged, or, conversely,
suddenly rising to the occasion when given responsibility. With this fixed in your
mind, you do some research into their past. You look at other actions you have
observed that fit into this pattern, now in retrospect. You pay close attention to
what they do in the present. You see their actions not as isolated incidents but as
parts of a compulsive pattern. If you ignore the pattern it is your own fault.

You must always keep in mind the primary corollary of this law: people
never do something just once. They might try to excuse themselves, to say they
lost their heads in the moment, but you can be sure they will repeat whatever
foolishness they did on another occasion, compelled by their character and habits. In fact, they will often repeat actions when it is completely against their
self-interest, revealing the compulsive nature of their weaknesses.

Cassius Severus was an infamous lawyer-orator who flourished in the time
of the Roman Emperor Augustus. He first gained attention with his fiery
speeches that attacked high-ranking Romans for their extravagant lifestyles.
He gained a following. His style was bombastic but full of humor that pleased
the public. Encouraged by the attention he received, he began to insult other
officials, always raising the tone of his attacks. The authorities warned him to
stop. The novelty wore off and the crowds grew thinner, but this only made
Severus try harder.

Finally the authorities had had enough—in AD 7 they ordered his books to
be burned and him to be banished to the island of Crete. To the dismay of the
Roman authorities, on Crete he simply continued his obnoxious campaign,
sending copies to Rome of his latest diatribes. They warned him yet again. He
not only ignored this, but he began to harangue and insult local Cretan officials, who wanted him put to death. In AD 24 the Senate wisely banished him
to the unpopulated rock of Serifos in the middle of the Aegean Sea. There he
would spend the last eight years of his life, and we can imagine him still concocting more insulting speeches that no one would hear.

It is hard for us to believe that people cannot control tendencies that are so
self-destructive, and we want to give them the benefit of the doubt, as the Romans did. But we must remember the wise words in the Bible: "Like a dog that
returns to his vomit is a fool that repeats his folly."

You can see eloquent signs of people's character in how they handle everyday affairs. If they are late in finishing simple assignments, they will be late
with larger projects. If they become irritated by little inconveniences, they will

tend to crumble under larger ones. If they are forgetful on small matters and inattentive to details, they will be so on more important ones. Look at how they treat employees in everyday settings and notice if there are discrepancies between the persona they present and their attitude toward underlings.

In 1969 Jeb Magruder came to San Clemente for a job interview in the Nixon administration. The man giving the interview was Bob Haldeman, chief of staff. Haldeman was very earnest, completely devoted to the Nixon cause, and impressed Magruder with his honesty, sharpness, and intelligence. But as they left the interview to get in a golf cart for a tour of San Clemente, Haldeman suddenly became frantic—there were no carts available. He railed at those in charge of the carts, and his manner was insulting and harsh. He was almost hysterical. Magruder should have seen this incident as a sign that Haldeman was not what he appeared, that he had control issues and a vicious streak, but charmed by the aura of power at San Clemente and wanting the job, he chose to ignore this, much to his later dismay.

In everyday life people can often do well at disguising their character flaws, but in times of stress or crisis these flaws can suddenly become very apparent. People under stress lose their normal self-control. They reveal their insecurities about their reputation, their fear of failure and lack of inner resilience. On the other hand, some people rise to the occasion and reveal strength under fire. There's no way to tell until the heat is on, but you must pay extra attention to such moments.

Similarly, how people handle power and responsibility will tell you a lot about them. As Lincoln said, "If you want to test a man's character, give him power." On the way to gaining power, people will tend to play the courtier, to seem deferential, to follow the party line, to do what it takes to make it to the top. Once at the top, there are fewer restraints and they will often reveal something about themselves you had not noticed before. Some people stay true to the values they had before attaining a high position—they remain respectful and empathetic. On the other hand, far more people suddenly feel entitled to treat others differently now that they have the power.

That is what happened to Lyndon Johnson once he attained a position of ultimate security in the Senate, as Senate majority leader. Tired of the years he had to spend playing the perfect courtier, he now relished the power he had to upset or humiliate those who had crossed him in the past. Now he would go up to such a senator and make a point of talking only to his assistant. Or he would get up and leave the floor when a senator he did not like was giving an

important speech, making other senators follow him. In general there are always signs of these character traits in the past if you look closely enough (Johnson had revealed such nasty signs in the earliest parts of his political career), but,
more important, you need to take notice of what people reveal once they are in
power. So often we think that power has changed people, when in fact it simply reveals more of who they are.

People's choice of spouse or partner says a lot about them. Some look for a
partner they can dominate and control, perhaps someone younger, less intelligent or successful. Some choose a partner they can rescue from a bad situation,
playing the savior role, another form of control. Yet others look for someone to
fill the mommy or daddy role. They want more pampering. These choices are
rarely intellectual; they reflect people's earliest years and attachment schemas.
They are sometimes surprising, as when people select someone who seems very
different and outwardly incompatible, but there is always an internal logic to
such choices. For instance, a person has a tremendous fear of being abandoned
by the one they love, reflecting anxieties from infancy, and so they select a
person who is noticeably inferior in looks or intelligence, knowing that person
will cling to them no matter what.

Another realm to examine is how people behave in moments away from
work. In a game or sport they might reveal a competitive nature that they cannot turn off. They have a fear of being overtaken in anything, even when they
are driving. They must be ahead, out in front. This can be channeled function-
ally into their work, but in off hours it reveals deep layers of insecurities. Look
at how people lose in games. Can they do so graciously? Their body language
will say a lot on that front. Do they try whatever they can to circumvent the
rules or bend them? Are they looking to escape and relax from work or to assert
themselves even in such moments?

In general, people can be divided into introverts and extroverts, and this
will play a large role in the character they develop. Extroverts are largely governed by external criteria. The question that dominates them is "What do others think of me?" They will tend to like what other people like, and the groups
they belong to frequently determine the opinions they hold. They are open to
suggestion and new ideas, but only if they are popular in the culture or asserted
by some authority they respect. Extroverts value external things—good
clothes, great meals, concrete enjoyment shared with others. They are in search
of new and novel sensations and have a nose for trends. They are not only

comfortable with noise and bustle but actively search it out. If they are bold, they love physical adventure. If they are not so bold, they love creature comforts. In any event, they crave stimulation and attention from others.

Introverts are more sensitive and easily exhausted by too much outward activity. They like to conserve their energy, to spend time alone or with one or two close friends. As opposed to extroverts, who are fascinated by facts and statistics for their own sake, introverts are interested in their own opinions and feelings. They love to theorize and come up with their own ideas. If they produce something, they do not like to promote it; they find the effort distasteful. What they make should sell itself. They like to keep a part of their life separate from others, to have secrets. Their opinions do not come from what others think or from any authority but from their inner criteria, or at least they think so. The bigger the crowd, the more lost and lonely they feel. They can seem awkward and mistrustful, uncomfortable with attention. They also tend to be more pessimistic and worried than the average extrovert. Their boldness will be expressed by the novel ideas they come up with and their creativity.

You might notice tendencies in both directions in individuals or yourself, but in general people trend in one or the other direction. It is important to gauge this in others for a simple reason: introverts and extroverts do not naturally understand each other. To the extrovert, the introvert has no fun, is stubborn, even antisocial. To the introvert, the extrovert is shallow, flighty, and overly concerned with what people think. Being one or the other is generally something genetic and will make two people see the same thing in a totally different light. Once you understand you are dealing with someone of the other variety than yourself, you must reassess their character and not foist your own preferences on them. Also, sometimes introverts and extroverts can work well together, particularly if people have a mix of both qualities and they complement each other, but more often than not they do not get along and are prone to constant misunderstandings. Keep in mind that there are generally more extroverts than introverts in the world.

Finally, it is critical that you measure the relative strength of people's character. Think of it in this way: such strength comes from deep within the core of the person. It could stem from a mixture of certain factors—genetics, secure parenting, good mentors along the way, and constant improvement (see the final section of this chapter). Whatever the cause, this strength is not something displayed on the outside in the form of bluster or aggression but manifests itself in overall resilience and adaptability. Strong character has a tensile quality like a good piece of metal—it can give and bend but still retains its overall shape and never breaks.

The strength emanates from a feeling of personal security and self-worth. This allows such people to take criticism and learn from their experiences. This means they do not give up so easily, since they want to learn how to get better. They are rigorously persistent. People of strong character are open to new ideas and ways of doing things without compromising the basic principles they adhere to. In adversity they can retain their presence of mind. They can handle chaos and the unpredictable without succumbing to anxiety. They keep their word. They have patience, can organize a lot of material, and complete what they start. Not continually insecure about their status, they can also subsume their personal interests to the good of the group, knowing that what works best for the team will in the end make their life easier and better.

People of weak character begin from the opposite position. They are easily overwhelmed by circumstances, making them hard to rely upon. They are slippery and evasive. Worst of all, they cannot be taught because learning from others implies criticism. This means you will continually hit a wall in dealing with them. They may appear to listen to your instructions, but they will simply revert to what they think is best.

We are all a mix of strong and weak qualities, but some people clearly veer in one or the other direction. As much as you can, you want to work and associate with strong characters and avoid weak ones. This has been the basis for almost all of Warren Buffett's investment decisions. He looks beyond the numbers to the CEOs he will be dealing with, and what he wants to gauge above all else is their resilience, their dependability, and their self-reliance. If only we used such measurements in those we hired, the partners we take in, and even the politicians we choose.

Although in intimate relationships there are certainly other factors that will guide our choices, strength of character should also be considered. This was largely what led Franklin Roosevelt to choose Eleanor as his wife. As a handsome young man of wealth, he could have chosen many other more beautiful young women, but he admired Eleanor's openness to new experiences and her remarkable determination. Looking far into the future, he could see the value of her character mattering more than anything else. And it ended up being a very wise choice.

In gauging strength or weakness, look at how people handle stressful moments and responsibility. Look at their patterns: what have they actually completed or accomplished? You can also test people. For instance, a good-natured joke at their expense can be quite revealing. Do they respond graciously to this, not so easily caught up in their insecurities, or do their eyes flash resentment or even anger? To gauge their trustworthiness as a team player, give them strategic information or share with them some rumor—do they quickly pass along the information to others? Are they quick to take one of your ideas and package it as their own? Criticize them in a direct manner. Do they take this to heart and try to learn and improve, or do they show overt signs of resentment? Give them an open-ended assignment with less direction than usual and monitor how they organize their thoughts and their time. Challenge them with a difficult assignment or some novel way of doing something, and see how they respond, how they handle their anxiety.

Remember: weak character will neutralize all of the other possible good qualities a person might possess. For instance, people of high intelligence but weak character may come up with good ideas and even do a job well, but they will crumble under pressure, or they will not take to kindly to criticism, or they will think first and foremost of their own agenda, or their arrogance and annoying qualities will cause others around them to quit, harming the general environment. There are hidden costs to working with them or hiring them. Someone less charming and intelligent but of strong character will prove more reliable and productive over the long run. People of real strength are as rare as gold, and if you find them, you should respond as if you had a discovered a treasure.

Toxic Types

Although each person's character is as unique as a fingerprint, we can notice throughout history certain types that keep recurring and that can be particularly pernicious to deal with. As opposed to the more obviously evil or manipulative characters that you can spot a mile away, these types are trickier. They often lure you in with an appearance that presents their weaknesses as something positive. Only over time do you see the toxic nature beneath the appearance, often when it is too late. Your best defense is to be armed with knowledge of these types, to notice the signs earlier on, and to not get involved or to disengage from them as quickly as possible.

The Hyperperfectionist: You are lured into their circle by how hard they work, how dedicated they are to making the best of whatever it is they produce. They put in longer hours than even the lowliest employee. Yes, they might explode and yell at people below them for not doing the job right, but that is because they want to maintain the highest standards, and that should be a good thing. But if you have the misfortune of agreeing to work with or for such a type, you will slowly discover the reality. They cannot delegate tasks; they have to oversee everything. It is less about high standards and dedication to the group than about power and control.

Such people often have dependency issues stemming from their family background, similar to Howard Hughes. Any feeling that they might have to depend on someone for something opens up old wounds and anxieties. They can't trust anyone. Once their back is turned, they imagine everyone slacking off. Their compulsive need to micromanage leads to people feeling resentful and secretly resistant, which is precisely what they fear the most. You will notice that the group they lead is not very well organized, since everything must flow through them. This leads to chaos and political infighting as the courtiers struggle to get closer to the king, who controls everything. Hyperperfectionists will often have health problems, as they work themselves to the bone. They like to blame others for everything that goes wrong—nobody is working hard enough. They have patterns of initial success followed by burnout and spectacular failures. It is best to recognize the type before getting enmeshed on any level. They cannot be satisfied by anything you do and will chew you up slowly with their anxieties, abusiveness, and desire to control.

The Relentless Rebel: At first glance such people can seem quite exciting. They hate authority and love the underdog. Almost all of us are secretly attracted to such an attitude; it appeals to the adolescent within us, the desire to snub our nose at the teacher. They don't recognize rules or precedents. Following conventions is for those who are weak and stodgy. These types will often have a biting sense of humor, which they might turn on you, but that is part of their authenticity, their need to deflate everyone, or so you think. But if you happen to associate with this type more closely, you will see that it is something they cannot control; it is a compulsion to feel superior, not some higher moral quality.

In their childhood a parent or father figure probably disappointed them. They came to mistrust and hate all those in power. In the end, they cannot accept any criticism from others because that reeks of authority. They cannot ever be told what to do. Everything must be on their terms. If you cross them in some way, you will be painted as the oppressor and be the brunt of their vicious humor. They gain attention with this rebel pose and soon become addicted to the attention. In the end it is all about power—no one shall be above them, and anyone who dares will pay the price. Look at their past history—they will tend to split with people on very bad terms, made worse by their insults. Do not be lured in by the hipness of their rebel pose. Such types are eternally locked in adolescence, and to try work with them will prove as productive as trying to lock horns with a sullen teenager.

The Personalizer: These people seem so sensitive and thoughtful, a rare and nice quality. They might seem a little sad, but sensitive people can have it rough in life. You are often drawn in by this air of theirs, and want to help. Also, they can appear quite intelligent, considerate, and good to work with. What you come to realize later on is that their sensitivity really only goes in one direction—inward. They are prone to take *everything* that people say or do as personal. They tend to brood over things for days, long after you have forgotten some innocuous comment that they have taken personally. As children, they had a gnawing feeling that they never got enough from their parents—love, attention, material possessions. As they get older, everything tends to remind them of what they didn't get. They go through life resenting this and wanting others to give them things without their having to ask. They are constantly on guard—are you paying them attention, do you respect them, are you giving them what they paid for? Being somewhat irritable and touchy, they inevitably push people away, which makes them even more sensitive. At some point they start to have a look of perpetual disappointment.

You will see in their life a pattern of many falling-outs with people, but they will always see themselves as the wronged party. Do not ever inadvertently insult such a type. They have a long memory and can spend years getting back at you. If you can recognize the type early enough, it's better to avoid them, as they will inevitably make you feel guilty for something.

The Drama Magnet: They will draw you in with their exciting presence. They have unusual energy and stories to tell. Their features are animated and they can be quite witty. They are fun to be around, until the drama turns ugly. As children, they learned that the only way to get love and attention that lasted was to enmesh their parents in their troubles and problems, which had to be large enough to engage the parents emotionally over time. This became a habit, their way of feeling alive and wanted. Most people shrink from any kind of confrontation, but they seem to live for it. As you get to know them better, you hear more stories of bickering and battles in their life, but they manage to always position themselves as the victim.

You must realize that their greatest need is to get their hooks into you by any means possible. They will embroil you in their drama to the point that you will feel guilty for disengaging. It is best to recognize them as early as possible, before you become enmeshed and dragged down. Examine their past for evidence of the pattern and run for the hills if you suspect you are dealing with such a type.

The Big Talker: You are impressed by their ideas, the projects that they are thinking about. They need help, they need backers, and you are sympathetic, but step back for a moment and examine their record for signs of past achievements or anything tangible. You might be dealing with a type that is not overtly dangerous but can prove maddening and waste your valuable time. In essence, these people are ambivalent. On the one hand they are secretly afraid of the effort and responsibility that go with translating their ideas into action. On the other hand, they crave attention and power. The two sides go to war within them, but the anxious part inevitably wins out and they slip away at the last moment. They come up with some reason for getting out of it, after you have committed to them. They themselves never finish anything. In the end, they tend to blame others for not realizing their visions—society, nebulous antagonistic forces, or bad luck. Or they try to find a sucker who will do all of the hard work in bringing to life their vague idea but who will take the blame if it all goes wrong.

Often such people had parents who were inconsistent, would turn on them suddenly for the smallest misdeed. Consequently their goal in life is to avoid situations in which they might open themselves up to criticism and judgment. They handle this by learning to talk well and impressing people with stories but running away when called to account, always with an excuse. Look carefully at their past for signs of this, and if they seem the type, be amused by their stories but take it no further.

The Sexualizer: They seem charged with sexual energy, in a way that is refreshingly unrepressed. They have a tendency to mix work with pleasure, to blur the usual boundaries for when it is appropriate to use this energy, and you might imagine that this is healthy and natural. But in truth it is compulsive and comes from a dark place. In their earliest years such people probably suffered sexual abuse in some way. This could have been directly physical or something more psychological, which the parent expressed through looks and touching that was subtle but inappropriate.

A pattern is deeply set from within and cannot be controlled—they will tend to see every relationship as potentially sexual. Sex becomes a means of self-validation, and when they are young, such types can lead an exciting, promiscuous life, as they will tend to find people to fall under their spell. But as they get older, any long periods without this validation can lead to depression and suicide, so they become more desperate. If they occupy positions of leadership, they will use their power to get what they want, all under the guise of being natural and unrepressed. The older they get, the more pathetic and frightening this becomes. You cannot help or save them from their compulsion, only save yourself from entanglement with them on any level.

The Pampered Prince/Princess: They will draw you in with their regal air. They are calm and ever so slightly imbued with a feeling of superiority. It is pleasant to meet people who appear confident and destined to wear a crown. Slowly you might find yourself doing favors for them, working extra hard for no pay, and not really understanding how or why. Somehow they express the need to be taken care of, and they are masters at getting others to pamper them. In childhood, their parents indulged them in their slightest whim and protected them from any kind of harsh intrusion from the outside world. There are also some children who incite this behavior in their parents by acting especially helpless. Whatever the cause, as adults their greatest desire is to replicate this early pampering. It remains their lost paradise. You will notice often that when they don't get what they want, they display baby-like behavior, pouting, or even tantrums.

This is certainly the pattern for all of their intimate relationships, and unless you have a deep need to pamper others, you will find the relationship maddening, always on their terms. They are not equipped to handle the harsh aspects of adult life and either manipulate a person into the pampering role or resort to drinking and drugs to soothe themselves. If you feel guilty for not helping them, it means you are hooked and should look to take care of yourself instead.

The Pleaser: You have never met anyone so nice and considerate. You almost can't believe how accommodating and charming they are. Then slowly you begin to have some doubts, but nothing you can put your finger on. Perhaps they don't show up as promised or don't do a job so well. It is subtle. The further this goes, however, the more it seems like they are sabotaging you or talking behind your back. These types are consummate courtiers, and they have developed their niceness not out of a genuine affection for their fellow humans but as a defense mechanism. Perhaps they had harsh and punishing parents who scrutinized their every action. Smiling and a deferential front was their way of deflecting any form of hostility, and it becomes their pattern for life. They also probably resorted to lying to their parents, and they are generally practiced and expert liars.

Just as when they were children, behind the smiles and flattery is a great deal of resentment at the role they have to play. They secretly yearn to harm or steal from the person they serve or defer to. You must be on your guard with people who actively exert so much charm and politeness, past the point of what is natural. They can turn out to be quite passive-aggressive, particularly hitting you when your guard is down.

The Savior: You cannot believe your good luck—you have met someone who will save you from your difficulties and troubles. Somehow they recognized your need for help and here they are with books to read, strategies to employ, the right foods to eat. In the beginning it is all quite seductive, but your doubts begin the moment you want to assert your independence and do things on your own.

In childhood, these types often had to become the caregivers of their own mother, father, or siblings. The mother, for instance, made her own needs the primary concern of the family. Such children compensate for the lack of care that they receive with the feeling of power that they derive from the inverted relationship. This sets a pattern: they gain their greatest satisfaction from rescuing people, from being the caregiver and savior. They have a nose for those in possible need of salvation. But you can detect the compulsive aspect of this behavior by their need to control you. If they are willing to let you stand on your own two feet after some initial help, then they are truly noble. If not, it is really about the power they can exercise. In any event, it is always best to cultivate self-reliance and tell saviors to save themselves.

The Easy Moralizer: They communicate a sense of outrage at this bit of injustice or that, and they are quite eloquent. With such conviction they find followers, including you. But sometimes you detect cracks in their righteous veneer. They don't treat their employees so well; they are condescending to their spouse; they may have a secret life or vice you catch glimpses of. As children, they were often made to feel guilty for their own strong impulses and desires for pleasure. They were punished and tried to repress these impulses. Because of this they develop some self-loathing and are quick to project negative qualities onto others or look enviously at people who are not so repressed. They don't like other people enjoying themselves. Instead of expressing their envy, they choose to judge and condemn. You will notice in the adult version a complete lack of nuance. People are good or evil, no middle ground. They are in fact at war with human nature, incapable of coming to terms with our less-than-perfect traits. Their morality is as easy and compulsive as drinking or gambling, and it requires no sacrifices on their part, just a lot of noble words. They thrive in a culture of political correctness.

In truth they are secretly drawn toward what they condemn, which is why they will inevitably have a secret side. You will certainly be the target of their inquisition at some point if you get too close to them. Notice their lack of empathy early on and keep your distance.

(For more toxic types, see the chapters on envy, 10; grandiosity, 11; and aggression, 16.)

The Superior Character

This law is simple and inexorable: you have a set character. It was formed out of elements that predate your conscious awareness. From deep within you, this character compels you to repeat certain actions, strategies, and decisions. The brain is structured to facilitate this: once you think and take a particular action, a neural pathway is formed that leads you to do it again and again. And in relation to this law, you can go in one of two directions, each one determining more or less the course of your life.

The first direction is ignorance and denial. You don't take notice of the patterns in your life; you don't accept the idea that your earliest years left a deep and lasting imprint that compels you to behave in certain ways. You imagine that your character is completely plastic, and that you can re-create yourself at will. You can follow the same path to power and fame as someone else, even though they come from very different circumstances. The concept of a set character can seem like a prison, and many people secretly want to be taken outside themselves, through drugs, alcohol, or video games. The result of such denial is simple: the compulsive behavior and the patterns become even more set into place. You cannot move against the grain of your character or wish it away. It is too powerful.

This was precisely the problem for Howard Hughes. He imagined himself a great businessman, establishing an empire that would outdo his father's. But by his nature, he was not a good manager of people. His real strength was more technical—he had a great feel for the design and engineering aspects of airplane production. If he had known and accepted this, he could have carved out a brilliant career as the visionary behind his own aircraft company and left the day-to-day operations to someone truly capable. But he lived with an image of himself that did not correlate with his character. This led to a pattern of failures and a miserable life.

The other direction is harder to take, but it is the only path that leads to true power and the formation of a superior character. It works in the following manner: You examine yourself as thoroughly as possible. You look at the deepest layers of your character, determining whether you are an introvert or extrovert, whether you tend to be governed by high levels of anxiety and sensitivity, or hostility and anger, or a profound need to engage with people. You look at your primal inclinations—those subjects and activities you are naturally drawn to. You examine the quality of attachments you formed with your parents, looking at your current relationships as the best sign of this. You look with rigorous honesty at your own mistakes and the patterns that continually hold you back. You know your limitations—those situations in which you do not do your best. You also become aware of the natural strengths in your character that have survived past adolescence.

Now, with this awareness, you are no longer the captive of your character, compelled to endlessly repeat the same strategies and mistakes. As you see yourself falling into one of your usual patterns, you can catch yourself in time and step back. You may not be able to completely eliminate such patterns, but with practice you can mitigate their effects. Knowing your limitations, you will not try your hand at things for which you have no capacity or inclination. Instead, you will choose career paths that suit you and mesh with your character. In general, you accept and embrace your character. Your desire is not to become someone else but to be more thoroughly yourself, realizing your true potential. You see your character as the clay that you will work with, slowly transforming your very weaknesses into strengths. You do not run away from your flaws but rather see them as a true source of power.

Look at the career of the actress Joan Crawford (1908–1977). Her earliest years would seem to mark her as someone extremely unlikely to make it in life. She never knew her father, who abandoned the family shortly after her birth. She grew up in poverty. Her mother actively disliked Joan and constantly beat her. As a child she learned that the stepfather she adored was not really her father, and shortly thereafter he too abandoned the family. Her childhood was an endless series of punishments, betrayals, and abandonments, which scarred her for life. As she began her career as a film actress at a very young age, she examined herself and her flaws with ruthless objectivity: she was hypersensitive and fragile; she had a lot of pain and sadness she could not get rid of or disguise; she wanted desperately to be loved; she had a continual need for a father figure.

Such insecurities could easily be the death of someone in a place as ruthless as Hollywood. Instead, through much introspection and work, she managed to transform these very weaknesses into the pillars of her highly successful career. She decided, for instance, to bring her own feelings of sadness and betrayal into all of the different roles she played, making women around the world identify with her; she was unlike so many of the other actresses, who were so falsely cheerful and superficial. She directed her desperate need to be loved toward the camera itself, and audiences could feel it. The film directors became father figures whom she adored and treated with extreme respect. And her most pronounced quality, her hypersensitivity, she turned outward instead of inward. She developed intensely fine antennae tuned to the likes and dislikes of the directors she worked with. Without looking at them or hearing a word they said, she could sense their displeasure with her acting, ask the right questions, and quickly incorporate their criticisms. She was a director's dream. She coupled all of this with her fierce willpower, forging a career that spanned over forty years, something unheard of for an actress in Hollywood.

This is the alchemy that you must use on yourself. If you are a hyperperfectionist who likes to control everything, you must redirect this energy into some productive work instead of using it on people. Your attention to detail and high standards are a positive, if you channel them correctly. If you are a pleaser, you have developed courtier skills and real charm. If you can see the source of this trait, you can control the compulsive and defensive aspect of it and use it as a genuine social skill that can bring you great power. If you are highly sensitive and prone to take things personally, you can work to redirect this into active empathy (see chapter 2), and transform this flaw into an asset to use for positive social purposes. If you have a rebellious character, you have a natural dislike of conventions and the usual ways of doing things. Channel this into some kind of innovative work, instead of compulsively insulting and alienating people. For each weakness there is a corresponding strength.

Finally, you need to also refine or cultivate those traits that go into a strong character—resilience under pressure, attention to detail, the ability to complete things, to work with a team, to be tolerant of people's differences. The only way to do so is to work on your habits, which go into the slow formation of your character. For instance, you train yourself to not react in the moment by repeatedly placing yourself in stressful or adverse situations in order to get used to them. In boring everyday tasks, you cultivate greater patience and attention to detail. You deliberately take on tasks slightly above your level. In completing them, you have to work harder, helping you establish more discipline and better work habits. You train yourself to continually think of what is best for the team. You also search out others who display a strong character and associate with them as much as possible. In this way you can assimilate their energy and their habits. And to develop some flexibility in your character, always a sign of strength, you occasionally shake yourself up, trying out some new strategy or way of thinking, doing the opposite of what you would normally do.

With such work you will no longer be a slave to the character created by your earliest years and the compulsive behavior it leads to. Even further, you can now actively shape your very character and the fate that goes with it.

> In anything, it is a mistake to think one can perform an action or behave in a certain way once and no more. (The mistake of those who say: "Let us slave away and save every penny till we are thirty, then we will enjoy ourselves." At thirty they will have a bent for avarice and hard work, and will never enjoy themselves any more . . . .) What one does, one will do again, indeed has probably already done in the distant past. The agonizing thing in life is that it is our own decisions that throw us into this rut, under the wheels that crush us. (The truth is that, even before making those decisions, we were going in that direction.) A decision, an action, are infallible omens of what we shall do another time, not for any vague, mystic, astrological reason but because they result from an automatic reaction that will repeat itself.
>
> —Cesare Pavese

5

Become an Elusive Object of Desire

$\diamond$

The Law of Covetousness

A bsence and presence have very primal effects upon us. Too much presence suffocates; a degree of absence spurs our interest. We are marked by the continual desire to possess what we do not have—the object projected by our fantasies. Learn to create some mystery around you, to use strategic absence to make people desire your return, to want to possess you. Dangle in front of others what they are missing most in life, what they are forbidden to have, and they will go crazy with desire. The grass is always greener on the other side of the fence. Overcome this weakness in yourself by embracing your circumstances, your fate.

The Object of Desire

In 1895 eleven-year-old Gabrielle Chanel sat by her mother's bedside for several days and watched her slowly die from tuberculosis at the age of thirty-three. Gabrielle's life had been hard, but now it could only get worse. She and her siblings had grown up in poverty, shuttled from one relative's house to another. Their father was an itinerant peddler of goods who hated any kind of ties or responsibility and was rarely at home. Their mother, who often accompanied her husband on the road, was the only comforting force in their lives.

As Gabrielle had feared, a few days after the mother's death her father showed up and deposited Gabrielle and her two sisters at a convent in central France. He promised to return for them quite soon, but they would never see him again. The nuns at the convent, housed in a former medieval monastery, took in all sorts of girls to care for, mostly orphans. They enforced strict discipline.

Within the somber walls of the monastery, which was sparsely decorated, the girls were to live a life of austerity and spiritual practice. They each had only two dresses they could wear, both alike and formless. Luxuries were forbidden. The only music was church music. The food was exceptionally plain. In her first few months there, Gabrielle tried to accommodate herself to this new world, but she felt impossibly restless.

One day, she discovered a series of romance novels that somehow had been smuggled into the convent, and soon they became her only salvation. They were written by Pierre Decourcelle, and almost all of them involved a Cinderella-like story—a young girl growing up in poverty, shunned and despised, suddenly finds herself whisked into a world of wealth through some clever plot twist. Gabrielle could completely identify with the protagonists, and she particularly loved the endless descriptions of the dresses that the heroines would wear. The world of palaces and châteaux seemed so very far away from her, but in those moments in which she drifted through novel after novel she could feel herself participating in the plot, and it gave her an overwhelming desire to make it come to life, even though it was forbidden for her to want such things and seemingly impossible to ever have them.

At the age of eighteen she left the convent for a boarding school, also run by nuns. There she was trained for a career as a seamstress. The school was in a small town, and as she explored it she quickly discovered a new passion to pursue, the theater. She loved everything about it—the costumes, the sets, the performers in makeup. It was a world of transformation, where somebody could become anybody. Now all she wanted was to be an actress and make her name in the theater. She took the stage name Coco and she tried everything—acting, singing, and dancing. She had a lot of energy and charisma, but she realized quickly enough that she lacked the talent for the kind of success she desired.

Coming to terms with this, she soon hit upon a new dream. Many of the actresses who could not make a living from their work had become courtesans who were supported by wealthy lovers. Such women had enormous wardrobes, could go where they pleased, and, although they were shunned by good society, they were not shackled with some despotic husband. As luck would have it, one of the young men who enjoyed her on the stage, Etienne Balsan, invited her to stay in his nearby château. He had inherited a family fortune and lived a life of total leisure. Gabrielle, now known as Coco to one and all, accepted the offer.

The château was filled with courtesans who floated in and out from all over Europe. Some of them were famous. They were all beautiful and worldly. It was a relatively simple life that centered on riding horses in the country, then lavish parties in the evening. The class differences were noticeable. Whenever aristocrats or important people came to the château, women like Coco were to eat with the servants and make themselves scarce.

With nothing to do and feeling restless yet again, she began to analyze herself and the future ahead of her. Her ambitions were great, but she was always searching for something beyond her grasp, continually dreaming about a future that was just not possible. At first it was the palaces in the romance novels, then it was a grand life on the stage, becoming another Sarah Bernhardt. Now her latest dream was just as absurd. The great courtesans were all voluptuous, beautiful women. Coco looked more like a boy. She had no curves and was not a classic beauty. It was more her presence and energy that charmed men, but that would not last. She always wanted what other people had, imagining it contained some hidden treasure. Even when it came to other women and their boyfriends or husbands, her greatest desire was to steal the man away, which she had done on several occasions. But whenever she got what she wanted, including the boyfriend or the life in a château, she inevitably felt disappointed by the reality. It was a mystery what in the end could satisfy her.

Then one day, without thinking of what exactly she was up to, she wandered into Balsan's bedroom and pilfered some of his clothes. She started to wear outfits that were totally her own invention—his open-collared shirts and tweed coats, paired with some of her own clothes, all topped with a man's straw boater hat. In wearing the clothes she noticed two things: She felt an incredible sense of freedom as she left behind the corsets, constricting gowns, and fussy headpieces women were wearing. And she reveled in the new kind of attention she received. The other courtesans now watched her with unconcealed envy. They were captivated by this androgynous style. These new outfits suited her figure well, and nobody had ever seen a woman dressed quite in this manner. Balsan himself was charmed. He introduced her to his tailor, and on her instructions the tailor custom-made for her a boy's riding costume with jodhpurs. She taught herself to ride horses, but not sidesaddle like the other women. She had always had an athletic bent to her character and within months had become an expert rider. Now she could be seen everywhere in her strange riding costume.

As she progressed with this new persona, it finally became clear to her the nature of her vague longings: what she wanted was the power and freedom that men possessed, which was reflected in the less constricting clothes that they wore. And she could sense that the other courtesans and women at the château could identify with this. It was something in the air, a repressed desire she had tapped into. Within a few weeks several of the courtesans began to visit her in her room and try on the straw hats that she had decorated with ribbons and feathers. Compared with the elaborate hats that women had to pin on their heads, these were simple and easy to wear. The courtesans now strode around town with Chanel's hats on their heads, and soon other women in the area were asking where they could buy them. Balsan offered her the use of his apartment in Paris, where she could begin to make many more of her hats and perhaps go into business. She happily took up the offer.

Soon another man entered her life—a wealthy Englishman named Arthur Capel, who was excited by the novelty of her look and her great ambitions. They became lovers. Capel started sending his aristocratic lady friends to Coco's studio, and soon her hats became a craze. Along with the hats she began to sell some clothes that she designed, all with the same androgynous look that she had worn herself, made out of the cheapest jersey fabric but seeming to offer a kind of freedom of movement so different from the prevailing styles. Capel encouraged her to open up a shop in the seaside town of Deauville, where all the fashionable Parisians spent their summers. It turned out to be the perfect idea: there in the relatively small town, filled with people-watchers and the most fashionable women of all, she could create a sensation.

She shocked the locals by swimming in the ocean. Women did not do such things, and swimming costumes for women were almost nonexistent, so she created her own out of the same jersey fabric. Within weeks women were at her store clamoring to buy them. She sauntered through Deauville wearing her own distinctive outfits—androgynous, easy to move in, and ever so slightly provocative as they hugged the body. She became the talk of the town. Women were desperate to find out where she got her wardrobe. She kept improvising with men's clothing to create new looks. She took one of Capel's sweaters and cut it open, added some buttons, and created a modern version of the cardigan, for women. This now became the rage. She cut her own hair to a short length, knowing how it suited her face, and suddenly this became the new trend. Sensing momentum, she gave her clothes without charge to beautiful and well-connected women, all sporting hairstyles similar to her own. Attending the most sought-after parties, these women, all looking like Chanel clones, spread the desire for this new style well beyond Deauville, to Paris itself.

By 1920 she had become one of the leading fashion designers in the world,

and the greatest trendsetter of her time. Her clothes had come to represent a
new kind of woman—confident, provocative, and ever so slightly rebellious.
Although they were cheap to make and still out of jersey material, she sold
some of her dresses at extremely high prices, and wealthy women were more
than willing to pay to share in the Chanel mystique. But quickly her old restlessness returned. She wanted something else, something larger, a faster way to
reach women of all classes. To realize this dream she decided upon a most unusual strategy—she would create and launch her own perfume.

At the time it was unusual for a fashion house to market its own perfume,
and unheard of to give it so much emphasis. But Chanel had a plan. This perfume would be as distinctive as her clothes yet more ethereal, literally something in the air that would excite men and women and infect them with the
desire to possess it. To accomplish this she would go in the opposite direction
from all the other perfumes out there, which were associated with some natural, floral scent. Instead, she wanted to create something that was not identifiable as a particular flower. She wanted it to smell like "a bouquet of abstract
flowers," something pleasant but completely novel. More than any other perfume, it would smell different on each woman. To take this further, she decided
to give it a most unusual name. Perfumes of the time had very poetic, romantic
titles. Instead, she would name it after herself, attaching a simple number, Chanel No. 5, as if it were a scientific concoction. She packaged the perfume in a
sleek modernist bottle and added to the label her new logo of interlocking C's.
It looked like nothing else out there.

To launch the perfume, she decided upon a subliminal campaign. She began
by spraying the scent everywhere in her store in Paris. It filled the air. Women
kept asking what it was and she would feign ignorance. She would then slip
bottles of the perfume, without labels, into the bags of her wealthiest and best-
connected clients. Soon women began to talk of this strange new scent, rather
haunting and impossible to identify as any known flower. The word of yet
another Chanel creation began to spread like wildfire and women were soon
showing up at her store begging to buy the new scent, which she now began to
place discreetly on shelves. In the first few weeks they could not stock enough.
Nothing like this had ever happened in the industry, and it would go on to
become the most successful perfume in history, making her a fortune.

Over the next two decades the house of Chanel reigned supreme in the
fashion world, but during World War II she flirted with Nazism, staying in
Paris during the Nazi occupation and visibly siding with the occupiers. She had

closed her store at the beginning of the war, and by the end of the war she had been thoroughly disgraced in the eyes of the French by her political sympathies. Aware and perhaps ashamed, she fled to Switzerland, where she would remain in self-imposed exile. By 1953, however, she felt the need not only for a comeback but for something even greater. Although she was now seventy, she had become disgusted at the latest trends in fashion, which she felt had returned to the old constrictions and fussiness of women's clothing that she had sought to destroy. Perhaps this also signaled a return to a more subservient role for women. To Chanel it would be the ultimate challenge—after some fourteen years out of business, she was now largely forgotten. No one thought of her anymore as a trendsetter. She would have to start almost completely over.

Her first move was to encourage rumors that she was planning a return, but she gave no interviews. She wanted to stimulate talk and excitement but surround herself with mystery. Her new show debuted in 1954, and an enormous crowd filled her store to watch it, mostly out of curiosity. Almost immediately there was a sense of disappointment. The clothes were mostly a rehash of her 1930s styles with a few new touches. The models were all Chanel look-alikes and mimicked her way of walking. To the audience, Chanel seemed a woman hopelessly locked in a past that would never return. The clothes seemed passé and the press pilloried her, dredging up at the same time her Nazi associations during the war.

For almost any designer this would have been a devastating blow, but she appeared remarkably unfazed by it all. As always, she had a plan and she knew better. She had decided well before the debut in Paris that the United States was to be the target of this new line of clothes. American women reflected her sensibility best of all—athletic, into ease of movement and unfussy silhouettes, eminently practical. And they had more money to spend than anyone else in the world. Sure enough, the new line created a sensation in the States. Soon the French began to tone down their criticisms. Within a year of her return she had reestablished herself as the most important designer in the world, and fashions now returned to the simpler and more classical shapes she had always promoted. When Jacqueline Kennedy began to wear her suits in many of her public appearances, it was the most apparent symbol of the power Chanel had reclaimed.

As she resumed her place at the top, she revealed another practice that was so against the times and the industry. Piracy was a great problem in fashion, as knockoffs of established designs would appear all over the world after a show.

Designers carefully guarded all of their secrets and fought through the courts any form of imitation. Chanel did the opposite. She welcomed all sorts of people into her shows and allowed them to take photographs. She knew this would only encourage the many people who made a living out of creating cheap versions of her clothes, but she wanted this. She even invited wealthy women to bring along their seamstresses, who would make sketches of the designs and then create replicas of them. More than making money, what she wanted most of all was to spread her fashions everywhere, to feel herself and her work to be objects of desire by women of all classes and nations. It would be the ultimate revenge for the girl who had grown up ignored, unloved, and shunned. She would clothe millions of women; her look, her imprint would be seen everywhere—as indeed it was a few years after her comeback.

Interpretation: The moment Chanel tried on Etienne Balsan's clothes and elicited a new kind of attention, something clicked in her brain that would forever change the course of her life. Prior to this she was always coveting something transgressive that stimulated her fantasies. It was not socially acceptable for a lowly orphan girl to aspire to mingle with the upper classes. Actress and courtesan were not suitable roles to pursue, especially for someone raised in a convent.

Now, as she rode around the château in her jodhpurs and boater hat, *she* was suddenly the object that other people coveted. And they were drawn to the transgressive aspect of her clothing, the deliberate flouting of gender roles. Instead of being locked in her imaginary world full of dreams and fantasies, she could be the one stimulating such fantasies in other people. All that was required was to reverse her perspective—to think of the audience first and to strategize how to play on their imagination. The objects she had desired since childhood were all somewhat vague, elusive, and taboo. That was their allure. That is the nature of human desire. She simply had to turn this around and incorporate such elements into the objects she created.

This is how she performed such magic: First, she surrounded herself and what she made with an aura of mystery. She never talked about her impoverished childhood. She made up countless contradictory stories about her past. Nobody really knew anything concrete about her. She carefully controlled the number of her public appearances, and she knew the value of disappearing for a while. She never revealed the recipe for her perfume or her creative process in general. Her oddly compelling logo was designed to stimulate interpretations. All of this gave endless space for the public to imagine and speculate about the Coco myth. Second, she always associated her designs with something vaguely transgressive. The clothes had a distinct masculine edge but remained decidedly feminine. They gave women the sense that they were crossing some gender boundaries—physically and psychologically loosening constrictions. The clothes also conformed more to the body, combining freedom of movement with sex. These were not your mother's clothes. To wear the overall Chanel look was to make a statement about youth and modernity. Once this took hold, it was hard for young women to resist the call.

Finally, from the beginning she made sure her clothes were seen everywhere. Observing other women wearing such clothes stimulated competitive desires to have the same and not be left out. Coco remembered how deeply she had desired men who were already taken. They were desirable because someone else desired them. Such competitive impulses are powerful in all of us, and certainly among women.

In truth, the boater hats she originally designed were nothing more than common objects anyone could buy in a department store. The clothes she first designed were made out of the cheapest materials. The perfume was a mix of ordinary flowers, such as jasmine, and chemicals, nothing exotic or special. It was pure psychological magic that transformed them into objects that stimulated such intense desires to possess them.

Understand: Just like Chanel, you need to reverse your perspective. Instead of focusing on what you want and covet in the world, you must train yourself to focus on others, on their repressed desires and unmet fantasies. You must train yourself to see how they perceive you and the objects you make, as if you were looking at yourself and your work from the outside. This will give you the almost limitless power to shape people's perceptions about these objects and excite them. People do not want truth and honesty, no matter how much we hear such nonsense endlessly repeated. They want their imaginations to be stimulated and to be taken beyond their banal circumstances. They want fantasy and objects of desire to covet and grope after. Create an air of mystery around you and your work. Associate it with something new, unfamiliar, exotic, progressive, and taboo. Do not define your message but leave it vague. Create an illusion of ubiquity—your object is seen everywhere and desired by others. Then let the covetousness so latent in all humans do the rest, setting off a chain reaction of desire.

At last I have what I wanted. Am I happy? Not really. But what's missing? My soul no longer has that piquant activity conferred by desire. . . . Oh, we shouldn't delude ourselves—pleasure isn't in the fulfillment, but in the pursuit.

—Pierre-Augustin Caron de Beaumarchais

Keys to Human Nature

By nature, we humans are not easily contented with our circumstances. By some perverse force within us, the moment we possess something or get what we want, our minds begin to drift toward something new and different, to imagine we can have better. The more distant and unattainable this new object, the greater is our desire to have it. We can call this the *grass-is-always-greener syndrome*, the psychological equivalent of an optical illusion—if we get too close to the grass, to that new object, we see that is not really so green after all.

This syndrome has very deep roots in our nature. The earliest recorded example can be found in the Old Testament, in the story of the exodus from Egypt. Chosen by God to bring the Hebrews to the Promised Land, Moses led them into the wilderness, where they would wander for forty years. In Egypt the Hebrews had served as slaves and their lives had been difficult. Once they suffered hardships in the desert, however, they suddenly grew nostalgic for their previous life. Facing starvation, God provided them with manna from heaven, but they could only compare it unfavorably to the delicious melons and cucumbers and meats they had known in Egypt. Not sufficiently excited by God's other miracles (the parting of the Red Sea, for example), they decided to forge and worship a golden calf, but once Moses punished them for this, they quickly dropped their interest in this new idol.

All along the way they griped and complained, giving Moses endless headaches. The men lusted after foreign women; the people kept looking for some new cult to follow. God himself was so irritated by their endless discontent that he barred this entire generation, including Moses, from ever entering the Promised Land. But even after the next generation established itself in the land of milk and honey, the grumbling continued unabated. Whatever they had, they dreamed of something better over the horizon.

Closer to home, we can see this syndrome at work in our daily lives. We continually look at other people who seem to have it better than us—their parents were more loving, their careers more exciting, their lives easier. We may be in a perfectly satisfying relationship, but our minds continually wander toward a new person, someone who doesn't have the very real flaws of our partner, or so we think. We dream of being taken out of our boring life by traveling to some culture that is exotic and where people are just happier than in the grimy city where we live. The moment we have a job, we imagine something better. On a political level, our government is corrupt and we need some real change, perhaps a revolution. In this revolution, we imagine a veritable utopia that replaces the imperfect world we live in. We don't think of the vast majority of revolutions in history in which the results were more of the same, or something worse.

In all these cases, if we got closer to the people we envy, to that supposed happy family, to the other man or woman we covet, to the exotic natives in a culture we wish to know, to that better job, to that utopia, we would see through the illusion. And often when we act on these desires, we realize this in our disappointment, but it doesn't change our behavior. The next object glittering in the distance, the next exotic cult or get-rich-quick scheme will inevitably seduce us.

One of the most striking examples of this syndrome is the view we take of our childhood as it recedes into the past. Most of us remember a golden time of play and excitement. As we get older, it becomes even more golden in our memory. Of course, we conveniently forget the anxieties, insecurities, and hurts that plagued us in childhood and more than likely consumed more of our mental space than the fleeting pleasures we remember. But because our youth is an object that grows more distant as we age, we are able to idealize it and see it as greener than green.

Such a syndrome can be explained by three qualities of the human brain. The first is known as *induction*, how something positive generates a contrasting negative image in our mind. This is most obvious in our visual system. When we see some color—red or black, for instance—it tends to intensify our perception of the opposite color around us, in this case green or white. As we look at the red object, we often can see a green halo forming around it. In general, the mind operates by contrasts. We are able to formulate concepts about something by becoming aware of its opposite. The brain is continually dredging up these contrasts.

What this means is that whenever we see or imagine something, our minds cannot help but see or imagine the opposite. If we are forbidden by our culture to think a particular thought or entertain a particular desire, that taboo instantly brings to mind the very thing we are forbidden. Every no sparks a corresponding yes. (It was the outlawing of pornography in Victorian times that created the first pornographic industry.) We cannot control this vacillation in the mind between contrasts. This predisposes us to think about and then desire exactly what we do not have.

Second, complacency would be a dangerous evolutionary trait for a conscious animal such as humans. If our early ancestors had been prone to feeling content with present circumstances, they would not have been sensitive enough to possible dangers that lurked in the most apparently safe environments. We survived and thrived through our continual conscious alertness, which predisposed us to thinking and imagining the possible negative in any circumstance. We no longer live in savannas or forests teeming with life-threatening predators and natural dangers, but our brains are wired as if we were. We are inclined therefore toward a continual negative bias, which often consciously is expressed through complaining and griping.

Finally, what is real and what is imagined are both experienced similarly in the brain. This has been demonstrated through various experiments in which subjects who imagine something produce electrical and chemical activity in their brains that is remarkably similar to when they actually live out what they are imagining, all of this shown through functional magnetic resonance imaging (fMRI). Reality can be quite harsh and is full of limits and problems. We all must die. Every day we get older and less strong. To become successful requires sacrifice and hard work. But in our imagination we can voyage beyond these limits and entertain all kinds of possibilities. Our imagination is essentially limitless. And what we imagine has almost the force of what we actually experience. And so we become creatures who are continually prone to imagining something better than present circumstances and feeling some pleasure in the release from reality that our imagination brings us.

All of this makes the grass-is-always-greener syndrome inevitable in our psychological makeup. We should not moralize or complain about this possible flaw in human nature. It is a part of the mental life of each one of us, and it has many benefits. It is the source of our ability to think of new possibilities and innovate. It is what has made our imagination such a powerful instrument. And on the flip side it is the material out of which we can move, excite, and seduce people.

Knowing how to work on people's natural covetousness is a timeless art that we depend on for all forms of persuasion. The problem we face today is not that people have suddenly stopped coveting but quite the opposite: that we are losing our connection to this art and the power that goes with it.

We see evidence of this in our culture. We live in an age of bombardment and saturation. Advertisers blanket us with their messages and brand presence, directing us here or there to click and buy. Movies bludgeon us over the head, attacking our senses. Politicians are masters at stirring up and exploiting our discontent with present circumstances, but they have no sense of how to spark our imagination about the future. In all of these cases subtlety is sacrificed, and all of this has an overall hardening effect on our imaginations, which secretly crave something else.

We see evidence of this in personal relationships as well. More and more people have come to believe that others should simply desire them for who they are. This means revealing as much as they can about themselves, exposing all of their likes and dislikes, and making themselves as familiar as possible. They leave no room for imagination or fantasy, and when the man or woman they want loses interest in them, they go online to rant at the superficiality of men or the fecklessness of women. Increasingly self-absorbed (see chapter 2), we find it harder than ever to get into the psychology of the other person, to imagine what they want from us instead of what we want from them.

Understand: People may point to all of this as evidence that we humans are becoming more honest and truthful, but human nature does not change within a few generations. People have become more obvious and forthright not out of some deep moral calling but out of increasing self-absorption and overall laziness. It requires no effort to simply be oneself or to blast one's message. And the lack of effort simply results in a lack of effect on other people's psychology. It means that people's interest in you will be paper thin. Their attention will quickly move on and you will not see the reason for this. Do not swallow the easy moralism of the day, which urges honesty at the expense of desirability. Go in the opposite direction. With so few people out there who understand the art of desirability, it affords you endless opportunities to shine and exploit people's repressed fantasies.

Strategies for Stimulating Desire

The key to making this law work for you is to objectify yourself and what you produce. Normally you are locked in your own thoughts and dreams. You imagine people should love and respect you for who you are. You believe that what you produce should naturally excite people. After all, you have invested a lot of effort and have high hopes for success. But others see none of this. To them, you are just a person among others, and as a person you inspire either curiosity and excitement or indifference, and, even hostility. They project onto you their own fantasies and preconceptions. Once made public, your work is also an object completely divorced from your own hopes and dreams, and it inspires emotions that are weak or strong. To the degree that you can see yourself and what you produce as objects that people perceive in their own manner, you have the power to alter their perceptions and create objects of desire.

The following are the three main strategies for creating such objects.

Know how and when to withdraw. This is the essence of the art. You have a presence that people see and interpret. If you are too obvious with this, if people can read you too easily and figure you out, if you show your needs too visibly, then they will unconsciously begin to have a degree of disrespect; over time they will lose interest. Your presence must have a touch of coldness to it, as if you feel like you could do without others. This signals to people that you consider yourself worthy of respect, which unconsciously heightens your value in their eyes. It makes people want to chase after you. This touch of coldness is the first form of withdrawal that you must practice. Add to this a bit of blankness and ambiguity as to who you are. Your opinions, values, and tastes are never too obvious to people. This gives them room to read into you what they want. Movie stars are masters of this. They turn their faces and their presence into screens upon which people can project their own fantasies. What you want in general is to create an air of mystery and to attract interpretations.

Once you sense that you have engaged people's imagination, that you have your hooks in them, then you must use physical absence and withdrawal. You are not so available. A day or week can go by without your presence. You create a feeling of emptiness inside them, a touch of pain. You occupy increasing amounts of their mental space in these absences. They come to want more of you, not less.

The musician Michael Jackson played this game to perfection on the social level. He was deeply aware of the dangers of saturating the market with his music and public appearances. He spread out the releases of his albums, making the public hungry for more. He carefully managed the frequency of his interviews and performances and never talked about the meaning of his lyrics or propagated any overt message. He occasionally had his publicists leak to the press some new story surrounding him, such as his use of hyperbaric chambers as a way to maintain eternal youthfulness. He would neither confirm nor deny these stories and the press would run wild. He was someone who sparked stories and rumors, but nothing concrete. Through this strategic elusiveness he made himself an object of continual desire—both to know him better and to possess his music.

With the work you produce you can create similar covetous effects. Always leave the presentation and the message relatively open-ended. People can read into your work several interpretations. Never define exactly how they should take or use it. This is why the work of great dramatists such as Shakespeare and Chekhov has lasted for so many centuries and always seem so fresh and exciting; each generation can read into their plays what they want to. These writers described timeless elements of human nature, but without judging or directing the audience to what they should feel or think. Take that as the model for whatever you produce.

Keep in mind the following: the more active our imagination becomes, the greater the pleasure we derive from it. When we were children, if we were given a game with explicit instructions and rules, we quickly lost interest. But if the game was something we invented or was loosely structured, allowing us to inject our own ideas and fantasies, we could sustain our interest for much longer. When we view an abstract painting that evokes dreams or fantasies, or see a film that is not easily interpreted, or hear a joke or advertisement that is ambiguous, *we* are the ones who do the interpreting, and we find it exciting to be able to exercise our imagination in this way. Through your work you want to stimulate this pleasure for people to the maximum degree.

Create rivalries of desire. Human desire is never an individual phenomenon. We are social creatures and what we want almost always reflects what other people want. This stems from our earliest years. We saw the attention that our parents could give us (the object we first coveted) as a zero-sum game. If our siblings received a lot of attention, then there would be less for us. We had to compete with them and with others to get attention and affection. When we saw our siblings or friends receive something—a gift or a favor—it sparked a competitive desire to have the same thing. If some object or person was not desired by others, we tended to see it as something indifferent or distasteful—there must be something wrong with it.

This becomes a lifelong pattern. For some it is more overt. In relationships they are interested only in men or women who are already taken, who are clearly desired by a third party. Their desire is to take away this loved object, to triumph over the other person, a dynamic that most certainly has roots in their childhood. If other people are making money through some new gimmick, they want not only to participate but to corner the market. For others it is subtler. They see people possessing something that seems exciting, and their desire is not to take but to share and participate in the experience. In either direction, when we see people or things desired by others, it drives up their value.

You must learn how to exploit this. If you can somehow create the impression that others desire you or your work, you will pull people into your current without having to say a word or impose yourself. They will come to you. You must strive to surround yourself with this social aura, or at least create the illusion.

You can create this effect in several ways. You manage it so that your object is seen or heard everywhere, even encouraging piracy if necessary, as Chanel did. You don't directly intervene. This will inevitably spark some kind of viral pull. You can speed up this process by feeding rumors or stories about the object through various media. People will begin to talk and the word of mouth will spread the effect. Even negative comments or controversy will do the trick, sometimes even better than praise. It will give your object a provocative and transgressive edge. Anyway, people are drawn toward the negative. Your silence or lack of overt direction of the message will allow people to run wild with their own stories and interpretations. You can also get important people or tastemakers to talk about it and fan the flames. What you are offering, they say, is new, revolutionary, something not seen or heard of before. You are trafficking in the future, in trends. At a certain point, enough people will feel the pull and will not want to be left out, which will pull in others. The only problem in this game is that in the world today you have much competition for these viral effects and the public is incredibly fickle. You must be a master not only at setting off these chain reactions but at renewing them or creating new ones.

As an individual you must make it clear that people desire you, that you have a past—not too much of a past to inspire mistrust but enough to signal that others have found you desirable. You want to be indirect in this. You want them to hear stories of your past. You want them to literally see the attention you receive from men or women, all of this without your saying a word. Any bragging or explicit signaling of this will neutralize the effect.

In any negotiating situation you must always strive to bring in a third or fourth party to vie for your services, creating a rivalry of desire. This will immediately enhance your value, not just in terms of a bidding war but also in the fact that people will see that others covet you.

Use induction. We may think we live in a time of great freedom compared with the past, but in fact we live in a world that is more regulated than ever before. Our every move is followed digitally. There are more laws than ever governing all aspects of human behavior. Political correctness, which has always existed, can be more intense because of how visible we have become on social media. Secretly most of us feel bothered or crushed by all of these constraints on our physical and mental movement. We yearn for what is transgressive and beyond the limits that are set for us. We can easily be pulled toward that repressed no or yes.

You want to associate your object with something ever so slightly illicit, unconventional, or politically advanced. Chanel did this with her overt androgynous appeal and flouting of gender roles. The fight between generations is always ripe material for this. What you offer is in bold contrast to the stodgy previous generation. John F. Kennedy did this by setting himself off against the 1950s and the Eisenhower era—a time of stultifying conformity. By contrast, voting for him meant youth, vigor, and a lost masculinity. In essence he played to the secret resentment of the father figure and the transgressive desire to get rid of him. This desire is always tacitly out there among the young, and it always has a taboo element attached.

One illicit desire that almost all people share is voyeurism. To peek inside the private lives of others violates strict social taboos on privacy, and yet everyone feels the pull to see what is going on behind people's doors. Theater and film depend upon these voyeuristic desires. They put us inside people's rooms, and we experience this almost as if we were literally spying on people. You can incorporate this into your work by giving the impression you are revealing secrets that should really not be shared. Some will be outraged but everyone will be curious. These could be secrets about yourself and how you accomplished what you did, or it could be about others, what happens behind the closed doors of powerful people and the laws that they operate by.

In any event, what you offer should be new, unfamiliar, and exotic, or at least presented as such. The contrast to what is out there, so numbingly conventional, will create a covetous pull.

Finally, dangle in front of people the prospect of grasping the unattainable or the impossible. Life is full of all kinds of irritating limits and difficulties. To become wealthy or successful requires great effort. We are locked inside our own character (see chapter 4) and cannot become someone else. We cannot recover our lost youth or the health that went with it. Every day brings us closer to death, the ultimate limit. Your object, however, offers the fantasy of a quick path to wealth and success, of recovering lost youth, of becoming a new person, and even of conquering death itself. People will grasp greedily at such things because they are considered so impossible. By the law of induction we can imagine all of these shortcuts and fantasies (just as we can imagine a unicorn), which gives us the desire to reach them, and imagining them is almost like experiencing them.

Remember: it is not possession but desire that secretly impels people. To possess something inevitably brings about some disappointment and sparks the desire for something new to pursue. You are preying upon the human need for fantasies and the pleasures of chasing after them. In this sense your efforts must be continually renewed. Once people get what they want or possess you, your value and their respect for you immediately begin to lower. Keep withdrawing, surprising, and stimulating the chase. As long as you do, you have the power.

The Supreme Desire

Our path must always be toward greater awareness of our nature. We must see within ourselves the grass-is-always-greener syndrome at work and how it continually impels us to certain actions. We need to be able to distinguish between what is positive and productive in our covetous tendencies and what is negative and counterproductive. On the positive side, feeling restless and discontented can motivate us to search for something better and to not settle for what we have. It enlarges our imagination as we consider other possibilities instead of the circumstances we face. As we get older, we tend to become more complacent, and renewing the restlessness of our earlier years can keep us youthful and our minds active.

This restlessness, however, must be under conscious control. Often our discontent is merely chronic; our desire for change is vague and a reflection of our boredom. This leads to a waste of precious time. We are unhappy with the way our career is going and so we make a big change, which requires learning new skills and acquiring new contacts. We enjoy the newness of it all. But several years later we again feel the stirring of discontent. This new path isn't right either. We would have been better off thinking about this more deeply, homing in on those aspects of our previous career that did not click and trying for a more gentle change, choosing a line of work related to the previous one but requiring an adaptation of our skills.

With relationships, we can spend our life searching for the perfect man or woman and end up largely alone. There is nobody perfect. Instead, it is better to come to terms with the flaws of the other person and accept them or even find some charm in their weaknesses. Calming down our covetous desires, we can then learn the arts of compromise and how to make a relationship work, which never come easily or naturally.

Instead of constantly chasing after the latest trends and modeling our desires on what others find exciting, we should spend our time getting to know our own tastes and desires better, so that we can distinguish what is something we truly need or want from that which has been manufactured by advertisers or viral effects.

Life is short and we have only so much energy. Led by our covetous desires, we can waste so much time in futile searches and changes. In general, do not constantly wait and hope for something better, but rather make the most of what you have.

Consider it this way: You are embedded in an environment that consists of the people you know and the places you frequent. This is your reality. Your mind is being continually drawn far away from this reality, because of human nature. You dream of traveling to exotic places, but if you go there, you merely drag with you your own discontented frame of mind. You search for entertainment that will bring you new fantasies to feed upon. You read books filled with ideas that have no relation to your daily life, that are full of empty speculations about things that only half exist. And none of this turmoil and ceaseless desire for what is most distant ever leads to anything fulfilling—it only stirs up more chimeras to pursue. In the end you cannot escape from yourself.

On the other hand, reality beckons you. To absorb your mind in what is nearest, instead of most distant, brings a much different feeling. With the people in your circle, you can always connect on a deeper level. There is much you will never know about the people you deal with, and this can be a source of endless fascination. You can connect more deeply to your environment. The place where you live has a deep history that you can immerse yourself in. Knowing your environment better will present many opportunities for power. As for yourself, you have mysterious corners you can never fully understand. In trying to know yourself better, you can take charge of your own nature instead of being a slave to it. And your work has endless possibilities for improvement and innovation, endless challenges for the imagination. These are the things that are closest to you and compose your real, not virtual world.

In the end what you really must covet is a deeper relationship to reality, which will bring you calmness, focus, and practical powers to alter what it is possible to alter.

> It is advisable to let everyone of your acquaintance—whether man or woman—feel now and then that you could very well dispense with their company. This will consolidate friendship. Nay, with most people there will be no harm in occasionally mixing a grain of disdain with your treatment of them; that will make them value your friendship all the more. . . . But if we really think very highly of a person, we should conceal it from him like a crime. This is not a very gratifying thing to do, but it is right. Why, a dog will not bear being treated too kindly, let alone a man!
>
> —Arthur Schopenhauer

6

Elevate Your Perspective

◇

The Law of Shortsightedness

*I*t is in the animal part of your nature to be most impressed by what you can see and hear in the present—the latest news reports and trends, the opinions and actions of the people around you, whatever seems the most dramatic. This is what makes you fall for alluring schemes that promise quick results and easy money. This is also what makes you overreact to present circumstances—becoming overly exhilarated or panicky as events turn one direction or the other. Learn to measure people by the narrowness or breadth of their vision; avoid entangling yourself with those who cannot see the consequences of their actions, who are in a continual reactive mode. They will infect you with this energy. Your eyes must be on the larger trends that govern events, on that which is not immediately visible. Never lose sight of your long-term goals. With an elevated perspective, you will have the patience and clarity to reach almost any objective.

Moments of Madness

All through the summer and early fall of 1719 the Englishman John Blunt (1665–1733), one of the lead directors of the South Sea Company, followed the latest news from Paris with increasing anxiety. The French were in the midst of a spectacular economic boom, fueled primarily by the success of the Mississippi Company, an enterprise started by the expatriate Scotsman John Law to exploit the riches in the Louisiana territories controlled by the French. Law sold shares in the company, and as its price kept rising, Frenchmen of all classes were cashing out and becoming fabulously wealthy. The word *millionaire* itself was coined in these months to refer to such nouveaux riches.

Such news made Blunt angry and envious. He was a loyal Englishman.

With the success of the Mississippi Company, Paris was drawing in investment capital from all over Europe. If this continued, France would soon become the finance capital of the world, surpassing Amsterdam and London. Such new-found power for the French could only spell disaster for England, its archenemy, particularly if another war broke out between them.

More personally, Blunt was a man of great ambition. He was the son of a humble shoemaker; from early on in his life he aimed to ascend to the highest levels of English society. His means of getting there, he believed, would be through the financial revolution sweeping Europe, which centered on the increasing popularity of joint-stock corporations like Law's and like the South Sea Company. As opposed to building wealth through the traditional means of owning land, which was expensive to manage and highly taxable, it was relatively easy to earn money through purchasing stock, and profits were tax free. Such investments were all the rage in London. Blunt had plans to turn the South Sea Company into the biggest and most prosperous joint-stock company in Europe, but John Law had stolen his thunder with a bold venture, and with the full backing of the French government. Blunt would simply have to come up with something bigger and better, for his sake and for the future of England.

The South Sea Company had been formed in 1710 as an enterprise that would handle and manage part of the English government's enormous debts, in exchange for which the company was to be granted a monopoly on all English trade with South America. Over the years the company did almost no trading but served as an informal bank for the government. Through his leadership of the company, Blunt had forged relationships with the wealthiest and most powerful Englishmen, most notably King George I (1660–1727) himself, who became one of its biggest investors and was named governor of the company. Blunt's motto in life had always been "Think big," and it had served him well. And so, as he racked his brain for a way to outdo the French, he finally hit upon a scheme in October of 1719 that was worthy of his motto and that he felt certain would change the course of history.

The greatest problem facing the English government, headed by the king, was the massive debts it had incurred over the course of thirty years during the wars that had been fought with France and Spain, all financed through borrowing. Blunt's proposal was simple and quite astounding: The South Sea Company would pay the government a nice fee in order to completely take over the debt, valued at a whopping £31 million. (The company would receive in exchange an annual interest payment on the debt.) The company would then privatize this £31 million debt and sell it as if it were a commodity, as shares in the South Sea Company—one share equaling £100 of debt. Those who had lent the government money could convert their IOUs into equivalent shares in the South Sea Company. The shares that were left over would be sold to the public.

The price for one share would start at £100. As with any stock, the price could rise and fall, but in this case, if played right, the price would only go up. The South Sea Company had an intriguing name and held out the possibility that it would also begin trading in the vast wealth in South America. It was also the patriotic duty of English creditors to participate in the scheme, since they would be helping to cancel the debt while potentially making much more money than the annual interest payments the government paid them. If the share price rose, as it almost certainly would, buyers could cash out for a profit and the company could afford to pay nice dividends. Like magic, debt could be transformed into wealth. This would be the answer to all of the government's problems, and it would assure Blunt lasting fame.

When King George first heard of Blunt's proposal in November of 1719, he was quite confused. He could not understand how such a negative (debt) could be instantly turned into a positive. Besides, this new jargon of finance went straight over his head. But Blunt spoke with such conviction that he found himself swept up in his enthusiasm. After all, he was promising to solve George's two greatest problems in one fell swoop, and it was hard to resist such a prospect.

King George was massively unpopular, one of the most unpopular English kings of all time. It was not totally his fault: he was not English by birth but German. His title previously had been the Duke of Brunswick and Elector of Hanover. When Queen Anne of England died in 1714, George was her closest living Protestant relative. But the moment he ascended the throne his new subjects found him not to their liking. He spoke English with a horrific accent, and his manners were so coarse, and he was always avid for more money. Despite his advanced age he was constantly chasing after women other than his wife, none of whom were particularly attractive. In the first years of his reign there were several coup attempts, and the public might have welcomed the change if they had succeeded.

George desperately wanted to prove to his new subjects that he could be a great king, in his own way. What he hated most of all was the crushing debts the government had incurred before he ascended the throne. George had an almost allergic reaction to any kind of debt, as if his own blood were being leeched.

Now here was Blunt offering him the chance to cancel the debt and bring prosperity to England, strengthening the monarchy in the process. It was almost too good to be true, and he threw his full weight behind the proposal. He assigned the chancellor of the exchequer, John Aislabie, the task of presenting the proposal to Parliament in January 1720. Parliament would have to approve it in the form of a bill. Almost immediately Blunt's proposal stirred up fierce opposition among several MPs, some of whom found it ludicrous. But in the weeks after Aislabie's speech, opponents of the bill watched in dismay as support for their side slowly withered away. Advance shares in the venture had been virtually gifted to the wealthiest and most powerful Englishmen, including prominent members of Parliament, who, sensing the sure profits they personally would gain, now gave their approval to the bill.

When the bill passed in April of that year, King George himself showed up at the South Sea House and deposited £100,000 for shares in the new venture. He wanted to display his confidence in it, but such a step was hardly necessary, as the buildup to the bill's passage had captured the public and interest in South Sea Company shares had already reached a fever pitch. The center of activity was an area of London known as Exchange Alley, where almost all stocks were sold. Now the narrow streets in and around the alley were clogged with traffic growing thicker by the day.

At first it was mostly the wealthy and influential who came in their fancy coaches to buy up shares. Among the buyers were also artists and intellectuals— including John Gay, Alexander Pope, and Jonathan Swift. Soon Sir Isaac Newton felt the pull and invested a good chunk of his savings, £7,000. A few weeks later, however, he felt doubt. The price was rising, but what rises can surely fall, and so he cashed out, doubling his initial investment.

Soon rumors began to circulate that the company was about to initiate trade in South America, where all kinds of riches lay buried in the mountains. This only added fuel to the fire, and people from all classes began to converge on London to buy up shares in the South Sea Company. Blunt, it was reported, was a financial alchemist who had found the secret of transforming debt into wealth. In the countryside farmers pulled up from under their beds their life savings in coins and sent their sons and nephews to buy as many shares as possible. The fever spread to women of all classes, who normally did not dabble in such things. Now actresses were rubbing elbows with duchesses in Exchange Alley. All the while, the price kept rising, over £300 and soon £400.

Like France before it, the country was now experiencing a spectacular boom. On May 28 the king celebrated his sixtieth birthday, and for someone who had been known for his frugality, it was the most lavish party anyone had ever seen, with enormous tubs full of claret and champagne. One woman at the party flaunted her new wealth by encrusting her dress with jewels worth over £5,000. Everywhere in London the wealthy were tearing down mansions and replacing them with houses that were even larger and grander. Porters and footmen were now quitting their jobs and buying expensive coaches and hiring porters and footmen of their own. One young actress made such a fortune, she decided to retire; she rented out an entire theater to say good-bye to her adoring fans. An aristocratic lady was astonished one evening at the opera to see that her former maid now occupied a more expensive box in the theater than her own. Jonathan Swift wrote in a letter to a friend, "I have enquired of some that have come from London, what is the religion there? They tell me it is South Sea stock. What is the policy of England? The answer is the same. What is the trade? South Sea still. And what is the business? Nothing but South Sea."

In this midst of this feverish buying and selling spree, there stood John Blunt at the pump, doing whatever he possibly could to stimulate the interest in South Sea shares and keep the price rising. He sold the stock in various subscriptions, offering generous terms of payment, sometimes requiring only a 20 percent advance to get in. For every £400 invested, Blunt would lend £300. He wanted to keep up the demand and make people feel that they might be missing out on their one chance for wealth. Soon the price had passed £500 and kept on rising. By June 15, he had set the subscription price at an astronomical £1,000, with only 10 percent down to get in and 10 percent installments spread out over four years. Few could resist such terms. That very month King George had Blunt knighted. Now a baronet, Sir John Blunt stood at the pinnacle of English society. Yes, he was rather unattractive to look at and he could be quite pompous. But he had made so many people so wealthy that he was now England's most cherished celebrity.

As the rich and powerful prepared to leave London for the summer months, the mood was downright giddy. Blunt affected a confident and carefree air, but underneath it he was beginning to feel worried, even panicky. There were so many things he had failed to foresee. He had inadvertently inspired a rash of new speculative ventures, some involving legitimate ideas and some patently absurd, such as the development of a wheel of perpetual motion. People were now feeling the fever and were pouring some of their money into these new joint-stock companies. Every £1 of cash that went into these was one £1 less that people had to spend on the South Sea Company, and that was a growing problem, since there was only so much cash in England, and there were limits to how far he could go by offering credit. Similarly, people were beginning to pour their money into land as a safe investment for the future, often cashing out their South Sea stock for such purposes. Blunt himself had been doing that very thing, unbeknownst to the public.

More troubling still, the French had lost faith in the Mississippi venture and were pulling out their money; cash had become scarce and the French economy had now fallen into a sudden depression. This would certainly affect the mood in London. Before people returned from their summer holidays, Blunt had to take action.

Working with Parliament, he got passed the Bubble Act of 1720, which banned all joint stocks not authorized by royal charter. This would put an end to rampant speculation. But this solution created consequences he did not foresee. Thousands of people had poured their savings into these new businesses, and as these were now outlawed, they had no way of getting their money back. Their only recourse was to sell South Sea shares. Many of those who had used credit to buy South Sea shares saw themselves facing installments they could no longer afford. They tried to cash out as well. The price of South Sea shares began to fall. That August crowds were forming outside the South Sea house as people felt desperate to sell.

Near the end of August Blunt became desperate himself. He decided to launch his fourth money subscription, once again at £1,000. Now the terms were even more generous than ever, and on top of it he was promising an astonishingly large Christmas dividend of 30 percent, to be followed by an annual dividend of 50 percent. Some were pulled back into the scheme by such alluring terms, including Sir Isaac Newton himself. But others, as if waking up from a dream, began to wonder about the whole thing: how could a company that had not traded for anything yet in South America, whose only tangible asset was the interest the government paid it on its debt, afford to dish out such large dividends? Now what had seemed like alchemy or magic appeared to be a downright hoax on the public. By early September the selling off had turned into a panic, as almost everyone rushed to convert paper shares into something real, into coin or metal of any kind.

As the panic for cash accelerated, the Bank of England was nearly brought down—it came close to running out of currency. It was now clear in England that the party was over. Many had lost their fortunes and life savings in the sudden downfall. Isaac Newton himself had lost some £20,000, and from then on the mere mention of finance or banks would make him ill. People were trying to sell whatever they could. Soon there was a wave of suicides, including that of Charles Blunt, Sir John's nephew, who slashed his throat after learning the exact nature of his losses.

Blunt himself was hounded in the streets and nearly killed by an assassin. He had to quickly escape London. He spent the rest of his life in the town of Bath, scraping by on the very modest means still left to him after Parliament seized almost all of the money he had earned through the South Sea scheme. Perhaps in his isolation he could contemplate the irony of it all—he had indeed changed the course of history and assured his fame for all time, as the man who had conjured up one of the most absurd and destructive schemes ever devised in the history of business.

Interpretation: John Blunt was a pragmatic, hard-nosed businessman with a single goal—to make a lasting fortune for himself and his family. In the summer of 1719, however, this highly realistic man caught a fever of sorts. When he began to read about what was going on in Paris, he was struck by the drama of it all. He read vivid stories about average Frenchmen suddenly making fortunes. He had never thought prior to this that investments in joint-stock companies could yield such quick results, but the evidence from France was irrefutable. He wanted to bring similar good fortune to England, and in crafting his plan he naturally imitated many of the features of Law's scheme, only increasing the scale of it.

What is striking here, however, is that one rather obvious question never seemed to cross his mind. The scheme would depend on the share price rising. If those who converted their government IOUs into shares had to pay £200 per share instead of £100, they would receive fewer shares, which would leave more shares for South Sea to sell to the public and make a nice profit. If the shares were purchased at £200 they were now worth more if the price continued to rise and were sold at some point. Seeing the price rise would lure more creditors to convert their shares and more people to buy in. Everyone would win only if the price kept rising. But how could the price keep rising if it was not based on any real assets, such as trade? If the price started to fall, as it inevitably would, panic would certainly set in, since people would lose faith in the scheme, and this could only set off a chain reaction of selling. How could Blunt not have foreseen this?

The answer is simple: Blunt's mental time frame had shrunk to the point where he lost the ability to look months down the road and consider consequences. Mesmerized by events in France and imagining all of the wealth and power he was on the verge of attaining, he could focus only on the present, making sure the scheme launched successfully. Its initial success only made him imagine it would trend this way for a long time. As it progressed, he certainly understood that he had to make the price rise even more quickly, and the only means of doing so was to lure in more investors through generous terms of credit. This would make the scheme even more precarious, one solution incurring several new dangers. The Bubble Act and the generous dividends carried even greater immediate risks, but by now his time frame had shrunk to a matter of days. If only he could keep the ship afloat another week, he would find some new solution. Finally, he ran out of time.

When people lose the connection between their actions and their consequences, they lose their hold on reality, and the further this goes the more it looks like madness. The madness that overcame Blunt soon infected the king, the Parliament, and eventually an entire nation of citizens renowned for their common sense. Once the English saw their compatriots making large sums of money, it became a fact—the scheme had to be a success. They too lost the ability to think a few months ahead. Look at what happened to Sir Isaac Newton, paragon of rationality. In the beginning he too caught the fever, but after a week his logical mind could see the holes in the scheme, and so he sold his shares. Then he watched others making much larger sums of money than his paltry £14,000 and it bothered him. By August he had to get back in, even though it was the absolute worst time to reinvest. Sir Isaac Newton himself had lost the ability to think past the day. As one Dutch banker observed of the scene in Exchange Alley, "[It resembled] nothing so much as if all the Lunatics had escaped out of the Madhouse at once."

Understand: We humans tend to live in the moment. It is the animal part of our nature. We respond first and foremost to what we see and hear, to what is most dramatic in an event. But we are not merely animals tied to the present. Human reality encompasses the past—every event is connected to something that happened before in an endless chain of historical causation. Any present problem has deep roots in the past. It also encompasses the future. Whatever we do has consequences that stretch far into the years to come.

When we limit our thinking to what our senses provide, to what is immediate, we descend to the pure animal level in which our reasoning powers are neutralized. We are no longer aware of why or how things come about. We imagine that some successful scheme that has lasted a few months can only get better. We no longer give thought to the possible consequences of anything we set in motion. We react to what is given in the moment, based on only a small piece of the puzzle. Naturally our actions then lead to unintended consequences, or even to disasters like the South Sea crash or the more recent crash of 2008.

To complicate matters, we are surrounded by others who are continually reacting, drawing us deeper into the present. Salesmen and demagogues play on this weakness in human nature to con us with the prospect of easy gains and instant gratification. Our only antidote is to train ourselves to continually detach from the immediate rush of events and elevate our perspective. Instead of merely reacting, we step back and look at the wider context. We consider the various possible ramifications of any action we take. We keep in mind our long-term goals. Often, in raising our perspective, we will decide that it is better to do nothing, to not react, and to let time go by and see what it reveals. (If Blunt had only waited a few months, he would have seen Law's scheme falling apart, and England would have been spared the ruin that came.) Such sanity and balance do not come naturally. They are powers we acquire through great effort, and they represent the height of human wisdom.

I can calculate the motion of heavenly bodies, but not the madness of people.

—Sir Isaac Newton

Keys to Human Nature

Almost all of us have experienced something similar to the following scenarios: Someone we need or depend on is not paying us proper attention, not returning our calls. Feeling frustrated, we express our feelings to him or double our efforts to get a response. Or we encounter a problem, a project that is not going well, and so we decide upon a strategy and take appropriate action. Or a new person appears in our life, and captivated by her fresh energy and charm, we become friends.

Then weeks go by and we are forced to reassess what had happened and how we had reacted. New information comes to light. That person who was not responding to us was himself overwhelmed with work. If only we had just waited and not been so impatient, we could have avoided pushing away a valuable ally. That problem we tried to solve was not really so urgent, and we made it worse by rushing an outcome. We needed to know more before acting. And that new friend ends up not being so charming; in fact, time reveals her to be a destructive sociopath whose friendship takes us years to heal from. A little more distance could have let us see the red flags before it was too late. Looking back on our life, we see that we have a tendency to be impatient and to over-react; we notice patterns of behavior over long periods of time that elude us in the moment but become clearer to us later on.

What this means is that in the present moment we lack perspective. With the passage of time, we gain more information and see more of the truth; what was invisible to us in the present now becomes visible in retrospect. Time is the greatest teacher of them all, the revealer of reality.

We can compare this to the following visual phenomenon: At the base of a mountain, in a thick forest, we have no ability to get our bearings or to map out our surroundings. We see only what is before our eyes. If we begin to move up the side of the mountain, we can see more of our surroundings and how they relate to other parts of the landscape. The higher we go, the more we realize that what we thought further below was not quite accurate, was based on a slightly distorted perspective. At the top of the mountain we have a clear panoramic view of the scene and perfect clarity as to the lay of the land.

For us humans, locked in the present moment, it as if we are living at the base of the mountain. What is most apparent to our eyes—the other people around us, the surrounding forest—gives us a limited, skewed vision of reality. The passage of time is like a slow ascent up the mountain. The emotions we felt in the present are no longer so strong; we can detach ourselves and see things more clearly. The further we ascend with the passage of time, the more information we add to the picture. What we saw three months after the fact is not quite as accurate as what we come to know a year later.

It would seem, then, that wisdom tends to come to us when it is too late, mostly in hindsight. But there is in fact a way for us humans to manufacture the effect of time, to give ourselves an expanded view in the present moment. We can call this the *farsighted perspective*, and it requires the following process.

First, facing a problem, conflict, or some exciting opportunity, we train ourselves to detach from the heat of the moment. We work to calm down our excitement or our fear. We get some distance.

Next, we start to deepen and widen our perspective. In considering the nature of the problem we are confronting, we don't just grab for an immediate explanation, but instead we dig deeper and consider other possibilities, other possible motivations for the people involved. We force ourselves to look at the overall context of the event, not just what immediately grabs our attention. We imagine as best we can the negative consequences of the various strategies we are contemplating. We consider how the problem or the apparent opportunity might play itself out over time, how other problems or issues not apparent in the moment might suddenly loom larger than what we are immediately dealing with. We focus on our long-term goals and realign our priorities in the present according to them.

In other words, this process involves *distance* from the present, a *deeper* look at the source of problems, a *wider* perspective on the overall context of the situation, and a look *further* into the future—including the consequences of our actions and our own long-term priorities.

As we go through this process, certain options and explanations will begin to seem more logical and realistic than others that grabbed us in the moment. We add to this the lessons we have learned over the years about our own patterns of behavior. In this way, though we cannot re-create the full effect that time has on our thinking, we can approximate it. Most often the passing months give us even more information and reveal better options for us to have taken. We are manufacturing this effect in the present by widening what we consider and opening our minds. We are moving up the mountain. Such an elevated perspective can calm us down and make it easier for us to maintain our presence of mind as events unfold.

Although this stands as an ideal, we must admit that such a perspective is rare among us humans. It seems to require an effort that is almost beyond us. The reason for this is simple: short-term thinking is hardwired into our system; we are built to respond to what is immediate and to seek out instant gratification. For our early human ancestors, it paid to notice what was potentially dangerous in the environment or what offered an opportunity for food. The human brain as it evolved was designed not to examine the full picture and context of an event but to home in on the most dramatic features. This worked well in a relatively simple environment and amid the simple social organization of the tribe. But it is not suited to the complex world we now live in. It makes us take notice mostly of what stimulates our senses and emotions, and miss much of the larger picture.

This has a decided impact on how we view the potential pleasure or pain involved in a situation. Our brains are designed to make us notice what could immediately harm us in our surroundings but not to pay great attention to other dangers looming in the future that are more abstract. This is why we tend to give much more attention to something like terrorism (immediate pain), which certainly deserves our scrutiny, than to global warming (distant pain), which in fact represents the greater danger since it puts the very survival of the planet at risk. But such a danger seems abstract in the present. By the time it becomes not abstract at all, it might be too late. We tend also to grab for things that offer immediate pleasure, even if we know about the negative long-term consequences. That is why people continue to smoke, drink, do drugs, or engage in any self-destructive behavior in which the destruction is not immediate and dramatic.

In a world that is complex, with myriad dangers that loom in the future, our short-term tendencies pose a continual threat to our well-being. And as our attention spans decrease because of technology, the threat is even greater. In many ways we are defined by our relationship to time. When we simply react to what we see and hear, when we swing from excitement and exuberance to fear and panic at each new piece of dramatic news, when we gear our actions toward gaining as much pleasure as possible in the moment without a thought for future consequences, we can say that we are giving in to our animal nature, to what is most primitive and potentially destructive in our neurological makeup.

When we strive to go against this grain, to consider more deeply the consequences of what we do and the nature of our long-term priorities, we are straining to realize our true human potential as the thinking animal. And just as short-term thinking can be contagious, one individual who embodies the wisdom of the farsighted perspective can have an immensely positive effect on the people around him or her. Such individuals make us aware of the larger picture and reveal a mind-set that we recognize as superior. We want to imitate them.

Throughout history there have been various icons of this wisdom to inspire and guide us: Joseph in the Old Testament, who could see into the hearts of men and foresee the future; Socrates of ancient Greece, who taught us how to be less foolish and more consequential in our thinking; the brilliant strategist Zhuge Liang of ancient China, who could predict every movement of the enemy; leaders such as Queen Elizabeth I and Abraham Lincoln, renowned for the success of their long-term strategizing; the very patient and prescient scientist Charles Darwin, who finally exposed the effects of deep time on the evolution of all living things; and Warren Buffett, the most successful investor in history, whose power is based on his farsighted perspective.

If possible, avoid deep contact with those whose time frame is narrow, who are in continual react mode, and strive to associate with those with an expanded awareness of time.

Four Signs of Shortsightedness and Strategies to Overcome Them

Most of us imagine that we engage in some form of long-term thinking; after all, we have goals and plans. But really we are fooling ourselves. We can see this most clearly when we talk to other people about *their* plans and strategies for the near and more distant future: we are often struck by their vagueness and the lack of deep thinking people generally give to such plans. They are more like hopes and wishes, and in the rush of immediate events, feeling pressure and the need to respond, such weak goals and plans are easily overwhelmed. Most of the time we are improvising and reacting to events with insufficient information. Basically we are in denial about this because it is hard to have perspective about our own decision-making process.

The best way to overcome this is to recognize the clear signs of shortsighted thinking in our own lives. As with most elements of human nature, awareness is the key. Only by seeing these signs can we combat them. The following are the four most common manifestations of short-term thinking:

1. **Unintended consequences.** History is littered with endless examples of this phenomenon. In ancient Rome, a group of men loyal to the Republic feared that Julius Caesar was going to make his dictatorship permanent and establish a monarchy. In 44 BC they decided to assassinate him, thereby restoring the Republic. In the ensuing chaos and power vacuum Caesar's great-nephew Octavius quickly rose to the top, assumed power, and permanently ended the Republic by establishing a de facto monarchy. After Caesar's death it

came out that he had never intended to create a monarchical system. The conspirators brought about precisely what they had tried to stop.

In nineteenth-century India, under British colonial rule, authorities decided there were too many venomous cobras in the streets of Delhi, making life uncomfortable for the British residents and their families. To solve this they offered a reward for every dead cobra residents would bring in. Soon enterprising locals began to breed cobras in order to make a living from the bounty. The government caught on to this and canceled the program. The breeders, resentful of the rulers and angered by their actions, decided to release their cobras back on the streets, thereby tripling the population from before the government program.

Other notorious examples would include the Eighteenth Amendment, establishing Prohibition in the United States in 1920, which was designed to stop the spread of alcoholism but only ended up increasing alcohol consumption by a substantial amount; and the surprise attack on Pearl Harbor by the Japanese in 1941, designed to decimate the U.S. naval force in one blow and bring America to its knees. Instead it shook the American public out of its deep isolationism, ensuring the total mobilization of the country's superior manpower and resources to not only defeat the Japanese but also to obliterate its military for good. The very success of the attack guaranteed the opposite of the intended result.

We can find less dramatic examples of this in our daily lives. We try to control a rebellious teenager by putting some restrictions on his behavior, only to make him even more rebellious and uncontrollable. We try to cheer up a depressed person by making her realize that her life is not that bad and that the sun is shining, only to find out we have made her even more depressed. She now feels guilty about her feelings, worthless, and more alone in her unhappiness. A wife tries to get her partner to open up more to her. With the hope of establishing more intimacy, she asks him what he is thinking, what happened during the course of the day, and so on. He interprets this as intrusiveness and closes up further, which makes the wife more suspicious and more prying, which closes him up even further.

The source of this age-old syndrome is relatively simple: alarmed by something in the present, we grab for a solution without thinking deeply about the context, the roots of the problem, the possible unintended consequences that might ensue. Because we mostly react instead of think, our actions are based on insufficient information—Caesar was not planning to start a monarchy; the poor people of Delhi despised their colonial rulers and would not take kindly to suddenly losing money; Americans would be willing to go to war if attacked. When we operate with such a skewed perspective, it results in all kinds of perverse effects. In all of these cases a simple move partway up the mountain would have made clear the possible negative consequences so obvious to us in hindsight: for example, offering a reward for dead cobras would naturally cause impoverished residents to breed them.

Invariably in these cases people's thinking is remarkably simple and lazy: kill Caesar and the Republic returns, action A leads to result B. A variation on this, one that is quite common in the modern world, is to believe that if people have good intentions, good things should be the result. If a politician is honest and means well, he or she will bring about the desired results. In fact, good intentions often lead to what are known as *cobra effects*, because people with the noblest intentions are often blinded by feelings of self-righteousness and do not consider the complex and often malevolent motivations of others.

Nonconsequential thinking is a veritable plague in the world today that is only growing worse with the speed and ease of access to information, which gives people the illusion that they are informed and have thought deeply about things. Look at self-destructive wars such as the 2003 invasion of Iraq, the attempts to shut down the American government for short-term political gain, the increasing number of financial bubbles from tech stocks to real estate. Related to this is a gradual disconnect from history itself, as people tend to view present events as if they were isolated in time.

Understand: Any phenomenon in the world is by nature complex. The people you deal with are equally complex. Any action sets off a limitless chain of reactions. It is never so simple as A leads to B. B will lead to C, to D, and beyond. Other actors will be pulled into the drama and it is hard to predict their motivations and responses. You cannot possibly map out these chains or get a complete handle on consequences. But by making your thinking more consequential you can at least become aware of the more obvious negative consequences that could ensue, and this often spells the difference between success and disaster. You want depth of thinking, to go to several degrees in imagining the permutations, as far as your mind can go.

Often, going through this process will convince you of the wisdom of doing nothing, of waiting. Who knows what would have resulted in history if the conspirators had thought this out and chosen to wait until Caesar died naturally or in battle?

While this mode of thinking is important for individuals, it can be even more crucial for large organizations, where there is a lot at stake for many people. In any group or team, put at least one person in charge of gaming out all of the possible consequences of a strategy or line of action, preferably someone with a skeptical and prudent frame of mind. You can never go too far in this process, and the time and money spent will be well rewarded as you avoid potential catastrophes and develop more solid plans.

2. **Tactical hell.** You find yourself embroiled in several struggles or battles. You seem to get nowhere but you feel like you have invested so much time and energy already that it would be a tremendous waste to give up. You have actually lost sight of your long-term goals, what you're really fighting for. Instead it has become a question of asserting your ego and proving you are right. Often we see this dynamic in marital spats: it is no longer about repairing the relationship but about imposing one's point of view. At times, caught in these battles, you feel defensive and petty, your spirit drawn downward. This is almost a sure sign that you have descended into tactical hell. Our minds are designed for strategic thinking—calculating several moves in advance toward our goals. In tactical hell you can never raise your perspective high enough to think in that manner. You are constantly reacting to the moves of this or that person, embroiled in their dramas and emotions, going around in circles.

The only solution is to back out temporarily or permanently from these battles, particularly if they are occurring on several fronts. You need some detachment and perspective. Get your ego to calm down. Remind yourself that winning an argument or proving your point really gets you nowhere in the long run. Win through your actions, not your words. Start to think again about your long-term goals. Create a ladder of values and priorities in your life, reminding yourself of what really matters to you. If you determine that a particular battle is in fact important, with a greater sense of detachment you can now plot a more strategic response.

More often than not you will realize that certain battles are not worth it in the end. They are a waste of valuable energy and time, which should be high on your scale of values. It is always better to walk away from a circular battle, no matter how deeply you feel personally invested in it. Your energy and your spirit are important considerations. Feeling petty and frustrated can have reverberating consequences for your ability to think strategically and reach your goals. Going through the process delineated above in the Keys will naturally elevate your perspective and put your mind on the strategic plane. And in life as in warfare, strategists will always prevail over tacticians.

3. Ticker tape fever. During the run-up to the 1929 crash on Wall Street, many people had become addicted to playing the stock market, and this addiction had a physical component—the sound of the ticker tape that electronically registered each change in a stock's price. Hearing that clicking noise indicated something was happening, somebody was trading and making a fortune. Many felt drawn to the sound itself, which felt like the heartbeat of Wall Street. We no longer have the ticker tape. Instead many of us have become addicted to the minute-by-minute news cycle, to "what's trending," to the Twitter feed, which is often accompanied by a ping that has its own narcotic effects. We feel like we are connected to the very flow of life itself, to events as they change in real time, and to other people who are following the same instant reports.

This need to know instantly has a built-in momentum. Once we expect to have some bit of news quickly, we can never go back to the slower pace of just a year ago. In fact, we feel the need for more information more quickly. Such impatience tends to spill over into other aspects of life—driving, reading a book, following a film. Our attention span decreases, as well as our tolerance for any obstacles in our path.

We can all recognize signs of this nervous impatience in our own lives, but what we don't recognize is the distorting effect it has on our thinking. The trends of the moment—in business or politics—are embedded in larger trends that play out over the course of weeks and months. Such larger spans of time tend to reveal the relative weaknesses and strengths of an investment, a strategic idea, a sports team, or a political candidate, which are often the opposite of what we see in the microtrends of the moment. In isolation, a poll or stock price do not tell us much about these strengths and weaknesses. They give us the deceptive impression that what is revealed in the present will only become more pronounced with time. It is normal to want to keep up with the latest news, but to base any kind of decision on these snapshots of the moment is to run the risk of misreading the larger picture.

Furthermore, people tend to react and overreact to any negative or positive change in the present, and it becomes doubly hard to resist getting caught up in their panic or exuberance.

Look at what Abraham Lincoln had to face in a much less technological age. At the outbreak of the Civil War, he looked at the larger picture—as he estimated it, the North should prevail because it had more men and more resources to draw on. The only danger was time. Lincoln would need time for the Union Army to develop itself as a fighting force; he also needed time to find the right generals who would prosecute the war as he desired. But if too much time passed and there were no big victories, public opinion might turn against the effort, and once the North became divided within itself, Lincoln's job would become impossible. He needed patience but also victories on the battlefield.

In the first year of the war the North suffered a great defeat at Bull Run, and suddenly almost everyone questioned the president's competency. Now even levelheaded Northerners such as the famous editor Horace Greeley urged the president to negotiate peace. Others urged him to throw everything the North had into an immediate blow to crush the South, even though the army was not ready for this.

On and on this went, the pressure continually mounting as the North failed to deliver a single solid victory until finally General Ulysses S. Grant finished off the siege at Vicksburg in 1863, followed soon by the victory at Gettysburg under General George Meade. Now suddenly Lincoln was hailed as a genius. But some six months later, as Grant got bogged down in his pursuit of the Confederate Army under General Robert E. Lee and the casualties mounted, the sense of panic returned. Once again Greeley urged negotiation with the South. Lincoln's reelection that year seemed doomed. He had become immensely unpopular. The war was taking too long. Feeling the weight of all this, in late August of 1864 Lincoln finally drafted a letter spelling out the terms of peace he would offer the South, but that very night he felt ashamed for losing his resolve and hid the letter in a drawer. The tide had to turn, he felt, and the South would be crushed. Only a week later, General William Tecumseh Sherman marched into Atlanta and all the doubts about Lincoln suddenly vanished for good.

Through long-term thinking Lincoln had correctly gauged the relative strengths and weaknesses of the two sides and how the war would eventually trend. Everyone else got caught up in the day-by-day reports of the progress of the war. Some wanted to negotiate, others to suddenly speed up the effort, but all of this was based on momentary swings of fortune. A weaker man would have given in to such pressures and the war would have ended very differently. The writer Harriet Beecher Stowe, who visited Lincoln in 1864, later wrote of him: "Surrounded by all sorts of conflicting claims, by traitors, by half-hearted, timid men, by Border States men and Free States men, by radical Abolitionists and Conservatives, he has listened to all, weighed the words of all, waited, observed, yielded now here and now there, but in the main kept one inflexible, honest purpose, and drawn the national ship through."

Lincoln provides the model for us all and the antidote to the fever. First and foremost we must develop patience, which is like a muscle that requires training and repetition to make it strong. Lincoln was a supremely patient man. When we face any kind of problem or obstacle, we must follow his example and make an effort to slow things down and step back, wait a day or two before taking action. Second, when faced with issues that are important, we must have a clear sense of our long-term goals and how to attain them. Part of this involves assessing the relative strengths and weaknesses of the parties involved. Such clarity will allow us to withstand the constant emotional overreactions of those around us. Finally, it is important to have faith that time will eventually prove us right and to maintain our resolve.

4. **Lost in trivia.** You feel overwhelmed by the complexity of your work. You feel the need to be on top of all the details and global trends so you can control things better, but you are drowning in information. It is hard to see the proverbial forest for the trees. This is a sure sign that you have lost a sense of your priorities—which facts are more important, what problems or details require more attention.

The icon for this syndrome would have to be King Philip II of Spain (1527–1598). He had a prodigious appetite for paperwork and for keeping on top of all facets of the Spanish government. This gave him a feeling of being in control, but in fact in the end it made him lose control. He fussed over the placement of toilets in his new palace at Escorial and their precise distance from the kitchen; he spent days deliberating on how exactly particular members of the clergy should be addressed and remunerated. But sometimes he would fail to pay proper attention to important reports on spies and national security issues. Poring over endless reports on the state of the Turkish army, he believed it showed signs of great weakness and decided to launch a war against the Turks. Somehow he had misjudged. The war would last eighteen years, have no definitive resolution, and bleed Spain of money.

A similar process occurred in relation to England. The king had to read every single report on the state of the English navy, the support of the people for Queen Elizabeth, every minute detail about the country's finances and shoreline defenses. Based on years of such study, in 1588 he decided to launch his armada against England, feeling certain that, having made the armada large enough, Spain would prevail. But he failed to pay enough attention to weather reports, the most critical factor of all—for storms at sea would spell the destruction of the armada. He also failed to realize that by the time he had compiled and assimilated enough information on the Turks or on England, the situation had actually changed. So while he seemed extremely detail oriented, he was never quite on top of anything. Over the years Philip strained his mind with so much reading that he had frequent headaches and dizzy spells. His thinking was definitely impaired, and he made decisions that ended up leading directly to the irreversible decline of the Spanish empire.

In some ways you are probably more like King Philip II than you would like to imagine. In your life you are more than likely paying attention to some details that seem immediately important to you, while ignoring the weather reports that will doom your project. Like Philip, you tend to take in information without considering your priorities, what really matters in the end. But the brain has its limits. Assimilating too much information leads to mental fatigue, confusion, and feelings of helplessness. Everything begins to seem equally important—the placement of toilets and a possible war with the Turks. What you need is a mental filtering system based on a scale of priorities and your long-term goals. Knowing what you want to accomplish in the end will help you weed out the essential from the nonessential. You do not have to know all the details. Sometimes you need to delegate—let your subordinates handle the information gathering. Remember that greater control over events will come from realistic assessments of the situation, precisely what is made most difficult by a brain submerged in trivia.

The Farsighted Human

Most of us live within a relatively narrow time frame. We generally associate the passage of time with something negative—aging and moving closer to death. Instinctively we recoil from thinking too deeply about the future and the past, for this reminds us of the passage of time. In relation to the future we may try to think about our plans a year or two from now, but our thinking is more like a daydream, a wish, than deep analysis. In relation to the past we may have a few fond or painful memories from childhood and later years, but in general the past baffles us. We change so much with each passing year that who we were five, ten, twenty years ago might seem like a stranger to us. We don't really have a cohesive sense of who we are, a feeling of connection between the five-year-old and thirty-five-year-old versions of ourselves.

Not wanting to go too far in either direction, we mostly live within the present. We react to what we see and hear and to what others are reacting to. We live for immediate pleasures to distract us from the passage of time and make us feel more alive. But we pay a price for all this. Repressing the thought of death and aging creates a continual underlying anxiety. We are not coming to terms with reality. Continually reacting to events in the present puts us on a roller coaster ride—up and down we go with each change in fortune. This can only add to our anxiety, as life seems to pass so quickly in the immediate rush of events.

Your task as a student of human nature, and someone aspiring to reach the greater potential of the human animal, is to widen your relationship to time as much as possible, and slow it down. This means you do not see the passage of time as an enemy but rather as a great ally. Each stage in life has its advantages—those of youth are most obvious, but with age comes greater perspective. Aging does not frighten you. Death is equally your friend (see chapter 18). It motivates you to make the most of each moment; it gives you a sense of urgency. Time is your great teacher and master. This affects you deeply in the present. Awareness that a year from now this current problem you are experiencing will hardly seem so important will help you lower your anxiety and adjust your priorities. Knowing that time will reveal the weaknesses of your plans, you become more careful and deliberative with them.

In relation to the future, you think deeply about your long-term goals. They are not vague dreams but concrete objectives, and you have mapped out a path to reach them. In relation to the past, you feel a deep sense of connection to your childhood. Yes, you are constantly changing, but these changes are on the surface and create the illusion of real change. In fact, your character was set in your earliest years (see chapter 4), along with your inclinations toward certain activities, your likes and dislikes. As you get older, this character only becomes more apparent. Feeling organically connected to who you were in the past gives you a strong sense of identity. You know what you like and dislike, you know who you are. This will help you maintain your self-love, which is so critical in resisting the descent into deep narcissism and in helping you to develop empathy (see chapter 2). Also, you will pay greater attention to the mistakes and lessons of the past, which those who are locked in the present tend to repress.

Like everyone, you enjoy the present and its passing pleasures. You are not a monk. You connect to the trends of the moment and to the current flow of life. But you derive even greater pleasure from reaching your long-term goals and overcoming adversity. This expanded relationship to time will have a definite effect on you. It will make you calmer, more realistic, more in tune with the things that matter. It will also make you a superior strategist in life, able to resist people's inevitable overreactions to what is happening in the present and to see further into the future, a potential power that we humans have only begun to tap into.

The years teach much which the days never know.

—*Ralph Waldo Emerson*

7

Soften People's Resistance by Confirming Their Self-opinion

———— ◇ ————

The Law of Defensiveness

*L*ife is harsh and people competitive. We naturally must look after our own interests. We also want to feel that we are independent, doing our own bidding. That is why when others try to persuade or change us, we become defensive and resistant. To give in challenges our need to feel autonomous. That is why to get people to move from their defensive positions you must always make it seem like what they are doing is of their own free will. Creating a feeling of mutual warmth helps soften people's resistance and makes them want to help. Never attack people for their beliefs or make them feel insecure about their intelligence or goodness—that will only strengthen their defensiveness and make your task impossible. Make them feel that by doing what you want they are being noble and altruistic—the ultimate lure. Learn to tame your own stubborn nature and free your mind from its defensive and closed positions, unleashing your creative powers.

The Influence Game

In December 1948, Senator Tom Connally of Texas received a visit from the newly elected second senator of the state, Lyndon Baines Johnson (1908–1973). Johnson had previously served as a Democratic congressman in the House of Representatives for twelve years, and had earned a reputation as a politician with high ambitions who was quite impatient to realize them. He could be brash, opinionated, and even a bit pushy.

Connally knew all of this, but he was willing to judge Johnson for himself.

He studied the young man closely (Connally was thirty-one years older). He had met him before and thought him rather astute. But after exchanging a few pleasantries, Johnson revealed his true motives: he was hoping to get a seat on one of the three most prestigious committees in the Senate—Appropriations, Finance, or Foreign Relations. Connally served on two of them as a senior member. Johnson seemed to suggest that as a fellow Texan Connally could help him get what he wanted. Connally felt that Johnson clearly did not understand how the senatorial system worked, and he decided to put him in his place right then and there.

Acting as if he were doing Johnson a great favor, he offered to help him get a seat on the Agriculture Committee, knowing full well Johnson would find this insulting—it was among the least coveted of all committees. Thrusting the knife in deeper, Connally said that he had followed Johnson's senatorial campaign and had heard him exclaim numerous times that he was a friend of the farmer. Here was his chance to prove it. The Agriculture Committee would be a perfect fit. Johnson could not hide his displeasure and squirmed uncomfortably in his chair. "And then, Lyndon," Connally concluded, "after you've been in the Senate for a while, then you get on the Foreign Relations or Finance Committee, and render a *real* public service." And by "for a while" Connally meant a good twelve to twenty years, the usual time it took for any senator to amass enough influence. It was called seniority and that was how the game was played. It had taken Connally himself nearly twenty years to get his plum committee positions.

Over the next few weeks, word quickly spread among senators that Johnson was someone to keep an eye on, a potential hothead. And so it was a pleasant surprise when many of them saw and met him for the first time, after he was officially inaugurated. He was not at all what they had expected. He was the picture of politeness, and very deferential. He would often come to visit them in their offices. He would announce himself to the secretary in the outer office, then patiently wait there until called in, sometimes for an hour. He didn't seem bothered by this—he busied himself by reading or taking notes. Once inside, he'd ask the senator about his wife and family or his favorite sports team—he had clearly done his homework on the senator in question. He could be quite self-deprecating. He'd often first introduce himself as "Landslide Lyndon," everyone knowing he had won his Senate seat by the slimmest of margins.

Mostly, however, he came to talk business and get advice. He'd ask a question or two about some bill or bit of senatorial procedure and would listen with a focus that was striking and charming, almost like a child. His large brown eyes would stay fixed on the senator in question, and with his chin resting on his hand, he would occasionally nod and every now and then ask another question. The senators could tell he was paying deep attention because invariably he would act on their advice or repeat their very words to someone else, always crediting the senator who had spoken them. He would leave with a gracious thank-you for their time and for the invaluable education they had provided. This was not the spirited hothead they had heard so much about, and the contrast redounded to his credit.

The senators saw him most often on the Senate floor, and unlike any other member of the institution, he attended every session and sat almost the whole time at his desk. He took copious notes. He wanted to learn everything about senatorial procedure—a dull affair, but one that seemed to captivate him. He was far, however, from being a dullard. When senators encountered him in the hallway or in the cloakroom, he always had a good joke to tell or some amusing anecdote. He had spent his early years in rural poverty, and although he was well educated, his language had some of the color and biting humor of the Texan farmer and migrant worker. The senators found him amusing. Even Tom Connally had to admit that he had somehow misread him.

Older senators, referred to at the time as Old Bulls, particularly came to appreciate Lyndon Johnson. Although they held positions of great authority based on their seniority, they often felt insecure about their age (some were in their eighties) and their physical and mental capacities. But here was Johnson visiting their offices frequently, intent on absorbing their wisdom.

One older Democratic senator in particular took to Johnson—Richard Russell of Georgia. He was only eleven years older than Johnson, but he had been serving in the Senate since 1933 and had become one of its most powerful members. They had gotten to know each other because Johnson had requested and received a seat on the Armed Services Committee, on which Russell was second in seniority. Russell crossed paths with Johnson in the cloakroom, in the corridors, on the Senate floor; he seemed to be everywhere. And although Johnson visited Russell in his office almost every day, Russell came to enjoy his presence. Like Russell, Johnson was mostly all business, and full of questions on arcane Senate procedures. He began to call Russell "the Old Master," and he would often say, "Well, that's a lesson from the Old Master. I'll remember that."

Russell was one of the few senators who had remained a bachelor. He never admitted he was lonely, but he spent almost all of his time at his Senate office, even on Sundays. As Johnson would often be in Russell's office discussing some matter until the evening, he would sometimes invite Russell over for dinner at his house, telling him that his wife, Lady Bird, was an excellent cook, particularly good with southern dishes. The first few times Russell politely refused, but finally he relented and he soon became a weekly regular at the Johnson house. Lady Bird was charming and he quickly took to her.

Slowly the relationship between Russell and Johnson deepened. Russell was a baseball fanatic, and to his delight, Johnson confessed a weakness for the sport as well. Now they would go together to night games of the Washington Senators. A day would not pass in which they did not see each other, as the two of them would often be the only senators in their offices working on the weekends. They seemed to have so many interests in common, including the Civil War, and they thought alike on so many issues dear to southern Democrats, such as their opposition to a civil rights bill.

Soon Russell could be heard touting the junior senator as "a can-do young man" with a capacity equal to his own for hard work. Johnson was the only junior senator over his long career whom he referred to as a "disciple." But the friendship went deeper than that. After attending a hunting party that Johnson had organized in Texas, Russell wrote to him, "Ever since I reached home I have been wondering if I would wake up and find that I had just been dreaming that I had made a trip to Texas. Everything was so perfect that it is difficult to realize that it could happen in real life."

In 1950 the Korean War broke out and there was pressure on the Armed Services Committee to form a subcommittee to investigate the military's preparedness for the war. Such a subcommittee had been formed during World War II and chaired by Harry Truman, and it was through that chairmanship that Truman had become famous and risen to power. The current chairman of the Armed Services Committee was Senator Millard Tydings of Maryland. Tydings would naturally assume the chairmanship of the subcommittee, since it would be a great platform for publicity.

Johnson approached Tydings with a proposal: Tydings was facing a reelection campaign that year, and Johnson offered to chair the subcommittee only up to the time of the election, allowing Tydings to focus on winning it. Then he would step aside and let Tydings have the position. Tydings, protective of the powers he had accrued, declined Johnson's offer. But then Dick Russell met with him and said something to cause Tydings to change his mind. Johnson was named the chairman, a stunning coup for a senator who had been on the job for only a year and a half, and he would hold on to the job for quite a while, as Tydings lost his reelection bid.

As chairman Johnson was suddenly receiving national public exposure, and journalists covering the Senate discovered that he was a master at handling the press. He carefully guarded the findings of the subcommittee, allowing no leaks to journalists. He surrounded its work with tremendous mystery and drama, giving the impression that the committee was uncovering some real dirt on the military. He doled out information and reports to a select group of powerful journalists who had written articles that he had approved of. The other journalists had to fight for any news crumbs he deigned to offer.

The junior senator began to fascinate the press corps—he was tough yet sympathetic to the journalists' job. And most important, he knew how to give them a good story. Soon some of them were writing about him as a zealous patriot, a future political force to be reckoned with. Now Russell could properly defend his elevation of Johnson—the senator from Texas had done a great job and had finally gotten the Senate some positive publicity.

In May and June of 1951, Johnson and Russell worked closely together on the recall of General MacArthur from Korea. Now Russell had a firsthand view of Johnson's staff, and he was astounded at how efficient it was, larger and better organized than his own. It made Russell feel out of step with the times. But Johnson, as if sensing his thoughts, began to help Russell build his own modern staff. He gave him complete access to the legal and public relations teams he had developed, showing Russell how helpful they could be. As Johnson worked with him on this, the bond between them grew even tighter. One day Russell told a reporter, "That Lyndon Johnson could be president, and would make a good one." The reporter was flabbergasted. It was so unlike Russell to ever pay such a compliment.

One spring day in 1951, Senator Hubert Humphrey of Minnesota was waiting to catch the subway to the Capitol when Lyndon Johnson suddenly approached him and suggested they ride together and talk. Such words were like music to Humphrey; he almost couldn't believe Johnson was sincere in the offer. Humphrey had joined the Senate at the same time as Johnson, and he had been considered the bigger star, a charismatic liberal who could be president one day. Humphrey, however, had a problem that had completely impeded his rise to the top: he believed so stridently in liberal causes that he had alienated almost everyone else. In his first speech to the Senate, Humphrey criticized the institution for its slow pace of change and its cozy atmosphere. Soon he was paid back in kind—relegated to the worst committees. The bills he introduced went nowhere. When he would walk into the Senate cloakroom, he would be shunned by almost everyone. As this ostracism got worse, Humphrey felt increasingly depressed and despondent. Sometimes driving home from work, he would pull over and cry. His career had taken a very wrong turn.

In the subway car together, Johnson praised him effusively. "Hubert," he told him, "you have no idea what a wonderful experience it is for me ride to the Senate chamber with you. There are so many ways I envy you. You are articulate, you have such a broad range of knowledge." Feeling relieved to hear this, Humphrey was then surprised by the vehemence of Johnson's criticisms that followed. "But goddammit, Hubert, you're spending so much time making speeches that there is no time left to get anything done." Humphrey needed to be more pragmatic, fit in better. When they finally parted, Johnson invited Humphrey to stop by his office one day for drinks. Humphrey soon became a regular visitor, and this southern senator, quite loathed by northern liberals as the darling of the conservative Russell, enthralled him.

First, Johnson was immensely entertaining. Everything he said was accompanied by some folksy anecdote, often of a bawdy nature but always teaching some wicked lesson. Sitting in his office, the drinks being lavishly poured, he would instigate bouts of laughter that would reverberate through the corridors. It was hard to resist a man who could put you in a good mood. He had incredible presence. As Humphrey later wrote, "He'd come on just like a tidal wave sweeping all over the place. He went through walls. He'd come through a door and he'd take the whole room over."

Second, he had such invaluable information to share. He taught Humphrey all of the intricacies of Senate procedure and the knowledge he had accrued about the psychological weaknesses of various senators through close observation. He had become the greatest vote counter in the history of the Senate, able to predict the results of almost any Senate vote with astounding accuracy. He shared with Humphrey his vote-counting method.

Finally, he taught Humphrey the power he could have by compromising, by being more pragmatic and less idealistic. He would share with him stories about FDR, Humphrey's hero. When Johnson was in the House of Representatives, he had become close friends with the president. FDR, according to Johnson, was a consummate politician who knew how to get things done by retreating tactically and even compromising. The subtext here was that Johnson was really a closet liberal who also idolized FDR and who wanted just as much as Humphrey to pass a civil rights bill. They were both on the same side, fighting for the same noble causes.

Working with Johnson, there was no limit to how high Humphrey could rise within the Senate and beyond. As Johnson had correctly guessed, Humphrey had presidential ambitions. Johnson himself could never become president, or so he said to Humphrey, because the nation was not ready for a president from the South. But he could help Humphrey get there. Together they would make an unbeatable team.

What sealed the deal for Humphrey, however, was how Johnson proceeded to make his life easier within the Senate. Johnson talked to his fellow southern Democrats about Humphrey's intelligence and humor, how they had misread him as a man. Having softened them up in this way, Johnson then reintroduced Humphrey to these senators, who found him charming. Most important of all, he got Russell to change his mind—and Russell could move mountains. Now that he was sharing drinks with the more powerful senators, Humphrey's loneliness faded away. He felt compelled to return the favor and to get many northern liberals to change their minds about Johnson, whose influence was now beginning to spread like an invisible gas.

In 1952 the Republicans swept into power with the election of Dwight D. Eisenhower as president, taking in the process control of the Senate and the House. One of the casualties in the election was Ernest McFarland of Arizona, the former Democratic leader in the Senate. Now that the leadership position was vacant, the scrambling for his replacement began.

Johnson suggested that Russell himself take the position, but Russell declined. He could have more power operating behind the scenes. Instead he told Johnson *he* should be the next leader, and Russell could make it happen. Johnson, acting surprised, said he would consider it, but only if Russell would remain the Old Master and advise Johnson every step of the way. He did not have to say another word. Within weeks, Russell had essentially helped secure him the position, and it was a remarkable coup. At the age of forty-four, Johnson was by far the youngest leader in the history of either party.

Several weeks into his new position, Johnson came to Russell with a most unusual request. Positions on key committees had been based for decades on seniority. But what this meant was that committee chairmen were often not up to the job. Men in their seventies and eighties had ideas that were rooted in the past. They did not have the stomach for a big fight. Now, with the Republicans in full control, they were planning on rolling back some of FDR's greatest achievements with the New Deal and in foreign policy. It was going to be a rough two years until midterm elections.

Johnson wanted the power as the leader of the Senate Democrats to alter the committee landscape. He was not advocating anything radical. He would shift here and there a few committees and chairmanships, bringing in some fresh blood, such as the newly elected Senator John Kennedy, and Hubert Humphrey, whom he wanted to get on the Foreign Relations Committee. These younger men would give a fresh public face to the party and bring some energy in combating the Republicans. Russell could see the wisdom in this, and he gave Johnson his tacit approval, but he also warned him: "You're dealing with the most sensitive thing in the Senate. . . . [You're] playing with dynamite."

Johnson approached other older senators. Some were easy to convince, such as Senator Robert Byrd, who had a great fondness for the new leader. Liberals came on board with these changes, thanks to the work of Humphrey, who now had tremendous power as the liaison between Johnson and the northerners. Others were much more recalcitrant. Johnson, however, would not give up the fight. With those who continued to resist, he went into a higher gear. He became relentless. He would spend hours in his office behind a closed door, talking to himself, rehearsing his arguments and the counterarguments of these stubborn senators until he was sure he had found the perfect approach. To some he argued pure pragmatism—the need to defeat the Republicans at all costs. With others he reached back to the glory years of FDR. To southern senators he made it clear that making the party more powerful and unified would make Johnson's job easier, and that as a fellow southerner he would be their ultimate ally in further fights.

He served them endless drinks in his office, pulled out the full arsenal of his wit and charm. He would telephone them at all hours. If the senator continued resisting, he would call again later in the evening. He never argued with vehemence or tried to force the issue. He saw their side. He offered numerous quid pro quos. Eventually, as one senator after another relented, he got the last holdouts to cave in. Somehow Johnson was now someone to fear; if they did not give in and remained one of the few holdouts, clearly he could make their lives miserable over the next few years.

When it finally became public, the Republicans and the press were astounded at what Lyndon Johnson had accomplished. In a matter of weeks, since assuming the leadership position, he had gained unprecedented powers. He, not the seniority system, controlled committee appointments. He was now the undisputed "Master of the Senate," and the byword among his colleagues was "Let Lyndon do it." Drawn into his sphere of influence was the most unlikely cast of characters—from Dick Russell to Hubert Humphrey. But the most astonished person of all must have been Senator Tom Connally himself. In four short years, Johnson had not only risen to the top but had gained control of the Senate Democrats through a slow and steady campaign of accumulating influence, far surpassing the power Connally had accrued in over twenty years of service.

Interpretation: From the beginning of his political career, Johnson had a single ambition—to one day become president of the United States. To get there he needed a relatively swift rise to prominence. The younger he reached leadership positions, the more time he would have to spread his name and gain leverage within the Democratic Party. Elected to the House of Representatives at the age of twenty-eight, he seemed on track to get what he wanted, but in the House his career got bogged down. The place was so big and complex, and he was not good at dealing with large groups. He was not an exciting public speaker. He was much more charming in one-on-one situations. He became frustrated and restless. Finally reaching the Senate at the age of forty, he brought with him his impatience, as evidenced by his meeting with Connally. But shortly before his inauguration, he toured the floor of the Senate and had an epiphany: the place was much smaller; it was more like a cozy club for gentlemen. Here he could work one on one and slowly gain power by accumulating influence.

To accomplish this, however, he had to transform himself. He was naturally aggressive; he would have to rein this in, slow down, and step back. He would have to stop talking so much and getting into heated arguments. Let other people do the talking; let them feel like the star of the show. Stop thinking of himself; instead, focus completely on his fellow senators as they talked and talked. Assume the inoffensive front of the junior senator learning the ropes, the serious and somewhat dull student of procedure and legislation. Behind this front he could observe people without seeming ambitious or aggressive. In this way he could slowly gain knowledge of the inner workings of the Senate— vote counting, how bills were actually passed—and insights into the various senators, their deepest insecurities and weaknesses. At some point, his deep understanding of the institution would translate into a commodity he could exchange for influence and favors.

After several months of this campaign, he was able to alter the reputation he had had in the House. He no longer seemed a threat, and with the senators' defenses down, Johnson could escalate his campaign.

He turned his attention to winning over key allies. As he had always believed, having one key ally at or near the top of the hierarchy could move mountains. Early on he spotted Senator Russell as the perfect target—lonely, a believer in a cause without any real disciples, and very powerful. Johnson genuinely liked Russell, and he was always in search of father figures, but his attention and approach were highly strategic. He made sure he got appointed to the Armed Services Committee, where he would have the most access to Russell. Their constant encounters in the hallway or the cloakroom were rarely accidental. Without making it obvious, he slowly increased the hours they spent together. Johnson had never liked baseball and could care less about the Civil War, but he quickly learned to cultivate an interest in both. He mirrored back to Russell his own conservative values and work ethic and made the lonely senator feel like he had not only a friend but a worshipping son and disciple.

Johnson was careful to never ask for favors. Instead he quietly did favors himself for Russell, helping him to modernize his staff. When Johnson finally wanted something, such as the chairmanship of the subcommittee, he would insinuate his desire rather than directly express it. Russell would come to see him as an extension of his own political ambitions, and at that point he would do almost anything for his acolyte.

Within a few years, word got around that Johnson was a masterful vote counter and had inside knowledge on various senators, the kind of information that could be extremely useful when trying to get a bill passed. Now senators would come to him for this information, and he would share it with the understanding that at some point he would expect favors in return. Slowly his influence was spreading, but he realized that his desire to have the dominant position within his party and the Senate had one major obstacle—the northern liberals.

Once again, Johnson chose the perfect target—Senator Humphrey. He read him as a man who was lonely, in need of validation, but who was also tremendously ambitious. The way to Humphrey's heart was threefold: make him feel liked, confirm his belief that he was presidential material, and give him the practical tools to realize his ambitions. As he had done with Russell, Johnson gave Humphrey the impression that he was secretly on his side, mirroring Humphrey's deepest values by sharing his adoration of FDR. After several months of this campaign, Humphrey would do almost anything for Johnson. Now with a bridgehead established to the northern liberals, Johnson had expanded his influence to all corners of the Senate.

By the time the leadership position opened up, Johnson had established tremendous credibility as someone who returned favors, who could get things done, and who had very powerful allies. His desire to get control over committee assignments represented a radical change in the system, but he carefully couched it as a way to enhance the Democratic Party and help individual senators in their various battles with Republicans. It was in their interest to hand over power to Lyndon Johnson. Step by step he had acquired such influence without ever appearing aggressive or even threatening. By the time those in the party realized what had happened, it was too late—he was in complete control of the chessboard, the Master of the Senate.

Understand: Influence over people and the power that it brings are gained in the opposite way from what you might imagine. Normally we try to charm people with our own ideas, showing ourselves off in the best light. We hype our past accomplishments. We promise great things about ourselves. We ask for favors, believing that being honest is the best policy. What we do not realize is that we are putting all of the attention on ourselves. In a world where people are increasingly self-absorbed, this only has the effect of making others turn more inward in return and think more of their own interests rather than ours.

As the story of Johnson demonstrates, the royal road to influence and power is to go the opposite direction: Put the focus on others. Let them do the talking. Let them be the stars of the show. Their opinions and values are worth emulating. The causes they support are the noblest. Such attention is so rare in this world, and people are so hungry for it, that giving them such validation will lower their defenses and open their minds to whatever ideas you want to insinuate.

Your first move then is always to step back and assume an inferior position in relation to the other. Make it subtle. Ask for their advice. People are dying to impart their wisdom and experience. Once you feel that they are addicted to this attention, you can initiate a cycle of favors by doing something small for them, something that saves them time or effort. They will instantly want to reciprocate and will return the favor without feeling manipulated or pushed. And once people do favors for you, they will continue to work on your behalf. In doing something for you, they have judged you worthy of this, and to stop helping you would mean to call into question their original judgment and their own intelligence, which people are very reluctant to do. Working slowly this way in a group, you will expand your influence without its seeming aggressive or even purposeful, the ultimate disguise for your ambitions.

The true spirit of conversation consists more in bringing out the cleverness of others than in showing a great deal of it yourself; he who goes away pleased with himself and his own wit is also greatly pleased with you. Most men . . . seek less to be instructed, and even to be amused, than to be praised and applauded.

—Jean de La Bruyère

Keys to Human Nature

From early on in life we humans develop a defensive and self-protective side to our personality. It begins in early childhood as we cultivate a sense of personal physical space that others should not violate. It later expands into a feeling of personal dignity—people should not coerce or manipulate us into doing things we don't want to. We should be free to choose what we desire. These are necessary developments in our growth as socialized humans.

As we get older, however, these defensive qualities often solidify into something much more rigid, and for good reason. People are continually judging and appraising us—are we competent enough, good enough, a team player? We never feel quite free of this scrutiny. One noticeable failure in our lives, and people's scrutiny will turn into negative judgments that can cripple us for a long time. Furthermore, we have the feeling that people are always trying to take from us—they want our time, our money, our ideas, our labor. In the face of all of this, we naturally become more self-absorbed and defensive—we have to look after our own interests, since nobody else will. We set up walls around ourselves to keep out intruders and those who want something from us.

By the time we reach our twenties, we have all developed systems of defense, but in certain circumstances our inner walls can come tumbling down. For instance, during a night of revelry with friends, perhaps after some drinking, we feel bonded with others and not judged by them. Our minds loosen up, and suddenly new and very interesting ideas come to us, and we're open to doing things we would normally never do. In another instance, perhaps we attend some public rally and hear an inspiring speaker advocating for a cause. Feeling on the same page as hundreds of others, caught up in the group spirit, we suddenly feel called to action and to work for the cause—something we might normally resist.

The most telling example, however, occurs when we fall in love and the feeling is reciprocated. The other person appreciates and reflects back to us our most positive qualities. We feel worthy of being loved. Under such a spell, we let go of our ego and our habitual stubbornness; we give the other person un-usual sway over our willpower.

What these moments have in common is that we feel inwardly secure—not judged but accepted by friends, the group, or the loved one. We see a reflection of ourselves in others. We can relax. At our core we feel validated. Not needing to turn inward and defensive, we can direct our minds outward, beyond our ego—to a cause, a new idea, or the happiness of the other.

Understand: Creating this feeling of validation is the golden key that will unlock people's defenses. And we cannot survive and thrive in this highly com-petitive world without possessing such a power.

We continually find ourselves in situations in which we need to move people from their resistant positions. We need their assistance, or we need the ability to alter their ugly behavior. If we flail about, improvising in the mo-ment, trying to plead, cajole, and even make people feel guilty, we are more than likely only making them more defensive. If we somehow succeed in get-ting what we want through these methods, their support is thin, with an undercurrent of resentment. We have taken from them—time, money, ideas— and they will close themselves off to further influence. And if we go through long stretches of time continually butting up against people's resistance and getting nowhere, we can face a very dangerous dynamic in life—mounting frustration at the apparent indifference of people. This subtly infects our atti-tude. When we find ourselves in situations needing to influence people, they sense our neediness and insecurity. We try too hard to please. We seem ever so slightly desperate, defeated before starting. This can turn into a negative self-fulfilling dynamic that will keep us marginalized without ever being aware of the source of the problem.

Before it is too late we must turn this dynamic around, as Johnson did at the age of forty. We must discover the power that we can possess by giving people the validation they crave and lowering their defenses. And the key to making this happen in a realistic and strategic manner is to fully understand a fundamental law of human nature.

This law is as follows: People have a perception about themselves that we shall call their *self-opinion*. This self-opinion can be accurate or not—it doesn't matter. What matters is how people perceive their own character and worthiness. And there are three qualities to people's self-opinion that are nearly universal: "I am autonomous, acting of my own free will"; "I am intelligent in my own way"; and "I am basically good and decent."

When it comes to the first universal (I am acting of my own free will), if we join a group, or believe something, or buy a product, it is because we *choose* to do so. The truth might be that we were manipulated or succumbed to peer pressure, but we will tell ourselves something else. If we ever feel consciously coerced—as in having to obey a boss—we either tell ourselves we have chosen to obey or we deeply resent being forced and manipulated. In the latter case, we might smile and obey, but we will find a way to secretly rebel. In other words, we feel the need to continually express and assert our free will.

With the second universal (I am intelligent), we may realize we are not on the level of an Einstein, but in our field, in our own way, we are intelligent. A plumber revels in his superior knowledge of the inner workings of a house and in his manual skills, which are a form of intelligence. He also thinks his political opinions come from solid common sense, another sign of intelligence, as he sees it. People are generally never comfortable with the thought that they could be gullible and less than intelligent. If they have to admit they are not smart in the conventional way, they will at least think they are cleverer than others.

With the third universal (I am a good person), we like to see ourselves as supporting the right causes. We treat people well. We are a team player. If we happen to be the boss and we like to instill discipline in the troops, we call it "tough love." We are acting for the good of others.

In addition to these universals, we find that people have more personalized self-opinions that serve to regulate their particular insecurities. For instance, "I'm a free spirit, one of a kind" or "I'm very self-reliant and don't need anybody's help" or "I am good-looking and I can depend on that" or "I am a rebel and disdain all authority." Implied in these various self-opinions is a feeling of superiority in this one area: "I am a rebel and you are less so." Many of these types of self-opinions are related to developmental issues in early childhood. For instance, the rebel type had a father figure who disappointed him; or perhaps he suffered from bullying and cannot bear any feeling of inferiority. He must despise all authority. The self-reliant type may have experienced a very distant mother, be haunted by feelings of abandonment, and have crafted a self-image of rugged independence.

Our self-opinion is primary: it determines so much of our thinking and our values. We will not entertain ideas that clash with our self-opinion. Let us say we see ourselves as particularly tough and self-reliant. We will then *gravitate* toward ideas and philosophies that are realistic, hard-core, and unforgiving of others' weaknesses. If in this scenario we also happen to be Christian, we will then *reinterpret* Christian religious doctrines to match our tough self-image, finding elements within Christianity that emphasize self-reliance, tough love, and the need to destroy our enemies. In general, we will choose to belong to groups that validate our feeling of being noble and smart. We might think we have particular ideas or values that stand on their own, but in fact they are dependent on our self-opinion.

When you try to convince people of something, one of three things will happen. First, you might inadvertently challenge a particular aspect of their self-opinion. In a discussion that might turn into an argument, you make them feel stupid or brainwashed or less than good. Even if you are subtle in your arguments, the implication is that you know better. If this happens, you make people even more defensive and resistant. Walls go up that will *never* come down.

Second, you can leave their self-opinion in a neutral position—neither challenged nor confirmed. This often happens if you try to be reasonable and calm in your approach, avoiding any emotional extremes. In this scenario people remain resistant and dubious, but you have at least not tightened them up, and you have some room to maneuver them with your rational arguments.

Third, you can actively confirm their self-opinion. In this case you are fulfilling one of people's greatest emotional needs. We can imagine that we are independent, intelligent, decent, and self-reliant, but only other people can truly confirm this for us. And in a harsh and competitive world in which we are all prone to continual self-doubt, we almost never get this validation that we crave. When you give it to people, you will have the magical effect that occurred when you yourself were drunk, or at a rally, or in love. You will make people relax. No longer consumed by insecurities, they can direct their attention outward. Their minds open, making them susceptible to suggestion and insinuation. If they decide to help you, they feel like they are doing this of their own free will.

Your task is simple: instill in people a feeling of inner security. Mirror their values; show that you like and respect them. Make them feel you appreciate their wisdom and experience. Generate an atmosphere of mutual warmth. Get them to laugh along with you, instilling a feeling of rapport. All of this works best if the feelings are not completely faked. By exercising your empathy, by getting inside their perspective (see chapter 2 for more on this), you are more likely to genuinely feel at least a part of such emotions. Practice this often enough and confirming people's self-opinion will become your default position—you will have a loosening-up effect on almost everyone you encounter.

One caveat: most people have a relatively high self-opinion, but some people have a low opinion of themselves. They tell themselves, "I am not worthy of good things" or "I am not such a nice person" or "I have too many problems and issues." Because they generally expect bad things to happen to them, they often feel relieved and justified when bad things do happen. In this way their low self-opinion serves to calm their insecurities about ever getting success in life. If your targets have a low self-opinion, the same rule applies. If you insist that they can easily better their lives by following your advice, this will clash with their belief that the world is against them and that they really do not deserve such good things. They will discount your ideas and resist you. Instead you must work from within their self-opinion, empathizing with the injustices in their life and the difficulties they have faced. Now, with them feeling validated and mirrored, you have some latitude to make gentle corrections and even apply some reverse psychology (see the section below).

Finally, the greatest obstacle you will face in developing these powers comes from a cultural prejudice against the very idea of influence: "Why can't we all just be honest and transparent with one another, and simply ask for what we want? Why can't we just let people be who they are and not try to change them? Being strategic is ugly and manipulative." First, when people tell you such things, you should be on guard. We humans cannot stand feelings of powerlessness. We need to have influence or we become miserable. The honestymongers are no different, but because they need to believe in their angelic qualities, they cannot square this self-opinion with the need to have influence. And so they often become passive-aggressive, pouting and making others feel guilty as a means of getting what they want. Never take people who say such things at face value.

Second, we humans cannot avoid trying to influence others. Everything we say or do is examined and interpreted by others for clues as to our intentions. We are silent? Perhaps it is because we are upset and want to make this clear. Or we are genuinely listening as a way of trying to impress with our politeness. No matter what we do, people will read into it attempts at influence, and they are not wrong in doing so. As social animals we cannot avoid constantly playing the game, whether we are conscious of this or not.

Most people do not want to expend the effort that goes into thinking about others and figuring out a strategic entry past their defenses. They are lazy. They want to simply be themselves, speak honestly, or do nothing, and justify this to themselves as stemming from some great moral choice.

Since the game is unavoidable, better to be skillful at it than in denial or merely improvising in the moment. In the end, being good at influence is actually more socially beneficial than the moral stance. By having this power, we can influence people who have dangerous or antisocial ideas. Becoming proficient at persuasion requires that we immerse ourselves in the perspective of others, exercising our empathy. We might have to abide by the cultural prejudice and nod our heads in agreement about the need for complete honesty, but inwardly we must realize that this is nonsense and practice what is necessary for our own well-being.

Five Strategies for Becoming a Master Persuader

The following five strategies—distilled from the examples of the greatest influencers in history—are designed to help you focus more deeply on your targets and create the kinds of emotional effects that will help lower people's resistance. It would be wise to put all five into practice.

1. Transform yourself into a deep listener. In the normal flow of a conversation, our attention is divided. We hear parts of what other people are saying, in order to follow and keep the conversation going. At the same time, we're planning what we'll say next, some exciting story of our own. Or we are even daydreaming about something irrelevant. The reason for this is simple: we are more interested in our own thoughts, feelings, and experiences than in those of the other person. If this were not the case, we would find it relatively easy to listen with full attention. The usual prescription is to talk less and listen more, but this is meaningless advice as long as we prefer our own internal monologue. The only solution is to somehow be *motivated* to reverse this dynamic.

Think of it this way: You know your own thoughts only too well. You are

rarely surprised. Your mind tends to circle obsessively around the same subjects. But each person you encounter represents an undiscovered country full of
surprises. Imagine for a moment that you could step inside people's minds and
what an amazing journey that could be. People who seem quiet and dull often
have the strangest inner lives for you to explore. Even with boors and fools, you
can educate yourself as to the origins and nature of their flaws. Transforming
yourself into a deep listener will not only prove more amusing as you open
your mind to their mind but will also provide the most invaluable lessons about
human psychology.

Once you are motivated to listen, the rest is relatively simple. You cannot
make the strategic purpose behind your listening too obvious. The other person has to feel it is a lively exchange, even though in the end they may do 80
percent of the talking. For this purpose, you must not barrage them with
questions that make it feel like a job interview. Instead, pay attention to their
nonverbal cues. You will see their eyes light up when certain topics are
mentioned—you must guide the conversation in that direction. People will
become chatty without realizing it. Almost everyone likes to talk about their
childhood, their family, the ins and outs of their work, or some cause that is
dear to them. An occasional question or comment plays off something they
have said.

You are deeply absorbed in what they say, but you must feel and appear relaxed in being so. You convey that you are listening by maintaining relatively
consistent eye contact and nodding as they talk. The best way to signal how
deeply you are listening is to occasionally say something that mirrors what
they have said, but in your own words and filtered through your own experience. In the end, the more they talk, the more they will reveal about their insecurities and unmet desires.

Your goal is to make them come away from the encounter feeling better
about themselves. You have let them be the star of the show. You have drawn
out of them the wittier, more fun-loving side of their personality. They will
love you for this and will look forward to the next encounter. As they become
increasingly relaxed in your presence, you will have great latitude for planting
ideas and influencing their behavior.

2. Infect people with the proper mood. As social animals, we are extremely susceptible to the moods of other people. This gives us the power to
subtly infuse into people the appropriate mood for influencing them. If you are
relaxed and anticipating a pleasurable experience, this will communicate itself

and have a mirror-like effect on the other person. One of the best attitudes to adapt for this purpose is one of complete indulgence. You do not judge other people; you accept them as they are.

In the novel *The Ambassadors*, the writer Henry James paints the portrait of this ideal in the form of Marie de Vionnet, an older French woman of impeccable manners who surreptitiously uses an American named Lambert Strether to help her in a love affair. From the very moment he meets her, Strether is captivated. She seems a "mix of lucidity and mystery." She listens deeply to what he says and, without responding, gives him the feeling she completely understands him. She envelops him in her empathy. She acts from the beginning as if they have become good friends, but it is in her manner, nothing she says. He calls her indulgent spirit "a beautiful conscious mildness," and it has a hypnotic power over him. Well before she even asks for his help, he is completely under her spell and will do anything for her. Such an attitude replicates the ideal mother figure—unconditional in her love. It is not expressed so much in words as in looks and body language. It works equally well on men and women and has an hypnotic effect on almost anyone.

A variation of this is to infect people with a warm feeling of rapport through laughter and shared pleasures. Lyndon Johnson was the master of this. Of course, he used alcohol, which flowed freely in his office, his targets never knowing that his own drinks were greatly watered down so he could retain control of himself. His bawdy jokes and colorful anecdotes created a comfortable club-like atmosphere for men. It was hard to resist the mood he set. Johnson could also be quite physical, often wrapping his arms around a man's shoulder, frequently touching him on the arm. Many studies on nonverbal cues have demonstrated the incredible power that a simple touch of people's hands or arms can have in any interaction, making them think positive things about you without their ever being aware of the source of their good opinion. Such gentle taps establish a feeling of visceral rapport, as long as you do not maintain eye contact, which will give it too much of a sexual connotation.

Keep in mind that your expectations about people are communicated to them nonverbally. It has been demonstrated, for instance, that teachers who expect greater things from their pupils can, without ever saying anything, have a positive effect on their work and grades. By feeling particularly excited when you're meeting someone, you will communicate this to him or her in a powerful way. If there is a person of whom you will eventually ask a favor, try imagining him or her in the best light—generous and caring—if that is possible.

Some have claimed to get great results by simply thinking the other person is handsome or good-looking.

3. Confirm their self-opinion. Recall the universal qualities of the self-opinions of people with a high self-opinion. Here's how to approach each one of them.

Autonomy. No attempt at influence can ever work if people feel in any way that they are being coerced or manipulated. They must *choose* to do whatever it is you want them to do, or they must at least experience it as their choice. The more deeply you can create this impression, the greater your chances of success.

In the novel *Tom Sawyer*, the twelve-year-old protagonist of the same name is portrayed as an extremely savvy boy, raised by his aunt, with an uncanny sensitivity to human nature. Despite his cleverness, Tom is always getting into trouble. The second chapter of the book begins with Tom being punished for getting in a fight. Instead of spending a hot summer Saturday afternoon messing around with his friends and swimming in the river, Tom has to whitewash the very large fence in the front of the house. As he starts the job, his friend Ben Rogers walks by, eating a delicious-looking apple. Ben is as mischievous as Tom, and seeing him at this tedious chore, he decides to torment him by asking him if he's planning on going for a swim that afternoon, knowing full well he can't.

Tom pretends to feign deep interest in his work. Now Ben is curious. He asks Tom if he's seriously more interested in painting the fence than in having some fun. Tom finally addresses him, while still keeping an eye on his work. His aunt would not give such a job to just anyone, he says. It is what people see first of their house when they pass by. This is a very important job that won't come up again for many years. In the past he and his friends painted something on fences and got into trouble; now he can do so freely. It is a challenge, a test of skill. And yes, he enjoys it. Swimming can be done any old weekend, but not this.

Ben asks if he can try his hand, to see what Tom means. After several pleas, Tom finally relents, only after Ben offers him his apple. Soon other boys approach and Tom does the same sell job on them, accumulating more pieces of fruit and toys. An hour later, we see Tom lying in the shade while a whole team of friends finishes the job for him. Tom used basic psychology to get what he wanted. First, he got Ben to reinterpret this job, not by saying anything but through his absorbed attention in the task and his body language: the task must be something interesting. Second, he framed the job as a test of skill and intelligence, a rare opportunity, something that would appeal to any competitive boy. And finally, as he knew, once the neighborhood boys saw others at the task, they would want to join in, making it a group activity. Nobody wanted to be left out. Tom could have pleaded with dozens of friends to help him and gotten nowhere. Instead he framed it in such a way that they *wanted* to do the work. They came to him, begging for the job.

Your attempts at influence must always follow a similar logic: how can you get others to perceive the favor you want to ask for as something they already desire? Framing it as something pleasurable, as a rare opportunity, and as something other people want to do will generally have the proper effect.

Another variation on this is to appeal directly to people's competitive instincts. In 1948 the director Billy Wilder was casting for his new film *A Foreign Affair*, which was to be set in Berlin just after the war. One of the main characters was a woman named Erika von Shluetow, a German cabaret singer with suspicious ties to various Nazis during the war. Wilder knew that Marlene Dietrich would be the perfect actress to play the part, but Dietrich had publicly expressed her intense dislike of anything having to do with the Nazis and had worked hard for various Allied causes. When first approached about the role, she found it too distasteful, and that was the end of the discussion.

Wilder did not protest or plead with her, which would have been futile, given Dietrich's famed stubbornness. Instead he told her he had found two perfect American actresses to play the part, but he wanted her opinion on which would be better. Would she view their tests? Feeling bad that she had turned down her old friend Wilder, Dietrich naturally agreed to this. But Wilder had cleverly tested two well-known actresses whom he knew would be quite terrible for the role, making a mockery of the part of a sexy German cabaret singer. The ploy worked like a charm. The very competitive Dietrich was aghast at their performances and immediately volunteered to do the part herself.

Finally, when giving people gifts or rewards as a possible means of winning them over to your side, it is always best to give smaller gifts or rewards than larger ones. Large gifts make it too apparent that you are trying to buy their loyalty, which will offend people's sense of independence. Some might accept large gifts out of need, but later they will feel resentful or suspicious. Smaller gifts have a better effect—people can tell themselves they deserve such things and are not being bought or bribed. In fact, such smaller rewards, spread out over time, will bind people to you in a much greater way than anything lavish.

Intelligence. When you disagree with another person and impose your contrary opinion, you are implying that you know better, that you have thought things through more rationally. People challenged in this way will then naturally become even more attached to their opinions. You can prevent this by being more neutral, as if this opposing idea is simply something you are entertaining and it could be wrong. But better still, you can go much further: you see *their* point of view and agree with it. (Winning arguments is rarely worth the effort.) With their intelligence flattered, you now have some room to gently alter their opinion or have lowered their defenses for a request for help.

The nineteenth-century British prime minister and novelist Benjamin Disraeli conceived of an even cleverer ploy when he wrote, "If you wish to win a man's heart, allow him to confute you." You do this by beginning to disagree with a target about a subject, even with some vehemence, and then slowly come to seeing their point of view, thereby confirming not only their intelligence but also their own powers of influence. They feel ever so slightly superior to you, which is precisely what you want. They will now be doubly vulnerable to a countermove of your own. You can create a similar effect by asking people for advice. The implication is that you respect their wisdom and experience.

In 1782 the French playwright Pierre-Augustin Caron de Beaumarchais put the finishing touches on his great masterpiece *The Marriage of Figaro*. The approval of King Louis XVI was required, and when he read the manuscript, he was furious. Such a play would lead to a revolution, he said: "This man mocks everything that must be respected in a government." After much pressure he agreed to have it privately performed in a theater at Versailles. The aristocratic audience loved it. The king allowed more performances, but he directed his censors to get their hands on the script and alter its worst passages before it was presented to the public.

To bypass this, Beaumarchais commissioned a tribunal of academics, intellectuals, courtiers, and government ministers to go over the play with him. A man who attended the meeting wrote, "M. de Beaumarchais announced that he would submit unreservedly to every cut and change that the gentlemen and even the ladies present might deem appropriate. . . . Everyone wanted to add something of his own. . . . M. de Breteuil suggested a witticism, Beaumarchais accepted it and thanked him. . . . 'It will save the fourth act.' Mme de Matignon contributed the color of the little page's ribbon. The color was adopted and became fashionable."

Beaumarchais was indeed a very clever courtier. By allowing others to make even the smallest changes to his masterpiece, he greatly flattered their egos and their intelligence. Of course, on the larger changes later requested by Louis's censors, Beaumarchais did not relent. By then he had so won over the members of his own tribunal that they stridently defended him, and Louis had to back down. Lowering people's defenses in this way on matters that are not so important will give you great latitude to move them in the direction you desire and get them to concede to your desires on more important matters.

Goodness. In our daily thoughts, we constantly comfort ourselves as to the moral nature of our actions. If we are employees of a company, we see ourselves as good team members. If we are bosses, we treat people well, or at least we pay and support them well. We help the right causes. In general, we do not like to see ourselves as selfish and narrowly focused on our own agenda. Just as important, we want others to see us in this light. Look at social media and how people will make a display of supporting the best causes. Few people give to charities anonymously—they want their names loudly advertised.

You must never inadvertently cast doubts on this saintly self-opinion. To make positive use of this trait in people, frame what you are asking them to do as part of a larger cause that they can participate in. They are not merely buying clothes but helping the environment or keeping jobs local. In taking these actions, people can feel better about themselves. Keep it subtle. If you are trying to get recruits for a job, let others spread the message about the cause. Make it appear prosocial and popular. Make people want to join the group, instead of having to plead with them. Pay great attention to the words and labels you use. It is better, for instance, to call someone a team member than an employee.

To put yourself in the inferior, one-down position, you can commit some relatively harmless faux pas, even offend people in a more pronounced way, and then ask for their forgiveness. By asking for this, you imply their moral superiority, a position people love to occupy. Now they are vulnerable to suggestion.

Finally, if you need a favor from people, do not remind them of what you have done for them in the past, trying to stimulate feelings of gratitude. Gratitude is rare because it tends to remind us of our helplessness, our dependence on others. We like to feel independent. Instead, remind them of the good things they have done for you in the past. This will help confirm their self-opinion: "Yes, I am generous." And once reminded, they will want to continue to live up to this image and do yet another good deed. A similar effect can come from suddenly forgiving your enemies and forging a rapprochement. In the emotional turmoil this creates, they will feel obligated to live up to the high opinion you have now shown toward them and will be extra motivated to prove themselves worthy.

4. Allay their insecurities. Everyone has particular insecurities—about their looks, their creative powers, their masculinity, their power status, their uniqueness, their popularity, et cetera. Your task is to get a bead on these insecurities through the various conversations you draw them into.

Once you've identified them, you must first be extra careful not to trigger them. People have grown sensitive antennae for any words or body language that might cast doubt on their physical appearance or their popularity, or whatever their insecurity may be. Be aware of this and be on guard. Second, the best strategy is to praise and flatter those qualities that people are most insecure about. We all crave this, even if we somehow see through the person who is praising us. That is because we live in a tough world in which we are continually judged, and yesterday's triumph is easily followed by tomorrow's failure. We never really feel secure. If the flattery is done right, we feel that the flatterer likes us, and we tend to like people who like us.

The key to successful flattery is to make it strategic. If I know that I am particularly awful at basketball, praising me for my basketball skills in any way will ring false. But if I am *uncertain* about my skills, if I imagine I am perhaps not really so bad, then any flattery on that score can work wonders. Look for those qualities people are uncertain about and offer reassurance. Lord Chesterfield advised his son in his letters (later published in 1774), "Cardinal Richelieu who was undoubtedly the ablest statesman of his time . . . had the idle vanity of being thought the best poet too: he envied the great Corneille his reputation. Those, therefore, who flattered skillfully, said little to him of abilities in state affairs, or at least but *en passant*, and as it might naturally occur. But the incense which they gave him, the smoke of which they knew would turn his head in their favour, was as a . . . poet."

If your targets are powerful and quite Machiavellian, they might feel somewhat insecure about their moral qualities. Flattering them about their clever manipulations might backfire, but obvious praise of their goodness would be too transparent, because they know themselves too well. Instead, some strategic flattery about how you have benefited from their advice and how their criticisms helped improve your performance will appeal to their self-opinion of being tough yet fair, with a good heart underneath the gruff exterior.

It is always better to praise people for their effort, not their talent. When you extol people for their talent, there is a slight deprecation implied, as if they were simply lucky for being born with natural skill. Instead, everyone likes to feel that they earned their good fortune through hard work, and that is where you must aim your praise.

With people who are your equals, you have more room to flatter. With those who are your superiors, it is best to simply agree with their opinions and validate their wisdom. Flattering your boss is too transparent.

Never follow up your praise with a request for help, or whatever it is you are after. Your flattery is a setup and requires the passage of some time. Do not appear too ingratiating in the first encounter or two. Better to show even a little coldness, which will give you room to warm up. After a few days you have grown to like this person, and then a few flattering words aimed at their insecurities will begin to melt their resistance. If possible, get third parties to pass along your compliments, as if they had simply overheard them. Never be too lavish in your praise or use absolutes.

A clever way to cover your tracks is to mix in some small criticisms of the person or their work, nothing that will trigger insecurities but enough to give your praise a more realistic hue: "I loved your screenplay, although I feel act two might need a little work." Do not say, "Your latest book is so much better than the last one." Be very careful when people ask you for their opinion about their work or something related to their character or their looks. They do not want the truth; they want support and confirmation given as realistically as possible. Be happy to supply this for them.

You must seem as sincere as possible. It would be best to choose qualities to praise that you actually admire, if at all possible. In any event, what gives people away is the nonverbal cues—praise along with stiff body language or a fake smile or eyes glancing elsewhere. Try to feel some of the good emotions you are expressing so any exaggeration will seem less obvious. Keep in mind that your target must have a relatively high self-opinion. If it is low, the flattery will not jibe with how they feel about themselves and will ring hollow, whereas for those of high self-opinion it will seem only natural.

5. Use people's resistance and stubbornness. Some people are particularly resistant to any form of influence. They are most often people with deeper levels of insecurity and low self-opinion. This can manifest itself in a rebellious attitude. Such types feel as if it is them against the world. They must assert their will at all costs and resist any kind of change. They will do the opposite of what people suggest. They will seek advice for a particular problem or symptom, only to find dozens of reasons of why the advice given won't work for them.

The best thing to do is to play a game of mental judo with them. In judo you do not counter people's moves with a thrust of your own but rather encourage their aggressive energy (resistance) in order to make them fall on their own. Here are some ways to put this into practice in everyday life.

Use their emotions: In the book *Change*, the therapist authors (Paul Watzlawick, John H. Weakland, and Richard Fisch) discuss the case of a rebellious teenager, suspended from school by the principal because he was caught dealing drugs. He was still to do his homework at home but was forbidden to be on campus. This would put a big dent in his drug-dealing business. The boy burned with the desire to get vengeance.

The mother consulted a therapist, who told her to do the following: explain to the son that the principal believed only students who attended class in person could do well. In the principal's mind, by keeping the boy away from school he was ensuring he would fail. If he did better by working at home than in class, this would embarrass the principal. Better to not try too hard this semester and get on the good side of the principal by proving him right. Of course, such advice was designed to play into his emotions. Now he desired nothing more than to embarrass the principal and so threw himself into his homework with great energy, the goal of the therapist all along. In essence, the idea is not to counter people's strong emotions but to move with them and find a way to channel them in a productive direction.

Use their language: The therapist Milton Erickson (see chapter 3) described the following case that he had treated: A husband came to him for advice, although he seemed quite set on doing what he wanted anyway. He and his wife came from very religious families and had married mostly to please their parents. The husband and wife were very religious as well. Their honeymoon, however, had been a disaster. They found sex very awkward and did not feel like they were in love. The husband decided it was not anyone's fault but that they should get "a friendly divorce." Erickson readily agreed with him and suggested exactly how to bring about this "friendly divorce." He instructed him to reserve a room at a hotel. They were to have one final "friendly" night together before the divorce. They were also to have one last "friendly" glass of champagne, one last "friendly" kiss between them, and so on. These instructions virtually ensured the wife's seduction by her husband. As Erickson had hoped, the husband followed his instructions, the couple had an exciting evening together, and they happily decided to remain married.

Erickson intuited that the husband did not really want a divorce and that the two of them felt awkward because of their religious backgrounds. They were both deeply insecure about their physical desires, yet resistant to any kind of change. Erickson used the husband's language and his desire for divorce but found a way to gently redirect the energy toward something much different. When you use people's words back at them, it has a hypnotic effect. How can they not follow what you suggest when it is exactly the words they have used?

Use their rigidity: A pawnbroker's son once came to the great eighteenth-century Zen master Hakuin with the following problem: he wanted to get his father to practice Buddhism, but the man pretended to be too busy with his bookkeeping to have time for even a single chant or prayer. Hakuin knew the pawnbroker—he was an inveterate miser who was only using this as an excuse to avoid religion, which he considered a waste of time. Hakuin advised the boy to tell his father that the Zen master himself would buy from him each prayer and chant that he did on a daily basis. It was strictly a business deal.

Of course the pawnbroker was very happy with the deal—he could shut his son up and make money in the process. Each day he presented Hakuin with his bill for the prayers, and Hakuin duly paid him. But on the seventh day he failed to show up. It seemed that he had gotten so caught up in the chanting that he had forgotten to count how many prayers he had done. A few days later he admitted to Hakuin he had become completely taken up with the chants, felt so much better, and did not need to be paid anymore. He soon became a very generous donor to Hakuin's temple.

When people are rigid in their opposition to something, it stems from deep fear of change and the uncertainty it could bring. They must have everything on their terms and feel in control. You play into their hands if you try with all your advice to encourage change—it gives them something to react against and justifies their rigidity. They become more stubborn. Stop fighting with such people and use the actual nature of their rigid behavior to effect a gentle change that could lead to something greater. On their own, they discover something new (like the power of Buddhist prayer), and on their own they might take this further, all set up by your judo maneuver.

Keep in mind the following: people often won't do what others ask them to do, because they simply want to assert their will. If you heartily agree with their rebellion and tell them to keep on doing what they're doing, it now means that if they do so they are following your advice, which is distasteful to them. They may very well rebel again and assert their will in the opposite direction, which is what you wanted all along—the essence of reverse psychology.

The Flexible Mind—Self-strategies

You find it frustrating when people resist your good ideas out of sheer stubbornness, but you are largely unaware of how the same problem—your own stubbornness—afflicts you and limits your creative powers.

As children our minds were remarkably flexible. We could learn at a rate that far surpasses our adult capacities. We can attribute much of the source of this power to our feelings of weakness and vulnerability. Sensing our inferiority in relation to those older than us, we felt highly motivated to learn. We were also genuinely curious and hungry for new information. We were open to the influence of parents, peers, and teachers.

In adolescence many of us had the experience of falling under the sway of a great book or writer. We became entranced by the novel ideas in the book, and because we were so open to influence, these early encounters with exciting ideas sank deeply into our minds and became part of our own thought processes, affecting us decades after we absorbed them. Such influences enriched our mental landscape, and in fact our intelligence depends on the ability to absorb the lessons and ideas of those who are older and wiser.

Just as the body tightens with age, however, so does the mind. And just as our sense of weakness and vulnerability motivated the desire to learn, so does our creeping sense of superiority slowly close us off to new ideas and influences. Some may advocate that we all become more skeptical in the modern world, but in fact a far greater danger comes from the increasing closing of the mind that afflicts us as individuals as we get older, and seems to be afflicting our culture in general.

Let us define the ideal state of the mind as one that retains the flexibility of youth along with the reasoning powers of the adult. Such a mind is open to the influence of others. And just as you use strategies to melt people's resistance, you must do the same on yourself, working to soften up your rigid mental patterns.

To reach such an ideal, we must first adopt the key tenet of the Socratic philosophy. One of Socrates's earliest admirers was a young man named Chaerephon. Frustrated that more Athenians did not revere Socrates as he himself did, Chaerephon visited the Oracle of Delphi and posed a question: "Is there a wiser man than Socrates in all of Athens?" The oracle answered no.

Chaerephon felt vindicated in his admiration of Socrates and rushed to tell his mentor the good news. Socrates, however, being a humble man, was not at all pleased to hear this and was determined to prove the oracle wrong. He visited many people, each eminent in their own field—politics, the arts, business—and asked them many questions. When they kept to knowledge of their field, they seemed quite intelligent. But then they would expatiate on all kinds of subjects about which they clearly knew nothing. On such subjects they merely spouted the conventional wisdom. They did not think through any of these ideas.

Finally Socrates had to admit that the oracle was indeed accurate—he was wiser than all the others because he was aware of his own ignorance. Over and over again he examined and reexamined his own ideas, seeing inadequacies and infantile emotions lodged within them. His motto in life had become "The unexamined life is not worth living." The charm of Socrates, what made him so devilishly fascinating to the youth of Athens, was the supreme openness of his mind. In essence, Socrates assumed the weaker, vulnerable position of the ignorant child, always asking questions.

Think of it this way: We like to scoff at the superstitious and irrational ideas that most people held in the seventeenth century. Imagine how those of the twenty-fifth century will scoff at ours. Our knowledge of the world is limited, despite the advances of science. Our ideas are conditioned by the prejudices instilled in us by our parents, by our culture, and by the historical period we live in. They are further limited by the increasing rigidity of the mind. A bit more humility about what we know would make us all more curious and interested in a wider range of ideas.

When it comes to the ideas and opinions you hold, see them as toys or building blocks that you are playing with. Some you will keep, others you will knock down, but your spirit remains flexible and playful.

To take this further, you can adopt a strategy promulgated by Friedrich Nietzsche: "He who really wants to get to *know* something new (be it a person, an event, a book) does well to entertain it with all possible love and to avert his eyes quickly from everything in it he finds inimical, repellent, false, indeed to banish it from mind: so that, for example, he allows the author of a book the longest start and then, like one watching a race, desires with beating heart that he may reach his goal. For with this procedure one penetrates to the heart of the new thing, to the point that actually moves it: and precisely this is what is meant by getting to know it. If one has gone this far, reason can afterwards make its reservations; that over-estimation, that temporary suspension of the critical pendulum, was only an *artifice* for luring forth the soul of the thing."

Even in writing that is inimical to your own ideas there is often something that rings true, which represents the "soul of the thing." Opening yourself up to its influence in this way should become part of your mental habits, allowing you to better understand things, even to criticize them properly. Sometimes, however, that "soul" will move you as well and gain some influence, enriching your mind in the process.

Upon occasion it is good to let go of your deepest set of rules and restrictions. The great fourteenth-century Zen master Bassui posted at the door of his temple a list of thirty-three rules his monks were to abide by or be thrown out. Many of the rules dealt with alcohol, which was strictly forbidden. One night, to totally disconcert his literal-minded monks, he showed up to a talk completely drunk. He never apologized or repeated it, but the lesson was simple: such rules are merely guidelines, and to demonstrate our freedom we must violate them from time to time.

Finally, when it comes to your own self-opinion, try to have some ironic distance from it. Make yourself aware of its existence and how it operates within you. Come to terms with the fact that you are not as free and autonomous as you like to believe. You do conform to the opinions of the groups you belong to; you do buy products because of subliminal influence; you can be manipulated. Realize as well that you are not as good as the idealized image of your self-opinion. Like everyone else, you can be quite self-absorbed and obsessed with your own agenda. With this awareness, you will not feel the need to be validated by others. Instead you will work at making yourself truly independent and concerned with the welfare of others, as opposed to staying attached to the illusion of your self-opinion.

There was something terribly enthralling in the exercise of influence. No other activity was like it. To project one's soul into some gracious form, and let it tarry there for a moment; to hear one's own intellectual views echoed back to one with all the added music of passion and youth; to convey one's temperament into another as though it were a subtle fluid or a strange perfume: there was a real joy in that—perhaps the most satisfying joy left to us in an age so limited and vulgar as our own, an age grossly carnal in its pleasures, and grossly common in its aims.

—*Oscar Wilde*, The Picture of Dorian Gray

8

Change Your Circumstances by Changing Your Attitude

———— ◇ ————

The Law of Self-sabotage

*E*ach of us has a particular way of looking at the world, of interpreting events and the actions of people around us. This is our attitude, and it determines much of what happens to us in life. If our attitude is essentially fearful, we see the negative in every circumstance. We stop ourselves from taking chances. We blame others for mistakes and fail to learn from them. If we feel hostile or suspicious, we make others feel such emotions in our presence. We sabotage our career and relationships by unconsciously creating the circumstances we fear the most. The human attitude, however, is malleable. By making our attitude more positive, open, and tolerant of other people, we can spark a different dynamic—we can learn from adversity, create opportunities out of nothing, and draw people to us. We must explore the limits of our willpower and how far it can take us.

The Ultimate Freedom

As a child, Anton Chekhov (1860–1904)—the future celebrated writer—faced each morning with a feeling of dread: would he be beaten that day by his father or somehow spared? Without warning, and sometimes without any apparent cause, his father, Pavel Yegorovich, would strike him hard several times with a cane or a whip or the back of his hand. What made it doubly confusing was that his father did not beat him out of any apparent malice or anger. He told Anton he was doing it out of love. It was God's will that children be beaten, to instill humility. That was how he had been raised, and look at what a fine man he had turned into. At the end of the beating, young Anton had to kiss his father's hand and ask to be forgiven. At least he was not alone in this ordeal—his four brothers and one sister all received the same treatment.

The beating was not the only thing he came to dread. In the afternoon he would hear his father's approaching footsteps outside their ramshackle wooden house, and he would tremble with fear. More often than not he was coming to the house at that hour to ask the child Anton to replace him in the grocery shop that he owned, in the backwater town of Taganrog, Russia, where the family lived. For most of the year, the shop was unbearably cold. While minding the counter, Anton would try to do his homework, but his fingers would quickly become numb and the ink in the pot for his pen would freeze up. In that mess of a store, which smelled of rancid meat, he would have to listen to the dirty jokes of the Ukrainian peasants who worked there, and witness the lewd behavior of the assortment of town drunks who wandered in for their shots of vodka. In the midst of all this, he had to make sure that every kopeck was accounted for, or he would get an added thrashing from his father. He would often be left there for hours while his father was getting drunk somewhere else.

His mother would try to intervene. She was a gentle soul who was no match for her husband. The boy was too young to work, she would say. He needed time for his studies. Sitting in the freezing shop was ruining his health. The father would thunder back that Anton was lazy by nature, and only through hard work could he become a respectable citizen.

There was no respite from the father's presence. On Sunday, the one day the shop was closed, he would wake the children up at four or five in the morning to rehearse their singing for the church choir, of which he was the director. Once home from the service, they would have to repeat it, ritual by ritual, on their own, then return for the noon mass. By the time it was over, they were all too exhausted to play.

In the moments he had to himself, Anton would wander around town. Taganrog was a grim place to grow up. The fronts of almost all of the houses were decaying and crumbling, as if they were already ancient ruins. The roads were not paved, and when the snow melted there was mud everywhere, with giant potholes that could swallow a child up to the neck. There were no streetlights. Prisoners would be tasked with finding the stray dogs on the streets and beating them to death. The only quiet and safe place was the surrounding graveyards, and Anton would visit them often.

On these walks, he would wonder about himself and the world. Was he really so worthless that he deserved the almost daily beatings from his father? Perhaps. And yet his father was a walking contradiction—he was lazy, a drunk, and quite dishonest with customers, despite his religious zeal. And the citizens of Taganrog were equally ridiculous and hypocritical. He would observe them at the cemetery, trying to act pious during the funeral service but then excitedly whispering to one another about the delicious cakes they would eat later at the home of the widow, as if that was why they had shown up.

His only recourse in the face of the pain and boredom he constantly felt was to laugh at it all. He became the family clown, imitating the characters of Taganrog and inventing stories about their private lives. Sometimes his humor turned aggressive. He played cruel practical jokes on other children in the neighborhood. Sent to the market by his mother, he often tormented the live duck or chicken that he carried home in a sack. He was becoming impish and quite lazy.

Then in 1875, everything changed for the Chekhov family. Anton's two older brothers, Alexander and Nikolai, had had enough of their father. They decided to move together to Moscow, Alexander to pursue a university degree and Nikolai to become an artist. This snubbing of his authority infuriated the father, but he could not stop them. At around the same time, Pavel Yegorovich had to finally confront his complete mismanagement of the grocery store—he had piled up debts over the years and now the bills came due. Facing bankruptcy and almost certainly time in the debtor's prison, he quietly slipped out of town one night, without telling his wife, and escaped to Moscow, intending to live with his sons.

The mother was forced to sell the family possessions to pay the debts. A boarder who lived with them offered to help the mother with their case against the creditors, but much to her surprise, he used his court connections to swindle the Chekhovs out of their house. Without a penny to her name, the mother was forced to leave for Moscow with the other children. Only Anton would stay to finish his studies and get his diploma. He was charged with selling all of the remaining family belongings and sending the money to Moscow as soon as possible. The former boarder, now owner of the house, gave Anton a corner of one room to live in, and so at the age of sixteen, with no money of his own and no family to look after him, Anton was suddenly left to fend for himself in Taganrog.

Anton had never really been alone before. His family had been his whole life, for better or worse. Now it was as if the bottom had dropped out. He had no one to turn to for help in any way. He blamed his father for this miserable fate, for being trapped in Taganrog. One day he felt angry and bitter, the next day depressed. But soon it became clear that he had no time for such sentiments. He had no money or resources, and yet somehow he had to survive. So he hired himself out as a tutor to as many families as possible. When they went on vacation he would often go hungry for days. His one jacket was threadbare; he had no galoshes for the heavy rains. He felt ashamed when he entered people's houses, shivering and his feet all wet. But at least he was now able to support himself.

He had decided to become a doctor. He had a scientific frame of mind, and doctors made a good living. To get into medical school he would have to study much harder. Frequenting the town library, the only place he could work in peace and quiet, he began to also browse the literature and philosophy sections, and soon he felt his mind soaring far beyond Taganrog. With books, he no longer felt so trapped. At night, he returned to his corner of a room to write stories and sleep. He had no privacy, but he could keep his corner neat and tidy, free of the usual disorder of the Chekhov household.

He had finally begun to settle down, and new thoughts and emotions came to him. Work was no longer something he dreaded; he loved absorbing his mind in his studies, and tutoring had made him feel proud and dignified—he *could* take care of himself. Letters came from his family—Alexander ranting and complaining about their father making everyone miserable again; Mikhail, the youngest son, feeling worthless and depressed. Anton wrote back to Alexander: stop obsessing over our father and start taking care of yourself. He wrote to Mikhail: "Why do you refer to yourself as my 'worthless, insignificant little brother'? Do you know where you should be aware of your worthlessness? Before God, perhaps . . . but not before people. Among people you should be aware of your worth." Even Anton was surprised by the new tone he was taking in these letters.

Then one day, several months after being abandoned, he wandered through the streets of Taganrog and suddenly felt welling up from within a tremendous and overwhelming sense of empathy and love for his parents. Where did this come from? He had never felt this before. In the days leading up to this moment he had been thinking long and hard about his father. Was he really to blame for all their problems? Pavel's father, Yegor Mikhailovich, had been born a serf, serfdom being a form of indentured slavery. The Chekhovs had been serfs for several generations. Yegor had finally been able to buy the family's freedom, and he set his three sons up in different fields, Pavel designated as the family merchant. But Pavel could not cope. He had an artistic temperament, could have been a talented painter or musician. He felt bitter at his fate—a grocery store and six children. His father had beaten him, and so he beat his children. Although no longer a serf, Pavel still bowed and kissed the hand of every local official and landowner. He remained a serf at heart.

Anton could see that he and his siblings were falling into the same pattern—bitter, secretly feeling worthless, and wanting to take their anger out on others. Now that he was alone and taking care of himself, Anton yearned to be free in the truest sense of the word. He wanted to be free of the past, free of his father. And here, as he walked the streets of Taganrog, the answer came to him from these new and sudden emotions. Understanding his father, he could accept and even love him. He was not some imposing tyrant but a rather helpless old man. With a bit of distance, he could feel compassion and forgive the beatings. He would not become enmeshed in all of the negative feelings his father inspired. And he could finally value as well his kind mother, and not blame her for being so weak. With his mind emptied of rancor and obsessive thoughts of his lost childhood, it was as if a great weight had been suddenly lifted off him.

He made a vow to himself: no more bowing and apologizing to people; no more complaining and blaming; no more disorderly living and wasting time. The answer to everything was work and love, work and love. He had to spread this message to his family and save them. He had to share it with mankind through his stories and plays.

Finally in 1879 Anton moved to Moscow to be with his family and to attend medical school, and what he saw there made him despondent. The Chekhovs and a few boarders were all crammed in a single room in the basement of a tenement, in the middle of the red-light district. The room had little ventilation and almost no light. Worst of all was the morale of the group. His mother was beaten down by the constant anxieties about money and the subterranean existence. His father drank even more and held some odd jobs that were quite a step down from owning a business. He continued to beat his children.

Anton's younger siblings were no longer in school (the family could not afford it) and felt completely useless. Mikhail in particular was even more depressed than ever. Alexander had gotten work as a writer for magazines, but he felt he deserved much better and started to drink heavily. He blamed his problems on his father for following him to Moscow and haunting his every move. Nikolai, the artist, slept till late, worked sporadically, and spent most of his time at the local tavern. The entire family was spiraling downward at an alarming rate, and the neighborhood they lived in only made it worse.

The father and Alexander had recently moved out. Anton decided he needed to do the opposite—move into the cramped room and become the catalyst for change. He would not preach or criticize but rather set the proper example. What mattered was keeping the family together and elevating their spirits. To his overwhelmed mother and sister he announced that he would take charge of the housework. Seeing Anton cleaning and ironing, his brothers now agreed to share in these duties. He scrimped and saved from his own medical school scholarship and got more money from his father and Alexander. With this money he put Mikhail, Ivan, and Maria back into school. He managed to find his father a better job. Using his father's money and his own savings, he was able to move the entire family to a much larger apartment with a view.

He worked to improve all aspects of their lives. He got his brothers and sister to read books he had chosen, and well into the night they would discuss and argue the latest findings in science and philosophical questions. Slowly they all bonded on a much deeper level, and they began to refer to him as Papa Antosha, the leader of the family. The complaining and self-pitying attitude he had first encountered had mostly disappeared. His two younger brothers now talked excitedly about their future careers.

Anton's greatest project was to reform Alexander, whom he considered the most gifted yet troubled member of the family. Once Alexander came home completely drunk, began to insult the mother and sister, and threatened to smash Anton's face in. The family had become resigned to these tirades, but Anton would not tolerate this. He told Alexander the next day that if he ever yelled at another family member, he would lock him out and disavow him as a brother. He was to treat his mother and sister with respect and not blame the father for his turning to drink and womanizing. He must have some dignity— dress well and take care of himself. That was the new family code.

Alexander apologized and his behavior improved, but it was a continual battle that demanded all of Anton's patience and love, for the self-destructive streak in the Chekhovs was deeply ingrained. It had led Nikolai to an early death from alcoholism, and without constant attention Alexander could easily follow the same path. Slowly Anton weaned him from drinking and helped him with his journalistic career, and eventually Alexander settled into a quiet and satisfying life.

Sometime in 1884, Anton had begun to spit blood, and it was apparent to him that he had the preliminary signs of tuberculosis. He refused to submit to the examination of a fellow doctor. He preferred not to know and to go on writing and practicing medicine without worrying about the future. But as he became increasingly famous for his plays and short stories, he began to experience a new kind of discomfort—the envy and petty criticisms of his fellow writers. They formed various political cliques and endlessly attacked one another, including Anton himself, who had refused to ally himself with any revolutionary cause. All of this made Anton feel increasingly disenchanted with the literary world. The elevated mood he had so carefully crafted in Taganrog was dissipating. He became depressed and considered giving up writing entirely.

Then, toward the end of 1889, he thought of a way to free himself from his growing depression. Since his days in Taganrog, the poorest and most abject members of society had fascinated him. He liked to write about thieves and con artists, and get inside their minds. The lowliest members of Russian society were its prisoners, who lived in ghastly conditions. And the most notorious prison in Russia was on Sakhalin Island, just north of Japan. It housed five penal colonies with hundreds of thousands of prisoners and their families. It was like a shadow state—nobody in Russia had any idea what really went on on the island. This could be the answer to his present misery. He would make the arduous trek across Siberia to the island. He would interview the most hardened criminals. He would write a detailed book on the conditions there. Far from the pretentious literary world, he would connect to something very real and reignite the generous mood he had crafted in Taganrog.

His friends and family tried to dissuade him. His health had gotten worse; the travel could kill him. But the more they tried to dissuade him, the more he felt certain it was the only way to save himself.

After a three-month journey he finally arrived at the island in July of 1890, and he immediately immersed himself in this new world. His task was to interview every possible prisoner, including the most vicious murderers. He investigated every aspect of their lives. He witnessed the most gruesome torture sessions of prisoners and followed convicts as they worked in the local mines, chained to wheelbarrows. Prisoners who completed their sentences would often have to stay on the island in labor camps, and so Sakhalin was full of wives waiting to join them in these camps. These women and their daughters would resort to prostitution to stay alive. Everything was designed to degrade people's spirits and drain them of every ounce of dignity. It reminded him of his family dynamic, on a much larger scale.

This was certainly the lowest rung of hell he could have visited, and it affected him deeply. He now longed to return to Moscow and write about what he had seen. His sense of proportion had been restored. He had finally freed himself of the petty thoughts and concerns that had weighed him down. Now he could get outside of himself and feel generous again. The book he wrote, *Sakhalin Island*, caught the attention of the public and led to substantial reforms of conditions on the island.

By 1897 his health had deteriorated, and he began to cough blood rather regularly. He could no longer disguise his tuberculosis from the world at large. The doctor who treated him advised that he retire from all work and leave Moscow for good. He needed rest. Perhaps by living in a sanatorium he could extend his life a few years. Anton would have none of this. He would live as if nothing had changed.

A cult had begun to form around Chekhov, comprising younger artists and adoring fans of his plays, all of which had made him one of Russia's most famous writers. They came to visit him in large numbers, and although he was clearly ailing, he radiated a calmness that astonished almost everyone. Where did it come from? Was he born this way? He seemed to absorb himself completely in their stories and problems. No one ever heard him talk about his illness.

In the winter of 1904, as his condition worsened, he suddenly had the desire to take an open-sleigh ride into the country. Hearing the bells of the sleigh and breathing the cold air had always been one of his greatest pleasures, and he needed to feel this one more time. It put him in such high spirits that he did not care anymore about the consequences, which were dire. He died a few months later.

Interpretation: The moment his mother left him to be alone in Taganrog, young Anton Chekhov felt trapped, as if he had been thrown into prison. He would be forced to work as much as he could outside his studies. He was now stuck in this hopelessly dull backwater with no support system, living in the corner of a small room. Bitter thoughts about his fate and about the childhood he had never had gnawed at him in his few free moments. But as the weeks went by, he noticed something very strange—he actually liked the work he did as a tutor, even though the pay was meager and he was continually running around town. His father had kept telling him he was lazy, and he had believed it, but now he was not so sure. Each day represented a challenge to find more work and put food on the table. He was succeeding in this. He was not some miserable worm who needed a beating. Besides, the work was a way to get outside himself and immerse his mind in the problems of his students.

The books he read took him far away from Taganrog and filled him with interesting thoughts that lingered in his mind for entire days. Taganrog itself was not so bad. Each shop, each house contained the oddest characters, supplying him endless material for stories. And that corner of the room—that was his kingdom. Far from feeling trapped, he now felt liberated. What had actually changed? Certainly not his circumstances, or Taganrog, or the corner of the room. What had changed was his attitude, which opened him up to new experiences and possibilities. Once he felt this, he wanted to take it further. The greatest remaining impediment to this sense of freedom was his father. No matter what he tried, he couldn't seem to get rid of deep feelings of bitterness. It was as if he could still feel the beatings and hear the endless pointed criticisms.

As a last resort, he tried to analyze his father as if he were a character in a story. This led him to think about his father's father and all the generations of Chekhovs. As he considered his father's erratic nature and his wild imagination, he could understand how *he* must have felt trapped by his circumstances, and why he turned to drinking and tyrannizing the family. He was helpless, more a victim than an oppressor. This understanding of his father laid the groundwork for the sudden rush of unconditional love he felt one day for his parents. As he glowed with this new emotion, he finally felt completely liberated from resentments and anger. The negative emotions from the past had finally fallen away from him. His mind could now be completely open. The sensation was so exhilarating that he had to share it with his siblings and free them as well.

What had brought Chekhov to this point was the crisis he had faced when left alone at such a young age. He experienced another such crisis some thirteen years later, when he became depressed about the pettiness of his fellow writers. His solution was to reproduce what had happened in Taganrog, but in reverse— he would be the one to abandon others and force himself to be alone and vulnerable. In this way he could reexperience the freedom and empathy he had felt in Taganrog. The early death sentence from tuberculosis was the last crisis. He would let go of his fear of death, and the bitter feelings that came with having his life cut short, by continuing to live at full tilt. This final and ultimate freedom gave him a radiance that almost everyone who met him in this period could feel.

Understand: The story of Anton Chekhov is really a paradigm for what we all face in life. We carry with us traumas and hurts from early childhood. In our social life, as we get older, we accumulate disappointments and slights. We too are often haunted by a sense of worthlessness, of not really deserving the good things in life. We all have moments of great doubt about ourselves. These emotions can lead to obsessive thoughts that dominate our minds. They make us curtail what we experience as a way to manage our anxiety and disappointments. They make us turn to alcohol or any kind of habit to numb the pain. Without realizing it, we assume a negative and fearful attitude toward life. This becomes our self-imposed prison. But this is not how it has to be. The freedom that Chekhov experienced came from a choice, a different way of looking at the world, a change in attitude. We can all follow such a path.

This freedom essentially comes from adopting a generous spirit—toward others and toward ourselves. By accepting people, by understanding and if possible even loving them for their human nature, we can liberate our minds from obsessive and petty emotions. We can stop reacting to everything people do and say. We can have some distance and stop ourselves from taking everything personally. Mental space is freed up for higher pursuits. When we feel generous toward others, they feel drawn to us and want to match our spirit. When we feel generous toward ourselves, we no longer feel the need to bow and scrape and play the game of false humility while secretly resenting our lack of success. Through our work and through getting what we need on our own, without depending on others, we can stand tall and realize our potential as humans. We can stop reproducing the negative emotions around us. Once we feel the exhilarating power from this new attitude, we will want to take it as far as possible.

Years later, in a letter to a friend, Chekhov tried to summarize his experience in Taganrog, referring to himself in the third person: "Write about how this young man squeezes the slave out of himself drop by drop and how one fine morning he awakes to find that the blood coursing through his veins is no longer the blood of a slave but that of a real human being."

The greatest discovery of my generation is the fact that human beings can alter their lives by altering their attitudes of mind.

—William James

Keys to Human Nature

We humans like to imagine that we have an objective knowledge of the world. We take it for granted that what we perceive on a daily basis is reality—this reality being more or less the same for everybody. But this is an illusion. No two people see or experience the world in the same way. What we perceive is our personal version of reality, one that is of our own creation. To realize this is a critical step in our understanding of human nature.

Imagine the following scenario: A young American must spend a year studying in Paris. He is somewhat timid and cautious, prone to feelings of depression and low self-esteem, but he's genuinely excited by this opportunity. Once there, he finds it hard to speak the language, and the mistakes he makes and the slightly derisory attitude of the Parisians make it even harder for him to learn. He finds the people not friendly at all. The weather is damp and gloomy. The food is too rich. Even Notre Dame Cathedral seems disappointing, the area around it so crowded with tourists. Although he has pleasurable moments, he generally feels alienated and unhappy. He concludes that Paris is overrated and a rather unpleasant place.

Now imagine the same scenario but with a young woman who is more extroverted and has an adventurous spirit. She's not bothered by making mistakes in French, nor by the occasional snide remark from a Parisian. She finds learning the language a pleasant challenge. Others find her spirit engaging. She makes friends more easily, and with more contacts her knowledge of French improves. She finds the weather romantic and quite suitable to the place. To her, the city represents endless adventures and she finds it enchanting.

In this case, two people see and judge the same city in opposite ways. As a matter of objective reality, the weather of Paris has no positive or negative qualities. Clouds simply pass by. The friendliness or unfriendliness of the Parisians is a subjective judgment—it depends on whom you meet and how they compare with the people where you come from. Notre Dame Cathedral is merely an agglomeration of carved pieces of stone. The world simply exists as it is—things or events are not good or bad, right or wrong, ugly or beautiful. It is we with our particular perspectives who add color to or subtract it from things and people. We focus on either the beautiful Gothic architecture or the annoying tourists. We, with our mind-set, can make people respond to us in a friendly or unfriendly manner, depending on our anxiety or openness. We shape much of the reality that we perceive, dictated by our moods and emotions.

Understand: Each of us sees the world through a particular lens that colors and shapes our perceptions. Let us call this lens our *attitude*. The great Swiss psychologist Carl Jung defined this in the following way: "Attitude is a readiness of the psyche to act or react in a certain way. . . . To have an attitude means to be ready for something definite, even though this something is unconscious; for having an attitude is synonymous with an *a priori* orientation to a definite thing."

What this means is the following: In the course of a day, our minds respond to thousands of stimuli in the environment. Depending on the wiring of our brain and our psychological makeup, certain stimuli—clouds in the sky, crowds of people—lead to stronger firings and responses. The stronger the response, the more we pay attention. Some of us are more sensitive to stimuli that others would mostly ignore. If we are unconsciously prone to feelings of sadness, for whatever reason, we are more likely to pick up signs that promote this feeling. If we have a suspicious nature, we are more sensitive to facial expressions that display any kind of possible negativity and to exaggerate what we perceive. This is the "readiness of the psyche to . . . react in a certain way."

We are never conscious of this process. We merely experience the aftereffects of these sensitivities and firings of the brain; they add up to an overall mood or emotional background that we might call depression, hostility, insecurity, enthusiasm, or adventurousness. We experience many different moods, but in an overall sense we can say that we have a particular way of seeing and interpreting the world, dominated by one emotion or a blend of several, such as hostility and resentment. This is our attitude. People with a largely depressive attitude can feel moments of joy, but they are more disposed toward experiencing sadness; they anticipate the feeling in their day-to-day encounters.

Jung illustrates this idea in the following way: Imagine that on a hike people come upon a brook that must be crossed to continue the journey. One person, without much thought, will simply leap across, touching a stone or two, not worried at all about possibly falling. He loves the sheer physical pleasure of the jump and doesn't care if he fails. Another person is excited as well, but it has less to do with the physical joy than with the mental challenge the brook represents. She will quickly calculate the most effective means of crossing and will gain satisfaction from figuring this out. Another person, of a cautious nature, will take more time to think it through. He takes no pleasure in the crossing; he is irritated by the obstruction, but he wants to continue the hike and he will do his best to safely cross. A fourth will simply turn back. She will see no need for crossing and will rationalize her fears by saying the hike has been long enough.

No one simply sees or hears the rushing of water over rocks. Our minds do not perceive just what is there. Each person sees and responds to the same brook differently, according to their particular attitude—adventurous, fearful, et cetera.

The attitude that we carry with us throughout life has several roots: First, we come into this world with certain genetic inclinations—toward hostility, greed, empathy, or kindness. We can notice these differences, for instance, in the case of the Chekhov children, who all had to respond to the same physical punishments of the father. At a very early age Anton revealed a more ironic attitude, prone to laughing at the world and seeing things with some detachment. This made it easier for him to reassess his father once he was on his own. The other children lacked this ability to distance themselves and were more easily enmeshed in the father's brutality. This would seem to indicate something different in the way Anton's brain was wired. Some children are greedier than others—they display from early on a greater need for attention. They tend to always see what is missing, what they are not getting from others.

Second, our earliest experiences and attachment schemas (see chapter 4) play a large role in shaping the attitude. We internalize the voices of the mother and father figure. If they were very authoritarian and judgmental, we will tend to be harsher on ourselves than others and have a more critical bent toward everything we see. Equally important are the experiences we have outside the family, as we get older. When we love or admire someone, we tend to internalize a part of their presence, and they shape how we see the world in a positive way. This could be teachers, mentors, or peers. Negative and traumatic experiences can have a constricting effect—they close our minds off to anything that might possibly make us reexperience the original pain. Our attitude is constantly being shaped by what happens to us, but vestiges of our earliest attitude always live on. No matter how far he progressed, Chekhov remained susceptible to feelings of depression and self-loathing.

What we must understand about the attitude is not only how it colors our perceptions but also how it actively determines what happens to us in life—our health, our relations with people, and our success. Our attitude has a self-fulfilling dynamic.

Look again at the scenario of the young man in Paris. Feeling somewhat tense and insecure, he reacts defensively to mistakes that he makes in learning the language. This makes it harder for him to learn, which in turn makes meeting people more difficult, which makes him feel more isolated. The more his energy lowers from depression, the more this cycle perpetuates itself. His insecurities can also push people away. The way we think about people tends to have a like effect upon them. If we feel hostile and critical, we tend to inspire critical emotions in other people. If we feel defensive, we make others feel defensive. The attitude of the young man tends to lock him into this negative dynamic.

The attitude of the young woman, on the other hand, triggers a positive dynamic. She is able to learn the language and meet people, all of which elevates her mood and energy levels, which makes her more attractive and interesting to others, on and on.

Although attitudes come in many varieties and blends, we can generally categorize them as negative and narrow or positive and expansive. Those with a negative attitude tend to operate from a basic position of fear toward life. They unconsciously want to limit what they see and experience to give them more control. Those with a positive attitude have a much less fearful approach. They are open to new experiences, ideas, and emotions. If the attitude is like our lens on the world, the negative attitude narrows the aperture of this lens, and the positive variety expands it as far as possible. We might move between these two poles, but generally we tend to see the world with a more closed or open lens.

Your task as a student of human nature is twofold: First, you must become aware of your own attitude and how it slants your perceptions. It is hard to observe this in your day-to-day life because it is so close to you, but there are ways to catch glimpses of it in action. You can see it in how you judge people once they are out of your presence. Are you quick to focus on their negative qualities and bad opinions, or are you more generous and forgiving when it comes to their flaws? You will see definite signs of your attitude in how you face adversity or resistance. Are you quick to forget or gloss over any mistakes on your part? Do you instinctively blame others for any bad things that happen to you? Do you dread any kind of change? Do you tend to keep to routines and to avoid anything unexpected or unusual? Do you get your back up when someone challenges your ideas and assumptions?

You will also catch signs of it in how people respond to you, particularly in a nonverbal way. Do you catch them being nervous or defensive in your presence? Do you tend to attract people who play the mother or father role in your life?

Once you have a good feel for the makeup of your own attitude, its negative or positive bent, you have much greater power to alter it, to move it more in the positive direction.

Second, you must not only be aware of the role of your attitude but also believe in its supreme power to alter your circumstances. You are not a pawn in a game controlled by others; you are an active player who can move the pieces at will and even rewrite the rules. View your health as largely dependent on your attitude. Feeling excited and open to adventure, you can tap into energy reserves you did not know that you had. The mind and the body are one, and your thoughts affect your physical responses. People can recover much more quickly from illness through sheer desire and willpower. You are not born with fixed intelligence and inherent limits. See your brain as a miraculous organ designed for continual learning and improvement, well into old age. The rich neural connections in your brain, your creative powers, are something you develop to the degree that you open yourself up to new experiences and ideas. View problems and failures as means to learn and toughen yourself up. You can get through anything with persistence. View the way people treat you as largely flowing from your own attitude, something you can control.

Do not be afraid to exaggerate the role of willpower. It is an exaggeration with a purpose. It leads to a positive self-fulfilling dynamic, and that is all you care about. See this shaping of your attitude as your most important creation in life, and never leave it to chance.

The Constricted (Negative) Attitude

Life is inherently chaotic and unpredictable. The human animal, however, does not react well to uncertainty. People who feel particularly weak and vulnerable tend to adopt an attitude toward life that narrows what they experience so that they can reduce the possibility of unexpected events. This negative, narrowing attitude often has its origins in early childhood. Some children have little comfort or support in facing a frightening world. They develop various psychological strategies to constrict what they have to see and experience. They build up elaborate defenses to keep out other viewpoints. They become increasingly self-absorbed. In most situations they come to expect bad things to happen, and their goals in life revolve around anticipating and neutralizing bad experiences to better control them. As they get older, this attitude becomes more entrenched and narrower, making any kind of psychological growth nearly impossible.

These attitudes have a self-sabotaging dynamic. Such people make others feel the same negative emotion that dominates their attitude, which helps confirm them in their beliefs about people. They do not see the role that their own actions play, how they often are the instigators of the negative response. They only see people persecuting them, or bad luck overwhelming them. By pushing people away, they make it doubly hard to have any success in life, and in their isolation their attitude gets worse. They are caught in a vicious cycle.

The following are the five most common forms of the constricted attitude. Negative emotions have a binding power—a person who is angry is more prone to also feel suspicion, deep insecurities, resentment, et cetera. And so we often find combinations of these various negative attitudes, each one feeding and accentuating the other. Your goal is to recognize the various signs of such attitudes that exist in you in latent and weakened forms, and to root them out; to see how they operate in a stronger version in other people, better understanding their perspective on life; and to learn how to handle people with such attitudes.

The Hostile Attitude. Some children exhibit a hostile attitude at a very early age. They interpret weaning and the natural separation from parents as hostile actions. Other children must deal with a parent who likes to punish and inflict hurt. In both cases, the child looks out on a world that seems fraught with hostility, and their answer is to seek to control it by becoming the source of the hostility themselves. At least then it is no longer so random and sudden. As they get older, they become adept at stimulating anger and frustration in others, which justifies their original attitude—"See, people are against me, I am disliked, and for no apparent reason."

In a relationship, a husband with a hostile attitude will accuse his wife of not really loving him. If she protests and becomes defensive, he will see this as a sign that she has to try hard to disguise the truth. If she is intimidated into silence, he sees that as a sign that he was right all along. In her confusion, she can easily begin to feel some hostility on her part, confirming his opinion. People with this attitude have many other subtle tricks up their sleeve for provoking the hostility they secretly want to feel directed at them—withdrawing their cooperation on a project at just the wrong moment, constantly being late, doing a poor job, deliberately making an unfavorable first impression. But they never see themselves as playing any kind of role in instigating the reaction.

Their hostility permeates everything they do—the way they argue and provoke (they are always right); the nasty undertone of their jokes; the greediness with which they demand attention; the pleasure they get out of criticizing others and seeing them fail. You can recognize them by how they are easily moved to anger in these situations. Their life, as they describe it, is full of battles, betrayals, persecutions, but seemingly not originating from them. In essence, they are projecting their own hostile feelings onto other people and are primed to read them in almost any apparently innocent action. Their goal in life is to feel persecuted and to desire some form of revenge. Such types generally have career problems, as their anger and hostility frequently flare up. This gives them something else to complain about and a basis on which to blame the world for being against them.

If you notice signs of this attitude in yourself, such self-awareness is a major step toward being able to get rid of it. You can also try a simple experiment: Approach people you are meeting for the first time, or only know peripherally, with various positive thoughts—"I like them," "They seem smart," et cetera. None of this is verbalized, but you do your best to feel such emotions. If they respond with something hostile or defensive, then perhaps the world is truly against you. More than likely you will not see anything that could be remotely construed as negative. In fact, you will see the opposite. Clearly, then, the source of any hostile response is you.

In dealing with the extremes of this type, struggle as best you can to not respond with the antagonism they expect. Maintain your neutrality. This will confound them and temporarily put a stop to the game they are playing. They feed off your hostility, so do not give them fuel.

The Anxious Attitude. These types anticipate all kinds of obstacles and difficulties in any situation they face. With people, they often expect some sort of criticism or even betrayal. All of this stimulates unusual amounts of anxiety before the fact. What they really fear is losing control of the situation. Their solution is to limit what can possibly happen, to narrow the world they deal with. This means limiting where they go and what they'll attempt. In a relationship, they will subtly dominate the domestic rituals and habits; they will seem brittle and demand extra careful attention. This will dissuade people from criticizing them. Everything must be on their terms. At work they will be ferocious perfectionists and micromanagers, eventually sabotaging themselves by trying to keep on top of too many things. Once outside their comfort zone—the home or the relationship they dominate—they become unusually fretful.

Sometimes they can disguise their need for control as a form of love and concern. When Franklin Roosevelt came down with polio in 1921, at the age of thirty-nine, his mother, Sara, did all she could to restrict his life and keep him to one room in the house. He would have to give up his political career and surrender to her care. Franklin's wife, Eleanor, knew him better. What he wanted and needed was to slowly get back to something resembling his old life. It became a battle between the mother and the daughter-in-law that Eleanor eventually won. The mother was able to disguise her anxious attitude and need to dominate her son through her apparent love, transforming him into a helpless invalid.

Another disguise, similar to such love, is to seek to please and cajole people in order to disarm any possible unpredictable and unfriendly action. (See chapter 4, Toxic Types, The Pleaser.)

If you notice such tendencies in yourself, the best antidote is to pour your energies into work. Focusing your attention outward into a project of some sort will have a calming effect. As long as you rein in your perfectionistic tendencies, you can channel your need to control into something productive. With people, try to slowly open yourself to their habits and pace of doing things, instead of the opposite. This can show you that you have nothing to fear by loosening control. Deliberately place yourself in the circumstances you most dread, discovering that your fears are grossly exaggerated. You are slowly introducing a bit of chaos into your overly ordered life.

In dealing with those with this attitude, try to not feel infected with their anxiety, and instead try to provide the soothing influence they so lacked in their earliest years. If you radiate calmness, your manner will have greater effect than your words.

The Avoidant Attitude. People with this attitude see the world through the lens of their insecurities, generally related to doubts about their competence and intelligence. Perhaps as children they were made to feel guilty and uncomfortable with any efforts to excel and stand out from siblings; or they were made to feel bad about any kind of mistake or possible misbehavior. What they came to dread most was the judgment of their parents. As these people get older, their main goal in life is to avoid any kind of responsibility or challenge in which their self-esteem might be at stake and for which they can be judged. If they do not try too hard in life, they cannot fail or be criticized.

To enact this strategy they will constantly seek escape routes, consciously or unconsciously. They will find the perfect reason for leaving a job early and changing careers, or breaking off a relationship. In the middle of some high-stakes project they will suddenly develop an illness that will cause them to leave. They are prone to all kinds of psychosomatic maladies. Or they become alcoholics, addicts of some sort, always falling off the wagon at the right time but blaming this on the "disease" they have, and their bad upbringing that caused their addiction. If it weren't for alcohol, they could've been a great writer or entrepreneur, so they say. Other strategies will include wasting time and starting too late on something, always with some built-in excuse for why that happened. They then cannot be blamed for the mediocre results.

These types find it hard to commit to anything, for a good reason. If they remained at a job or in a relationship, their flaws might become too apparent to others. Better to slip away at the right moment and maintain the illusion—to themselves and to others—of their possible greatness, if only . . . Although they are generally motivated by the great fear of failing and the judgments that ensue, they are also secretly afraid of success—for with success come responsibilities and the need to live up to them. Success might also trigger their early fears about standing out and excelling.

You can easily recognize such people by their checkered careers and their short-term personal relationships. They may try to disguise the source of their problems by seeming saintly—they look down on success and people who have to prove themselves. Often they will present themselves as noble idealists, propagating ideas that will never come to pass but that will add to the saintly aura they wish to project. Having to enact ideals might expose them to criticism or failure, so they choose those that are too lofty and unrealistic for the times they live in. Do not be fooled by the holier-than-thou front they present. Look at their actions, the lack of accomplishments, the great projects they never start on, always with a good excuse.

If you notice traces of this attitude in yourself, a good strategy is to take on a project of even the smallest scale, taking it all the way to completion and embracing the prospect of failure. If you fail, you will have already cushioned the blow because you anticipated it, and inevitably it will not hurt as much as you had imagined. Your self-esteem will rise because you finally tried something and finished it. Once you diminish this fear, progress will be easy. You will want to try again. And if you succeed, all the better. Either way, you win.

When you find others with this attitude, be very wary of forming partnerships with them. They are masters at slipping away at the wrong moment, at getting you to do all of the hard work and take the blame if it fails. At all costs avoid the temptation to help or rescue them from their negativity. They are too good at the avoidance game.

The Depressive Attitude. As children, these types did not feel loved or respected by their parents. For helpless children, it is too much to imagine that their parents could be wrong or flawed in their parenting. Even if unloved, they still are dependent on them. And so their defense is to often internalize the negative judgment and imagine that they are indeed unworthy of being loved, that there is something actually wrong with them. In this way they can maintain the illusion that their parents are strong and competent. All of this occurs quite unconsciously, but the feeling of being worthless will haunt such people their entire lives. Deep down they will feel ashamed of who they are and not really know why they feel this way.

As adults they will anticipate abandonment, loss, and sadness in their experiences and see signs of potentially depressing things in the world around them. They are secretly drawn to what is gloomy in the world, to the seamy side of life. If they can manufacture some of the depression they feel in this way, it at least is under their control. They are consoled by the thought that the world is a dreary place. A strategy they will employ throughout their lives is to temporarily withdraw from life and from people. This will feed their depression and also make it something they can manage to some extent, as opposed to traumatic experiences imposed upon them.

An excellent example of this type was the talented German composer and conductor Hans von Bülow (1830–1894). In 1855 von Bülow met and fell in love with Cosima Liszt (1837–1930), the charismatic daughter of the composer Franz Liszt. Cosima was drawn to von Bülow's air of sadness. He lived with his domineering and hostile mother, and Cosima had great sympathy for him. She wanted to rescue von Bülow and transform him into a great composer. They were soon married. As time went on, Cosima could see that he felt quite inferior in relation to her intelligence and strong will. Soon he began to question her love for him. He continually withdrew from her during his bouts of depression. When she became pregnant, he suddenly developed some mysterious ailment that prevented him from being with her. Without warning he could become quite cold.

Feeling unloved and neglected, she began an affair with the famous composer Richard Wagner, who was a friend and colleague of von Bülow's. Cosima had the feeling that von Bülow had unconsciously encouraged their affair. When she eventually left von Bülow to live with Wagner, von Bülow bombarded her with letters, blaming himself for what had happened; he was unworthy of her love. He would then go on about the bad turn in his career, his various illnesses, his suicidal tendencies. Although he criticized himself, she could not help but feel guilty and depressed for somehow being responsible. Recounting all of his woes seemed like his subtle way of wounding her. She compared each letter to "a sword twisted in my heart." And they kept coming, year after year, until he remarried and repeated the same pattern with his new wife.

These types often have a secret need to wound others, encouraging behavior such as betrayal or criticism that will feed their depression. They will also sabotage themselves if they experience any kind of success, feeling deep down that they don't deserve it. They will develop blocks in their work, or take criticism to mean they should not continue with their career. Depressive types can often attract people to them, because of their sensitive nature; they stimulate the desire to want to help them. But like von Bülow, they will start to criticize and wound the ones who wish to help, then withdraw again. This push and pull causes confusion, but once under their spell it is hard to disengage from them without feeling guilty. They have a gift for making other people feel depressed in their presence. This gives them more fuel to feed off.

Most of us have depressive tendencies and moments. The best way to handle them is to be aware of their necessity—they are our body's and mind's way of compelling us to slow down, to lower our energies and withdraw. Depressive cycles can serve positive purposes. The solution is to realize their usefulness and temporary quality. The depression you feel today will not be with you in a week, and you can ride it out. If possible, find ways to elevate your energy level, which will physically help lift you out of the mood. The best way to handle recurrent depression is to channel your energies into work, especially the arts. You are used to withdrawing and being alone; use such time to tap into your unconscious. Externalize your unusual sensitivity and your dark feelings into the work itself.

Never try to lift up depressive people by preaching to them about the wonderfulness of life. Instead, it is best to go along with their gloomy opinion of the world while subtly drawing them into positive experiences that can elevate their moods and energy without any direct appeal.

The Resentful Attitude. As children, these types never felt they got enough parental love and affection—they were always greedy for more attention. They carry this sense of dissatisfaction and disappointment with them throughout their lives. They are never quite getting the recognition they deserve. They are experts at scanning people's faces for signs of possible disrespect or disdain. They see everything in relation to themselves; if someone has more than they do, it is a sign of injustice, a personal affront. When they feel this lack of respect and recognition, they do not explode in anger. They are generally cautious and like to control their emotions. Instead, the hurt incubates inside them, the sense of injustice growing stronger as they reflect on this. They do not easily forget. At some point they will take their revenge in some shrewdly plotted act of sabotage or passive aggression.

Because they have a continual feeling of being wronged, they tend to project this on to the world, seeing oppressors everywhere. In this way, they often become the leader of those who feel disaffected and oppressed. If such types get power, they can become quite vicious and vengeful, finally able to vent their resentments on various victims. In general, they carry themselves with an air of arrogance; they are above others even if no one recognizes this. They carry their head a little too high; they frequently have a slight smirk or look of disdain. As they get older, they are prone to pick petty battles, unable to completely contain their resentments that have accumulated over time. Their bitter attitude pushes a lot of people away, and so they often end up congregating with others who have this attitude, as their form of community.

The Roman emperor Tiberius (42 BC–AD 37) is perhaps the most classic example of this type. As a child, his tutor noticed something wrong with the boy. "He is a pitcher molded with blood and bile," the tutor once wrote to a friend. The writer Suetonius, who knew Tiberius, described him as follows: "He carried himself with his head held proudly high. . . . He was almost always silent, never saying a word except now and again. . . . And even then he did so with extreme reluctance, at the same time always making a disdainful gesture with his fingers." Emperor Augustus, his stepfather, had to continually apologize to the Senate for "his displeasing manners, full of haughtiness." Tiberius hated his mother—she never loved him enough. He never felt appreciated by Augustus, or his soldiers, or the Roman people. When he became emperor, he slowly and methodically took revenge on those who he felt had slighted him, and such revenge would be cold and cruel.

As he got older, he became increasingly unpopular. His enemies were legion. Feeling the hatred of his subjects, he retired to the island of Capri, where he spent the last eleven years of his reign, almost completely avoiding Rome. He was known to repeat to others in his last years, "After me, let fire destroy the earth!" At his death Rome exploded with celebration, the crowds voicing their feelings with the famous phrase "Into the Tiber [River] with Tiberius!"

If you notice resentful tendencies within yourself, the best antidote is to learn to let go of hurts and disappointments in life. It is better to explode into anger in the moment, even it if it's irrational, than to stew on slights that you have probably hallucinated or exaggerated. People are generally indifferent to your fate, not as antagonistic as you imagine. Very few of their actions are really directed at you. Stop seeing everything in personal terms. Respect is something that must be earned through your achievements, not something given to you simply for being human. You must break out of the resentful cycle by becoming more generous toward people and human nature.

In dealing with such types, you must exercise supreme caution. Although they might smile and seem pleasant, they are actually scrutinizing you for any possible insult. You can recognize them by their history of past battles and sudden breaks with people, as well as how easily they judge others. You might try to slowly gain their trust and lower their suspicions; but be aware that the longer you are around them, the more fuel you will give them for something to resent, and their response can be quite vicious. Better to avoid this type if possible.

The Expansive (Positive) Attitude

Some fifty years ago, many medical experts began to think of health in a new and revolutionary way. Instead of focusing on specific problems, such as digestion or skin ailments or the condition of the heart, they decided it was much better to look at the human body as a whole. If people improved their diet and their exercise habits, this would have a beneficial effect on all of the organs, because the body is an interconnected whole.

This seems obvious to us now, but such an organic way of thinking has great application to our psychological health as well. Now more than ever people focus on their specific problems—their depression, their lack of motivation, their social inadequacies, their boredom. But what governs all of these seemingly separate problems is our attitude, how we view the world on a daily basis. It is how we see and interpret events. Improve the overall attitude and everything else will elevate as well—creative powers, the ability to handle stress, confidence levels, relationships with people. It was an idea first promulgated in the 1890s by the great American psychologist William James, but it remains a revolution waiting to happen.

A negative, constricting attitude is designed to narrow down the richness of life at the cost of our creative powers, our sense of fulfillment, our social pleasures, and our vital energies. Without wasting another day under such conditions, your goal is to break out, to expand what you see and what you experience. You want to open the aperture of the lens as wide as you can. Here is your road map.

How to view the world: See yourself as an explorer. With the gift of consciousness, you stand before a vast and unknown universe that we humans have just begun to investigate. Most people prefer to cling to certain ideas and principles, many of them adopted early on in life. They are secretly afraid of what is unfamiliar and uncertain. They replace curiosity with conviction. By the time they are thirty, they act as if they know everything they need to know.

As an explorer you leave all that certainty behind you. You are in continual search of new ideas and new ways of thinking. You see no limits to where your mind can roam, and you are not concerned with suddenly appearing inconsistent or developing ideas that directly contradict what you believed a few months before. Ideas are things to play with. If you hold on to them for too long, they become something dead. You are returning to your childlike spirit and curiosity, from before you had an ego and being right was more important than connecting to the world. You explore all forms of knowledge, from all cultures and time periods. You want to be challenged.

By opening the mind in this way, you will unleash unrealized creative powers, and you will give yourself great mental pleasure. As part of this, be open to exploring the insights that come from your own unconscious, as revealed in your dreams, in moments of tiredness, and in the repressed desires that leak out in certain moments. You have nothing to be afraid of or to repress there. The unconscious is merely one more realm for you to freely explore.

How to view adversity: Our life inevitably involves obstacles, frustrations, pain, and separations. How we come to handle such moments in our early years plays a large role in the development of our overall attitude toward life. For many people, such difficult moments inspire them to restrict what they see and experience. They go through life trying to avoid any kind of adversity, even if this means never really challenging themselves or getting much success in their careers. Instead of learning from negative experiences, they want to repress them. Your goal is to move in the opposite direction, to embrace all obstacles as learning experiences, as means to getting stronger. In this way you embrace life itself.

By 1928 the actress Joan Crawford had a reasonably successful career in Hollywood, but she was feeling increasingly frustrated by the limited roles she was receiving. She saw other less talented actresses vault ahead of her. Perhaps the problem was that she was not assertive enough. She decided she needed to voice her opinion to one of the most powerful production chiefs on the MGM lot, Irving Thalberg. Little did she realize that Thalberg viewed this as impudence and that he was vindictive by nature. He therefore cast her in a Western, knowing that was the last thing she wanted and that such a fate was a dead end for many an actress.

Joan had learned her lesson and decided to embrace her fate. She made herself love the genre. She became an expert rider. She read up on the Old West and became fascinated by its folklore. If that's what it took to get ahead, she decided to become the leading actress of Westerns. At the very least this would expand her acting skills. This became her lifelong attitude toward work and the supreme challenges an actress faced in Hollywood, where careers were generally very short. Every setback was a chance to grow and develop.

In 1946 twenty-year-old Malcolm Little (later known as Malcolm X) began serving an eight-to-ten-year prison sentence for burglary. Prison generally has the effect of hardening the criminal and narrowing his already narrow view of the world. Instead, Malcolm decided to reassess his life. He began to spend time in the prison library and fell in love with books and learning. As he saw it now, prison afforded him the best possible means of changing himself and his attitude toward life. With so much time on his hands, he could study and earn himself a degree. He could develop the discipline he had always been missing. He could train himself to become an expert speaker. He embraced the experience without any bitterness and emerged stronger than ever. Once he left prison, he saw any difficulty, large or small, as a means to test and toughen himself.

Although adversity and pain are generally beyond your control, you have the power to determine your response and the fate that comes from that.

How to view yourself: As we get older, we tend to place limits on how far we can go in life. Over the years we internalize the criticisms and doubts of others. By accepting what we think to be the limits of our intelligence and creative powers, we create a self-fulfilling dynamic. They become our limits.

You do not need to be so humble and self-effacing in this world. Such humility is not a virtue but is rather a value that people promote to help keep you down. Whatever you are doing now, you are in fact capable of much more, and by thinking that, you will create a very different dynamic.

In ancient times, many great leaders, such as Alexander the Great and Julius Caesar, felt that they were descended from gods and part divine. Such self-belief would translate into high levels of confidence that others would feed off and recognize. It became a self-fulfilling prophecy. You do not need to indulge in such grandiose thoughts, but feeling that you are destined for something great or important will give you a degree of resilience when people oppose or resist you. You will not internalize the doubts that come from such moments. You will have an enterprising spirit. You will continually try new things, even taking risks, confident in your ability to bounce back from failures and feeling destined to succeed.

When Chekhov had the epiphany about the ultimate freedom he could create for himself, he had what the American psychologist Abraham Maslow called a "peak experience." These are moments in which you are lifted out of the daily grind and you sense that there is something larger and more sublime in life that you have been missing. In the case of Chekhov it was sparked by a crisis, by loneliness, and it led to the sensation of complete acceptance of people and the world around him. These moments can come from exerting yourself past what you thought were your limits; they can come from overcoming great obstacles, climbing a mountain, taking a trip to a very different culture, or the deep bonding that comes from any form of love. You want to deliberately go in search of such moments, stimulate them if you can. They have the effect, as they did with Chekhov, of altering your attitude for good. They expand what you think about your possibilities and about life itself, and the memory is something you will always return to for supreme inspiration.

In general, this way of looking at yourself runs counter to the cool, ironic attitude that many people like to assume in the postmodern world—never too ambitious, never too positive about things or life, always affecting a nonchalant and very false humility. Such types see the positive, expansive attitude as Pollyannaish and simpleminded. But really their cool attitude is a clever mask for their great fears—of embarrassing themselves, of failing, of showing too much emotion. As with all such trends in culture, the cool attitude will eventually fade away, a remnant of the early twenty-first century. Moving in the opposite direction, you are much more progressive.

How to view your energy and health: Although we are all mortal and subject to illnesses beyond our control, we must recognize the role that will-power plays in our health. We have all felt this to some degree or another. When we fall in love or feel excited by our work, suddenly we have more energy and recover quickly from any illnesses. When we are depressed or unusually stressed, we become prey to all kinds of ailments. Our attitude plays an enormous role in our health, one that science has begun to explore and will examine in more depth in the coming decades. In general, you can safely push yourself beyond what you think are your physical limits by feeling excited and challenged by a project or endeavor. People get old and prematurely age by accepting physical limits to what they can do, making it a self-fulfilling cycle. Those who age well continue to engage in physical activity, only moderately adjusted. You have wellsprings of energy and health you have yet to tap into.

How to view other people: First you must try to get rid of the natural tendency to take what people do and say as something personally directed at you, particularly if what they say or do is unpleasant. Even when they criticize you or act against your interests, more often than not it stems from some deep earlier pain they are reliving; you become the convenient target of frustrations and resentments that have been accumulating over the years. They are projecting their own negative feelings. If you can view people this way, you will find it easier to not react and get upset or become embroiled in some petty battle. If the person is truly malicious, by not becoming emotional yourself you will be in a better place to plot the proper countermove. You will save yourself from accumulating hurts and bitter feelings.

See people as facts of nature. They come in all varieties, like flowers or rocks. There are fools and saints and sociopaths and egomaniacs and noble warriors; there are the sensitive and the insensitive. They all play a role in our social ecology. This does not mean we cannot struggle to change the harmful behavior of the people who are close to us or in our sphere of influence; but we cannot reengineer human nature, and even if we somehow succeeded, the result could be a lot worse than what we have. You must accept diversity and the fact that people are what they are. That they are different from you should not be felt as a challenge to your ego or self-esteem but as something to welcome and embrace.

From this more neutral stance, you can then try to understand the people you deal with on a deeper level, as Chekhov did with his father. The more you do this, the more tolerant you will tend to become toward people and toward human nature in general. Your open, generous spirit will make your social interactions much smoother, and people will be drawn to you.

FINALLY, THINK OF THE MODERN CONCEPT OF ATTITUDE IN TERMS OF THE ANCIENT concept of the *soul*. The concept of the soul is found in almost all indigenous cultures and in premodern civilizations. It originally referred to external *spiritual forces* permeating the universe and contained in the individual human in the form of the soul. The soul is not the mind or the body but rather the overall spirit we embody, our way of experiencing the world. It is what makes a person an individual, and the concept of the soul was related to the earliest ideas of personality. Under this concept, a person's soul could have depths. Some people possessed a greater degree of this spiritual force, had more of a soul. Others had a personality lacking in this force and were somewhat soulless.

This has great relevance to our idea of the attitude. In our modern conception of the soul, we replace this external spiritual force with life itself, or what can be described as the *life force*. Life is inherently complex and unpredictable, its powers far beyond anything we can ever completely comprehend or control. This life force is reflected in nature and human society by the remarkable diversity we find in both realms.

On the one side we find people whose goal in life is to inhibit and control this life force. This leads them to self-destructive strategies. They have to limit their thoughts and remain true to ideas that have lost their relevance. They have to limit what they experience. Everything is about them and their petty needs and personal problems. They often become obsessed with a particular goal that dominates all of their thoughts—such as making money or getting attention. All of this renders them dead inside as they close themselves off to the richness of life and the variety of human experience. In this way they veer toward the soulless, an internal lack of depth and flexibility.

Your goal must be to always move in the opposite direction. You rediscover the curiosity you once had as a child. Everything and everyone is a source of fascination to you. You keep learning, continually expanding what you know and what you experience. With people you feel generous and tolerant, even with your enemies and with those trapped in the soulless condition. You do not enslave yourself to bitterness or rancor. Instead of blaming others or circumstances, you see the role that your own attitude and actions played in any failure. You adapt to circumstances instead of complaining about them. You accept and embrace uncertainty and the unexpected as valuable qualities of life. In this way, your soul expands to the contours of life itself and fills itself with this life force.

Learn to measure the people you deal with by the depth of their soul, and if possible associate as much as you can with those of the expansive variety.

> This is why the same external events or circumstances affect no two people alike; even with perfectly similar surroundings every one lives in a world of his own. . . . The world in which a man lives shapes itself chiefly by the way in which he looks at it, and so it proves different to different men; to one it is barren, dull, and superficial; to another rich, interesting, and full of meaning. On hearing of the interesting events which have happened in the course of a man's experience, many people will wish that similar things had happened in their lives too, completely forgetting that they should be envious rather of the mental aptitude which lent those events the significance they possess when he describes them.
>
> —*Arthur Schopenhauer*

9

Confront Your Dark Side

◇

The Law of Repression

*P*eople are rarely who they seem to be. Lurking beneath their polite, affable exterior is inevitably a dark, shadow side consisting of the insecurities and the aggressive, selfish impulses they repress and carefully conceal from public view. This dark side leaks out in behavior that will baffle and harm you. Learn to recognize the signs of the Shadow before they become toxic. See people's overt traits—toughness, saintliness, et cetera—as covering up the opposite quality. You must become aware of your own dark side. In being conscious of it you can control and channel the creative energies that lurk in your unconscious. By integrating the dark side into your personality, you will be a more complete human and will radiate an authenticity that will draw people to you.

The Dark Side

On November 5, 1968, Republican Richard Nixon accomplished perhaps the greatest comeback in American political history, narrowly defeating his Democratic rival, Hubert Humphrey, to become the thirty-seventh president of the United States. Only eight years earlier he had lost his first attempt at the presidency to John F. Kennedy in a devastating fashion. The election was extremely close, but clearly some voting shenanigans in Illinois, orchestrated by the Democratic Party machine in Chicago, played a role in his defeat. Two years later he lost badly in the race to become the governor of California. Bitter at how the press had hounded and provoked him throughout the race, he addressed the media the day after this defeat and concluded by saying, "Just think of how much you're going to be missing. You won't have Nixon to kick around anymore, because, gentlemen, this is my last press conference."

The response to these words was overwhelmingly negative. He was accused of wallowing in self-pity. *ABC News* ran a half-hour special called "The Political Obituary of Richard Nixon." A *Time* magazine article on him concluded: "Barring a miracle, Richard Nixon can never hope to be elected to any political office again."

By all accounts his political career should have been over in 1962. But Richard Nixon's life had been an endless series of crises and setbacks that had only made him more determined. As a young man his dream was to attend an Ivy League school, the key to attaining power in America. Young Richard was exceptionally ambitious. His family, however, was relatively poor and could not afford to pay for such an education. He overcame this seemingly insuperable barrier by transforming himself into a superior student, earning the nickname "Iron Butt" for his inhuman work habits, and managed to land a scholarship to the law school at Duke University. To keep the scholarship he had to remain at the top of his class, which he did through the kind of hard work few others could endure.

After several years in the U.S. Senate, in 1952 Dwight D. Eisenhower had chosen him to be his running mate as vice president on the Republican ticket, but quickly regretted the choice. Nixon had kept a secret fund from the Republican Party that he had supposedly used for private purposes. In fact he was innocent of the charges, but Eisenhower did not feel comfortable with him, and this was the excuse to get rid of him. Cutting him loose in this way would almost certainly ruin Nixon's political career. Once again he rose to the challenge, appearing on live television and delivering the speech of his life, defending himself against the charges. It was so effective, the public clamored for Eisenhower to keep him on the ticket. He went on to serve eight years as vice president.

And so, the crushing defeats of 1960 and 1962 would again be the means of toughening himself up and resurrecting his career. He was like a cat with nine lives. Nothing could kill him. He laid low for a few years, then came charging back for the 1968 election. He was now the "new Nixon," more relaxed and affable, a man who liked bowling and corny jokes. And having learned all the lessons from his various defeats, he ran one of the smoothest and savviest campaigns in modern history and made all of his enemies and doubters eat crow when he defeated Humphrey.

In becoming president, he had seemingly reached the apex of power. But in his mind there was yet one more challenge to overcome, perhaps the greatest of all. Nixon's liberal enemies saw him as a political animal, one who would resort to any kind of trickery to win an election. To the East Coast elites who hated him, he was the hick from Whittier, California, too obvious in his ambition. Nixon was determined to prove them all wrong. He was not who they thought he was. He was an idealist at heart, not a ruthless politician. His beloved mother, Hannah, was a devout Quaker who had instilled in him the importance of treating all people equally and promoting peace in the world. He wanted to craft a legacy as one of the greatest presidents in history. For the sake of his mother, who had died earlier that year, he wanted to embody her Quaker ideals and show his detractors how deeply they had misread him.

His political icons were men like French president Charles de Gaulle, whom he had met and greatly admired. De Gaulle had crafted a persona that radiated authority and love of country. Nixon would do the same. In his notebooks he began to refer to himself as "RN"—the world leader version of himself. RN would be strong, resolute, compassionate yet completely masculine. The America he was to lead was riven by antiwar protests, riots in the cities, a rising crime rate. He would end the war and work toward world peace; at home he would bring prosperity to all Americans, stand for law and order, and instill a sense of decency the country had lost. Accomplishing this, he would take his place among the presidents he revered—Abraham Lincoln and Woodrow Wilson. And he would will this into existence, as he always had done.

In his first months he moved quickly. He assembled a top-notch cabinet, including the brilliant Henry Kissinger as his national security adviser. For his personal staff he preferred clean-cut young men who would be fiercely loyal to him and serve as tools to realize his great ambitions for America. This would include Bob Haldeman, his chief of staff; John Ehrlichman, in charge of domestic policy; John Dean, the White House counsel; and Charles Colson, a White House aide.

He didn't want intellectuals around him; he wanted go-getters. But Nixon was not naive. He understood that in politics loyalty was ephemeral. And so early on in his administration he installed a secret voice-activated taping system throughout the White House that only a select few would know about. In this way he could keep discreet tabs on his staff and preemptively discover any possible turncoats or leakers among them. It would provide evidence he could use later on if anyone tried to misrepresent any conversations with him. And

best of all, once his presidency was over, the edited tapes could be used to demonstrate his greatness as a leader, the clear and rational way he came to his decisions. The tapes would secure his legacy.

As the first few years went by, Nixon worked to execute his plan. He was
an active president. He signed bills to protect the environment, the health of
workers, and the rights of consumers. On the foreign front, he struggled to
wind down the war in Vietnam, with limited success. But soon he laid the
groundwork for his first visit to the Soviet Union and his celebrated trip to
China and signed into law an agreement with the Soviets to limit the prolif-
eration of nuclear weapons. This was just the start of what he would bring
about.

And yet despite the relative smoothness of these first years, something
strange began to stir within Richard Nixon. He could not shake these feelings
of anxiety, something he had been prone to his entire life. It started to come out
in his closed-door meetings with his personal staff, late at night over some
drinks. Nixon would begin to share with them stories from his colorful past,
and in the process he would go over some of his old political wounds, and bitterness would rise up from deep within.

He was particularly obsessed with the Alger Hiss case. Alger Hiss was an
important staffer in the State Department who in 1948 had been accused of
being a communist spy. Hiss denied the charges. Dapper and elegant, he was
the darling of the liberals. Nixon, at the time a junior congressman from California, smelled a phony. While other congressmen decided to leave Hiss alone,
Nixon, representing the House Un-American Activities Committee, kept investigating. In an interview with Hiss, as Nixon reminded him of the law
against perjury, Hiss replied, "I am familiar with the law. I attended Harvard
Law School. I believe yours was Whittier?" (a reference to the lowly under-
graduate college Nixon had attended).

Relentless in his pursuit of Hiss, Nixon was successful in getting him in-
dicted for perjury, and Hiss went to prison. This victory made Nixon famous
but, as he told his staff members, it earned him the eternal wrath of East Coast
elites, who saw him as the unctuous upstart from Whittier. In the 1950s these
elites, many of them Harvard graduates, quietly kept Nixon and his wife, Pat,
out of their social circles, limiting Nixon's political contacts. Their allies in the
press ridiculed him mercilessly for any misstatement or possible misdeed. Yes,
Nixon was no angel. He liked winning, but the hypocrisy of these liberals

galled him—Bobby Kennedy was the king of political dirty tricks, and yet what reporter publicized this?

As he went deeper and deeper into these stories night after night with his staff, he reminded them that this past was still very much alive. The old enemies were still at work against him. There was CBS correspondent Daniel Schorr, who seemed to hate Nixon with unusual zeal. His reports from Vietnam always managed to highlight the worst aspects of the war and make Nixon look bad. There was Katharine Graham, the owner of the *Washington Post*, a newspaper that seemed to have a personal vendetta against him going back many years. She was the doyenne of the Georgetown social scene, which had snubbed him and Pat for years. Worst of all, there was Larry O'Brien, now the chairman of the Democratic Party, who as a key adviser in the Kennedy administration had managed to get Nixon audited by the IRS. As Nixon saw it, O'Brien was the evil genius of politics, a man who would do anything to prevent Nixon's reelection in 1972.

His enemies were everywhere and they were relentless—planting negative stories in the press, procuring embarrassing leaks from within the bureaucracy, spying on him, ready to pounce on the slightest whiff of scandal. And what, he would ask his staff, are we doing on our side? If his team did nothing to respond to this, they would have only themselves to blame. His legacy, his ambitions were at stake. As the stories began to pile up of antiwar demonstrations and leaks about his administration's Vietnam War effort, Nixon became red-hot with anger and frustration, the talk with his staff heating up on both sides. Once, as Colson talked about getting revenge on some particularly nettlesome opponents, Nixon chimed in, "One day we will get them—we'll get them on the ground where we want them. And then we'll stick our heels in, step on them hard and twist—right, Chuck, right?"

When informed that many of the staff at the Bureau of Labor Statistics were Jews, he felt that was probably the reason for some bad economic numbers coming from there. "The government is full of Jews," he told Haldeman. "Most Jews are disloyal." They were the mainstay of the East Coast establishment that worked so hard against him. Another time he told Haldeman, "*Please* get me the names of the Jews, you know, the big Jewish contributors to the Democrats. . . . Could we please investigate some of the cocksuckers?" Auditing them would be in order. He had other harsh ideas for how to hurt Katharine Graham and embarrass Daniel Schorr.

Nixon also began to feel increasingly anxious about his public image, so critical to his legacy. He badgered his staff, and even Henry Kissinger, to promote to the press his strong leadership style. In interviews, they should refer to him as Mr. Peace, and Kissinger should not be getting so much credit. He wanted to know what the elites at the parties in Georgetown were saying about him. Were they finally changing their minds in any way about Richard Nixon?

Despite his nervousness, by 1972 it was clear that events were lining up well for him. His Democratic opponent in his reelection bid would be Senator George McGovern, a diehard liberal. Nixon was ahead in the polls, but he wanted much more. He wanted a complete landslide and mandate from the public. Certain that men like O'Brien had some tricks up their sleeve, he began to rail at Haldeman to do some spying and get some dirt on the Democrats. He wanted Haldeman to assemble a team of "nutcutters" to do the necessary dirty work with maximum efficiency. He would leave the details up to him.

Much to his chagrin, in June of that year Nixon read in the *Washington Post* of a botched break-in at the Watergate Hotel, in which a group of men had attempted to plant bugs in the offices of Larry O'Brien. This led to the arrest of three men—James McCord, E. Howard Hunt, and G. Gordon Liddy—with ties to the committee for the reelection of President Nixon. The break-in was so badly done that Nixon suspected it was all a setup by the Democrats. This was not the efficient team of nutcutters he had advocated.

A few days later, on June 23, he discussed the break-in with Haldeman. The FBI was investigating the case. Some of the men arrested were former CIA operatives. Perhaps, Haldeman proposed, they could get top brass in the CIA to put pressure on the FBI to drop the investigation. Nixon approved. He told Haldeman, "I'm not going to get that involved." Haldeman responded, "No, sir. We don't want you to." But Nixon then added, "Play it tough. That's the way they play and that's the way we're going to play it." Nixon put his counsel, John Dean, in charge of the internal investigation, with clear instructions that he should stonewall the FBI and cover up any connections to the White House. Anyway, Nixon had never directly ordered the break-in. Watergate was a trifle, nothing to tarnish his reputation. It would fade away, along with all the other dirty political deeds never discovered or recorded in the history books.

And indeed he was correct, for the time being—the public paid little attention to the break-in. Nixon went on to have one of the biggest landslides in electoral history. He swept every state except Massachusetts and the District of Columbia. He even won over a large percentage of Democrats. He now had four more years to solidify his legacy and nothing to stop him. His popularity numbers had never been higher.

Watergate, however, kept coming back to life and would not leave him alone. In January 1973, the Senate decided to launch an investigation. In March, McCord finally spilled the beans, implicating various members of the White House staff in the ordering of the break-in. Hunt began demanding hush money to not reveal what he knew. The way out of this mess was simple and clear—hire an outside lawyer to do an internal investigation of the break-in, with the full cooperation of Nixon and his team, and bring all the details to light. Nixon's reputation would suffer, some would go to prison, but it would keep him politically alive, and he was the master of coming back from the dead.

Nixon, however, could not take such a step. There would be too much immediate damage. The thought of coming clean about what he knew and had ordered frightened him to death. In meetings with Dean he continued to discuss the cover-up, even suggesting where they could come up with hush money. Dean cautioned him to not get so involved, but Nixon seemed oddly fascinated by the growing mess he had created, and unable to pull himself away.

Soon he was forced to fire Haldeman and Ehrlichman, both of whom had been deeply implicated in the break-in. It was an ordeal to get him to personally fire them, and when it came to delivering the news to Ehrlichman, he broke down and sobbed. But it seemed that nothing he did could stop the momentum of the Watergate investigation, which got closer and closer to Nixon, making him feel like a trapped rat.

On July 19, 1973, he received the worst news of all: the Senate committee investigating Watergate had learned of the secret taping system installed in the White House, and they demanded that the tapes be handed over to them as evidence. All Nixon could think about was the intense embarrassment that would ensue if the tapes went public. They would make him the laughingstock of the world. Think of the language that he had used and the many harsh things he had advocated. His image, his legacy, all the ideals he had striven to realize, it would all be ruined in one fell stroke. He thought of his mother and his own family—they had never heard him speak as he had done in the privacy of his own office. It was as if he were another person on those tapes. Alexander Haig, who was now his chief of staff, told Nixon he had to tear out the taping system and destroy the tapes immediately, before receiving an official subpoena.

Nixon seemed paralyzed: Destroying the tapes would be an admission of guilt; perhaps the tapes would exonerate him, as they would prove he had never directly ordered the break-in. But the thought of any of these tapes becoming public terrified him. He went back and forth on this in his mind, but in the end he decided to not destroy them. By invoking executive privilege he would resist handing them over.

Finally, as pressure mounted, in April 1974 Nixon decided to release edited transcripts of the tapes in the form of a 1,200-page book and hope for the best. The public was horrified by what it read. Yes, many had thought him slippery and devious, but the forceful language, the swearing, the sometimes hysterical, paranoid tone of his conversation, and the utter lack of compunction or hesitation in ordering various illegal acts revealed a side of Nixon they had never suspected. Even members of his family were shocked. When it came to Watergate, he seemed very weak and indecisive, not at all the de Gaulle image he wanted to project. He never once showed the slightest desire to get at the truth and punish the wrongdoers. Where was the man of law and order?

On July 24 came the final blow: the Supreme Court ordered him to hand over the tapes themselves, and among them would be the recorded conversation of June 23, 1972, in which he had approved of using the CIA to quash the FBI investigation. This was the "smoking gun" that revealed his involvement in the cover-up from early on. Nixon was doomed, and although it was against everything he believed in, by early August he decided to resign.

The morning after he delivered his resignation speech to the country, Nixon addressed his staff one last time, and fighting to control his emotions, he concluded, "Never get discouraged, never be petty; always remember, others may hate you, but those who hate you don't win unless you hate them, and then you destroy yourself." Along with his family, he then got into the helicopter that was to take him into political exile.

Interpretation: For those who worked closely with Richard Nixon, the man was an enigma. According to his chief speechwriter, Ray Price, there were two Nixons, one light, one dark. The light Nixon was "exceptionally considerate, exceptionally caring, sentimental, generous of spirit, kind." The dark Nixon was "angry, vindictive, ill-tempered, mean-spirited." He saw both sides as being "at constant war with one another." But perhaps the most perceptive observer of Nixon, the one closest to figuring out the enigma, was Henry Kissinger, who made a point of studying him closely so that he could manage and even play him for his own purposes. And according to Kissinger, the key to

Nixon and his split personality must somehow lie in his childhood. "Can you imagine," Kissinger once observed, "what this man would have been like if somebody had loved him?"

As an infant, Nixon seemed to be unusually needy. He was a notorious cry-baby; it took great effort to soothe him, and he was continually bursting into sobs. He wanted more attention, more fussing after him, and he was quite ma-nipulative if he did not get these things. His parents did not like this aspect of their child. Growing up in the pioneer days of southern California, they pre-ferred to have a stoic, self-reliant child. Nixon's father could be physically abu-sive and cold. His mother was more caring but frequently depressed and very moody. She had to deal with the business failures of her husband and two sickly brothers of Richard who died at young ages. She had to frequently leave Rich-ard alone for months to attend to his brothers, which Richard must have expe-rienced as some kind of abandonment.

In dealing with his difficult parents, the personality of Nixon was formed. Seeking to overcome and disguise his vulnerabilities, he created a persona that served him well, first with his family and later with the public. For this persona he accentuated his own strengths and developed new ones. He became su-premely tough, resilient, fierce, decisive, rational, and not someone to mess with, particularly in debate. (According to Kissinger, "There was nothing he feared more than to be thought weak.") But the weak and vulnerable child within does not miraculously disappear. If its needs have never been met or dealt with, its presence sinks into the unconscious, into the shadows of the per-sonality, waiting to come out in strange ways. It becomes the dark side.

With Nixon, whenever he experienced stress or unusual levels of anxiety, this dark side would stir from deep within in the form of potent insecurities ("nobody appreciates me"), suspicions (enemies everywhere), sudden outbursts and tantrums, and powerful desires to manipulate and harm those he believed had crossed him.

Nixon repressed and denied this side of himself with vehemence, even up to the very end in his last words to his staff. He frequently told people he never cried, or held grudges, or cared what others thought of him—the opposite of the truth. For much of the time he played his role well as RN. But when the shadow stirred, strange behavior emerged, giving people who saw him on a regular basis the impression they were indeed dealing with two Nixons. To Kissinger, it was like seeing the unloved child come back to life.

Nixon's dark side finally became something tangible in form of the tapes.

Nixon knew that everything he said was being recorded, and yet he never held back or filtered what he was saying. He insulted close friends behind their backs, indulged in wild bouts of paranoia and revenge fantasies, waffled over the simplest decisions. He was a man who greatly feared the slightest internal leak and suspected betrayal in almost anyone around him, and yet he entrusted his fate to tapes that he believed would never be made public in an unedited form. Even when it seemed that they could become public and he was advised to destroy them, he held on to them, mesmerized by this other Nixon that had emerged. It was as if he secretly desired his own punishment, the child and the dark side taking revenge for being so deeply denied.

Understand: The story of Nixon is closer to you and your reality than you might like to imagine. Like Nixon, you have crafted a public persona that accentuates your strengths and conceals your weaknesses. Like him, you have repressed the less socially acceptable traits you naturally possessed as a child. You have become terribly nice and pleasant. And like him, you have a dark side, one that you are loath to admit or examine. It contains your deepest insecurities, your secret desires to hurt people, even those close to you, your fantasies of revenge, your suspicions about others, your hunger for more attention and power. This dark side haunts your dreams. It leaks out in moments of inexplicable depression, unusual anxiety, touchy moods, sudden neediness, and suspicious thoughts. It comes out in offhand comments you later regret.

And sometimes, as with Nixon, it even leads to destructive behavior. You will tend to blame circumstances or other people for these moods and behavior, but they keep recurring because you are unaware of their source. Depression and anxiety come from not being your complete self, from always playing a role. It requires great energy to keep this dark side at bay, but at times unpleasant behavior leaks out as a way to release the inner tension.

Your task as a student of human nature is to recognize and examine the dark side of your character. Once subjected to conscious scrutiny, it loses its destructive power. If you can learn to detect the signs of it in yourself (see the following sections for help on this), you can channel this darker energy into productive activity. You can turn your neediness and vulnerability into empathy. You can channel your aggressive impulses into worthwhile causes and into your work. You can admit your ambitions, your desires for power, and not act so guiltily and stealthily. You can monitor your suspicious tendencies and the projection of your own negative emotions onto others. You can see that selfish and harmful impulses dwell within you as well, that you are not as angelic or strong as you imagine. With this awareness will come balance and greater tolerance for others.

It might seem that only those who project continual strength and saintliness can become successful, but that is not at all the case. By playing a role to such an extent, by straining to live up to ideals that are not real, you will emit a phoniness that others pick up. Look at great public figures such as Abraham Lincoln and Winston Churchill. They possessed the ability to examine their flaws and mistakes and laugh at themselves. They came across as authentically human, and this was the source of their charm. The tragedy of Nixon was that he had immense political talent and intelligence; if only he had also possessed the ability to look within and measure the darker sides to his character. It is the tragedy that confronts us all to the extent that we remain in deep denial.

This longing to commit a madness stays with us throughout our lives. Who has not, when standing with someone by an abyss or high up on a tower, had a sudden impulse to push the other over? And how is it that we hurt those we love although we know that remorse will follow? Our whole being is nothing but a fight against the dark forces within ourselves. To live is to war with trolls in heart and soul. To write is to sit in judgment on oneself.

—Henrik Ibsen

Keys to Human Nature

If we think about the people we know and see on a regular basis, we would have to agree that they are usually quite pleasant and agreeable. For the most part, they seem pleased to be in our company, are relatively up-front and confident, socially responsible, able to work with a team, take good care of themselves, and treat others well. But every now and then with these friends, acquaintances, and colleagues, we glimpse behavior that seems to contradict what we normally see.

This can come in several forms: Out of nowhere they make a critical, even cruel comment about us, or express a rather harsh assessment of our work or personality. Is this what they really feel and were struggling to conceal? For a moment they are not so nice. Or we hear of their unpleasant treatment of family or employees behind closed doors. Or out of the blue they have an affair with the most unlikely man or woman, and it leads to bad things. Or they put their money in some absurd and risky financial scheme. Or they do something rash that puts their career in jeopardy. Or we catch them in some lie or manipulative act. We can also notice such moments of acting out, or behaving against reputation, in public figures and celebrities, who then go through lengthy apologies for the strange moods that came over them.

What we glimpse in these moments is the dark side of their character, what the Swiss psychologist Carl Jung called the Shadow. The Shadow consists of all the qualities people try to deny about themselves and repress. This repression is so deep and effective that people are generally unaware of their Shadow; it operates unconsciously. According to Jung, this Shadow has a thickness to it, depending on how deep the level of repression and the number of traits that are being concealed. Nixon would be said to have a particularly thick Shadow. When we experience those moments when people reveal the dark side, we can see something come over their face; their voice and body language is altered—almost as if another person is confronting us, the features of the upset child suddenly becoming visible. We *feel* their shadow as it stirs and emerges.

The Shadow lies buried deep within, but it becomes disturbed and active in moments of stress, or when deep wounds and insecurities are triggered. It also tends to emerge more as people get older. When we are young, everything seems exciting to us, including the various social roles we must play. But later in life we tire of the masks we have been wearing, and the leakage is greater.

Because we rarely see the Shadow, the people we deal with are somewhat strangers to us. It is as if we only see a two-dimensional, flattened image of people—their pleasant social side. Knowing the contours of their Shadow makes them come to life in three dimensions. This ability to see the rounded person is a critical step in our knowledge of human nature. Armed with this knowledge, we can anticipate people's behavior in moments of stress, understand their hidden motives, and not get dragged under by any self-destructive tendencies.

The Shadow is created in our earliest years and stems from two conflicting forces that we felt. First, we came into this world bursting with energy and intensity. We did not understand the difference between acceptable and unacceptable behavior; we only experienced natural impulses. Some of these impulses were aggressive. We wanted to monopolize our parents' attention and receive much more of it than our siblings. We experienced moments of great affection but also powerful dislikes and hatreds, even of our parents for not meeting our needs. We wanted to feel superior in some way and appreciated for it—in appearance, strength, or smartness. We could be remarkably selfish if we were denied what we wanted, and turn devious and manipulative to get it. We could even find some pleasure in hurting people, or fantasize about getting revenge. We experienced and expressed the full gamut of emotions. We were not the innocent angels people imagine children to be.

At the same time, we were completely vulnerable and dependent on our parents for survival. This dependence lasted for many years. We watched our parents with eagle eyes, noting every signal of approval and disapproval on their faces. They would chastise us for having too much energy and wish we could sit still. They sometimes found us too willful and selfish. They felt that other people were judging them by the behavior of their children, so they wanted us to be nice, to put on a show for others, to act like the sweet angel. They urged us to be cooperative and play fairly, even though at times we wished to behave differently. They encouraged us to tone down our needs, to be more of what they needed in their stressful lives. They actively discouraged our tantrums and any form of acting out.

As we got older, these pressures to present a particular front came from other directions—peers and teachers. It was fine to show some ambition, but not too much of it or we might seem antisocial. We could exude confidence, but not too much or we would seem to be asserting our superiority. The need to fit into the group became a primary motivation, and so we learned to tamp down and restrain the dark side of our personality. We internalized all of the ideals of our culture—being nice, having prosocial values. Much of this is essential for the smooth functioning of social life, but in the process a large part of our nature moved underground, into the Shadow. (Of course, there are some who never learned to control these darker impulses and end up acting them out in real life—the criminals in our midst. But even criminals struggle to appear nice a great deal of the time and justify their behavior.)

Most of us succeed in becoming a positive social animal, but at a price. We end up missing the intensity that we experienced in childhood, the full gamut of emotions, and even the creativity that came with this wilder energy. We secretly yearn to recapture it in some way. We are drawn toward what is outwardly forbidden—sexually or socially. We may resort to alcohol or drugs or any stimulant, because we feel our senses dulled, our minds too restrained by convention. If we accumulate a lot of hurts and resentments along the way, which we strive to conceal from others, the Shadow grows thicker. If we experience success in our lives, we become addicted to positive attention, and in the inevitable down moments when the drug of such attention wears off, the Shadow will be disturbed and activated.

Concealing this dark side requires energy; it can be draining to always present such a nice, confident front. And so the Shadow wants to release some of the inner tension and come back to life. As the poet Horace once said, *Naturam expellas furca, tamen usque recurret* ("You can throw out Nature with a pitchfork, but she'll always come back"). You must become adept at recognizing such moments of release in others and interpreting them, seeing the outlines of the Shadow that now come forward. The following are some of the most notable signs of such release.

Contradictory behavior: This is the most eloquent sign of all. It consists of actions that belie the carefully constructed front that people present. For instance, a person who preaches morals is suddenly caught out in a very compromising situation. Or someone with a tough exterior reveals insecurities and hysteria at the wrong moment. Or a person who preaches free love and open behavior suddenly becomes quite domineering and authoritarian. The strange, contradictory behavior is a direct expression of the Shadow. (For more on such signs and how to interpret them, see the section on page 248.)

Emotional outbursts: A person suddenly loses his or her habitual self-control and sharply expresses deep resentments or says something biting and hurtful. In the aftermath of such a release, they may blame it on stress; they may say they did not mean any of it, when in fact the opposite is the case—the Shadow has spoken. Take what they said at face value. On a less intense level, people may suddenly become unusually sensitive and touchy. Some of their deepest fears and insecurities from childhood have somehow become activated, and this makes them hyperalert to any possible slight and ripe for smaller outbursts.

Vehement denial: According to Freud, the only way that something unpleasant or uncomfortable in our unconscious can reach the conscious mind is through active denial. We express the very opposite of what is buried within. This could be a person fulminating against homosexuality, when in fact he or she feels the opposite. Nixon engaged in such denials frequently, as when he told others, in the strongest terms, that he never cried, or held grudges, or gave in to weakness, or cared what people thought of him. You must reinterpret the denials as positive expressions of Shadow desires.

"Accidental" behavior: People might talk of quitting some addiction, or not working so damned hard, or staying away from a self-destructive relationship. They then fall into the behavior they spoke of trying to avoid, blaming it on an uncontrollable illness or dependency. This salves their conscience for indulging their dark side; they simply can't help it. Ignore the justifications and see the Shadow operating and releasing. Also remember that when people are drunk and behave differently, often it is not the alcohol that is speaking but the Shadow.

Overidealization: This can serve as one of the most potent covers for the Shadow. Let us say we believe in some cause, such as the importance of transparency in our actions, particularly in politics. Or we admire and follow the leader of just such a cause. Or we decide that some new type of financial investment—mortgage-backed securities, for instance—represents the latest and most sophisticated path to wealth. In these situations we go much further than simple enthusiasm. We are charged with powerful conviction. We gloss over any faults, inconsistencies, or possible downsides. We see everything in black-and-white terms—our cause is moral, modern, and progressive; the other side, including doubters, is evil and reactionary.

We now feel sanctioned to do everything for the cause—lie, cheat, manipulate, spy, falsify scientific data, get revenge. Anything the leader does is justified. In the case of the investment, we feel justified in taking what normally would be seen as great risks, because this time the financial tool is different and new, not subject to the usual rules. We can be as greedy as we like without worrying about the consequences.

We tend to be dazzled by the strength of people's convictions and interpret excessive behavior as simply overzealousness. But we should look at it in another light. By overidealizing a cause, person, or object, people can give free rein to the Shadow. That is their unconscious motivation. The bullying, the manipulations, the greed that comes out for the sake of the cause or product should be taken at face value, the overly strong conviction providing simple cover for repressed emotions to play themselves out.

Related to this, in arguments people will use their powerful convictions as a perfect way to disguise their desires to bully and intimidate. They trot out statistics and anecdotes (which can always be found) to buttress their case, then proceed to insult or impugn our integrity. It's just an exchange of ideas, they say. Pay attention to the bullying tone, and do not be fooled. Intellectuals might be subtler. They will lord it over us with obscure language and ideas we cannot decode, and we are made to feel inferior for our ignorance. In all cases, see this as repressed aggression finding a way to leak out.

Projection: This is by far the most common way of dealing with our Shadow, because it offers almost daily release. We cannot admit to ourselves certain desires—for sex, for money, for power, for superiority in some area—and so instead we project those desires onto others. Sometimes we simply imagine and completely project these qualities out of nothing, in order to judge and condemn people. Other times we find people who express such taboo desires in some form, and we exaggerate them in order to justify our dislike or hatred.

For instance, we accuse another person in some conflict of having authoritarian desires. In fact, they are simply defending themselves. We are the ones who secretly wish to dominate, but if we see it in the other side first, we can vent our repressed desire in the form of a judgment and justify our own authoritarian response. Let us say we repressed early on assertive and spontaneous impulses so natural to the child. Unconsciously we wish to have back such qualities, but we cannot overcome our internal taboos. We look out for those who are less inhibited, more assertive and open with their ambition. We exaggerate these tendencies. Now we can despise them, and in thinking about them, give vent to what we cannot admit to ourselves or about ourselves.

The great nineteenth-century German composer Richard Wagner frequently expressed anti-Semitic sentiments. He blamed Jews for ruining Western music with their eclectic tastes, sentimentality, and emphasis on technical brilliance. He yearned for a more pure German music, which he would create. Most of what he blamed Jews for in music was completely made up. Yet Wagner, strangely enough, had many of the same qualities that he seemed to hate in Jews. His tastes were quite eclectic. He had sentimental tendencies. Many of the pianists and conductors he worked with were Jewish, because of their technical proficiency.

Remember: behind any vehement hatred is often a secret and very unpalatable envy of the hated person or people. It is only through such hate that it can be released from the unconscious in some form.

Consider yourself a detective when it comes to piecing together people's Shadow. Through the various signs you pick up, you can fill in the outlines of their repressed desires and impulses. This will allow you to anticipate future leakage and odd Shadow-like behavior. Rest assured such behavior never occurs just once, and it will tend to pop up in different areas. If, for instance, you pick up bullying tendencies in the way someone argues, you will also see it in other activities.

You might entertain the notion that this concept of the Shadow is somewhat antiquated. After all, we live in a much more rational, scientifically oriented culture today. People are more transparent and self-aware than ever, we might say. We are much less repressed than our ancestors, who had to deal with all sorts of pressures from organized religion. The truth, however, might very well be the opposite. In many ways we are more split than ever between our conscious, social selves and our unconscious Shadow. We live in a culture that enforces powerful codes of correctness that we must abide by or face the shaming that is now so common on social media. We are supposed to live up to ideals of selflessness, which are impossible for us because we are not angels. All of this drives the dark side of our personalities even further underground.

We can read signs of this in how deeply and secretly we are all drawn to the dark side in our culture. We thrill at watching shows in which various Machiavellian characters manipulate, deceive, and dominate. We lap up stories in the news of those who have been caught acting out in some way and enjoy the ensuing shaming. Serial killers and diabolical cult leaders enthrall us. With these shows and the news we can always become moralistic and talk of how much we despise such villains, but the truth is that the culture constantly feeds us these figures because we are hungry for expressions of the dark side. All of this provides a degree of release from the tension we experience in having to play the angel and seem so correct.

These are relatively harmless forms of release, but there are more dangerous ones, particularly in the realm of politics. We find ourselves increasingly drawn to leaders who give vent to this dark side, who express the hostility and resentment we all secretly feel. They say things we would dare not say. In the safety of the group and rallied to some cause, we have license to project and vent our spleen on various convenient scapegoats. By idealizing the leader and the cause, we are now free to act in ways we would normally shy away from as individuals. These demagogues are adept at exaggerating the threats we face, painting everything in black-and-white terms. They stir up the fears, insecurities, and desires for revenge that have gone underground but are waiting at any moment to explode in the group setting. We will find more and more such leaders as we experience greater degrees of repression and inner tension.

The writer Robert Louis Stevenson expressed this dynamic in the novel *The Strange Case of Dr. Jekyll and Mr. Hyde,* published in 1886. The main character, Dr. Jekyll, is a well-respected and wealthy doctor/scientist with impeccable manners, so much like the paragons of goodness in our culture. He invents a concoction that transforms him into Mr. Hyde, the embodiment of his Shadow, who proceeds to murder and rape and indulge in the wildest of sensual pleasures. Stevenson's idea is that the more civilized and moral we outwardly become, the more potentially dangerous is the Shadow, which we so fiercely deny. As the character Dr. Jekyll describes it, "My devil had long been caged, he came out roaring."

The solution is not more repression and correctness. We can never alter human nature through enforced niceness. The pitchfork doesn't work. Nor is the solution to seek release for our Shadow in the group, which is volatile and dangerous. Instead the answer is to see our Shadow in action and become more self-aware. It is hard to project onto others our own secret impulses or to overidealize some cause, once we are made aware of the mechanism operating within us. Through such self-knowledge we can find a way to integrate the dark side into our consciousness productively and creatively. (For more on this, see the last section of this chapter.) In doing so we become more authentic and complete, exploiting to the maximum the energies we naturally possess.

Deciphering the Shadow: Contradictory Behavior

In the course of your life you will come upon people who have very emphatic traits that set them apart and seem to be the source of their strength—unusual confidence, exceptional niceness and affability, great moral rectitude and a saintly aura, toughness and rugged masculinity, an intimidating intellect. If you look closely at them, you may notice a slight exaggeration to these traits, as if they were performing or laying it on just a little too thick. As a student of human nature, you must understand the reality: the emphatic trait generally rests on top of the opposite trait, distracting and concealing it from public view.

We can see two forms of this: Early on in life some people sense a softness, vulnerability, or insecurity that might prove embarrassing or uncomfortable. They unconsciously develop the opposite trait, a resilience or toughness that lies on the outside like a protective shell. The other scenario is that a person has a quality that they feel might be antisocial—for instance, too much ambition or an inclination to be selfish. They develop the opposite quality, something very prosocial.

In both cases, over the years they hone and perfect this public image. The underlying weakness or antisocial trait is a key component of their Shadow— something denied and repressed. But as the laws of human nature dictate, the deeper the repression, the greater the volatility of the Shadow. As they get older or experience stress, there will be cracks in the façade. They are playing a role to the extreme, and it is tiring. Their real self will rebel in the form of moods, obsessions, secret vices, and behavior that is quite contrary to their image and is often self-destructive.

Your task is simple: be extra wary around people who display such emphatic traits. It is very easy to get caught up in the appearance and first impression. Watch for the signs and emergence of the opposite over time. It is much easier to deal with such types once you understand them. The following are seven of the most common emphatic traits that you must learn to recognize and manage appropriately.

The Tough Guy: He projects a rough masculinity that is intended to intimidate. He has a swagger and an air that signals he is not to be messed with. He tends to boast about past exploits—the women he has conquered, the brawls, the times he's outnegotiated opponents. Although he seems extremely convincing in telling such stories, they feel exaggerated, almost hard to believe. Do not be fooled by appearances. Such men have learned to conceal an underlying softness, an emotional vulnerability from deep within that terrifies them. On occasion you will see this sensitive side—they may cry, or have a tantrum, or suddenly show compassion. Embarrassed by this, they will quickly cover it up with a tough or even cruel act or comment.

For the baseball player Reggie Jackson, Yankees manager Billy Martin was just such a brawling type. Jackson could recognize the softness behind the bluster in Martin's touchiness when it came to his ego, his changing moods (not very masculine), and emotional outbursts that revealed glaring insecurities. Such men will often make terrible decisions under the impact of the emotions that they have tried to conceal and repress but that inevitably surface. Although they like to dominate women, they will often end up with a wife who clearly dominates them, a secret wish of theirs.

You must not let yourself be intimidated by the front, but also be careful to not stir up their deep insecurities by seeming to doubt their tall tales or masculine nature. They are notoriously touchy and thin-skinned, and you might detect a micropout on their face if you trigger their insecurities, before they cover it up with a fierce scowl. If they happen to be a rival, they are easy to bait into an overreaction that reveals something less than tough.

The Saint: These people are paragons of goodness and purity. They support the best and most progressive causes. They can be very spiritual if that is the circle they travel in; or they are above the corruption and compromises of politics; or they have endless compassion for every type of victim. This saintly exterior developed early on as a way to disguise their strong hunger for power and attention or their strong sensual appetites. The irony is that often by projecting this saintly aura to the nth degree they will gain great power, leading a cult or political party. And once they are in power, the Shadow will have space to operate. They will become intolerant, railing at the impure, punishing them if necessary. Maximilien Robespierre (nicknamed the Incorruptible), who rose to power in the French Revolution, was just such a type. Under his reign, the guillotine was never busier.

They are also secretly drawn to sex, to money, to the limelight, and to what is expressly taboo for their particular saintliness. The strain and the temptations are too much—they are the gurus who sleep with their students. They will appear the saint in public, but their family or spouse will see the demonic side in private. (See the story of the Tolstoys in chapter 2.) There are genuine saints out there, but they do not feel the need to publicize their deeds or grab power. To distinguish between the real and the fake, ignore their words and the aura they project, focusing on their deeds and the details of their life—how much they seem to enjoy power and attention, the astonishing degree of wealth they have accumulated, the number of mistresses, the level of self-absorption. Once you recognize this type, do not become a naive follower. Keep some distance. If they are enemies, simply shine a light on the clear signs of hypocrisy.

As a variation on this, you will find people who propound a philosophy of free love and anything goes; but in fact they are after power. They prefer sex with those who are dependent on them. And of course anything goes, as long as it's on their terms.

The Passive-Aggressive Charmer: These types are amazingly nice and accommodating when you first meet them, so much so that you tend to let them into your life rather quickly. They smile a lot. They are upbeat and always willing to help. At some point, you may return the favor by hiring them for a job or helping them in their careers. You will detect along the way some cracks in the veneer—perhaps they make a somewhat critical comment out of the blue, or you hear from friends that they have been talking about you behind your back. Then something ugly occurs—a blowup, some act of sabotage or betrayal—so unlike that nice, charming person you first befriended.

The truth is that these types realize early on in life that they have aggressive, envious tendencies that are hard to control. They want power. They intuit that such inclinations will make life hard for them. Over many years they cultivate the opposite façade—their niceness has an almost aggressive edge. Through this stratagem they are able to gain social power. But they secretly resent having to play such a role and be so deferential. They can't maintain it. Under stress or simply worn out by the effort, they will lash out and hurt you. They can do this well now that they know you and your weak spots. They will, of course, blame you for what ensues.

Your best defense is to be wary of people who are too quick to charm and befriend, too nice and accommodating at first. Such extreme niceness is never natural. Keep your distance and look for some early signs, such as passive-aggressive comments. If you notice that—somewhat out of character—they indulge in malicious gossip about someone, you can be sure the Shadow is speaking and that you will be the target of such gossip one day.

The Fanatic: You are impressed by their fervor, in support of whatever cause. They speak forcefully. They allow for no compromise. They will clean things up, restore greatness. They radiate strength and conviction, and because of this they gain followers. They have a flair for drama and capturing attention. But at the key moment when they could possibly deliver what they have promised, they unexpectedly slip up. They become indecisive at the wrong moment, or burn themselves out and fall ill, or take such ill-conceived actions that it all falls apart. It's as if they have suddenly lost belief, or secretly wanted to fail.

The truth is that such types have massive insecurities from early on in life. They have doubts about their self-worth. They never felt loved or admired enough. Riddled with fears and uncertainty, they cover this up with the mask of great belief, in themselves and in their cause. You will notice in their past some shifts in their belief system, sometimes radical. That is because it is not the particular belief that matters but the intense conviction, and so they will shift this around to fit the times. Belief in something is like a drug for them. But the doubts return. They secretly know they cannot deliver the goods. And so under stress they become the opposite—indecisive and secretly doubtful. They suddenly fire their assistants and managers to give the impression of action, but unconsciously they are sabotaging themselves with unnecessary change. They have to blow it all up, somehow and yet blame others.

Never be taken in by the strength of people's convictions and their flair for drama. Always operate by the rule that the greater the stridency in what they say, the deeper the underlying insecurities and doubts. Do not become a follower. They will make a fool of you.

The Rigid Rationalist: All of us have irrational tendencies. It is the lasting legacy of our primitive origins. We will never get rid of them. We are prone to superstitions, to seeing connections between events that have no connection. We are fascinated by coincidences. We anthropomorphize and project our feelings onto other people and the world around us. We secretly consult astrology charts. We must simply accept this. In fact, we often resort to irrationality as a form of relaxation—silly jokes, meaningless activities, occasional dabbling in the occult. Always being rational can be tiresome. But for some people, this makes them terribly uncomfortable. They experience this primitive thinking as softness, as mysticism, as contrary to science and technology. Everything must be clear and analytical in the extreme. They become devout atheists, not realizing that the concept of God cannot be proven or disproven. It is a belief either way.

The repressed, however, always return. Their faith in science and technology has a religious air to it. When it comes to an argument, they will impose their ideas with extra intellectual heft and even a touch of anger, which reveals the stirring of the primitive within and the hidden emotional need to bully. At the extreme, they will indulge in a love affair that is most irrational and contrary to their image—the professor running off with the young model. Or they will make some bad career choice, or fall for some ridiculous financial scheme, or indulge in some conspiracy theory. They are also prone to strange shifts in mood and emotional outbursts as the Shadow stirs. Bait them into just such overreactions to prick their bubble of intellectual superiority. True rationality should be sober and skeptical about its own powers and not publicize itself.

The Snob: These types have a tremendous need to be different from others, to assert some form of superiority over the mass of mankind. They have the most refined aesthetic tastes when it comes to art, or film criticism, or fine wines, or gourmet food, or vintage punk rock records. They have amassed impressive knowledge of these things. They put a lot of emphasis on appearances—they are more "alternative" than others, their tattoos are more unique. In many cases, they seem to come from very interesting backgrounds, perhaps with some exciting ancestry. Everything surrounding them is extraordinary. Of course, it later comes out that they were exaggerating or downright lying about their background. Beau Brummell, the notorious snob and dandy of the early nineteenth century, actually came from a staunch middle-class background, the opposite of what he peddled. The family of Karl Lagerfeld, the current Chanel creative director, did not inherit its money but made it in the most bourgeois fashion, contrary to the stories he has told.

The truth is that banality is part of human existence. Much of our lives is spent doing the most boring and tedious tasks. For most of us, our parents had normal, unglamorous jobs. We all have mediocre sides to our character and skills. Snobs are especially sensitive about this, greatly insecure about their origins and possible mediocrity. Their way of dealing with this is to distract and deceive with appearances (as opposed to real originality in their work), surrounding themselves with the extraordinary and with special knowledge. Underneath it all is the real person waiting to come out—rather ordinary and not so very different.

In any case, those who are truly original and different do not need to make a great show of it. In fact, they are often embarrassed by being so different and learn to appear more humble. (As an example of this, see the story of Abraham Lincoln in the section below.) Be extra wary of those who go out of their way to make a show of their difference.

The Extreme Entrepreneur: At first glance these types seem to possess very positive qualities, especially for work. They maintain very high standards and pay exceptional attention to detail. They are willing to do much of the work themselves. If mixed with talent, this often leads to success early on in life. But underneath the façade the seeds of failure are taking root. This first appears in their inability to listen to others. They cannot take advice. They need no one. In fact, they mistrust others who do not have their same high standards. With success they are forced to take on more and more responsibility.

If they were truly self-reliant, they would know the importance of delegating on a lower level to maintain control on the higher level, but something else is stirring within—the Shadow. Soon the situation becomes chaotic. Others must come in and take over the business. Their health and finances are ruined and they become completely dependent on doctors or outside financiers. They go from complete control to total dependence on others. (Think of the pop star Michael Jackson near the end of his life.)

Often their outward show of self-reliance disguises a hidden desire to have others take care of them, to regress to the dependency of childhood. They can never admit this to themselves or show any signs of such weakness, but unconsciously they are drawn to creating enough chaos that they break down and are forced into some form of dependency. There are signs beforehand: recurring health issues, the sudden microneeds to be pampered by people in their daily lives. But the big sign comes as they lose control and fail to take steps to halt this. It is best to not get too entangled with such types later on in their careers, as they have a tendency to bring about much collateral damage.

The Integrated Human

In the course of our lives we inevitably meet people who appear to be especially comfortable with themselves. They display certain traits that help give this impression: they are able to laugh at themselves; they can admit to certain shortcomings in their character, as well as to mistakes they have made; they have a playful, sometimes impish edge to them, as if they have retained more of the child within; they can play their role in life with a little bit of distance (see the last section of chapter 3). At times they can be charmingly spontaneous.

What such people signal to us is a greater authenticity. If most of us have lost a lot of our natural traits in becoming socialized adults, the authentic types have somehow managed to keep them alive and active. We can contrast them easily with the opposite type: people who are touchy, who are hypersensitive to any perceived slight, and who give the impression of being somewhat uncomfortable with themselves and having something to hide. We humans are masters at smelling the difference. We can almost *feel* it with people in their nonverbal behavior—the relaxed or tense body language, the flowing or halting tone of voice; the way the eyes gaze and let you in; the genuine smile or lack of it.

One thing is for certain: we are completely drawn to the authentic types and unconsciously repulsed by their opposite. The reason for this is simple: we all secretly mourn for the child part of our character we have lost—the wildness, the spontaneity, the intensity of experience, the open mind. Our overall energy is diminished by the loss. Those who emit that air of authenticity signal to us another possibility—that of being an adult who has managed to integrate the child and the adult, the dark and the light, the unconscious and the conscious mind. We yearn to be around them. Perhaps some of their energy will rub off on us.

If Richard Nixon in many ways epitomizes the inauthentic type, we find many examples of the opposite to inspire us—in politics, men like Winston Churchill and Abraham Lincoln; in the arts, people like Charlie Chaplin and Josephine Baker; in science, someone like Albert Einstein; in social life in general, someone like Jacqueline Kennedy Onassis. And these types indicate for us the path to follow, which largely centers on self-awareness. Conscious of our Shadow, we can control, channel, and integrate it. Aware of what we have lost, we can reconnect to that part of ourselves that has sunk into the Shadow.

The following are four clear and practical steps for achieving this.

See the Shadow. This is the most difficult step in the process. The Shadow is something we deny and repress. It is so much easier to dig up and moralize about the dark qualities of others. It is almost unnatural for us to look inward at this side of ourselves. But remember that you are only half a human if you keep this buried. Be intrepid in this process.

The best way to begin is to look for indirect signs, as indicated in the sections above. For instance, take note of any particular one-sided, emphatic traits in yourself. Assume that the opposite trait lies buried deep within, and from there try to see more signs of this trait in your behavior. Look at your own emotional outbursts and moments of extreme touchiness. Somebody or something has struck a chord. Your sensitivity to a remark or imputation indicates a Shadow quality that is stirring, in the form of a deep insecurity. Bring it into the light.

Look deeply at your tendencies to project emotions and bad qualities onto people you know, or even entire groups. For instance, say you really loathe narcissistic types or pushy people. What is happening is that you are probably brushing up against your own narcissistic tendencies and secret desire to be more assertive, in the form of a vehement denial or hatred. We are particularly sensitive to traits and weaknesses in others that we are repressing in ourselves. Look at moments in your youth (late teens, early twenties) in which you acted in a rather insensitive or even cruel manner. When you were younger, you had less control of the Shadow and it came out more naturally, not with the repressed force of later years.

Later in his career, the writer Robert Bly (born 1926) began to feel depressed. His writing had become sterile. He started to think more and more about the Shadow side of his character. He was determined to find signs of it and consciously scrutinize it. Bly was the bohemian type of artist, very much active in the counterculture of the 1960s. His artistic roots went back to the

Romantic artists of the early nineteenth century, men and women who extolled spontaneity and naturalness. In much of Bly's own writing, he railed at advertising men and businesspeople—as he saw it, they were so calculating, planning everything to the extreme, afraid of the chaos of life, and quite manipulative.

And yet, as he looked inward, Bly could catch glimpses of such calculating, manipulative qualities in himself. He too secretly feared moments of chaos in life, liked to plan things out and control events. He could be quite malicious with people he perceived to be so different, but in fact there was a part of the stockbroker and advertising man within him. Perhaps it was the deeper part of himself. Others told him that they saw him as rather classical in his taste and in his writing (constructing things well), something that bothered him, since he thought the opposite. But as he became increasingly honest with himself, he realized they were right. (People can often see our Shadow better than we can, and it would be wise to elicit their frank opinions on the subject.)

Step by step he unearthed the dark qualities within—rigid, overly moralistic, et cetera—and in doing so he felt reconnected with the other half of his psyche. He could be honest with himself and channel the Shadow creatively. His depression lifted, as well as the writer's block.

Take this process deeper by reexamining the earlier version of yourself. Look at traits in childhood that were drummed out of you by your parents and peers—certain weaknesses or vulnerabilities or forms of behavior, traits you were made to feel ashamed of. Perhaps your parents did not like your introspective tendencies or your interest in certain subjects that were not of their taste. They instead steered you toward careers and interests that suited them. Look at emotions you were once prone to, things that sparked a sense of awe or excitement that has gone missing. You have become more like others as you have gotten older, and you must rediscover the lost authentic parts of yourself.

Finally, look at your dreams as the most direct and clear view of your Shadow. Only there will you find the kinds of behavior you have carefully avoided in conscious life. The Shadow is talking to you in various ways. Don't look for symbols or hidden meanings. Pay attention instead to the emotional tone and overall feelings that they inspire, holding on to them throughout the day. This could be unexpected bold behavior on your part, or intense anxiety spurred by certain situations, or sensations of being physically trapped or of soaring above it all, or exploring a place that is forbidden and beyond the boundaries. The anxieties could relate to insecurities you are not confronting;

the soaring and exploring are hidden desires trying to rise to consciousness. Get in the habit of writing your dreams down and paying deep attention to their feeling tone.

The more you go through this process and see the outlines of your Shadow, the easier it will become. You will find more signs as your tense muscles of repression loosen up. At a certain point, the pain of going through this turns into excitement at what you're uncovering.

Embrace the Shadow. Your natural reaction in uncovering and facing up to your dark side is to feel uncomfortable and maintain only a surface awareness of it. Your goal here must be the opposite—not only complete acceptance of the Shadow but the desire to integrate it into your present personality.

From an early age Abraham Lincoln liked to analyze himself, and a recurrent theme in his self-examinations was that he had a split personality—on the one hand an ambitious almost cruel streak to his nature, and on the other a sensitivity and softness that made him frequently depressed. Both sides of his nature made him feel uncomfortable and odd. On the rough side, for instance, he loved boxing and thoroughly thrashing his opponent in the ring. In law and politics he had a rather scathing sense of humor.

Once he wrote some anonymous letters to a newspaper, attacking a politician he thought of as a buffoon. The letters were so effective that the target went mad with rage. He found out that Lincoln was the source of them and challenged him to a duel. This became the talk of the town and proved quite embarrassing to Lincoln. He managed to get out of the duel, but he vowed to never indulge his cruel streak again. He recognized the trait in himself and would not deny it. Instead he would pour his aggressive, competitive energy into winning debates and elections.

On his soft side, he loved poetry, felt tremendous affection for animals, and hated witnessing any kind of physical cruelty. He hated drinking and what it did to people. At his worst, he was prone to fits of deep melancholy and brooding over death. All in all, he felt himself to be far too sensitive for the rough-and-tumble world of politics. Instead of denying this side of himself, he channeled it into incredible empathy for the public, for the average man and woman. Caring deeply about the loss of lives in the war, he put all his efforts into ending it early. He did not project evil onto the South but rather empathized with its plight and planned on a peace that was not retributive.

He also incorporated it into a healthy sense of humor about himself, making frequent jokes about his ugliness, high-pitched voice, and brooding nature.

By embracing and integrating such opposing qualities into his public persona, he gave the impression of tremendous authenticity. People could identify with him in a way never seen before with a political leader.

Explore the Shadow. Consider the Shadow as having depths that contain great creative energy. You want to explore these depths, which include more primitive forms of thinking and the darkest impulses that come out of our animal nature.

As children, our minds were much more fluid and open. We would make the most surprising and creative associations between ideas. But as we get older, we tend to tighten this down. We live in a sophisticated, high-tech world dominated by statistics and ideas gleaned from big data. Free associations between ideas, images from dreams, hunches, and intuitions seem irrational and subjective. But this leads to the most sterile forms of thinking. The unconscious, the Shadow side of the mind, has powers we must learn to tap into. And in fact some of the most creative people in our midst actively engage this side of thinking.

Albert Einstein based one of his theories of relativity on an image from a dream. The mathematician Jacques Hadamard made his most important discoveries while boarding a bus or taking a shower—hunches that came out of nowhere, or what he claimed to be his unconscious. Louis Pasteur made his great discovery about immunization based on a rather free association of ideas after an accident in his laboratory. Steve Jobs claimed that his most effective ideas came from intuitions, moments when his mind roamed most freely.

Understand: The conscious thinking we depend on is quite limited. We can hold on to only so much information in short- and long-term memory. But the unconscious contains an almost limitless amount of material from memories, experiences, and information absorbed in study. After prolonged research or work on a problem, when we relax our minds in dreams or while we are performing unrelated banal activities, the unconscious begins to go to work and associate all sorts of random ideas, some of the more interesting ones bubbling to the surface. We all have dreams, intuitions, and free associations of ideas, but we often refuse to pay attention to them or take them seriously. Instead you want to develop the habit of using this form of thought more often by having unstructured time in which you can play with ideas, widen the options you consider, and pay serious attention to what comes to you in less conscious states of mind.

In a similar vein, you want to explore from within your own darkest impulses, even those that might seem criminal, and find a way to express them in your work or externalize them in some fashion, in a journal for instance. We all have aggressive and antisocial desires, even toward those we love. We also have traumas from our earliest years that are associated with emotions we prefer to forget. The greatest art in all media somehow expresses these depths, which causes a powerful reaction in us all because they are so repressed. Such is the power of the films of Ingmar Bergman or the novels of Fyodor Dostoyevsky, and you can have the same power by externalizing your dark side.

Show the Shadow. Most of the time we secretly suffer from the endless social codes we have to adhere to. We have to seem so nice and agreeable, always going along with the group. We better not show too much confidence or ambition. Seem humble and similar to everyone else; that's how the game is played. In following this path we gain comfort by fitting in, but we also become defensive and secretly resentful. Being so nice becomes a habit, which easily turns into timidity, lack of confidence, and indecision. At the same time, our Shadow will show itself, but unconsciously, in explosive fits and starts, and often to our detriment.

It would be wise to look at those who are successful in their field. Inevitably we will see that most of them are much less bound by these codes. They are generally more assertive and overtly ambitious. They care much less what others think of them. They flout the conventions openly and proudly. And they are not punished but greatly rewarded. Steve Jobs is a classic example. He showed his rough, Shadow side in his way of working with others. Our tendency in looking at people like Jobs is to admire their creativity and subtract their darker qualities as unnecessary. If only he had been nicer, he would have been a saint. But in fact the dark side was inextricably interwoven with his power and creativity. His ability to not listen to others, to go his own way, and be a bit rough about it were key parts of his success, which we venerate. And so it is with many creative, powerful people. Subtract their active Shadow, and they would be like everyone else.

Understand: You pay a greater price for being so nice and deferential than for consciously showing your Shadow. First, to follow the latter path you must begin by respecting your own opinions more and those of others less, particularly when it comes to your areas of expertise, to the field you have immersed yourself in. Trust your native genius and the ideas you have come up with. Second, get in the habit in your daily life of asserting yourself more and compromising less. Do this under control and at opportune moments. Third, start caring less what people think of you. You will feel a tremendous sense of liberation. Fourth, realize that at times you must offend and even hurt people who block your path, who have ugly values, who unjustly criticize you. Use such moments of clear injustice to bring out your Shadow and show it proudly. Fifth, feel free to play the impudent, willful child who mocks the stupidity and hypocrisy of others.

Finally, flout the very conventions that others follow so scrupulously. For centuries, and still to this day, gender roles represent the most powerful convention of all. What men and women can do or say has been highly controlled, to the point where it seems almost to represent biological differences instead of social conventions. Women in particular are socialized to be extra nice and agreeable. They feel continual pressure to adhere to this and mistake it for something natural and biological.

Some of the most influential women in history were those who deliberately broke with these codes—performers like Marlene Dietrich and Josephine Baker, political figures such as Eleanor Roosevelt, businesswomen such as Coco Chanel. They brought out their Shadow and showed it by acting in ways that were traditionally thought of as masculine, blending and confusing gender roles.

Even Jacqueline Kennedy Onassis gained great power by playing against the type of the traditional political wife. She had a pronounced malicious streak. When Norman Mailer first met her in 1960 and she seemed to poke fun at him, he saw that "something droll and hard came into her eyes as if she were a very naughty eight-year-old indeed." When people displeased her, she showed it rather openly. She seemed to care little what others thought of her. And she became a sensation because of the naturalness she exuded.

In general, consider this a form of exorcism. Once you show these desires and impulses, they no longer lie hidden in corners of your personality, twisting and operating in secret ways. You have released your demons and enhanced your presence as an authentic human. In this way, the Shadow becomes your ally.

> Unfortunately there is no doubt about the fact that man is, as a whole, less good than he imagines himself or wants to be. Everyone carries a shadow, and the less it is embodied in the individual's conscious life, the blacker and denser it is.
>
> —Carl Jung

10

Beware the Fragile Ego

$\Diamond$

The Law of Envy

*W*e humans are naturally compelled to compare ourselves with one another. We are continually measuring people's status, the levels of respect and attention they receive, and noticing any differences between what we have and what they have. For some of us, this need to compare serves as a spur to excel through our work. For others, it can turn into deep envy—feelings of inferiority and frustration that lead to covert attacks and sabotage. Nobody admits to acting out of envy. You must recognize the early warning signs— praise and bids for friendship that seem effusive and out of proportion; subtle digs at you under the guise of good-natured humor; apparent uneasiness with your success. It is most likely to crop up among friends or your peers in the same profession. Learn to deflect envy by drawing attention away from yourself. Develop your sense of self-worth from internal standards and not incessant comparisons.

Fatal Friends

In late 1820, Mary Shelley (1797–1851), author of the novel *Frankenstein*, and her twenty-eight-year-old husband, the poet Percy Bysshe Shelley, moved to Pisa, Italy, after having spent several years traveling through the country. Mary had had a rough time of it lately. Her two young children had both died from fevers while in Italy. Mary had been particularly close to her son William, and his death had pushed her into a profound depression. She had recently given birth to another child, a boy named Percy, but she felt continually anxious about his health. The guilt and gloom she felt surrounding the death of her children had finally caused some friction between her and her husband. They had been so close, had experienced so much together, that they could almost read each other's thoughts and moods. Now her husband was drifting away, interested in other women. She was hoping that in Pisa they could finally settle down, reconnect, and do some serious writing.

In early 1821, a young English couple named Jane and Edward Williams arrived in Pisa, and their first stop in town was to visit the Shelleys. They were close friends with one of Percy Shelley's cousins. They were thinking of living in Pisa, and they were clearly starstruck at meeting the famous couple. Mary was used to these kinds of visitors; she and her husband were so notorious that curious bohemians from all over Europe would come to gawk at them and try to make their acquaintance.

Certainly the Williamses, like all the other visitors, would have known about the Shelleys' past. They would have known that Mary had two of the most illustrious intellectual parents in all of England. Her mother, Mary Wollstonecraft (1759–1797) was perhaps the first great feminist writer in history, renowned for her books and scandalous love affairs. She had died giving birth to Mary. Mary's father was William Godwin (1756–1836), a celebrated writer and philosopher who advocated many radical ideas, including the end of private property. Famous writers would come to see the child Mary, for she was an object of fascination, with striking red hair like her mother, the most intense eyes, and an intelligence and imagination far beyond her years.

The Williamses would have almost certainly known about her meeting the poet Percy Shelley when she was sixteen and their infamous love affair. Shelley, of aristocratic origins and due to inherit a fortune from his wealthy father, had married a young beauty named Harriet, but he left her for Mary, and along with Mary's stepsister Claire, they traveled through Europe, living together and creating a scandal everywhere they went. Shelley was an ardent believer in free love and an avowed atheist. His wife Harriet subsequently committed suicide, which Mary would forever feel guilty about, even later imagining that the children she had had with Shelley were somehow cursed. Shortly after the death of Harriet, Mary and Percy got married.

The Williamses would undoubtedly know about the Shelleys' relationship with the other great rebel of the time, the poet Lord Byron. They had all spent time together in Switzerland, and it was there, inspired by a midnight discussion of horror stories, that Mary got the inspiration for her great novel *Frankenstein*, written when she was nineteen. Lord Byron had his own scandals and numerous love affairs. The three of them became a magnet for endless rumors, Lord Byron now living in Italy as well. The English press had dubbed them "the League of Incest and Atheism."

At first Mary paid scant attention to the new English couple on the scene, even after a few dinners together. She found Jane Williams a bit dull and pretentious. As Mary wrote to her husband, who was away for a few weeks: "Jane is certainly very pretty but she wants animation and sense; her conversation is nothing particular and she speaks in a slow, monotonous tone." Jane was not well read. She loved nothing more than to arrange flowers, play the pedal harp, sing songs from India, where she had lived as a child, and pose rather prettily. Could she be that superficial? Every now and then Mary would catch Jane staring at her with an unpleasant look, which she quickly covered over with a cheerful smile. More important, a common friend who had known the Williamses in their travels across Europe had warned Mary in a letter to keep her distance from Jane.

Edward Williams, however, was quite charming. He seemed to worship Shelley and to want to be like him. He had aspirations to be a writer. He was so eager to please and be of service. And then one day he told Mary the story of the romance between him and Jane, and Mary was quite moved.

The Williamses were not actually married. Jane Cleveland, who came from the middle class, had married a high-ranking English soldier, only to find out he was an abusive brute. When she met the handsome Edward Williams—a military man who had lived in India, as Jane had—she fell instantly in love. In 1819, although Jane was still married to her first husband, she and Edward left for the Continent, posing as a married couple. Like the Shelleys, they also had lived in Switzerland and had come to Italy for adventure and the good weather. Jane was now expecting her second child with Edward, just as Mary was now pregnant again. It seemed, in a fateful way, that they had much in common. More important, Mary empathized deeply with their love affair and how much they had sacrificed for each other.

Then Jane had her second child. Now the two women could bond as young mothers. Finally someone to talk to about the difficulties of raising infants in a foreign land, something Mary's husband could care less about. Besides, the Shelleys had no English friends, since English expatriates in Italy avoided them like the plague. It would be such a relief to have some daily companionship in this moment of turbulence in her life. Mary quickly became dependent on Jane's company and forgot any misgivings she might have had about her.

Shelley seemed to warm up to the couple as well. Edward was so officious in offering to help Shelley in any way. Edward loved sailing and boasted of his navigational skills. Sailing was an obsession of Shelley's, despite the fact he had never learned to swim. Perhaps Edward could help him design the perfect sailing boat. And Jane began to intrigue him the more he spent time around her. Jane was so different from Mary. She never argued. She only looked at him admiringly and seconded everything he said. She was so cheerful. He could be her teacher, instructing her in poetry, and she could be his new muse, a role his depressed wife could not fill anymore. He bought Jane a guitar and loved to listen to the songs from India she seemed to know so well. She had a beautiful voice. He wrote poems in her honor and slowly became infatuated.

Mary noticed all this. She knew well her husband's pattern. He was always looking for a woman very different from the one he was with to inspire him and break the monotony of a relationship. His first wife, Harriet, had been more like Jane, pretty and simple, and so he fell for the much more complicated Mary. Now the pattern was repeating as he fell for the simpler Jane. But how could she take Jane seriously as a rival? She was so ordinary. He was simply poeticizing her; he would eventually see her as she was and grow bored. Mary did not fear losing him.

In 1822 the Shelleys and Williamses, now rather inseparable, decided to move together into a house further north along the coast, overlooking the Bay of Lerici. From the beginning Mary hated the place and begged her husband to find something else. It was so isolated. It was not easy to find supplies. The local peasants seemed rather brutal and unfriendly. The two couples would be completely dependent on their servants. Nobody besides Mary seemed interested in running the household, least of all Jane, who had proven to be quite lazy. But worse than everything, Mary had terrible forebodings about the place. She feared greatly for the fate of her child Percy, only three years old. She smelled disaster in the walls of the isolated villa that they occupied. She became nervous and hysterical. She knew she was putting everyone off with her behavior, but she could not quell her anxiety. Shelley reacted by spending more and more time with Jane.

Several months after settling at the villa, Mary had a miscarriage and nearly died. Her husband attended to her for several weeks, and she recovered. But just as quickly he seemed to become enamored with a new plan that terrified Mary. He and Edward had designed a boat, one that was beautiful to look at, sleek, and fast. In June of that year some old friends of the Shelleys had arrived in

Italy—Leigh Hunt and his wife. Hunt was a publisher who championed young poets, and Shelley was his favorite. Shelley planned to sail up the coast with Edward to meet the Hunts. Mary was desperate for him not to go. Shelley tried to reassure her: Edward was an expert navigator, and the boat he had built was more than seaworthy. Mary did not believe this. The boat seemed flimsy for the rough waters of the area.

Nevertheless Shelley and Edward left on July 1, with a third crewmember. On July 8, as they started on their homeward journey, they ran into one of the storms endemic to the region. Their boat had indeed been badly designed, and went under. A few days later the bodies of all three were found.

Almost immediately Mary was seized with remorse and guilt. She played in her mind every angry word she had addressed to her husband, every critique of his work, every doubt she had instilled in him about her love. It was all too much, and she determined then and there that she would devote the rest of her life to making Shelley's poetry famous.

At first Jane seemed extremely broken up by the tragedy, but she recovered more quickly than Mary. She had to be practical. Mary might have a nice inheritance from Shelley's family. Jane had nothing. She decided she would return to London and somehow find a way to support her two children. Mary empathized with her plight. She gave her a list of important contacts in England, including Shelley's best friend from his youth, Thomas Hogg, a lawyer. Hogg had his own issues—he was always falling in love with the people closest to Shelley, first Shelley's sister, then Shelley's first wife, and finally Mary herself, whom he tried to seduce. But that had been years ago, they remained good friends, and as a lawyer Hogg could be of some help to Jane.

Mary decided to stay in Italy. She had hardly any friends left, but the Hunts were still in Italy. Much to her dismay, however, Leigh Hunt had become surprisingly cold to her. In this, her most vulnerable moment, he had apparently lost all sympathy for her, and she could not figure out why. This only added to her misery. Certainly he must know how deeply she had loved her husband and the depth of her mourning? She was not one to show her emotions as openly as Jane, but deep inside she suffered more than anyone. Other former friends were now acting cold as well. Only Lord Byron stood by her, and they grew closer.

Soon it became apparent that Shelley's parents, who had been shocked by their son's libertine ways, would not recognize Percy as their grandson, certainly as long as he was in the care of Mary. There would be no money for her. She thought the only answer was to return to London. Perhaps if the Shelley family met Percy and saw what a devoted mother she was, they might change their minds. She wrote to Jane and to Hogg for their advice. The two of them had now become close friends. Hogg seemed to think she should wait before returning; his letter was remarkably cold. Here was yet another person who had suddenly become distant. But it was the response of Jane that most surprised her. She advised giving up Percy and not coming to England. As Mary tried to explain how impossible that would be for her emotionally, Jane became even more adamant in her opinion. She expressed this in practical terms— Mary would not be welcomed in London, the Shelley family would turn against her even more—but it seemed so unsympathetic.

In the months together in Italy after the deaths of their husbands, they had grown quite close. Jane was the last real link to Mary's husband left in her life. She had forgiven Jane for any indiscretions with her husband. Losing Jane's friendship would be like experiencing another death. She decided she would in fact return to London with her son and rekindle the friendship with Jane.

Mary returned to London in August of 1823, only to find that she had become quite a celebrity. *Frankenstein* had been turned into a play that emphasized the horror elements in the book. And it was quite a sensation. The story and the name "Frankenstein" now had seeped into popular culture. Mary's father, who had become a bookseller and publisher, came out with a new edition of *Frankenstein*, with Mary clearly identified as the author. (The first edition was published anonymously.) Mary, her father, and Jane went to see the play version, and it was clear now to all of them what an object of fascination Mary had become to the public—this was the slight, very gentle woman who had written such a powerful horror story?

When Lord Byron died in Greece shortly after Mary's return to London, Mary became even more famous, for she had been one of Byron's closest friends. All of the principal English intellectuals wanted to meet her, to find out more about her, Lord Byron, and her husband. Even Jane was now back to her friendly self, although at times she seemed to withdraw from Mary.

Despite her fame, Mary was unhappy. She did not want the attention, because it came with endless gossip about her past and insinuations about her morality. She was tired of being looked at and judged. She wanted to hide herself and raise her son. She decided she would move close to where Jane was living, in a more remote part of London. There Percy would be reunited with Jane's children. They could live for each other and share their memories, recapture the past. Jane was so cheerful, and Mary needed cheering up. In return, she would do whatever it took to take care of Jane.

In the summer of 1824 the two women saw much of each other. It was now apparent that Hogg had been courting Jane, but he was such an awkward and unpleasant man, Mary could hardly imagine Jane reciprocating his attentions. Besides, it was so soon after the death of her husband. But then one evening in January it became clear to Mary that she had been deceived for quite a while. It was somewhat late at night, at Jane's house. She and Percy had stuck around, Percy to play some games with Jane's children and Mary to talk some more. Hogg had arrived and Jane finally exploded at Mary, with a look Mary had never seen before on her friend's face. She asked Mary to leave so abruptly and rudely that it was clear she and Hogg had been having an affair and Jane could no longer conceal her irritation with Mary. She had noticed for some time that Jane had become increasingly cold and less interested in being with her. Now she understood this better.

They remained friends. Mary empathized with her plight as a lonely widow, her need for a husband. Jane was now pregnant with Hogg's child. Mary struggled to get over her resentment and to help Jane as best she could. They saw less and less of each other.

To distract her from her loneliness, Mary befriended a beautiful young woman named Isabel Robinson who needed help—she had given birth to an illegitimate child and her father would certainly disown her if he discovered the truth. For weeks Mary conspired to help her, planning to send Isabel to Paris to live with a "man" who would act as the father—the man in this case being a woman known as Miss Dods, a notorious lesbian who loved to dress as a man and could easily pass for one.

Mary delighted in furthering this plot, but before accompanying Isabel to Paris, one afternoon she received the shock of her life: Isabel confided to her in complete detail the stories that Jane had been telling her for months about Mary— that Shelley had never really loved his wife; that he had admired her but had had no feelings for her; that she was not the woman he had needed or wanted; that Jane was in fact the great love of his life. Jane had even hinted to Isabel that Mary had made him so unhappy that he had secretly wanted to die the day he left on his fatal sailing venture, and that Mary was somehow responsible for his death.

Mary could hardly believe this, but Isabel had no reason to make up such a story. And as she thought about it more deeply, suddenly things began to make sense—the sudden coldness of Hogg, Leigh Hunt, and others who must have heard these stories; the looks Jane occasionally threw at Mary when she was the center of attention in a group; that look on her face when she threw Mary out of her house; the vehemence with which she wanted Mary to stay away from London and give up her child, which meant giving up their inheritance. All these years she had been not a friend but a competitor, and now it seemed clear that it was not Mary's husband who had pursued Jane but Jane who had actively seduced him with her poses, her coquettish looks, her guitar, her put-on soft manner. She was false to the core. It was, after the death of Mary's husband, the harshest blow of all.

Not only did Jane believe these monstrous stories, but she had made others believe them. Mary knew how well her husband had loved her over so many years, and after so many shared experiences. To spread the story that she had somehow caused his death was beyond hurtful; it was like a knife being plunged into an old wound. She wrote in her journal: "My friend has proved false & treacherous. Have I not been a fool?"

After several months of brooding over this, Mary finally confronted her. Jane burst into tears, creating a scene. She wanted to know who had spread this awful story of her betrayal, which she denied. She accused Mary of being cold and unaffectionate. But for Mary, it was as if she had finally woken up from a dream. She could now see the fake outrage, the phony love, the way Jane confused matters with her drama. There was no going back.

Over the ensuing years Mary would not cut off ties with Jane, but now their relationship was totally on her terms. Mary could only feel some strange satisfaction to see Jane's life slowly fall apart, the relationship with Hogg turning into a disaster. As Mary became more and more famous for her novels and her publishing of Shelley's poems, she mingled with the greatest writers and politicians of her time and slowly cut off contact with Jane. She could never trust her again. As she wrote some years later about this affair in her journal: "Life is not ill till we wish to forget. Jane first inspired me with that miserable feeling, staining past years as she did—taking sweetness from memory and giving it instead a serpent's tooth."

Interpretation: Let us look at the many transformations that envy causes in the mind, as we can clearly see in the example of Jane Williams. When Jane first met Mary, she had conflicting emotions. On the one hand, there was much to like and admire about Mary. She had pleasant manners, was clearly brilliant, and felt deeply attached to her son. She could be quite generous. On the other hand, she made Jane feel deeply inferior; Jane lacked so many of the things that Mary had, but which she felt she deserved—attention for her own talents, for her willingness to sacrifice for love, for her charming nature. Inevitably, along with the attraction to Mary came envy—the desire to have the same things as Mary, the sense of being entitled to have them, but the apparent inability to get them easily or legitimately. With envy comes the secret desire to hurt, wound, or steal from the envied person, to right the unfairness that comes with his or her supposed superiority.

There were many reasons for Jane to conceal and even repress the envy stirring within her. First, it is socially toxic to display envy. It reveals deep insecurity along with hostility, a very ugly brew, which is certain to push people away. Second, she and her husband depended on the Shelleys for their future livelihood, since Jane was determined to get Edward attached to Shelley as a friend, assistant, and sailing expert. Shelley was notoriously generous with money. Acting in a hostile manner toward Mary would have put that all in jeopardy. Finally, envy is a painful emotion, an admission of our own inferiority, something rather unbearable for us humans. It is not an emotion we want to sit with and brood over. We like to conceal it from ourselves and not be aware that it motivates our actions.

Considering all this, Jane took the natural next step: she befriended Mary, returning Mary's friendly advances and then some. A part of her liked the woman and felt flattered at the attention shown to her by someone so famous. Jane was avid for attention. How could she now imagine herself as feeling envy toward Mary, if she had chosen to become her friend? But the more time she spent around Mary, the more the imbalance between them became apparent. It was Mary who had the illustrious, handsome husband, the possible large inheritance, the deep friendship with Lord Byron, and the rich imagination that made her so talented. And so the more time she spent with Mary, the stronger her envious feelings became.

To conceal this envy from herself and others now required the next logical step: she had to mentally convert Mary into an unsympathetic character. Mary was not so talented; she was merely lucky; if it weren't for her famous parents and the men around her, she never would have gotten to her fortunate position; she did not deserve her fame; she was an irritating person to be around, moody, depressive, clinging, no fun; she was not nice or loving toward her husband and was not much of a woman. As Jane went through this process, hostility began to overwhelm friendly feelings. She felt more than justified in actively seducing Percy Shelley and concealing her true feelings from Mary. Most devastating to Mary's marital relationship, every time her husband complained to Jane about Mary, Jane would reinforce this with some new story or observation, deepening the rift between them.

Of course, in turning Mary into someone so unlikable, Jane had to willfully ignore the context—the recent loss of two beloved children to illness, Shelley's own coldness toward his wife, and his pursuit of other women. But in order for enviers to feel entitled to take harmful action, they must create a narrative: everything the other person does reveals some negative trait; they do not deserve their superior position. Now Jane had what she had wanted—the adoring attention of Percy Shelley along with the complete alienation of him from his wife. Once Shelley died, she could vent her envy by spreading the malicious story that Mary did not seem particularly sad at the loss, something so troubling to those who heard this, including Leigh Hunt, that they distanced themselves from Mary.

Once Jane was back in London and Mary joined her there, the pattern repeated. A part of Jane was still drawn to Mary; over the years they had shared much. But the more time she spent around her, the more she had to see Mary's growing fame, her circle of illustrious friends, her generous nature toward other women who had been mistreated, her total devotion to her son and to the memory of her husband. None of this jibed with the narrative, and so Jane had to take yet another step in her mind: "Mary is false, still living off the legacy of her husband and others, motivated by her neediness, not by her generosity. If only other people could see this." So she stole Mary's friend Hogg, a weaker imitation of the original sin of stealing her husband. And she continued to spread stories about Mary, but this time with the added vicious twist that Jane was the last great love of Shelley's life, that he had never loved his wife, and that Mary had driven him to suicide. Telling such lurid stories in London would do maximum damage to Mary's reputation.

It is hard to calculate the pain she inflicted over the years on Mary—the quarrels with Mary's husband exacerbated by Jane, the sudden mysterious coldness of Mary's closest friends, the push and pull Jane played on Mary, always stepping back when Mary wanted more closeness, and finally the revelation of the ultimate betrayal, and the thought, which would haunt Mary for years, that so many had believed Jane's story. Such can be the hidden pain inflicted by one great envier.

Understand: Envy occurs most commonly and painfully among friends. We assume that something in the course of the relationship caused the friend to turn against us. Sometimes all we experience is the betrayal, the sabotage, the ugly criticisms they throw at us, and we never understand the underlying envy that inspired these actions.

What we need to grasp is something paradoxical: people who feel envy in the first place are often motivated to become our friends. Like Jane, they feel a mix of genuine interest, attraction, and envy, if we have some qualities that make them feel inferior. Becoming our friend, they can disguise the envy to themselves. They will often go even further, becoming extra attentive and impatient to secure our friendship. But as they draw closer, the problem gets worse. The underlying envy is continually stirred. The very traits that might have stimulated feelings of inferiority—the good position, the solid work ethic, the likability—are now being witnessed on a daily basis.

And so as with Jane, a narrative is gradually constructed: the envied person is lucky, overly ambitious, not nearly so great. As our friends, enviers can discover our weak points and what will wound the most. From within a friendship they are better positioned to sabotage us, steal our spouse, spread mayhem. Once they attack us, we tend to feel guilty and confused: "Perhaps I deserve some of their criticisms." If we respond angrily, this only feeds the narrative of our unlikable nature. Because we were friends, we feel doubly wounded and betrayed, and the deeper the wound, the greater the satisfaction for the envier. We can even speculate that the envier is unconsciously drawn to befriending the envied person in order to have this wounding power.

Although such fatal friends are elusive and tricky, there are always warning signs. Learn to pay deeper attention to your first impressions. (If only Mary had done so.) Often we intuit that the other person is false but then forget this as they make friendly overtures. We always feel better about people who seem to like us, and enviers know this well. Rely upon the opinions of friends and neutral third parties. Many friends of Mary found Jane conniving and even a bit scary. The envy of the friend will also tend to leak out in sudden looks and disparaging comments. Enviers will give puzzling advice—something that seems against our interests but well reasoned on their part. They want us to make mistakes and will often try to find a way to lead us into them. Any success or increase in attention that we experience will cause greater leakage of their true feelings.

It is not a question of becoming paranoid but simply of being alert once you pick up some signs of possible envy. Learn to spot the types particularly prone to feeling envy (see the next section for more on this) before you become too enmeshed in their drama. It is hard to measure what you will gain by avoiding an envy attack, but think of it this way: the pain inflicted by one envier friend can resonate and poison you for years.

Every time a friend succeeds, I die a little.

—Gore Vidal

Keys to Human Nature

Of all the human emotions, none is trickier or more elusive than envy. It is very difficult to actually discern the envy that motivates people's actions or to even know that we have suffered an envy attack from another. This is what makes it so frustrating to deal with and so dangerous.

The reason for this elusiveness is simple: we almost never directly express the envy we are feeling. If we feel anger toward people because of something they said or did, we may try to disguise our anger for various reasons, but we are aware that we are feeling hostile. Eventually the anger will leak out in some nonverbal behavior. And if we act upon our anger, the target will feel it for what it is and more often than not know what caused the anger in that moment. But envy is very different.

All of us feel envy, the sensation that others have more of what we want—possessions, attention, respect. We deserve to have as much as they do yet feel somewhat helpless to get such things. But as discussed above, envy entails the admission to ourselves that we are inferior to another person in something we value. Not only is it painful to admit this inferiority, but it is even worse for others to see that we are feeling this.

And so almost as soon as we feel the initial pangs of envy, we are motivated to disguise it to ourselves—it is not envy we feel but unfairness at the distribution of goods or attention, resentment at this unfairness, even anger. Furthermore, the other person is not really superior but simply lucky, overly ambitious, or unscrupulous. That's how they got to where they are. Having convinced ourselves that envy is not motivating us but something else, we also make it very difficult for others to detect the underlying envy. They see only our anger, indignation, hostile criticisms, poisonous praise, and so on.

In ancient times, those who felt intense envy might have acted upon it through violence, forcefully taking what the other had or even resorting to murder. In the Old Testament, Cain murdered Abel out of envy; the brothers of Joseph threw him in a ditch in the desert to die because their father seemed to favor him; on several occasions King Saul tried to kill the younger David, so handsome and naturally gifted, finally going mad with envy.

Today, however, people are much more political and indirect, able to control any overt aggressive impulses and disguise what they're feeling. Instead of violence, enviers are likely to sabotage our work, ruin a relationship, sully our reputation, torment us with criticisms that are aimed at our most basic insecurities. This allows them to maintain their social position while causing harm, their targets not even suspecting envy as the motivation. They can justify these actions to themselves as righting the perceived imbalance or unfairness.

If someone is angry with us and acts on it, we can analyze the anger this person is feeling and figure out a way to defuse it or defend ourselves. But if we cannot see the underlying envy, we are inevitably confused by the hostile action of the envier, and this confusion doubles the pain we experience. "Why are people suddenly being so cold to me?" "Why did that project fail so unexpectedly?" "Why have I been fired?" "Why is this person against me?"

Your task as a student of human nature is to transform yourself into a master decoder of envy. You are ruthless in your analysis and your determination to get to the root of what motivates people. The signs that people emit of envy are harder to discern, but they exist, and you can master the language with some effort and subtle discernment. Think of it as an intellectual challenge. By being able to decode it, you will not feel so confused. You will understand in hindsight that you suffered an envy attack, which will help you get over it. You might be able to see in advance the warning signs of such an attack and either defuse or deflect it. And knowing the hidden pain that comes from one well-aimed envy attack, you will spare yourself the emotional damage that can last for years. This will not make you paranoid but only better able to weed out the false and fatal friends (or colleagues) from the real ones, the ones you can truly trust.

Before immersing yourself in the subtleties of the emotion, it is important to distinguish between *passive* and *active* envy. All of us in the course of a day will inevitably feel some pangs of envy, as we unconsciously monitor the people around us and sense that they might have more. It is a fact of social life that there are always people who are superior to us in wealth, intelligence, likability, and other qualities. If these pangs rise to the level of consciousness and are a bit acute, we might say something hurtful or mean-spirited as a way to vent the emotion. But generally as we experience this passive form of envy, we do not do anything that would in any meaningful way harm the relationship with a friend or colleague. In detecting signs of passive envy in others (for instance, little put-downs and offhand comments), you should simply tolerate this as a fact of being a social animal.

Sometimes, however, this passive envy turns active. The underlying sense of inferiority is too strong, leading to hostility that cannot be vented by a comment or put-down. Sitting with one's envy over a long period of time can be painful and frustrating. Feeling righteous indignation against the envied person, however, can be invigorating. Acting on envy, doing something to harm the other person, brings satisfaction, as it did to Jane, although the satisfaction is short-lived because enviers always find something new to envy.

Your goal is to detect the signs of this more acute form of envy before it turns dangerous. You can do this in three ways: by learning the signs of envy that manage to leak through, by being aware of the types of people who are more prone to acting on envy, and by understanding the circumstances and actions that might trigger active envy in people. You can never see all of the actions motivated by envy; people are simply too good at disguising it. But using all three decoding devices will increase your chances of detection.

Signs of Envy

Although the signs are subtle, envious feelings tend to leak out and can be detected if you are observant. Seeing one such sign in isolation might indicate passive or weak envy. You want to look for combinations or repetitions of the following signs, a pattern, before moving to alert mode.

Microexpressions: When people first experience envy, they have not yet fooled themselves into thinking it is something else, and so they are more prone to leakage than later on. That is why first impressions are often the most accurate and should be given added weight in this case. Envy is most associated with the eyes. The root of the Latin word for envy, *invidia*, means "to look through, to probe with the eyes like a dagger." The early meaning of the word was associated with the "evil eye" and the belief that a look could actually convey a curse and physically harm someone.

The eyes are indeed a telling indicator, but the envious microexpression affects the entire face. You will notice the envier's eyes momentarily boring into you, with a look that suggests disdain and a touch of hostility. It is the look of a child who feels cheated. With this look the corners of the mouth will often be turned down, the nose in a sneering, somewhat upturned position, the chin jutting out. Although the look will be a little too direct and held a little too long, it still will not last more than a second or two. It is usually followed with a strained, fake smile. Often you will see the look by accident, as you suddenly turn your head their direction, or you will feel their eyes burning into you without directly looking at them.

The German philosopher Arthur Schopenhauer (1788–1860) devised a quick way to elicit these looks and test for envy. Tell suspected enviers some good news about yourself—a promotion, a new and exciting love interest, a book contract. You will notice a very quick expression of disappointment. Their tone of voice as they congratulate you will betray some tension and strain. Equally, tell them some misfortune of yours and notice the uncontrollable microexpression of joy in your pain, what is commonly known as schadenfreude. Their eyes light up for a fleeting second. People who are envious cannot help feeling some glee when they hear of the bad luck of those they envy.

If you see such looks in the first few encounters with someone, as Mary did with Jane, and they happen more than once, be on the lookout for a dangerous envier entering your life.

Poisonous praise: A major envy attack is often preceded by little envy bites—offhand comments expertly designed to get under your skin. Confusing, paradoxical praise is a common form of this. Let us say you have completed a project—a book, a film, some creative venture—and the initial response from the public is quite positive. Enviers will make a comment praising the money you will now be making, implying that that is the main reason you have worked on it. You want praise for the work itself and the effort that went into it, and instead they imply that you have done it for the money, that you have sold out. You feel confused—they have praised you, but in a way that makes you uncomfortable. These comments will also come at moments chosen to cause maximum doubt and damage, for instance just when you have heard the good news and feel a flush of joy.

Similarly, in noting your success, they may bring up the least likable parts of your audience, the kinds of fans or consumers who do not reflect well on you. "Well, I'm sure Wall Street executives are going to love this." This is thrown in among other normal comments, but the guilt by association lingers in your mind. Or they will praise something once you have lost it—a job, a house in a nice neighborhood, a spouse who has left you. "That was such a beautiful house. What a shame." It's all said in a way that seems compassionate but has a discomforting effect. Poisonous praise almost always indicates envy. They feel the need to praise, but what dominates is the underlying hostility. If they have a habit of praising in this way, if you experience it several times, it is probably an indication of something more intense stirring within them.

Backbiting: If people like to gossip a lot, particularly about common acquaintances, you can be sure they will gossip about you. And gossip is a frequent cover for envy, a convenient way to vent it by sharing malicious rumors and stories. When they talk about others behind their backs, you will see their eyes light up and their voice become animated—it gives them a joy comparable to schadenfreude. They will elicit any kind of negative report about a common acquaintance. A frequent theme in their gossip is that no one's really that great, and people aren't what they pretend to be.

If you ever get wind of a story they have spread about you, subtly or not so subtly negative, only one such instance should be enough to raise your antennae. What indicates active envy in this case is that they are your friend and they feel the need to vent their underlying hostility to a third party rather than keep it to themselves. If you notice that friends or colleagues are suddenly cooler to you than before for no apparent reason, such gossiping might be the source and would be worth ferreting out. In any event, serial gossipers do not make loyal and trustworthy friends.

The push and pull: As we saw in the Jane Williams story, enviers often use friendship and intimacy as the best way to wound the people they envy. They display unusual eagerness to become your friend. They saturate you with attention. If you are in any way insecure, this will have great effect. They praise you a little too effusively too early on. Through the closeness they establish they are able to gather material on you and find your weak points. Suddenly, after your emotions are engaged, they criticize you in pointed ways. The criticism is confusing, not particularly related to anything you have done, but still you feel guilty. They then return to their initial warmth. The pattern repeats. You are trapped between the warm friendship and the occasional pain they inflict.

In criticizing you, they are experts at picking out any possible flaws in your character or words you might have regretted, and giving them great emphasis. They are like lawyers building a case against you. When you've had enough and decide to defend yourself or criticize them or break off the friendship, they can now ascribe to you a mean or even cruel streak and tell others of this. You will notice in their past other intense relationships with dramatic breakups, always the other person's fault. And at the source of this pattern, something hard to discern, is that they choose to befriend people whom they envy for some quality, then subtly torture them.

In general, criticism of you that seems sincere but not directly related to anything you have actually done is usually a strong sign of envy. People want to bully and overwhelm you with something negative, both wounding you and covering any tracks of envy.

Envier Types

According to the psychoanalyst Melanie Klein (1882–1960), certain people are prone to feeling envy their entire lives, and this begins in early infancy. In the first few weeks and months of life, the mother and infant are almost never out of each other's presence. But as they get older, infants must deal with the mother's absence for longer periods of time, and this entails a painful adjustment. Some infants, however, are more sensitive to the mother's occasional withdrawal. They are greedy for more feeding and more attention. They become aware of the presence of the father, with whom they must compete for the mother's attention. They may also become aware of other siblings, who are seen as rivals. Klein, who specialized in the study of infancy and early childhood, noticed that some children feel greater degrees of hostility and resentment toward the father and siblings for the attention they are receiving at their (the enviers') expense, and toward the mother for not giving them enough.

Certainly there are parents who create or intensify such envy by playing favorites, by withdrawing on purpose to make the child more dependent. In any event, infants or children experiencing such envy will not feel grateful and loved for the attention they do get but instead feel continually deprived and unsatisfied. A pattern is set for their entire lives—they are children and later adults for whom nothing is ever quite good enough. All potentially positive experiences are spoiled by the sensation that they should have more and better. Something is missing, and they can only imagine that other people are cheating them out of what they should have. They develop an eagle eye for what others have that they don't. This becomes their dominant passion.

Most of us experience moments in childhood in which we feel another person is getting more of the attention that we deserve, but we are able to counterbalance this with other moments in which we experience undeniable love, and gratitude for it. As we get older, we can transfer such positive emotions to a series of people—siblings, teachers, mentors, friends, lovers, and spouses. We alternate between wanting more and feeling relatively satisfied and grateful. Those prone to envy, however, do not experience life the same way. Instead, they transfer their initial envy and hostility to a series of others whom they see as disappointing or hurting them. Their moments of satisfaction and gratitude are rare or nonexistent. "I need, I want more," they are always telling themselves.

Because envy is a painful sensation, these types will enact lifelong strategies to mitigate or repress these feelings that gnaw at them. They will denigrate anything or anyone good in the world. This means there aren't really people out there worth envying. Or they will become extremely independent. If they do not need people for anything, that will expose them to fewer envy scenarios. At an extreme they will devalue themselves. They don't deserve good things in life and so have no need to compete with others for attention and status. According to Klein, these common strategies are brittle and will break down under stress—a downturn in their career, bouts of depression, wounds to their ego. The envy they experienced in their earliest years remains continually latent and ready to be directed at others. They are literally looking for people to envy so they can reexperience the primal emotion.

Depending on their psychological makeup, they will tend to conform to certain envying types. It is of great benefit to be able to recognize such types early on, because they are the ones most likely to turn active with their envy. The following are five common varieties of enviers, how they tend to disguise themselves, and their particular forms of attack.

The Leveler: When you first meet them, levelers can seem rather entertaining and interesting. They tend to have a wicked sense of humor. They are good at putting down those who are powerful and deflating the pretentious. They also seem to have a keen nose for injustice and unfairness in this world. But where they differ from people with genuine empathy for underdogs is that levelers cannot recognize or appreciate excellence in almost anyone, except those who are dead. They have fragile egos. Those who have achieved things in life make them feel insecure. They are highly sensitive to feelings of inferiority. The envy they initially feel for those who are successful is quickly covered up by indignation. They rail at high achievers for gaming the system, for being far too ambitious, or simply for being lucky and not really deserving praise. They have come to associate excellence with unfairness, as a way to soothe their insecurities.

You will notice that though they can put others down, they do not take easily to any jokes at their expense. They often celebrate low culture and trash, because mediocre work does not stir their insecurities. Besides their cynical humor, you can recognize this type by how they talk about their own life: they love to tell stories of the many injustices inflicted on them; they are always blameless. These types make excellent professional critics—they can use this medium to tear down those they secretly envy and be rewarded for it.

Their main goal is to bring everyone down to the same mediocre level they occupy. This sometimes means leveling not only achievers and the powerful but also those who are having too good a time, who seem to be enjoying themselves too much, or who have too great a sense of purpose, which levelers lack.

Be wary around such types, particularly in the workplace, because they will make you feel guilty for your own impulse to excel. They will begin with passive-aggressive comments that taint you with the ugly word "ambition." You might be a part of the oppressor class. They will criticize you in ugly and hurtful ways. They may follow this up with active sabotage of your work, which they justify to themselves as a form of retributive justice.

The Self-entitled Slacker: In the world today many people rightfully feel entitled to have success and the good things in life, but they usually understand that this will require sacrifice and hard work. Some people, however, feel they deserve attention and many rewards in life as if these are *naturally* due to them. These self-entitled slackers are generally quite narcissistic. They will make the briefest outline for a novel or screenplay they want to write, or an "idea" for a brilliant business, and feel that that is enough to attract praise and attention. But deep down, these slackers feel insecure about their ability to get what they want; that is why they have never really developed the proper discipline. When they find themselves around high achievers who work very hard and have earned true respect for their work, this will make them aware of the doubts about themselves they have been trying to repress. They will move quickly from envy to hostility.

Christopher Wren (1632–1723) was one of the great geniuses of his age, a renowned scientist and one of the leading architects of the time, his most famous work being St. Paul's Cathedral in London. Wren was also generally beloved by almost everyone who worked with him. His enthusiasm, his obvious skill, and the long hours he gave on the job made him popular with both the public and the workers on his projects. One man, however, came to deeply envy him—William Talman, a lower-level architect appointed as Wren's assistant on several important jobs. Talman believed that their roles should have been reversed; he had an extremely high opinion of himself, a rather sour attitude, and a pronounced lazy streak.

When a couple of accidents occurred on two of Wren's projects, killing some workmen, Talman went into overdrive, accusing his boss of being negligent. He dug up every other possible misdeed in Wren's long career, trying to make the case that he did not deserve his lofty reputation. For years he waged a campaign to besmirch Wren's reputation, calling him careless with lives and money and generally overrated. He so muddied the waters that the king finally gave some important commissions to the much less talented Talman, infuriating Wren. Talman proceeded to steal and incorporate many of Wren's innovations. The ugly battle with Talman had a debilitating emotional effect on Wren that lasted years.

Be extra careful in the work environment with those who like to maintain their position through charm and being political, rather than by getting things done. They are very prone to envying and hating those who work hard and get results. They will slander and sabotage you without any warning.

The Status Fiend: As social animals we humans are very sensitive to our rank and position within any group. We can measure our status by the attention and respect we receive. We are constantly monitoring differences and comparing ourselves with others. But for some people status is more than a way of measuring social position—it is the most important determinant of their self-worth. You will notice such fiends by the questions they ask about how much money you make, whether you own your home, what kind of neighborhood it's in, whether you occasionally fly business class, and all of the other petty things that they can use as points of comparison. If you are of a higher social status than they are, they will conceal their envy by appearing to admire your success. But if you are a peer or happen to work with them, they will be sniffing for any sign of favoritism or privileges they don't have, and they will attack you in underhanded ways, undermining your position within the group.

For baseball Hall of Famer Reggie Jackson (b. 1946), his Yankee teammate Graig Nettles fit this type. To Jackson, Nettles seemed extremely attentive to the credit and accolades others were getting that he was not. He was always discussing and comparing salaries. What embittered Nettles was the size of

Jackson's salary and the attention he got from the media. Jackson had earned the salary and attention he received through his batting prowess and colorful personality, but the envious Nettles saw it differently. He thought Jackson simply knew how to play the media and cozy up to the Yankees owner George Steinbrenner. Jackson, he decided, was a manipulator. His envy leaked out in wicked jokes at Jackson's expense, poisonous praise, and hostile looks. He turned much of the Yankee clubhouse against Jackson and made his life miserable. As Jackson wrote of him in his autobiography, "I always had the feeling he was behind me, ready to turn the knife." He also felt there was some tacit racism in Nettles's envy, as if a black athlete could not possibly earn a salary that much larger than his own.

Recognize status fiends by how they reduce everything to material considerations. When they comment on the clothes you wear or the car you drive, they seem to focus on the money these things must have cost, and as they talk about such things, you will notice something childish in their demeanor, as if they were reliving a family drama in which they felt cheated by a sibling who had something better. Don't be fooled by their driving an older car or dressing shabbily. These types will often try to assert their status in the opposite direction, by being the consummate monk, the idealistic hippie, while secretly yearning for the luxuries they cannot get through hard work. If you are around such types, try to downplay or conceal what you have that might trigger envy, and talk up their possessions, skills, and status in whatever way you can.

The Attacher: In any court-like environment of power, you will inevitably find people who are drawn to those who are successful or powerful, not out of admiration but out of secret envy. They find a way to attach themselves as friends or assistants. They make themselves useful. They may admire their boss for some qualities, but deep down they believe they are entitled to have some of the attention he or she is getting, without all the hard work. The longer they are around the high achiever, the more this feeling gnaws at them. They have talent, they have dreams—why should the person they work for be so favored? They are good at concealing the undercurrent of envy through excessive fawning. But these types attach themselves because it gives them some kind of satisfaction to spoil and wound the person who has more. They are drawn to the powerful out of a desire to harm them in some way.

Yolanda Saldivar (b. 1960) is an extreme example of the type. She started a major fan club for the popular Tejano singer Selena, then ingratiated herself into Selena's business by becoming manager of her clothing stores and accumulated more power. No one was more sycophantic to the singer. But feeling deeply envious of the fame of Selena and turning quite hostile, she began to embezzle funds from the business, which she felt more than justified in doing. When confronted about this by Selena's father, her response was to plot to murder Selena herself, which she finally did in 1995.

These types have a trait that is quite common to all enviers: they lack a clear sense of purpose in their life (see chapter 13 for more on this). They do not know their calling; they could do many things, they think, and often try different jobs. They wander around and feel empty inside. They naturally envy those who act with a sense of purpose, and will go so far as to attach themselves to such a person's life, partly wishing to get some of what they themselves are missing and partly desiring to harm the other person.

In general, be wary of those who are too eager to attach themselves to your life, too impatient to make themselves useful. They try to draw you into a relationship not by their experience and competence but by the flattery and attention they give you. Their form of attack is to gather information on you that they can leak out or spread as gossip, harming your reputation. Learn to hire and work with those who have experience rather than just a pleasing manner.

The Insecure Master: For some people, reaching a high position validates their self-opinion and boosts their self-esteem. But there are some who are more anxious. Holding a high position tends to increase their insecurities, which they are careful to conceal. Secretly they doubt whether they are worthy of the responsibility. They look at others who might have more talent, even those below them, with an envious eye.

You will work for such bosses under the assumption that they are self-assured and confident. How else could they have become the boss? You will work extra hard to impress them, show them you're a person on the way up, only to find yourself after several months suddenly demoted or fired, which makes little sense, since you had clearly delivered results. You did not realize you were dealing with the insecure variety and had inadvertently triggered their self-doubts. They secretly envy your youth, your energy, your promise, and the signs of your talent. Even worse if you are socially gifted and they are not. They will justify the firing or demotion with some narrative they have concocted; you will never discover the truth.

Michael Eisner, all-powerful CEO of Disney for twenty years, is just such a type. In 1995 he fired his number two man, Jeffrey Katzenberg, head of the film studio, ostensibly because of his abrasive personality, saying he was not a team player. In truth, Katzenberg had had far too much success in his position; the films he oversaw became the main source of Disney's revenue. He had the golden touch. Never admitting this to himself, Eisner clearly envied Katzenberg for his talent and transmuted this into hostility. This pattern repeated itself time and again with new creative people he brought in.

Pay attention to those above you for signs of insecurity and envy. They will inevitably have a track record of firing people for strange reasons. They will not seem particularly happy with that excellent report you turned in. Always play it safe by deferring to bosses, making them look better, and earning their trust. Couch your brilliant ideas as their ideas. Let them get all the credit for your hard work. Your time to shine will come, but not if you inadvertently stimulate their insecurities.

Envy Triggers

Although certain types are more prone to envy, you must also be aware that there are circumstances that will tend to trigger envy in almost anyone. You must be extra alert in such situations.

The most common trigger is a sudden change in your status, which alters your relationship to friends and peers. This is particularly true among people in your own profession. This has been known for a long time. As Hesiod noted in the eighth century BC, "The potter envies the potter, the craftsman the craftsman, the writer the writer." If you experience success, those in your field who have similar aspirations but who are still struggling will naturally feel envious. You should be reasonably tolerant of this because if the tables were reversed, you would probably feel the same. Do not take so personally their faint praise and veiled criticisms. But be aware that among some of these peers envy can turn active and dangerous.

Renaissance artists who suddenly got commissions became targets for envious rivals, who could turn quite vicious. Michelangelo clearly envied the younger and talented Raphael and did what he could to sully his reputation and block his commissions. Writers are notoriously envious of other writers, particularly those with more lucrative deals.

The best you can do in such situations is to have some self-deprecating humor and to not rub people's faces in your success, which, after all, might contain some elements of luck. In fact, when discussing your success with others who might envy you, always emphasize or play up the element of luck. For those closest to you, offer to help them in their struggles as best you can, without appearing patronizing. In a similar vein, never make the mistake of praising a writer in front of another writer, or an artist in front of an artist, unless the person being praised is dead. If you detect signs of a more active envy in peers, get as far away from them as possible.

Keep in mind that people who are getting older, with their careers on the decline, have delicate egos and are quite prone to experiencing envy.

Sometimes it is people's natural gifts and talents that will stir up the most intense forms of envy. We can strive to become proficient in a field, but we cannot reengineer our physiology. Some people are born with better looks, more raw athletic skill, an unusually vivid imagination, or an open and generous nature. If people with natural gifts also possess a good work ethic and have some luck in life, envy will follow them wherever they go. Often making it worse for such types, they also tend to be quite naive. They themselves do not feel envy toward others, so they cannot understand the emotion at all. Unaware of the dangers, they naturally display their talents and attract even more envy. Mary Shelley was all of this—gifted with a brilliant imagination and superior intellectual capabilities, and also quite naive. What is worse, envying types secretly loathe those who are immune to feeling envy. It makes their envious nature doubly apparent to themselves and stirs the desire to hurt and wound.

If you have any natural gifts that elevate you above others, you must be aware of the dangers and avoid flaunting such talents. Instead you want to strategically reveal some flaws to blunt people's envy and mask your natural superiority. If you are gifted in the sciences, make it clear to others how you wish you had more social skills. Show your intellectual clumsiness at subjects outside your expertise.

John F. Kennedy seemed almost too perfect to the American public. So handsome, intelligent, and charismatic, and with such a beautiful wife—it was hard to identify with or like him. As soon as he made his big mistake in the failed invasion of Cuba (known as the Bay of Pigs) early on in his administration, and took full responsibility for the debacle, his poll numbers skyrocketed. The mistake had humanized him. Although this was not done by design, you can have a similar effect by discussing the mistakes you have made in the past and showing some selective awkwardness in certain areas that do not diminish your overall reputation.

Women who achieve success and fame are more prone to attracting envy and hostility, although this will always be veiled as something else—such women are said to be too cold, or ambitious, or unfeminine. Oftentimes we choose to admire people who achieve great things, admiration being the opposite of envy. We do not feel personally challenged or insecure in the face of their excellence. We might also emulate them, use them as spurs toward trying to achieve more. But unfortunately this is rarely the case with successful women. A high-achieving woman inflicts greater feelings of inferiority in both other women and men ("I'm inferior to a woman?"), which leads to envy and hostility, not admiration.

Coco Chanel, the most successful businesswoman of her era, especially considering her origins as an orphan (see chapter 5), suffered from such envy her entire life. In 1931, at the height of her power, she met Paul Iribe, an illustrator and designer whose career was on the decline. Iribe was an expert seducer and they had much in common. But several months into their relationship, he began to criticize her for her extravagance and torment her about her other flaws as he saw them. He wanted to control all aspects of her life. Lonely and desperate for a relationship, she hung on, but she later wrote of Iribe, "My growing celebrity eclipsed his declining glory. . . . Iribe loved me with the secret hope of destroying me." Love and envy are not mutually exclusive.

Successful women will have to bear this burden until such entrenched underlying values are changed. In the meantime, they will have to be even more adept at deflecting envy and playing the humble card.

Robert Rubin (b. 1938), two-term secretary of the treasury under Bill Clinton, was a grand master when it came to masking his excellence and defusing envy. He had begun his career at Goldman Sachs in 1966, slowly rising through the ranks to become its cohead in 1990. He was one of the key figures who transformed Goldman Sachs into the most powerful investment bank on Wall Street. He was a hard worker and brilliant at finance, but as he became more powerful within Goldman, he also became more deferential in all of his interactions. In meetings in which he was clearly the most knowledgeable person, he would make a point of asking for the opinions of the most junior associate in attendance, and of listening to what he or she had to say with rapt attention. When people who worked for him asked him what should be done in relation to some crisis or problem, he would look at them calmly and ask first, "What do you think?" He would take their answer quite seriously.

As one colleague at Goldman later said of him, "There is no one better at the humility shtick than Bob. The line, 'just one's man opinion' was something he would utter a dozen times a day." What is remarkable is how Rubin earned the admiration of so many people and how few had anything bad to say about him, considering the competitive environment within the company. This reveals the power you have to short-circuit envy by placing attention on other people instead of yourself and engaging with them on a meaningful level.

If you find yourself under an envy attack, your best strategy is to control your emotions. It is much easier to do this once you realize that envy is the source. The envier feeds upon your overreaction as material to criticize you, justify their actions, and entangle you in some further drama. At all costs, maintain your composure. If possible, get some physical distance as well—fire them, cut off contact, whatever is possible. Do not imagine you can somehow repair the relationship. Your generosity in trying this will only intensify their feelings of inferiority. They will strike again. By all means defend yourself from any public attacks or gossip that they spread, but do not harbor revenge fantasies. The envier is miserable. The best strategy is let to them stew in their "cold poison" from a distance, without any future means of wounding you, as Mary did to Jane. Their chronic unhappiness is punishment enough.

Finally, you might imagine that envy is a somewhat rare occurrence in the modern world. After all, it is a primitive, childish emotion, and we live in such sophisticated times. Furthermore, not many people discuss or analyze envy as a major social factor. But the truth is that envy is more prevalent now than ever before, largely because of social media.

Through social media we have a continual window into the lives of friends, pseudofriends, and celebrities. And what we see is not some unvarnished peek into their world but a highly idealized image that they present. We see only the most exciting images from their vacations, the happy faces of their friends and children, accounts of their continual self-improvement, the fascinating people they are meeting, the great causes and projects they are involved in, the examples of success in their endeavors. Are we having as much fun? Are our lives as seemingly fulfilled as theirs? Are we perhaps missing out on something? We generally believe, and for good reason, that we are all entitled to share in the good life, but if our peers seem to have more, someone or something must be to blame.

What we experience in this case is a generalized feeling of dissatisfaction. Low-grade envy sits inside us, waiting to be triggered into the more acute variety if something we read or see intensifies our insecurities. Such diffuse envy among large groups of people can even become a political force, as demagogues can stir it against certain individuals or groups of people who have or seem to have it easier than others. People can be unified through their underlying envy, but as with the personal variety, nobody will admit to this, nor will it ever be seen as such. Public envy can be quickly turned against public figures, especially in the form of schadenfreude when they experience some misfortune. (Witness the piling on of hostility toward Martha Stewart once she seemed to run afoul of the law.) Gossip about the powerful becomes an industry.

What this means is simple: we will find more and more people around us prone to feeling passive envy that can turn into the virulent form if we are not careful. We must be prepared to feel its effects coming from friends, colleagues, and the public if we are in the public eye. In such an overheated social environment, learning to recognize the signs and being able to identify envier types is an absolutely critical skill to develop. And since we are now all more susceptible to feeling envy ourselves, we must also learn how to manage this emotion within ourselves, transforming it into something positive and productive.

Beyond Envy

Like most humans, you will tend to deny that you ever experience envy, at least strong enough to act on. You are simply not being honest with yourself. As described above, you are only conscious of the indignation or resentment you feel that covers up the initial pangs of envy. You need to overcome the natural resistance to seeing the emotion as it first stirs within you.

We all compare ourselves with others; we all feel unsettled by those who are superior in some area that we esteem; and we all react to this by feeling some form of envy. (It is wired into our nature; studies have shown that monkeys feel envy.) You can begin with a simple experiment: next time you hear or read about the sudden success of someone in your field, notice the inevitable feeling of wanting the same (the pang) and the subsequent hostility, however vague, toward the person you envy. It happens quickly and you can easily miss the transition, but try to catch it. It is natural to go through this emotional sequence and there should be no guilt attached. Monitoring yourself and seeing more such instances will only help you in the slow process of moving beyond envy.

Let us be realistic, however, and realize that it is almost impossible to rid ourselves of the compulsion to compare ourselves with others. It is too ingrained in our nature as a social animal. Instead, what we must aspire to is to slowly transform our comparing inclination into something positive, productive, and prosocial. The following are five simple exercises to help you in achieving this.

Move closer to what you envy. Envy thrives on relative closeness—in a corporate environment where people see each other every day, in a family, in a neighborhood, in any group of peers. But people tend to hide their problems and to put their best face forward. We only see and hear of their triumphs, their new relationships, their brilliant ideas that will land them a gold mine. If we moved closer—if we saw the quarrels that go on behind closed doors or the horrible boss that goes with that new job—we would have less reason to feel envy. Nothing is ever so perfect as it seems, and often we would see that we are mistaken if we only looked closely enough. Spend time with that family you envy and wish you had as your own, and you will begin to reassess your opinion.

If you envy people with greater fame and attention, remind yourself that with such attention comes a lot of hostility and scrutiny that is quite painful. Wealthy people are often miserable. Read any account of the last ten years of the life of Aristotle Onassis (1906–1975), one of the wealthiest men in history, married to the glamorous Jacqueline Kennedy, and you will see that his wealth brought him endless nightmares, including the most spoiled and unloving of children.

The process of moving closer is twofold: on the one hand, try to actually look behind the glittering façades people present, and on the other hand, simply imagine the inevitable disadvantages that go along with their position. This is not the same as leveling them down. You are not diminishing the achievements of those who are great. You are mitigating the envy you might feel for things in people's personal lives.

Engage in downward comparisons. You normally focus on those who seem to have more than you, but it would be wiser to look at those who have less. There are always plenty of people to use for such a comparison. They live in harsher environments, deal with more threats to their lives, and have deeper levels of insecurity about the future. You can even look at friends who have it much worse than you. This should stimulate not only empathy for the many who have less but also greater gratitude for what you actually possess. Such gratitude is the best antidote to envy.

As a related exercise, you can write up all the positive things in your life that you tend to take for granted—the people who have been kind and helpful to you, the health that you presently enjoy. Gratitude is a muscle that requires exercise or it will atrophy.

Practice *Mitfreude*. Schadenfreude, the experience of pleasure in the pain of other people, is distinctly related to envy, as several studies have demonstrated. When we envy someone, we are prone to feel excitement, even joy, if they experience a setback or suffer in some way. But it would be wise to practice instead the opposite, what the philosopher Friedrich Nietzsche called *Mitfreude*—"joying with." As he wrote, "The serpent that stings us means to hurt us and rejoices as it does so; the lowest animal can imagine the *pain* of others. But to imagine the joy of others and to rejoice at it is the highest privilege of the highest animals."

This means that instead of merely congratulating people on their good fortune, something easy to do and easily forgotten, you must instead actively try to feel their joy, as a form of empathy. This can be somewhat unnatural, as our first tendency is to feel a pang of envy, but we can train ourselves to imagine how it must feel to others to experience their happiness or satisfaction. This not only cleans our brain of ugly envy but also creates an unusual form of rapport. If we are the targets of *Mitfreude*, we *feel* the other person's genuine excitement at our good fortune, instead of just hearing words, and it induces us to feel the same for them. Because it is such a rare occurrence, it contains great power to bond people. And in internalizing other people's joy, we increase our own capacity to feel this emotion in relation to our own experiences.

Transmute envy into emulation. We cannot stop the comparing mechanism in our brains, so it is best to redirect it into something productive and creative. Instead of wanting to hurt or steal from the person who has achieved more, we should desire to raise ourselves up to his or her level. In this way, envy becomes a spur to excellence. We may even try to be around people who will stimulate such competitive desires, people who are slightly above us in skill level.

To make this work requires a few psychological shifts. First, we must come to believe that we have the capacity to raise ourselves up. Confidence in our overall abilities to learn and improve will serve as a tremendous antidote to envy. Instead of wishing to have what another has and resorting to sabotage out of helplessness, we feel the urge to get the same for ourselves and believe we have the ability to do so. Second, we must develop a solid work ethic to back this up. If we are rigorous and persistent, we will be able to overcome almost any obstacle and elevate our position. People who are lazy and undisciplined are much more prone to feeling envy.

Related to this, having a sense of purpose, a feel for your calling in life, is a great way to immunize yourself against envy. You are focused on your own life and plans, which are clear and invigorating. What gives you satisfaction is realizing your potential, not earning attention from the public, which is fleeting. You have much less need to compare. Your sense of self-worth comes from within, not from without.

Admire human greatness. Admiration is the polar opposite of envy—we are acknowledging people's achievements, celebrating them, without having to feel insecure. We are admitting their superiority in the arts or sciences or in business without feeling pain from this. But this goes further. In recognizing the greatness of someone, we are celebrating the highest potential of our species. We are experiencing *Mitfreude* with the best in human nature. We share the pride that comes from any great human achievement. Such admiration elevates us above the pettiness of our day-to-day life and will have calming effect.

Although it is easier to admire without any taint of envy those who are dead, we must try to include at least one living person in our pantheon. If we are young enough, such objects of admiration can also serve as models to emulate, at least to some degree.

Finally, it is worth cultivating moments in life in which we feel immense satisfaction and happiness divorced from our own success or achievements. This happens commonly when we find ourselves in a beautiful landscape—the mountains, the sea, a forest. We do not feel the prying, comparing eyes of others, the need to have more attention or to assert ourselves. We are simply in awe of what we see, and it is intensely therapeutic. This can also occur when we contemplate the immensity of the universe, the uncanny set of circumstances that had to come together for us to be born, the vast reaches of time before us and after us. These are sublime moments, and as far removed from the pettiness and poisons of envy as possible.

> For not many men . . . can love a friend who fortune prospers
> without envying; and about the envious brain
> cold poison clings and doubles all the pain
> life brings him. His own woundings he must nurse,
> and feel another's gladness like a curse.
>
> —Aeschylus

11

Know Your Limits

◇

The Law of Grandiosity

*W*e humans have a deep need to think highly of ourselves. If that opinion of our goodness, greatness, and brilliance diverges enough from reality, we become grandiose. We imagine our superiority. Often a small measure of success will elevate our natural grandiosity to even more dangerous levels. Our high self-opinion has now been confirmed by events. We forget the role that luck may have played in the success, or the contributions of others. We imagine we have the golden touch. Losing contact with reality, we make irrational decisions. That is why our success often does not last. Look for the signs of elevated grandiosity in yourself and in others—overbearing certainty in the positive outcome of your plans; excessive touchiness if criticized; a disdain for any form of authority. Counteract the pull of grandiosity by maintaining a realistic assessment of yourself and your limits. Tie any feelings of greatness to your work, your achievements, and your contributions to society.

The Success Delusion

By the summer of 1984, Michael Eisner (b. 1942), president of Paramount Pictures, could no longer ignore the restlessness that had been plaguing him for months. He was impatient to move on to a bigger stage and shake the foundations of Hollywood. This restlessness had been the story of his life. He had begun his career at ABC, and never settling too comfortably within one department, after nine years of various promotions he had risen to the position of head of prime-time programming. But television began to seem small and constricting to him. He needed a larger, grander stage. In 1976 Barry

Diller—a former boss at ABC and now the chairman of Paramount Pictures—offered him the job of heading Paramount's film studio, and he jumped at the chance.

Paramount had long been in the doldrums, but working with Diller, Eisner transformed it into the hottest studio in Hollywood, with a string of remarkably successful films—*Saturday Night Fever, Grease, Flashdance*, and *Terms of Endearment*. Although Diller certainly played a part in this turnaround, Eisner saw himself as the main driving force behind the studio's success. After all, he had invented a surefire formula for creating profitable films.

The formula depended on keeping costs down, an obsession of his. To do so, a film had to begin with a great concept, one that was original, easy to summarize, and dramatic. Executives could hire the most expensive writers, directors, and actors for a film, but if the underlying concept was weak, all the money in the world would be wasted. Films with a strong concept, however, would market themselves. A studio could churn these relatively inexpensive films out in volume, and even if they were only moderate hits, they would ensure a steady flow of income. This thinking went against the grain of the blockbuster mentality of the late 1970s, but who could argue with the undeniable profits Eisner had generated for Paramount? Eisner immortalized this formula in a memo that soon spread around Hollywood and became gospel.

But after so many years of sharing the limelight with Diller at Paramount, trying to please corporate CEOs, and pushing back against marketing directors and finance people, Eisner had had enough. If only he could run his own studio, unfettered. With the formula he had created and with his relentless ambition, he could forge the greatest and most profitable entertainment empire in the world. He was tired of other people piggybacking on his ideas and success. Operating on top and alone, he could control the show and take all the credit.

As Eisner contemplated this next critical move in his career that summer of '84, he finally settled upon the perfect target for his ambitions—the Walt Disney Company. At first glance, this would seem a puzzling choice. Since the death of Walt Disney in 1966, the Walt Disney film studio seemed frozen in time, getting weirder with each passing year. The place operated more like a stodgy men's club. Many executives stopped working after lunch and spent their afternoons in card games, or would lounge about in the steam room on site. Hardly anyone was ever fired. The studio produced one animated film about every four years and in 1983 produced a meager three live-action films. They had not had a single hit film since *The Love Bug* in 1968. The Disney lot in

Burbank almost seemed like a ghost town. The actor Tom Hanks, who worked on the lot in 1983, described it as "a Greyhound bus station in the 1950s."

Given its dilapidated condition, however, this would be the perfect place for Eisner to work his magic. The studio and the corporation could only move up. Its board members were desperate to turn it around and avoid a hostile takeover. Eisner could dictate the terms of his leadership position. Presenting himself to Roy Disney (Walt's nephew and the largest shareholder of Disney stock) as the company's savior, he laid out a detailed and inspiring plan for a dramatic turnaround (greater than Paramount's), and Roy was won over. With Roy's blessing the board approved the choice, and in September 1984 Eisner was named chairman and CEO of the Walt Disney Company. Frank Wells, the former head of Warner Bros., was named president and chief operating officer. Wells would focus on the business side. In all matters Eisner was the boss; Wells was there to help and serve him.

Eisner wasted no time. He embarked on a major restructuring of the company, which led to the departure of over a thousand employees. He started filling the executive ranks with Paramount people, most notably Jeffrey Katzenberg (b. 1950), who had worked as Eisner's right-hand man at Paramount and was now named chairman of Walt Disney Studios. Katzenberg could be abrasive and downright rude, but no one in Hollywood was more efficient or worked harder. He simply got things done.

Within months Disney began to churn out a remarkable series of hits, adhering to Eisner's formula. Fifteen of its first seventeen films (such as *Down and Out in Beverly Hills* and *Who Framed Roger Rabbit*) generated profits, a run of success almost unheard of for any studio in Hollywood.

One day, as Eisner explored the Burbank lot with Wells, they entered the Disney library and discovered hundreds of cartoons from the golden era that had never been shown. There on endless shelves were stored all of the great Disney classic animated hits. Eisner's eyes lit up at the sight of this treasure. He could reissue all of these cartoons and animated films on video (the home video market was in the midst of exploding) and it would be pure profit. Based on these cartoons, the company could create stores to market the various Disney characters. Disney was a virtual gold mine waiting to be exploited, and Eisner would make the most of this.

Soon the stores opened, the videos sold like crazy, the film hits kept pumping profit into the company, and Disney's stock price soared. It had replaced Paramount as the hottest film studio in town. Wanting to cultivate a more public presence, Eisner decided to revive the old *The Wonderful World of Disney*, an hourlong television show from the fifties and sixties hosted by Walt Disney himself. This time Eisner would be the host. He was not a natural in front of the camera, but he felt audiences would grow to like him. He could be comforting to children, like Walt himself. In fact, he began to feel the two of them were somehow magically connected, as if he were more than just the head of the corporation but rather the natural son and successor to Walt Disney himself.

Despite all his success, however, the old restlessness returned. He needed a new venture, a bigger challenge, and soon he found it. The Walt Disney Company had plans to create a new theme park in Europe. The last one to open, Tokyo Disneyland in 1983, had been a success. Those in charge of theme parks had settled upon two potential sites for the new Disneyland—one near Barcelona, Spain, the other near Paris. Although the Barcelona site made more economic sense, since the weather there was much better, Eisner chose the French site. This was going to be more than a theme park. This was going to be a cultural statement. He would hire the best architects in the world. Unlike the usual fiberglass castles at the other theme parks, at Euro Disney—as it came to be known—the castles would be built out of pink stone and feature handcrafted stained-glass windows with scenes from various fairy tales. It would be a place even snobby French elites would be excited to visit. Eisner loved architecture, and here he could be a modern-day Medici.

As the years went by, the cost of Euro Disney mounted. Letting go of his usual obsession with the bottom line, Eisner felt that if he built it right, the crowds would come and the park would eventually pay for itself. But when it finally opened as planned in 1992, it quickly became clear that Eisner had not understood French tastes and vacation habits. The French were not so willing to wait in line for rides, particularly in bad weather. As in the other theme parks, no beer or wine was served on the premises, and that seemed like sacrilege to the French. The hotel rooms were too expensive for a family to stay there more than a night. And despite all the attention to detail, the pink stone castles still looked like kitschy versions of the originals.

Attendance was only half of what Eisner had anticipated. The debts Disney had incurred in the construction had ballooned, and the money coming in from visitors could not even service the interest on them. It was shaping up to be a disaster, the first ever in his glorious career. As he finally came to terms with this reality, he decided that Frank Wells was to blame. It was his job to oversee the financial health of the project, and he had failed. Whereas before Eisner had only had the best things to say about their working relationship, now he often complained about his second-in-command and contemplated firing him.

In the middle of this growing debacle, Eisner felt a new threat on the horizon—Jeffrey Katzenberg. He had once referred to Katzenberg as his golden retriever—so loyal and hardworking. It was Katzenberg who had overseen the string of early hits for the studio, including the biggest hit of all, *Beauty and the Beast*, the film that had initiated the renaissance of Disney's animation department. But something about Katzenberg was making him increasingly nervous. Perhaps it was the memo that Katzenberg had written in 1990, in which he dissected the string of flops Disney had recently produced in live action. "Since 1984, we have slowly drifted away from our original vision of how to run a business," he wrote. Katzenberg criticized the studio's decision to go for bigger-budget films such as *Dick Tracy*, trying to make "event movies." Disney had fallen for "the blockbuster mentality" and had lost its soul in the process.

The memo made Eisner uncomfortable. *Dick Tracy* was Eisner's own pet project. Was Katzenberg indirectly criticizing his boss? When he thought about it, it seemed like this was a clear imitation of his own infamous memo at Paramount, in which he had advocated for less expensive, high-concept films. Now it occurred to him that Katzenberg saw himself as the next Eisner. Maybe he was angling to take Eisner's job, to subtly undermine his authority. This began to eat away at him. Why was Katzenberg now cutting him out of story meetings?

The animation department soon became the primary generator of profits for the studio, with new hits such as *Aladdin* and now *The Lion King*, which had been Katzenberg's baby—he had come up with the story idea and developed it from start to finish. Magazine articles now began to feature Katzenberg as if he were the creative genius behind Disney's resurgence in the genre. What about Roy Disney, the vice chairman of animation? What about Eisner himself, who was in charge of everything? To Eisner, Katzenberg was now playing the media, building himself up. An executive had reported to Eisner that Katzenberg was going around saying, "I'm the Walt Disney of today." Suspicion soon turned into hatred. Eisner could not stand to be around him.

Then, in March of 1994, Frank Wells was killed in a helicopter accident while on a skiing trip. To reassure shareholders and Wall Street, Eisner soon announced that he would take over Wells's position as president. But suddenly here was Katzenberg pestering him with phone calls and memos, reminding Eisner that he had promised him the president's job if Wells ever left the company. How insensitive, so soon after the tragedy. He stopped returning Katzenberg's phone calls.

Finally, in August 1994, Eisner fired Jeffrey Katzenberg, shocking almost everyone in Hollywood. He had fired the most successful studio executive in town. *The Lion King* had become one of the most profitable films in Hollywood history. It was Katzenberg who was behind Disney's acquisition of Miramax, considered a great coup with the ensuing success of *Pulp Fiction*. It seemed like madness on his part, but Eisner did not care. Finally freed of Katzenberg's shadow, he could relax and now take Disney to the next level, on his own and with no more distractions.

To prove he had not lost his touch, he soon dazzled the entertainment world by engineering Disney's purchase of ABC. The sheer audacity of this coup once again made him the center of attention. Now he was forging an entertainment empire beyond what anyone had ever attempted or imagined. This move, however, created a problem for him. The company had virtually doubled in size. It was too complex, too big for one man. Only a year earlier he had undergone open-heart surgery, and he could not handle the added stress.

He needed another Frank Wells, and his thoughts soon turned to his old friend Michael Ovitz, one of the founders and the head of Creative Artists Agency. Ovitz was the greatest deal maker in Hollywood history, perhaps the most powerful man in town. Together they could dominate the field. Many within the business warned him against this hire—Ovitz was not like Frank Wells; he was not a finance guy or a master of detail, as Ovitz himself would have admitted. Eisner ignored such advice. People were being too conventional in their thinking. He decided to lure Ovitz away from CAA with a very lucrative package and offer him the title of president. He assured Ovitz in several discussions that although Ovitz would be second in command, they would eventually run the company as coleaders.

In a phone call Ovitz finally agreed to all of the terms, but the moment Eisner hung up, he realized he had made the biggest mistake of his life. What had he been thinking? They might have been the closest of friends, but how would two such larger-than-life men ever be able to work together? Ovitz was power hungry. This would be the Katzenberg problem times two. It was too late, however. He had gotten the board's approval for the hire. His own reputation, his decision-making process as a CEO, was at stake. He would have to make it work.

He quickly decided upon a strategy—he would narrow Ovitz's responsibilities, keep a tight leash on him, and make him prove himself as president. By doing so Ovitz could earn Eisner's trust and get more power. From day one Eisner wanted to signal to Ovitz who was boss. Instead of moving him into Frank Wells's old office on the sixth floor at Disney headquarters, next to Eisner's, Eisner put him in a rather unimpressive office on the fifth floor. Ovitz liked to spread money around with gifts and lavish parties to charm people; Eisner had his team monitor every penny that Ovitz spent on such things, and watch his every move. Was Ovitz contacting other executives behind Eisner's back? He would not nurture another Katzenberg at his breast.

Soon the following dynamic developed: Ovitz would approach him with some potential deal, and Eisner would not discourage him from exploring it. But once it came time to agree to the deal, Eisner would give a firm no. Slowly word spread through the industry that Ovitz had lost his touch and could no longer close a deal. Ovitz began to panic. He wanted desperately to prove he had been worthy of the choice. He offered to move to New York to help manage ABC, since the merger of the two companies was not working out so smoothly, but Eisner said no. He told his lieutenants to keep their distance from Ovitz. He was not a man to be trusted—he was the son of a liquor salesman in the San Fernando Valley, and like his father, Ovitz was just a smooth salesman. He was addicted to attention from the media. Within the company, Ovitz had become completely isolated.

As the months dragged on in this saga, Ovitz could see what was happening, and he complained bitterly to Eisner. He had left his agency for Disney; he had staked his reputation on what he would do as president, and Eisner was destroying his reputation. Nobody respected him any longer in the business. Eisner's treatment of Ovitz was downright sadistic. In Eisner's mind, however, Ovitz had failed the test he had laid out; he had not proven himself to be patient; he was no Frank Wells. In December of 1996, after a mere fourteen months on the job, Ovitz was fired, taking with him an enormous severance package. It was a dizzying and rapid fall from grace.

Finally liberated from this great mistake, Eisner began to consolidate power within the company. ABC was not doing so well. He would have to intervene and take some control. He began to attend programming meetings; he talked of his own golden days at ABC and of the great shows he had created there, such as *Laverne & Shirley* and *Happy Days*. ABC needed to go back to that earlier philosophy and create high-concept shows for the family.

As the internet began to take off, Eisner had to get involved in a big way. He nixed the purchase of Yahoo!, pushed by his executives. Instead Disney would start its own internet portal, called Go. Over the years he had learned the lesson—it was always best to design and run your own show. Disney would dominate the internet. He had proven himself a turnaround genius twice before, and with Disney now in a slump, he would do it a third time.

Soon, however, a wave of disasters hit the corporation, one after another. After being fired, Katzenberg had sued Disney for the bonus—based on performance—he was due under his contract. When he had been president, Ovitz had tried to settle the suit before it went to court and had gotten Katzenberg to agree to $90 million, but at the last minute Eisner had nixed this, certain he did not owe Katzenberg anything. In 2001 the judge ruled in Katzenberg's favor, and they had to settle for a whopping $280 million. Disney had poured vast resources into the creation of Go, and it was a terrific flop that had to be shut down. The costs from Euro Disney were still bleeding the company. Disney had a partnership with Pixar, and together they had produced such hits as *Toy Story*. But now the CEO of Pixar, Steve Jobs, made it clear he would never work with Disney again, deeply resenting Eisner's micromanaging. ABC was underperforming. Most of the movies Disney produced were not just flops but expensive flops, culminating in the biggest one of all, *Pearl Harbor*, which opened in May of 2001.

Suddenly it seemed that Roy Disney had lost faith in Eisner. The stock price was plummeting. He told Eisner it would be best for him to resign. What ingratitude, what hubris! He, Eisner, was the man who had singlehandedly brought the company back from the dead. He had saved Roy from disaster and made him a fortune, Roy who had been considered Walt's idiot nephew. And now, in Eisner's darkest hour, Roy was going to betray him? Eisner had never felt more enraged. He quickly struck back, forcing Roy to resign from the board. This only seemed to embolden Roy. He organized a shareholder revolt known as Save Disney, and in March of 2004 the shareholders voted a stinging rebuke of Eisner's leadership.

Soon the board decided to strip Eisner of his position as chairman of the board. The empire he had forged was falling apart. In September of 2005, with hardly an ally to lean on and feeling alone and betrayed, Eisner officially resigned from Disney. How had it all unraveled so quickly? They would come to miss him, he told friends, and he meant all of Hollywood; there would never be another like him.

_____

Interpretation: We can say that at a certain point in his career Michael Eisner succumbed to a form of delusion when it came to power, his thinking so divorced from reality that he made business decisions with disastrous consequences. Let us follow the progress of this particular form of delusion as it emerged and took over his mind.

At the beginning of his career at ABC, young Eisner had a solid grasp on reality. He was fiercely practical. He understood and exploited to the maximum his strengths—his ambitious and competitive nature, his intense work ethic, his keen sense for the entertainment tastes of the average American. Eisner had a quick mind and the ability to encourage others to think creatively. Leaning on these strengths, he rose quickly up the ladder. He possessed a high degree of confidence in his talents, and the series of promotions he received at ABC confirmed this self-opinion. He could afford to be a little cocky, because he had learned a lot on the job and his skills as a programmer had improved immensely. He was on a fast track toward the top, which he reached at the age of thirty-four by being named head of prime-time programming at ABC.

As a person of high ambition, he soon felt that the world of television was somewhat constricting. There were limits to the kinds of entertainment he could program. The film world offered something looser, greater, and more glamorous. It was natural, then, for him to accept the position at Paramount. But at Paramount something occurred that began the subtle process of the unbalancing of his mind. Because the stage was bigger and he was the head of the studio, he began to receive attention from the media and the public. He was featured on the cover of magazines as the hottest film executive in Hollywood. This was qualitatively different from the attention and satisfaction that had come from the promotions at ABC. Now he had millions of people admiring him. How could their opinions be wrong? To them he was a genius, a new kind of hero altering the landscape of the studio system.

This was intoxicating. It inevitably elevated his estimation of his skills. But it came with a great danger. The success that Eisner had had at Paramount was not completely of his own doing. When he had arrived at the studio, several films were already in preproduction, including _Saturday Night Fever_, which would spark the turnaround. Barry Diller was the perfect foil to Eisner. He would argue with him endlessly about his ideas, forcing Eisner to sharpen them. But puffed up by the attention he was receiving, Eisner had to imagine that he deserved the accolades he received strictly for his own efforts, and so naturally he subtracted from his success the elements of good timing and the contributions of others. Now his mind was subtly divorcing itself from reality. Instead of rigorously focusing on the audience and how to entertain people, he started to increasingly focus on himself, believing in the myth of his greatness as promulgated by others. He imagined he had the golden touch.

At Disney the pattern repeated and grew more intense. He basked in the glow of his amazing success there, quickly forgetting the incredible good luck he had had in inheriting the Disney library at the time of the explosion of home video and family entertainment. He discounted the critical role that Wells had played in balancing him out. With his sense of grandeur growing, he faced a dilemma. He had become addicted to the attention that came from creating a splash, doing something big. He could not content himself with simple success and rising profits. He had to add to the myth to keep it alive. Euro Disney would be the answer. He would show the world he was not just a corporate executive but rather a renaissance man.

In building the park, he refused to listen to experienced advisers who recommended the Barcelona site and advocated a modest theme park to keep the costs down. He did not pay attention to French culture but directed everything from Burbank. He operated under the belief that his skills as the head of a film studio could be transferred to theme parks and architecture. He was certainly overestimating his creative powers, and now his business decisions revealed a large enough detachment from reality to qualify as delusional. Once this mental imbalance takes hold, it can only get worse, because to come back down to earth is to admit that one's earlier high self-opinion was wrong, and the human animal will almost never admit that. Instead, the tendency is to blame others for every failure or setback.

In the grips now of his delusion, he made his most serious mistake of all—the firing of Jeffrey Katzenberg. The Disney system depended on a steady flow of new animated hits, which fed the stores and theme parks with new characters, merchandise, rides, and avenues for publicity. Katzenberg clearly had developed the knack for creating such hits, exemplified by the unprecedented success of The Lion King. Firing him put the entire assembly line at risk. Who would take over? Certainly not Roy Disney or Eisner himself? Furthermore, he had to know that Katzenberg would take his skills elsewhere, which he did when he cofounded a new studio, DreamWorks. There he churned out more animated hits. The new studio drove up the price for skilled animators, vastly increasing the cost of producing an animated film and threatening Disney's entire profit system. But instead of a firm grip on this reality, Eisner was more focused on the competition for attention. Katzenberg's rise threatened his elevated self-opinion, and he had to sacrifice profit and practicality to soothe his ego.

The downward spiral had begun. The acquisition of ABC, under the belief that bigger is better, revealed his growing detachment from reality. Television was a dying business model in the age of new media. It was not a realistic business decision but a play for publicity. He had created an entertainment behemoth, a blob without any clear identity. The hiring and firing of Ovitz revealed an even greater level of delusion. People had become mere instruments for Eisner to use. Ovitz was considered the most feared and powerful man in Hollywood. Perhaps Eisner was unconsciously driven by the desire to humiliate Ovitz. If he had the power to make Ovitz beg for crumbs, *he* must be the most powerful man in Hollywood.

Soon all of the problems that stemmed from his delusional thought process began to cascade—the continually rising costs of Euro Disney, the Katzenberg bonus, the lack of hits in both film divisions, the continual drain on resources from ABC, the Ovitz severance package. The board members could no longer ignore the falling stock price. The firing of Katzenberg and Ovitz made Eisner the most hated man in Hollywood, and as his fortunes fell, all of his enemies came out of the woodwork to hasten his destruction. His fall from power was fast and spectacular.

Understand: The story of Michael Eisner is much closer to you than you think. His fate could easily be yours, albeit most likely on a smaller scale. The reason is simple: we humans possess a weakness that is latent in us all and will push us into the delusional process without our ever being aware of the dynamic. The weakness stems from our natural tendency to overestimate our skills. We normally have a self-opinion that is somewhat elevated in relation to reality. We have a deep need to feel ourselves superior to others in something—intelligence, beauty, charm, popularity, or saintliness. This can be a positive. A degree of confidence impels us to take on challenges, to push past our supposed limits, and to learn in the process. But once we experience success on any level—increased attention from an individual or group, a promotion, funding for a project—that confidence will tend to rise too quickly, and there will be an ever-growing discrepancy between our self-opinion and reality.

Any success that we have in life inevitably depends on some good luck, timing, the contributions of others, the teachers who helped us along the way, the whims of the public in need of something new. Our tendency is to forget all of this and imagine that any success stems from our superior self. We begin to assume we can handle new challenges well before we are ready. After all, people have confirmed our greatness with their attention, and we want to keep it coming. We imagine we have the golden touch and that we can now magically transfer our skills to some other medium or field. Without realizing it, we become more attuned to our ego and our fantasies than to the people we work for and our audience. We grow distant from those who are helping us, seeing them as tools to be used. And with any failures that occur we tend to blame others. Success has an irresistible pull to it that tends to cloud our minds.

Your task is the following: After any kind of success, analyze the components. See the element of luck that is inevitably there, as well as the role that other people, including mentors, played in your good fortune. This will neutralize the tendency to inflate your powers. Remind yourself that with success comes complacency, as attention becomes more important than the work and old strategies are repeated. With success you must raise your vigilance. Wipe the slate clean with each new project, starting from zero. Try to pay less attention to the applause as it grows louder. See the limits to what you can accomplish and embrace them, working with what you have. Don't believe bigger is better; consolidating and concentrating your forces is often the wiser choice. Be wary of offending with your growing sense of superiority—you will need your allies. Compensate for the drug-like effect of success by keeping your feet planted firmly on the ground. The power you will build up in this slow and organic way will be more real and lasting. Remember: the gods are merciless with those who fly too high on the wings of grandiosity, and they will make you pay the price.

Existence alone had never been enough for him; he had always wanted more. Perhaps it was only from the force of his desires that he had regarded himself as a man to whom more was permitted than to others.

—Fyodor Dostoyevsky, *Crime and Punishment*

Keys to Human Nature

Let us say that you have a project to realize, or an individual or group of people you wish to persuade to do something. We could describe a realistic attitude toward reaching such goals in the following way: Getting what you want is rarely easy. Success will depend on a lot of effort and some luck. To make your project work, you will probably have to jettison your previous strategy—circumstances are always changing and you need to keep an open mind. The people you are trying to reach never respond exactly as you might have imagined or hoped. In fact, people will generally surprise and frustrate you in their reactions. They have their own needs, experiences, and particular psychology that are different from your own. To impress your targets, you will have to focus on them and their spirit. If you fail to accomplish what you want, you will have to examine carefully what you did wrong and strive to learn from the experience.

You can think of the project or task ahead of you as a block of marble you must sculpt into something precise and beautiful. The block is much larger than you and the material is quite resistant, but the task is not impossible. With enough effort, focus, and resiliency you can slowly carve it into what you need. You must begin, however, with a proper sense of proportion—goals are hard to reach, people are resistant, and you have limits to what you can do. With such a realistic attitude, you can summon up the requisite patience and get to work.

Imagine, however, that your brain has succumbed to a psychological disease that affects your perception of size and proportion. Instead of seeing the task you are facing as rather large and the material resistant, under the influence of this disease you perceive the block of marble as relatively small and malleable. Losing your sense of proportion, you believe it won't take long to fashion the block into the image you have in your mind of the finished product. You imagine that the people you are trying to reach are not naturally resistant but quite predictable. You know how they'll respond to your great idea—they'll love it. In fact, they need you and your work more than you need them. They should seek you out. The emphasis is not on what you need to do to succeed but on what you feel you deserve. You can foresee a lot of attention coming your way with this project, but if you fail, other people must be to blame, because you have gifts, your cause is the right one, and only those who are malicious or envious could stand in your way.

We can call this psychological disease *grandiosity*. As you feel its effects, the normal realistic proportions are reversed—your self becomes larger and greater than anything else around it. That is the lens through which you view the task and the people you need to reach. This is not merely deep narcissism (see chapter 2), in which everything must revolve around you. This is seeing yourself as enlarged (the root of the word *grandiosity* meaning "big" or "great"), as superior and worthy of not only attention but of being adored. It is a feeling of being not merely human but godlike.

You may think of powerful, egotistical leaders in the public eye as the ones who contract such a disease, but you would be very wrong in that assumption. Certainly we find many influential people, such as Michael Eisner, with high-grade versions of grandiosity, where the attention and accolades they receive create a more intense enlargement of the self. But there is a low-grade, everyday version of the disease that is common to almost all of us because it is a trait embedded in human nature. It stems from our deep need to feel important, esteemed by people, and superior to others in something.

You are rarely aware of your own grandiosity because by its nature it alters your perception of reality and makes it hard to have an accurate assessment of yourself. And so you are unaware of the problems it might be causing you at this very moment. Your low-grade grandiosity will cause you to overestimate your own skills and abilities and to underestimate the obstacles that you face. And so you will take on tasks that are beyond your actual capacity. You will feel certain that people will respond to your idea in a particular way, and when they don't, you will become upset and blame others.

You may become restless and suddenly make a career change, not realizing that grandiosity is at the root—your present work is not confirming your greatness and superiority, because to be truly great would require more years of training and the development of new skills. Better to quit and be lured by the possibilities a new career offers, allowing you to entertain fantasies of greatness. In this way, you never quite master anything. You may have dozens of great ideas that you never attempt to execute, because that would cause you to confront the reality of your actual skill level. Without being aware of it, you might become ever so slightly passive—you expect other people to understand you, give you what you want, treat you well. Instead of earning their praise, you feel entitled to it.

In all of these cases, your low-grade grandiosity will prevent you from learning from your mistakes and developing yourself, because you begin with the assumption that you are already large and great, and it is too difficult to admit otherwise.

Your task as a student of human nature is threefold: First, you must understand the phenomenon of grandiosity itself, why it is so embedded in human nature, and why you will find many more grandiose people in the world today than ever before. Second, you need to recognize the signs of grandiosity and know how to manage the people who display them. And third and most important, you must see the signs of the disease in yourself and learn not only how to control your grandiose tendencies but also how to channel this energy into something productive (see "Practical Grandiosity," on page 315, for more on this).

According to the renowned psychoanalyst Heinz Kohut (1913–1981), grandiosity has its roots in the earliest years of our life. In our first months, most of us bonded completely with our mother. We had no sense of a separate identity. She met our every need. We came to believe that the breast that gave us food was actually a part of ourselves. We were omnipotent—all we had to do was feel hungry or feel any need, and the mother was there to meet it, as if we had magical powers to control her. But then, slowly, we had to go through a second phase of life in which we were forced to confront the reality—our mother was a separate being who had other people to attend to. We were not omnipotent but rather weak, quite small, and dependent. This realization was painful and the source of much of our acting out—we had a deep need to assert ourselves, to show we were not so helpless, and to fantasize about powers we did not possess. (Children will often imagine the ability to see through walls, to fly, or to read people's minds, and that is why they are drawn to stories of superheroes.)

As we get older, we may not be physically small anymore, but our sense of insignificance only gets worse. We come to realize we are one person not just in a larger family, school, or city but in an entire globe filled with billions of people. Our lives are relatively short. We have limited skills and brainpower. There is so much we cannot control, particularly with our careers and global trends. The idea that we will die and be quickly forgotten, swallowed up in eternity, is quite intolerable. We want to feel significant in some way, to protest against our natural smallness, to expand our sense of self. What we experienced at the age of three or four unconsciously haunts us our entire lives. We alternate between moments of sensing our smallness and trying to deny it. This makes us prone to finding ways to imagine our superiority.

Some children do not go through that second phase in early childhood in which they must confront their relative smallness, and these children are more vulnerable to deeper forms of grandiosity later in life. They are the pampered, spoiled ones. The mother and the father continue to make such children feel like they are the center of the universe, shielding them from the pain of confronting the reality. Their every wish becomes a command. If ever attempts are made to instill the slightest amount of discipline, the parents are met with a tantrum. Furthermore, such children come to disdain any form of authority. Compared with themselves and what they can get, the father figure seems rather weak.

This early pampering marks them for life. They need to be adored. They become masters at manipulating others to pamper them and shower them with attention. They naturally feel greater than anyone above them. If they have any talent, they might rise quite far, as their sense of being born with a crown on their head becomes a self-fulfilling prophecy. Unlike others, they never really alternate between feelings of smallness and greatness; they know only the latter. Certainly Eisner came from such a background, as he had a mother who met his every need, completed his homework for him, and sheltered him from his cold and sometimes cruel father.

In the past, we humans were able to channel our grandiose needs into religion. In ancient times, our sense of smallness was not just something bred into us by the many years we spent dependent on our parents; it also came from our weakness in relation to the hostile powers in nature. Gods and spirits represented these elemental powers of nature that dwarfed our own. By worshipping them we could gain their protection. Connected to something much larger than ourselves, we felt enlarged. After all, the gods or God cared about the fate of our tribe or city; they cared about our individual soul, a sign of our own significance. We did not merely die and disappear. Many centuries later, in a similar manner, we channeled this energy into worshipping leaders who represented a great cause and promoted a future utopia, such as Napoleon Bonaparte and the French Revolution, or Mao Zedong and communism.

Today, in the Western world, religions and great causes have lost their binding power; we find it hard to believe in them and to satisfy our grandiose energy through identification with a greater power. The need to feel larger and significant, however, does not simply disappear; it is stronger than ever. And absent any other channels, people will tend to direct this energy toward themselves. They will find a way to expand their sense of self, to feel great and superior. Although rarely conscious of this, what they are choosing to idealize and worship is the self. Because of this, we find more and more grandiose individuals among us.

Other factors have also contributed to increases in grandiosity. First, we find more people who experienced pampering attention in their childhood than ever in the past. Feeling like they were once the center of the universe becomes a hard thing to shake. They come to believe that anything they do or produce should be seen as precious and worthy of attention. Second, we find increasing numbers of people who have little or no respect for authority or experts of any kind, no matter the experts' level of training and experience, which they themselves lack. "Why should their opinion be any more valid than my own?" they might tell themselves. "Nobody's really that great; people with power are just more privileged." "My writing and music are just as legitimate and worthy as anyone else's." Without a sense of anyone rightly being above them and deserving authority, they can position themselves among the highest.

Third, technology gives us the impression that everything in life can be as fast and simple as the information we can glean online. It instills the belief that we no longer have to spend years learning a skill; instead, through a few tricks and with a few hours a week of practice we can become proficient at anything. Similarly, people believe that their skills can easily be transferred: "My ability to write means I can also direct a film." But more than anything it is social media that spreads the grandiosity virus. Through social media we have almost limitless powers to expand our presence, to create the illusion that we have the attention and even adoration of thousands or millions of people. We can possess the fame and ubiquity of the kings and queens in the past, or even of the gods themselves.

With all of these elements combined, it is harder than ever for any of us to maintain a realistic attitude and a proportionate sense of self.

In looking at the people around you, you must realize that their grandiosity (and yours) can come in many different forms. Most commonly people will try to satisfy the need by gaining social prestige. People may claim they are interested in the work itself or in contributing to humanity, but often deep down what is really motivating them is the desire to have attention, to have their high self-opinion confirmed by others who admire them, to feel powerful and inflated. If they are talented, such types can get the attention they need for several years or longer, but inevitably, as in the story of Eisner, their need for accolades will lure them into overreaching.

If people are disappointed in their careers yet still believe they are great and unrecognized, they may turn to various compensations—drugs, alcohol, sex with as many partners as possible, shopping, a superior, mocking attitude, et cetera. Those with unsatisfied grandiosity will often become filled with manic energy—one moment telling everyone about the great screenplays they will write or the many women they will seduce, and the next moment falling into depression as reality intrudes.

People still tend to idealize leaders and worship them, and you must see this as a form of grandiosity. By believing someone else will make everything great, followers can feel something of this greatness. Their minds can soar along with the rhetoric of the leader. They can feel superior to those who are not believers. On a more personal level, people will often idealize those they love, elevating them to god or goddess status and by extension feeling some of this power reflected back on them.

In the world today, you will also notice the prevalence of negative forms of grandiosity. Many people feel the need to disguise their grandiose urges not only from others but also from themselves. They will frequently make a show of their humility—they are not interested in power or feeling important, or so they say. They are happy with their small lot in life. They do not want a lot of possessions, do not own a car, and disdain status. But you will notice they have a need to display this humility in a public manner. It is grandiose humility—their way to get attention and to feel morally superior.

A variation on this is the *grandiose victim*—they have suffered a lot and been the victim numerous times. Although they may like to frame it as being simply unlucky and unfortunate, you will notice that they often have a tendency to fall for the worst types in intimate relationships, or put themselves in circumstances in which they are certain to fail and suffer. In essence, they are compelled to create the drama that will turn them into a victim. As it turns out, any relationship with them will have to revolve around their needs; they have suffered too much in the past to attend to your needs. They are the center of the universe. Feeling and expressing their misfortune gives them their sense of importance, of being superior in suffering.

You can measure the levels of grandiosity in people in several simple ways. For instance, notice how people respond to criticism of them or their work. It's normal for any of us to feel defensive and a bit upset when criticized. But some people become enraged and hysterical, because we have called into doubt their sense of greatness. You can be sure that such a person has high levels of grandiosity. Similarly, such types might conceal their rage behind a martyred, pained expression meant to make you feel guilty. The emphasis is not on the criticism itself and what they need to learn but on their sense of grievance.

If people are successful, notice how they act in more private moments. Are they able to relax and laugh at themselves, letting go of their public mask, or have they so overidentified with their powerful public image that it carries over into their private life? In the latter case, they have come to believe in their own myth and are in the grip of powerful grandiosity.

Grandiose people are generally big talkers. They take credit for anything that is even tangential to their work; they invent past successes. They talk of their prescience, how they foresaw certain trends or predicted certain events, none of which can be verified. All such talk should make you doubly dubious. If people in the public eye suddenly say something that gets them into trouble for being insensitive, you can ascribe that to their potent grandiosity. They are so attuned to their own great opinions that they assume everyone else will interpret them in the right spirit and agree with them.

Higher grandiose types generally display low levels of empathy. They are not good listeners. When the attention is not on them, they have a faraway look in their eyes and their fingers twitch with impatience. Only when the spotlight is on them do they become animated. They tend to see people as extensions of themselves—tools to be used in their schemes, sources of attention. Finally, they exhibit nonverbal behavior that can only be described as grandiose. Their gestures are big and dramatic. At a meeting, they take up a lot of personal space. Their voice tends to be louder than others, and they speak at a fast pace, giving no one else time to interrupt.

With those who exhibit moderate amounts of grandiosity, you should be indulgent. Almost all of us alternate between periods in which we feel superior and great and others in which we come back down to earth. Look for such moments of realism in people as signs of normalcy. But with those whose self-opinion is so high they cannot allow for any doubts, it is best to avoid relationships or entanglements. In intimate relationships, they will tend to demand adoring one-sided attention. If they are employees, business partners, or bosses, they will oversell their skills. Their levels of confidence will distract you from the deficiencies in their ideas, work habits, and character. If you cannot avoid such a relationship, be aware of their tendency to feel certain about the success of their ideas, and maintain your skepticism. Look at the ideas themselves and don't get caught up in their seductive self-belief. Don't entertain the illusion that you can confront them and try to bring them down to earth; you may trigger a rage response.

If such types happen to be your rivals, consider yourself lucky. They are easy to taunt and bait into overreactions. Casting doubts on their greatness will make them apoplectic and doubly irrational.

Finally, you will need to manage your own grandiose tendencies. Grandiosity has some positive and productive uses. The exuberance and high self-belief that come from it can be channeled into your work and help inspire you. (See "Practical Grandiosity," on page 315, for more on this.) But in general it would be best for you to accept your limitations and work with what you have, rather than fantasize about godlike powers you can never attain. The greatest protection you can have against grandiosity is to maintain a realistic attitude. You know what subjects and activities you are naturally attracted to. You cannot be skilled at everything. You need to play to your strengths and not imagine you can be great at whatever you put your mind to. You must have a thorough understanding of your energy levels, of how far you can reasonably push yourself, and of how this changes with age. And you must have a solid grasp on your social position—your allies, the people with whom you have the greatest rapport, the natural audience for your work. You cannot please everyone.

This self-awareness has a physical component to it that you must be sensitive to. When you are doing activities that mesh with your natural inclinations, you feel ease in the effort. You learn faster. You have more energy and you can withstand the tedium that comes with learning anything important. When you take on too much, more than you can handle, you feel not only exhausted but also irritable and nervous. You are prone to headaches. When you have success in life, you will naturally feel a touch of fear, as if the good fortune could disappear. You sense with this fear the dangers that can come from rising too high (almost like vertigo) and feeling too superior. Your anxiety is telling you to come back down to earth. You want to listen to your body as it signals to you when you are working against your strengths.

In knowing yourself, you accept your limits. You are simply one person among many in the world, and not naturally superior to anyone. You are not a god or an angel but a flawed human like the rest of us. You accept the fact that you cannot control the people around you and no strategy is ever foolproof. Human nature is too unpredictable. With this self-knowledge and acceptance of limits you will have a sense of proportion. You will search for greatness in your work. And when you feel the pull to think more highly of yourself than is reasonable, this self-knowledge will serve as a gravity mechanism, pulling you back down and directing you toward the actions and decisions that will best serve your particular nature.

Being realistic and pragmatic is what makes us humans so powerful. It is how we overcame our physical weakness in a hostile environment so many thousands of years ago, and learned to work with others and form powerful communities and tools for survival. Although we have veered away from this pragmatism, as we no longer have to rely on our wits to survive, it is in fact our true nature as the preeminent social animal on the planet. In becoming more realistic, you are simply becoming more human.

The Grandiose Leader

If people with high levels of grandiosity also possess some talent and a lot of assertive energy, they can rise to positions of great power. Their boldness and confidence attract attention and give them a larger-than-life presence. Mesmerized by their image, we often fail to see the underlying irrationality in their decision-making process and so follow them straight into some disaster. They can be very destructive.

You must realize a simple fact about these types—they depend on the attention we give them. Without our attention, without being adored by the public, they cannot have their high self-opinion validated, and in such cases the very confidence they depend on withers. To awe us and distract us from the reality, they employ certain theatrical devices. It is imperative for us to see through their stage tricks, to demythologize them and scale them back down to human size. In doing so, we can resist their allure and avoid the dangers they represent. The following are six common illusions they like to create.

I am destined. Grandiose leaders often try to give the impression that they were somehow destined for greatness. They tell stories of their childhood and youth that indicate their uniqueness, as if fate had singled them out. They highlight events that showed from early on their unusual toughness or creativity, either making such stories up or reinterpreting the past. They relate tales from earlier in their career in which they overcame impossible odds. The future great leader was already in gestation at a young age, or so they make it seem. When you hear such things you must become skeptical. They are trying to forge a myth, which they themselves probably have come to believe in. Look for the more mundane facts behind the tales of destiny and, if possible, publicize them.

I'm the common man/woman. In some cases grandiose leaders may have risen from the lower classes, but in general they either come from relatively privileged backgrounds or because of their success have lived removed from the cares of everyday people for quite some time. Nevertheless it is absolutely essential to present themselves to the public as highly representative of the average man and woman out there. Only through such a presentation can they attract the attention and the adoration of large enough numbers to satisfy themselves.

Indira Gandhi, the prime minister of India from 1966 to 1977 and 1980 to 1984, came from political royalty, her father Jawaharlal Nehru having been the first prime minister of the country. She was educated in Europe and lived for most of her life far apart from the poorer segments of India. But as a grandiose leader who later became quite dictatorial, she positioned herself as one with the people, their voice speaking through her. She altered her language when speaking in front of large crowds and used homely metaphors when she visited small villages. She would wear her sari as local women wore them and would eat with her fingers. She liked to present herself as "Mother Indira," who ruled over India in a familiar, motherly manner. And this style she assumed was highly effective in winning elections, even though it was pure stagecraft.

The trick grandiose leaders play is to place the emphasis on their cultural tastes, not on the actual class they come from. They may fly first class and wear the most expensive suits, but they counteract this by seeming to have the same culinary tastes as the public, enjoy the same movies as others, and avoid at all costs the whiff of cultural elitism. In fact, they will go out of their way to ridicule the elites, even though they probably depend on such experts to guide them. They are simply just like the common folk out there, but with a lot more money and power. The public can now identify with them despite the obvious contradictions. But the grandiosity of this goes beyond merely gaining more attention. These leaders become vastly enlarged by this identification with the masses. They are not merely one man or woman but embody an entire nation or interest group. To follow them is to be loyal to the group itself. To criticize them is to want to crucify the leader and betray the cause.

Even in the prosaic corporate world of business we find such religious-style identification: Eisner, for instance, liked to present himself as embodying the entire Disney spirit, whatever that meant. If you notice such paradoxes and primitive forms of popular association, stand back and analyze the reality of what is going on. You will find at the core something quasi-mystical, highly irrational, and quite dangerous in that the grandiose leader now feels licensed to do whatever he or she wants in the name of the public.

I will deliver you. These types often rise to power in times of trouble and crisis. Their self-confidence is comforting to the public or to shareholders. They will be the ones to deliver the people from the many problems they are facing. In order to pull this off, their promises have to be large yet vague. By being large they can inspire dreams; by being vague, nobody can hold the person to account if they don't come to pass, since there are no specifics to get hold of. The more grandiose the promises and visions of the future, the more grandiose the faith they will inspire. The message must be simple to digest, reducible to a slogan, and promising something large that stirs the emotions. As part of this strategy these types require convenient scapegoats, often the elites or outsiders, to tighten the group identification and to stir the emotions even further. The movement around the leader begins to crystallize around hatred of these scapegoats, who begin to stand for every bit of pain and injustice each person in the crowd has ever experienced. The leader's promise to bring these invented enemies down increases the leader's power exponentially.

What you will find here is that they are creating a cult more than leading a political movement or a business. You will see that their name, image, and slogans must be reproduced in large numbers and assume a godlike ubiquity. Certain colors, symbols, and perhaps music are used to bind the group identity and appeal to the basest human instincts. People who now believe in the cult are doubly mesmerized and ready to excuse any kind of action. At such a point nothing will dissuade true believers, but you must maintain your internal distance and analytic powers.

I rewrite the rules. A secret wish of humans is to do without the usual rules and conventions in place in any field—to gain power just by following our own inner light. When grandiose leaders claim to have such powers, we are secretly excited and wish to believe them.

Michael Cimino was the director of the Academy Award–winning film *The Deer Hunter* (1978). To those who worked with and for him, however, he was not simply a film director but rather a special genius on a mission to disrupt the rigid, corporate Hollywood system. For his next film, *Heaven's Gate* (1980), he negotiated a contract that was completely unique in Hollywood history, one that allowed him to increase the budget as he saw fit and to create precisely the film he had envisioned, with no strings attached. On the set, Cimino spent weeks rehearsing the actors in the right kind of roller-skating he needed for one scene. One day he waited hours before rolling cameras, just so the perfect kind of cloud could pass into frame. The costs soared and the film he initially turned in was over five hours long. In the end, *Heaven's Gate* was one of the greatest disasters in Hollywood history, and it virtually destroyed Cimino's career. It seemed that the traditional contract had actually served a purpose—to rein in the natural grandiosity of any film director and make him or her work within limits. Most rules do have common sense and rationality behind them.

As a variation on this, grandiose leaders will often rely on their intuitions, disregarding the need for focus groups or any form of scientific feedback. They have a special inside connection to the truth. They like to create the myth that their hunches have led to fantastic successes, but close scrutiny will reveal that their hunches miss as often as they hit. When you hear leaders present themselves as the consummate maverick, able to do away with rules and science, you must see this only as a sign of madness, not divine inspiration.

I have the golden touch. Those with heightened grandiosity will try to create the legend that they have never really failed. If there were failures or setbacks in their career, it was always the fault of others who betrayed them. U.S. Army general Douglas MacArthur was a genius at deflecting blame; to hear him say it, in his long career he had never lost a battle, although in fact he had lost many. But by trumpeting his successes and finding endless excuses, such as betrayals, for his losses, he created the myth of his magical battlefield powers. Grandiose leaders inevitably resort to such marketing magic.

Related to this is the belief that they can easily transfer their skills—a movie executive can become a theme park designer, a businessman can become the leader of a nation. Because they are magically gifted, they can try their hand at anything that attracts them. This is often a fatal move on their part, as they attempt things beyond their expertise and quickly become overwhelmed with the complexity and chaos that come from their lack of experience. In dealing with such types, look carefully at their record and notice how many glaring failures they have had. Although people under the influence of their grandiosity will probably not listen, publicize the truth of their record in as neutral a manner as possible.

I'm invulnerable. The grandiose leader takes risks. This is what often attracts attention in the first place, and combined with the success that often attends the bold, they seem larger than life. But this boldness is not really under control. They must take actions that create a splash in order to keep the attention coming that feeds their high self-opinion. They cannot rest or retreat, because that would cause a lapse in publicity. To make things worse, they come to feel invulnerable because so many times in the past they have gotten away with risky maneuvers, and if they faced setbacks, they managed to overcome them through more audacity. Furthermore, these daring activities make them feel alive and on edge. It becomes a drug. They need bigger stakes and rewards to maintain the feeling of godlike invulnerability. They can work twenty hours a day when under this form of pressure. They can walk through fire.

In fact they *are* rather invulnerable, until that fatal hubristic maneuver in which they finally go too far and it all crashes down. This could be MacArthur's grandiose tour of the United States after the Korean War, in which his irrational need for attention became painfully apparent; or Mao's fatal decision to unleash the Cultural Revolution; or Stan O'Neal, CEO of Merrill Lynch, sticking with mortgage-backed securities when everyone else was getting out, essentially destroying one of the oldest financial institutions in the country. Suddenly the aura of being invulnerable is shattered. This occurs because their decisions are determined not by rational considerations but by the need for attention and glory, and eventually reality catches up, in one hard blow.

In general, in dealing with the grandiose leader, you want to try to deflate the sacred, glorious image they have forged. They will overreact and their followers will become rabid, but slowly a few followers may have second thoughts. Creating a viral disenchantment is your best hope.

Practical Grandiosity

Grandiosity is a form of primal energy we all possess. It impels us to want something more than we have, to be recognized and esteemed by others, and to feel connected to something larger. The problem is not with the energy itself, which can be used to fuel our ambitions, but with the direction it takes. Normally grandiosity makes us imagine we are greater and more superior than is actually the case. We can call this *fantastical grandiosity* because it is based on our fantasies and the skewed impression we get from any attention we receive. The other form, which we shall call *practical grandiosity*, is not easy to achieve and does not come naturally to us, but it can be the source of tremendous power and self-fulfillment.

Practical grandiosity is based not on fantasy but on reality. The energy is channeled into our work and our desire to reach goals, to solve problems, or to improve relationships. It impels us to develop and hone our skills. Through our accomplishments we can feel greater. We attract attention through our work. The attention we receive in this way is gratifying and keeps us energized, but the greater sense of gratification comes from the work itself and from overcoming our own weaknesses. The desire for attention is under control and subordinate.

Our self-esteem is raised, but it is tied to real achievements, not to nebulous, subjective fantasies. We feel our presence enlarged through our work, through what we contribute to society.

Although the precise way to channel the energy will depend on your field and skill level, the following are five basic principles that are essential for attaining the high level of fulfillment that can come from this reality-based form of grandiosity.

Come to terms with your grandiose needs. You need to begin from a position of honesty. You must admit to yourself that you do want to feel important and be the center of attention. This is natural. Yes, you want to feel superior. You have ambitions like everyone else. In the past, your grandiose needs may have led you into some bad decisions, which you can now acknowledge and analyze. Denial is your worst enemy. Only with this self-awareness can you begin to transform the energy into something practical and productive.

Concentrate the energy. Fantastical grandiosity will make you flit from one fantastic idea to another, imagining all the accolades and attention you'll receive but never realizing any of them. You must do the opposite. You want to get into the habit of focusing deeply and completely on a single project or problem. You want the goal to be relatively simple to reach, and within a time frame of months and not years. You will want to break this down into mini steps and goals along the way. Your objective here is to enter a state of flow, in which your mind becomes increasingly absorbed in the work, to the point at which ideas come to you at odd hours. This feeling of flow should be pleasurable and addicting. You don't allow yourself to engage in fantasies about other projects on the horizon. You want to absorb yourself in the work as deeply as possible. If you do not enter this state of flow, you are inevitably multitasking and stopping the focus. Work on overcoming this.

This could be a project you work on outside your job. It is not the number of hours you put in but the intensity and consistent effort you bring to it.

Related to this, you want this project to involve skills you already have or are in the process of developing. Your goal is to see continual improvement in your skill level, which will certainly come from the depth of your focus. Your confidence will rise. That should be enough to keep you advancing.

Maintain a dialogue with reality. Your project begins with an idea, and as you try to hone this idea, you let your imagination take flight, being open to various possibilities. At some point you move from the planning phase to execution. Now you must actively search for feedback and criticism from people you respect or from your natural audience. You want to hear about the flaws and inadequacies in your plan, for that is the only way to improve your skills. If the project fails to have the results you imagined, or the problem is not solved, embrace this as the best way to learn. Analyze what you did wrong in depth, being as brutal as possible.

Once you have feedback and have analyzed the results, you then return to this project or start a new one, letting your imagination loose again but incorporating what you have learned from the experience. You keep cycling endlessly through this process, noticing with excitement how you are improving by doing so. If you stay too long in the imagination phase, what you create will tend to be grandiose and detached from reality. If you only listen to feedback and try to make the work a complete reflection of what others tell you or want, the work will be conventional and flat. By maintaining a continual dialogue between reality (feedback) and your imagination, you will create something practical and powerful.

If you have any success with your projects, that is when you must step back from the attention you are receiving. Look at the role that luck may have played, or the help you received from others. Resist falling for the success delusion. As you now focus on the next idea, see yourself back at square one. Each new project represents a new challenge and a fresh approach. You might very well fail. You need the same level of focus as you had on the last project. Never rest on your laurels or let up in your intensity.

Seek out calibrated challenges. The problem with fantastical grandiosity is that you imagine some great new goal you will achieve—that brilliant novel you will write, that lucrative start-up you will create. The challenge is so great that you may start, but you will soon peter out as you realize you are not up to it. Or if you are the ambitious, assertive type, you might try to go all the way, but you will end up in the Euro Disney syndrome, overwhelmed, failing in a large fashion, blaming others for the fiasco, and never learning from the experience.

Your goal with practical grandiosity is to continually look for challenges just above your skill level. If the projects you attempt are below or at your skill level, you will become easily bored and less focused. If they are too ambitious, you will feel crushed by your failure. However, if they are calibrated to be more challenging than the last project, but to a moderate degree, you will find yourself excited and energized. You must be up to this challenge so your focus levels will rise as well. This is the optimum path toward learning. If you fail, you will not feel overwhelmed and you will learn even more. If you succeed, your confidence increases, but it is tied to your work and to having met the challenge. Your sense of accomplishment will satisfy your need for greatness.

Let loose your grandiose energy. Once you have tamed this energy, made it serve your ambitions and goals, you should feel safe to let it loose upon occasion. Think of it as a wild animal that needs to roam free now and then or it will go mad from restlessness. What this means is that you occasionally allow yourself to entertain ideas or projects that represent greater challenges than you have considered in the past. You feel increasingly confident and you want to test yourself. Consider developing a new skill in an unrelated field, or writing that novel you once considered a distraction from the real work. Or simply give freer rein to your imagination when in the planning process.

If you are in the public eye and must perform before others, let go of the restraint you have developed and let your grandiose energy fill you with high levels of self-belief. This will animate your gestures and give you greater charisma. If you are a leader and your group is facing difficulties or a crisis, let yourself feel unusually grandiose and confident in the success of your mission, to lift up and inspire the troops. That was the kind of grandiosity that made Winston Churchill such an effective leader during World War II.

In any event, you can allow yourself to feel ever so godlike because you have come so far with your improved skills and actual achievements. If you have taken the time to properly work through the other principles, you will naturally return back down to earth after a few days or hours of grandiose exuberance.

FINALLY, AT THE SOURCE OF OUR INFANTILE GRANDIOSITY WAS A FEELING OF INTENSE connection to the mother. This was so complete and satisfying that we spend much of our time trying to recapture that feeling in some way. It is the source of our desire to transcend our banal existence, to want something so large we cannot express what it is. We have glimmers of that original connection in intimate relationships and in moments of unconditional love, but these are rare and fleeting. Entering a state of flow with our work or cultivating deeper levels of empathy with people (see chapter 2) will give us more such moments and satisfy the urge. We feel oneness with the work or with other people. We can take this even further by experiencing a deeper connection to life itself, what Sigmund Freud called "the oceanic feeling."

Consider this in the following way: The formation of life itself on the planet

Earth so many billions of years ago required a concatenation of events that were highly improbable. The beginning of life was a tenuous experiment that could have expired at any moment early on. The evolution since then of so many forms of life is astounding, and at the end point of that evolution is the only animal we know to be conscious of this entire process, the human.

Your being alive is an equally unlikely and uncanny event. It required a very particular chain of events leading to the meeting of your parents and your birth, all of which could have gone very differently. At this moment, as you read this, you are conscious of life along with billions of others, and only for a brief time, until you die. Fully taking in this reality is what we shall call the Sublime. (For more on this, see chapter 18.) It cannot be put into words. It is too awesome. Feeling a part of that tenuous experiment of life is a kind of reverse grandiosity—you are not disturbed by your relative smallness but rather ecstatic at the sense of being a drop in this ocean.

> Then, overwhelmed by the afflictions I suffered in connection with my sons, I sent again and inquired of the god what I should do to pass the rest of my life most happily; and he answered me: "Knowing thyself, O Croesus—thus shall you live and be happy." . . . [But] spoiled by the wealth I had and by those who were begging me to become their leader, by the gifts they gave me and by the people who flattered me, saying that if I would consent to take command they would all obey me and I should be the greatest of men—puffed up by such words, when all the princes round about chose me to be their leader in the war, I accepted the command, deeming myself fit to be the greatest; but, as it seems, I did not know myself. For I thought I was capable of carrying on war against you; but I was no match for you. . . . Therefore, as I was thus without knowledge, I have my just deserts.
>
> —*Xenophon*, The Education of Cyrus

12

Reconnect to the Masculine or Feminine Within You

---⬦---

The Law of Gender Rigidity

All of us have masculine and feminine qualities—some of this is genetic, and some of it comes from the profound influence of the parent of the opposite sex. But in the need to present a consistent identity in society, we tend to repress these qualities, overidentifying with the masculine or feminine role expected of us. And we pay a price for this. We lose valuable dimensions to our character. Our thinking and ways of acting become rigid. Our relationships with members of the opposite sex suffer as we project onto them our own fantasies and hostilities. You must become aware of these lost masculine or feminine traits and slowly reconnect to them, unleashing creative powers in the process. You will become more fluid in your thinking. In bringing out the masculine or feminine undertone to your character, you will fascinate people by being authentically yourself. Do not play the expected gender role, but rather create the one that suits you.

The Authentic Gender

As a young girl, Caterina Sforza dreamed of great deeds that she would be a part of as a member of the illustrious Sforza family of Milan. Born in 1463, Caterina was the daughter out of wedlock of a beautiful Milanese noblewoman and Galeazzo Maria Sforza, who became Duke of Milan upon the death of his father in 1466. As duke, Galeazzo ordered that his daughter be brought into the castle, Porta Giovia, where he lived with his new wife, and that she be raised like any legitimate member of the Sforza family. His wife, Caterina's step-mother, treated her as one of her own. The girl was to have the finest education.

The man who had served as Galeazzo's tutor, the famous humanist Francesco Filelfo, would now serve as Caterina's tutor. He taught her Latin, Greek, philosophy, the sciences, and even military history.

Often alone, Caterina would wander almost daily into the vast castle library, one of the largest in Europe. She had her favorite books that she would read over and over. One of these was a history of the Sforza family, written by Filelfo himself in the style of Homer. There, in this enormous volume with its elaborate illustrations, she would read about the remarkable rise to power of the Sforza family, from *condottiere* (captains in mercenary armies) to ruling the duchy of Milan itself. The Sforzas were renowned for their cleverness and bravery in battle. Along with this, she loved to read books that recounted the chivalric tales of real-life knights in armor, and the stories of great leaders in the past; among these, one of her favorites was *Illustrious Women* by Boccaccio, which related the deeds of the most celebrated women in history. And as she whiled away her time in the library, all of these books converging in her mind, she would daydream about the future glory of the family, somehow herself in the midst of it all. And at the center of these fantasies was the image of her father, a man who to her was as great and legendary as anyone she had read about.

Although the encounters with her father were often brief, to Caterina they were intense. He treated her as an equal, marveling at her intelligence and encouraging her in her studies. From early on, she identified with her father—experiencing his traumas and triumphs as if they were her own. As were all the Sforza children, girls included, Caterina was taught sword fighting and underwent rigorous physical training. As part of this side of her education, she would go on hunting expeditions with the family in the nearby woods of Pavia. She was trained to hunt and kill wild boars, stags, and other animals. On these excursions she would watch her father with awe. He was a superior horseman, riding with such impetuosity, as if nothing could harm him. In the hunt, taking on the largest animals, he showed no signs of fear. At court, he was the consummate diplomat yet always maintained the upper hand. He confided in her his methods—think ahead, plot several moves in advance, always with the goal of seizing the initiative in any situation.

There was another side to her father, however, that deepened her identification with him. He loved spectacle; he was like an artist. She would never forget the time the family toured the region and visited Florence. They brought with them various theater troupes, the actors wearing outlandish costumes. They dined in the country inside the most beautifully colored tents. On the march, the brightly caparisoned horses and the accompanying soldiers—all decked in the Sforza colors, scarlet and white—would fill the landscape. It was a hypnotic and thrilling sight, all orchestrated by her father. He delighted in always wearing the latest in Milanese fashions, with his elaborate and bejeweled silk gowns. She came to share this interest, clothes and jewels becoming her passion. He might seem so virile in battle, but she would see him crying like a baby as he listened to his favorite choral music. He had an endless appetite for all aspects of life, and her love and admiration for him knew no bounds.

And so in 1473, when her father informed the ten-year-old Caterina of the marriage he had arranged for her, her only thought was to fulfill her duty as a Sforza and please her father. The man Galeazzo had chosen for her was Girolamo Riario, the thirty-year-old nephew of Pope Sixtus IV, a marriage that would forge a valuable alliance between Rome and Milan. As part of the arrangement, the pope purchased the city of Imola, in Romagna, which the Sforzas had taken decades before, christening the new couple the Count and Countess of Imola. Later the pope would add the nearby town of Forlì to their possessions, giving them control of a very strategically located part of northeastern Italy, just south of Venice.

In her initial encounters with him, Caterina's husband seemed a most unpleasant man. He was moody, self-absorbed, and high-strung. He appeared interested in her only for sex and could not wait for her to come of age. Fortunately, he continued to live in Rome and she stayed in Milan. But a few years later some disgruntled noblemen in Milan murdered her beloved father, and the power of the Sforzas seemed in jeopardy. Her position as the marriage pawn solidifying the partnership with Rome was now more important than ever. She quickly installed herself in Rome. There she would have to play the exemplary wife and keep on the good side of her husband. But the more she saw of Girolamo, the less she respected him. He was a hothead, making enemies wherever he turned. She had not imagined that a man could be so weak, and compared with her father he failed by every measure.

She turned her attention to the pope. She worked hard to gain his favor and that of his courtiers. Caterina was now a beautiful young woman with blond hair, a novelty in Rome. She ordered the most elaborate gowns to be sent from Milan. She made sure to never be seen wearing the same outfit twice. If she sported a turban with a long veil, it suddenly became the latest craze. She reveled in the attention she received as the most fashionable woman in Rome,

Botticelli using her as a model for some of his greatest paintings. Being so well read and cultivated, she was the delight of the artists and writers in town, and the Romans began to warm up to her.

Within a few years, however, everything unraveled. Her husband instigated a feud with one of the leading families in Italy, the Colonnas. Then in 1484 the pope suddenly died, and without his protection Caterina and her husband were in grave danger. The Colonnas were plotting their revenge. The Romans hated Girolamo. And it was almost a certainty that the new pope would be a friend of the Colonnas, in which case Caterina and her husband would lose everything, including the towns of Forlì and Imola. Considering the weak position of her own family in Milan, the situation began to look desperate.

Until a new pope was elected, Girolamo was still the captain of the papal armies, now stationed just outside Rome. For days Caterina watched her husband, who was paralyzed with fear and unable to make a decision. He dared not enter Rome, fearing battle with the Colonnas and their many allies in the crowded streets. He would wait it out, but with time their options seemed to narrow, and the news kept getting worse—mobs had sacked the palace they lived in; what few allies they had in Rome had now deserted them; the cardinals were congregating to elect the new pope.

It was August and the sweltering heat made Caterina—seven months pregnant with her fourth child—feel faint and continually nauseated. But as she contemplated the impending doom, the thought of her father began to occupy her mind; it was as if she could feel his spirit inhabiting her. Thinking as he would think about the predicament she faced, she felt a rush of excitement as she formulated an audacious plan. Without telling a soul of her intentions, in the dark of night she mounted a horse and snuck out of camp, riding as fast as she could to Rome.

As she had expected, in her condition no one recognized her and she was allowed to enter the city. She headed straight for the Castel Sant'Angelo, the most strategic point in Rome—just across the Tiber River from the city center and close to the Vatican. With its impregnable walls and its cannons that could be aimed at all parts of Rome, the person who controlled the castle controlled the city. Rome was in tumult, mobs filling the streets everywhere. The castle was still held by a lieutenant loyal to Girolamo. Identifying herself, Caterina was let into Sant'Angelo.

Once inside, in the name of her husband she took possession of the castle, throwing out the lieutenant, whom she did not trust. Sending word out through the castle to soldiers who swore loyalty to her, she managed to smuggle in more troops. With the cannons of Sant'Angelo now pointing at all roads leading to the Vatican, she made it impossible for the cardinals to meet in one location and elect the new pope. To make her threats real, she had her soldiers fire the cannons as a warning. She meant business. Her terms for surrendering the castle were simple—that all of the property of the Riarios be guaranteed to remain in their hands, including Forlì and Imola.

A few evenings after she had taken over Sant'Angelo, wearing some armor over her gown, she marched along the ramparts of the castle. It gave her a feeling of great power, so far above the city, looking down at the frantic men below, helpless to fight against her, a single woman hobbled by pregnancy. When an envoy of the cardinal who was organizing the conclave to elect the new pope was sent to negotiate with her and seemed reluctant to agree to her conditions of surrender, she shouted down from the ramparts, so all could hear, "So [the cardinal] wants a battle of wits with me, does he? What he doesn't understand is that I have the brains of Duke Galeazzo and I am as brilliant as he!"

As she waited for their response, she knew she controlled the situation. Her only fear was that her husband would surrender and betray her, or that the August heat would make her too ill to wait it out. Finally, sensing her resolve, a group of cardinals came to the castle to negotiate, and they acceded to her demands. The following morning, as the drawbridge was lowered to let the countess leave the castle, she noticed an enormous crowd pushing close to her. Romans of all classes had come to catch a glimpse of the woman who had controlled Rome for eleven days. They had taken the countess for a rather frivolous young woman addicted to clothes, the pope's little pet. Now they stared at her in astonishment— she was wearing one of her silk gowns, with a heavy sword dangling from a man's belt, her pregnancy more than evident. They had never seen such a sight.

Their titles now secure, the count and countess moved to Forlì to rule their domain. With no more funds coming from the papacy, Girolamo's main concern was how to get more money. And so he increased the taxes on his subjects, stirring up much discontent in the process. He quickly made enemies of the powerful Orsi family in the region. Fearing plots against his life, the count holed himself up in their palace. Slowly Caterina took over much of the day-to-day ruling of their realm. Thinking ahead, she installed a trusted ally as the new commander of the castle Ravaldino, which dominated the area. She did everything she could to ingratiate herself with the locals, but in a few short years her husband had done too much damage.

On April 14, 1488, a group of men, clad in armor and led by Ludovico Orsi, stormed into the palace and stabbed the count to death, throwing his body out the window and into the city square. The countess, dining with her family in a nearby room, heard the shouts and quickly shuffled her six children into a safer room in the palace's tower. She bolted the door and from a window, under which several of her most trusted allies had gathered, she shouted instructions to them: they were to notify the Sforzas in Milan and her other allies in the region and urge them to send armies to rescue her; under no circumstances should the keeper of Ravaldino ever surrender the castle. Within minutes the assassins had broken into her room, taking her and her children captive.

Several days later, Ludovico Orsi and his fellow conspirator Giacomo del Ronche marched Caterina up to Ravaldino—she was to order the castle's commander to surrender it to the assassins. As the commander she had installed, Tommaso Feo, looked down from the ramparts, Caterina seemed to fear for her life. Her voice breaking with emotion, she begged Feo to give up the fortress, but he refused.

As the two of them continued their dialogue, Ronche and Orsi sensed the countess and Feo were playing some sort of game, talking in code. Ronche had had enough of this. Pressing the sharp edge of his lance tight against her chest, he threatened to run her through unless she got Feo to surrender, and he gave her the sternest glare. Suddenly the countess's expression changed. She leaned further into the blade, her face inches from Ronche, and with a voice dripping with disdain, she told him, "Oh, Giacomo del Ronche, don't you try to frighten me. . . . You can hurt me, but you can't scare me, because I am the daughter of a man who knew no fear. Do what you want: you have killed my lord, you can certainly kill me. After all, I'm just a woman!" Confounded by her words and demeanor, Ronche and Orsi decided they had to find other means to pressure her.

Several days later Feo communicated with the assassins that he would indeed hand over the fortress, but only if the countess would pay him his back wages and sign a letter absolving him of any guilt for such surrender. Once again, Orsi and Ronche led her to the castle and watched her closely as she seemed to negotiate with Feo. Finally Feo insisted that the countess enter the fortress to sign the document. He feared the assassins were trying to trick him and he insisted she enter alone. Once the letter was signed, he would do as he had promised.

The conspirators, feeling they had no choice, granted his request but gave the countess a brief time frame to conclude the business. For a fleeting moment, just as she disappeared over the drawbridge into Ravaldino, she turned with a sneer and gave the Italian equivalent of "the finger" to Ronche and Orsi. The entire drama of the past few days had been planned and staged by her and Feo, with whom she had communicated through various messengers. She knew that the Milanese had sent an army to rescue her and she only had to play for time. A few hours later Feo stood on the ramparts and yelled down that he was holding the countess hostage and that was that.

The enraged assassins had had enough. The next day they returned to the castle with her six children and called Caterina to the ramparts. With daggers and spears pointed at them in the most menacing fashion, and with the children wailing and begging for mercy, they ordered Caterina to surrender the fortress or they would kill them all. Surely they had already proven they were more than willing to shed blood. She might be fearless and the daughter of a Sforza, but no mother could possibly watch her children die before her eyes. Caterina wasted no time. She shouted down: "Do it then, you fools! I am already pregnant with another child by Count Riario and I have the means to make more!" at which she lifted her skirts, as if to emphasize her meaning.

Caterina had foreseen the maneuver with the children and had calculated that the assassins were weak and indecisive—they should have killed her and her family on that first day, amid the mayhem. Now they would not dare to kill them in cold blood: the assassins knew that the Sforzas, on their way to Forlì, would take terrible revenge on them if they ever did such a deed. And if she surrendered now, she and her children would all be imprisoned, and some poison would find its way into their food. She didn't care what they thought of her as a mother. She had to keep stalling. To emphasize her resolve, after refusing to surrender, she had the cannons of the castle fire at the Orsi palace.

Ten days later a Milanese army arrived to rescue her, and the assassins scattered. The countess was quickly restored to power, the new pope himself confirming her rule as regent until her eldest son, Ottaviano, came of age. And as word of all that she had done—and what she had yelled down to the assassins from the ramparts of Ravaldino—spread throughout Italy, the legend of Caterina Sforza, the beautiful warrior countess of Forlì, began to take on a life of its own.

Within a year after the death of her husband, the countess had taken a lover, Giacomo Feo, the brother of the commander she had installed in Ravaldino. Giacomo was seven years younger than Caterina, and he was the polar opposite of Girolamo—handsome and virile, he had come from the lower classes, having served as the stable boy to the Riario family. Most important, he not only loved Caterina, he worshipped her and showered her with attention. The countess had spent her whole life mastering her emotions and subordinating her personal interests to practical matters. Suddenly feeling herself overwhelmed by Giacomo's affection, she lost her habitual self-control and fell hopelessly in love.

She made Giacomo the new commander of Ravaldino. As he now had to live in the castle, she built a palace for herself inside it and soon barely left its confines. Giacomo was decidedly insecure about his status. Caterina had him knighted, and in a secret ceremony they married. To allay his self-doubts, she increasingly handed over to him governing powers of Forlì and Imola, and began to retire from public affairs. She ignored the warnings of courtiers and diplomats that Giacomo was out for himself and was in over his head. She did not listen to her sons, who feared Giacomo had plans to get rid of them. In her eyes, her husband could do no wrong. Then one day in 1495, as she and Giacomo left the castle for a picnic, a group of assassins surrounded her husband and killed him before her eyes.

Caught off guard by this action, Caterina reacted with fury. She rounded up the conspirators and had them executed and their families imprisoned. In the months after this, she fell into a deep depression, even contemplating suicide. What had happened to her over the past few years? How had she lost her way and given up her power? What had happened to her girlhood dreams and the spirit of her father that was her own? Something had clouded her mind. She turned to religion and she returned to ruling her realm. Slowly she recovered.

Then one day she received a visit from Giovanni de' Medici, a thirty-year-old member of the famous family and one of Florence's leading businessmen. He had come to forge commercial ties between the cities. More than anyone else, he reminded her of her father. He was handsome, clever, extremely well read, and yet there was a softness to his character. Finally here was a man who was her equal in knowledge, power, and refinement. The admiration was mutual. Soon they were inseparable, and in 1498 they married, uniting two of the most illustrious families in Italy.

Now she could finally dream of creating a great regional power, but events beyond her control would spoil her plans. That same year Giovanni died from illness. And before she had time to grieve for him, she had to deal with the latest and most dangerous threat of all to her realm: The new pope, Alexander VI (formerly known as Roderigo Borgia), had his eye on Forlì. He wanted to extend the papal domains through conquest, his son Cesare Borgia serving as the commander of the papal forces. Forlì would be a key acquisition for the pope, and he began to maneuver to politically isolate Caterina from her allies.

To prepare for the imminent invasion, Caterina forged a new alliance with the Venetians and built an elaborate series of defenses within Ravaldino. The pope tried to pressure her to surrender her domain, making her all kinds of promises in return. She knew better than to trust a Borgia. But by the fall of 1499, it seemed that the end had finally come. The pope had allied himself with France, and Cesare Borgia had appeared in the region with an army of twelve thousand, fortified by the addition of two thousand experienced French soldiers. They quickly took Imola and easily entered the city of Forlì itself. All that remained was Ravaldino, which by late December was surrounded by Borgia's troops.

On December 26, Cesare Borgia himself rode up to the castle on his white horse, dressed all in black—quite a sight. As Caterina looked down from the ramparts and contemplated the scene, she thought of her father. It was the anniversary of his assassination. He represented everything she valued, and she would not disappoint him. She was the most like him of all his children. As he would have done, she had thought ahead—her plan was to play for time until her remaining allies could come to her defense. She had cleverly fortified Ravaldino in a way that would allow her to keep retreating behind barricades if the walls were breached. In the end, they would have to take the castle from her by force, and she was more than prepared to die in defense of it, sword in hand.

As she listened to Borgia address her, it was clear he had come to flatter and flirt—everyone knew his reputation as a devilish seducer, and many in Italy thought Caterina had rather loose morals. She listened and smiled, occasionally reminding him of her past deeds and her reputation as a Sforza—if he wanted her to surrender, he would have to do better. He persisted in his courtship and asked to parley with her personally.

She appeared to finally succumb to his charm; she was a woman, after all. She ordered the drawbridge to be lowered and started walking toward him. He continued to press his case, and she gave him certain looks and smiles that indicated she was falling under his spell. Now only inches away, he reached for her arm, and she playfully withdrew it. They should discuss matters in the castle, she said with a coy expression, and began to walk back, inviting him to follow. As he stepped onto the drawbridge to catch up with her, it began to rise, and he leaped back to the other side just in time. Enraged and embarrassed by the trick she had tried to play, he swore revenge.

During the next few days he unleashed a torrent of cannon fire at the castle walls, finally opening a breach. Borgia's troops flooded in, led by the more experienced French. It was now hand-to-hand combat, and at the front of her remaining troops was Caterina. The head of the French troops, Yves d'Allegre, stared at her in amazement as the beautiful countess—her ornamented cuirass over her dress—charged at his men from the front line, handling her sword deftly, without a trace of fear.

She and her men were about to withdraw further into the castle, hoping to prolong the battle for days, as she had planned, when one of her own soldiers grabbed her from behind and, his sword at her throat, marched her over to the other side. Borgia had put a price on her head, and the soldier had betrayed her for the reward. The siege was over, and Borgia himself took possession of his great prize. That night he raped her and kept her confined in his rooms, trying to make it seem to the world that the infamous warrior countess had willingly succumbed to his charms.

Even under duress she refused to sign away her domain, and so she was brought to Rome and soon thrown into the dreaded prison at Castel Sant'-Angelo. For one long year, in a small and windowless cell, she endured her loneliness and the endless tortures devised by the Borgias. Her health deteriorated and she seemed destined to die in prison, defiant to the end, but the chivalric French captain Yves d'Allegre had fallen under her spell. He persisted in demanding, in the name of the French king, to have her freed, and he finally succeeded, getting her safe passage to Florence.

In retirement from public life, Caterina began to receive letters from men from all parts of Europe. Some had seen her over the years; most had only heard of her. They obsessed over her story, confessed their love, and begged for some memento, some relic to worship. One man who had caught a glimpse of her when she had first come to Rome wrote to her, "If I sleep, it seems that I am with you; if I eat, I leave my food and talk to you. . . . You are engraved in my heart."

Weakened by her year in prison, the countess died in 1509.

Interpretation: In Caterina Sforza's time, the roles that a woman could play were severely restricted. Her primary role was to be the good mother and wife, but if unmarried, she could devote her life to religion, or in rare cases she could become a courtesan. It was as if a circle had been drawn around each and every woman, and she dared not explore beyond that circle. It was in a woman's earliest years and education that she internalized these restrictions. If she studied only a limited number of subjects and practiced only certain skills, she couldn't expand her role even if she wanted to. Knowledge was power.

Caterina stands out as a remarkable exception, and it was because she benefited from a unique confluence of circumstances. The Sforzas were new to power. They had discovered in their rise to the top that a strong and capable wife could be of great assistance. They developed the practice of training their daughters in hunting and sword fighting as a way to toughen them up and make them fearless—important qualities to have as marriage pawns. Caterina's father, however, took this further. Perhaps he saw in his daughter a female reflection of himself. Giving her his own tutor signaled some sort of identification he felt between them.

And so a unique experiment began in the castle at Porta Giovia. Isolated from the outside world and allowed a tremendous degree of freedom, Caterina could develop herself in any direction she desired. Intellectually she could explore all forms of knowledge. She could indulge herself in all of her natural interests—in her case, fashion and the arts. In her physical training, she could give free rein to her own bold and adventurous spirit. In this early education, she could bring out the many different sides of her character.

And so when she entered public life at the age of ten, she naturally drifted beyond that restricted circle imposed on women. She could play many roles. As a dutiful Sforza, she could be the loyal wife. Naturally empathetic and caring, she could be the devoted mother. She felt great pleasure in being the most fashionable and beautiful young woman at the papal court. But when the actions of her husband appeared to doom her and her family, she felt herself called to play another role. Trained to think for herself and inspired by her father, she could turn into the daring soldier, bringing an entire city under her control. She could become the keen strategist, plotting several moves ahead in a crisis. She could lead her troops, sword in hand. As a young girl she had fantasized about playing these various roles, and it felt natural and deeply satisfying to do so in real life.

We could say of Caterina that she had a feminine spirit with a pronounced masculine undertone, the reverse of her father. And these feminine and masculine traits were blended together, giving her a unique style of thinking and acting. When it came to ruling, she displayed a high degree of empathy, something quite unusual for the time. When plague struck Forlì, she comforted the sick, at great risk to her own life. She was willing to suffer the worst conditions in prison to safeguard the inheritance for her children, a rare act of self-sacrifice for a person of power. But at the same time she was a shrewd and tough negotiator, and she had no tolerance for the incompetent or the weak. She was ambitious and proud of it.

In conflicts, she always strategized to outwit her aggressive male opponents and avoid bloodshed. With Cesare Borgia, she tried to lure him onto the drawbridge using her feminine wiles; later, she tried to lure him deeper and deeper into the castle, trapping him in a protracted battle, giving her allies plenty of time to rescue her. She nearly succeeded in both efforts.

This ability to play many different roles, to blend the masculine with the feminine, was the source of her power. The only time she relinquished this was in her marriage to Giacomo Feo. When she fell in love with Feo, she was in a highly vulnerable position. The pressures on her had been immense—dealing with a hopeless and abusive husband, surviving the numerous pregnancies that had worn her down, holding together the tenuous political alliances she had built up. And so suddenly experiencing Feo's adoring attention, it was natural for her to seek a respite from her burdens, to relinquish power and control for love. But in narrowing herself down to the role of the devoted wife, she had to repress her naturally expansive character. She had to expend her energy in placating her husband's insecurities. In the process she lost all initiative and paid the price, experiencing a deep depression that nearly killed her. She learned her lesson and afterward would remain true to herself for the rest of her life.

Perhaps what is most surprising about the story of Caterina Sforza is the effect she had on the men and women of her time. We would expect that people would have condemned her as a witch or virago and shunned her for all her flouting of gender conventions. Instead, she fascinated almost everyone who came in contact with her. Women admired her strength. Isabella d'Este, the ruler of Mantua and her contemporary, found her inspiring and wrote after her capture by Borgia, "If the French criticize the cowardliness of our men, at least they should praise the daring and valor of the Italian woman." Men of all types—artists, soldiers, priests, nobility, servants—obsessed over her. Even those who wanted to destroy her, like Cesare Borgia, felt an initial attraction and the desire to possess her.

Men could talk battle and strategy with her and feel like they were talking to an equal, not like the other women in their lives, with whom they could barely converse. But more important, they sensed a freedom in her that was exciting. They also had to play a gender role, one that was not as constricting as a woman's role but had its disadvantages. They were expected to be always in control, tough and indomitable. Secretly they were drawn to this dangerous woman with whom they could lose control. She was not a feminine doll, all passive and existing only to please men. She was unrepressed and authentic, which inspired in them the desire to let go as well, to move past their own constricted roles.

Understand: You might like to imagine that much has changed when it comes to gender roles, that the world of Caterina Sforza is too distant from our own to be relevant. But in thinking so you would be greatly mistaken. The specific details of gender roles might fluctuate according to culture and time period, but the pattern is essentially the same and is as follows: We are all born as complete beings, with many sides to us. We have qualities of the opposite sex, both genetically and from the influence of the parent of the other gender. Our character has natural depths and dimensions to it. When it comes to boys, studies have shown that an early age they are actually more emotionally reactive than girls. They have high degrees of empathy and sensitivity. Girls have an adventurous and exploratory spirit that is natural to them. They have powerful wills, which they like to exert in transforming their environment.

As we get older, however, we have to present to the world a consistent identity. We have to play certain roles and live up to certain expectations. We have to trim and lop off natural qualities. Boys lose their rich range of emotions and, in the struggle to get ahead, repress their natural empathy. Girls have to sacrifice their assertive sides. They are supposed to be nice, smiling, deferential, always considering other people's feelings before their own. A woman can be a boss, but she must be tender and pliant, never too aggressive.

In this process, we become less and less dimensional; we conform to the expected roles of our culture and time period. We lose valuable and rich parts to our character. Sometimes we can realize this only when we encounter those who are less repressed and we feel fascination with them. Certainly Caterina Sforza had such an effect. There are also many male counterparts to this in history—the nineteenth-century British prime minister Benjamin Disraeli, Duke Ellington, John F. Kennedy, David Bowie, all men who displayed an unmistakable feminine undertone and intrigued people all the more for this.

Your task is to let go of the rigidity that takes hold of you as you overidentify with the expected gender role. Power lies in exploring that middle range between the masculine and the feminine, in playing against people's expectations. Return to the harder or softer sides of your character that you have lost or repressed. In relating to people, expand your repertoire by developing greater empathy, or by learning to be less deferential. When confronting a problem or resistance from others, train yourself to respond in different ways—attacking when you normally defend, or vice versa. In your thinking, learn to blend the analytical with the intuitive in order to become more creative (see the final section of this chapter for more on this).

Do not be afraid to bring out the more sensitive or ambitious sides to your character. These repressed parts of you are yearning to be let out. In the theater of life, expand the roles that you play. Don't worry about people's reactions to any changes in you they sense. You are not so easy to categorize, which will fascinate them and give you the power to play with their perceptions of you, altering them at will.

It is the terrible deception of love that it begins by engaging us in play not with a woman of the external world but with a doll fashioned in our brain—the only woman moreover that we have always at our disposal, the only one we shall ever possess.

—Marcel Proust

Keys to Human Nature

We humans like to believe that we are consistent and mature, and that we have reasonable control over our lives. We make decisions based on rational considerations, on what will benefit us the most. We have free will. We know who we are, more or less. But in one particular aspect of life these self-opinions are all easily shattered—when we fall in love.

When in love, we become prey to emotions we cannot control. We make choices of partners we cannot rationally explain, and often these choices end up being unfortunate. Many of us will have at least one successful relationship in our lives, but we will tend to have many more that were decidedly unsuccessful, that ended unhappily. And often we repeat the same types of bad choices of partners, as if compelled by some inner demon.

We like to tell ourselves in retrospect that when we were in love, a type of temporary madness overcame us. We think of such moments as representing the exception, not the rule, to our character. But let us entertain for the moment the opposite possibility—in our conscious day-to-day life, we are sleepwalking, unaware of who we really are; we present a front of reasonableness to the world, and we mistake the mask for reality. When we fall in love, we are actually being *more* ourselves. The mask slips off. We realize then how deeply unconscious forces determine many of our actions. We are more connected to the reality of the essential irrationality in our nature.

Let us look at some of the common changes that occur when we are in love.

Normally our minds are in a state of distraction. The deeper we fall in love, however, the more our attention is completely absorbed in one person. We become obsessive.

We like to present a particular appearance to the world, one that highlights our strengths. When in love, however, opposite traits often come to the fore. A person who is normally strong and independent can suddenly become rather helpless, dependent, and hysterical. A nurturing, empathetic person can suddenly become tyrannical, demanding, and self-absorbed.

As adults we feel relatively mature and practical, but in love we can suddenly regress to behavior that can only be seen as childish. We experience fears and insecurities that are greatly exaggerated. We feel terror at the thought of being abandoned, like a baby who has been left alone for a few minutes. We have wild mood swings—from love to hate, from trust to paranoia.

Normally we like to imagine that we are good judges of other people's character. Once infatuated or in love, however, we mistake the narcissist for a genius, the suffocator for a nurturer, the slacker for the exciting rebel, the control freak for the protector. Others can often see the truth and try to disabuse us of our fantasies, but we won't listen. And what is worse, we will often continue to make the same types of mistaken judgments again and again.

In looking at these altered states, we might be tempted to describe them as forms of possession. We are normally rational person A, but under the influence of an infatuation, irrational person B begins to emerge. At first, A and B can fluctuate and even blend into each other, but the deeper we fall in love, the more it is person B who dominates. Person B sees qualities in people that are not there, acts in ways that are counterproductive and even self-destructive, is quite immature, with unrealistic expectations, and makes decisions that are often mysterious later on to person A.

When it comes to our behavior in these situations, we never really completely understand what is happening. Too much of our unconscious is at play, and we have no rational access to its processes. But the eminent psychologist Carl Jung—who analyzed over the course of his very long career thousands of men and women with stories of painful love affairs—offered perhaps the most profound explanation for what happens to us when we fall in love. According to Jung, we *are* actually possessed in such moments. He gave the entity (person B) that takes hold of us the name *anima* (for the male) and *animus* (for the female). This entity exists in our unconscious but comes to the surface when a person of the opposite sex fascinates us. The following is the origin of the *anima* and the *animus*, and how they operate.

We all possess hormones and genes of the opposite sex. These *contrasexual* traits are in the minority (to a greater or lesser extent, depending on the individual), but they are within us all and they form a part of our character. Equally significant is the influence on our psyche of the parent of the opposite sex, from whom we absorb feminine or masculine traits.

In our earliest years we were completely open and susceptible to the influence of others. The parent of the opposite sex was our first encounter with someone dramatically different from us. As we related to their alien nature, much of our personality was formed in response, becoming more dimensional and multifaceted. (With the parent of the same sex there is often a level of comfort and immediate identification that does not require the same adaptive energy).

For instance, small boys are often comfortable expressing emotions and traits that they've learned from the mother, such as overt affection, empathy, and sensitivity. Small girls, conversely, are often comfortable expressing traits they've learned from the father, such as aggression, boldness, intellectual rigor, and physical prowess. Each child may also naturally possess these opposite-gender traits in him- or herself. In addition, each parent will also have a shadow side that the child must assimilate or deal with. For instance, a mother may be narcissistic rather than empathetic, and a father may be domineering or weak rather than protective and strong.

Children must adapt to this. In any event, the boy and the girl will internalize the positive and the negative qualities of the parent of the opposite sex in ways that are unconscious and profound. And the association with the parent of the opposite sex will be charged with all kinds of emotions—physical and sensual connections, tremendous feelings of excitement, fascination, or disappointment at what one was not given.

Soon, however, comes a critical period in our early lives in which we must separate from our parents and forge our identity. And the simplest and most powerful way to create this identity is around gender roles, the masculine and the feminine. The boy will tend to have an ambivalent relationship to his mother that will mark him for life. On the one hand he craves the security and adoring attention she gives him; on the other hand he feels threatened by her, as if she might suffocate him in her femininity and he would lose himself. He fears her authority and her power over his life. From a certain age forward, he feels the need to differentiate himself. He needs to establish his own sense of masculine identity. Certainly the physical changes that occur as he gets older will fuel this identity with the masculine, but in the process he will tend to overidentify with the role (unless he identifies with the feminine role instead), playing up his toughness and independence to emphasize his separation from the mother. The other sides to his character—the empathy, the gentleness, the need for connection, which he absorbed from the mother or were naturally a part of him—will tend to become repressed and sink into the unconscious.

The girl may have an adventurous spirit and may incorporate the willpower and determination of her father into her own personality. But as she gets older, she will most likely feel pressure to conform to certain cultural norms and to forge her identity around what is considered feminine. Girls are supposed to be nice, sweet, and deferential. They are supposed to put the interests of others before their own. They are supposed to tame any wild streaks, to look pretty and to be objects of desire. For the individual girl, these expectations turn into voices she hears in her head, continually judging her and making her doubt her self-worth. These pressures may be subtler in our day and age, but they still exert a powerful influence. The more exploratory, aggressive, and darker sides of her character—both naturally occurring and absorbed from the father— will tend to become repressed and sink into the unconscious, if she adopts a more traditionally feminine role.

The unconscious feminine part of the boy and the man is what Jung calls the *anima*. The unconscious masculine part of the girl and woman are the *animus*. Because they are parts of ourselves that are deeply buried, we are never really aware of them in our daily life. But once we become fascinated with a person of the opposite sex, the anima and animus stir to life. The attraction we feel toward another might be purely physical, but more often the person who draws our attention unconsciously bears some resemblance—physical or psychological—to our mother or father. Remember that this primal relationship is full of charged energy, excitement, and obsessions that are repressed but yearning to come out. A person who triggers these associations in us will be a magnet for our attention, even though we are not aware of the source of our attraction.

If the relationship to the mother or father was mostly positive, we will tend to project onto the other person the desirable qualities that our parent had, in the hope of reexperiencing that early paradise. Take, for instance, a young man whose mother nurtured and adored him. He may have been a sweet, loving little boy, devoted to his mother and reflecting her nurturing energy, but he repressed these traits in himself as he grew into an independent man with a masculine image to uphold. In the woman who triggers an association with his mother he will see the capacity to adore him that he secretly craves. This feeling of getting what he wants will intensify his excitement and physical attraction. She will supply him the qualities he never developed in himself. He is falling in love with his own anima, in the form of the desired woman.

If the feelings toward the mother or father were mostly ambivalent (their attention inconsistent), we will often try to fix the original relationship by falling in love with someone who reminds us of our imperfect parent figure, in the hope that we can subtract their negative qualities and get what we never quite got in our earliest years. If the relationship was mostly negative, we may go in search of someone with the opposite qualities to that parent, often of a dark, shadowy nature. For instance, a girl who had a father who was too strict, distant, and critical perhaps had the secret desire to rebel but didn't dare to. As a young woman she might be drawn to a rebellious, unconventional young man who represents the wild side she was never able to express, and is the polar opposite of her father. The rebel is her animus, now externalized in the form of the young man.

In any case, whether the association is positive, negative, or ambivalent, powerful emotions are triggered, and feeling ourselves transported to the primal relationship in our childhood, we act in ways that are often contrary to the persona we present. We become hysterical, needy, obsessive, controlling. The anima and animus have their own personalities, and so when they come to life we act like person B. Because we are not really relating to women and men as they are, but rather to our projections, we will eventually feel disappointed in them, as if they are to blame for not being what we had imagined. The relationship will often tend to fall apart from the misreading and miscommunications on both sides, and not aware of the source of this, we will go through precisely the same cycle with the next person.

There are infinite variations on these patterns, because everyone has very particular circumstances and mixes of the masculine and feminine. For instance, there are men who are more psychologically feminine than women and women who are more psychologically masculine than men. If they are heterosexual, the man will be drawn to masculine women who have the qualities he never developed in himself. He has more of an animus than an anima. The woman will be drawn to feminine men. There are many such contrasexual couples, some more overt than others, and they can be successful if both sides get what they want—a famous historical example would be the composer Frédéric Chopin and the writer George Sand, Sand being more like the husband and Chopin like the wife. If they are homosexual, the man or woman will still be in search of the contrasexual qualities undeveloped from within. In general, people are imbalanced, overidentifying with the masculine or feminine and drawn to the polar opposite.

Your task as a student of human nature is threefold: First you must try to observe the anima and the animus as they manifest themselves in others, particularly in their intimate relationships. By paying attention to their behavior and patterns in these situations, you will have access to their unconscious that is normally denied to you. You will see the parts of themselves they have repressed, and you can use such knowledge to great effect. Pay special attention to those who are hypermasculine or hyperfeminine. You can be sure that below the surface lurks a very feminine anima for the man and a very masculine animus for the woman. When people go extra far in repressing their feminine or masculine qualities, these will tend to leak out in a caricatured form.

The hypermasculine man, for instance, will be secretly obsessed with clothes and his looks. He will display an unusual interest in people's appearances, including other men, and make rather snippy judgments about them. Richard Nixon desperately tried to project a macho image to those who worked for him as president, but he was constantly commenting on and fussing over the color of the suits they wore and the drapes in his office. The hypermasculine man will express strong opinions about cars, technology, or politics that are not based on real knowledge, and when called on this, he will become rather hysterical in his defense, throw a tantrum, or pout. He is always trying to contain his emotions, but they can often have a life of their own. For instance, without wanting to, he will suddenly become quite sentimental.

The hyperfeminine woman will often be concealing a great deal of repressed anger and resentment at the role she has been forced to play. Her seductive, girlish behavior with men is actually a ploy for power, to tease, entrap, and hurt the target. Her masculine side will leak out in passive-aggressive behavior, attempts to dominate people in relationships in underhanded ways. Underneath the sweet, deferential façade, she can be quite willful and highly judgmental of others. Her willfulness, always under the surface, will come out in rather irrational stubbornness in petty matters.

Your second task is to become aware of the projecting mechanism within yourself. (See the next section for common types of projections.) Projections have a positive role to play in your life, and you could not stop them even if you wanted to, because they are so automatic and unconscious. Without them, you would not find yourself paying deep attention to a person, becoming fascinated with him or her, idealizing, and falling in love. But once the relationship develops, you need to have the power and awareness to withdraw the projections, so that you can begin to see women and men as they really are. In doing so, perhaps you will realize how truly incompatible you are, or the opposite. Once connected to the real person, you can continue to idealize him or her, but this will be based on actual positive qualities he or she possesses. Perhaps you can find his or her faults charming. You can accomplish all of this by becoming aware of your own patterns and the types of qualities you tend to project onto others.

This also has relevance to relationships with the opposite sex that are not intimate. Imagine that in an office situation a colleague criticizes your work or postpones a meeting you asked for. If that person happens to be of the opposite sex, all kinds of emotions—resentments, fears, disappointments, hostility—will be stirred up, along with various projections, whereas with someone of your own gender there would be much less of a reaction. Seeing this dynamic in everyday life, you will be better able to control it and have smoother relationships with those of the opposite sex.

Your third task is to look inward, to see those feminine or masculine qualities that are repressed and undeveloped within you. You will catch glimpses of your anima or animus in your relationships with the opposite sex. That assertiveness you desire to see in a man, or empathy in a woman, is something you need to develop within yourself, bringing out that feminine or masculine undertone. What you are doing in essence is integrating into your everyday personality the traits that are within you but are repressed. They will no longer operate independently and automatically, in the form of possession. They will become part of your everyday self, and people will be drawn to the authenticity they sense in you. (For more on this, see the final section of this chapter.)

FINALLY, WHEN IT COMES TO GENDER ROLES, WE LIKE TO IMAGINE A CONTINUAL LINE of progress leading to perfect equality, and to believe that we are not far from reaching this ideal. But this is hardly the truth. Although on one level we can see definite progress, on another level, one that is deeper, we can see increasing tension and polarization between the sexes, as if the old patterns of inequality between men and women exert an unconscious influence upon us.

This tension can sometimes feel like a war, and it stems from a growing psychological distance between the genders, in which people of the opposite sex seem like alien creatures, with habits and patterns of behavior we cannot begin to fathom. This distance can turn into hostility among some. Although we can see this in both men and women, the hostility is stronger among men. Perhaps this is related to the latent hostility many men feel toward the mother figure, and the feeling of dependency and weakness she unconsciously triggers. The male sense of masculinity often has a defensive edge that reveals underlying insecurities. Such insecurity has only become more acute with shifting gender roles, and it increases the suspiciousness and hostility between men and women.

This outer conflict between the genders, however, is merely a reflection of an unresolved inner conflict. As long as the inner feminine or masculine is denied, the outer distance will only grow. When we bridge this distance from within, our attitude toward the opposite sex changes as well. We feel a deeper connection. We can talk and relate to them as if relating to parts of ourselves. The polarity between the sexes still exists and still causes us to be attracted and fall in love, but now it includes the desire to get closer to the feminine or the masculine. This is much different from the polarization between the genders, in which distance and hostility eventually come to the fore in the relationship and push people further away. The inner connection will vastly improve the outer connection and should be the ideal we aim for.

Gender Projection—Types

Although there are infinite variations, below you will find six of the more common types of gender projections. You must use this knowledge in three ways:

First, you must recognize in yourself any tendency toward one of these forms of projection. This will help you understand something profound about your earliest years and make it much easier for you to withdraw your projections on other people. Second, you must use this as an invaluable tool for gaining access to the unconscious of other people, to seeing their anima and animus in action.

And finally, you must be attentive to how others will project onto you their needs and fantasies. Keep in mind that when you are the target of other people's projections, the temptation is to want to live up to their idealization of you, to be their fantasy. You get caught up in their excitement and you want to believe you are as great, strong, or empathetic as they imagine. Without realizing it, you begin to play the role they want you to play. You become the mother or father figure they crave. Inevitably, however, you will come to resent this— you cannot be yourself; you are not appreciated for your true qualities. Better to be aware of this dynamic before it entraps you.

The Devilish Romantic: For the woman in this scenario, the man who fascinates her—often older and successful—might seem like a rake, the type who cannot help but chase after young women. But he is also romantic. When he's in love, he showers the woman with attention. She decides she will seduce him and become the target of his attention. She will play to his fantasies. How can he not want to settle down with her and reform himself? She will bask in his love. But somehow he is not as strong, masculine, or romantic as she had imagined. He is a bit self-absorbed. She does not get the desired attention, or it does not last very long. He cannot be reformed, and leaves her.

This is often the projection of women who had rather intense, even flirtatious relationships with the father. Such fathers often find their wives boring, and the young daughter more charming and playful. They turn to the daughter for inspiration; the daughter becomes addicted to their attention and adept at playing the kind of girl that daddy wants. It gives her a sense of power. It becomes her lifelong goal to recapture this attention and the power that goes with it. Any association with the father figure will spark the projecting mechanism, and she will invent or exaggerate the man's romantic nature.

A prime example of this type would be Jacqueline Kennedy Onassis. Jack Bouvier, her father, adored his two daughters, but Jacqueline was his favorite. Jack was devilishly handsome and dashing. He was a narcissist obsessed with his body and the fine clothes that he wore. He considered himself macho, a real risk taker, but underneath the façade he was in fact quite feminine in his tastes and totally immature. He was also a notorious womanizer. He treated Jackie more like a playmate and lover than a daughter. For Jackie, he could do no wrong. She took perverse pride in his popularity with women. In the frequent fights between her mother and father, she always took his side. Compared to the fun-loving father, the mother was prudish and rigid.

Spending so much time in his company, even after her parents divorced, and thinking of him constantly, Jackie deeply absorbed his energy and spirit. As a young woman, she turned all of her attention to older, powerful, and unconventional men, with whom she could re-create the role she had played with her father—always the little girl in need of his love, but also quite flirtatious. And she was continually disappointed in the men she had chosen. John F. Kennedy was the closest to her ideal, for in so many ways he was just like her father in looks and in spirit. Kennedy, however, would never give her the attention she craved. He was too self-absorbed. He was too busy having affairs with other women. He was not really the romantic type. She was continually frustrated in this relationship, but she was trapped in this pattern, later marrying Aristotle Onassis, an older, unconventional man of great power who seemed so dashing and romantic but who would treat her horribly and cheat on her continually.

Women in this scenario have become trapped by the early attention paid to them by the father. They have to be continually charming, inspiring, and flirtatious to elicit that attention later on. Their animus is seductive, but with an aggressive, masculine edge, having absorbed so much of the father's energy. But they are in a continual search for a man who does not exist. If the man were completely attentive and tirelessly romantic, they would grow bored with him. He would be seen as too weak. They are secretly drawn to the devilish side of their fantasy man and to the narcissism that comes with it. Women trapped in this projection will grow resentful over the years about how much energy they have to expend playing to men's fantasies and how little they get in return. The only way out of the trap for such women is to see the pattern itself, to stop mythologizing the father, and to focus instead on the damage he has caused by the inappropriate attention he paid to them.

The Elusive Woman of Perfection: He thinks he has found the ideal woman. She will give him what he's been missing in his prior relationships, whether that's some wildness, some comfort and compassion, or a creative spark. Although he has had few actual encounters with the woman in question, he can imagine all kinds of positive experiences with her. The more he thinks of her, the more he's certain he cannot live without her. When he talks of this perfect woman, you will notice there's not a lot of concrete detail about what makes her so perfect. If he does manage to forge a relationship, he will quickly become disenchanted. She's not who he thought she was; she misled him. He then moves on to the next woman to project his fantasy onto.

This is a common form of male projection. It contains all of the elements he thinks he never got from his mother, never got from the other women in his life. This ideal mate will haunt his dreams. She will not appear to him in the form of someone he knows; she is a woman fashioned in his imagination—often young, elusive, but promising something great. In real life, certain types of women will tend to trigger this projection. She is usually quite hard to pin down and conforms to what Freud called the narcissistic woman—self-contained, not really needing a man or anybody to complete her. She can be a bit cold at the core and a blank screen upon which men can project whatever they want. Alternatively, she can seem to be a free spirit, full of creative energy but without a clear sense of her own identity. For men she serves as a muse, a great spark to their imagination, a lure to loosen up their own rigid mind.

The men prone to this projection often had mothers who were not totally there for them. Perhaps such a mother expected the son to give *her* the attention and validation she was not getting from her husband. Because of this reversal, when the boy becomes a man, he feels a great emptiness inside that he constantly needs to fill. He cannot exactly verbalize what he wants or what he missed, hence the vagueness of his fantasy. He will spend his life searching for this elusive figure and never settle on a flesh-and-blood female. It's always the next one who will be perfect. If he falls for the narcissistic type, he will repeat the problem he experienced with his mother, falling for a woman who cannot give him what he wants. His own anima is a bit dreamy, introspective, and moody, which is the behavior he will tend to exhibit when in love.

Men of this type must recognize the nature of their pattern. What they really need is to find and interact with a real woman, accept her inevitable flaws, and give more of themselves. They often prefer to chase their fantasy, because in such a scenario they are in control and have the freedom to leave when reality sets in. To break the pattern, such men will have to give up some of this control. When it comes to their need for a muse, they must learn to find such inspiration from within, to bring out more of the anima within themselves. They are too alienated from their own feminine spirit and need to loosen up their own thought processes. Not needing this wildness from their fantasy woman, they will better relate to the actual women in their life.

The Lovable Rebel: For the woman who is drawn to this type, the man who intrigues her has a noticeable disdain for authority. He is a nonconformist. Unlike the Devilish Romantic, this man will often be young and not so successful. He will also tend to be outside her usual circle of acquaintances. To have a relationship with him would be ever so slightly taboo—certainly her father would not approve, and perhaps not her friends or colleagues. If a relationship does ensue, however, she will see a totally different side to him. He can't hold down a good job, not because he's a rebel but because he's lazy and ineffectual. Despite the tattoos and shaved head, he's quite conventional, controlling, and domineering. The relationship will break apart, but the fantasy will remain.

The woman with this projection often had a strong, patriarchal father who was distant and strict. The father represents order, rules, and conventions. He was often quite critical of his daughter—she was never good or pretty or smart enough. She internalized this critical voice and hears it in her head all the time. As a girl she dreamed of rebelling and asserting herself against the father's control, but too often she was reduced to obeying and playing the deferential daughter. Her desire to rebel was repressed and went into her animus, which is quite angry and resentful. Instead of developing the rebelliousness herself, she looks to externalize it in the form of the rebellious male. If she senses a man might be like this, based on his appearance, she will project fantasies that are charged and sexual. Oftentimes she chooses a man who is relatively young because this makes him less threatening, less of a patriarch. But his youth and immaturity make it almost impossible to form a stable relationship, and her angry side will come out as she grows disenchanted.

Once a woman recognizes she is prone to this projection, she must come to terms with a simple fact: what she really wants is to develop the independence, assertiveness, and power to disobey in herself. It is never too late to do so, but these qualities must be built up and developed in small steps, everyday challenges in which she practices saying no, breaking some rules, et cetera. Becoming more assertive, she can begin to have relationships that are more equal and satisfying.

The Fallen Woman: To the man in question, the woman who fascinates him seems so different from those he has known. Perhaps she comes from a different culture or social class. Perhaps she is not as educated as he is. There might be something dubious about her character and her past; she is certainly less physically restrained than most women. He thinks she's earthy. She seems to be in need of protection, education, and money. He will be the one to rescue and elevate her. But somehow the closer he gets to her, the less it turns out as he had expected.

In *Swann's Way*, volume 1 of the novel *In Search of Lost Time* by Marcel Proust, the protagonist, Charles Swann—based on a real person—is an aesthete, a connoisseur of art. He is also a Don Juan who is deathly afraid of any relationship or form of commitment. He has seduced many women of his class. But then he meets a woman named Odette, who is from a decidedly different social circle. She is uneducated, a bit vulgar, and some would say she is a courtesan. She intrigues him. Then one day, while staring at a reproduction of a biblical scene from a Botticelli fresco, he decides she resembles a woman in the painting. Now he is fascinated and begins to idealize her. Odette must have had a hard life, and she deserves better. Despite his fear of commitment, he will marry her and educate her in the finer things of life. What he doesn't realize is that she does not at all resemble the woman he fantasizes about. She is extremely clever and strong willed, much stronger than he is. She will end up making him her passive slave, as she continues to have affairs with other men and women.

Men of this type often had strong mother figures in their childhood. They became good, obedient boys, excellent students at school. Consciously they are attracted to well-educated women, to those who seem good and perfect. But unconsciously they are drawn to women who are imperfect, bad, of dubious character. They secretly crave what is the opposite of themselves. It is the classic split of the mother/whore—they want the mother figure for a wife but feel a much stronger physical attraction to the whore, the Fallen Woman, the type who likes to display her body. They have repressed the playful, sensual, and earthy sides of the character they had as boys. They are too rigid and civilized. The only way they can relate to these qualities is through women who appear to be so different from themselves. Like Swann, they find a way to idealize them with some highbrow reference that has no relation to reality. They project onto such women weakness and vulnerability. They tell themselves they want to help and protect them. But what really attracts them is the danger and naughty pleasures these women seem to promise. Underestimating the strength of such women, they often end up as their pawns. Their anima is passive and masochistic.

Men who engage in this kind of projection need to develop the less conventional sides of their character. They need to move outside their comfort zone and try new experiences on their own. They require more challenges, and even a bit of danger that will help loosen them up. Perhaps they need to take more risks at work. They also need to develop the more physical and sensual side of their character. Not having to get what they crave by looking for the Fallen Woman type, they can actually begin to satisfy their urges with any type of woman, not passively waiting for her to lead them astray but actively initiating the guilty pleasures.

The Superior Man: He seems brilliant, skilled, strong, and stable. He radiates confidence and power. He could be a high-powered businessman, a professor, an artist, a guru. Even though he may be older and not so physically attractive, his self-assurance gives him an attractive aura. For the woman attracted to this type, a relationship with him would give her an indirect feeling of strength and superiority.

In the novel *Middlemarch* (1872) by George Eliot, the main character, Dorothea Brooke, is a nineteen-year-old orphan raised by her wealthy uncle. Dorothea is quite beautiful and would be a desirable match for marriage. In fact, a local young man named Sir James Chettam is actively courting her. But one evening she meets the much older Edward Causabon, a wealthy landowner who has devoted his life to scholarly pursuits, and he intrigues her. She starts to pay him attention and he courts her, much to the horror of her sister and uncle. To them he is ugly, with moles on his face and a sallow complexion. He slurps his food and talks very little. But to Dorothea his face is full of a spiritual quality. He is too above people to care about etiquette. He talks little because no one would understand him. Being married to him would be like being married to Pascal or Kant. She'll learn Greek and Latin and help him complete his great masterpiece, *The Key to All Mythologies*. And he will help educate and elevate her. He will be the father she has been unconsciously missing. Only after being married to him does she discover the truth—he's dead inside, and very controlling. He sees her as a glorified secretary. She becomes trapped in a loveless marriage.

Although the relationship details might be quite different now, this type of projection is all too common among women. It stems from feelings of inferiority. The woman in this case has internalized the voices of the father and others who have been so critical of her, who have lowered her self-esteem by telling her who she is and how she should behave. Not having ever developed her own strength or confidence, she will tend to search for these qualities in men and exaggerate any traces of them. Many of the men who respond to her sense her low self-esteem and find this alluring. They like the adoring attention of a woman, often younger, whom they can lord over and control. This would be the classic professor seducing the student. Because such men are rarely as brilliant, clever, and self-assured as she imagines, the woman either is disappointed and leaves or is trapped in her low self-esteem, bending to his manipulations and blaming herself for any problems.

What such a woman needs to do is first realize that the source of her insecurity is the critical opinions of others, which she has accepted and internalized. It does not stem from her inherent lack of intelligence or worthiness. She must actively work at developing her assertiveness and self-confidence through her actions—taking on projects, starting a business, mastering a craft. With men, she must see herself as their natural equal, as potentially strong and creative as they are, or even more so. With genuine self-confidence she will then be able to gauge the true worth and character of the men she meets.

The Woman to Worship Him: He's driven and ambitious, but his life is hard. It's a harsh, unforgiving world out there, and it's not easy to find any comfort. He feels something missing in his life. Then along comes a woman who is attentive to him, warm, and engaging. She seems to admire him. He feels overwhelmingly drawn to her and her energy. This is the woman to complete him, to help comfort him. But then, as the relationship develops, she no longer seems quite so nice and attentive. She certainly has stopped admiring him. He concludes that she has deceived him or has changed. Such a betrayal makes him angry.

This male projection generally stems from a particular type of relationship with the mother—she adores her son and showers him with attention. Perhaps this is to compensate for never quite getting what she wants from her husband. She fills the boy with confidence; he becomes addicted to her attention and craves her warm, enveloping presence, which is what she wants.

When he grows up, he is often quite ambitious, always trying to live up to the expectations of his mother. He pushes himself hard. He chooses a certain type of woman to pursue and then subtly positions her to play the mother role—to comfort, adore, and pump up his ego. In many instances, the woman will come to understand how he has manipulated her into this role, and she will resent it. She will stop being so soothing and reverential. He will blame her for changing, but in fact he is the one projecting qualities that were never exactly there and trying to make her conform to his expectations. The ensuing breakup will be very painful for the man, because he has invested energy from his earliest years and will feel this as abandonment from the mother figure. Even if he is successful in getting the woman to play the role, he himself will feel resentment at his dependency on her, the same dependency and ambivalence he had toward his mother. **He may** sabotage the relationship or withdraw. His anima has a sharp, recriminating edge, always ready to complain and blame.

The man in this case must see the pattern of these relationships in his life. What this should signal to him is that he needs to develop from within more of the mothering qualities that he projects onto women. He must see the nature of his ambition as stemming from his desire to please his mother and live up to her expectations. He tends to drive himself too hard. He must learn to comfort and soothe himself, to withdraw from time to time and be satisfied with his accomplishments. He needs to be able to care for himself. This will drastically improve his relationships. He will give more, instead of waiting to be adored and taken care of. He will relate to women as they are, and in the end they will perhaps feel unconsciously impelled to provide more of the comfort he needs, without being pushed into this.

The Original Man/Woman

A common experience for us humans is that at a certain point in life—often near the age of forty—we go through what is known as a midlife crisis. Our work has become mechanical and soulless. Our intimate relationships have lost their excitement and spirit. We crave change, and we look for it through a new career or relationship, some new experiences, even some danger. Such changes may give us a short-term therapeutic jolt, but they leave the real source of the problem untouched, and the malaise will return.

Let us look at this phenomenon from a different angle—as a crisis of identity. As children, we had a rather fluid sense of self. We absorbed the energy of everyone and everything around us. We felt a very wide range of emotions and were open to experience. But in our youth we had to shape a social self, one that was cohesive and would allow us to fit into a group. To do so we had to trim and tighten up our freer-flowing spirit. And much of this tightening revolved around gender roles. We had to repress masculine or feminine aspects of ourselves, in order to feel and present a more consistent self.

In our late teens and into our twenties, we continually adjust this identity in order to fit in—it is still a work in progress, and we derive some pleasure in forging this identity. We feel our lives can go in many directions, and the many possibilities enchant us. But as the years go by, the gender role we play gets more and more fixed, and we begin to sense that we have lost something essential, that we are almost strangers to who we were in our youth. Our creative energies have dried up. Naturally we look outward for the source of this crisis, but it comes from within. We have become imbalanced, too rigidly identified with our role and the mask we present to others. Our original nature incorporated more of the qualities that we absorbed from the mother or father, and of the traits of the opposite sex that are biologically a part of us. At a certain point, we inwardly rebel at the loss of what is so essentially a part of us.

In primitive cultures around the world, the wisest man or woman in the tribe was the shaman, the healer who could communicate with the spirit world. The male shaman had an inner woman or wife whom he listened to closely and who guided him. The female shaman had the inner husband. The shamans' power came from the depth of their communication with this inner figure, which was experienced as a real woman or man from within. The shaman figure reflects a profound psychological truth that our most primitive ancestors had access to. In fact, in the myths of many ancient cultures—Persian, Hebrew, Greek, Egyptian—original humans were believed to be both male and female; this made them so powerful that the gods feared them and split them in half.

Understand: The return to your original nature contains elemental power. By relating more to the natural feminine or masculine parts within you, you will unleash energy that has been repressed; your mind will recover its natural fluidity; you will understand and relate better to those of the opposite sex; and by ridding yourself of the defensiveness you have in relation to your gender role, you will feel secure in who you are. This return requires that you play with styles of thinking and acting that are more masculine or feminine, depending on your imbalance. But before describing such a process, we must first come to terms with a deeply ingrained human prejudice about the masculine and the feminine.

For millennia, it has been men who largely defined masculine and feminine roles and who imposed value judgments on them. Feminine styles of thinking were associated with irrationality, and feminine ways of acting seen as weak and inferior. We may have outwardly progressed in terms of inequality between the genders, but inwardly these judgments still have profound roots in us. The masculine style of thinking is still esteemed as superior, and femininity is still experienced as soft and weak. Many women have internalized these judgments. They feel that being equal means being able to be as tough and aggressive as men. But what is truly needed in the modern world is to see the masculine and the feminine as completely equal in potential reasoning power and strength of action, but in different ways.

Let us say there are feminine and masculine styles when it comes to thinking, taking action, learning from experience, and relating to other people. These styles have been reflected in the behavior of men and women for thousands of years. Some are related to physiological differences, some stem mostly from culture. Certainly there are men who have more feminine styles and women more masculine styles, but almost all of us are imbalanced to one side or the other. Our task is to open ourselves up to the opposite. We have only our rigidity to lose.

Masculine and feminine styles of thinking: Masculine thinking tends toward focusing on what separates phenomena from one another and categorizing them. It looks for contrasts between things to better label them. It wants to take things apart, like a machine, and analyze the separate parts that go into the whole. Its thought process is linear, figuring out the sequence of steps that goes into an event. It prefers to look at things from the outside, with emotional detachment. The masculine way of thinking tends to prefer specialization, to dig deep into something specific. It feels pleasure in uncovering the order in phenomena. It likes to build elaborate structures, whether in a book or a business.

Feminine thinking orients itself differently. It likes to focus on the whole, how the parts connect to one another, the overall gestalt. In looking at a group of people, it wants to see how they relate to one another. Instead of freezing phenomena in time in order to examine them, it focuses on the organic process itself, how one thing grows into another. In trying to solve a puzzle, the feminine style will prefer to meditate on several aspects, absorb the patterns, and let answers or solutions come to the individual over time, as if they needed to be cooked. This form of thinking leads to insights when the hidden connections between things suddenly become visible in intuitive flashes. As opposed to specialization, it is more interested in how different fields or forms of knowledge can connect to one another. In studying another culture, for instance, it will want to get closer to it, to understand how it is experienced from within. It is more sensitive to information from the senses, not merely from abstract reasoning.

For too long the masculine style has been seen as more rational and scientific, but this does not reflect the reality. All of the greatest scientists in history have displayed a powerful mix of the masculine and feminine styles. The biologist Louis Pasteur's greatest discoveries came from his ability to open his mind to as many explanations as possible, to let them cook in his mind, in order to see the connections between wide-ranging phenomena. Einstein attributed all of his greatest discoveries to intuitions, in which long hours of thinking gave way to sudden insights about the interconnection of certain facts. The anthropologist Margaret Mead used the latest abstract models from her time to rigorously analyze indigenous cultures, but she combined this with months of living within it and gaining a feel from the inside position.

In business, Warren Buffett is an example of someone who blends the two styles. When he considers buying a company, he breaks it down into its component parts and analyzes them in statistical depth, but he also tries to get a feel for the overall gestalt of the business, how the employees relate to one another, the spirit of the group as instilled by the man or woman at the top—a lot of the intangibles most businesspeople ignore. He looks at a company from both the outside and the inside.

Almost all people will lean more toward one style of thinking. What you want for yourself is to create balance by leaning more in the other direction. If you are more on the masculine side, you want to widen the fields you look at, finding connections between different forms of knowledge. In looking for solutions, you want to consider more possibilities, give greater time to the deliberative process, and allow for freer associations. You need to take seriously the intuitions that come to you after much deliberation, and not discount the value of emotions in thinking. Without a sense of excitement and inspiration, your thinking can become stale and lifeless.

If you lean more in the feminine direction, you need to be capable of focusing and digging into specific problems, tamping down the impulse to widen your search and multitask. You have to find pleasure in boring into one aspect of a problem. Reconstructing a causal chain and continually refining it will give depth to your thinking. You tend to see structure and order as dull affairs, giving greater emphasis to expressing an idea and feeling inspired by it. Instead, you need to derive pleasure in paying deep attention to the structure of a book, argument, or project. Being creative and clear with the structure will give your material its power to influence people. Sometimes you need to gain greater emotional distance to understand a problem, and you must force yourself to do so.

Masculine and feminine styles of action: When it comes to taking action, the masculine tendency is to move forward, explore the situation, attack, and vanquish. If there are obstacles in the way, it will try to push through them, this desire aptly expressed by the ancient military leader Hannibal—"I will either find a way or make a way." It derives pleasure from staying on the offensive and taking risks. It prefers to maintain its independence and room to maneuver.

When confronted with a problem or the need to take action, the feminine style often prefers to first withdraw from the immediate situation and contemplate more deeply the options. It will often look for ways to avoid the conflict, to smooth out relations, to win without having to go to battle. Sometimes the best action is nonaction—let the dynamic play itself out to understand it better; let the enemy hang itself by its aggressive actions.

This was the style of Queen Elizabeth I, whose primary strategy was to wait and see: when confronted with an imminent invasion by Spain's vast seafaring armada, she decided to not commit to a strategy until she knew exactly when the armada was launched and the weather conditions of the moment, working to slow down its advance and let the bad weather destroy it, with minimal loss of life. Instead of charging forward, the feminine style lays traps for the enemy. Independence is not an essential value in action; in fact, it is better to focus on interdependent relationships and how one move might harm an ally and cause ripple effects to an alliance.

In the West, this feminine style of strategizing and acting is instinctively judged as weak and timid. But in other cultures the style is viewed quite differently. To Chinese strategists, wu-wei, or nonaction, is often the height of wisdom and aggressive action a sign of stupidity because it narrows one's options. There is in fact tremendous strength contained within the feminine style— patience, resilience, and flexibility. To the great samurai warrior Miyamoto Musashi, the ability to stand back and wait, to let the opponent tire himself out mentally before counterattacking, was critical for success.

For those with the aggressive, masculine inclination, balance would come from training yourself to step back before taking any action. Consider the possibility that it is better to wait and see how things play out, or even to not respond at all. Taking action without proper consideration reveals weakness and a lack of self-control. For balance, always try to consider the interdependent relationships you are involved in and how each group or individual will be affected by any action. If you find yourself blocked in your career later in life, you must learn the power of withdrawing and reflecting on who you are, your needs, your strengths and weaknesses, your true interests before making any important decisions. This could require weeks or months of introspection.

Some of the greatest leaders in history honed their best ideas while in prison. As the French would say, *reculer pour mieux sauter* ("step back in order to leap forward").

For those with the feminine style, it is best to accustom yourself to various degrees of conflict and confrontation, so that any avoidance of it is strategic and not out of fear. This requires baby steps, confronting people in small ways in everyday situations before handling larger conflicts. Drop the need to always consider the other side's feelings; sometimes there are bad people who need to be thwarted, and being empathetic only empowers them. You need to be comfortable saying no and turning people down. Sometimes when you try to smooth things out, it is not out of empathy or strategy but out of an aversion to displeasing people. You have been trained to be deferential, and you need to get rid of this impulse. You need to reconnect to the bold and adventurous spirit you once had and widen your strategic options to both offense and defense. Sometimes you can overthink things and come up with too many options. Action for its own sake can be therapeutic, and taking aggressive action can discomfit your opponents.

Masculine and feminine styles of self-assessment and learning: As studies have shown, when men make mistakes they tend to look outward and find other people or circumstances to blame. Men's sense of self is deeply tied to their success, and they do not like to look inward if they fail. This makes it difficult to learn from failures. On the other hand, men will tend to feel that they are completely responsible for any success in life. This will make them blind to the element of luck and the help of others, which will feed their grandiose tendencies (see chapter 11 for more on this). Similarly, if there is a problem, the masculine style is to try to figure it out on one's own—to ask for assistance would be an admission of weakness. In general, men will overestimate their abilities and display confidence in their skills that are often not warranted by circumstances.

For women, it is the opposite: When there is failure, they tend to blame themselves and look inward. If there is success, they are more prone to look at the role of others in helping them. They find it easy to ask for assistance; they do not see this as a sign of personal inadequacy. They tend to underestimate their skills and are less prone to the grandiose confidence that often fuels men.

For those with the masculine style, when it comes to learning and improving yourself, it is best to reverse the order—to look inward when you make mistakes and to look outward when you have success. You will be able to benefit from experience by dropping the feeling that your ego is so tied to the success of each action or decision you make. Develop this reversal as a habit. Don't be afraid of asking for help or feedback; instead, make this a habit as well. Weakness comes from the inability to ask questions and to learn. Lower your self-opinion. You are not as great or skilled as you imagine. This will spur you to *actually* improve yourself.

For those with the feminine style, it is easy to beat yourself up after failures or mistakes. The introspection can go too far. The same can be said of ascribing success to others. Women more than men will suffer from low self-esteem, which is not natural but acquired. They often have internalized critical voices from others. Jung called these *animus voices*: all the men over the years who have judged women for their looks and intelligence. You want to catch these voices as they occur and rid yourself of them. Because failures or criticisms might affect you too deeply, you can become afraid to try something again, which narrows your learning possibilities. You need to adopt more of the masculine self-confidence, without the attendant stupidity. In your daily encounters, try to drop or minimize your emotional responses to events and see them from a greater distance. You are training yourself to not take things so personally.

Masculine and feminine styles of relating to people and leadership: As with male chimpanzees, in a group setting the masculine style is to require a leader, and to either aspire to that role or gain power by being the most loyal follower. Leaders will designate various deputies to do their bidding. Men form hierarchies and punish those who fall out of line. They are highly status conscious, hyperaware of their place in the group. Leaders will tend to use some element of fear to keep the group cohesive. The masculine style of leadership is to identify clear goals and reach them. It puts emphasis on results, however they are achieved.

The feminine style is more about maintaining the group spirit and keeping the relationships smoothed out, with fewer differences among individuals. It is more empathetic, considering the feelings of each member and trying to involve them more in the decision-making process. Results are important, but the way they are achieved, the process, is equally important.

For those with the masculine style, it is important to enlarge your concept of leadership. When you think more deeply about the individuals on the team and strategize to involve them more, you can have superior results, engaging the energy and creativity of the group. Studies have shown that boys are as empathetic as girls, highly attuned, for instance, to the emotions of the mother.

But empathy is slowly drummed out of men as they come to develop their assertive style. Some of the greatest male leaders in history, however, managed to retain and develop their empathy. A leader such as Sir Ernest Henry Shackleton (see chapter 2) was no less of a man for his constant consideration of the emotions of each of the men he was responsible for—he was simply a stronger and more effective leader. The same could be said of Abraham Lincoln.

For those of the feminine style, you must not be afraid of assuming a strong leadership role, particularly in times of crisis. Considering the feelings of everyone and incorporating the ideas of too many will weaken you and your plans. Although women are certainly better listeners, sometimes it is best to know when to stop listening and go with the plan you have opted for. Once you recognize the fools, the incompetents, and the hyperselfish in the group, it is best to fire them and to even find pleasure in getting rid of those who bring the whole group down. Instilling a touch of fear in your lieutenants is not always a bad thing.

FINALLY, LOOK AT IT THIS WAY: WE ARE COMPELLED BY NATURE TO WANT TO MOVE closer to what is feminine or masculine, in the form of an attraction to another person. But if we are wise, we realize we are equally compelled to do so inwardly. For centuries men have looked to women as muses, sources of inspiration. The truth is that the muse, for both genders, lies within. Moving closer to your anima or animus will bring you closer to your unconscious, which contains untapped creative treasures. The fascination you feel in relation to the feminine or masculine in others you will now feel in relation to your work, to your own thought process, and to life in general. Just as with shamans, that inner wife or husband will become the source of uncanny powers.

> What is most beautiful in virile men is something feminine; what is most beautiful in feminine women is something masculine.
>
> —*Susan Sontag*

13

Advance with a Sense of Purpose

———————— ◇ ————————

The Law of Aimlessness

*U*nlike animals, with their instincts to guide them past dangers, we humans have to rely upon our conscious decisions. We do the best we can when it comes to our career path and handling the inevitable setbacks in life. But in the back of our minds we can sense an overall lack of direction, as we are pulled this way and that way by our moods and by the opinions of others. How did we end up in this job, in this place? Such drifting can lead to dead ends. The way to avoid such a fate is to develop a sense of purpose, discovering our calling in life and using such knowledge to guide us in our decisions. We come to know ourselves more deeply—our tastes and inclinations. We trust ourselves, knowing which battles and detours to avoid. Even our moments of doubt, even our failures have a purpose— to toughen us up. With such energy and direction, our actions have unstoppable force.

The Voice

Growing up in a staunchly middle-class black neighborhood in Atlanta, Georgia, Martin Luther King Jr. (1929–1968) had a pleasant and carefree childhood. His father, Martin Sr., was the pastor of the large and thriving Ebenezer Baptist Church in Atlanta, so the Kings were relatively well off. His parents were loving and devoted to their children. Home life was stable and comfortable and included Grandmother King, who doted on young Martin Jr. He had a wide circle of friends. The few encounters he had with racism outside the neighborhood marred this idyllic childhood but left him relatively unscathed. Martin Jr., however, was exceptionally sensitive to the feelings of those around him. And as he got older, he sensed something from his father that began to trigger some inner tension and discomfort.

His father was a strict disciplinarian who set solid boundaries of behavior for the three King children. When Martin Jr. misbehaved in any way, his father whipped him, telling the boy this was the only way to turn him into a real man. The whippings continued until he was fifteen. Once his father caught Martin Jr. at a church social dancing with a girl, and his scolding of the boy in front of his friends was so vehement, Martin Jr. strove to never repeat the experience by causing his father's displeasure. But none of this discipline came with the slightest hint of hostility. Martin Sr.'s affection for his son was too real and palpable for the boy to feel anything but guilt for disappointing him.

And such feelings of guilt were all the more stressful for Martin Jr. because of the high hopes the father placed on his son. As a boy, Martin Jr. displayed an unusual way with words; he could talk his friends into almost anything, and his eloquence was quite precocious. He was certainly bright. A plan formed in Martin Sr.'s mind that his elder son would follow in his father's footsteps—attending Morehouse College in Atlanta, becoming ordained as a minister, serving as copastor at Ebenezer, and then eventually inheriting the father's position, just as Martin Sr. had inherited it from his father-in-law.

Sometimes the father shared this plan, but more than anything else the boy could feel the weight of his father's expectations in the prideful way he looked at him and treated him. And it made him anxious. He deeply admired his father—he was a man of very high principle. But Martin Jr. could not avoid sensing the growing differences between them in taste and temperament. The son was more easygoing. He loved attending parties, wearing nice clothes, dating girls, and dancing. As he got older, he developed a pronounced serious and introspective side and was drawn to books and learning. It was almost as if there were two people inside of him—one social, the other solitary and reflective. His father, on the other hand, was not complicated at all.

When it came to religion, Martin Jr. had his doubts. His father's faith was strong but simple. He was a fundamentalist who believed in a literal interpretation of the Bible. His sermons were aimed at the emotions of his parishioners, and they responded in kind. Martin Jr., on the other hand, had a cool temperament. He was rational and practical. His father seemed more concerned with helping people in the afterlife, whereas the son was more interested in life on earth and how it could be improved and enjoyed.

The thought of becoming a minister intensified these inner conflicts. At times he could imagine himself following his father's career path. As someone deeply sensitive to any form of suffering or injustice, serving as a minister could be the perfect way to channel his desire to help people. But could he be a minister with such tenuous religious faith? He hated any kind of confrontation with his father, with whom it was impossible to argue. He developed the strategy of always saying yes to whatever his father said. His way of dealing with the tension inside him was to postpone any decision that might cause a rift. And so, when he graduated from high school at the age of fifteen, he decided to attend Morehouse, delighting his father. But in his mind he had a plan—he would study everything that interested him and decide on his own the path he would take.

In the first few months he thought of a career in medicine, then sociology, then law. He kept changing his mind about a major, excited by all the subjects now open to him. He took a class in Bible studies, and he was pleasantly surprised at the profound, earthy wisdom in the book. There were professors at Morehouse who approached Christianity from a very intellectual angle, and he found this quite appealing. By his last year at Morehouse he had changed his mind yet again: he would become ordained as a minister, and he would enroll at Crozer Theological Seminary, located in Pennsylvania, for a divinity degree. Now his father was quite ecstatic. He understood it was best to let Martin Jr. explore religion on his own, as long as he ended up at Ebenezer.

At Crozer, Martin Jr. discovered a whole other side to Christianity, one that emphasized social commitment and political activism. He read all of the major philosophers, devoured the works of Karl Marx, and became fascinated with the story of Mahatma Gandhi. Finding the life of an academic a pleasant one, he decided to continue his studies at Boston University, where he gained a reputation among his professors as a brilliant scholar in the making. But as he prepared to graduate in 1954 from Boston University with a PhD in systematic theology, he could no longer postpone the inevitable. His father had lined up for him an irresistible offer—a position as copastor at Ebenezer and a part-time teaching position at Morehouse, where he could continue the academic studies he loved.

Martin had recently married, and his wife, Coretta, wanted them to stay in the North, where life would be easier than in the troubled South. He could get a teaching job at almost any university he wanted. It was tempting to fall for either option—Ebenezer or teaching at a northern university. They would certainly lead to a comfortable life.

In the past few months, however, he had had a different vision of his future. He could not rationally explain where this came from, but it was clear to him: He would return to the South, where he felt a primal connection to his roots.

He would become the minister of a large congregation in a good-sized city, a place where he could help people, serve the community, and make a practical difference. But it would not be in Atlanta, as his father had planned. He was not destined to be a professor or merely a preacher molded by his father. He would have to resist the easy path. And this vision had become too strong for him to deny it any longer—he would have to displease his father, breaking the news as gently as possible.

Several months before graduating, he heard of an opening at Dexter Avenue Baptist Church in Montgomery, Alabama. He visited the church and gave a sermon there, impressing the church's leaders. He found the congregation at Dexter more solemn and thoughtful than at Ebenezer, which suited his own temperament. Coretta tried to dissuade him from such a choice. She had grown up not far from Montgomery, and she knew how fiercely segregated the city was, and the many ugly tensions below the surface. Martin would encounter there a virulent racism he had never experienced in his relatively sheltered life. To Martin Sr., Dexter and Montgomery spelled trouble. He added his voice to Coretta's. But when Dexter offered Martin Jr. the job, he did not experience his usual ambivalence and need to think things over. For some reason, he felt certain about the choice; it seemed fateful and right.

Established at Dexter, Martin Jr. worked hard at imposing his authority (he knew he looked a bit too young for the position). He devoted a great deal of time and effort to his sermons. Preaching became his passion, and he soon gained a reputation as the most formidable preacher in the area. But unlike many other pastors, his sermons were full of ideas, inspired by all of the books he had read. He managed to make these ideas relevant to the day-to-day lives of his congregation. The key theme he had begun to develop was the power of love to transform people, a power that was desperately underused in the world and that blacks would have to adopt in relation to their white oppressors in order to change things.

He became active in the local chapter of the NAACP, but when he was offered the position of president of the chapter, he turned it down. Coretta had just given birth to their first child, and his responsibilities as a father and as a minister were great enough. He would remain very active in local politics, but his duty was to his church and family. He reveled in the simple and satisfying life he was now leading. His congregation adored him.

In early December of 1955, Dr. King (as he was now known) watched with

great interest as a protest movement began to take shape in Montgomery. An
older black woman named Rosa Parks had refused to give up her seat on the bus
to a white man, as prescribed by the local law for segregated buses. Parks, an
active member of the local NAACP chapter, had spent years fuming at this
treatment of black people and at the abusive behavior of bus drivers. Finally she
had had enough. For her defiance of the law she was arrested. This served as a
catalyst for activists in Montgomery, and they decided upon a one-day boycott
of Montgomery buses to show their solidarity. Soon the boycott stretched into
a week, then several weeks as organizers managed to create a substitute system
of transportation. One of the organizers of the boycott, E. D. Nixon, asked
King to take a leading role in the movement, but he was reluctant. He had so
little time to spare from his congregation work. He would do what he could to
lend his support.

As the boycott gained momentum, it became clear to its leaders that the
local chapter of the NAACP was not big enough to handle it. They decided
they would form a new organization, to be called the Montgomery Improvement Association. Because of his youth, his eloquence, and what seemed to be
his natural leadership skills, at a local town meeting those who had formed the
MIA nominated King to be its president. It was an offer they half expected him
to refuse—they knew of his past hesitations. King, however, could feel the
energy in the room and their faith in him. Without his usual careful premedita-
tion, he suddenly decided to accept.

As the boycott continued, the white administrators who controlled the city
became increasingly adamant in their refusal to end the segregated practices on
the city's buses. The tension was escalating—several blacks involved in the
boycott movement had been shot at and assaulted. In the speeches he now delivered to large crowds at the MIA meetings, King developed his theme of non-
violent resistance, invoking the name of Gandhi. They would defeat the other
side through peaceful protests and justified boycotts; they would take the campaign further, aiming at complete integration in Montgomery's public places.
Now the local authorities saw King as a dangerous man, an interloper from
outside the state. They initiated a whispering campaign, inventing all sorts of
rumors to be spread about King's youthful indiscretions, insinuating he was a
communist.

Almost every night he received phone calls threatening his life and that of
his family, and such threats were not to be taken lightly in Montgomery. A
normally reserved man, he did not like all of the attention from the press, which

had now become national. There was so much bickering within the MIA leadership, and the whites in power were so devilishly tricky. It was all so much more than he had bargained for when he had decided to become the MIA leader.

Several weeks after assuming the leadership position, King was arrested while driving, ostensibly for speeding, and placed in a cell full of the most hardened criminals. Once bail was posted, a trial was set for two days later, and who could guess what trumped up charges they might come up with? The night before his trial he received yet another phone call: "Nigger, we are tired of you and your mess now. And if you aren't out of this town in three days we're going to blow your brains out, and blow up your house." Something in the tone of the caller's voice sent chills down his spine—this seemed more than just a threat.

He tried to sleep that night but couldn't, the man's voice on the phone call replaying in his mind. He went into the kitchen to make some coffee and calm himself down. He was shaking. He was losing his nerve and his confidence. Couldn't he just find a way to gracefully bow out of his leadership position and return to the comfortable life of being just a minister? As he examined himself and contemplated his past, he realized that up until these weeks he had never really known true adversity. His life had been relatively easy and happy. His parents had given him everything. He had not known what it was like to feel such intense anxiety.

And as he went deeper with these thoughts, he realized that he had simply inherited religion from his father. He had never personally communicated with God or felt His presence from within. He thought of his newborn daughter and the wife he loved. He couldn't take much more of this. He couldn't call his father for advice or solace—it was well past midnight. He felt a wave of panic.

Suddenly it came to him—there was only one way out of this crisis. He bowed over the cup of coffee and prayed with a sense of urgency he had never felt before: "Lord, I must confess that I'm weak now. I'm faltering. I'm losing my courage. And I can't let the people see me like this, because if they see me weak and losing my courage, they will begin to get weak." At that moment, clear as could be, he heard a voice from within: "Martin Luther, stand up for righteousness. Stand up for justice. Stand up for truth. And lo, I will be with you, even until the end of the world." The voice—that of the Lord, he felt sure—promised to never leave him, to come back to him when he needed it. Almost immediately he felt a sense of tremendous relief, the burden of his doubts and anxiety lifted from his shoulders. He could not help but cry.

Several nights later, while King was attending an MIA meeting, his house was bombed. By sheer luck, his wife and daughter were unharmed. When informed of what had happened, he remained calm. He felt that nothing could rattle him now. Addressing an angry crowd of black supporters who had congregated outside his home, he said, "We are not advocating violence. We want to love our enemies. I want you to love our enemies. Be good to them. Love them and let them know you love them." After the bombing, his father pleaded with him to return with his family to Atlanta, but with Coretta's support, he refused to leave.

Over the following months there would be many challenges as he struggled to keep the boycott alive and maintain the pressure on the local government. Finally, toward the end of 1956, the Supreme Court affirmed a lower court decision ending bus segregation in Montgomery. On the morning of December 18, King was the first passenger to board the bus and sit wherever he liked. It was a great victory.

Now came national attention and fame, and with it endless new problems and headaches. The death threats continued. The older black leaders in the MIA and the NAACP came to resent the attention he now received. The infighting and the clash of egos became almost intolerable. King decided to start a new organization, to be called the Southern Christian Leadership Conference, its purpose to take the movement beyond Montgomery. For King, however, the infighting and envy only followed him.

In 1959 he returned to his hometown to serve as copastor at Ebenezer and to lead various SCLC campaigns from the headquarters in Atlanta. For some in the movement he was too charismatic, too domineering, and his campaigns too ambitious; for others he was too weak, too willing to compromise with white authorities. The criticism from both sides was relentless. But what added most of all to King's burdens was the slippery and infuriating tactics of the whites in power, who had no intention of accepting any substantial changes in segregation laws or in practices that discouraged blacks from registering to vote. They negotiated with King and agreed to compromises, then as soon as the boycotts and sit-ins stopped, they found all kinds of loopholes in the agreements and backtracked.

In one campaign King led in Albany, Georgia, to desegregate the city, the mayor and police chief made a show of exaggerated calmness, making it seem as if King and the SCLC were the unreasonable group, just stirring up trouble from the outside.

The campaign in Albany was largely a failure, and it left King depressed and exhausted. It was now the pattern in his life that in such moments he yearned for the simpler, easier days of the past—his happy childhood, his pleasant years at the university, the first year and a half at Dexter. Perhaps he should retire from the leadership role and devote his time to preaching, writing, and lecturing. Such thoughts tugged him at him with greater frequency.

Then, toward the end of 1962, he received yet another request for his services: Fred Shuttlesworth, one of the leading black activists in Birmingham, Alabama, begged King and the SCLC to help him in his efforts to desegregate stores in the downtown area. Birmingham was one of the most fiercely segregated cities in the country. Rather than comply with federal laws to desegregate public places, such as swimming pools, they merely closed them down. Any form of protest against the segregation practices was met with powerful violence and terrorism. The city had come to be known as "Bombingham." And overseeing this bastion of the segregated South was the police chief, Bull Connor, who seemed to relish the chance to use force—whips, attack dogs, high-pressure fire hoses, billy clubs.

This would certainly be the most dangerous campaign so far. Everything inside King leaned toward turning it down. The old doubts and fears returned to him. What if people were killed, and the violence touched him and his family? What if he failed? He suffered more sleepless nights as he agonized over this.

Then the voice from seven years before returned to him, as loud and clear as ever: he had been tasked to stand up for justice, not to think of himself but to think of the mission. How foolish to be afraid again. Yes, it was his mission to go to Birmingham. But as he mulled this over, he could not help thinking more deeply about what the voice had told him. Standing up for justice meant bringing it about in some real and practical way, not talking or settling for useless compromises. His fears of disappointing people and failing had made him too cautious. He would have to be more strategic and more courageous this time. He would have to raise the stakes and he would have to win. No more fears or doubts.

He accepted Shuttlesworth's offer, and as he planned the campaign with his team, he made it clear to them they would need to learn from past mistakes. King laid out to them the nature of the predicament they faced. The Kennedy administration had proven to be incredibly cautious when it came to civil rights. The president feared alienating congressional southern Democrats, upon whom he depended. He would make great promises but keep dragging his feet.

What they needed to do in Birmingham was to provoke a national crisis, one that was bloody and ugly. The racism and segregation in the South were largely invisible to moderate whites. Birmingham seemed like just another sleepy southern town. Their goal must be to make the racism so visible to the whites watching television that it would strike their consciences, and with a growing sense of outrage, pressure would be placed on the Kennedy administration that it could no longer resist. Most of all, King was counting on the cooperation of Bull Connor in his plans—his overreaction to the intensity of their campaign would be the key to the whole drama they were hoping to enact.

In April 1963 King and his team put their plan into action. They attacked on multiple fronts with sit-ins and demonstrations. Although reluctant because of his fear of jails, King got himself arrested. This would garner more publicity and stir the local population to emulate him. But the campaign had a fatal weakness that became apparent only as it evolved: local black support for the movement was tepid. Many blacks in Birmingham resented Shuttlesworth's autocratic style; others reasonably feared the violence Connor would unleash. King depended on large and boisterous crowds, but what he got was far from that. The national press, not smelling a story, started to leave.

Then one of the leaders on his team, James Bevel, had an idea—they would enlist the participation of students in local schools. King had his fears and argued they should not bring in anyone under the age of fourteen, but Bevel reminded him of the high stakes and the need for numbers, and King relented. Many of those inside the organization and sympathizers were shocked that King could be so pragmatic and strategic in using such young people, but the campaign had a higher purpose, and it was no time to be so delicate.

The students responded with great enthusiasm. It was just what the movement needed. They filled the streets of Birmingham, more daring and boisterous than their parents. Soon they were filling up the jails. The press returned en masse. Out came the high-pressure fire hoses, the attack dogs, and the night sticks, striking teenagers and even children. Soon television screens around America were broadcasting the tense, dramatic, and bloody scenes that ensued. Enormous crowds now showed up for King's speeches, drumming up support for the cause. Federal authorities were forced to intervene to lessen the tension.

King had learned his lesson from before—he had to keep up the pressure to the very end. Representatives of the white power structure reluctantly opened negotiations with King. At the same time, he sanctioned the demonstrators to continue their downtown marches, coming from all directions and stretching Connor's police force to the breaking point. Frightened local merchants had had enough and asked the white negotiators to work on a comprehensive settlement with the black leaders, essentially desegregating the downtown stores and agreeing to the hiring of black employees.

It was his greatest triumph so far; he had realized his ambitious goal. It did not matter now if the white authorities backtracked, as they inevitably would; Kennedy was caught in the trap, his own conscience pricked by what he had seen in Birmingham. Shortly after the settlement, he addressed the nation on television, explaining the need for immediate progress in civil rights and proposing some ambitious new laws. This led to the Civil Rights Act of 1964, which paved the way for the Voting Rights Act of 1965. It made King the undisputed leader of the civil rights movement, and soon a winner of the Nobel Peace Prize. Money now poured into the SCLC, and the movement seemed to have ineluctable momentum. But as before, the troubles and burdens for King only seemed to increase with each new victory.

In the years following Birmingham he sensed a powerful reaction forming among conservatives and Republicans against the gains of the movement. They would work to halt further progress. He learned that the FBI had placed listening devices in his hotel rooms and had spied on him for years; they were now leaking stories and rumors to various newspapers. He watched as America descended into cycles of violence, starting with the assassination of Kennedy.

He saw a new generation of black activists emerge under the banner of Black Power, and they criticized his adherence to nonviolence as weak and antiquated. When King moved the campaign to Chicago to try to stop discriminatory housing practices there, he brokered a settlement with local authorities, but black activists around the country harshly criticized him—he had settled for far too little. Shortly after this, an audience at a Chicago Baptist church loudly booed him, drowning out his talk with chants of "Black Power."

He grew depressed and despondent. In early 1965, he saw images of the Vietnam War in a magazine, and it sickened him. Something was deeply wrong with America. That summer he toured the Watts neighborhood in Los Angeles after the violent riots that had scorched the area. The sight of so much poverty and devastation overwhelmed him. Here in the heart of one of the most affluent cities in America, the center of the fantasy industry, was an enormous neighborhood where large numbers of people lived in poverty and felt no hope for the future. And they were largely invisible. America had a cancer in its system—extreme inequalities in wealth, and the willingness to spend vast sums of money on an absurd war, while blacks in inner cities were left to rot and riot.

His depression now mixed with growing anger. In his conversations with friends, people noticed a new edge to him. In one retreat with his staff, he said, "All too many people have seen power and love as polar opposites. . . . [But] the two fulfill each other. Power without love is reckless, and love without power is sentimental." At another retreat, he talked of new tactics. He would never abandon nonviolence as the means, but the civil disobedience campaign would have to be altered and intensified. "Nonviolence must mature to a new level . . . mass civil disobedience. There must be more than a statement to the larger society, there must be a force that interrupts its functioning at some key point." The movement was not about integrating blacks into the values of American society but about actively altering those values at their root.

He would add to the civil rights movement the need to address poverty in inner cities and to protest the Vietnam War. On April 4, 1967, he expressed this widening of the struggle in a speech that got lots of attention, almost all negative. Even his most ardent supporters criticized it. Including the Vietnam War would only alienate the public from the cause of civil rights, they said. It would anger the Johnson administration, whose support they depended upon. It was not part of his mandate to speak so broadly.

He had never felt so alone, so attacked by his many critics. By early 1968 his depression had become deeper than ever. He felt the end was near—some among his many enemies were going to kill him for all that he had said and done. He was exhausted by the tension and felt spiritually at a loss. In March of that year, a pastor in Memphis, Tennessee, invited King to his city, hoping he could help support a strike by black sanitation workers, who had been treated horribly. There had been marches, boycotts, and protests, and the police had responded brutally. The situation was explosive. King put them off—he felt depleted. But as so often happened in these circumstances, he realized it was his duty to do what he could, and so he agreed. On March 18 he addressed an enormous crowd in Memphis, and their enthusiastic response cheered him up. He heard that voice once again supporting and urging him forward. Memphis would have to be a key part of his mission.

For the next few weeks he kept returning to Memphis to lend his support and assistance, against the fierce resistance of the local authorities. On Wednesday evening, April 4, he addressed another crowd: "We got some difficult days ahead. But it really doesn't matter with me now, because I've been to the mountaintop. . . . Like anybody, I would like to live a long life. . . . But I'm not concerned about that now. I just want to do God's will. And He's allowed me to go up to the mountain, and I've looked over, and I've seen the promised land. I may not get there with you. But I want you to know tonight, that we, as a people will get to the promised land."

The speech left him revitalized and in a good mood. The next day he expressed some concern about an upcoming march that could turn violent but said fear should not stop them from proceeding. "I'd rather be dead than afraid," he told an aide. That evening, he dressed and prepared for a dinner at a restaurant with his aides, and running late, he finally appeared on the balcony outside his motel room when a rifle shot rang out and a single bullet pierced his neck. He died within an hour.

Interpretation: Martin Luther King Jr. was a complex man with several sides to his character. There was the pleasure-loving King, who loved nice clothes, food, dances, women, and mischievous behavior. There was the practical King, always wanting to solve people's problems and think things through thoroughly. There was the sensitive, introspective King, a side that increasingly inclined him toward spiritual pursuits. These sides were often in conflict from within, as he succumbed to passing moods. This was what often caused him to agonize over decisions. Associates would often be troubled by how deeply he considered his options and how often he doubted himself, imagining that he was not worthy of the role that he had been called upon to play.

His relationship to his father reflected this complexity. On the one hand, he truly loved and respected him, enough to consider becoming a minister and emulating his style of leadership. On the other hand, he became aware from a very early age of the dangers that would ensue if he allowed himself to be overwhelmed by his father's dominating presence. His younger brother, A.D. King, lacked such awareness, a fact that caused him much pain in his life. A.D. became a minister, but he never could assert his independence. His career was erratic as he moved from one church to another. He developed an alcohol problem and later in life revealed a definite self-destructive streak that troubled his older brother. A.D. lived in their father's shadow.

Something from deep within Martin Jr. impelled him to create some distance and autonomy. This meant not mindlessly rebelling against his father, which in the end would simply have revealed how defined he had been by him in reverse. It meant understanding the differences between them and using these differences as levers to create space. It meant taking the best from his father—his discipline, his high sense of principle, his caring nature. And it meant going his own way when something from deep within urged him to do so. He taught himself to listen to such intuitions, which led to his decision to begin his public career in Montgomery and to accept the MIA leadership position. In such moments, it was as if he could foresee his destiny and drop his habit of overthinking things.

Then, a few weeks after becoming the MIA leader, as he began to feel the increasing tension that went with the position, the many sides of his character suddenly took over and led to an inner crisis. There was the self-doubting King, the fearful King, the practical King frustrated by the endless obstacles and infighting, the King who yearned for a simpler and more pleasant life. This inner conflict paralyzed him. And as all of that reached a peak the night he entered his kitchen, suddenly those inclinations and intuitions that had guided him before in his life transformed into an actual voice, the voice of God, clarifying his destiny and offering continual support. He could hear this voice so clearly from within that it would echo and reverberate throughout his life.

From then on, in conversations and speeches, he would continually refer to this "voice" that now guided him. And with this voice the doubts, fears, and debilitating inner conflicts would disappear. He could feel integrated on a whole new level. Certainly the moods and anxieties would return, but so would the voice, making his mission clear to him.

People were often surprised, and sometimes perturbed, by how strategic he had become as his leadership role expanded to a national level. During and after every civil rights campaign, he would conduct deep analysis of the actions and reactions of the other side, learning lessons and honing tactics. For some, this did not square with his position as a spiritual leader—for instance, his decision to use children and teenagers in Birmingham as a means to fill the city jails. Ministers were not supposed to think like that. But to King, such pragmatism was intimately connected to his mission. To merely inspire people with speeches was sentimental, and he hated that. To not think deeply about results was to merely seek attention for appearing righteous, and to gratify the ego. He wanted to effect change, to dramatically and palpably alter the conditions of blacks in the South.

And so he came to understand that the game was about gaining leverage against the whites in power, who resisted change at every step. He had to use sit-ins and boycotts to maximize the pain they felt, even during the negotiating process. He had to maximize the attention from the press and bring into the living rooms of white America the ugly reality of life in the South for blacks. His strategic objective was their conscience. He had to keep the movement unified in the face of the increasing desire for violence among younger blacks. And as the voice reminded him of his ultimate purpose, to stand up for and bring about real justice, he naturally felt compelled to widen the struggle into a mass civil disobedience campaign.

In a sense, King would serve as the voice for black America, assuming a role similar to that of the voice that had guided him. He would strive to bring unity to the cause and keep the movement focused on practical results instead of debilitating infighting.

His bouts of depression, which became more intense in the later years, stemmed from his deep sensitivity not only to the people around him (the envy and continual criticisms he faced) but to the zeitgeist. Before others did, he sensed the mood in America, the grim reality of the war in Vietnam, the despair in the inner cities, the restlessness of the young and their hunger to escape reality through drugs, the cowardice of the political leadership. He linked this with his own sense of doom—he *knew* he would be assassinated. Such moods would overwhelm him. But the voice he had heard so many years before in Montgomery allowed him to squelch his fears and rise above the depression. Whenever he felt connected to his mission and purpose in life, he would experience a profound sense of fulfillment. He was doing what he was called to do, and he would not have traded this life for any other. In his last days, the connection grew deeper: he would bring change to the people of Memphis, but his fate would cut this short.

Understand: In many ways, the dilemma that King faced is the dilemma that all of us face in life, because of a profound element in human nature. We are all complex. We like to present a front to the world that is consistent and mature, but we know inside that we are subject to many different moods and wear many different faces, depending on circumstances. We can be practical, social, introspective, irrational, depending on the mood of the moment. And this inner chaos actually causes us pain. We lack a sense of cohesion and direction in life. We could choose any number of paths, depending on our shifting emotions, which pull us this way and that. Why go here instead of there? We wander through life, never quite reaching the goals that we feel are so important to us, or realizing our potential. The moments in which we feel clarity and purpose are fleeting. To soothe the pain from our aimlessness, we might enmesh ourselves in various addictions, pursue new forms of pleasure, or give ourselves over to some cause that interests us for a few months or weeks.

The only solution to the dilemma is King's solution—to find a higher sense of purpose, a mission that will provide us our own direction, not that of our parents, friends, or peers. This mission is intimately connected to our individuality, to what makes us unique. As King expressed it: "We have a responsibility to set out to discover what we are made for, to discover our life's work, to discover what we are called to do. And after we discover that, we should set out to do it with all the strength and all of the power that we can muster." This "life's work" is what we were intended to do, as dictated by our particular skills, gifts, and inclinations. It is our calling in life. For King, it was an impulse to find his own particular path, to fuse the practical with the spiritual. Finding this higher sense of purpose gives us the integration and direction we all crave.

Consider this "life's work" something that speaks to you from within—a voice. This voice will often warn you when you are getting involved in unnecessary entanglements or when you are about to follow career paths that are unsuited to your character, by the uneasiness that you feel. It directs you toward activities and goals that mesh with your nature. When you are listening to it, you feel like you have greater clarity and wholeness. If you listen closely enough, it will direct you toward your particular destiny. It can be seen as something spiritual or something personal, or both.

It is not the voice of your ego, which wants attention and quick gratification, something that further divides you from within. Rather, it absorbs you in your work and what you have to do. It is sometimes hard to hear, as your head is full of the voices of others telling you what you should and should not do. Hearing it involves introspection, effort, and practice. When you follow its guidance, positive things tend to happen. You have the inner strength to do what you must and not be swayed by other people, who have their own agendas. Hearing this voice will connect you to your larger goals and help you avoid detours. It will make you more strategic, focused, and adaptive. Once you hear it and understand your purpose, there will be no going back. Your course has been set, and deviating from it will cause anxiety and pain.

He who has a why to live can bear with almost any how.

—Friedrich Nietzsche

Keys to Human Nature

In the world today, we humans face a particular predicament: As soon as our schooling ends, we suddenly find ourselves thrown into the work world, where people can be ruthless and the competition is fierce. Only a few years before, if we were lucky, our parents met many of our needs and were there to guide us; in some cases, they were overprotective. Now we find ourselves on our own, with little or no life experience to rely upon. We have to make decisions and choices that will affect our entire future.

In the not-so-distant past, people's career and life choices were somewhat limited. They would settle into the particular jobs or roles available to them and stay there for decades. Certain older figures—mentors, family members, religious leaders—could offer some direction if needed. But such stability and help is hard to find today, as the world changes ever more quickly. Everyone is caught up in the harsh struggle to make it; people have never been so preoccupied with their own needs and agendas. The advice of our parents might be totally antiquated in this new order. Facing this unprecedented state of affairs, we tend to react in one of two ways.

Some of us, excited by all the changes, actually embrace this new order. We are young and full of energy. The smorgasbord of opportunities offered by the digital world dazzles us. We can experiment, try many different jobs, have many different relationships and adventures. Commitments to a single career or person feel like unnecessary restrictions on this freedom. Obeying orders and listening to authority figures is old-fashioned. Better to explore, have fun, and be open. A time will come when we will figure out what exactly to do with our lives. In the meantime, maintaining the freedom to do as we wish and go where we please becomes our main motivation.

Some of us, however, react the opposite way: Frightened of the chaos, we quickly opt for a career that is practical and lucrative, hopefully related to some of our interests, but not necessarily. We settle on an intimate relationship. We may even continue to cling to our parents. What motivates us is to somehow establish the stability that is so hard to find in this world.

Both paths, however, tend to lead to some problems further down the road. In the first case, trying so many things out, we never really develop solid skills in one particular area. We find it hard to focus on a specific activity for too long because we are so used to flitting around and distracting ourselves, which makes it doubly hard to learn new skills if we want to. Because of this our career possibilities begin to narrow. We become trapped into moving from one job to another. We might now want a relationship that lasts, but we haven't developed the tolerance for compromise, and we cannot help but bristle at the restrictions to our freedom that a lasting relationship will represent. Although we might not like to admit it to ourselves, our freedom can begin to wear on us.

In the second case, the career we committed to in our twenties might begin to feel a bit lifeless in our thirties. We chose it for practical purposes, and it has little connection to what actually interests us in life. It begins to feel like just a job. Our minds disengage from the work. And now that smorgasbord of opportunities in the modern world begins to tempt us as we reach midlife. Perhaps we need some new, exciting career or relationship or adventure.

In either case, we do what we can to manage our frustrations. But as the years go by, we start to experience bouts of pain that we cannot deny or repress. We are generally unaware of the source of our discomfort—the lack of purpose and true direction in our lives.

This pain comes in several forms.

We feel increasingly *bored*. Not really engaged in our work, we turn to various distractions to occupy our restless minds. But by the law of diminishing returns, we need to continually find new and stronger forms of diversion—the latest trend in entertainment, travel to an exotic location, a new guru or cause to follow, hobbies that are taken up and abandoned quickly, addictions of all kinds. Only when we are alone or in down moments do we actually experience the chronic boredom that motivates many of our actions and eats away at us.

We feel increasingly *insecure*. We all have dreams and a sense of our own potential. If we have wandered aimlessly through life or gone astray, we begin to become aware of the discrepancy between our dreams and reality. We have no solid accomplishments. We feel envious of those who do. Our ego becomes brittle, placing us in a trap. We are too fragile to take criticism. Learning requires an admission that we don't know things and need to improve, but we feel too insecure to admit this, and so our ideas become set and our skills stagnate. We cover this up with an air of certainty and strong opinions, or moral superiority, but the underlying insecurity cannot be shaken.

We often feel *anxious* and *stressed* but are never quite certain as to why. Life involves inevitable obstacles and difficulties, but we have spent much of our time trying to avoid anything painful. Perhaps we didn't take on responsibilities that would open us to failure. We steered clear of tough choices and stressful situations. But then they crop up in the present—we are forced to finish something by a deadline, or we suddenly become ambitious and want to realize a dream of ours. We have not learned in the past how to handle such situations, and the anxiety and stress overwhelm us. Our avoidance leads to a low-grade, continual anxiety.

And finally, we feel *depressed*. All of us want to believe that there is some purpose and meaning to our life, that we are connected to something larger than ourselves. We want to feel some weight and significance to what we have done. Without that conviction, we experience an emptiness and depression that we will ascribe to other factors.

Understand: This feeling of being lost and confused is not anyone's fault. It is a natural reaction to having been born into times of great change and chaos. The old support systems of the past—religions, universal causes to believe in, social cohesion—have mostly disappeared, at least in the Western world. Disappearing also are the elaborate conventions, rules, and taboos that once channeled behavior. We are all cast adrift, and it is no wonder that so many people lose themselves in addictions and depression.

The problem here is simple: By our nature we humans crave a sense of direction. Other living organisms rely upon elaborate instincts to guide and determine their behavior. We have come to depend upon our consciousness. But the human mind is a bottomless pit—it provides us with endless mental spaces to explore. Our imagination can take us anywhere and conjure up anything. At any moment, we could choose to go in a hundred different directions. Without belief systems or conventions in place, we seem to have no obvious compass points to guide our behavior and decisions, and this can be maddening.

Fortunately there is one way out of this predicament, and it is by nature available to each and every one of us. There is no need to look for gurus or to grow nostalgic for the past and its certainties. A compass and guidance system does exist. It comes from looking for and discovering the *individual* purpose to our lives. It is the path taken by the greatest achievers and contributors to the advancement of human culture, and we only have to see the path to take it. Here's how it works.

Each human individual is radically unique. This uniqueness is inscribed in us in three ways—the one-of-a-kind configuration of our DNA, the particular way our brains are wired, and our experiences as we go through life, experiences that are unlike any other's. Consider this uniqueness as a seed that is planted at birth, with potential growth. And this uniqueness has a purpose.

In nature, in a thriving ecosystem we can observe a high level of diversity among species. With these diverse species operating in a balance, the system is rich and feeds off itself, creating newer species and more interrelationships. Ecosystems with little diversity are rather barren, and their health is much more tenuous. We humans operate in our own cultural ecosystem. Throughout history we can see that the healthiest and most celebrated cultures have been the ones that encouraged and exploited the greatest internal diversity among individuals—ancient Athens, the Chinese Sung Dynasty, the Italian Renaissance, the 1920s in the Western world, to name a few. These were periods of tremendous creativity, high points in history. We can contrast this with the conformity and cultural sterility in dictatorships.

By bringing our uniqueness to flower in the course of our life, through our particular skills and the specific nature of our work, we contribute our share to this needed diversity. This uniqueness actually transcends our individual existence. It is stamped upon us by nature itself. How can we explain why we are drawn to music, or to helping other people, or to particular forms of knowledge? We have inherited it, and it is there for a purpose.

Striving to connect to and cultivate this uniqueness provides us a path to follow, an internal guidance system through life. But connecting to this system does not come easily. Normally the signs of our uniqueness are clearer to us in early childhood. We found ourselves naturally drawn to particular subjects or activities, despite the influence of our parents. We can call these *primal inclinations*. They speak to us, like a voice. But as we get older, that voice becomes drowned out by parents, peers, teachers, the culture at large. We are told what to like, what is cool, what is not cool. We start to lose a sense of who we are, what makes us different. We choose career paths unsuited to our nature.

To tap into the guidance system, we must make the connection to our uniqueness as strong as possible, and learn to trust that voice. (For more on this, see "Discover your calling in life" in the next section.) To the degree we manage to do so, we are richly rewarded. We have a sense of direction, in the form of an overall career path that meshes with our particular inclinations. We have a calling. We know which skills we need and want to develop. We have goals and subgoals. When we take detours from our path or become involved in entanglements that distract us from our goals, we feel uncomfortable and quickly get back on course. We may explore and have adventures, as is natural for us when we are young, but there is a relative direction to our exploring that frees us from continual doubts and distractions.

This path does not require that we follow one simple line, or that our inclinations be narrowly focused. Perhaps we feel the pull of several types of knowledge. Our path involves mastering a variety of skills and combining them in highly inventive and creative ways. This was the genius of Leonardo da Vinci, who combined his interests in art, science, architecture, and engineering, having mastered each one of them. This way of following the path goes well with our modern, eclectic tastes and our love of wide exploration.

When we engage this internal guidance system, all of the negative emotions that plague us in our aimlessness are neutralized and even turned around into positive ones. For instance, we may feel *boredom* in the process of accumulating skills. Practice can be tedious. But we can embrace the tedium, knowing of the tremendous benefits to come. We are learning something that excites us. We do not crave constant distractions. Our minds are pleasantly absorbed in the work. We develop the ability to focus deeply, and with such focus comes momentum. We retain what we absorb because we are engaged emotionally in learning. We then learn at a faster rate, which leads to creative energy. With a mind teeming with fresh information, ideas begin to come to us out of nowhere. Reaching such creative levels is intensely satisfying, and it becomes ever easier to add new skills to our repertoire.

With a sense of purpose, we feel much less *insecure*. We have an overall sense that we are advancing, realizing some or all of our potential. We can begin to look back at various accomplishments, small or large. We got things done. We may have moments of doubt, but they are generally related more to the quality of our work than to our self-worth—did we do our best job? Focusing more on the work itself and its quality than on what people think of us, we can distinguish between practical and malicious criticism. We have an inner resiliency, which helps us bounce back from failures and learn from them. We know who we are, and this self-awareness becomes our anchor in life.

With this guidance system in place, we can turn *anxiety* and *stress* into productive emotions. In trying to reach our goals—a book, a business, winning a political campaign—we have to manage a great deal of anxiety and uncertainty, making daily decisions on what to do. In the process, we learn to control our levels of anxiety—if we think too much about how far we have to go, we might feel overwhelmed. Instead we learn to focus on smaller goals along the way, while also retaining a degree of urgency. We develop the ability to regulate our anxiety—enough to keep us going and keep improving the work, but not so much as to paralyze us. This is an important life skill.

We develop a high tolerance for stress as well, and even feed off of it. We humans are actually built to handle stress. Our restless and energetic minds thrive best when we are mentally and physically active, our adrenaline pumping. It is a known phenomenon that people tend to age more quickly and deteriorate more rapidly right after they retire. Their minds have nothing to feed on. Anxious thoughts return. They become less active. Maintaining some stress and tension, and knowing how to handle it, can improve our health.

And finally, with a sense of purpose we are less prone to *depression*. Yes, low moments are inevitable, even welcome. They make us withdraw and reassess ourselves, as they did for King. But more often we feel excited and lifted above the pettiness that so often marks daily life in the modern world. We are on a mission. We are realizing our life's work. We are contributing to something much larger than ourselves, and this ennobles us. We have moments of great fulfillment that sustain us. Even death can lose its sting. What we have accomplished will outlive us, and we do not have that debilitating feeling of having wasted our potential.

Think of it this way: In military history, we can identify two types of armies—those that fight for a cause or an idea, and those that fight largely for money, as part of a job. Those that go to war for a cause, such as the armies of Napoleon Bonaparte fighting to spread the French Revolution, fight with greater intensity. They tie their individual fate to that of the cause and the nation. They are more willing to die in battle for the cause. Those in the army who are less enthusiastic get swept up in the group spirit. The general can ask more of his soldiers. The battalions are more unified, and the various battalion leaders are more creative. Fighting for a cause is known as a *force multiplier*—the greater the connection to the cause, the higher the morale, which translates into greater force. Such an army can often defeat one that is much larger but less motivated.

We can say something similar about your life: operating with a high sense of purpose is a force multiplier. All of your decisions and actions have greater power behind them because they are guided by a central idea and purpose. The many sides to your character are channeled into this purpose, giving you more sustained energy. Your focus and your ability to bounce back from adversity give you ineluctable momentum. You can ask more of yourself. And in a world where so many people are meandering, you will spring past them with ease and attract attention for this. People will want to be around you to imbibe your spirit.

Your task as a student of human nature is twofold: First, you must become aware of the primary role that a sense of purpose plays in human life. By our nature, the need for purpose has a gravitational pull to it that no one can resist. Look at the people around you and gauge what is guiding their behavior, seeing patterns in their choices. Is the freedom to do what they please their primary motivation? Are they mostly after pleasure, money, attention, power for its own sake, or a cause to join? These are what we shall call *false purposes*, and they lead to obsessive behavior and various dead ends. (For more on *false purposes*, see the last section of this chapter.) Once you identify people as motivated by a false purpose, you should avoid hiring or working with them, as they will tend to draw you downward with their unproductive energy.

You will also notice some people who are struggling to find their purpose in the form of their calling in life. Perhaps you can help them or you can help each other. And finally, you may recognize a few people who have a relatively high sense of purpose. This could be someone young who seems destined for greatness. You will want to befriend them and become infected with their enthusiasm. Others will be older, with a string of accomplishments to their name. You will want to associate with them in any way possible. They will draw you upward.

Your second task is to find *your* sense of purpose and elevate it by making the connection to it as deep as possible. (See the next section for more on this.) If you are young, use what you find to give an overall framework to your restless energy. Explore the world freely, accumulate adventures, but all within a certain framework. Most important, accumulate skills. If you are older and have gone astray, take the skills you have acquired and find ways to gently channel them in the direction that will eventually mesh with your inclinations and spirit. Avoid sudden and drastic career changes that are impractical.

Keep in mind that your contribution to the culture can come in many forms. You don't have to become an entrepreneur or figure largely on the world's stage. You can do just as well operating as one person in a group or organization, as long as you retain a strong point of view that is your own and use this to gently exert your influence. Your path can involve physical labor and craft—you take pride in the excellence of the work, leaving your particular stamp on the quality. It can be raising a family in the best way possible. No calling is superior to another. What matters is that it be tied to a personal need and inclination, and that your energy move you toward improvement and continual learning from experience.

In any event, you will want to go as far as you can in cultivating your uniqueness and the originality that goes with it. In a world full of people who seem largely interchangeable, you cannot be replaced. You are one of a kind. Your combination of skills and experience is not replicable. That represents true freedom and the ultimate power we humans can possess.

Strategies for Developing a High Sense of Purpose

Once you commit yourself to developing or strengthening your sense of purpose, then the hard work begins. You will face many enemies and obstacles impeding your progress—the distracting voices of others who instill doubts about your calling and your uniqueness; your own boredom and frustrations with the work itself and your slow progress; the lack of trustworthy criticism from people to help you; the levels of anxiety you must manage; and finally, the burnout that often accompanies focused labor over long periods. The following five strategies are designed to help you move past these obstacles. They are in a loose order, the first being the essential starting point. You will want to put them all into practice to ensure continual movement forward.

Discover your calling in life. You begin this strategy by looking for signs of primal inclinations in your earliest years, when they were often the clearest. Some people can easily remember such early indications, but for many of us it requires some introspection and some digging. What you are looking for is moments in which you were unusually fascinated by a particular subject, or certain objects, or specific activities and forms of play.

The great nineteenth- and early-twentieth-century scientist Marie Curie could distinctly recall the moment when she was four years old and entered her father's office, suddenly mesmerized by the sight of all sorts of tubes and measuring devices for various chemistry experiments placed behind a polished glass case. Her whole life she would feel a similar visceral thrill whenever she entered a laboratory. For Anton Chekhov, it was attending his first play in a theater as a boy in his small town. The whole atmosphere of make-believe thrilled him. For Steve Jobs, it was passing an electronics store as a child and seeing the wondrous gadgets in the window, marveling at their design and complexity. For Tiger Woods, it was, at the age of two, watching his father hit golf balls into a net in the garage and being unable to contain his excitement and desire to imitate him.

For the writer Jean-Paul Sartre, it was a childhood fascination with printed words on a page, and the possible magical meanings each word possessed.

These moments of visceral attraction occurred suddenly and without any prodding from parents or friends. It would be hard to put into words why they occurred; they are signs of something beyond our personal control. The actress Ingrid Bergman expressed it best, when talking of the fascination she had with performing in front of her father's movie camera at a very early age: "I didn't choose acting. It chose me."

Sometimes these moments can come when we are older, as when Martin Luther King Jr. realized his mission in life as he got pulled into the Montgomery bus boycott. And sometimes they can occur while observing other people who are masters in their field.

As a young man, the future Japanese film director Akira Kurosawa felt particularly aimless. He tried painting, then apprenticed as an assistant director on films, a job he hated. He was ready to quit when he got assigned to work for the director Kajiro Yamamoto in 1936. Watching this great master at work, suddenly his eyes were opened to the magical possibilities of film, and he realized his calling. As he later described this, "It was like the wind in a mountain pass blowing across my face. By this I mean that wonderfully refreshing wind you feel after a painfully hard climb. The breath of that wind tells you you are reaching the pass. Then you stand in the pass and look down over the panorama as it opens up. When I stood behind Yama-san in his director's chair next to the camera, I felt my heart swell with that same feeling—'I've made it at last.'"

As another sign, examine moments in your life when certain tasks or activities felt natural and easy to you, similar to swimming with a current. In performing such activities, you have a greater tolerance for the tedium of practicing. People's criticisms don't discourage you so easily; you want to learn. You can contrast this with other subjects or tasks that you find deeply boring and unfulfilling, which frustrate you.

Related to this, you will want to figure out the particular form of intelligence that your brain is wired for. In his book *Frames of Mind*, the psychologist Howard Gardner lists certain forms of intelligence for which people usually have one particular gift or affinity. This could be mathematics and logic, physical activity, words, images, or music. We could also add to this social intelligence, a superior sensitivity to people. When you are engaged in the activity that feels right, it will correspond to that form of intelligence for which your brain is most suited.

From these various factors you should be able to spot the outline of your calling. In essence, in going through this process you are discovering yourself, what makes you different, what predates the opinions of others. You are reacquainting yourself with your natural likes and dislikes. Later in life we often lose contact with our own preferences for things, deeply influenced by what others are doing and by the culture. You are subtracting such external influences. The deeper you make this connection to your calling, the more you will be able to resist the bad ideas of others. You will engage that internal guidance system. Put some time into the process, working with a journal if necessary. You are developing the habit of assessing and listening to yourself, so that you can continually monitor your progress and adjust this calling to the various stages in your life.

If you are young and just starting out in your career, you will want to explore a relatively wide field related to your inclinations—for instance, if your affinity is words and writing, try all the different types of writing until you hit upon the right fit. If you are older and have more experience, you will want to take the skills you have already developed and find a way to adapt them more in the direction of your true calling. Remember that the calling could be combining several fields that fascinate you. For Jobs, it was the intersection of technology and design. Keep the process open-ended; your experience will instruct you as to the way.

Do not try to bypass the work of discovering your calling or imagine that it will simply come to you naturally. Although it may come to a few people early in life or in a lightning-bolt moment, for most of us it requires continual introspection and effort. Experimenting with the skills and options related to your personality and inclinations is not only the single most essential step in developing a high sense of purpose, it is perhaps the most important step in life in general. Knowing in a deep way who you are, your uniqueness, will make it that much easier to avoid all of the other pitfalls of human nature.

Use resistance and negative spurs. The key to success in any field is first developing skills in various areas, which you can later combine in unique and creative ways. But the process of doing so can be tedious and painful, as you become aware of your limitations and relative lack of skill. Most people, consciously or unconsciously, seek to avoid tedium, pain, and any form of adversity. They try to put themselves in places where they will face less criticism and minimize their chances of failure. You must choose to move in the opposite direction. You want to embrace negative experiences, limitations, and even pain as the perfect means of building up your skill levels and sharpening your sense of purpose.

When it comes to exercise, you understand the importance of manageable levels of pain and discomfort, because they later yield strength, stamina, and other positive sensations. The same will come to you by actually embracing the tedium in your practice. Frustration is a sign that you are making progress as your mind becomes aware of higher levels of skill that you have yet to attain.

You want to use and embrace any kind of deadline. If you give yourself a year to finish a project or start up a business, you will generally take a year or more. If you give yourself three months, you will finish it that much sooner, and the concentrated energy with which you work will raise your skill level and make the end result that much better. If necessary, manufacture reasonably tight deadlines to intensify your sense of purpose.

Thomas Edison knew he could take far too long to realize his inventions, and so he developed the habit of talking about their future greatness to journalists, overselling his ideas. With publicity, he would now be put in the position of having to make it happen, and relatively soon, or be ridiculed. He would now have to rise to the occasion, and he almost always did. The great eighteenth-century Zen master Hakuin took this further. He became greatly frustrated by the particular koans (paradoxical anecdotes designed to spark enlightenment) presented to him by his master. His lack of progress made him feel desperate, so he told himself, in all seriousness, "If I fail to master one of these koans in seven days, I will kill myself." This worked for him and kept on working for him, until he attained total enlightenment.

As you progress on your path, you will be subject to more and more of people's criticisms. Some of them might be constructive and worth paying attention to, but many of them come from envy. You can recognize the latter by the person's emotional tone in expressing their negative opinions. They go a little too far, speak with a bit too much vehemence; they make it personal, instilling doubts about your overall ability, emphasizing your personality more than the work; they lack specific details about what and how to improve. Once recognized, the trick is not to internalize these criticisms in any form.

Becoming defensive is a sign they have gotten to you. Instead, use their negative opinions to motivate you and add to your sense of purpose.

Absorb purposeful energy. We humans are extremely susceptible to the moods and energy of other people. For this reason, you want to avoid too much contact with those who have a low or false sense of purpose. On the other hand, you always want to try to find and associate with those who have a high sense of purpose. This could be the perfect mentor or teacher or partner on a project. Such people will tend to bring out the best in you, and you will find it easier and even refreshing to receive their criticisms.

This was the strategy that brought Coco Chanel (see chapter 5) so much power. She began life from a position of great weakness—an orphan with little or no resources in life. She realized in her early twenties that her calling was to design clothes and to start her own apparel line. She desperately needed guidance, however, particularly when it came to the business side. She looked for people who could help her find her way. At the age of twenty-five she met the perfect target, a wealthy older English businessman named Arthur "Boy" Capel. She was attracted to his ambition, his well-rounded experience, his knowledge of the arts, and his ruthless practicality.

She latched onto him with great vehemence. He was able to instill in her the confidence that she could become a famous designer. He taught her about business in general. He offered her tough criticisms that she could accept because of her deep respect for him. He helped guide her in her first important decisions in setting up her business. From him she developed a very honed sense of purpose that she retained her entire life. Without his influence, her path would have been too confusing and difficult. Later in life, she kept returning to this strategy. She found other men and women who had skills she lacked or needed to strengthen—social graciousness, marketing, a nose for cultural trends—and developed relationships that allowed her to learn from them.

In this case, you want to find people who are pragmatic and not merely those who are charismatic or visionaries. You want their practical advice, and to absorb their spirit of getting things done. If possible, collect around you a group of people from different fields, as friends or associates, who have similar energy. You will help elevate one another's sense of purpose. Do not settle for virtual associations or mentors. They will not have the same effect.

Create a ladder of descending goals. Operating with long-term goals will bring you tremendous clarity and resolve. These goals—a project or business to create, for instance—can be relatively ambitious, enough to bring out the best in you. The problem, however, is that they will also tend to generate anxiety as you look at all you have to do to reach them from the present vantage point. To manage such anxiety, you must create a ladder of smaller goals along the way, reaching down to the present. Such objectives are simpler the further down the ladder you go, and you can realize them in relatively short time frames, giving you moments of satisfaction and a sense of progress. Always break tasks into smaller bites. Each day or week you must have microgoals. This will help you focus and avoid entanglements or detours that will waste your energy.

At the same time, you want to continually remind yourself of the larger goal, to avoid losing track of it or getting too mired in details. Periodically return to your original vision and imagine the immense satisfaction you will have when it comes to fruition. This will give you clarity and inspire you forward. You will also want a degree of flexibility built into the process. At certain moments you reassess your progress and adjust the various goals as necessary, constantly learning from experience and adapting and improving your original objective.

Remember that what you are after is a series of practical results and accomplishments, not a list of unrealized dreams and aborted projects. Working with smaller, embedded goals will keep you moving in such a direction.

Lose yourself in the work. Perhaps the greatest difficulty you will face in maintaining a high and consistent sense of purpose is the level of commitment that is required over time and the sacrifices that go with this. You have to handle many moments of frustration, boredom, and failure, and the endless temptations in our culture for more immediate pleasures. The benefits listed above in the Keys are often not immediately apparent. And as the years pile up, you can face burnout.

To offset this tedium, you need to have moments of flow in which your mind becomes so deeply immersed in the work that you are transported beyond your ego. You experience feelings of profound calmness and joy. The psychologist Abraham Maslow called these "peak experiences"—once you have them, you are forever changed. You will feel the compulsion to repeat them. The more immediate pleasures the world offers will pale in comparison. And when you feel rewarded for your dedication and sacrifices, your sense of purpose will be intensified.

These experiences cannot be manufactured, but you can set the stage for them and vastly increase your odds. First, it is essential to wait until you are further along in the process—at least more than halfway through a project, or after several years of study in your field. At such moments, your mind will be naturally filled with all kinds of information and practice, ripe for a peak experience.

Second, you must plan on giving yourself uninterrupted time with the work—as many hours in the day as possible, and as many days in the week. For this purpose, you have to rigorously eliminate the usual level of distractions, even plan on disappearing for a period of time. Think of it as a type of religious retreat. Steve Jobs would close the door to his office, spend the entire day holed up in the room, and wait until he fell into a state of deep focus. Once you become adept at this, you can do it almost anywhere. Einstein would notoriously go into such a deep state of absorption that he would lose himself in the city streets or while sailing on a lake.

Third, the emphasis must be on the work, never on yourself or the desire for recognition. You are fusing your mind with the work itself, and any intrusive thoughts from your ego or doubts about yourself or personal obsessions will interrupt the flow. Not only will you find this flow immensely therapeutic, but it will also yield uncannily creative results.

For the time period that the actress Ingrid Bergman was engaged in a particular film project, she poured every ounce of her energy into it, forgetting everything else about her life. Unlike other actors, who gave greater importance to the money they earned or the attention they received, Bergman saw only the opportunity to completely embody the role she was to play and bring it to life. For this purpose, she would engage with the writers and the director involved, actively altering the role itself and some of the dialogue, making it more real; they would trust her in this, because her ideas were almost always excellent and were based on deep thinking about the character.

Once she had gone far enough in the writing and thinking process, she would go through days or weeks feeling herself fuse with the role, and not interacting with others. In doing so, she could forget about all the pain in her life—the loss of her parents when she was young, her abusive husband. These were the moments of genuine joy in her life, and she translated such peak experiences to the screen. Audiences could sense something profoundly realistic in her performances, and they identified unusually intensely with the characters she played. Knowing she would periodically have such experiences, and the results that went with them, kept her moving past the pain and sacrifices that she demanded of herself.

Look at this as a form of religious devotion to your life's work. Such devotion will eventually yield moments of union with the work itself, and a type of ecstasy that is impossible to verbalize until you have experienced it.

The Lure of False Purposes

The gravitational pull we feel toward finding a purpose comes from two elements in human nature. First, unable to rely on instincts as other animals do, we require some means of having a sense of direction, a way to guide and restrict our behavior. Second, we humans are aware of our puniness as individuals in a world with billions of others in a vast universe. We are aware of our mortality, and how we will eventually be swallowed up in the eternity of time. We need to feel larger than just the individuals we are, and connected to something that transcends us.

Human nature being what it is, however, many people seek to create purpose and a feeling of transcendence on the cheap, to find it in the easiest and most accessible way, with the least amount of effort. Such people give themselves over to *false purposes*, those that merely supply the illusion of purpose and transcendence. We can contrast them with real purposes in the following way: The real purpose comes from within. It is an idea, a calling, a sense of mission that we feel personally and intimately connected to. It is our own; we may have been inspired by others, but nobody imposed it upon us and nobody can take it away. If we are religious, we don't merely accept the orthodoxy; we go through rigorous introspection and make our belief inward, true to ourselves. False purposes come from external sources—belief systems that we swallow whole, conformity to what other people are doing.

The real purpose leads us upward, to a more human level. We improve our skills and sharpen our minds; we realize our potential and contribute to society. False purposes lead downward, to the animal side of our nature—to addictions, loss of mental powers, mindless conformity, and cynicism.

It is critical that we become aware of these false forms of purpose. Inevitably all of us at some point in our lives fall for them because they are so easy, popular, and cheap. If we can eliminate the impulse toward these lower forms, we will naturally gravitate toward the higher, in our unavoidable search for meaning and purpose. Here are five of the most common forms of false purposes that have appealed to humans since the beginning of civilization.

The pursuit of pleasure: For many of us, work is just an irritating necessity of life. What really motivates us is avoiding pain, and finding as much pleasure as possible in our time outside work. The pleasures we pursue can take various forms—sex, stimulants, entertainment, eating, shopping, gambling, technological fads, games of all sorts.

No matter the objects of the pursuit, they tend to lead to a dynamic of diminishing returns. The moments of pleasure we get tend to get duller through repetition. We need either more and more of the same or constantly new diversions. Our need often turns into an addiction, and with the dependency comes a diminishing of health and mental powers. We become possessed by the objects we crave and lose ourselves. Under the influence of drugs or alcohol, for instance, we can temporarily feel transported beyond the banality of our lives.

This form of false purpose is very common in the world today, largely because of the cornucopia of distractions we can choose from. But it goes against a basic element of human nature: to have deeper levels of pleasure, we have to learn to limit ourselves. Reading a variety of books for entertainment, in rapid succession, leads to a diminishing sense of satisfaction with each book; our minds are overwhelmed and overstimulated; and we must reach for a new one right away. Reading one excellent book and absorbing ourselves in it has a relaxing and uplifting effect as we discover hidden riches within it. In the moments when we are not reading, we think of the book again and again.

All of us require pleasurable moments outside work, ways to relieve our tension. But when we operate with a sense of purpose, we know the value of limiting ourselves, opting for depth of experience rather than overstimulation.

Causes and cults: People have a profound need to believe in something, and in the absence of great unifying belief systems, this void is easily filled by all kinds of microcauses and cults. We notice that such groups tend not to last very long. Within ten years they already seem passé. During their brief existence, their adherents will substitute extreme conviction and hyperbelief for a clear vision of what they are after. For this purpose, enemies are quickly found and are said to be the source of all that is wrong in the world. Such groups become the means for people to vent their personal frustrations, envy, and hatred. They also get to feel superior, as part of some clique with special access to the truth.

We can recognize a microcause or cult by the vagueness of what its disciples want. They cannot describe the kind of world or society they desire in concrete, practical terms. Much of their raison d'être revolves around negative definitions—get rid of these people or those practices and the world will become a paradise. They have no sense of strategy or defined ways of reaching their nebulous goals, which is a clear sign that their group is merely about the release of emotions.

Often such groups will depend on large public gatherings in which people can become intoxicated by numbers and shared feelings. Wily rulers throughout history have used this to great effect. People in a crowd are highly suggestible. Through short, simple phrases, with lots of repetition, they can be made to chant back slogans and swallow the most absurd and irrational ideas. In a crowd people can feel relieved of any personal responsibility, which can lead to violence. They feel transported beyond themselves and not so puny, but such enlargement is an illusion. They are actually made smaller by losing their will and their individual voice.

Allying ourselves with a cause can be an important part of our sense of purpose, as it was for Martin Luther King Jr. But it must emerge from an internal process in which we have thought deeply about the subject and are committing ourselves to the cause as part of our life's work. We are not simply a cog in the machinery of such a group but active contributors, bringing our uniqueness into play and not mimicking the company line. We are not joining out of a need to gratify our ego or to vent ugly emotions, but rather out of a hunger for justice and truth that springs from deep within our own sense of purpose.

Money and success: For many people, the pursuit of money and status can supply them with plenty of motivation and focus. Such types would consider figuring out their calling in life a monumental waste of time and an antiquated notion. But in the long run this philosophy often yields the most impractical of results.

First, more often than not such types enter the field in which they can make the most money the fastest. They aim for the biggest paychecks. Their career choices have slight or no connection to their actual inclinations. The fields they choose will tend to be crowded with other insatiable hunters of money and success, and so the competition is fierce. If they are zealous enough, they might do quite well for a while, but as they get older, they begin to feel restless and ever so slightly bored. They try different avenues for money and success; they need new challenges. They have to keep finding ways to motivate themselves. Often they make big mistakes in their obsessive pursuit of money because their thinking is so short term, as we saw with those who went all in on the derivatives frenzy leading up to the crash of 2008.

Second, money and success that last come from remaining original and not mindlessly following the path that others are following. If we make money our primary goal, we never truly cultivate our uniqueness, and eventually someone younger and hungrier will supplant us.

And finally, what often motivates people in this quest is to simply have more money and status than other people, and to feel superior. With that standard, it is difficult to know when they have enough, because there are always people with more. And so the quest is endless and exhausting. And since the connection to their work is not personal, such people become alienated from themselves; the pursuit feels soulless; they are workaholics without a true calling. They may become depressed or manic, and they will often lose what they have gained if they become manic enough.

We all know the effects of "hyperintention": If we want and need desperately to sleep, we are less likely to fall asleep. If we absolutely must give the best talk possible at some conference, we become hyperanxious about the result, and the performance suffers. If we desperately need to find an intimate partner or make friends, we are more likely to push them away. If instead we relax and focus on other things, we are more likely to fall asleep or give a great talk or charm people. The most pleasurable things in life occur as a result of something not directly intended and expected. When we try to manufacture happy moments, they tend to disappoint us.

The same goes for the dogged pursuit of money and success. Many of the most successful, famous, and wealthy individuals do not begin with an obsession with money and status. One prime example would be Steve Jobs, who amassed quite a fortune in his relatively short life. He actually cared very little for material possessions. His singular focus was on creating the best and most original designs, and when he did so, good fortune followed him. Concentrate on maintaining a high sense of purpose, and the success will flow to you naturally.

Attention: People have always pursued fame and attention as a way to feel enlarged and more important. They become dependent on the number of people applauding, the size of the army they command, the crowd of courtiers that serve them. But this false sense of purpose has become greatly democratized and widespread through social media. Now almost any one of us can have the quantity of attention that past kings and conquerors could only dream about. Our self-image and self-esteem become tied to the attention we receive on a daily basis. In social media, this often requires becoming increasingly outrageous to capture eyeballs. It is an exhausting and alienating quest, as we become more of a clown than anything else. And each moment that the attention ebbs ever so slightly, a gnawing pain eats away at us: Are we losing it? Who is siphoning off the flow of attention that was ours?

As with money and success, we have a much greater chance of attracting attention by developing a high sense of purpose and creating work that will naturally draw people to it. When the attention is unexpected, as with the success we suddenly have, it is all the more pleasurable.

Cynicism: According to Friedrich Nietzsche, "Man would rather have the void as purpose than be void of purpose." Cynicism, the feeling that there is no purpose or meaning in life, is what we shall call having "the void as purpose." In the world today, with growing disenchantment with politics and the belief systems of the past, this form of the false purpose is becoming increasingly common.

Such cynicism involves some or all of the following beliefs: Life is absurd, meaningless, and random. Standards of truth, excellence, or meaning are completely old-fashioned. Everything is relative. People's judgments are simply interpretations of the world, none better than another. All politicians are corrupt, so it's not really worth it to get involved; better to abstain or choose a leader who will deliberately tear it all down. People who are successful get there through gaming the system. Any form of authority should be naturally mistrusted. Look behind people's motives and you will see that they are selfish. Reality is quite brutal and ugly; better to accept this and be skeptical. It's really hard to take anything so seriously; we should just laugh and have a good time. It's all the same.

This attitude presents itself as cool and hip. Its adherents display a somewhat apathetic and sardonic air that gives them the appearance that they see through it all. But the attitude is not what it seems. Behind it is the adolescent pose of appearing to not care, which disguises a great fear of trying and failing, of standing out and being ridiculed. It stems from sheer laziness and offers its believers consolation for their lack of accomplishments.

As hunters for purpose and meaning, we want to move in the opposite direction. Reality is not brutal and ugly—it contains much that is sublime, beautiful, and worthy of wonder. We see this in the great works of other achievers. We want to have more encounters with the Sublime. Nothing is more awe-inspiring than the human brain itself—its complexity, its untapped potential. We want to realize some of that potential in our lives, not wallow in the cynical slacker attitude. We see a purpose behind everything that we experience and see. In the end, what we want is to fuse the curiosity and excitement we had toward the world as children, when almost everything seemed enchanting, with our adult intelligence.

> The whole law of human existence consists in nothing other than a man's always being able to bow before the immeasurably great. If people are deprived of the immeasurably great, they will not live and will die in despair. The immeasurable and infinite are as necessary for man as the small planet he inhabits.
>
> —*Fyodor Dostoyevsky*

14

Resist the Downward Pull of the Group

◇

The Law of Conformity

We have a side to our character that we are generally unaware of—our social personality, the different person we become when we operate in groups of people. In the group setting, we unconsciously imitate what others are saying and doing. We think differently, more concerned with fitting in and believing what others believe. We feel different emotions, infected by the group mood. We are more prone to taking risks, to acting irrationally, because everyone else is. This social personality can come to dominate who we are. Listening so much to others and conforming our behavior to them, we slowly lose a sense of our uniqueness and the ability to think for ourselves. The only solution is to develop self-awareness and a superior understanding of the changes that occur in us in groups. With such intelligence, we can become superior social actors, able to outwardly fit in and cooperate with others on a high level, while retaining our independence and rationality.

An Experiment in Human Nature

As a young boy growing up in communist China, Gao Jianhua (b. 1952) dreamed of becoming a great writer. He loved literature, and his teachers commended him for his essays and poems. In 1964 he gained admittance to the Yizhen Middle School (YMS), not far from where his family lived. Located in the town of Yizhen, several hundred miles north of Beijing, YMS was labeled a "key school"—over 90 percent of its students went on to college. It was difficult to get into and quite prestigious. At YMS, Jianhua was a quiet and studious boy; he had ambitions of graduating in six years with a top record, good enough to get into Beijing University, from where he would launch the writing career he dreamed about.

Students at YMS lived on campus, and life there could be rather dull, since the Communist Party regulated almost every aspect of life in China, including education. There were daily military drills, propaganda classes, manual labor duty, and regular classes, which could be rigorous.

At YMS, Jianhua developed a close friendship with a classmate named Fangpu, perhaps the most zealous communist at school. Pale and thin and wearing glasses, Fangpu looked the type of the intellectual revolutionary. He was four years older than Jianhua, but they had bonded over their common love of literature and their desire to become writers. They had their differences—Fangpu's poetry centered on political issues; he worshipped Chairman Mao Zedong and wanted to emulate not only his writings but also his revolutionary career. Jianhua, on the other hand, had little interest in politics, even though his father was a respected communist war veteran and government official. But they enjoyed their literary discussions, and Fangpu treated Jianhua like a younger brother.

In May of 1966, as Jianhua was engrossed in his studies, preparing for the final exams to end his second year, Fangpu paid him a visit, and he seemed unusually animated. He had been scouring the Beijing newspapers to keep up with trends in the capital, and recently he had read of a literary debate started by several renowned intellectuals that he had to share with Jianhua.

These intellectuals had accused well-known, respected writers of hiding counterrevolutionary messages in their plays, films, and magazine articles. They based these accusations on careful readings of certain passages in the writers' work that could be seen as veiled criticisms of Mao himself. "Certain people are using art and literature to attack the party and socialism," said Fangpu. This debate is about the future of the revolution, he said, and Mao must be behind it all. To Jianhua it all seemed a bit tedious and academic, but he trusted his older friend's instincts, and he promised to follow the events in the newspaper.

Fangpu's words proved prophetic: within a week, papers throughout China had picked up the story of the raging debate. Teachers at YMS began to talk about some of the newspaper articles in their classes. One day the school's Communist Party secretary, a paunchy man named Ding Yi, called for an assembly and gave a speech recounting almost verbatim an editorial against the counterrevolutionary writers. Something was definitely in the air. The students now had to devote so many hours every day to discussing the latest turns in the debate.

Throughout Beijing, posters with large headlines had appeared everywhere attacking the "antiparty black line," meaning those who were secretly trying to put the brakes on the communist revolution. Ding supplied the students with materials for making their own posters, and the students happily threw themselves into the task. They largely copied the posters from Beijing; Jianhua's friend Zongwei, a talented artist, made the most attractive posters of all, with his elegant calligraphy. Within days, almost all of the walls of the school were covered with posters, and Secretary Ding roamed around the campus reading them, smiling and approving of the work. To Jianhua it was all quite novel and exciting, and he loved the new look of the campus walls.

The campaign in Beijing focused on local intellectuals everyone knew, but in Yizhen this seemed rather distant. If China was being infiltrated by all kinds of counterrevolutionaries, that meant that they had also probably infiltrated the school itself, and the only logical place for the students to look for such class enemies was among their teachers and school officials. They began to scrutinize their lectures and lessons for hidden messages, much as the intellectuals had done with the work of famous writers.

The geography teacher Liu always talked about the beautiful landscapes of China but hardly ever mentioned the inspiring words of Mao. Could that mean something? The physics teacher Feng had an American father who had served in the U.S. Navy; was he secretly an imperialist? Li, the teacher of Chinese, had fought initially on the side of the nationalists against the communists during the revolution, but in the last year had switched sides. The students had always trusted his version of events, and he was Jianhua's favorite teacher because he had such a flair for telling stories. But in retrospect he seemed a bit old-fashioned and bourgeois. Could he still be a counterrevolutionary nationalist at heart? Soon a few posters appeared that questioned the fervor of some of these teachers. Secretary Ding found this a trivial application of the debate, and he ordered a ban on all posters attacking teachers.

By June the movement sweeping Beijing, and soon all of China, had acquired a name—the Great Socialist Cultural Revolution. It was indeed Mao himself who had instigated it all by setting up the newspaper articles, and he was to be the ongoing leader of the new movement. He feared that China had been slipping back into its feudal past. Old ways of thinking and acting had returned. Bureaucracies had become breeding grounds for a new type of elite. Peasants remained relatively powerless.

He wanted a wake-up call to revive the revolutionary spirit. He wanted the younger generation to experience revolution firsthand by making it themselves.

He proclaimed to young people that it was "right to rebel," but the word he used in Chinese for this was *zao fan*, which literally means to turn everything upside down. It was young people's duty, he said, to question authority. Those who secretly worked to pull China back into its past he called "revisionists," and he implored students to help him uncover the revisionists and root them out of the new revolutionary China.

Taking these pronouncements of Mao as a call to action, Fangpu created the most audacious poster anyone had yet seen—it was a direct attack on Secretary Ding himself. Ding was not only the school's party secretary but also a veteran of the revolution and a highly respected figure. According to Fangpu, however, his prohibition on criticizing teachers proved he was a revisionist, bent on suppressing the questioning spirit Mao had encouraged. This created quite a stir. The students had been reared to unquestioningly obey those in authority, particularly respected party members. Fangpu had broken this taboo. Had he gone too far?

A few days after the appearance of Fangpu's poster, some strangers arrived on campus from Beijing. They were part of "work teams" sent to schools around China to help supervise and maintain some discipline over the burgeoning Cultural Revolution. The work team at YMS ordered Fangpu to publicly apologize to Secretary Ding. At the same time, however, they lifted the ban on posters that criticized teachers. As in schools around China, they also suspended all classes and exams at YMS. Students were to devote themselves to making revolution, under their watchful eye.

Suddenly feeling free of the yoke of the past and all the habits of obedience drummed into them, the students at YMS began to brazenly attack those teachers who had demonstrated less than revolutionary zeal or had been unkind to students.

Jianhua felt compelled to join the campaign, but this was difficult—he happened to like almost all of his teachers. He did not want to seem, however, like a revisionist. Besides, he respected the wisdom and authority of Mao. He decided to make a poster attacking Teacher Wen, who had criticized him once for not being sufficiently interested in politics, which had bothered him at the time. He made his criticism of her as gentle as possible. Others took this up and went further with their attacks on Teacher Wen, and Jianhua felt bad.

To satisfy the students' growing anger, some teachers began to confess to some minor revolutionary sins, but this made the students feel they were hiding even more. They had to apply more pressure to get them to reveal the truth, and a student nicknamed "Little Bawang" (*bawang* meaning "overseer," referring to his love of giving orders) had an idea on how to do this. He had read Mao's description of how during the revolution in the 1940s peasants had captured the most notorious landlords and paraded them through their villages with enormous dunce caps on their heads and heavy wooden boards—with inscriptions describing their crimes—hung around their necks. To avoid such public humiliation, certainly the teachers would come clean and confess. The students agreed to try this, and their first target for such treatment was to be Teacher Li, Jianhua's favorite.

Teacher Li was accused of faking his switch to communism. Stories began to come out of his telling other teachers about his visits to brothels in Shanghai. Clearly he had a secret life, and Jianhua now felt disappointed in Li. China before the communist revolution had been a cruel place, and if Li was working to bring that back, he could only hate him. Unwilling to confess to any crimes, Li was the first to be paraded through school with the dunce cap and board around his neck. Along the way some students poured a bucket of poster paste over his head. Jianhua followed the parade from a distance, trying to repress his uneasiness at the humiliation of his teacher.

Led by Little Bawang, the students imposed the same fate on more teachers, the dunce caps becoming unbearably tall and the boards heavier. Imitating their revolutionary brothers and sisters in Beijing, the students initiated "struggle meetings" in which they forced certain teachers into the jet-plane position— a student standing on either side, pushing teachers to their knees, pulling their hair back with a jerk, then holding their arms out and back, like the wings of a jet plane. It was a most painful position, but it seemed to work, as after an hour or two of this, with students jeering at them, many teachers began to confess. The students were right in their suspicions—the school had been teeming with revisionists, right under their noses!

Soon the students' attention turned to the vice principal, Lin Sheng, who they discovered was the son of a notorious landlord. He was the third-highest official at school, which made this bit of news all the more salacious. Jianhua had been sent to his office once for misbehavior, and Sheng had been quite lenient with him, which he had appreciated at the time. The students locked Lin Sheng in a room, where he was to stay between the struggle meetings, but one morning Jianhua, serving as the guard on duty, opened the room to discover the vice principal had hung himself. Once again Jianhua struggled to repress his discomfort, but he had to admit the suicide made it seem as if Lin Sheng was indeed guilty of something.

One day, in the midst of all this, Jianhua ran into Fangpu, who was bursting with excitement. Since his forced public apology over his poster attacking Ding, he had been laying low. He had spent his time devouring the writings of Mao and Marx and plotting his next move. Word had come from Beijing that the work teams were to be withdrawn from all schools. Students were to form their own committee, choose a school official to be its head, and run the school itself through the committee. Fangpu planned on becoming the student leader of the committee. And he was going to wage open revolution against Secretary Ding. Jianhua could only admire his bravery and persistence.

Through Little Bawang, who had forced more and more confessions from teachers, Fangpu learned that Secretary Ding had had affairs with at least two female teachers, revealing his audacious hypocrisy. He was the one continually ranting against Western decadence and was always admonishing the male and female students at Yizhen to keep their distance from each other. Bawang and Fangpu ransacked his office and found that he had been hoarding food coupons and possessed a fancy radio and bottles of nice wine, all hidden away.

Now posters attacking Ding filled the walls. Even Jianhua felt indignant at his behavior. Soon Ding Yi was paraded through school and then through the town of Yizhen, on his head the most enormous dunce cap, decorated with drawings of monsters, and a very heavy drum hung around his neck. As he drummed with one hand while holding the cap with the other, he had to chant, "I am Ding Yi, ox demon and snake spirit." Citizens of Yizhen, who knew Secretary Ding, gaped at the spectacle. The world had indeed been turned upside down.

By the middle of the summer, most of the teachers had fled. When it came time to form the committee to run the school, only a few remained to serve as chairman of the committee, and with Fangpu as the student leader, a little-known and rather harmless teacher named Deng Zeng was named chairman. Now the work team left YMS, and Deng and the committee were in charge.

And as the students progressed in making revolution, Jianhua began to feel increasingly excited. He and his friend Zongwei carried old spears and swords as they patrolled the school looking for spies, and it was just like in the novels he loved to read. He and the other students marched in columns into town, waving enormous red flags, carrying large posters of Chairman Mao and copies of his little red book, chanting slogans, banging on drums, and crashing cymbals. It was so dramatic, and it felt like they were indeed participating in revolution. One day, they marched through Yizhen tearing down store and street signs that were vestiges of prerevolutionary China. Mao would be proud of them.

In Beijing, some students had formed groups to support and defend Mao in his Cultural Revolution; they called themselves Red Guards, and their members wore bright red armbands. Mao gave his personal approval to this, and now Red Guard units began to appear in schools and universities around the country. Only the purest and most fervent revolutionaries could be admitted to the Red Guards, and competition was fierce to join their ranks. Because of his father's illustrious past, Jianhua became a member of the Red Guards, and now he basked in the admiring glances of fellow students and local citizens who noticed the bright red armband that never left him.

There was one wrinkle, however, in these exciting events: On a visit home to see his family in the nearby town of Lingzhi, Jianhua discovered that local students had accused his father of being a revisionist. He cared more about farming and economics than about making revolution, said the students. They had gotten him dismissed from his government position; he had had to suffer through various struggle meetings in the jet-plane position. The family was in disgrace. Although he loved and admired his father and worried for him, he could not help but feel anxious that, if news of this disgrace reached his school, he might lose his red armband and be ostracized. He would have to be careful when talking about his family.

When he returned to school several weeks later, he noticed some radical changes that had already occurred: Fangpu had consolidated power. He had formed a new group called the East-Is-Red Corps; he and his team had kicked out Chairman Deng and were now running the school themselves. They had started their own newspaper, called *Battlefield News*, to promote and defend their actions. Jianhua also learned that another teacher had died under suspicious circumstances.

One day, Fangpu visited Jianhua and invited him to be a star reporter for *Battlefield News*. Fangpu looked different—he had put on weight, was not so pale, and was trying to grow a beard. It was a tempting offer from his friend, but something made Jianhua put him off, and Fangpu did not like this, although he tried to disguise his annoyance with a forced smile. Fangpu was beginning to frighten Jianhua.

Students were now joining the East-Is-Red Corps en masse, but within a few weeks a rival group, calling themselves the Red Rebels, emerged on campus. Their leader was Mengzhe, a student whose parents were peasants and who advocated revolution that was more tolerant, based on reason and not violence, which he felt was the purer form of Maoism. He gained some adherents, including Jianhua's older brother, Weihua, who was a student at YMS. Mengzhe's growing popularity infuriated Fangpu; he called him a royalist, a sentimentalist, and secret counterrevolutionary. He and his followers destroyed the Red Rebels' office and threatened to do worse. It would certainly cause a complete rift with Fangpu, but Jianhua contemplated joining the Red Rebels. He was attracted to their idealism.

Just as the tension between the two sides was escalating into outright war, a representative from the Chinese military arrived on campus and announced that the army was now in charge. Mao had dispatched army units throughout the country to take control of schools. The increasing chaos and violence that was engulfing YMS was going on all over China, not only in schools but in factories and government offices as well; the Cultural Revolution was spinning out of control. Soon thirty-six soldiers arrived on campus, part of an army unit known as the 901; they ordered that all factions disband and that classes resume. There would be military drilling and discipline would be reestablished.

Too much had changed, however, in the eight months since this had all begun. The students could not accept such a sudden return to discipline. They sulked and did not turn up at classes. Fangpu took charge of the campaign to get rid of the soldiers: he put up posters accusing the 901 of being enemies of the Cultural Revolution. One day, he and his followers attacked one of the army officers with a slingshot and wounded him. Just as the students feared reprisals, the 901 unit was suddenly recalled from campus without any explanation.

The students were now completely on their own, and it seemed a frightening prospect. They quickly allied themselves with one of the two groups. Some joined the East-Is-Red Corps because it was larger and offered better positions; others joined the Red Rebels because they hated Fangpu and Little Bawang; and others thought one group or the other was more revolutionary. Jianhua joined the Red Rebels, as did his friend Zongwei.

Each side felt certain it represented the true spirit of the Cultural Revolution, and as they yelled at one another and argued, fistfights broke out, and there was nobody to stop them. Soon students were bringing bats and sticks to the fights, and the injuries mounted. One day some members of the East-Is-Red

Corps captured some Red Rebels and held them prisoners. The Red Rebels could not find out anything about their fate.

In the middle of this tense moment, the Red Rebels discovered that one of their members, a female student named Yulan, was actually a spy for the other side. Infuriated by such tactics, they tied Yulan up and began to beat her, to find out if there were more spies. Much to the dismay of Jianhua, who considered this a betrayal of their ideals, they battered and bruised her, but she revealed nothing. Soon Yulan was exchanged for the prisoners held by the East-Is-Red Corps, but now the antipathy between the two sides had reached a breaking point.

A few weeks later, the East-Is-Red Corps suddenly left school en masse and established their headquarters in a building in town that they seized. Mengzhe decided to form a team of guerrilla fighters who would operate in Yizhen at night to keep an eye on the Corps and do some sabotage work. Jianhua was assigned to them as a reporter. It was an exciting job. As they encountered the enemy in town, battles with slingshots erupted. Then the Corps captured one of the Rebel guerrillas, named Heping. A few days later, he was discovered in a hospital, dead. The Corps had taken him for a ride in a jeep in the desert, with a sock in his mouth, and he had suffocated along the way. Now even Mengzhe had had enough and vowed revenge for this horrible deed. Jianhua could only agree with him.

As the skirmishes spread throughout the town, citizens fled and entire buildings were abandoned, and looters scoured them for goods. The Red Rebels were soon on the offensive. Working with local craftsmen, they manufactured the highest-quality swords and spears. Casualties mounted. Finally the Rebels encircled the Corps's stronghold in town and prepared for a final offensive. The Corps fled, leaving behind a small band of student soldiers in the building. The Rebels demanded their surrender, and suddenly, from a third-floor window, there was the young student Yulan screaming out, "I'd rather die than surrender to you!" With the Corps's bright red flag in her hand, she shouted, "Long live Chairman Mao!" and jumped. Jianhua found her lifeless body wrapped up in the flag on the ground. Her devotion to the cause astounded and impressed him.

Now in control, the Red Rebels established their headquarters at the school and prepared their defenses for a counteroffensive from the Corps. They built a makeshift munitions factory on campus. Some students had learned how to make grenades and various powerful explosive devices. An inadvertent explosion killed several of them, but the work went on. Zongwei, the artist, had had enough; somehow the noble origins of the Red Rebels had been lost, and he feared the expanding violence; he fled Yizhen for good. Jianhua lost respect for his friend. How could Zongwei forget those who had been injured or died for their cause? To give up now would be to say it was all in vain. He would not be a coward like his friend. Besides, the East-Is-Red Corps was downright evil and was capable of doing anything to take power. They had betrayed the revolution.

As life at the school settled down and the Red Rebels built up their defenses, Jianhua visited his family, whom he had not seen for a while. When he finally returned one night to school, however, he could not believe his eyes: his Red Rebel comrades were nowhere in sight; their flag was no longer flying above the school. Everywhere there were armed soldiers. Finally he found a few comrades hiding in a school building, and they told him what had happened: Mao was reasserting his authority once and for all; he was picking sides in various local conflicts to help create some order; and the military in the county had come down on the side of the East-Is-Red Corps as the more truly revolutionary group. The repercussions of this could be awful.

Jianhua and several other comrades decided they would try to escape and regroup in the mountains, where Mengzhe had apparently fled, but there was a blockade throughout the county and they were forced back to school, which had become more of a prison, overseen by the East-Is-Red Corps.

Now the Rebels could only expect the worst. To the Corps, they were a bunch of counterrevolutionaries who had beaten and killed their comrades. Then one day, as the Red Rebel members on campus were huddled together in a room, the leaders of the East-Is-Red Corps, including Fangpu and Little Bawang, entered with grenades tied to their belts. Fangpu carried a blacklist of all those who were to be taken from the room, clearly for some nefarious purpose. Fangpu appeared friendly toward Jianhua and told him it was not too late to change sides, but Jianhua could no longer see Fangpu in the same light. His friendliness made him seem even more sinister.

That night they could hear the screams of their blacklisted comrades from another building. Then news reached them that Corps members had found Mengzhe, beaten him up, and marched him back to school, where he was under arrest as well. In the room next to where Jianhua and his friends now slept, they observed Little Bawang and his team covering the windows with blankets. They were transforming it into a torture chamber. Soon they noticed former Red

Rebels limping about on campus, afraid to talk to anyone. Then it was Jianhua's turn to be taken into the room. He was blindfolded and tied to a chair in a most uncomfortable position. They wanted him to sign a withdrawal statement, and as he hesitated to do so, they began to beat him with a chair leg. Jianhua screamed, "You can't do this to me. We're classmates. We're all class brothers. . . ."

Little Bawang would have none of this. Jianhua had to confess his crimes, the part he had played in the various battles in town, and name names of other Red Rebels hiding somewhere on campus. The blows on his legs became more intense, and then they began to hit him over the head. Still blindfolded, he feared for his life and in a panic suddenly spilled the name of a fellow Red Rebel, Dusu. Finally they carried Jianhua, unable to walk, out of the room. He quickly felt intense regret that he had named Dusu. What a coward he had been. He tried to warn Dusu, but it was too late. The torturing of other Red Rebels continued in the room next door, including his brother Weihua, beaten to a bloody pulp. Mengzhe had his head shaved, and when they saw him next, his face was covered in the most hideous bruises.

One day Jianhua was told his old friend and comrade Zongwei had been captured, and when Jianhua went to see him he was unconscious, his bare legs full of large punctures, blood oozing everywhere. They had flailed him with steel hooks for refusing to admit his crimes. How could the rather harmless Zongwei inspire such savagery? Jianhua ran to get the doctor, but when they returned it was too late: Zongwei died in his friend's arms. The dead body was quickly carted away, and a cover story was created for how he had died. Jianhua was ordered to remain silent. A female teacher who refused to affirm in an affidavit the official East-Is-Red Corps version of his death was beaten and gang-raped by Little Bawang and his followers.

In the months to come, Fangpu extended his powers everywhere, as he essentially ran the school and classes resumed. *Battlefield News* was the only newspaper allowed. The school itself had been renamed East-Is-Red Middle School. With the Corps's power secure, the torture chamber was dismantled. Classes largely consisted of reciting quotes from Mao. Every morning they assembled before a giant poster of Chairman Mao and, brandishing their little red books, chanted to his long life.

The East-Is-Red members began a scrupulous rewriting of the past. They held an exhibition to celebrate their victories, full of doctored photographs and fake news reports, all to bolster their side of events. An enormous statue of Chairman Mao, five times larger than life, was now installed at the school gate, towering over everything else. The former members of the Red Rebels had to wear white armbands that described their various crimes. They were made to kowtow before the Mao statue several times a day while classmates kicked them from behind. The former Red Rebels had become like the reviled teachers, cowed and obedient.

Jianhua was forced to do the most menial labor, and having had enough of this, in early summer of 1968 he returned to his hometown. His father sent him and his brother to a farm deep in the mountains where they could be safe and work as laborers. In September, determined to finish his studies, Jianhua returned to school. The few months away had given him some perspective, and now when he looked at the East-Is-Red Middle School, it appeared in a very different light: everywhere he saw signs of unbelievable destruction—classrooms completely torn up with no desks or chairs, the walls full of peeling posters and crumbling plaster; the science labs devoid of all equipment; piles of rubble around the campus; unmarked graves; the music hall blown up by a bomb; and hardly a reputable teacher or official left to resume their education.

All of this destruction in a few short years, and for what? What did Heping and Yulan and Zongwei and so many others die for? What had they been fighting over? What had they learned? He could no longer figure it out, and the waste of their young lives filled him with disgust and despair.

Soon Jianhua and his brother joined the army, to escape the school and bury their memories. Over the following years, as he drove an army truck delivering stone and cement, he and his comrades watched the slow disassembling of the Cultural Revolution, all of its former leaders falling into disgrace. After the death of Mao in 1976, the Communist Party itself finally condemned the Cultural Revolution as a national catastrophe.

Interpretation: The above story and characters come from the book *Born Red* (1987) by Gao Yuan. (After the Cultural Revolution, the author changed his name from Gao Jianhua to Gao Yuan.) It is his nonfiction account of the events he participated in at his school during the Cultural Revolution.

In essence, the Cultural Revolution was Mao's attempt to try to alter human nature itself. According to Mao, through millennia of capitalism in various forms, humans had become individualistic and conservative, bound to their social class. Mao wanted to wipe the slate clean and start over. As he explained it, "A clean sheet of paper has no blotches, and so the newest and most beautiful pictures can be painted on it." To get his blank canvas, Mao would have to shake things up on a mass scale by uprooting old habits and ways of thinking and by eradicating people's mindless respect for those in authority. Once he accomplished this, Mao could start to paint something bold and new on the clean sheet. The result would be a fresh generation that could begin to forge a classless society not weighed down by the past.

The events depicted in Born Red reveal in a microcosm the result of Mao's experiment—how human nature cannot be uprooted; try to alter it and it merely reemerges in different shapes and forms. The results of hundreds of thousands of years of evolution and development cannot be radically reengineered by some scheme, particularly when it involves the behavior of humans in groups, which inevitably conforms to certain ancient patterns. (Although it might be tempting to see what happened at YMS as mostly relevant to group adolescent behavior, young people often represent human nature in a more naked and purer form than adults, who are cleverer at disguising their motivations. In any case, what happened at the school occurred throughout China—in government offices, factories, within the army, and among Chinese of all ages—in an eerily similar way.) Here's exactly how Mao's experiment failed and what it shows about human nature.

Mao had the following specific strategy to enact his bold idea: Focus people's attention on a legitimate enemy—in this case, revisionists, those who consciously or unconsciously were clinging to the past. Encourage people, particularly the young, to actively fight against this reactionary force, but also against any entrenched forms of authority. In struggling against these conservative enemies, the Chinese would be able to free themselves from old patterns of thinking and acting; they would finally get rid of elites and ranking systems; and they would unify as a revolutionary class with utmost clarity as to what they were fighting for.

His strategy, however, had a fatal flaw at its core: when people operate in groups, they do not engage in nuanced thinking and deep analysis. Only individuals with a degree of calmness and detachment can do so. People in groups feel emotional and excited. Their primary desire is to fit in to the group spirit. Their thinking tends to be simplistic—good versus evil, with us or against us. They naturally look for some type of authority to simplify matters for them. Deliberately creating chaos, as Mao did, only makes the group more certain to fall into these primitive patterns of thinking, since it is too frightening for humans to live with too much confusion and uncertainty.

Look at how the students at YMS responded to Mao's call for action: When first confronted with the Cultural Revolution, they merely transformed Mao himself into the new authority to guide them. They swallowed his ideas with very little personal reflection. They imitated the actions of others in Beijing in the most conventional way. Looking for revisionists, they tended to base their judgments on appearances—the clothes the teachers wore, the special food or wine they drank, their manners, their family background. Such appearances could be quite deceptive. Teacher Wen was radical in her beliefs but was judged a revisionist based on her fondness for Western-style fashion.

In the old order, the students were supposed to give total obedience to their all-powerful teachers. Suddenly freed from all that, they remained just as emotionally tied to the past. The teachers still seemed all-powerful, but now as scheming counterrevolutionaries. The students' repressed resentment at having to be so obedient now boiled over into anger and the desire to be the ones doing the punishing and oppressing. When the teachers confessed to crimes they mostly had never committed, to avoid the escalating punishments, that only seemed to confirm the students in their paranoia. They had shifted roles from obedient students to oppressors, but their thinking had become even more simplistic and irrational, the opposite of Mao's intentions.

In the power vacuum that Mao had now created, another timeless group dynamic emerged: those who were naturally more assertive, aggressive, and even sadistic (in this case Fangpu and Little Bawang) pushed their way forward and assumed power, while those who were more passive (Jianhua, Zongwei) quietly receded into the background, becoming followers. The aggressive types at YMS now formed a new class of elites, doling out perks and privileges. Similarly, amid all the confusion the Cultural Revolution had spawned, the students became even more obsessed with status within the group. Who was in the red category among them, and who in the black, they wondered? Was it better now to come from the peasantry or the proletariat? How could they finagle membership in the Red Guards and garner that beautiful red armband that signified revolutionary elite status? Instead of naturally inclining toward a new egalitarian order, the students kept straining to occupy superior positions.

Once all forms of authority were removed and the students ran the school, there was nothing to stop the next and most dangerous development in group dynamics—the split into tribal factions. By nature, we humans reject attempts by anyone to completely monopolize power, as Fangpu tried to do. This cuts off opportunities for other ambitious, aggressive people. It also creates large groupings in which individual members can feel somewhat lost. Almost automatically, groups will split into rival smaller factions and tribes. In the rival tribe, a new, charismatic leader (Mengzhe in this case) can assume power and members can identify more easily with the smaller number of comrades. The bonds are tight and made even tighter by the struggle against the tribal enemy. People may think they are joining because of the different ideas or goals of this tribe or the other, but what they want more than anything is the sense of belonging and a clear tribal identity.

Look at the actual differences between the East-Is-Red Corps and the Red Rebels. As the battle between them intensified, it was hard to say what they were fighting for, except to assume power over the other group. One strong or vicious act of one side called for a reprisal from the other, and any type of violence seemed totally justified. There could be no middle ground, nor any questioning of the rightness of their cause. The tribe is always right, and to say otherwise is to betray it, as Zongwei did.

Mao had wanted to forge a unified Chinese citizenry, clear as to its goals, and instead the entire country descended into tribal battles completely disconnected from the original purpose of the Cultural Revolution. To make matters worse, the crime rate soared and the economy had ground to a halt, as hardly anyone felt compelled to work or manufacture anything. The masses had become even lazier and more resentful than under the old order.

By the spring of 1968, Mao's only recourse was to install a police state. Hundreds of thousands were thrown into prisons. The army virtually took over. To help restore order and respect for authority, Mao converted himself into a cult figure, his image to be worshipped and his words to be repeated like revolutionary prayers. It is interesting to note how Fangpu's form of repression at YMS—the torture, the rewriting of history, the control of all media—mirrored what Mao was doing throughout the country. The new revolutionary society that Mao (and Fangpu) had wanted now actually resembled the most repressive, superstitious regimes of feudal China. As Jianhua's father, a victim of the Cultural Revolution himself, kept telling his son, "A thing turns into its opposite if pushed too far."

Understand: We will tend to imagine that this story is an extreme example that has little relevance to our own lives and the groups we belong to. After all, we navigate through worlds full of sophisticated people in high-tech offices, where everyone is seemingly so polite and civilized. We see ourselves in a similar way: we have our progressive ideals and our independent thinking. But much of this is an illusion. If we looked at ourselves closely and honestly, we would have to admit that the moment we enter our workspace or any group, we undergo a change. We easily slip into more primitive modes of thinking and behaving, without realizing it.

Around others, we naturally tend to feel insecure as to what they think of us. We feel pressure to fit in, and to do so, we begin to shape our thoughts and beliefs to the group orthodoxies. We unconsciously imitate others in the group—in appearances, verbal expressions, and ideas. We tend to worry a lot about our status and where we rank in the hierarchy: "Am I getting as much respect as my colleagues?" This is the primate part of our nature, as we share this obsession with status with our chimpanzee relatives. Depending on patterns from early childhood, in the group setting we become more passive or more aggressive than usual, revealing the less developed sides of our character.

When it comes to leaders, we generally don't see them as ordinary people. We tend to feel somewhat awed and intimidated in their presence, as if they possessed some mythical extra powers. When we contemplate our group's main rival or enemy, we can't help but get a little heated and angry and exaggerate any negative qualities. If others in the group are feeling anxious or outraged by something, we often get swept up in the group mood. All of these are subtle indications that we are under the influence of the group. If we are experiencing the above transformations, we can be sure the same is going on with our colleagues.

Now imagine some outside threat to our group's well-being or stability, a crisis of sorts. All of the above reactions would be intensified by the stress, and our apparently civilized, sophisticated group could become quite volatile. We would feel greater pressure to prove our loyalty and go along with anything the group advocated. Our thinking about the rival/enemy would become even more simplistic and heated. We would be subject to more powerful waves of viral emotions, including panic or hatred or grandiosity. Our group could split up into factions with tribal dynamics. Charismatic leaders could easily emerge to exploit this volatility. If pushed far enough, the potential for aggression lies under the surface of almost any group. But even if we hold back from overt violence, the primitive dynamic that takes over can have grave consequences, as the group overreacts and makes decisions based on exaggerated fears or uncontrollable excitement.

To resist this downward pull that groups inevitably exert on us, we must conduct a very different *experiment in human nature* from Mao's, with a simple goal in mind—to develop the ability to detach ourselves from the group and create some mental space for true independent thinking. We begin this experiment by accepting the reality of the powerful effect that the group has on us. We are brutally honest with ourselves, aware of how our need to fit in can shape and warp our thinking. Does that anxiety or sense of outrage that we feel come completely from within, or is it inspired by the group? We must observe our tendency to demonize the enemy and control it. We must train ourselves to not blindly venerate our leaders; we respect them for their accomplishments without feeling the need to deify them. We must be especially careful around those who have charismatic appeal, and try to demystify and pull them down to earth. With such awareness, we can begin to resist and detach.

As part of this experiment we must not only accept human nature but work with what we have to make it productive. We inevitably feel the need for status and recognition, so let's not deny it. Instead, let's cultivate such status and recognition through our excellent work. We must accept our need to belong to the group and prove our loyalty, but let's do it in more positive ways—by questioning group decisions that will harm it in the long run, by supplying divergent opinions, by steering the group in a more rational direction, gently and strategically. Let's use the viral nature of emotions in the group but play on a different set of emotions: by staying calm and patient, by focusing on results and cooperating with others to get practical things done, we can begin to spread this spirit throughout the group. And by slowly mastering the primitive part of our character within the heated environment of the group, we can emerge as individuals who are truly independent and rational—the end point of our experiment.

When people are free to do as they please, they usually imitate each other.

—Eric Hoffer

Keys to Human Nature

At certain moments in life, we humans may experience an energy that is powerful, with sensations unlike any other, but this energy is something we rarely discuss or analyze. We can describe it as an intense feeling of belonging to a group, and we often experience it in the following situations.

Let us say we find ourselves in a large audience for a concert, sporting event, or political rally. At a certain point, waves of excitement, anger, or joy move through us, shared by thousands of others. These emotions rise in us automatically. We cannot experience this when alone or with just a few people. In this larger group setting, we might be led to say or do things we would never have said or done on our own.

In a similar vein, perhaps we have to give a talk before a group. If we are not too nervous and the crowd is on our side, we experience a swelling of emotion from deep within. We're feeding off the audience. Our voice changes to a pitch and tone we never have in daily life; our gestures and body language become unusually animated. We might also experience this from the other side, when we listen to a charismatic speaker. That person seems to be invested with some sort of special force that commands our respect and fills us with increasing excitement.

Or perhaps we find ourselves working in a group with a critical goal to reach within a short time frame. We feel compelled to do more than we normally can, to work extra hard. We feel a charge of energy that comes from feeling connected to others who are working with the same urgent spirit. A point is reached at which members of the group do not even have to talk—we're all on the same page and can even anticipate the thoughts of our colleagues.

The above feelings are not registered rationally; they come to us in automatic bodily sensations—goose bumps, racing heartbeat, extra vitality and power. Let us call us this energy the *social force*, a type of invisible force field that affects and binds a group of people through shared sensations and creates an intense feeling of connection.

If we confront this force field as outsiders, it tends to induce anxiety. For instance, we find ourselves traveling to a place with a culture very different from our own. Or we begin a job at a workplace where people seem to have their own way of relating to one another, with a secret language of sorts. Or we walk through a neighborhood of a much different social class than what we're used to—much wealthier or poorer. In these moments, we are aware that we don't belong, that others are looking at us as outsiders, and from deep within we feel uneasy and unusually alert, although in fact we may have nothing really to fear.

We can observe several interesting elements to the social force: First, *it exists inside us and outside us at the same time.* When we experience the bodily sensations mentioned above, we are almost certain that others on our side are feeling the same. We feel the force within, but we think of it as outside ourselves as well. This is an unusual sensation, perhaps equivalent to what we feel when we are in love and experience a shared energy that passes between ourselves and the love object.

We can also say *this force differs, depending on the size and chemistry of the particular group.* In general, the larger the group, the more intense is the effect. When we are among a very large group of people who seem to share our ideas or values, we feel quite a rush of increased strength and vitality, as well as a communal warmth or heat that comes from feeling that we belong. There is something awesome and sublime about this force multiplied in a large crowd. This increase in energy and excitement can easily shift to anger and violence in the presence of an enemy. The particular mix of people shapes the effect as well. If the leader is charismatic and bursting with energy, it filters through the group or gathered masses. If a large number of individuals have a particular emotional tendency toward anger or joy, that will alter the collective mood.

And finally, *we are drawn to this force.* We feel attracted to numbers—a stadium full of partisan supporters of a team, choirs of people singing, parades, carnivals, concerts, religious assemblies, and political conventions. In these situations, we are reliving what our ancestors invented and refined—the gathering of the clan, massed soldiers parading in columns before the city walls, early theatrical and gladiatorial spectacles. Subtracting the minority who feel frightened by such gatherings, we generally have a love of partisan crowds for their own sake. They make us feel alive and vital. This can become an addiction— we feel compelled to expose ourselves to this energy again and again. Music and dance epitomize this aspect of the social force. The group experiences the rhythm and melody as one, and music and dance are among the earliest forms we created to satisfy this urge, to externalize the force.

We can observe one other aspect to the social force, in its reverse form: when we experience a prolonged period of isolation. We know from the accounts of prisoners in solitary confinement and explorers isolated in remote regions (see Richard E. Byrd's account of his harrowing five months in isolation in Antarctica, in his book *Alone*) that they begin to feel disconnected from reality and sense that their personalities are disintegrating. They become prone to elaborate hallucinations. What they miss most of all is not simply the presence of people near them but the eyes of others looking back at them. We formed our whole concept of ourselves in our first months as we looked at our mothers; her return gaze gave us a sense that we existed; she told us who we were by how she looked at us. As adults, we experience the same kind of nonverbal validation and sense of self through the eyes of others who look at us. We are never aware of this; it would take prolonged isolation to understand the phenomenon.

This is the social force at its most basic level—only the eyes of other people can reassure us that we are real and whole and that we belong.

The social force can make itself felt in our virtual worlds and virtual crowds. It is less intense than being in an actual crowd, but we can feel the presence of others in a phantom-like way through the screen (inside us and outside us), and we continually consult our smartphones as a kind of substitute pair of eyes upon us.

The social force among humans is merely a more complex version of what all social animals experience. Social animals are continually *attuned* to the emotions of others within the group, aware of their role in the pack and anxious to fit in. (Among higher primates, this includes imitating those higher up in the rank as a show of inferiority.) They display elaborate physical cues that allow the group to communicate and cooperate. They have grooming rituals to tighten their bonds, and hunting in packs has a similar effect. They experience a shared energy when simply assembled together.

We humans may seem much more sophisticated, but the same dynamic occurs in us as well, on a completely subverbal level. We sense and feel what others in the group are feeling. We have an urgent need to fit in and play our role in the group. We are prone to unconsciously imitate gestures and expressions, particularly from leaders. We still like to hunt in packs, through social media or wherever it is acceptable to vent our anger. We have our own rituals to tighten group bonds—religious or political assemblies, spectacles, warfare. And we most definitely experience a collective energy that passes through any group of like-minded people.

What is most peculiar about this force as it exists within us is how little we discuss or analyze something that is so obviously common to our experience. Some of this may come from the fact that it is hard to study these sensations in a rigorously scientific manner. But there is also something willful about this ignorance; deep down, this phenomenon troubles us. Our automatic reactions in a group, or our propensity to imitate others, reminds us of the most primitive aspects of our nature, our animal roots. We want to imagine ourselves not only as civilized and sophisticated but also as individuals with conscious control of much of what we do. Our group behavior tends to shatter this myth, and historical examples such as the Cultural Revolution frighten us with our own possibilities. We do not like to see ourselves as social animals operating under particular compulsions. It offends our self-opinion as a species.

Understand: The social force is neither positive nor negative. It is simply a physiological part of our nature. Many aspects of this force that evolved so long ago are quite dangerous in the modern world. For instance, the deep suspicion we tend to feel toward outsiders to our group, and our need to demonize them, evolved among our earliest ancestors because of the tremendous dangers of infectious diseases and the aggressive intentions of rival hunter-gatherers. But such group reactions are no longer relevant in the twenty-first century. In fact, with our technological prowess, they can be the source of our most violent and genocidal behavior. In general, to the degree that the social force tends to degrade our ability to think independently and rationally, we can say it exerts a downward pull into more primitive ways of behaving, unsuited to modern conditions.

The social force, however, can be used and shaped for *positive* purposes, for high-level cooperation and empathy, for an upward pull, which we experience when we create something together in a group.

The problem we face as social animals is not that we experience this force, which occurs automatically, but that we are in denial of its existence. We become influenced by others without realizing it. Accustomed to unconsciously following what others say and do, we lose the ability to think for ourselves. When faced with critical decisions in life, we simply imitate what others have done or listen to people who parrot conventional wisdom. This can lead to many inappropriate decisions. We also lose contact with what makes us unique, the source of our power as individuals (see chapter 13 for more on this).

Some people, aware of these tendencies in our nature, may choose to rebel and become nonconformists. But this can be equally mindless and self-destructive. We are social creatures. We depend on our ability to work with others. Rebelling for its own sake will simply marginalize us.

What we need more than anything is *group intelligence*. This intelligence includes a thorough understanding of the effect that groups have on our thinking and emotions; with such awareness, we can resist the downward pull. It also includes understanding how human groups operate according to certain laws and dynamics, which can make it easier to navigate through such spaces. With such intelligence, we can do a delicate dance—we can become gifted social actors and outwardly fit in, while inwardly maintaining some distance and some mental space to think for ourselves. With this degree of independence, we can make decisions in life that are appropriate to who we are and our circumstances.

To acquire this intelligence, we must study and master the two aspects of the social force outlined above—the individual effect of groups on us and the patterns and dynamics that groups will almost always tend to fall into.

The Individual Effect

The desire to fit in: Let us say that you enter a group, as part of a new job for instance. As you try to adjust to the environment, you become aware that people are scrutinizing and judging you as the outsider. On a nonverbal level, you feel their eyes probing you for clues. You begin to wonder: Do I fit in? Have I said the right things? What do they think of me? *The first and primary effect on you in any group is the desire to fit in and cement your sense of belonging.* The more you fit in, the less you pose a challenge to the group and its values. This will minimize the scrutiny you face and the anxiety that comes with it.

The first way you do this is through appearances. You dress and present yourself more or less as the others do in the group. There are always a small percentage of people who like to stand out in their look but manage to conform when it comes to ideas and values. Most of us, however, are uncomfortable looking too different, and we do what we can to blend in. We adopt the clothes and looks that say the right thing—I'm serious, I work hard, I may have style but not so much of it that I stand out.

The second and more important way you fit in is by adopting the ideas, beliefs, and values of the group. You may begin to use similar verbal expressions as others, a sign of what's happening below the surface. Your own ideas slowly shape themselves to those of the group. Some people may outwardly rebel against such conformity, but they are usually the types who are eventually fired or marginalized. You may hold on to a few peculiar beliefs or opinions that you largely keep to yourself, but not on issues important to the group. The longer you are in the group, the stronger and more insidious this effect.

If you observed this group from the outside, you would notice an overall uniformity of thinking that is quite surprising, considering that as individuals we all differ quite a bit from one another in temperament and background. This is a sign of the subtle molding and conformity that takes place. You might have joined a group *because* you share their ideas and values, but you will find over time that the parts of your thinking that were a little different from others, reflecting your uniqueness, are slowly trimmed way, like a shrub made to match the others, so that on almost all issues you agree with the group.

You are not aware of all this as it is happening to you. It occurs unconsciously. In fact, you will tend to vociferously deny such conformity has ever taken place. You will imagine that you have come upon these ideas on your own, that you have *chosen* to believe this and think that. You don't want to confront the social force operating on you and causing you to blend in and enhance your sense of belonging. In the long run, it is much better to confront your conformity to the group ethos, so that you can become aware of it as it happens and control the process to some degree.

The need to perform: Stemming from this first effect is the second effect—*in the group setting, we are always performing.* It is not just that we conform in appearances and thinking but that we exaggerate our agreement and *show* others that we belong. In the group, we become actors, molding what we say and do so that others accept and like us and see us as loyal team members. Our performances change depending on the size of the group and its particular makeup—bosses or colleagues or friends. We might begin with a degree of inner distance in these performances, aware, for instance, that we are being unusually obsequious around the boss. But over time, in acting the part we begin to feel what we are showing; the inner distance melts away, and the mask we wear fuses into our personality. Instead of thinking to smile in appropriate moments, we automatically paste on the smile.

As part of this performance, we minimize our flaws and display what we consider our strengths. We put on confidence. We *act* more altruistic. Studies have shown that we are much more likely to give money or help someone cross the road when others are looking at us. In the group, we make sure that people see we support the right causes; we post our progressive opinions prominently on social media. We also make sure others see us working hard and putting in extra hours. When we are alone, we often rehearse in our minds things we will say or do for our next performance.

Do not imagine that it is better to simply be your natural self or to rebel against this. There is nothing more *unnatural* than curbing this need to perform, which even chimpanzees display to a high degree. If you want to seem natural, as if you are comfortable with yourself, you have to *act* the part; you have to train yourself to not feel nervous and to shape your appearance so that in your naturalness you don't offend people or the group values. Those who sulk and refuse to perform end up marginalized, as the group unconsciously expels such types.

In any event, you should feel no shame about this need; there is nothing you can do about it anyway, since in the group we unconsciously mold our behavior to fit in. Better to be aware, to retain that inner distance, and to transform yourself into a conscious and superior actor, capable of altering your expression to fit the subgroup and impressing people with your positive qualities.

Emotional contagion: When we were babies, we were highly sensitive to the moods and emotions of our mother; her smiles elicited our own, her anxiety made us tense. We evolved this high degree of empathy to the emotions of the mother as a survival mechanism long ago. Like all social animals, we are primed from an early age to sense and pick up the emotions of others, particularly those close to us. This is the third effect of the group on us—*the contagiousness of emotions.*

When we are alone, we are aware of our shifting moods, but the moment we enter the group and feel the eyes of others upon us, we become aware on unconscious levels of *their* moods and emotions, which, if strong enough, can displace our own. In addition, among those whom we feel comfortable and sense that we belong, we are less defensive and more vulnerable to the contagious effect.

Certain emotions are more contagious than others, anxiety and fear being the strongest of all. Among our ancestors, if one person sensed a danger, it was important that others feel this as well. But in our present environment, where the threats are less immediate, it is more like a low-grade anxiety that passes quickly through the group, triggered by possible or imagined dangers. Other highly contagious emotions are joy and excitement, tiredness and apathy, and intense anger and hatred. Desire is also highly contagious. If we see that others want to possess something or follow some new trend, we are easily infected with the same impulse.

All of these effects have a self-fulfilling dynamic: If three people are feeling anxious, there must be a good reason for it. Now we become the fourth, and it gains a reality that others find compelling. The more people who feel it, the more others will catch it and the more intense it becomes within us as individuals.

You can observe this in yourself by looking at your own emotions in the moment and trying to decipher the effect others might have had on them. Is the fear you are feeling related to something confronting you in an immediate sense, or is it more secondhand, derived from what you have heard or sensed from others? Try to catch this as it occurs. Discern which emotions are the most contagious for you, and how your emotions shift with the various groups and subgroups you pass through. Awareness of this gives you the power to control it.

Hypercertainty: When we are on our own and think about our decisions and plans, we naturally feel doubts. Have we chosen the right career path? Did we say the right thing to get the job? Are we adopting the best strategy? But when we are in the group, this doubting, reflective mechanism is neutralized. Let us say the group has to decide on an important strategy. We feel the urgency to act. Arguing and deliberating is tiring, and where will it end? We feel the pressure to decide and get behind the decision. If we dissent, we might be marginalized or excluded, and we recoil from such possibilities. Furthermore, if everyone seems to agree that this is the right course of action, we are compelled to feel confident about the decision. And so the fourth effect on us is *to make us feel more certain about what we and our colleagues are doing, which makes us all the more prone to taking risks.*

This is what happens in financial crazes and bubbles—if everyone is betting on the price of tulips or South Sea stock (see chapter 6) or subprime mortgages, it must be a sure thing. Those who raise doubts are simply being too cautious. As individuals, it is hard to resist what others seem so certain about. We don't want to miss out. Furthermore, if we were among just a few who bought this stock, and it failed, we would feel ridiculous and ashamed, sadly responsible for being such a sucker. But covered by thousands doing the same, we are shielded from feeling accountable, which increases the likelihood we will take such risks in the group setting.

If as individuals we had some plan that was clearly ridiculous, others would warn us and bring us back down to earth, but in a group the opposite happens—everyone seems to validate the scheme, no matter how delusional (such as invading Iraq and expecting to be greeted as liberators), and there are no outsiders to splash some cold water on us.

Whenever you feel unusually certain and excited about a plan or idea, you must step back and gauge whether it is a viral group effect operating on you. If you can detach yourself for a moment from your excitement, you might notice how your thinking is used to rationalize your emotions, to confirm the certainty you *want* to feel. Never relinquish your ability to doubt, reflect, and consider other options—your rationality as an individual is your only protection against the madness that can overcome a group.

Group Dynamics

Since the beginning of recorded history, we can observe certain patterns that human groups fall into almost automatically, as if they were subject to particular mathematical or physical laws. The following are the most common dynamics that you must study in the groups that you belong to or pass through.

Group culture: When we travel to another country, we are aware of the differences in culture from our own. Not only do the inhabitants have their own language, but they also have customs, ways of looking at the world and thinking, that are different from our own. This is more pronounced among nations which have long traditions, but to a subtler extent we can see the same thing happening with a company or office. It is all part of the social force blending and knitting the group together based on the particular chemistry of its members.

When looking at your own group and its culture, think in terms of style and the overall mood that prevails. Is it loosely structured, with an easygoing style? Or is it organized top down, its members afraid of stepping out of line or breaking discipline? Do its members feel superior and separate from the rest of the world, displaying an elitist attitude, or does the group pride itself on its populism? Does it see itself as cutting-edge or more traditionalist?

Does information flow easily throughout the group, giving it an open feel, or does the leadership control and monopolize this flow? Does it have a masculine feel to it—a hypercompetitive edge and a more rigid chain of command— or does it have a more fluid, feminine spirit that emphasizes cooperation over hierarchy? Does it seem riddled with dysfunction and disunity, its members more concerned with their egos than with getting actual results, or does it emphasize productivity and the quality of the work? To answer these questions, don't pay much attention to what the group says about itself, but rather examine its actions and the emotional tone that prevails within.

Its style can have degrees of the above qualities, or combinations of them, but the group will always have some type of identifiable culture and spirit. Two things to keep in mind: First, the culture will often center on an ideal that the group imagines for itself—liberal, modern, progressive, ruthlessly competitive, tasteful, et cetera. The group may not live up to this ideal, but to the degree that it tries to, the ideal operates as a myth that binds the group's members. Second, this culture will often reflect the founders of the group, particularly if they have a strong personality. With their own rigid or loose style, they have put their stamp on the group, even if it numbers in the thousands. But leaders who enter a group or company that has its set culture will often find themselves completely absorbed by this culture, even though they might think of altering it.

The U.S. Department of Defense, housed in the Pentagon, emerged from World War II with a very strong, hawkish spirit. Both presidents Kennedy and Johnson had their own views on the Pentagon and altering its culture; they both wanted to avoid entangling the U.S. in the Vietnam War. But this aggressive culture ended up altering *their* ideas and dragging them into the war. Many film directors in Hollywood have thought of doing things their own way, only to find themselves swallowed up by an entrenched culture that emphasizes top-down control and micromanagement by producers, with their interminable notes. This culture has existed for close to ninety years, and no individual has been able to alter it.

Better to be aware and realize that the larger the group and the more established the culture over time, the more likely it will control you than the other way around.

One thing to keep in mind: no matter the type of culture, or how disruptive it might have been in its origins, the longer a group exists and the larger it grows, the more conservative it will become. This is an inevitable result of the desire to hold on to what people have made or built, and to rely on tried-and-true ways to maintain the status quo. This creeping conservatism will often be the death of the group, because it slowly loses the ability to adapt.

Group rules and codes: For any human group, disorder and anarchy are too distressing. And so standards of conduct and rules for how to do things quickly evolve and become set. These rules and codes are never written down but are implicit. Violate them in some way and you risk becoming a nonentity or even being fired, without necessarily knowing the cause. In this way, the group imposes its own order without the need for active policing. The codes will regulate acceptable appearances, how much free talk is encouraged in meetings, the quality of obedience in relation to bosses, the expected work ethic, et cetera.

When you are new to a group, you must pay extra attention to these tacit codes. Look at who's rising and who's falling within the group—signs of the standards that govern success and failure. Does success stem more from results or from political schmoozing? Look at how hard people work when not being observed by bosses. You could work too hard or do a job too well and find yourself fired for making others look bad. There are inevitably sacred cows within the group—people or beliefs never to be criticized. Consider all of these as trip wires you must avoid at all costs. Sometimes a particular member of higher standing serves as the de facto policeman or policewoman for these rules and codes. Identify such individuals and avoid any friction with them. It's not worth it.

The group court: Observe any community of chimpanzees at the zoo, and you will notice the existence of an alpha male and other chimpanzees adapting their behavior to him, fawning, imitating, and struggling to forge closer ties. This is the prehuman version of the court. We humans created a more elaborate version in aristocratic courts, dating from the earliest civilizations. In the aristocratic court, the subordinate members depended on the king or queen's favor to survive and thrive; the object of the game was to get closer to the man or woman on top without alienating the other courtiers, or to gang up and depose the leader, always a risky venture.

Today the court will form around the film executive, the head of an academic department, the CEO of a business venture, the political boss, the owner of an art gallery, a critic or artist who has cultural power. In a large group, there will be subcourts formed around subleaders. The more powerful the leader, the more intense is the gamesmanship. The courtiers may look different now, but their behavior and strategies are pretty much the same. You must take note of a few of these behavioral patterns.

First, courtiers have to gain the attention of leaders and ingratiate themselves in some way. The most immediate way to do this is through flattery, since leaders inevitably have large egos and a hunger to have their high self-opinion validated. Flattery can do wonders, but it comes with risks. If it is too obvious, the flatterer looks desperate, and it is easy to see through the strategy. The best courtiers know how to tailor their flattery to the particular insecurities of the leader and to make it less direct. They focus on flattering qualities in the leader that no one else has bothered to pay attention to but that need extra validation. If everyone praises the leader's business acumen but not his or her cultural refinement, you will want to aim at the latter. Mirroring the leader's ideas and values, without using their exact words, can be a highly effective form of indirect flattery.

Keep in mind that forms of acceptable flattery will differ in each court. In Hollywood, it must be more effusive than in academia or in Washington DC. Adapt your flattery to the group spirit, and make it as indirect as possible.

Of course, it is always wise to impress bosses with your efficiency and to make them dependent on your usefulness, but be careful of taking this too far: if they feel you are too good at what you do, they may come to fear their dependence on you and wonder about your ambition. Make them feel comfortable in the superiority they believe they possess.

Second, you must pay great attention to the other courtiers. Standing out too much, being seen as too brilliant or charming, will stir up envy, and you will die by a thousand bites. You want as many courtiers on your side as possible. Learn to downplay your successes, to listen (or seem to listen) deeply to the ideas of others, strategically giving them credit and praise in meetings, paying attention to *their* insecurities. If you must take action against particular courtiers, make it as indirect as possible, working to slowly isolate them in the group, never appearing too aggressive. Courts are always supposed to seem civilized. Be aware that the best courtiers are consummate actors and that their smiles and professions of loyalty mean very little. In the court, it does not pay to be naive. Without being paranoid, try to question people's motives.

Third, you need to be aware of the types of courtiers you will find in most courts and the particular dangers they can pose. One aggressive but clever courtier with little conscience can quickly dominate the group. (For more on the types of courtiers, see the next section.)

Keep in mind that there is no way to opt out of the court dynamic. Trying to act superior to the political games or the need to flatter will only make you look suspicious to others; nobody likes the holier-than-thou attitude. All you'll get for your "honesty" is to be marginalized. Better to be the consummate courtier and find some pleasure in the game of court strategy.

The group enemy: As mentioned above, our ancestors had a reflexive fear at the sight of any outsiders to their group. This fear easily slid into hatred. The basis for this fear may well have been real, but the existence of rival tribes also had a positive side effect—it united and tightened the group. It also fit in well with the way the human brain processes information, through binary pairs of opposites—light and dark, good and evil, us versus them. Today, in our modern sophisticated world, you will notice this very ancient dynamic continually at play: any group will reflexively focus on some hated enemy, real or imagined, to help bring the tribe together. As Anton Chekhov once noted, "Love, friendship, respect do not unite people as much as common hatred for something."

Since time immemorial, leaders have exploited this enemy reflex for power, using the existence of the rival or enemy to justify almost anything and to distract from their own shortcomings. The enemy will be described as "amoral," "irrational," "untrustworthy," or "aggressive," the implication being that "our" group is the opposite. No side ever likes to admit it is not pure in its ethics, or has aggressive intentions, or is governed by emotion—it is *always* the other side. In the end, the need to feel a part of the tribe and against the other side is more important than the actual differences, which tend to be greatly exaggerated.

Look at the group you belong to, and you will inevitably see some sort of enemy or bogeyman to push against. What you require is the ability to detach yourself from this dynamic and to see the "enemy" as it is, minus the distortions. You will not want to overtly display your skepticism—you might be seen as disloyal. Instead, keep your mind open so that you can resist the downward pull and overreactions that come from such tribal emotions. Take this even a step further by learning from the enemy, adapting some of its superior strategies.

Group factions: Over enough time, individuals in a group will begin to split off into factions. The reason for this dynamic is simple: In a group, we get a narcissistic boost from being around those who share our values. But in a group over a certain size, this becomes too abstract. The differences among the members become noticeable. Our power to influence the group as individuals is reduced. We want something more immediate, and so we form subgroups and cliques with those who seem even more like us, giving us back that narcissistic boost. In this subgrouping, we now have power to divvy up, which increases its members' sense of self-importance. Eventually the faction will experience its own splits from within, on and on. This splitting occurs unconsciously, almost as if it were responding to mechanical laws of group fission.

If a faction gets strong enough, its members will start to give precedence to its interests over that of the greater group. Some leaders try to exploit this dynamic by playing one faction off the other, in the form of divide and conquer: the more the factions fight, the weaker they become, and the greater the power in the hands of the man or woman on top. Mao Zedong was a master at this game, but it is a dangerous one, because too much time tends to be wasted dealing with petty internal squabbles, and it can be hard to keep them all down. If left alone, factions can become so powerful they take over and depose or control the leaders themselves. Better to tighten the whole group by creating a positive culture that excites and unifies its members, making factions less attractive. (For more on this, see the last section of this chapter.)

One faction to pay particular attention to is the one that is formed by those in the higher echelons, which we can identify as the *elites* in the group. Although elites themselves sometimes split into rival factions, more often than not, when push comes to shove, they will unite and work to preserve their elite status. The clan tends to look after its own, all the more so among the powerful. They will inevitably manage to bend the group rules to ensure they tilt in their favor. In these democratic times, they will try to cover this up by posturing that what they are doing is for the greater good of the group. If the elites prosper, so will everyone else, they say. But you will never actually see the elite faction doing things that will lessen their power, or making true sacrifices. Somehow it is always those not among the elites who must make the sacrifices. Try not to fall for their rationalizations or cover stories, and to see this faction for what it is.

YOUR TASK AS A STUDENT OF HUMAN NATURE IS TWOFOLD: FIRST, YOU MUST BECOME a consummate observer of yourself as you interact with groups of any size. Begin with the assumption that you are not nearly as much of an individual as you imagine. To a great extent, your thoughts and belief system are heavily influenced by the people who raised you, your colleagues at work, your friends, and the culture at large. Be ruthlessly frank with yourself. Look at how your ideas and beliefs alter the longer you stay at a job or within a particular group. You are under subtle pressure to get along and to fit in, and you will respond to this without being aware.

To see this clearly, think of how many times you have promoted an idea that is contrary to what the group wants on some fundamental issue and held on to this idea for a long period. It will probably be quite rare. Look at the bad decisions the group has taken, and how often you went along with them. If this conformity becomes too ingrained in you, you will lose the ability to reason on your own, your most prized possession as a human. As a thought experiment, sometimes try entertaining an idea that is the very opposite of the group you belong to or the conventional wisdom. See if there is any value in deliberately going against the grain.

We are all permeable to the influence of the group. What makes us more permeable is our insecurities. The less we are certain about our self-worth as individuals, the more we are unconsciously drawn toward fitting in and blending ourselves into the group spirit. Gaining the superficial approval of group members by displaying our conformity, we cover up our insecurities to ourselves and to others. But this approval is fleeting; our insecurities gnaw at us, and we must continually get people's attention to feel validated. Your goal must be to lower your permeability by raising your self-esteem. If you feel strong and confident about what makes you unique—your tastes, your values, your own experience—you can more easily resist the group effect. Furthermore, by relying upon your work and accomplishments to anchor your self-opinion, you won't be so tied to constantly seeking approval and attention.

It is not that you become self-absorbed or cut off from the group—outwardly you do what you can to fit in, but inwardly you subject the ideas and beliefs of the group to constant scrutiny, comparing them with your own, adapting parts or all of those that have merit and rejecting others that go against your experience. You are putting the focus on the ideas themselves, not on where they come from.

Your second task is to become a consummate observer of the groups you belong to or interact with. Consider yourself an anthropologist studying the strange customs of an alien tribe. Look deeply at the culture of your group, how it "feels" from within, the feeling contrasted to other groups you have worked with or belonged to. You are catching the social force as it molds the group into an organism, the sum greater than its parts.

Most people intuitively sense the rules and codes of behavior in the group. You want to take this further by observing these rules in action and making your knowledge of them more conscious: Why do they exist? What do they say about the group? Gaining a deeper appreciation of the culture and codes will make it much easier to navigate the social space and maintain a degree of detachment. You will not try to change what cannot be changed. When it comes to the inevitable factions that emerge, it is better to keep yourself unaligned and let others fight over you. You do not need to belong to a faction to derive a narcissistic boost. What you want within the group is strategic options and room to maneuver, to have many allies and widen your power base.

Your goal in this second task is to maintain as tight a grip on reality as possible. Groups tend to share beliefs and ways of looking at the world that are one-sided. They give greater weight to information that fits into their preconceived notions. They exaggerate qualities of rivals or enemies. They become overoptimistic about their plans. Taken far enough, the group can hold beliefs that are quite delusionary, and its actions can border on madness. Observing the group with a degree of distance will help you be aware of the distorting effect on your perception that can come from being so embedded within a group. Your strategies and decisions will be all the more effective for this.

Just as groups tend to exert a downward pull on our emotions and behavior, we can also experience or imagine the opposite—a group that exerts an upward pull. We shall call this ideal the *reality group*. It consists of members who feel free to contribute their diverse opinions, whose minds are open, and whose focus is on getting work done and cooperating on a high level. By maintaining your individual spirit and your grip on reality, you will help create or enrich this ideal team of people. (For more on this, see "The Reality Group" on page 431.)

This ability to observe the group and detach ourselves is more critical now than ever for several reasons. In the past, people's sense of belonging to certain groups was more stable and secure. To be a Baptist or a Catholic or a communist or a French citizen provided one with a strong sense of identity and pride. With the diminishing power of these large-scale belief systems, we have lost this inner security, and yet we retain the same profound human need to belong. So many of us are searching for groups to join, hungry for the approval of others who share our values. We are more permeable than ever. This makes us eager to become a member of the latest cult or political movement. It makes us highly susceptible to the influence of some unscrupulous populist leader who preys upon this need.

Instead of forming large-scale groups, we now form tribes of diminishing size, to get a greater narcissistic boost. We view larger groups with suspicion. Social media abets this dynamic by making it easier to spread the narrowly focused views and values of the tribe and making them viral. But these tribes don't last long; they are continually disappearing or regrouping or splitting apart. And so the ancient need to belong is never satisfied and drives us mad.

Tribalism has its roots in the deepest and most primitive parts of our nature, but it is now coupled with much greater technological prowess, which makes it all the more dangerous. What allowed us thousands of years ago to bind our group tightly and survive could now easily lead to our extinction as a species. The tribe feels its very existence at stake by the presence of the enemy. There is little middle ground. Battles can be more intense and violent between tribes.

The future of the human race will likely depend on our ability to transcend this tribalism and to see our fate as interconnected with everyone else's. We are one species, all descendants of the same original humans, all brothers and sisters. Our differences are mostly an illusion. Imagining differences is part of the madness of groups. We must see ourselves as one large reality group and experience a deep sense of belonging to it. To solve the man-made problems threatening us will require cooperation on a much higher level and a practical spirit missing from the tribe. This does not mean the end of diverse cultures and the richness that comes with them. In fact, the reality group encourages inner diversity.

We must come to the conclusion that the primary group we belong to is that of the human race. That is our inevitable future. Anything else is regressive and far too dangerous.

The Court and Its Courtiers

Any type of court obviously revolves around the leader, the courtiers' power depending on the relative closeness of their relationship with this leader. Although leaders come in many varieties, one dynamic is fairly universal: the courtiers (minus the cynical types, see below) will tend to idealize those in power. They will see their leaders as smarter, cleverer, more perfect than is the reality. This will make it easier for them to justify their fawning behavior.

This dynamic is similar to what we all experienced in childhood: we idealized our parents in order to feel more secure about the power they had over us. It was too frightening to imagine our parents as weak or incompetent. Dealing with authority figures in the court tends to regress us to our childhood and the family dynamic. The way we adapted to our parents' power and the presence of our siblings will play itself out again in adult form in the court. If we felt the deep need to please our parents in every way in order to feel more secure, we will become the pleaser type in the court. If we resented our siblings for the parental attention they drew away from us, and tried to dominate these siblings, we will be the envious type and resort to passive aggression. We may want to monopolize the leaders' attention as we once tried to do with our mother or father.

And so we can say that courtiers tend to fall into certain types, depending on deep patterns stemming from childhood. Some of these types can become quite dangerous if they accumulate power within the court, and they are usually adept at disguising their negative qualities in order to rise from within. It is best to be able to identify them as early as possible and take necessary defensive action. The following are seven of the more common types you will find.

The Intriguer: These individuals can be particularly difficult to recognize. They seem intensely loyal to the boss and to the group. No one works harder or is more ruthlessly efficient. But this is a mask they wear; behind the scenes they are continually intriguing to amass more power. They generally have a disdain for the boss that they are careful to conceal. They feel they could do the job better, and they yearn to prove this. Perhaps they had competitive issues in childhood with the father figure.

In the court of Richard Nixon, Alexander Haig (1924–2010) epitomized this type. A graduate of West Point and a decorated war hero in Vietnam, he was hired as one of several assistants to Henry Kissinger, Nixon's national security adviser. Kissinger's own little court was filled with men with brilliant academic backgrounds. Haig could not compete on this level; he stayed away from policy arguments. Instead, he so expertly tailored himself to the desires and needs of Kissinger that he quickly rose from within. He organized Kissinger's desk, streamlined his schedule, and would do the lowliest task, even helping his boss dress for an important evening. He silently suffered Kissinger's numerous and volcanic temper tantrums. But what Kissinger did not realize was the depth of Haig's ambitions and his contempt for his boss. He was continually playing to the real boss in the game, Nixon himself.

While Kissinger was out most evenings attending some party, Nixon would see the light on in Haig's office at all hours. Nixon, a workaholic himself, could not help but admire this. Of course, Haig made sure he worked evenings when Nixon was there and would notice him. Soon Nixon was borrowing him for his own tasks. In 1973, as the Watergate scandal blossomed, Nixon appointed Haig as his chief of staff. This infuriated Kissinger—not only did he feel Haig had used him for his own purposes, but he was now having to report to Haig as a superior. To make matters worse, Haig had seen up close all of Kissinger's weaknesses and had a lot of dirt on him, and Kissinger was certain he would be sharing this information with Nixon, who loved such gossip. To colleagues Haig could be chummy and even disarming. But behind the scenes he undercut almost everyone in his path, wiretapping their phones, putting his name on their ideas and memos.

As the Watergate crisis deepened and Nixon fell into a depression, Haig slowly took over operations, with a zeal that surprised and disgusted many. For several months, he became the de facto president. This pattern repeated through-out his career. As Ronald Reagan's secretary of state, after the assassination at-tempt on the president in 1981, Haig told reporters, "I am in control here."

In identifying this type, you must look behind the efficient and loyal front and even the charm. Keep your eye instead on their maneuvers and their impa-tience to rise from within. Look at their past record for signs of intrigue. They are masters at making leaders, and others, dependent on their efficiency as means of binding them and securing their own position. Pay attention to that little extra zeal they display to please the boss and make themselves useful. Re-alize that when they are looking at you, they are thinking of how they can use you as a tool or stepping-stone. Imagining themselves blessed with brilliance, they have little compunction in doing whatever is necessary to advance them-selves. It is best to keep your distance and not become one of their pawns, nor their enemy.

The Stirrer: This type is generally riddled with insecurities but adept at disguising them from those in the court. They feel deep wells of resentment and envy for what others seem to have that they don't, part of their childhood pattern. Their game is to infect the group with doubts and anxieties, stirring up trouble, which puts them at the center of action and may allow them to get closer to the leader. They will often target another courtier who triggers their envy, and they will spread rumors and innuendo about the courtier in question, playing upon the latent envy of other courtiers. They will be full of secret in-formation for the leader about those who might be less than perfectly loyal. The more turmoil and emotions they can stir up, the better they can take ad-vantage of the situation.

If a rebellion of some sort suddenly erupts within the court, you can be sure they had a finger in it. All it takes is one good Stirrer in a court to create endless drama and discord, making life intolerable for everyone. They actually get a secret pleasure from doing so. They will cover their tracks by being hyperrigh-teous and indignant about the "betrayals" of others. They project such a front of loyalty and devotion to the cause that it is hard to suspect them of being so manipulative.

If you notice courtiers who "innocently" share with you some rumor, be wary—they could be of this type, and you may be the target of such rumors at some point. If you feel the group succumbing to viral anxiety about some vague threat, try to locate the source of this—you might have a Stirrer in your midst. They can be tricky—they can project an extra cheery and optimistic front to conceal the churning negativity within. Always look behind the mask and notice the secret delight they have when something bad happens. When dealing with a known Stirrer, do not directly or indirectly insult or show disrespect. Even though they are quite insensitive to the feelings of those they malign, they are hypersensitive to any sign of disrespect to them, and since they have fewer compunctions than you, they will make your life miserable through their passive-aggressive campaigns.

The Gatekeeper: The goal of the game for these types is gaining exclusive access to leaders, monopolizing the flow of information to them. They may resemble the Intriguer in their willingness to use people to get to this position, but unlike that type, their objective is not to take over power. They are motivated not by a secret disdain for others but by their intense adoration for the person on top. They often rise to the position by fawning over the genius and perfection of the leader, whom they idealize. (There might even be a slight sexual edge to their attraction.) They ingratiate themselves with leaders by giving them a great deal of narcissistic supply. As Gatekeepers, they keep away irritating courtiers and buffer leaders from petty political struggles, which seems to make them quite useful.

In gaining such proximity, they also get to see the leaders' dark sides and learn of their weaknesses; this unconsciously binds leaders even more tightly to Gatekeepers, whom they might fear alienating. Having such power over the admired leader is their endgame. This type can also become the policeman or policewoman in the court, making sure the group adheres to the ideas and beliefs of the leader.

Once such types are installed in power, they are extremely dangerous—running afoul of them in any way will cut off key access to the one player on the board who matters the most, and other perks. Recognize them early on by their shameless sycophancy toward the boss. These types obviously wear a very different face to other courtiers from what they present to leaders, and you can try to gather evidence to reveal their duplicity to the leader before it is too late. But they generally are masters at understanding and playing to the insecurities of bosses and come to know them better than you do. They can easily turn your efforts around. In general, it is best to recognize their power and remain on their good side. If you're a leader, beware of such types. They will tend to isolate you from the group, and isolation is dangerous.

The Shadow Enabler: Leaders are often in a difficult position. They have to bear the responsibility for what happens to the group and the stress that goes with that. At the same time, they must maintain a reputation that is above re-proach. More than others, they have to keep their Shadow side (see chapter 9) under wraps. This could be extramarital desires they have had to repress, or paranoia about the loyalty of everyone around them, or the craving to do some violence against a hated enemy. Unconsciously their Shadow is yearning to come out. In steps the Enabler, one of the cleverest and most diabolical court-iers of all.

These types often are closer to their own Shadow, aware of their own dark-est yearnings. In childhood they probably felt these desires deeply but had to repress them, which made such desires all the more powerful and obsessive. As adults, they search for complicit partners with whom they can bring the Shadow out into the open. They are masters at detecting repressed desires in others, including leaders. They may begin in conversation to broach somewhat taboo subjects, but in a nonthreatening, jocular way. The leader falls into the spirit and opens up a bit. Having established contact with the leader's Shadow, the Enabler then takes this further, with suggestions of possible actions for lead-ers, ways to vent their frustrations, with the Enabler handling it all and serving as protection.

Charles Colson, special counsel to President Nixon, carved out just such a role for himself. He knew his boss to be quite paranoid about all of the enemies supposedly surrounding him. Nixon was also quite insecure about his own masculinity and yearned to punish his purported enemies and display some swagger. He felt deeply frustrated in not being able to act on these desires. Col-son played on his worst instincts, allowing Nixon to vent his feelings in meet-ings and then insinuating ways to act on them, such as revenge schemes against hated reporters. Nixon found this too tempting and too therapeutic to resist. Colson shared some of these hidden sadistic desires himself, and so this was the perfect way for him to live out his own Shadow.

In any court, there are inevitably those with a low character, who live for scheming and knocking heads. They are not overtly violent or evil but simply have fewer compunctions than others. If they are Enablers and inveigle their way into a position close to the boss, there is little you can do against them. It is too dangerous to cross such types, unless what they are planning is so dark that it is worth risking your own position to stop them. Take heart that their careers are generally short. They often serve as the fall guy if what they advocated, or acted on, becomes public. Be aware that they may try to play the game with you. Do not take the first step into any dubious actions they are trying to draw you into. Your clean reputation is the most important thing you possess. Maintain a polite distance.

The Court Jester: Almost every court has its Jester. In the past they wore a cap and bells, but today they come in different varieties and looks. They can be the court cynic and scoffer, who has license to poke fun at almost everyone and everything, including sometimes the leaders themselves, who tolerate this because it shows their apparent lack of insecurity and sense of humor. Another variety is the domesticated rebel. Such types are allowed to go against the dress code, display looser behavior, and espouse unconventional opinions. They can be a bit flamboyant. In meetings, unlike anyone else, they are allowed to come up with wild opinions contrary to the group. Such nonconformists prove that the leaders encourage the free exchange of opinions, at least in appearance.

These types fall into such roles because secretly they have a fear of responsibility and a dread of failing. They know that as Jesters they are not taken seriously and are given little actual power. Their humor and antics give them a place in the court without the stress of actually having to get things done. Their "rebelliousness" never really represents a threat or challenge to the status quo. In fact, they make it so others in the group can feel a bit superior to the in-house oddball, more comfortable in conforming to the norm.

Never take their existence as a sign that you can freely imitate their behavior. There is rarely more than one Jester per court for a reason. If you feel the pull to rebel against the norms of the group, better to keep it as subtle as possible. Often the modern court will tolerate differences in appearances but not so much in ideas and political correctness. Better to reserve your nonconformity for your private life, or until you have amassed more power.

The Mirrorer: These types are often among the most successful courtiers of all, because they are capable of playing the double game to the hilt—they are adept at charming leaders *and* fellow courtiers, maintaining a broad base of support. Their power is based on the idea that everyone at heart is a narcissist. They are masters at reflecting back to people their own moods and ideas, making them feel validated without sensing the manipulation, as opposed to using overt flattery.

In the court of Franklin Delano Roosevelt, Frances Perkins, FDR's secretary of labor and longtime adviser, was the consummate player of this game. She had high levels of empathy and could sense Roosevelt's moods. She would adapt to them. She knew he loved to hear stories, so any idea she presented to him she would present with some type of story line, and this would charm him. She listened to whatever he said with much more attention than anyone else and could later refer verbatim to something "brilliant" he had said, which proved how deeply she had listened.

If she was going to recommend an action that might meet some resistance, she would couch it as one of his own ideas from the past, but with a slight modification of her own. She could decipher the meaning of his various types of smiles, knowing when she could go further with her idea and when to stop in her tracks. And she made certain to confirm his idealized image of himself as the noble warrior fighting on behalf of the disenfranchised. To other courtiers, she presented herself in the most nonthreatening manner, never making a show of her influence over her boss and applying the same type of charm to everyone who crossed her path. In this way she made it hard to feel threatened or envious of her powers.

This is a role you might want to consider playing in the court because of the power it brings, but to pull it off you will have to be a great reader of people, sensitive to their nonverbal cues. You want to be able to mirror their moods, not just their ideas. This will cast a spell over them and lower their resistance. With leaders, you must be aware of their idealized opinion of themselves and always confirm it in some way, or even encourage them to live up to it. Those on top are lonelier and more insecure than you imagine, and they will lap this up. As mentioned before, overt flattery can be dangerous because people can see through it, but even if they see through your mirroring, they will remain charmed and want more.

The Favorite and the Punching Bag: These two types occupy the highest and lowest rungs of the court. Every king or queen must have his or her Favorite within the court. As opposed to the other types, whose power generally depends on efficiency and demonstrations of abject loyalty, the Favorite's rise in power is often based on cultivating a more personal, friend-like relationship. Early on, they act relaxed and chummy with the leader, without seeming disrespectful. Many leaders are secretly dying to not have to be so formal and in control. Sometimes leaders who are lonely will pick out one person to occupy this position. With the Favorite, they will gladly share secrets and bestow favors. This, of course, will stir up the envy of other courtiers.

This position is fraught with danger. First, it depends on the friendly feelings of leaders, and such feelings are inevitably fickle. People are more sensitive to the words or actions of friends, and if they feel somehow disappointed or betrayed in any way, they can go from liking to hating the former friend. Second, the Favorite receives so much privileged treatment that they often become arrogant and entitled. Leaders might tire of their spoiled behavior. Courtiers are already envious of the Favorite, but their increased arrogance only alienates them further. When Favorites fall from grace—and history is littered with such stories—the fall is hard and painful. No one comes to their defense, and because their rise did not depend on any special skill, they often have nowhere else to go. Try to avoid being lured into taking this position. Make your power dependent on your accomplishments and your usefulness, not on the friendly feelings people have for you.

Much as in any children's playground, in the court there is almost always a person who plays the role of the Punching Bag, whom everyone feels encouraged to laugh at in some way and feel superior to. People today are more politically correct and careful, and yet this human need for a Punching Bag is too embedded in our nature. People will base their feeling of superiority on the Punching Bag's supposed incompetence, or unorthodox opinions, or lack of sophistication, whatever makes them seem different and somehow inferior. Much of their ridicule will be behind the back of the targets, but they will sense it. Do not engage in this dynamic. It will coarsen and debase you. See everyone in the court as your potential ally. Within the ruthless environment of the court, try to befriend the Punching Bag, showing a different way of behaving and taking the fun out of this cruel game.

The Reality Group

When a group of people fails in some enterprise, we often see the following dynamic play itself out: The first reaction is to look at the actors involved and affix blame. Perhaps it was the overambitious leader who led the group into failure, or the incompetent lieutenant, or the very shrewd adversary. Perhaps some bad luck was involved as well. The leader or lieutenant may be fired and a new team brought in. Leadership learns a few lessons from the experience, and these are shared. Everyone in the group feels satisfied and ready to move on. Then, a few years down the line, nearly the same problem and the same type of failure recurs, and the same tired solutions are recycled.

The reason for this common pattern is simple: what is really at fault is the dysfunctional dynamic of the group, which tends to produce incompetent lieutenants and grandiose leaders. And unless it is fixed, the problems keep recurring with different faces.

In a dysfunctional culture, the members are often confused about their roles and the overall direction of the group. Amid such confusion, people start to think more of their own interests and agendas, and they form factions. Worried more about their status than the health of the group, their egos become touchy, and they obsess over who's getting more. In this contentious atmosphere, the bad apples—the Stirrers, the men and women of low character—find numerous ways to stir trouble and promote themselves. Those who excel at schmoozing and playing politics but little else often thrive, rise to the top, and become lieutenants. Mediocrity is preferred and rewarded.

Leaders find themselves dragged down by all the internal dissension and gamesmanship. Feeling vulnerable, they surround themselves with courtiers who tell them what they want to hear. Inside this court cocoon, leaders hatch ill-conceived and grandiose plans, which are encouraged by the spineless courtiers. Firing the leader or lieutenants won't change anything. The next ones will simply find themselves infected and transformed by the dysfunctional culture.

What we must do to avoid this trap is to alter our perspective: instead of instantly focusing on individuals and the drama of the failed action, we must focus on the overall group dynamic. Fix the dynamic, create a productive culture, and not only will we avoid all of the above evils but we will trigger a much different, upward pull within the group.

What creates a functional, healthy dynamic is the ability of the group to maintain a tight relationship to reality. The reality for a group is as follows: It exists in order to get things done, to make things, to solve problems. It has certain resources it can draw upon—the labor and strengths of its members, its finances. It operates in a particular environment that is almost always highly competitive and constantly changing. The healthy group puts primary emphasis on the work itself, on getting the most out of its resources and adapting to all of the inevitable changes. Not wasting time on endless political games, such a group can accomplish ten times more than the dysfunctional variety. It brings out the best in human nature—people's empathy, their ability to work with others on a high level. It remains the ideal for all of us. We shall call this ideal *the reality group*.

Certainly, a true reality group is a rare occurrence in history—to some degree we saw it in action with the famed battalions of Napoleon Bonaparte, or the early years of IBM under Thomas Watson, or the initial cabinet Franklin Roosevelt formed, or the film team assembled by the great director John Ford that worked with him for decades, or the Chicago Bulls under basketball coach Phil Jackson. From these examples, and others, we can learn some valuable lessons about the components of the reality group and how leaders can shape one.

The following are five key strategies for achieving this, all of which should be put into practice. Keep in mind that if you inherit a culture that is firmly set and dysfunctional, your job is harder and it will take more time. You need to be resolute in the changes you want to effect and have patience, being careful that the culture does not slowly assimilate you. Think of it as war, and the enemy is not individuals but the dysfunctional group dynamic.

Instill a collective sense of purpose. That social force that compels people to want to belong and to fit in you want to capture and channel for a higher purpose. You accomplish this by establishing an ideal—your group has a definite purpose, a positive mission that unites its members. This could be creating a product that is superior and unique, that makes life easier or brings pleasure; or improving conditions for those in need; or solving some seemingly intractable problem. This is the ultimate reality of the group, why it was formed in the first place. This purpose is not vague or implied but clearly stated and publicized. No matter the type of work, you want to emphasize excellence and creating something of the highest possible quality. Making money or being successful should be a natural result of this ideal and not the goal itself.

To make this work, the group must practice what you preach. Any signs of hypocrisy or noticeable discrepancy between the ideal and the reality will destroy your efforts. You want to establish a track record of results that reflect the group's ideal. Groups will tend to lose connection to their original purpose, particularly with any success. You want to keep reminding the group of its mission, adapting it if necessary but never drifting from this core.

We often like to reduce the behavior of people to base motives—greed, selfishness, the desire for attention. Certainly we all have a base side. But we also possess a nobler, higher side that often is frustrated and cannot find expression in the ruthless world today. Making people feel an integral part of a group creating something important satisfies a deep yet rarely met human need. Once members experience this, they are motivated to keep the healthy dynamic alive and vital. With its relatively high esprit de corps, the group will police itself. People who are petty and all about ego will stand out and be isolated. With clarity about what the group represents and the role they are to play, members are less likely to form factions. Everything becomes easier and smoother if you instill this collective purpose.

Assemble the right team of lieutenants. As the leader of a reality group, you need the ability to focus on the larger picture and the overall goals that matter. You have only so much mental energy, and you must marshal it wisely. The greatest obstacle to this is your fear of delegating authority. If you succumb to micromanaging, your mind will become clouded by all the details you try to keep on top of and the battles among the courtiers. Your own confusion then filters down through the group, ruining the effect of the first strategy.

What you need to do from the outset is to cultivate a team of lieutenants, imbued with your spirit and the collective sense of purpose, whom you can trust to manage the execution of ideas. To achieve this, you must have the right standards—you do not base your selection on people's charm, and never hire friends. You want the most competent person for the job. You also give great consideration to their character. Some people can be brilliant, but in the end their poisonous personalities and egos make them a drain on the group's spirit. (For more on judging character, see chapter 4.)

You select for this team people who have skills that you lack, each individual with their particular strengths. They know their roles. You also want this team of lieutenants to be diverse in temperament, background, and ideas. They show a willingness to speak up and take initiative, all within the framework of the group's purpose. They can even challenge some rules that seem outdated. Feeling a part of a team but able to bring their own creativity to the tasks will bring out the best in them, and this spirit will spread throughout the group.

For this team of lieutenants, and for the group as a whole, you want to make sure that members are treated more or less equally—no one has special privileges; rewards and punishments are doled out fairly and evenly. If particular individuals are not living up to the ideal, you get rid of them. Now if you bring in new lieutenants, they naturally are absorbed into the healthy dynamic. You are also leading from the front. If there are sacrifices to be made, you share in them as much as any member. In doing all of this, you will make it harder for people to feel envious and resentful, which can sow divisions and make people political.

Let information and ideas flow freely. As the group evolves, your greatest danger is the slow formation of a bubble around you. The lieutenants, trying to ease your burdens, may eventually isolate you from what is happening throughout the group and filter the information they provide you. Without realizing it, they tell you what they believe will please you and keep out the noise that is important to hear. Your perspective on reality slowly becomes distorted and your decisions reflect this.

Without becoming overwhelmed by details, you need to establish a very different dynamic. Consider the open communication of ideas and information—about rivals, about what is happening on the streets or among your audience—the lifeblood of the group. This was the secret to the success of Napoleon Bonaparte on the battlefield. He personally reviewed the concise reports sent to him by his field marshals, lieutenants, and others all the way down the chain of command, including even foot soldiers. This gave him several lines of perspective as to the performance of the army and the actions of the enemy. He wanted as much unfiltered information as possible before deciding on a strategy. He kept such reports to a reasonably small number, but their diversity is what gave him such a clear picture.

To achieve this, you want to encourage frank discussion up and down the line, with members trusting that they can do so. You listen to your foot soldiers. You want your meetings to be lively, with people not overly concerned about bruising egos and causing offense; you want a diversity of opinions. To allow for such openness, you must be careful in these discussions to not signal your own preference for a particular option or decision, as this will subtly tip the team into following your lead. Even bring in experts and outsiders to broaden the group's perspective.

The more expansive the deliberation process, the greater the connection to reality, and the better your decisions. Of course, you can take too much time in this process, but most people sin in the opposite direction, making hurried decisions on highly filtered information. You also want to establish as much transparency as possible: when decisions are made, you share with the team how they came about and for what purpose.

Extend this open communication to the ability for the group to criticize itself and its performance, particularly after any mistakes or failures. Try to turn this into a positive and lively experience, with the focus not on scapegoats but on the overall functioning of the group, which was not up to par. You want the group to keep learning and improving. Learning from mistakes will make the team that much more confident moving forward.

Infect the group with productive emotions. In the group setting, people are naturally more emotional and permeable to the moods of others. You must work with human nature and turn this into a positive by infecting the group with the proper set of emotions. People are more susceptible to the moods and attitudes of the leader than of anyone else. Productive emotions would include calmness. Phil Jackson, the most successful basketball coach in history, noticed that a lot of other coaches would try to rev up the team before a game, get them excited and even angry. He found it much more productive to instill a sense of calmness that helped the players execute the game plan and not over-react to the ups and downs in the game. As part of this strategy, always keep the group focused on completing concrete tasks, which will naturally ground and calm them.

Infect the group with a sense of resolution that emanates from you. You are not upset by setbacks; you keep advancing and working on problems. You are persistent. The group senses this, and individuals feel embarrassed for becoming hysterical over the slightest shift in fortune. You can try to infect the group with confidence, but be careful that this does not slip into grandiosity. Your confidence and that of the group mostly stems from a successful track record. Periodically change up routines, surprise the group with something new or challenging. This will wake them up and stir them out of the complacency that can settle into any group that achieves success.

Most important, showing a lack of fear and an overall openness to new ideas will have the most therapeutic effect of all. The members will become less de-fensive, which encourages them to think more on their own, and not operate as automatons.

Forge a battle-tested group. It is essential that you know your group well, its strengths and weaknesses and the maximum you can expect of it. But ap-pearances can be deceiving. In their day-to-day work, people can seem moti-vated, connected, and productive. But add some stress or pressure or even a crisis, and suddenly you see a whole other side of them. Some begin to think more about themselves and disconnect from the group spirit; others become far too anxious and infect the group with their fears. Part of the reality you need to be on top of is the *actual* strength of your team.

You want to be able to gauge the relative inner toughness of people before you are thrust into a crisis. Give various members some relatively challenging tasks or shorter deadlines than usual, and see how they respond. Some people rise to the occasion and even do better under such stress; consider such people a treasure to hoard. Lead the team itself into an action that is novel and slightly riskier than usual. Observe carefully how individuals react to the slight amount of chaos and uncertainty that unfold from this. Of course, in the aftermath of any crises or failures, use such moments as a way to review people's inner strength or lack of it. You can tolerate a few fearful types who have other virtues, but not too many.

In the end, you want a group that has been through a few wars, dealt with them reasonably well, and now is battle-tested. They do not wilt at the sign of new obstacles and in fact welcome them. With such a group, you can slowly expand the limits of what you can ask of them, and the members feel a powerful upward pull to meet challenges and prove themselves. Such a group can move mountains.

FINALLY, WE LIKE TO FOCUS ON THE PSYCHOLOGICAL HEALTH OF INDIVIDUALS, AND how perhaps a therapist could fix any problems they might have. What we don't consider, however, is that being in a dysfunctional group can actually make individuals unstable and neurotic. The opposite is true as well: by participating in a high-functioning reality group, we can make ourselves healthy and whole. Such experiences are memorable and life-changing. We learn the value of cooperating on a higher level, of seeing our fate as intertwined with those around us. We develop greater empathy. We gain confidence in our own abilities, which such a group rewards. We feel connected to reality. We are brought into the upward pull of the group, realizing our social nature on the high level it was intended for. It is our duty as enlightened humans to create as many such groups as possible, making society healthier in the process.

> Madness is something rare in individuals—but in groups, parties, peoples, and ages it is the rule.
>
> —*Friedrich Nietzsche*

15

Make Them Want to Follow You

◇

The Law of Fickleness

*A*lthough styles of leadership change with the times, one constant remains: people are always ambivalent about those in power. They want to be led but also to feel free; they want to be protected and enjoy prosperity without making sacrifices; they both worship the king and want to kill him. When you are the leader of a group, people are continually prepared to turn on you the moment you seem weak or experience a setback. Do not succumb to the prejudices of the times, imagining that what you need to do to gain their loyalty is to seem to be their equal or their friend; people will doubt your strength, become suspicious of your motives, and respond with hidden contempt. Authority is the delicate art of creating the appearance of power, legitimacy, and fairness while getting people to identify with you as a leader who is in their service. If you want to lead, you must master this art from early on in your life. Once you have gained people's trust, they will stand by you as their leader, no matter the bad circumstances.

The Entitlement Curse

On the morning of Saturday, January 14, 1559, English people of all ages and classes began gathering in the streets of London. It was the day before the coronation of their new ruler, the twenty-five-year-old Elizabeth Tudor, to be known as Queen Elizabeth I. By tradition, the new monarch always led a ceremonial procession through the city. For most, it would be the first time they had ever seen Elizabeth.

Some in the crowd were anxious—England was in bad financial shape, the government heavily in debt; beggars were everywhere in the streets of large cities, and thieves roamed the countryside. Worst of all, the country had just been through a virtual civil war between Catholics and Protestants. Elizabeth's father, Henry VIII (1491–1547), had created the Church of England and had moved to transform England into a Protestant country. The daughter from Henry's first marriage became Queen Mary I in 1553, and she tried to return England to the Catholic fold, initiating a kind of English inquisition and earning the nickname "Bloody Mary." After Mary's death in late 1558, Elizabeth was next in line to succeed her, but was this the time for England to be ruled by a woman who was so young and inexperienced?

Others were cautiously hopeful: like the majority of the English, Elizabeth was a solid Protestant and would return the country to the Church of England. But optimistic or pessimistic, no one on either side really knew much about her. After Henry VIII had Elizabeth's mother and his second wife, Anne Boleyn, executed on trumped-up charges when Elizabeth was not yet three, Elizabeth had been shunted from stepmother to stepmother, and her presence within the court had been minimal. The English people knew that her childhood had been difficult and that Queen Mary had detested her, even throwing Elizabeth into the Tower of London in 1554. (She had wanted to have Elizabeth executed on charges of conspiring against the Crown but could not gather enough evidence.) How had these experiences affected the young Elizabeth? Was she as impetuous as her father or as arrogant as her half-sister, Mary? With so much at stake, they were beyond curious to know more about her.

For the English, the procession was a day for celebration and merriment, and Elizabeth did not disappoint on that score. It was quite a spectacle—colorful tapestries on the exterior walls of houses, banners and streamers from every window, musicians and jesters roaming the streets entertaining the crowd.

As a light snow fell, the queen-to-be herself now appeared on the streets, and wherever she passed the crowd grew hushed. Carried in an open litter, she wore the most beautiful golden royal robe and the most magnificent jewels. She had a charming face and the liveliest dark eyes. But as the procession moved along and various pageants were performed for her benefit, the English saw something they had never witnessed before or could even begin to imagine: the queen seemed to enjoy mingling with the crowds, tears filling her eyes as she listened attentively to the poorest of Londoners with their petitions and blessings for her reign.

When she talked, her manner of speaking was natural and even a bit folksy. She fed off the growing excitement in the crowd, and her affection for the people in the streets was all too apparent. One older and quite poor woman handed her a withered sprig of rosemary for good luck, and Elizabeth clutched it the entire day.

One witness wrote of Elizabeth, "If ever any person had either the gift or the style to win the hearts of people, it was this Queen. . . . All her faculties were in motion, and every motion seemed a well-guided action: her eye was set upon one, her ear listened to another, her judgment ran upon a third, to a fourth she addressed her speech; her spirit seemed to be everywhere, and yet so entire in herself as it seemed to be nowhere else. Some she pitied, some she commended, some she thanked, at others she pleasantly and wittily jested . . . and distributing her smiles, looks, and graces . . . that thereupon the people again redoubled the testimony of their joys, and afterwards, raising everything to the highest strain, filled the ears of all men with immoderate extolling of their Prince."

That night the city of London was abuzz with stories of the day. In taverns and homes, people commented on Elizabeth's strange and electrifying presence. Kings and queens would often appear before the public, but they were surrounded with such pomp and eager to maintain their distance. They expected the people to obey and worship them. But Elizabeth seemed eager to win *the people's* love, and it had charmed everyone who had seen her that day. As word spread of this throughout the country, affection for their new queen began to swell among the English, and they entertained some hope for the new reign.

BEFORE HER CORONATION, ELIZABETH HAD MADE IT KNOWN TO SIR WILLIAM CECIL that she would choose him as her most trusted minister. Cecil, thirteen years older than the queen, had served as an important councillor under Edward VI, Elizabeth's half-brother, who had ruled after the death of Henry VIII in 1547 from age nine until his death at age fifteen. Cecil had known Elizabeth since she was fourteen; they shared similar intellectual interests and were both solid Protestants; they had many lively conversations and a friendly rapport. For his part, Cecil understood her well. She was extremely intelligent, was very well read, and spoke many languages fluently. They would often play chess, and he was impressed with her patient style and how she often laid elaborate traps for his pieces.

He knew that Elizabeth had been schooled in hardship. She had lost not only her mother when she was so young but also her most beloved stepmother, Catherine Howard, when she was eight. Catherine was Henry's fifth wife and a cousin of Anne Boleyn. Henry had had her beheaded on trumped-up charges of adultery. Cecil also knew that the few months Elizabeth had spent in the Tower of London had had a traumatic effect on her, since she had expected to be executed at any moment. She had emerged from all of these experiences as a remarkably affable young woman, but Cecil knew that behind the exterior she was willful, temperamental, and even devious.

Cecil was also certain about one more thing: ruling was not for women. Queen Mary I had been England's first true female ruler, and she had proven to be a disaster. All the government ministers and administrators were men, and a woman could not stand up to the rough-and-tumble of dealing with them, and with male foreign diplomats. Women were too emotional and unsteady. Elizabeth might have a very capable mind, but she did not have the resilience for the job. And so Cecil had formed a plan: Slowly he and his cohorts would take over the reins, the queen advising but mostly following her ministers' guidance. And as quickly as possible they would get her married, preferably to a Protestant, and her husband would take over and rule as the king.

Almost from the beginning of her reign, however, Cecil realized that his plan would not be so easy to enact. The queen was headstrong and had plans of her own. In one way, he could not help but be impressed. Her first day on the job, she held a meeting and made it clear to her future councillors that she knew more than they did about the financial state of the country; she was determined to make the government solvent. She appointed Cecil as her secretary of state, and she began meeting with him several times a day, giving him no spare hour to rest.

Unlike her father, who had let his ministers run things so he could devote himself to hunting and pursuing young women, Elizabeth was completely hands-on; Cecil was astounded at how many hours she put into the job, working well past midnight. She was exacting in what she expected from him and the other ministers, and occasionally she could be quite intimidating. If he pleased her with what he said or did, the queen was all smiles and a touch coquettish. But if something turned out wrong or if he disagreed too vociferously, she would shut him out for days, and he would return home to stew in his anxiety. Had he lost her trust? On occasion, she looked at him harshly or even upbraided him in the thunderous style of her father. No, the queen would not be easy to manage, and slowly he found himself working harder than ever to impress her.

As part of his plan for the men to slowly take over power, he made sure that all correspondence from foreign governments would be first routed to his desk.

He would keep the queen in the dark on several important matters. Then he discovered that the queen had learned of this and behind his back had ordered all diplomatic correspondence to go through her. It was like a chess game, and she was playing several moves ahead. He got angry and accused her of undermining him in his work, but she stood her ground and had a very logical response: unlike Cecil, she spoke and read all of the major European languages and understood their nuances, and it would be better for all if she personally conducted diplomacy and brought the ministers up to date on foreign affairs. It was useless to argue, and he soon realized that when it came to handling such correspondence and meetings with diplomats, Elizabeth was a master negotiator.

Slowly his resistance wore down. Elizabeth would remain in charge, at least for the first few years of her reign. But then she would marry and produce the necessary heir for England, and her husband would take over. It was unnatural for her to continue in this role as an unwed ruler. It was rumored that she had confided in several friends that she would never marry, and that she had an overwhelming fear of marriage based on what she had seen with her father. But Cecil could not take this seriously. She kept telling everyone that all that mattered was the greater good of England, but to keep England without an heir apparent was to risk a future civil war. Surely she could see the logic in this.

His goal was simple: to get the queen to agree to marry a foreign prince in order to forge an alliance that would benefit England in its weakened state. Preferably this would be a Protestant prince, but as long as he was not a Catholic fanatic, Cecil would approve the choice. The French were dangling before her a marriage with their fourteen-year-old king, Charles IX, and the Habsburgs were promoting a marriage with Archduke Charles of Austria. Cecil's great fear was that she would marry the one man whom she had actually fallen in love with, Robert Dudley, the Earl of Leicester, a man beneath her in station who would stir up all kinds of dissension and intrigue within the English court.

As representatives of different countries pressed their cases, Elizabeth would seem to favor one, then grow cold. If the Spanish were suddenly creating trouble on the Continent, she would begin marriage negotiations with the French to make King Philip II of Spain suddenly fear a French-English alliance and back off, or with Archduke Charles of Austria to strike fear in both the French and Spanish. Year after year she played this game. She confessed to Cecil she had no desire to be a wife, but when Parliament threatened to cut off funds if she did not promise to marry, Elizabeth would soften and negotiate with one of her suitors. Then, once the funds from Parliament had been secured, she would find some other excuse to break off the marriage talk—the prince or king or archduke was too young, too fervently Catholic, not her type, too effeminate, on and on. Not even Dudley could break her resolve and get her to marry him.

After a few years of this, his frustration mounting, Cecil finally saw through the game. There was nothing he could do, but at the same time he had come to realize that Queen Elizabeth I was almost certainly a more capable ruler than any of the foreign matches. She was so frugal with expenses that the government was no longer in debt. As Spain and France ruined themselves with endless wars, Elizabeth prudently kept England out of the conflicts, and soon the country was prospering. Although she was Protestant, she treated the English Catholics well, and the bitter feelings from the religious wars a decade before were now mostly gone. "There was never so wise a woman born as Queen Elizabeth," he would later write, and so he eventually dropped the marriage issue, and the country itself slowly became used to the idea of the Virgin Queen, married to her subjects.

Over the years, however, one issue would continue to eat away at the people's affection for the queen, and even made Cecil begin to doubt her competence: the fate of Mary, Queen of Scots, cousin to Elizabeth. Mary was a staunch Catholic, while Scotland had become largely Protestant. Mary was next in line to be Queen of England, and many Catholics asserted that Mary was in fact the rightful queen. The Scots themselves came to despise Mary for her religious sentiments, for her adulterous affairs, and for her apparent implication in the murder of her husband, Lord Darnley. In 1567 she was forced to abdicate the Scottish throne in favor of her infant son, James VI. The following year she escaped imprisonment in Scotland and fled to England, putting herself in the hands of her cousin.

Elizabeth had every reason to despise Mary and return her to Scotland. She was the polar opposite of Elizabeth—selfish, flighty, and immoral. She was a fervent Catholic, and around her she would attract all those in England and abroad who wanted to depose Elizabeth and put a Catholic on the throne. She could not be trusted. But to the dismay of Cecil, her councillors, and the English people, Elizabeth allowed Mary to stay in the country under a mild form of house arrest. Politically this seemed to make no sense. It infuriated the Scots and threatened relations between the two countries.

As Mary began to secretly conspire against Elizabeth, and calls arose from all sides to have her executed for treason, inexplicably Elizabeth refused to take what appeared to be the rational step. Was it simply a case of one Tudor protecting another? Did she fear the precedent of executing a queen, and what it might mean for her own fate? In any event, it made her look weak and selfish, as if what mattered were protecting a fellow queen.

Then, in 1586, Mary became involved with the most audacious plot to have Elizabeth murdered, upon which Mary would have become Queen of England. She had secret backing from the pope and the Spanish, and there was now incontrovertible proof of her involvement in the plot. This outraged the public, who could well imagine the bloody civil war that would have ensued if the plot had gone forward. This time the pressure on Elizabeth was too great—no matter if Mary had been a queen, she had to be executed. But yet again Elizabeth hesitated.

A trial convicted Mary, but Elizabeth could not bring herself to sign the death warrant. To Cecil and those in the court who saw her daily, the queen had never appeared so distraught. Finally, in February of the next year, she caved to the pressure and signed the death warrant. Mary was beheaded the next day. The country erupted in celebration; Cecil and his fellow ministers breathed a sigh of relief. There would be no more conspiracies against Elizabeth, which would make the lack of an heir easier to bear. Despite her apparent mishandling of the situation, the English people quickly forgave her. She had proven that she could put the welfare of the country over personal considerations, and her reluctance only made the final decision seem all the more heroic.

KING PHILIP II OF SPAIN HAD KNOWN ELIZABETH FOR MANY YEARS, HAVING BEEN married to her half-sister, Queen Mary I. When Mary had imprisoned Elizabeth in the Tower of London, Philip had managed to soften her stance and get Elizabeth released. He found the young Elizabeth quite charming, and he admired her intelligence. But over the years he began to dread and despise her. She was the main obstacle to his goal of reestablishing the dominance of Catholicism, and he would have to humble her. In his mind, she was not the legitimate Queen of England. He began sneaking Jesuit priests into England to spread the Catholic faith and secretly foment rebellion. He built up his navy and stealthily prepared for what was known as the Enterprise of England, a massive invasion that would overwhelm the island and restore it to Catholicism. The execution of Mary, Queen of Scots, was the final straw—it was time for the invasion.

Philip felt supremely confident in the success of the Enterprise. Over the years, he had taken the measure of his great rival. She was crafty and clever, but she had one overwhelming disadvantage—she was a woman. As such, she was unsuited to lead a war. In fact, she seemed to be afraid of armed conflict, always negotiating and finding ways to avoid it. She had never paid much attention to her military. The English navy was relatively small, its ships not nearly as large and powerful as the great Spanish galleons. England's army was quite pitiful compared with Spain's. And Philip had the gold from the New World to help finance the effort.

He planned for the invasion to take place in the summer of 1587, but that year Sir Francis Drake raided the Spanish coast and destroyed many of its ships in the harbor of Cádiz, while seizing great treasures of gold. Philip postponed the invasion to the following year, the costs slowly mounting for maintaining his army and building more galleons.

Philip had overseen every detail of the invasion. He would launch an invincible armada of some 130 ships, manned by over thirty thousand men. They would easily destroy the English navy, link up with a large Spanish force in the Netherlands, cross the Channel, and sweep their way to London, where they would capture the Queen and put her on trial for the execution of Mary Queen of Scots; he would then put his own daughter on the throne of England.

Finally, the armada was launched in May of 1588, and by July the Spanish fleet was maneuvering around the southwestern coast of England. The Spanish galleons had perfected a certain form of warfare: they were so large they would maneuver close to the enemy ships, grapple, and board them with a virtual army. But they had never done battle with the much smaller and faster English ships, with their long-range cannons, and in waters much rougher than the Mediterranean. They did not do well.

On July 27, the armada anchored at Calais, just a few miles from where the Spanish army awaited them. In the middle of the night, the English sent five unmanned "fireships"—loaded with flaming wood and pitch—toward the anchored galleons. With the high winds that evening, the fire spread quickly from ship to ship. The Spanish galleons tried to regroup farther out to sea, but their formation was loose and scattered, and the fast English ships fired at them like ducks in the water. As the winds changed again, the Spanish were forced to retreat northward, into the stormiest parts of the North Sea. Trying to round England and retreat to Spain, they lost most of their ships and over twenty thousand Spanish soldiers died. The English had lost no ships and had only around a hundred casualties. It was one of the most lopsided victories in military history.

For Philip, it was the most humiliating moment in his life. He retired into his palace, where he holed himself up for months contemplating the disaster. The armada had left Spain utterly bankrupt, and in the years to come England would prosper while Spain became the second-rate power. Somehow Elizabeth had outwitted him. To the other leaders in Europe who hated her, she now seemed invincible and a ruler to be feared. Pope Sixtus V, who had excommunicated her and had given his blessing to the armada, now exclaimed, "Just look how well she governs! She is only a woman, only mistress of half an island, and yet she makes herself feared by Spain, by France, by the Empire, by all!"

NOW IN ENGLAND THERE AROSE A VERITABLE CULT AROUND THE VIRGIN QUEEN. She was now referred to as "Her Sacred Majesty." To catch a glimpse of her riding through London or passing on her barge on the Thames seemed like a religious experience.

One group, however, proved less susceptible to this powerful aura—the new generation of young men now filling the royal court. To them, the queen was showing her age. They respected her accomplishments, but they saw her more as a domineering mother figure. England was a rising power. These young men yearned to make a name for themselves on the battlefield and so earn public acclaim. Yet Elizabeth continually thwarted this desire. She refused to finance a large-scale campaign to finish off Philip, or to aid the French in their fight against the Spanish. They saw her as tired and felt it was time for their spirited, masculine generation to lead England. And the young man who came to epitomize this new spirit was Robert Devereux, 2nd Earl of Essex.

Born in 1566, Essex was handsome and high-strung. He knew the queen had a weakness for young men, and he quickly charmed her, becoming her new favorite. He genuinely liked and admired her, but at the same time he resented the power she possessed over his fate. He began to test her: he asked for favors, mostly money. She gave these to him. She seemed to enjoy spoiling him. And as the relationship progressed, Essex began to see her as a woman he could manipulate. He started to criticize her rather boldly in front of other courtiers, and the queen let him get away with it. She drew a line, however, when he asked for high political positions for himself and his friends, and then he would fly into a rage. It was humiliating to depend on the whims of a woman! But days later he would calm down and return to his charm offensive.

Kept away from political power, he saw that his only chance for fame and glory was to lead an English army to victory. Elizabeth allowed him to lead some smaller military expeditions on the Continent. His record was mixed— he was brave but not very good at strategy. Then, in 1596, he persuaded her to let him lead a Drake-like raid on the Spanish coast. This time his boldness paid off, and the campaign was a success. To the English people, now somewhat drunk on their new status as a European power, Essex represented their new swagger, and he became their darling. Essex wanted more of this and kept asking the queen for another chance in battle. He attributed her reluctance to the many enemies he had made in the court, men who envied him.

In 1598 news reached the court that a band of Irish rebels under Hugh O'Neill, 2nd Earl of Tyrone, was moving through English-controlled territory in Ireland and wreaking havoc. Now Essex offered his services to lead a force to crush Tyrone. He pleaded and persisted, and Elizabeth finally relented. Feeling confident of his powers over the queen, he requested for the campaign the largest army yet assembled by the English. Elizabeth granted his wish. For the first time, he felt truly appreciated by her. She did have a strange ability to make him want to please her. He expressed his gratitude and promised to finish the job quickly. Ireland would be the means for him to rise to the top.

Once he was there, however, the troubles mounted. It was the winter of 1599; the weather was awful and the terrain hopelessly boggy. He could not advance his enormous force. The Irish were elusive and masters at guerrilla warfare. While the English remained hobbled in their camps, thousands of soldiers died from disease and just as many began to desert. Essex could only imagine his many enemies at court talking behind his back. He felt certain the queen and several ministers were somehow plotting his downfall.

He had to test her again—he asked for reinforcements. The queen agreed, but she ordered him to finally find and fight Tyrone. Suddenly the pressure was too much, and he blamed the queen and her envious courtiers for trying to rush him. He felt humiliated by the position he was in, and by the end of the summer he had decided upon a plan that would put an end once and for all to his misery—he would secretly negotiate a truce with Tyrone, then return to England and march on London with his troops. He would force the queen to get rid of his enemies within the court and secure his position as her lead councillor.

He would be forceful but respectful of her position; seeing him in person and with his troops, the queen would certainly relent.

After a swift march through England, he suddenly showed up one morning in her bedchamber, his uniform caked in mud. The queen, caught by surprise and not knowing if he had come to arrest her and launch a coup, retained her composure. She offered him her hand to kiss and told him they would talk of Ireland later that day. Her calmness discomfited him; it was not what he had expected. She possessed a strange kind of power over him. Somehow the tables had been turned, and now he agreed to postpone their talk to the afternoon. Within hours, he found himself taken by her soldiers and placed under house arrest.

Counting on his influence over the queen and how often she had forgiven him, he wrote her letter after letter, apologizing for his actions. She did not respond. This had never happened before, and it frightened him. Finally, in August of 1600, she freed him. Grateful for this and plotting his comeback, he asked just one favor—to restore to him the monopoly he had possessed over the sale of sweet wines in England; he was hopelessly in debt and this was his principal source of income. Much to his chagrin, she refused to honor his request. She was playing some game, trying to teach him a lesson or tame him, but that would never happen. She had pushed him too far.

He retired to his house in London and gathered around him all of the disgruntled noblemen in England. Together he would lead them on a march to the queen's residence and take over the country. He predicted that thousands of Englishmen, who still adored him, would rally to his cause and swell the ranks of his troops. In early February 1601, he finally put his plan into action. To his utter dismay, Londoners stayed in their houses and ignored him. Sensing the foolhardiness of the venture, his fellow soldiers quickly deserted. Virtually alone, he retreated to his house. He knew this was the end for him, but at least he would remain defiant.

That afternoon, soldiers came to arrest Essex. Elizabeth arranged for a quick trial, and Essex was found guilty of treason. This time Elizabeth did not hesitate to sign the death warrant. During his trial, Essex maintained the most insolent air. He would go to his death denying his guilt and refusing to ask forgiveness.

The night before he was to be beheaded, the queen sent her own chaplain to prepare him for the end. Confronted with this representative of Elizabeth, who relayed her last words to him, Essex broke down. All those moments in which he had sensed her authority but had tried to resist its power, including that morning in her bedchamber when she had stood before him so regal and self-possessed, suddenly overwhelmed him. He confessed his crimes to the chaplain. In his mind, he mixed the image of his imminent judgment before God with the majesty of the queen, and he felt the full weight of his betrayal. He could see her face before him, and it frightened him.

He told the chaplain, "I must confess to you that I am the greatest, the vilest, and most unthankful traitor that ever has been in the land." The queen was right to execute him, he said. He requested a private execution so as not to inflame the public. In his last words, he asked God to preserve the queen. He went to his death with a submissiveness and quiet dignity that no one had seen or suspected in him before.

Interpretation: When Elizabeth Tudor became queen, she understood her supremely fragile position. Unlike her father or almost any other English monarch, she had zero credibility as a ruler, and no respect or authority to draw upon. The country was in a weakened state. She was too young, with no political experience or prior proximity to power to learn from. Yes, by merely occupying the throne she could expect some obedience, but such loyalty was thin and could change with the slightest mistake or crisis. And within months or years she would be forced to marry, and as she knew, being married could lead to all sorts of problems if she did not quickly produce a male heir.

What made this even more troubling was that Elizabeth was ambitious and highly intelligent; she felt more than capable of ruling England. She had a vision of how she could solve its many problems and transform it into a European power. Marriage would not only be bad for her but for the country as well. Most likely she would have to marry a foreign prince, whose allegiance would be to his country of origin. He would use England as a pawn in the Continent's power games and drain its resources even further. But given all the odds against her, how could she hope to rule England on her own? She decided the only way forward was to turn her weak position into an advantage, forging her own type of credibility and authority, one that in the end would give her powers far greater than any previous king.

Her plan was based on the following logic: Kings and queens of her time ruled with a tremendous sense of entitlement due to their bloodline and semi-divine status. They expected complete obedience and loyalty. They did not have to do anything to earn this; it came with the position. But this sense of entitlement had its consequences. Their subjects would pay homage, but the emotional connection to such rulers was in most cases not very deep. The English people could feel the distance separating themselves from the monarch, and how little their rulers really considered them.

This feeling of entitlement also blunted their political effectiveness. The government ministers were cowed and intimidated by someone like Henry VIII, and so their energy went into appeasing the king rather than using their own intelligence and creative powers. With this sense of entitlement, rulers paid less attention to the details of governing, which were too boring; wars of conquest became their chief means of getting glory and providing riches for the aristocracy, even though such wars drained a country's resources. These rulers could be incredibly selfish—Henry VIII had Elizabeth's mother executed so he could marry his latest mistress, not caring how tyrannical this made him seem to the English. Mary, Queen of Scots, had her husband murdered so she could marry her lover.

It would be easy for Elizabeth to delude herself and simply expect the loyalty that came with her august position. But she was too smart to fall into that trap. She would deliberately go in the opposite direction. She would feel no sense of entitlement. She would keep in mind the weakness of her actual position. She would not passively expect loyalty; she would turn active. She would earn the trust and credibility she required through her actions over time. She would demonstrate that she was not selfish, that everything she did was motivated by what was for the greater good of the country. She would be alert and relentless in this task. She would alter the way people (her subjects, her ministers, her foreign rivals) perceived her—from an inexperienced and weak woman to a figure of authority and great power. By forging much deeper ties with her ministers and the commoners, she would overcome people's natural fickleness and channel their energies for the purpose of rebuilding England.

Her first appearances before the English people were cleverly crafted to set the stage for a new type of leadership. Surrounded by all the usual royal pomp, she mixed in a common touch, making her seem both comforting and regal. She was not faking this. Having felt powerless in her youth, she could identify with the poorest charwoman of England. She indicated through her attitude that she was on their side, sensitive to their opinions of her. She wanted to earn their approval. She would build on this empathy throughout her reign, and the bonds between her and subjects became much more intense than with any previous ruler.

With her ministers, the task was more delicate and difficult. It was a group of power-hungry men, with their egos and need to feel smarter than and superior to a woman. She depended on their help and goodwill to run the country, but if she revealed too much dependence on them, they would walk all over her. And so, from the first days of her rule, she made the following clear: she was all business; she would work harder than all of them; she would reduce expenditures for the court, sacrificing her own income in the process; and all activity was to be directed toward lifting England out of the hole it had fallen into. She showed early on her superior knowledge of the finances of the country and the tough side of herself in any negotiation. Upon occasion, she would flash her anger if a minister seemed to be furthering a personal agenda, and such outbursts could be quite intimidating.

Mostly, though, she was warm and empathetic, attuned to the various moods of these men. Soon they wanted to please her and win her approval. To not work hard or smart enough could mean isolation and some coldness, and unconsciously they wanted to avoid this. They respected the fact that she lived up to her own high standards. In this way, she slowly placed these ministers into the same position that she had found herself in: needing to gain her trust and respect through their actions. Now, instead of a cabal of conspiring, selfish ministers, the queen had a team working to further her agenda, and the results soon spoke for themselves.

By these methods, Elizabeth acquired the credibility she needed, but she made one major mistake—her handling of Mary, Queen of Scots. Elizabeth had become somewhat entitled herself, feeling in this case that she knew better than her ministers and that her personal qualms about executing a fellow queen trumped everything else. She paid a price for this policy, as she felt the people's respect for her draining away, and it pained her. Her sense of the greater good was what guided her, but in this case the greater good would be served by having Mary executed. She was violating her own principles.

It took some time, but she realized her mistake. She tasked the head of her secret service to lure Mary into her most far-reaching conspiracy to get rid of Elizabeth. Now with solid evidence of Mary's complicity, Elizabeth could take the dreaded step. In the end, going against her own feelings for the sake of the country, in essence admitting her mistake, gained her even more trust from the English. It was the kind of response to public opinion that almost no rulers of the time were capable of.

When it came to her foreign rivals, particularly Philip II, Elizabeth was not naive and understood the situation: Nothing she had done had earned her any respect or respite from their endless conspiracies to get rid of her. They disrespected her as an unmarried queen and as a woman who seemed to fear conflict and warfare. She largely ignored all of this and kept to her mission of securing England's finances. But when the invasion of England seemed imminent, she knew it was time to finally prove herself as the great strategist that she was. She would play on Philip's underestimating of her craftiness and her toughness as a leader.

If war was necessary, she would do it as economically and efficiently as possible. She invested large sums in creating the most elaborate spy system in Europe, which allowed her to know in advance Spain's plans for the invasion, including the date of the launch. With such knowledge, she could commission and pay for an army at the last minute, saving huge sums of money. She financed Sir Frances Drake's raids on the coast of Spain and its galleons at sea. This allowed her to enrich England's coffers and delay the launching of the armada, which made it all the more expensive for Philip.

When it seemed certain the launch would occur within a few months, she quickly built up the English navy, commissioning smaller and faster ships, cheaper to build in bulk and well suited to the English seas. Unlike Philip, she left battle strategy in the hands of her admirals, but she overruled them on one score—she wanted them to fight the armada as close to England as possible. This would play into English hands, as the Spanish galleons were not suited for the stormy northern seas, and the English soldiers, fighting with their backs to their country, would fight all the harder. In the end, Spain was bankrupted and never to return to her former glory, while England under Elizabeth was now the rising power. But after this great victory, she resisted the calls to take the battle to Spain and deal the country a fatal blow. She was not interested in war for glory or conquest but only to safeguard the country's interests.

After the defeat of the armada, her authority and credibility seemed invulnerable, but Elizabeth would never let her guard down. She knew that with age and success would naturally come that dreaded sense of entitlement and the insensitivity that went with it. As a woman ruling the country by herself, she could not afford such a letdown. She retained her receptiveness to the moods of those around her, and she could sense that the younger men now filling the court had a much different attitude toward her. Their respect was for her position as queen, but it did not run much deeper than that. Once again she would have to struggle against masculine egos, but this time without her own youthful charms and coquetry to fall back on.

Her goal with Essex was to tame and channel his spirit for the good of the country, as she had done with her ministers. She indulged him in his endless desires for money and perks, trying to calm his insecurities, but when it came to giving him any political power, she set limits. He had to prove himself, to rise to her level, before she would grant him such powers. When he threw tantrums, she remained calm and steady, unconsciously proving to him her superiority and the need for self-control. When it became clear he could not be tamed, she let him go far enough with his conspiring to ruin his reputation and allow her to get rid of this cancer. And when he faced death for his crime, it was not simply the image of God that terrified him but that of the queen, whose aura of authority finally overwhelmed this most insolent and self-entitled of men.

Understand: Although there are no longer powerful kings and queens in our midst, more of us than ever operate as if we consider ourselves royalty. We feel entitled to respect for our work, no matter how little we have actually accomplished. We feel people should take our ideas and projects seriously, no matter how little thought went into them or how meager our track record. We expect people to help us in our careers, because we are sincere and have the best intentions. Some of this modern form of entitlement might come from being especially spoiled by our parents, who made us feel that anything we did was golden. Some of it might come from the technology that so dominates our lives and spoils us as well. It gives us immense powers without our having to exert any real effort. We have come to take such powers for granted and expect everything in life to be so fast and easy.

Whatever the cause, it infects all of us, and we must see this sense of entitlement as a curse. It makes us ignore the reality—people have no inherent reason to trust or respect us just because of who we are. It makes us lazy and contented with the slightest idea or the first draft of our work. Why do we have to raise our game or strain to improve ourselves when we feel we are already so great? It makes us insensitive and self-absorbed. By feeling that others owe us trust and respect, we negate their willpower, their ability to judge for themselves, and this is infuriating. We may not see it, but we inspire resentment.

And if we become leaders or subleaders, the effect of this curse only gets worse. Unconsciously, we tend to sit back and expect people to come to us with their loyalty and respect for the high position we occupy. We grow defensive and prickly if our ideas are challenged, putting our intelligence and wisdom into question, even on the smallest of matters. We expect certain perks and privileges, and if there are sacrifices to be made, we somehow feel we should be exempted. If we make a mistake, it is always the fault of someone else, or circumstances, or some momentary inner demon beyond our control. We are never really to blame.

We are not aware of how this affects those whom we lead, because we notice only people's smiles and nods of approval at what we say. But they see through us. They feel the entitlement we project, and over time it diminishes their respect and disconnects them from our influence. At a certain tipping point, they may turn against us with a suddenness that is shocking.

Like Elizabeth, we must realize that we are actually in a weak position, and we must struggle to adopt the opposite attitude: We expect nothing from the people around us, from those whom we lead. We are not defensive or sitting back but completely active—everything we get from others, and most definitely their respect, must be earned. We have to continually prove ourselves. We have to show that our primary consideration is not ourselves and our sensitive egos but the welfare of the group. We must be responsive and truly empathetic to people's moods, but with limits—to those who show themselves to be mostly self-promoting, we are tough and merciless. We practice what we preach, working harder than others, sacrificing our own interests if necessary, and being accountable for any mistakes. We expect the members of the group to follow our lead and prove themselves in return.

With such an attitude, we will notice a very different effect. People will open themselves to our influence; as we move toward them, they move toward us. They want to win our approval and respect. With such an emotional connection, we are more easily forgiven for mistakes. The group energy is not squandered on endless infighting and the clashing of egos but is directed toward reaching goals and accomplishing great things. And in achieving such results, we can forge an aura of authority and power that only grows with time. What we say and do seems to carry extra weight, and our reputation precedes us.

That . . . is the road to the obedience of compulsion. But there is a shorter way to a nobler goal, the obedience of the will. When the interests of mankind are at stake, they will obey with joy the man whom they believe to be wiser than themselves. You may prove this on all sides: you may see how the sick man will beg the doctor to tell him what he ought to do, how a whole ship's company will listen to the pilot.

—Xenophon

Keys to Human Nature

We humans like to believe that the emotions we experience are simple and pure: we love certain people and hate others, we respect and admire this individual and have nothing but disdain for another. The truth is that this is almost never the case. *It is a fundamental fact of human nature that our emotions are almost always ambivalent, rarely pure and simple.* We can feel love and hostility at the same time, or admiration and envy.

This ambivalence began in our childhood and set the pattern for the rest of our lives. If our parents were relatively attentive and loving, we remember our childhood fondly, as a golden period. What we conveniently forget is that even with such parents we tended to feel resentful of our dependence on their love and care. In some cases, we felt smothered. We yearned to assert our willpower, to show we could stand on our own. Feeling too dependent on their attention could open up tremendous anxieties about our vulnerability if they were gone. And so we inevitably felt some hostility and desire to disobey, along with our affection.

If they were not kind and caring, later in life we resent them and can remember only their coldness and our present antipathy. But we forget that in our childhood we tended to gloss over their negative traits and find ways to love them despite their treatment, and to somehow blame ourselves for not deserving their affection. Given the fact that we depended on them for our survival, to feel they truly did not care would have stirred up far too much anxiety. Mixed with moments of anger and frustration were feelings of need and love.

And so as children, when one emotion dominated us, the other lay underneath, a continual ambivalent undertone. As adults, we experience similar ambivalence with our friends and intimate partners, particularly if we feel dependent on them and vulnerable.

Part of the reason for this essential ambivalence is that strong, pure emotions are frightening. They represent a momentary loss of control. They seem to negate our willpower. We unconsciously balance them with contrary or conflicting emotions. And part of it stems from the fact that our moods are continually shifting and overlapping. Whatever the cause, we are not aware of our own ambivalence because contemplating the complexity of our emotions is baffling, and we prefer to rely on simple explanations for who we are and what

we are feeling. We do the same with the people around us, reducing our interpretations of their feelings to something simple and digestible. It would take
effort, and much honesty on our part, to catch our own underlying ambivalence in action.

Nowhere is this fundamental aspect of human nature more evident than in
our relationship toward leaders, whom we unconsciously associate with parental figures. This ambivalence toward leaders operates in the following way.

On the one hand, we intuitively recognize the need for leaders. In any
group, people have their narrow agendas and competing interests. The members feel insecure about their own position and work to secure it. Without leaders who stand above these competing interests and who see the larger picture,
the group would be in trouble. Hard decisions would never be made. No one
would be guiding the ship. Therefore, we crave leadership and unconsciously
feel disoriented, even hysterical, without someone fulfilling this role.

On the other hand, we also tend to fear and even despise those who are
above us. We fear that those in power will be tempted to use the privileges of
their position to accumulate more power and enrich themselves, a common
enough occurrence. We are also willful creatures. We don't feel comfortable
with the inferiority and dependence that comes with serving under a leader.
We want to exercise our own will and feel our autonomy. We secretly envy the
recognition and privileges that leaders possess. This essential ambivalence tips
toward the negative when leaders show signs of abuse, insensitivity, or incompetence. No matter how powerful the leaders, no matter how much we might
admire them, below the surface sits this ambivalence, and it makes people's
loyalties notoriously fickle and volatile.

Those in power will tend to notice only the smiles of their employees and
the applause they receive at meetings, and they will mistake such support for
reality. They do not realize that people almost always show such deference to
those above them, because their personal fate is in the hands of such leaders and
they cannot afford to show their true feelings. And so leaders are rarely aware
of the underlying ambivalence that is there even when things are going well. If
leaders make some mistakes, or if their power seems shaky, suddenly they will
see the mistrust and loss of respect that had been invisibly building up, as the
members of the group or the public turn on them with an intensity that is surprising and shocking. Look at the news to see how quickly leaders in any field
can lose support and respect, and how quickly they are judged by their latest
success or failure.

We might be tempted to believe that such fickleness is more of a modern phenomenon, a product of the fiercely democratic times we live in. After all, our ancestors were much more obedient than we moderns, or so we think. But this was hardly the case. Far back in time, among indigenous cultures and early civilizations, once-revered chiefs and kings were routinely put to death if they showed signs of aging or weakness; or if they lost a battle; or if a sudden drought occurred, meaning the gods no longer blessed them; or if they were seen as favoring their own clan at the expense of the group. These executions were moments of great celebration, a time to release all of the pent-up hostility toward leaders. (See *The Golden Bough*, by James Frazer, for innumerable examples of this.)

Perhaps unconsciously our ancestors feared any one individual lasting long in power, because they sensed the corrupting aspect of power; and with someone new and fresh, they could control him better. In any case, underneath their obedience lay tremendous wariness. We may not execute our chiefs anymore, but we do so symbolically in our elections and in the media, taking joy in witnessing the ritualistic fall of the powerful. We may not blame them for a lack of rainfall, but we will blame them for any downturn in the economy, even though most of what happens in the economy is beyond their control. As with the rainfall, they seem to have lost the blessings of good fortune, of the gods. When it comes to our ambivalence and mistrust, we have not changed as much as we think.

Throughout history, however, certain notable leaders have been able to erect a bulwark against this volatility, to earn a type of solid respect and support that allowed them to accomplish great things over time. We think of Moses, or the ancient Indian emperor Asoka, or Pericles (see chapter 1), or the Roman general Scipio Africanus, or Queen Elizabeth I. In more modern times we can think of Abraham Lincoln, or Martin Luther King Jr., or Warren Buffett, or Angela Merkel, or Steve Jobs. We shall call such power *authority*, reverting to the original significance of the word, which comes from the Latin *auctoritas*, the root meaning "to increase or augment."

To the ancient Romans, those who had founded their republic possessed tremendous wisdom. Their ancestors had demonstrated this wisdom by how strong and long-lasting were the institutions they had established, and how they had transformed their provincial town into the preeminent power in the known world. To the extent that Roman senators and leaders returned to this basic wisdom and embodied the ideals of the founders, they had *authority*—an augmented presence, an increased prestige and credibility. Such leaders did not have to resort to speeches or to force. Roman citizens willingly followed their lead and accepted their ideas or advice. Their every word and deed seemed to carry extra weight. This gave them greater leeway in making hard decisions; they were not judged merely by their latest success.

The Romans were notoriously fractious and mistrustful of those in power. Their politics could easily descend into civil war, which in fact happened on several occasions. Having leaders who exuded authority was a way to control this combativeness, to get things done, to maintain a degree of unity. And it required that such leaders embody the highest of ideals, ones that transcended the pettiness of daily political life.

This Roman model, which represents an adherence to a higher purpose, remains the essential ingredient for all true forms of authority. And this is how we must operate if we wish to establish such authority in the world today.

First and foremost, we must understand the fundamental task of any leader—to provide a far-reaching vision, to see the global picture, to work for the greater good of the group and maintain its unity. That is what people crave in their leaders. We have to avoid ever seeming petty, self-serving, or indecisive. Showing signs of that will stir up the ambivalence. Focusing on the future and the larger picture should consume much of our thinking. Based on this vision, we must set practical goals and guide the group toward them. We need to become masters of this visionary process through practice and experience. Attaining such mastery will give us tremendous confidence in ourselves, as opposed to the fake confidence of those who are merely grandiose. And when we exude this confidence, people will be drawn to us and want to follow our lead.

At the same time, however, we must see leadership as a dynamic relationship we have with those being led. We have to understand that our slightest gesture has an unconscious effect on individuals. And so we must pay great attention to our attitude, to the tone that we set. We need to attune ourselves to the shifting moods of the members of the group. We must never assume we have their support. Our empathy must be visceral—we can *feel* when members are losing respect for us. As part of the dynamic, we need to realize that when we show our respect and trust toward those below us, such feelings will flow back to us. The members will open up to our influence. We must try as much as possible to engage people's willpower, to make them identify with the group's mission, to want to actively participate in realizing our higher purpose.

This empathy, however, must never mean becoming needlessly soft and pliant to the group's will. That will only signal weakness. When it comes to our primary task—that of providing a vision for the group and leading it toward the appropriate goals—we must be stern and immovable. Yes, we can listen to the ideas of others and incorporate the good ones. But we must keep in mind that we have a greater command of the overall details and global picture. We must not succumb to political pressures to seem fairer, and so dilute our vision. This vision of ours is beyond politics. It represents truth and reality. We have to be resilient and tough when it comes to realizing it, and merciless with those who try to sabotage this vision or work against the greater good. Toughness and empathy are not incompatible, as Queen Elizabeth I demonstrated.

When leaders fail to establish these twin pillars of authority—vision and empathy—what often happens is the following: Those in the group feel the disconnect and distance between them and leadership. They know that deep down they are viewed as replaceable pawns. They sense the overall lack of direction and the constant tactical reactions to events. And so, in subtle ways, they begin to feel resentful and to lose respect. They listen less attentively to what such leaders say. They spend more hours in the day thinking of their own interests and future. They join or form factions. They work at half or three-quarter speed.

If such leaders, sensing all of this, become more forceful and demanding, the members become more passive-aggressive. If the leaders become pliant and plead for more support, the members feel even less respect, as if the group were now leading the leader. In this way, the members create endless forms of friction for leaders, who might now feel like they have to drag the group up a hill. This friction, caused by their own inattentiveness, is why so many leaders get so little done and are so mediocre.

On the other hand, if we intuitively or consciously follow the path of establishing authority, as described above, we have a much different effect on the group dynamic. The ambivalence of the members or the public does not go away—that would violate human nature—but it becomes manageable. People will still waver and have moments of doubt or envy, but they will more quickly forgive us for any mistakes and move past their suspicions. We have established enough trust for that to happen. Besides, the members have come to dread what could occur if we no longer were the leaders—the disunity, the lack of clarity, the bad decisions. Their need for us is too strong.

Now we are no longer dealing with the invisible friction from the group but the opposite. The members feel engaged in the larger mission. We are able to channel their creative energy, instead of having to drag them along. With this loyalty in place, it is easier to reach goals and realize our vision. This gives us the augmented presence of authority, in which everything we say and do has added weight.

It is always within our capacity to reach this ideal, and if the members lose respect and trust in us, we must see this as our own fault.

YOUR TASK AS A STUDENT OF HUMAN NATURE IS THREEFOLD: FIRST, YOU MUST MAKE yourself a consummate observer of the phenomenon of authority, using as a measuring device the degree of influence people wield without the use of force or motivational speeches. You begin this process by looking at your own family and gauging which parent, if any, exercised greater authority over you and your siblings. You look at the teachers and mentors in your life, some of whom distinguished themselves by the powerful effect they had on you. Their words and the example they set still reverberate in your mind. You observe your own bosses in action, looking at their effect not only on you and other individuals but also on the group as a whole. Lastly, you look at the various leaders in the news. In all these cases, you want to determine the source of their authority or lack of it. You want to discern moments when their authority waxes or wanes, and figure out why.

Second, you want to develop some of the habits and strategies (see the next section) that will serve you well in projecting authority. If you are an apprentice who aspires to a position of leadership, developing these strategies early on will give you an impressive and appealing aura in the present, making it seem as if you were destined to be powerful. If you are already in a leadership position, these strategies will strengthen your authority and connectedness to the group.

As part of this process, you need to reflect on the effect you have on people: Are you constantly arguing, trying to impose your will, finding much more resistance than you expect to your ideas and projects? Do people nod as they listen to your advice and then do the opposite? If you are just starting out, sometimes this cannot be helped—people generally don't respect the ideas of those lower down in the hierarchy; the same ideas promulgated by a boss would have a different effect. But sometimes it could stem from your own actions, as you violate many of the principles described above.

Do not take people's smiles and expressions of assent for reality. Notice their tension as they do so; pay particular attention to their actions. Take any grumbling as a reflection on your authority. In general, you want to heighten your sensitivity to others, looking in particular at those moments when you can *feel* people's disrespect, or your authority on the wane. But keep in mind that there are always bad apples within any group, people who will grumble and not be won over by you no matter what you do. They live to be passive-aggressive and undermine anyone in a leadership position. Don't bother with empathy; nothing will work on them. The art is to recognize them as quickly as possible and either fire or marginalize them. Having a group that is tight and committed will also make it much easier to control such malevolent types.

Third and most important, you must not fall for the counterproductive prejudices of the times we live in, in which the very concept of authority is often misunderstood and despised. Today we confuse authority with leaders in general, and since so many of them in the world seem more interested in preserving their power and enriching themselves, naturally we have doubts about the very concept itself. We also live in fiercely democratic times. "Why should we ever have to follow a person of authority, and assume such an inferior role?" we might ask ourselves. "People in power should simply get the job done; authority is a relic of kings and queens. We have progressed far beyond that."

This disdain for authority and leadership has filtered its way throughout our culture. We no longer recognize authority in the arts. Everyone is a legitimate critic, and standards should be personal—nobody's taste or judgment should be seen as superior. In the past, parenting was considered the model of authority, but parents no longer want to see themselves as authority figures whose role is to inculcate children with particular values and culture. Instead, parents like to see themselves more as equals, with a bit more knowledge and experience, whose role is really to validate their children's feelings and make sure they are continually entertained and occupied. They are more like older friends. This same leveling dynamic applies to teachers and students, where learning must be fun.

In this atmosphere, leaders begin to believe that they are more like caretakers, there to stand back and enable the group to make the right decisions, doing everything by consensus. Or they entertain the idea that what matters more than anything else is crunching numbers, absorbing the mass of information available today. Data and algorithms will determine the direction to take and are the real authority.

All of these ideas and values have unintended consequences. Without authority in the arts, there is nothing to rebel against, no prior movement to overturn, no deep thinking to assimilate and later even reject. There is only an amorphous world of trends that flicker away with increasing speed. Without parents as authority figures, we cannot go through the critical stage of rebellion in adolescence, in which we reject their ideas and discover our own identity. We grow up lost, constantly searching outside ourselves for that identity. Without teachers and masters whom we acknowledge as superior and worthy of respect, we cannot learn from their experience and wisdom, perhaps even seeking later on to surpass them with new and better ideas.

Without leaders who dedicate much mental energy to foreseeing trends and guiding us to long-term solutions, we are lost. And as this situation becomes the norm, because we humans have always needed some form of authority as a guide, we tend to fall for certain fake forms of authority that proliferate in times of chaos and uncertainty.

This could be the strongman, who gives the illusion of leadership and direction but has no real vision of where to go, just ideas and actions that serve his ego and enhance his sense of control. This could be the panderer, the leader who cleverly mimics what the public wants to hear, creating the illusion of being sensitive to the group and giving it what it wants. This could be the chummy leader, who affects the style and mannerisms of everyone else, offering what seems to be the ultimate in fairness, fun, and consensus. This could also be the authority of the group, which becomes that much more powerful in the age of social media: what other people are saying and doing must be true and respected, by dint of sheer numbers. But all of these false forms only lead to more turmoil, chaos, and bad decisions.

As students of human nature, we must recognize the myriad dangers of our prejudice against authority figures. To acknowledge people of authority in the world is not an admission of our own inferiority but rather an acceptance of human nature and the need for such figures. People of authority should not be seen as self-serving or tyrannical—in fact, those are the qualities that diminish their authority. They are not relics of the past but people who fulfill a necessary function and whose style adapts with the times. Authority can be an eminently democratic phenomenon. We must realize that much of what is behind progressive ideas of consensus, the minimal leader, and the parent as friend, is actually a great fear of responsibility, of the tough choices that must be made, of standing out and taking the heat. We must move in the opposite direction, embracing the risks and dangers that come with leadership and authority.

In the world today, we humans have become more self-absorbed, more tribal and tenacious in holding on to our narrow agendas; we have become consumed by the barrage of information inundating us; we are even more fickle when it comes to leaders. And so the need for true figures of authority— with an elevated perspective, a high attunement to the group, and a feel for what unifies it—has never been greater. And because of that, we are tasked with establishing our authority and assuming such a necessary role.

Strategies for Establishing Authority

Remember that the essence of authority is that people willingly follow your lead. They choose to adhere to your words and advice. They want your wisdom. Certainly at times you may have to use force, rewards and punishments, and inspiring speeches. It is only a matter of degree. The less your need of such devices, the greater your authority. And so you must think of continually striving to engage people's willpower and overcome their natural resistances and ambivalence. That is what the following strategies are designed to do. Put them all into practice.

Find your authority style: Authenticity. The authority you establish must emerge naturally from your character, from the particular strengths you possess. Think of certain archetypes of authority: one of them suits you best. A notable archetype is the *Deliverer*, such as Moses or Martin Luther King Jr., an individual determined to deliver people from evil. Deliverers have an acute dislike of any kind of injustice, particularly those that affect the group they identify with. They have so much conviction, and most often such a way with words, that people are drawn to them.

Another archetype would be the *Founder*. These are the ones who establish a new order in politics or business. They generally have a keen sense of trends and a great aversion to the status quo. They are unconventional and independent minded. Their greatest joy is to tinker and invent something new. Many people naturally rally to the side of Founders, because they represent some form of progress. Related to this archetype would be the *Visionary Artist*, such as Pablo Picasso or the jazz artist John Coltrane or the film director David Lynch. These artists learn the conventions in their field and then turn them upside down. They crave some new style and they create it. With their skill, they always find an audience and followers.

Other archetypes could include the *Truth Seeker* (people who have no tolerance for lies and politicking); the *Quiet Pragmatist* (they want nothing more than to fix things that are broken, and have infinite patience); the *Healer* (they have a knack for finding what will fulfill and unify people); the *Teacher* (they have a way of getting people to initiate action and learn from their mistakes). You must identify with one of these archetypes, or any others that are noticeable in culture.

By bringing out a style that is natural to you, you give the impression that it is something beyond you, as if your sense of justice or nose for trends came from your DNA or were a gift from the gods. You cannot help but fight for your cause or create a new order. Without this naturalness, it might seem that your attempt at authority is too opportunistic and manipulative, that your support for some cause or trend is a mere ploy for power. The earlier you recognize this style the better; you will have more time to hone it, to adapt it to changes in yourself and in the culture, to bring out new facets to impress and fascinate people. And having left signs of this style from the beginning of your career, it will seem all the more like a higher power that you cannot help but follow.

Focus outwardly: the Attitude. We humans are self-absorbed by nature and spend most of our time focusing inwardly on our emotions, on our wounds, on our fantasies. You want to develop the habit of reversing this as much as possible. You do this in three ways. First, you hone your listening skills, absorbing yourself in the words and nonverbal cues of others. You train yourself to read between the lines of what people are saying. You attune yourself to their moods and their needs, and sense what they are missing. You do not take people's smiles and approving looks for reality but rather sense the underlying tension or fascination.

Second, you dedicate yourself to earning people's respect. You do not feel entitled to it; your focus is not on your feelings and what people owe you because of your position and greatness (an inward turn). You earn their respect by respecting their individual needs and by proving that you are working for the greater good. Third, you consider being a leader a tremendous responsibility, the welfare of the group hanging on your every decision. What drives you is not getting attention but bringing about the best results possible for the most people. You absorb yourself in the work, not your ego. You feel a deep and visceral connection to the group, seeing your fate and theirs as deeply intertwined.

If you exude this attitude, people will feel it, and it will open them up to your influence. They will be drawn to you by the simple fact that it is rare to encounter a person so sensitive to people's moods and focused so supremely on results. This will make you stand out from the crowd, and in the end you will gain far more attention this way than by signaling your desperate need to be popular and liked.

Cultivate the third eye: the Vision. In 401 BC, ten thousand Greek mercenary soldiers, fighting on behalf of the Persian prince Darius in his attempt to take over the empire from the king, his brother, suddenly found themselves on the losing side of the battle, and now trapped deep in the heart of Persia. When the victorious Persians tricked the leaders of the mercenaries into coming to a meeting to discuss their fate and then executed them all, it became clear to the surviving soldiers that they would be either executed as well or sold into slavery by the next day. That night they wandered through their camp bemoaning their fate.

Among them was the writer Xenophon, who had gone along with the soldiers as a kind of roving reporter. Xenophon had studied philosophy as a student of Socrates. He believed in the supremacy of rational thinking, of seeing the entire picture, the general idea behind the fleeting appearances of daily life. He had practiced such thinking skills over several years.

That night he had a vision of how the Greeks could escape their trap and return home. He saw them moving swiftly and stealthily through Persia, sacrificing everything for speed. He saw them leaving right away, using the element of surprise to gain some distance. He thought ahead—of the terrain, the route to take, the many enemies they would face, how they could help and use citizens who revolted against the Persians. He saw them getting rid of their wagons, living off the land and moving quickly, even in winter. In the space of a few hours, he had conjured up the details of the retreat, all inspired by his overall vision of their fast zigzag route to the Mediterranean and home.

Although he had no military experience, his vision was so complete, and he communicated it with such confidence, that the soldiers nominated him as their de facto leader. It took several years and involved many ensuing challenges, each time Xenophon applying his global vision to determine a strategy, but in the end, he proved the power of such rational thinking by leading them to safety despite the immense odds against them.

This story embodies the essence of all authority and the most essential element in establishing it. Most people are locked in the moment. They are prone to overreacting and panicking, to seeing only a narrow part of the reality facing the group. They cannot entertain alternative ideas or prioritize. Those who maintain their presence of mind and elevate their perspective above the moment tap into the visionary powers of the human mind and cultivate that third eye for unseen forces and trends. They stand out from the group, fulfill the true function of leadership, and create the aura of authority by seeming to possess the godlike ability to read the future. And this is a power that can be practiced and developed and applied to any situation.

As early in life as possible, you train yourself to disconnect from the emotions roiling the group. You force yourself to raise your vision, to imagine the larger picture. You strain to see events in themselves, uncolored by people's partisan opinions. You entertain the perspective of the enemy; you listen to the ideas of outsiders; you open your mind to various possibilities. In this way, you gain a feel for the gestalt, or overall shape of the situation. You game out the possible trends, how things might play out in the future, and in particular how things could go wrong. You have infinite patience for this exercise. The more deeply you go into it, the more you can acquire the power to discern the future in some form.

Those who faced Napoleon Bonaparte on the battlefield often had the impression he read their minds and knew of their plans, but he had merely thought forward more thoroughly than the other side. The great German thinker and writer Johann Wolfgang von Goethe seemed to have the uncanny ability to predict future trends, but it came from years of study and global thinking.

Once you have your vision, you then slowly work backward to the present, creating a reasonable and flexible way to reach your goal. The more thinking that goes into this process, the more confident you will feel about your plan, and this confidence will infect and convince others. If people doubt your vision, you stay inwardly firm. Time will prove you right. If you fall short of your goals, take this as a sign you have not gone far enough with your thinking.

Lead from the front: the Tone. As the leader, you must be seen working as hard as or even harder than everyone else. You set the highest standards for yourself. You are consistent and accountable. If there are sacrifices that need to be made, you are the first to make them for the good of the group. This sets the proper tone. The members will feel compelled to raise themselves up to your level and gain your approval, much like Elizabeth's ministers. They will internalize your values and subtly imitate you. You will not have to yell and lecture them to make them work harder. They will want to.

It is important that you set this tone from the beginning. First impressions are critical. If you try later on to show you want to lead from the front, it will look forced and lack credibility. Equally important is to show some initial toughness; if people get the impression early on that they can maneuver you, they will do so mercilessly. You set limits that are fair. If members don't rise to the high levels you uphold, you punish them. Your tone in speaking or writing is peremptory and bold. People always respect strength in the leader, as long as it does not stir up fears of the abuse of power. If such toughness is not natural to you, develop it, or you will not last very long in the position. You will always have plenty of time to reveal that softer, kinder side that is really you, but if you start soft, you signal that you are a pushover.

Begin this early on in your career by developing the highest possible standards for your own work (see the next section for more on this) and by training yourself to be constantly aware of how your manner and tone affect people in the subtlest of ways.

Stir conflicting emotions: the Aura. Most people are too predictable. To mix well in social situations, they assume a persona that is consistent—jovial, pleasing, bold, sensitive. They try to hide other qualities that they are afraid to show. As the leader, you want to be more mysterious, to establish a presence that fascinates people. By sending mixed signals, by showing qualities that are ever so slightly contrary, you cause people to pause in their instant categorizations and to think about who you really are. The more they think about you, the larger and more authoritative your presence.

So, for instance, you are generally kind and sensitive, but you show an undertone of harshness, of intolerance toward certain types of behavior. This is the pose of parents, who demonstrate their love while indicating limits and boundaries. The child is trapped between affection and a touch of fear, and from that tension comes respect. In general, try to keep your bursts of anger or recriminations as infrequent as possible. Because you are mostly quiet and empathetic, when your anger flares, it really stands out and has the power to make people truly intimidated and contrite.

You can mix prudence with an undertone of boldness that you occasionally display. You deliberate long on problems, but once a decision is made, you act with great energy and audacity. Such boldness comes out of nowhere and creates a strong impression. Or you can blend the spiritual with an undertone of earthy pragmatism. Those were the paradoxical qualities of Martin Luther King Jr. that fascinated people. Or you can be folksy and regal, like Queen Elizabeth I. Or you can blend the masculine and the feminine. (See chapter 12 for more on this.)

Related to this, you must learn to balance presence and absence. If you are too present and familiar, always available and visible, you seem too banal. You give people no room to idealize you. But if you are too aloof, people cannot identify with you. In general, it is best to lean slightly more in the direction of absence, so that when you do appear before the group, you generate excitement and drama. If done right, in those moments when you are not available, people will be thinking of you. Today people have lost this art. They are far too present and familiar, their every move displayed on social media. That might make you relatable, but it also makes you seem just like everyone else, and it is impossible to project authority with such an ordinary presence.

Keep in mind that talking too much is a type of overpresence that grates and reveals weakness. Silence is a form of absence and withdrawal that draws attention; it spells self-control and power; when you do talk, it has a greater effect. In a similar fashion, if you commit a mistake, do not overexplain and overapologize. You make it clear you accept responsibility and are accountable for any failures, and then you move on. Your contrition should be relatively quiet; your subsequent actions will show you have learned the lesson. Avoid appearing defensive and whiny if attacked. You are above that.

Develop this aura early on, as a way to enthrall people. Do not make the mix too strong, or you will seem insane. It is an undertone that makes people wonder in a good way. It is a matter not of faking qualities you do not have, but rather of bringing out more of your natural complexity.

Never appear to take, always to give: the Taboo. Taking something from people they have assumed they possessed—money, rights or privileges, time that is their own—creates a basic insecurity and will call into question your authority and all the credit you have amassed. You make the members of the group feel uncertain about the future in a most visceral manner. You stir up doubts about your legitimacy as a leader: "What more will you take? Are you abusing the power that you have? Have you been fooling us all along?" Even the hint of this will harm your reputation. If sacrifices are necessary, you are the first to make them, and they are not simply symbolic. Try to frame any loss of resources or privileges as temporary, and make it clear how quickly you will restore them. Follow the path of Queen Elizabeth I and make the husbanding of resources your primary concern, so that you never end up in this position. Make it so that you can afford to be generous.

Related to this, you must avoid overpromising to people. In the moment, it might feel good to let them hear of the great things you will do for them, but people generally have an acute memory for promises, and if you fail to deliver, it will stick in their mind, even if you try to blame others or circumstances. If this happens a second time, your authority begins to sharply erode. Not giving what you promised to deliver will feel like something you have taken away. Everyone can talk a good game and promise, and so you seem like just anyone else we encounter, and the disappointment can be profound.

Rejuvenate your authority: Adaptability. Your authority will grow with each action that inspires trust and respect. It gives you the luxury to remain in power long enough to realize great projects. But as you get older, the authority you established can become rigid and stodgy. You become the father figure who starts to seem oppressive by how long he has monopolized power, no matter how deeply people admired him in the past. A new generation inevitably emerges that is immune to your charm, to the aura you have created. They see you as a relic. You also have the tendency as you get older to become ever so slightly intolerant and tyrannical, as you cannot help but expect people to follow you. Without being aware, you start to feel entitled, and people sense this. Besides, the public wants newness and fresh faces.

The first step in avoiding this danger is to maintain the kind of sensitivity that Elizabeth displayed throughout her life, noting the moods behind people's words, gauging the effect you have on newcomers and young people. Losing that empathy should be your greatest fear, as you will begin to cocoon yourself in your great reputation.

The second step is to look for new markets and audiences to appeal to, which will force you to adapt. If possible, expand the reach of your authority. Without making a fool of yourself by attempting to appeal to a younger crowd that you cannot really understand, try to alter your style somewhat with the passing years. In the arts, this has been the secret to success of people like Pablo Picasso, or Alfred Hitchcock, or Coco Chanel. Such flexibility in those who are in their fifties and beyond will give you a touch of the divine and immortal—your spirit remains alive and open, and your authority is renewed.

The Inner Authority

We all have a higher and a lower self. At certain moments in life, we can definitely feel one part or the other as the stronger. When we accomplish things, when we finish what we start, we can sense the outlines of this higher self. We feel it as well when we think of others before ourselves, when we let go of our ego, when instead of merely reacting to events, we step back and think and strategize the best way forward. But equally we know all too well the stirrings of the lower self, when we take everything personally and become petty, or when we want to escape reality through some addictive pleasure, or when we waste time, or when we feel confused and unmotivated.

Although we most often float between these two sides, if we look at ourselves closely, we have to admit that the lower half is the stronger one. It is the more primitive and animal part of our nature. If nothing impels us to do otherwise, we naturally become indolent, crave quick pleasures, turn inward, and brood over petty matters. It often takes great effort and awareness to tame this lower half and bring out the higher side; it is not our first impulse.

The key to making the struggle between the two sides more even and to perhaps tip the scales toward the higher is to cultivate what we shall call the *inner authority*. It serves as the voice, the conscience of our higher self. This voice is already there; we hear it at times, but it is weak. We need to increase the frequency with which we hear it and its volume. Think of this voice as dictating a code of behavior, and every day we must make ourselves listen to it. It tells us the following.

You have a responsibility to contribute to the culture and times you live in. Right now, you are living off the fruits of millions of people in the past who have made your life incomparably easier through their struggles and inventions. You have benefited from an education that embodies the wisdom of thousands of years of experience. It is so easy to take this all for granted, to imagine that it all just came about naturally and that you are entitled to have all of these powers. That is the view of spoiled children, and you must see any signs of such an attitude within you as shameful. This world needs constant improvement and renewal. You are here not merely to gratify your impulses and consume what others have made but to make and contribute as well, to serve a higher purpose.

To serve this higher purpose, you must cultivate what is unique about you. Stop listening so much to the words and opinions of others, telling you who you are and what you should like and dislike. Judge things and people for yourself. Question what you think and why you feel a certain way. Know yourself thoroughly—your innate tastes and inclinations, the fields that naturally attract you. Work every day on improving those skills that mesh with your unique spirit and purpose. Add to the needed diversity of culture by creating something that reflects your uniqueness. Embrace what makes you different.

Not following this course is the real reason you feel depressed at times. Moments of depression are a call to listen again to your inner authority.

In a world full of endless distractions, you must focus and prioritize. Certain activities are a waste of time. Certain people of a low nature will drag you down, and you must avoid them. Keep your eye on your long- and short-term goals, and remain concentrated and alert. Allow yourself the luxury of exploring and wandering creatively, but always with an underlying purpose.

You must adhere to the highest standards in your work. You strive for excellence, to make something that will resonate with the public and last. To fall short of this is to disappoint people and to let down your audience, and that makes you feel ashamed. To maintain such standards, you must develop self-discipline and the proper work habits. You must pay great attention to the details in your work and place a premium value on effort. The first thought or idea that comes to you is most often incomplete and inadequate. Think more thoroughly and deeply about your ideas, some of which you must discard. Do not become attached to your initial ideas, but rather treat them roughly. Keep in mind that your life is short, that it could end any day. You must have a sense of urgency to make the most of this limited time. You don't need deadlines or people telling you what to do and when to finish. Any motivation you need comes from within. You are complete and self-reliant.

When it comes to operating with this inner authority, we can consider Leonardo da Vinci our model. His motto in life was *ostinato rigore*, "relentless rigor." Whenever Leonardo was given a commission, he went well beyond the task, poring over every detail to make the work more lifelike or effective. No one had to tell him to do this. He was ferociously diligent and hard on himself. Although his interests ranged far and wide, when he attacked a particular problem, it was with complete focus. He had a sense of a personal mission—to serve mankind, to contribute toward its progress. Impelled by this inner authority, he pushed beyond all of the limits that he had inherited—being an illegitimate son with little direction or education early on in his life. Such a voice will likewise help us push beyond the obstacles that life places in our path.

It might seem at first glance that having such a voice from within could lead to a rather harsh and unpleasant life, but in fact it is the opposite. There is nothing more disorienting and depressing than to see the years pass by without a sense of direction, grasping to reach goals that keep changing, and squandering our youthful energies. Much as the outer authority helps keep the group unified, its energy channeled toward productive and higher ends, the inner authority brings you a sense of cohesion and force. You are not gnawed by the anxiety that comes with living below your potential.

Feeling the higher self in ascendance, you can afford to indulge that lower self, to let it out at moments to release tension and not become a prisoner of your Shadow. And most important, you no longer need the comfort and guidance of a parent or leader. You have become your own mother and father, your own leader, truly independent and operating according to your inner authority.

> The select man, the excellent man is urged, by interior necessity, to appeal from himself to some standard beyond himself, superior to himself, whose service he freely accepts. . . . We distinguished the excellent man from the common man by saying that the former is one who makes great demands on himself, and the latter the one who makes no demands on himself, but contents himself with what he is, and is delighted with himself. Contrary to what is usually thought, it is the man of excellence . . . who lives in essential servitude. Life has no savor for him unless he makes it consist in service to something transcendental. Hence he does not look upon the necessity of serving as an oppression. When, by chance, such necessity is lacking, he grows restless and invents some new standard, more difficult, more exigent, with which to coerce himself. This is life lived as a discipline—the noble life.
>
> —José Ortega y Gasset

16

See the Hostility Behind
the Friendly Façade

◇

The Law of Aggression

On the surface, the people around you appear so polite and civilized. But beneath the mask, they are all inevitably dealing with frustrations. They have a need to influence people and gain power over circumstances. Feeling blocked in their endeavors, they often try to assert themselves in manipulative ways that catch you by surprise. And then there are those whose need for power and impatience to obtain it are greater than others. They turn particularly aggressive, getting their way by intimidating people, being relentless and willing to do almost anything. You must transform yourself into a superior observer of people's unsatisfied aggressive desires, paying extra attention to the chronic aggressors and passive aggressors in our midst. You must recognize the signs—the past patterns of behavior, the obsessive need to control everything in their environment—that indicate the dangerous types. They depend on making you emotional—afraid, angry—and unable to think straight. Do not give them this power. When it comes to your own aggressive energy, learn to tame and channel it for productive purposes—standing up for yourself, attacking problems with relentless energy, realizing great ambitions.

The Sophisticated Aggressor

In late 1857, Maurice B. Clark, a twenty-eight-year-old Englishman living in Cleveland, Ohio, made the most important decision yet in his young life: he would quit his comfortable job as a high-level buyer and seller for a produce firm and start his own business in the same line. He had the ambition of becoming yet another new millionaire in this bustling city, and he had nothing but confidence in his powers to get there: he was a born hustler with a nose for making money.

Clark had fled England some ten years earlier, fearing imminent arrest for having struck his employer and knocked him unconscious. (He always had a bit of a temper.) He had emigrated to the United States, traveled west from New York, landed all kinds of odd jobs, and then ended up in Cleveland, where he quickly rose through the ranks of merchants. Cleveland was something of a boomtown, located on a river and Lake Erie and serving as a key transportation hub connecting the East to the West. There would never be a better time for Clark to push his way forward and make a fortune.

There was only one problem—he did not have enough money to start the business. He would need a collaborator with some capital, and as he thought about this, he came up with a possible business partner, a young man named John D. Rockefeller whom Clark had befriended at a commercial college both had attended a few years before.

At first glance, it seemed an odd choice. Rockefeller was only eighteen years old. He was working as a bookkeeper at a fairly large produce-shipping firm named Hewitt and Tuttle, and he was in so many ways the polar opposite of Clark: Clark loved to live well, with a taste for fine things, gambling, and the ladies; he was feisty and combative. Rockefeller was fiercely religious, unusually sober and mild-mannered for his age. How could they possibly get along? And Clark had calculated that his partner would have to put up at least $2,000 to get the company under way. How would a bookkeeper from a family of limited means have such savings? On the other hand, in his two years at Hewitt and Tuttle, Rockefeller had earned a reputation as one of the most fiercely efficient and honest clerks in town, a man who could be relied upon to account for every penny spent and keep the company in the black. More important, as Rockefeller was so young, Clark could dominate the relationship. It was worth asking him.

To Clark's surprise, when he suggested the partnership, Rockefeller not only jumped at the opportunity with uncharacteristic zeal but quickly came up with the $2,000, somehow borrowing the funds. Rockefeller quit his job and the new company, called Clark and Rockefeller, opened for business in April 1858.

In its first years Clark and Rockefeller was a thriving enterprise. The two men balanced each other out, and there was much business to be had in Cleveland. But as time went on, Clark began to feel increasingly irritated by the young man, and even a bit contemptuous of him. He was more straitlaced than Clark had imagined; he had no discernible vices. His main pleasure seemed to come from the accounting books that he kept so well and finding ways to save money. Although still so young, he already had a slumped posture from poring over his ledgers day and night. He dressed like a middle-aged banker, and acted that way as well. Clark's brother James, who worked in the office, dubbed him "the Sunday-school superintendent."

Slowly Clark began to see Rockefeller as too dull and dreary to be one of the faces of the company. Clark brought in a new partner from an elite Cleveland family and dropped Rockefeller's name from the company title, hoping that would draw even more business. Surprisingly, Rockefeller did not seem to object to this; he was all in favor of making more money and cared little about titles.

Their produce business was booming, but soon word spread through Cleveland of a new commodity that could spark the region's equivalent of a gold rush—the recent discovery of rich veins of oil in nearby western Pennsylvania. In 1862 a young Englishman named Samuel Andrews—an inventor/entrepreneur who had known Clark in England—visited their offices and pleaded with Clark to become partners in the oil business. He bragged of the limitless potential in oil—the lucrative series of products that could be made out of the material and the cheapness of producing them. With just a little capital they could start their own refinery and make a fortune.

Clark's response was lukewarm—it was a business that experienced tremendous ups and downs, prices continually rising and falling, and with the Civil War now raging, it seemed a bad time to commit so fully. It would be better to get involved on some lower level. But then Andrews gave his pitch to Rockefeller, and something seemed to spark to life in the young man's eyes. Rockefeller convinced Clark that they should fund the refinery—he would personally ensure its success. Clark had never seen Rockefeller so enthusiastic about anything. It must mean something, he thought, and so he relented to the pressure from the two men. In 1863 they formed a new refining business called Andrews, Clark and Company.

That same year, twenty other refineries sprouted up in Cleveland, and the competition was fierce. To Clark, it was quite amusing to watch Rockefeller in action. He spent hours in the refinery, sweeping the floors, polishing the metal, rolling out barrels, stacking hoops. It was like a love affair. He worked well into the night trying to figure out ways to streamline the refinery and squeeze more money out of it. It had become the principal generator of profit for their firm, and Clark could not help but be pleased that he had agreed to fund it. Oil, however, had become Rockefeller's obsession, and he constantly bombarded

Clark with new ideas for expansion, all at a time when the price of oil was fluctuating more than ever. Clark told him to go more slowly; he found the chaos
in the oil business unnerving.

Increasingly, Clark found it hard to hide his irritation: Rockefeller was getting a bit puffed up with the success of the refinery. Clark had to remind the
former bookkeeper of whose idea it had been all along to start their business.
Like a refrain, he kept telling Rockefeller, "What in the world would you have
done without *me*?" Then he discovered that Rockefeller had borrowed $100,000
for the refinery without consulting him, and he angrily ordered Rockefeller to
never go behind his back again and to stop looking to expand the business. But
nothing he said or did seemed to stop him. For someone so quiet and unassum-
ing, Rockefeller could be annoyingly relentless, like a child. A few months after
Clark had berated him, Rockefeller hit him with another request to sign for a
big loan, and Clark finally exploded: "If that's the way you want to do business,
we'd better dissolve, and let you run your own affairs to suit yourself."

Clark had no desire to break up the partnership at this point—it was too
profitable, and despite the qualities that grated on his nerves, he needed Rockefeller as the man to look after the dull details of their growing enterprise. He
simply wanted to intimidate Rockefeller with this threat, which seemed to be
the only way to get him to back off on his tireless quest to quickly grow the
refinery business. As usual, Rockefeller said little and seemed to defer.

Then, the following month, Rockefeller invited Clark and Andrews to his
house to discuss future plans. And despite all of Clark's previous admonitions,
Rockefeller outlined even bolder ideas for expanding the refinery, and once
again Clark could not control himself. "We'd better split up!" he yelled. Then
something odd happened—Rockefeller agreed to this and got Clark and Andrews to affirm that they were all in favor of dissolving the partnership. He did
this without the slightest trace of anger or resentment.

Clark had played a lot of poker, and he felt certain Rockefeller was bluffing,
trying to force his hand. If he refused to budge on the young man's desire to
expand the business, Rockefeller would have to back down. He could not afford to be on his own; he needed Clark more than the other way around. He
would be forced to realize his rashness and ask to resume the partnership. In
doing so, Rockefeller would be humbled. Clark could set the terms and demand that Rockefeller follow his lead.

To his amazement, however, the next day Clark read in the local newspaper
the announcement of the dissolution of their business, the notice obviously

placed there by Rockefeller himself. When Clark confronted him later that day, Rockefeller calmly replied he was merely putting into action what they had agreed upon the day before, that it had been Clark's idea to start with, and that he thought Clark was right. He suggested they hold an auction and sell the company to the highest bidder. Something about his dull, businesslike manner was infuriating. At this point, agreeing to the auction was not the worst option. Clark would outbid him and be rid of this insufferable upstart once and for all.

On the day of the auction in February 1865, Clark used a lawyer to represent his side, while Rockefeller represented himself, yet another sign of his arrogance and lack of sophistication. The price kept ticking upward, and finally Rockefeller bid $72,500, a rather ridiculous and shocking price to pay, a sum that Clark could not possibly afford. How would Rockefeller have so much money, and how could he possibly run this business without Clark? He clearly had lost any business sense that he had had. If that was what he was willing to pay, and he had the funds, let him have it and good riddance. As part of the sale, Rockefeller got the refinery but had to let go of the produce business with no compensation. Clark was more than satisfied, although it bothered him that Andrews had decided to go along with Rockefeller and remain his partner.

In the months to come, however, Maurice Clark began to reassess what had happened: he started to have the uneasy feeling that Rockefeller had been planning this for months, perhaps more than a year. Rockefeller must have courted bankers and secured bank loans well before the auction, to be able to afford the high price. He must have also secured Andrews to his side in advance. He could detect a gloating look in Rockefeller's eye the day the refinery became his, something he had never seen before in the sober young man. Was that quiet and dull appearance of his merely an act? As the years revealed the immense wealth Rockefeller would accumulate through this first move, Clark could not help but entertain the thought he had somehow been played.

COLONEL OLIVER H. PAYNE WAS THE EQUIVALENT OF CLEVELAND ARISTOCRACY. He came from an illustrious family that included one of the founders of the city itself. He had attended Yale University and had become a decorated Civil War hero. And after the war he had started several successful business enterprises. He had one of the finest mansions in town on Euclid Avenue, nicknamed Millionaire's Row. But he had larger ambitions, perhaps politics; he thought of himself as presidential material.

One of his thriving businesses was a refinery, which was the second biggest in town. But toward the end of 1871, Payne began to hear strange rumors of some kind of agreement between a few refinery owners and the largest railroads: the railroads would lower their rates for the particular refineries that had joined this secret organization, in exchange for a guaranteed volume of traffic. Those outside this organization would find their rates rising, making business difficult if not impossible. And the chief refinery owner, and the only one in Cleveland, behind this agreement was apparently none other than John D. Rockefeller.

Rockefeller had expanded to two refineries in Cleveland and had renamed the company Standard Oil. Standard Oil was now the country's largest refining business, but the competition remained stiff, even within Cleveland and its now twenty-eight refineries, including those of Standard Oil. Because of this booming business, more and more millionaires had built their mansions on Euclid Avenue. But if Rockefeller controlled entrée into this new organization, he could do great damage to his competitors. It was in the midst of these rumors that Rockefeller arranged for a very private meeting between him and Payne at a Cleveland bank.

Payne knew Rockefeller well. They had been born two weeks apart, had gone to the same high school, and lived near each other on Euclid Avenue. He admired Rockefeller's business savvy but also feared him. Rockefeller was the kind of man who could not stand to lose in anything. If someone passed him by in a horse-drawn carriage, Rockefeller would have to whip his horses and overtake it. They worshipped in the same church; Payne knew he was a man of high principle, but he was also quite mysterious and secretive.

In their meeting, Rockefeller confided in Payne: he was the first outsider to be told of the existence of this secret organization, to be called the Southern Improvement Company (SIC). Rockefeller claimed it was the railroads that had come up with the idea of the SIC to increase their profits, and that he had really had no choice but to enter into the agreement. He did not invite Payne to join the SIC. Instead he offered to buy out Payne's refinery at a very nice price, to give Payne a hefty amount of Standard Oil stock that would certainly mint him a fortune, and to bring him in as a high-level executive with an illustrious title. He would make far more money this way than by trying to compete with Standard Oil.

Rockefeller said all of this in the politest tone. He was going to keep expanding and bring some much-needed order to the anarchic oil industry. It was a crusade of his, and he was inviting Payne to be a fellow crusader from within Standard Oil. It was a compelling way to present his case, but Payne hesitated. He had moments of exasperation in dealing with this unpredictable business, but he had not thought of selling the refinery. It was all so sudden. Sensing his indecision, Rockefeller gave him a look of great sympathy and offered Payne the chance to examine Standard Oil's ledgers, to convince him of the futility of resistance. Payne could hardly turn that down, and what he saw in a few short hours astounded him: Standard Oil had considerably higher profit margins than his own. Nobody had suspected to what extent Standard Oil was outpacing its rivals. For Payne, it was enough, and he accepted Rockefeller's offer.

News of the sale of Payne's refinery, as well as the growing rumors of the existence of the SIC, completely rattled the other refinery owners in town. With Payne's refinery in his pocket, Rockefeller was in a very strong position.

Within weeks, J. W. Fawcett of Fawcett and Critchley, another major refinery in town, received a visit from Rockefeller. His pitch was ever so slightly more ominous than what he had delivered to Payne: the business was too unpredictable; Cleveland was farther away from the oil-producing towns, and the refiners had to pay more for crude oil to be shipped there; they were at a continual disadvantage; with the prices of oil continuing to fluctuate, many of them would go bust; Rockefeller was going to consolidate them and give Cleveland some leverage with the railroads; he was doing them all a favor, relieving them of the tremendous burdens of the business and giving them money before they went broke, which with the SIC was certain to happen.

The price he offered for Fawcett's refinery was certainly less generous than what he had paid Payne, as were the shares and the position within Standard Oil that went along with the proposition, and Fawcett was quite reluctant to sell, but a glance at Standard Oil's books overwhelmed him, and he surrendered to Rockefeller's terms.

Now more and more refinery owners received a visit from Rockefeller, and one after another succumbed to the pressure, since holding out put them in a weaker negotiating position, as the price Rockefeller offered for their refineries kept getting lower. One holdout owner was Isaac Hewitt, Rockefeller's former boss when he was a fledgling bookkeeper. Selling the refinery at such a low price could ruin Hewitt. He begged Rockefeller for mercy and to be left alone with his business. Rockefeller, ever gentle and polite, told him that he could not possibly compete with Standard Oil moving forward. "I have ways of making money you know nothing about," he explained. Hewitt sold his refinery for more than half the price he had wanted.

By the middle of March, the existence of the SIC had become public and the pressure had mounted for such an organization to be disbanded or suffer legal consequences. The railroads relented, and so did Rockefeller, who did not seem all that upset at this news. The matter was settled, the SIC disappeared, but in the months to come some people in Cleveland began to wonder if all was not what it had appeared to be. The SIC had never really taken effect; it had remained just a rumor, and Standard Oil, it seemed, was the principal source of that rumor. In the meantime, Rockefeller had effected what had become known as the Cleveland Massacre—in just a few months, he had bought out twenty of the twenty-six refineries outside his control. Many elegant mansions of former millionaires on Euclid Avenue were now being sold or boarded up, as Rockefeller had carefully knocked them out of the business. He had acted as if the railroads were calling all the shots with the SIC, but perhaps it had been the other way around.

IN THE YEARS TO COME, THOSE IN THE RAILROAD BUSINESS BEGAN TO GREATLY FEAR the growing power of Standard Oil. After the Cleveland Massacre, Rockefeller applied the same tactics to refineries in Pittsburgh, Philadelphia, and New York. His method was always the same: aiming first for the biggest refineries in the respective town, showing them his books, which were now even more impressive, getting a few big fish to surrender, and instilling panic in the others. Those who held out he would ruthlessly undersell and drive out of the market. By 1875, Rockefeller controlled all of the major refining centers in the United States and virtually monopolized the worldwide market for kerosene, the principal product used for lighting.

Such power gave him far too much leverage over railroad rates, but to make matters worse, Rockefeller had begun to dominate the pipeline business, the other way of transporting oil. He built up a whole series of pipelines throughout Pennsylvania and had gained control of several railroads that helped ship the oil the rest of the way to the East Coast, giving him his own transportation networks. If he continued unimpeded in this campaign, his position would be impregnable. And nobody was more afraid of this prospect than Tom Scott, president of the Pennsylvania Railroad, at the time the largest and most power-ful corporation in America.

Scott had led a most distinguished life. During the Civil War, he had served as Lincoln's assistant secretary of war, in charge of ensuring the smooth func-tioning of the railroads in aiding the North's effort. As head of the Pennsylva-nia Railroad, he had ambitions of endlessly expanding the company's reach, but Rockefeller stood in the way, and it was time to do battle with Standard Oil.

Scott had all the necessary resources to take on Rockefeller, and he had a plan. For the past few years, anticipating Rockefeller's maneuvers, he had built up his own enormous network of pipelines that would work in conjunction with his railroad to move oil to refineries. He would ramp up the construction of new pipelines and purchase new refineries that sprang up, creating his own rival network, ensuring his railroad enough business to check Rockefeller's progress, then work to weaken him further. But as it became clear what he was up to, Rockefeller's response was totally unexpected and rather shocking: Stan-dard Oil shut down almost all its Pennsylvania refineries, giving Scott's pipe-lines and railroads virtually no oil to ship. If they managed to get their hands on some oil, Rockefeller rigorously undersold them to any refineries outside his system, and he seemed to not care how low the price would go. He also made it hard for Scott to get his hands on the oil the company needed to lubri-cate train engines and wheels.

Pennsylvania Railroad had overextended itself in this campaign and was losing money at a rapid rate, but Rockefeller had to be losing just as much. He seemed to be aiming for mutual suicide. Scott was in too deep to back out of this war, and so he was forced to cut costs by firing hundreds of railroad work-ers and reducing wages for those who remained. Scott's workers retaliated with a general railroad strike that quickly turned violent and bloody, as workers spread throughout the state destroying thousands of Pennsylvania Railroad freight cars. Scott retaliated brutally, but the strike persisted and the sharehold-ers in the Pennsylvania Railroad were growing quite nervous. All the while, Rockefeller seemed unperturbed and continued with his pressure campaign, as if he had nothing to lose.

Scott had had enough. Somehow Rockefeller could absorb these huge losses, but he could not. He had literally run out of money. Not only did he agree to put a stop to his campaign, but he had to sell to Rockefeller the lion's share of his refineries, storage tanks, steamships, and pipelines. Scott would never recover from this humiliating and rather sudden defeat: a year later he suffered a stroke, and within a few years he died at the age of fifty-eight.

ALTHOUGH IT APPEARED THAT ROCKEFELLER'S CONTROL OF THE OIL BUSINESS WAS now complete, a businessman and engineer named Byron Benson had an idea about how to poke a hole in his expanding empire. Rockefeller could call the shots with his immense resources, but he could not compete with technological progress. What gave Rockefeller an advantage was that pipelines were relatively short, at most thirty miles long. He could dominate by creating pipeline networks all across Pennsylvania and by controlling many of the railroads operating between the refineries and the pipelines. Even if someone had an independent pipeline, at some point he would depend on Standard Oil to transport the oil the rest of the way.

What if, however, Benson could design something new—one long, continuous pipeline that would run from the oil fields of western Pennsylvania to the Eastern Seaboard? In that way he could deliver oil directly to the few independent East Coast refineries that remained and guarantee low prices for them, bypassing Rockefeller's network. This would halt Rockefeller's momentum, and with more of these long-range pipelines, rivals to Standard Oil could begin to compete on fairer terms.

It would not be easy. The pipeline would require some novel engineering to make the oil flow upward over the hills and mountains that would inevitably be in the way, but Benson had been working on this. And because Rockefeller had made so many enemies and so many feared his growing monopoly, Benson was able to raise very large sums of money from investors, more than enough to cover the high cost of building such a pipeline.

Benson named his enterprise the Tidewater Pipeline Company, and in 1878 construction began. But almost immediately he had to deal with an insidious campaign to halt the work on the pipeline. Benson depended on railroad tank cars to transport the heavy materials to the construction site, but it seemed that over the years Rockefeller had bought up the lion's share of such cars and had virtually cornered the market. Wherever he turned to find tank cars, Benson ran into Standard Oil subsidiaries that controlled them. Benson had to find other means of moving the material, and this added to his costs and wasted valuable time. All of this only made him more determined to finish the job and outwit Rockefeller.

This, however, was only the beginning. Benson needed to make his route to the sea as easy as possible, to save money, and that would mean running it through Maryland. But now word reached him that, through lots of generous bribes, Rockefeller had gotten the Maryland legislature to give an exclusive pipeline charter to Standard Oil. This meant Tidewater would have to pass through the hillier and even mountainous areas farther north in Pennsylvania, making the route more circuitous and the job more expensive.

Then, however, came the most threatening blow of all: Rockefeller suddenly went on a real estate buying spree, purchasing large tracts of farmland in Pennsylvania, right in the way of Tidewater's advance to the sea. No price seemed too high for Standard Oil to pay. Benson did what he could to fight back and buy his own land, but rumors began to spread among the farmers in the area of the danger if they sold parts of their land to Tidewater—being so long, the pipeline would be subject to leaks that could ruin their crops. Clearly, Standard Oil was the source of the rumors, and they had an effect.

To Benson, Rockefeller was like a relentless, invisible demon attacking him from all directions, ratcheting up the costs and the pressure. But Benson could be just as relentless. If Rockefeller bought out an entire valley, Benson made the pipeline change course, even if it meant going over more hills. The route became a ridiculous zigzag, but the pipeline kept inching its way east and finally reached the coast in May of 1879.

Once the pipeline went into operation, however, no one could predict if its elaborate pumping system could move the oil up steep climbs. Slowly the first flow of crude oil made its way through the pipeline, ascending even the highest mountain, and after seven days the first drops reached the end point. The Tidewater Pipeline was considered one of the great engineering feats of the day, and Benson became an overnight hero. Finally someone had outwitted and outfought Standard Oil.

To Benson's amazement, however, Rockefeller now only ratcheted up the pressure. Tidewater had bled money and had little left in reserve, but here was Rockefeller drastically reducing rates on Standard Oil's own pipelines and railroads, transporting oil virtually for free. Tidewater could not find a drop of oil to ship, and this was bringing the company to its knees. By March of 1880 Benson had had enough, and he struck a deal with Standard Oil on the most favorable terms he could get, joining the two companies. But this was only a preliminary move. In the months to come, Rockefeller bought up more and more shares in Tidewater, bringing it completely under his control. Like so many others before him, in trying to fight against Rockefeller, Benson had only made him stronger and more invincible. How could anyone hope to fight against such an indomitable force?

In the 1880s the demand for kerosene to light houses and offices exploded, and Rockefeller controlled the market. And in cities and towns across America, local grocers and retailers began to notice a revolutionary new system introduced by Standard Oil. The company had set up storage tanks in all corners of the country and financed tank wagons to transport the kerosene to almost every town. Not only would Standard Oil salesmen personally sell the company's kerosene to stores, but they would also go from house to house, selling heaters and stoves directly to homeowners, at the lowest prices.

This threatened the business of many local retailers, and when they protested, Standard Oil representatives would tell them that they would stop the practice if the retailers sold exclusively Standard Oil products. For those who refused, Standard Oil would start its own grocery store in the area and, with cheap prices, drive the rebellious store owners out of business. In some areas, furious retailers would turn to a rival company, such as Republic Oil, which specialized in selling to retailers who hated Rockefeller. Little did they know that Standard Oil had secretly set up and owned Republic Oil.

With all of these practices Rockefeller had created a growing number of enemies, but none of them was as dogged and fanatical as George Rice, a man who had managed to maintain a small, independent refinery in Ohio. He tried to get lawmakers to investigate the company's practices. He published a newsletter called *Black Death*, which compiled all the muckraking articles on Rockefeller. And to somehow find a way to make a profit and snub his nose at Rockefeller, he decided he would personally travel and sell his own oil in several towns, bypassing the new system that had cornered the market.

It was hard to imagine that Standard Oil could possibly care about him; the amount of oil he was trying to sell was miniscule and his success was quite limited. But when he managed to sell a mere seventy barrels of kerosene to a retailer in Louisville, suddenly he learned that the railroad that had agreed, while he was on the road, to ship his oil to him now refused to carry his product. He knew who was behind this, but he managed to find other, more expensive means to get shipments of oil.

He moved to another town near Louisville, only to find Standard Oil salesmen there who had anticipated his presence and carefully kept underselling him. He found himself pushed to ever-smaller towns farther south, but once again there were the Standard Oil men blocking his way, and soon he could not sell a drop of oil. It was as if they had spies everywhere and were tracking his progress. But more than anything, he felt the ubiquitous presence of Rockefeller himself, who clearly knew of his little campaign and was out to crush this tiniest of competitors at all costs. Finally realizing what he was truly up against, Rice gave up the fight and returned home.

IN THE EARLY 1900S, AFTER ROCKEFELLER HAD RESIGNED AS HEAD OF STANDARD OIL, he began to fascinate the American public. He was by far the wealthiest man in the world, the first billionaire on the planet, but the stories of the way he had conducted his battles and the monopoly he had forged made them wonder about his character. He was a notorious recluse, and few knew anything concrete about him. Then some among his many enemies initiated a series of court cases to break up the Standard Oil monopoly. Rockefeller was forced to testify, and to the public's amazement, he was not at all like the devil they had imagined. As one newspaper writer reported: "He seems the embodiment of sweetness and light. His serenity could not be disturbed. . . . At times his manner was mildly reproachful, at others tenderly persuasive, but never did he betray an ill temper or vexation."

As he emerged as the world's most generous philanthropist, and as the public came to appreciate the cheap oil he provided, they changed their opinion of him. After all, as the major shareholder in Standard Oil he had immense influence, and he had agreed to the breakup of the Standard Oil monopoly. Little did they know that behind the scenes he operated as he always had done: finding loopholes in the law, keeping the monopoly together through secret agreements, and maintaining his control. He would not allow anyone to block his path, and certainly not the government.

Interpretation: The story of the rise to power of John D. Rockefeller has to be considered one of the most remarkable in history. In a relatively short period of time (some twenty years), he rose from the bottom of society (his family had suffered periods of poverty) to become the founder and owner of the largest corporation in America, and shortly after that to emerge as the wealthiest man in the world. In the process, as so often happens in such cases, his story became shrouded in all kinds of myths. He was either a demon or a god of capitalism. But lost in all of these emotional responses is the answer to a simple question: how did one man—with little help—accumulate so much power in so little time?

If we examine him closely, we must conclude that it wasn't through supreme intelligence or some particular talent or creative vision. He had some of those qualities, but nothing strong enough to account for his outrageous success. In truth, what we can attribute it to more than anything is the sheer relentless force of will that he possessed to utterly dominate every situation and rival he encountered, and to exploit every opportunity that crossed his path. We shall call this *aggressive energy*. Such energy can have productive purposes (see the last section in the chapter for more on this), and certainly Rockefeller had some achievements that benefited the society of his time. But as so often happens with highly aggressive people, this energy pushed him to monopolize virtually all power in a complex industry. It made him wipe out all rivals and any possible competition, bend laws to his benefit, standardize all practices according to his desires, and in the end, depress innovation in the field.

Let us divorce Rockefeller's story from the usual emotional responses and simply look at him dispassionately, as a kind of specimen to help us understand the nature of highly aggressive individuals and what makes large numbers of people submit to their will. In this way we can also learn some valuable lessons about human nature and how we can begin to counter those who continually work to monopolize power, often to the detriment of the rest of us.

Rockefeller grew up in peculiar circumstances. His father, William, was a notorious con artist. And from the very beginning, the father set a rather unpleasant pattern for the family: He would leave his wife, Eliza, and four children (John being the eldest) for months on end in their flimsy cabin in western New York and travel the region plying his various con games. During this time, the family would have barely enough money to survive. Eliza had to find a way to make every penny count. Then the father would reappear with wads of cash and gifts for the family. He was amusing (a great storyteller) but at times rather cruel and even violent. Then he would leave again, and the pattern would reset. It was impossible to predict when he would return, and the members of the family were continually on edge when he was there and when he was not.

As a teenager, John had to go to work to help bring some stability to the family's finances. And as he advanced in his career, he could not escape the anxieties that had plagued him in his childhood. He had a desperate need to make everything orderly and predictable in his environment. He immersed himself deeply in his accounting books—nothing was more predictable than the pluses and minuses on a ledger sheet. At the same time, he had great ambitions for making a fortune; his father had instilled in him an almost visceral love of money.

And so, when he first learned of what could be accomplished with an oil refinery, he saw his great opportunity. But his attraction to the oil business may seem at first glance rather strange. It was a Wild West environment, totally anarchic; fortunes could be made or lost in a matter of months. In many ways, the oil business was like his father—exciting, promising sudden riches, but treacherously unpredictable. Unconsciously he was drawn to it for those very reasons—he could relive his worst fears from childhood and surmount them by establishing rigorous control over the oil industry. It would be like conquering the father himself. The chaos would only spur him to greater heights, as he would have to work doubly hard to tame its wildness.

And so, in these first years of business, we can see the motivating factor that would drive all his subsequent actions—the overwhelming need for control. The more complicated and difficult this task, the more relentless the energy he would summon to achieve such a goal. And out of this need came a second one, almost as important—to justify his aggressive actions to the world and to himself. Rockefeller was a deeply religious man. He could not live with the thought that what drove his actions was a desire to control people and acquire the vast sums of money necessary for such a purpose. That would have been to see himself in too ugly and soulless a light.

To repress such a thought, he constructed what we shall call the *aggressor's narrative*. He had to convince himself that his quest for power served some higher purpose. There was a belief at the time among Protestants that to make a lot of money was a sign of grace from God. With wealth, the religious individual could give back to the community and help support the local parish. But Rockefeller took this further. He believed that establishing order in the oil business was a divine mission, like ordering the cosmos. He was on a crusade to bring cheap prices and predictability to American households. Turning Standard Oil into a monopoly blended seamlessly with his deep religious convictions.

Sincerely believing in this crusade, it did not bother his conscience to ruthlessly manipulate and ruin his rivals, to bribe legislators, to run roughshod over laws, to form fake rival enterprises to Standard Oil, to spark and use the violence of a strike (with Pennsylvania Railroad) that would help him in the long run. Belief in this narrative made him all the more energetic and aggressive, and for those who faced him, it could be confusing—perhaps there was some good in what he was doing; perhaps he was not a demon after all.

Finally, to realize his dream of control, Rockefeller transformed himself into a superior reader of men and their psychology. And the most important quality for him to gauge in the various rivals he faced was their relative willpower and resiliency. He could sense this in people's body language and in the patterns of their actions. Most people, he determined, are rather weak. They are mostly led by their emotions, which change by the day. They want things to be rather easy in life and tend to take the path of least resistance. They don't have a stomach for protracted battles. They want money for the pleasures and comforts it can bring, for their yachts and mansions. They want to look powerful, to satisfy their ego. Make them afraid or confused or frustrated, or offer them an easy way out, and they would surrender to his stronger will. If they got angry, all the better. Anger burns itself out quickly, and Rockefeller always played for the long term.

Look at how he played each of the antagonists in his path. With Clark, he carefully fed his arrogance and deliberately made him irritable, so that he would quickly agree to the auction just to get rid of Rockefeller, without thinking too deeply about the consequences.

Colonel Payne was a vain and greedy man. Give him plenty of money and a nice title, and he would be satisfied and surrender to Rockefeller his refinery. For the other refinery owners, instill fears about the uncertain future, using the SIC as a convenient bogeyman. Make them feel isolated and weak, and sow some panic. Yes, his refineries were more profitable, as shown by his books, but the other owners failed to reason that Rockefeller himself was just as vulnerable as they were to the ups and downs of the business. If only they had united in opposition to his campaign, they could have countered him, but they were made too emotional to think straight, and they surrendered their refineries with ease.

When it came to Scott, Rockefeller saw him as a hothead, enraged by Standard Oil's threat to his preeminent position in business. Rockefeller welcomed the war with Scott and prepared for it by amassing vast amounts of cash. He would simply outlast him. And the angrier he made Scott with his unorthodox tactics, the more imprudent and rash Scott became, going so far as to try to crush the railroad strike, which only made his position weaker. With Benson, Rockefeller recognized the type—the man enamored with his own brilliance and wanting attention as the first one to defeat Standard Oil. Putting up obstacles in his path would only make him try harder, while weakening his finances. It would be simple to buy him off in the end, when he had grown tired of Rockefeller's relentless pressure.

As an extra measure, Rockefeller would always strategize to make his opponents feel rushed and impatient. Clark had only one day to plan for the auction. The refinery owners faced imminent doom in a few months unless they sold to him. Scott and Benson had to hurry up in their battles or face running out of money. This made them more emotional and less able to strategize.

Understand: Rockefeller represents a type of individual that you will likely come across in your field. We shall call this type the *sophisticated aggressor,* as opposed to the *primitive aggressor.* Primitive aggressors have very short fuses. If someone triggers in them feelings of inferiority or weakness, they explode. They lack any self-control, and so they tend to not get very far in life, inevitably bullying and hurting too many people. Sophisticated aggressors are much trickier. They rise to top positions and can stay there because they know how to cloak their maneuvers, to present a distracting façade, and to play upon people's emotions. They know that most people do not like confrontation or long struggles, and so they can intimidate or wear people down. They depend on our docility as much as on their own aggression.

The sophisticated aggressors that you encounter do not have to be as spectacularly successful as a Rockefeller. They can be your boss, a rival, or even a scheming colleague on the way up. You can recognize them by one simple sign: they get to where they're going primarily through their aggressive energy, not through their particular talents. They value amassing power more than the quality of their work. They do whatever is necessary to secure their position and crush any kind of competition or challenge. They do not like to share power.

In dealing with this type, you will tend to become angry or fearful, enlarging their presence and playing into their hands. You obsess over their evil character and fail to pay close attention to what they are actually up to. What you often end up surrendering to is the appearance or illusion of strength that they project, their aggressive reputation. The way to handle them is to lower the emotional temperature. Start by looking at the individual, not the myth or legend. Understand their primary motivation—to gain control over the environment and the people around them. As with Rockefeller, this need for control covers up vast layers of anxieties and insecurities. You must see the frightened child within, terrified by anything unpredictable. In this way you can cut them down to size, diminishing their ability to intimidate you.

They want to control your thoughts and reactions. Deny them this power by focusing on their actions and your strategies, not your feelings. Analyze and anticipate their real goals. They want to instill in you the idea that you have no options, that surrender is inevitable and the best way out. But you always have options. Even if they are your boss and you must surrender in the present, you can maintain your inner independence and plot for the day in which they make a mistake and are weakened, using your knowledge of their vulnerable points to help take them down.

See through their narrative and their shrewd attempts at distraction. They will often present themselves as holier-than-thou or as the victim of other people's malice. The louder they proclaim their convictions, the more certain you can be they're hiding something. Be aware that they can sometimes seem charming and charismatic. Do not be mesmerized by such appearances. Look at their patterns of behavior. If they have taken from people in the past, they will continue to do so in the present. Never bring on such types as partners, no matter how friendly and charming they might seem. They like to piggyback on your hard work, then wrest control. Your realistic appraisal of their actual strength and their aggressive intentions is your best defense.

When it comes to taking action against aggressors, you must be as sophisticated and crafty as they are. Do not try to fight with them directly. They are too relentless, and they usually have enough power to overwhelm you in direct confrontation. You must outwit them, finding unexpected angles of attack. Threaten to expose the hypocrisy in their narrative or the past dirty deeds they have tried to keep hidden from the public. Make it seem that a battle with you will be costlier than they had imagined, that you are also willing to play a little dirty, but only in defense. If you are particularly clever, appear relatively weak and exposed, baiting them into a rash attack that you have prepared for. Often the wisest strategy is to band together with others who have suffered at their hands, creating strength and leverage in numbers.

Keep in mind that aggressors often get their way because you fear that in fighting them, you have too much to lose in the present. But you must calculate instead what you have to lose in the long term—decreasing options for power and expansion in your own field, once they assume a dominating position; your own dignity and sense of self-worth by not standing up to them. Surrender and docility can become a habit with devastating consequences for your well-being. Use the existence of aggressors as a spur to your own fighting spirit and to build your own confidence. Standing up to and outwitting aggressors can be one of the most satisfying and ennobling experiences we humans can have.

> Men are not gentle, friendly creatures wishing for love, who simply defend themselves if attacked. . . . A powerful desire for aggression has to be reckoned as part of their . . . endowment.
>
> —Sigmund Freud

Keys to Human Nature

We like to think of ourselves as relatively peaceful and agreeable members of society. We are social animals to the core, and we need to convince ourselves that we are loyal to and cooperative with the communities we belong to. But on occasion, all of us have acted in ways that go against this self-opinion. Perhaps it came in a moment when we felt that our job security was threatened, or that someone was blocking our career advancement. Or perhaps we believed we were not getting the attention and recognition that we deserved for our work. Or maybe it came in a moment of financial insecurity. Or perhaps it occurred in an intimate relationship in which we felt particularly frustrated in our attempt to get the other to change his or her behavior, or we sensed that he or she was going to abandon us.

Out of frustration, anger, insecurity, fear, or impatience we suddenly found ourselves becoming unusually assertive. We did something a bit extreme to hold on to our job; we tried to push a colleague out of our way; we reached for some dubious scheme to secure easy and fast money; we went too far in trying to get attention; we turned belligerent and controlling with our partner; we became vindictive and attacked someone on social media. In such moments, we crossed a line and became aggressive. Most often, when we act this way, we rationalize our behavior to ourselves and to others: we had no choice; we felt threatened; we were being treated unfairly; people were being unresponsive and harming us; we did not start it. In this way we are able to maintain our self-opinion as the peaceful creatures we imagine ourselves to be.

Although we will rarely notice this, we can also observe a subtler example of our aggressive tendencies coming to the fore. When we face intimidating types who are more aggressive than we are, we often find ourselves acting more submissive than usual, and maybe a bit sycophantic if they have power. But when we face people clearly weaker and meeker than us, often the lion in us unconsciously emerges. Perhaps we decide to help them, but mixed in with this is a feeling of contempt and superiority. We become rather aggressive in trying to help them, ordering their life, being forceful with our advice. Or if we have little sympathy for them, we might feel compelled to use them in some way for our own purposes, and maybe push them around. All of this occurs unconsciously; we generally do not experience this as aggressiveness, but nonetheless, as we compare our inner strength with others', we cannot help but lower and raise our aggression level.

We can notice this split—between what we think of ourselves and how we actually act at times—in the behavior of our friends, colleagues, and those in the news. In our workplace, inevitably certain people push their way forward and grab more power. Perhaps they take credit for our work, or steal our ideas, or push us off a project, or ally themselves rather vigorously with those in power. We can see on social media the delight people take in feeling outraged, in attacking and bringing down others. We can see the energy with which the press exposes the slightest flaw in those in power, and the feeding frenzy that ensues. We can observe the rampant violence in our films and games, all masquerading as entertainment. And all the while nobody admits to being aggressive. In fact, more than ever people *seem* so modest and progressive. The split is profound.

What this means is the following: All of us understand that humans have been capable of much violence and aggression in the past and in the present. We know that out there in the world there are sinister criminals, greedy and unscrupulous businesspeople, belligerent negotiators, and sexual aggressors. But we create a sharp dividing line between those examples and us. We have a powerful block against imagining any kind of continuum or spectrum when it comes to our own aggressive moments and those of the more extreme variety in others. We in fact define the word to describe the stronger manifestations of aggression, excluding ourselves. It is always the other who is belligerent, who starts things, who is aggressive.

This is a profound misconception of human nature. Aggression is a tendency that is latent in every single human individual. It is a tendency wired into our species. We became the preeminent animal on this planet precisely because of our aggressive energy, supplemented by our intelligence and cunning.

We cannot separate this aggressiveness from the way we attack problems, alter the environment to make our lives easier, fight injustice, or create anything on a large scale. The Latin root of the word *aggression* means "to step forward," and when we assert ourselves in this world and try to create or change anything, we are tapping into this energy.

Aggression can serve positive purposes. At the same time, under certain circumstances, this energy can push us into antisocial behavior, into grabbing too much or pushing people around. These positive and negative aspects are two sides of the same coin. And although some individuals are clearly more aggressive than others, all of us are capable of slipping into that negative side. There is a continuum of human aggression, and we are all on the spectrum.

Being unaware of our true nature causes us many problems. We can turn aggressive in the negative sense without realizing what is happening, and then pay the consequences for going too far. Or, feeling uncomfortable with our own assertive impulses and knowing the trouble they can stir, we might try to repress our aggressiveness and appear to be paragons of humility and goodness, only to become more passive-aggressive in our behavior. This energy cannot be denied or repressed; it will emerge in some way. But with awareness, we can begin to control and channel it for productive and positive purposes. To do so, we must understand the source of all human aggression, how it turns negative, and why some people become more aggressive than others.

The Source of Human Aggression

Unlike any other animal, we humans are aware of our own mortality, and that we could die at any moment. Consciously and unconsciously this thought haunts us throughout our lives. We are aware that our position in life is never secure—we can lose our job, our social status, and our money, often for reasons beyond our control. The people around us are equally unpredictable—we can never read their thoughts, anticipate their actions, or totally rely on their support. We are dependent on others, who often don't come through. We have certain innate desires for love, excitement, and stimulation, and it is often beyond our control to satisfy these desires in the way we would like. In addition, we all have certain insecurities that stem from wounds in our childhood. If events or people trigger these insecurities and reopen old wounds, we feel particularly vulnerable and weak.

What this means is that we humans are continually plagued by feelings of helplessness that come from many sources. If this feeling is strong enough or lasts for too long, it can become unbearable. We are willful creatures who crave power. This desire for power is not evil or antisocial; it is a natural response to the awareness of our essential weakness and vulnerability. In essence, what drives much of our behavior is to have control over circumstances, to feel the connection between what we do and what we get—to feel that we can influence people and events to some extent. This mitigates our sense of helplessness and makes the unpredictability of life tolerable.

We satisfy this need by developing solid work skills that help us secure our career status and give us a feeling of control over the future. We also try to develop social skills that allow us to work with other people, earn their affection, and have a degree of influence over them. When it comes to our needs for excitement and stimulation, we generally choose to satisfy them through various activities—sports, entertainment, seduction—that our culture provides or accepts.

All of these activities help us to have the control that we crave, but they require that we recognize certain limits. To gain such power in our work and relationships, we must be patient. We cannot force things. It takes time to secure our career position, to develop genuine creative powers, to learn how to influence people and charm them. It also requires abiding by certain social codes and even laws. We cannot do just anything to get ahead in our careers; we cannot force people to do our bidding. We can call these codes and laws *guardrails* that we carefully stay within in order to gain power while remaining liked and respected.

In certain moments, however, we find it hard to accept these limits. We cannot advance in our careers or make a lot of money as quickly as we would like. We cannot get people to work with us to the degree that we want them to, so we feel frustrated. Or perhaps an old wound from childhood is suddenly reopened. If we anticipate that a partner could be ending the relationship, and we have a great fear of being abandoned stemming from parental coldness, we could easily overreact and try to control him or her, using all of our manipulative powers and turning quite aggressive. (Feelings of love often turn to hostility and aggression in people, because it is in love that we feel most dependent, vulnerable, and helpless.)

In these cases, our hunger for more money, power, love, or attention overwhelms any patience we might have had. We might then be tempted to go outside the guardrails, to seek power and control in a way that violates tacit codes and even laws. But for most of us, when we cross the line, we feel uncomfortable and perhaps remorseful. We scurry back to within the guardrails, to our normal ways of trying for power and control. Such aggressive acts can occur at moments in our lives, but they do not become a pattern.

This is not the case, however, with more chronically aggressive types. The sense of helplessness or frustration that we may feel upon occasion plagues them more deeply and more often. They feel chronically insecure and fragile and must cover this with an inordinate amount of power and control. Their need for power is too immediate and strong for them to accept the limits, and overrides any sense of compunction or social responsibility.

It is possible that there is a genetic component to this. The psychoanalyst Melanie Klein, who specialized in the study of infants, noticed that some babies were decidedly more anxious and greedier than others. From their very first days, they would suckle on the mother's breast as if they were attacking it and wanting to suck it dry. They needed more coddling and attention than others. Their crying and tantrums were almost impossible to stop. They felt a higher degree of helplessness that verged on continual hysteria.

Such babies were in the minority, but she noticed them often enough. She speculated that those who are chronically aggressive could be adult versions of the greedy baby. They are simply born with a greater need to control everything around them. They brood more over feelings of hurt or envy—"Why should other people have more than me?" When they feel like they are losing control to any degree, their tendency is to exaggerate the threat, to overreact and grab for much more than is necessary.

It is also true that early family life can play a decisive role. According to the psychoanalyst and writer Erich Fromm, if parents are too domineering, if they repress their children's need for power and independence, such children are often the types who later like to dominate and tyrannize others. If they were beaten as children, they often resort to beating and physical abuse as adults. In this way, they turn the enforced passivity in their childhood into something active as adults, giving them the feeling of control they sorely lacked in their earliest years, through aggressive behavior.

Whatever the cause of their tendencies, these types do not scurry back within the guardrails but rather continually resort to aggressive behavior. They have an unusually strong will and little patience to satisfy their desires through the socially acceptable channels. They find the normal ways of gaining stimulation too dull. They need something stronger and more immediate. If they are the primitive type, they may turn to criminal behavior or simply become the overt bully; if they are more sophisticated, they will learn to control this behavior to some extent and use it when necessary.

What this means is that human aggression stems from an underlying insecurity, as opposed to simply an impulse to hurt or take from others. Before any impulse to take aggressive action, aggressors are unconsciously processing feelings of helplessness and anxiety. They often perceive threats that are not really there, or exaggerate them. They take action to preempt the perceived attack of another, or to grab for things in order to dominate a situation they feel may elude their control. (Such feelings also provoke the positive type of aggression as well. Feeling the need to fight an injustice or create something important is preceded by feelings of anxiety and insecurity. It remains an attempt at control for positive purposes.) When we look at any chronic aggressor around us, we must search for the underlying insecurity, the deep wound, the reverberating feelings of helplessness from their earliest years.

We can notice the following interesting phenomenon: people who are domineering often are extremely intolerant of any kind of dissent. They need to be surrounded by sycophants and constantly be reminded of their greatness and superiority. If such types have political power, they work to tamp down any negative publicity and control what people say about them. We must see this hypersensitivity to criticism as a sign of great inner weakness. A person who is truly strong from within can endure criticism and open discussion without feeling personally threatened. Generally, aggressors and authoritarian types are expert at concealing this profound inner weakness by constantly projecting toughness and conviction. But we must train ourselves to look past their façade and see the inner fragility. This can greatly help us control any feelings of fear or intimidation, which aggressors love to stimulate.

There are other qualities of the chronically aggressive that we must understand. First, aggressors have less tolerance for feelings of helplessness and anxiety than the rest of us. What might cause us to feel frustrated or insecure will often trigger in them a much more powerful reaction, and rage. This is perhaps why chronic aggression is much more common among men than women. Men find it harder to manage feelings of dependency and helplessness, something psychologists have noted in male infants. Men are generally more insecure about their status in the work world and elsewhere. They have a greater need to continually assert themselves and gauge their effect on others. Their self-esteem is tied to feelings of power, control, and respect for their opinions. And so it often takes less to trigger the aggressive response in men. In any event, we must always be aware that the chronic aggressor is more thin-skinned than we are, and if we know we are dealing with this type, we must be particularly careful to not inadvertently trigger their rage response by challenging their self-esteem or criticizing them.

Another common aspect of aggressive behavior is that it can easily become an addiction. In acting out their desires in an overt and immediate way, in getting the best of people through their maneuvers, aggressors receive a jolt of adrenaline that can become addictive. They feel stimulated and excited, and the more socially acceptable ways of relieving boredom can seem tepid in comparison. (Certainly the thrill of getting easy money, whether as Wall Street brokers peddling dubious investments or as criminals stealing what they can, has an immensely addictive quality.) At first glance, this might seem self-destructive, as each aggressive outburst creates more enemies and unintended consequences. But aggressors are often adept at upping the ante with even more intimidating behavior, so that few will challenge them.

This often leads to the phenomenon of the aggressor's trap: the more power they get, and the larger their empire, the more points of vulnerability they create; they have more rivals and enemies to worry about. This sparks in them the need to be more and more aggressive and gain more and more power. (Certainly Rockefeller fell victim to this dynamic.) They also come to feel that to stop acting in this way would make them seem weak. No matter what aggressors might say to us or how they try to disguise their intentions, we must realize that their past pattern of behavior will inevitably continue in the present, because they are both addicted and trapped. We must never be naive in dealing with them. They will be relentless. If they take a step back, it is only momentary. They are rarely capable of changing this essential pattern in their behavior.

We must also be aware that aggressors see the people around them as objects to use. They might have some natural empathy, but because their need for power and control is so strong, they cannot be patient enough to rely solely upon charm and social skills. To get what they want, they have to use people, and this becomes a habit that degrades any empathy they once had. They need adherents and disciples, so they train themselves to listen, to occasionally praise others, and to do favors for people. The charm they may display upon occasion, however, is only for effect and has little human warmth to it. When they are listening to us, they are gauging the strength of our will and seeing how we can serve their purposes down the road. If they praise us or do us a favor, it is a way to further entrap and compromise us. We can see this in the nonverbal cues, in the eyes that look through us, in how thinly they are engaged in our stories. We must always try to make ourselves immune to any attempt at charm on their part, knowing what purpose it serves.

It is interesting to note that despite all of the socially negative qualities that aggressors inevitably reveal, they are frequently able to attract enough followers to help them in their quest for power. The people who are attracted to such aggressors often have their own deep-seated issues, their own frustrated aggressive desires. They find the confidence and sometimes brazenness of the aggressor quite exciting and appealing. They fall in love with the narrative. They become infected with the leader's aggression and get to act it out on others, perhaps those below them. But such an environment is tiring, and those serving the aggressor are constantly taking hits to their self-esteem. With most aggressors, the turnover is high and the morale low. As the ancient Greek dramatist Sophocles once wrote, "Whoever makes his way into a tyrant's court becomes his slave, although he went there a free man."

YOUR TASK AS A STUDENT OF HUMAN NATURE IS THREEFOLD: FIRST, YOU MUST STOP denying the reality of your own aggressive tendencies. You are on the aggressive spectrum, like all of us. Of course, there are some people who are lower down on this spectrum. Perhaps they lack confidence in their ability to get what they want; or they may simply have less energy. But a lot of us are in the mid-to-upper range on the spectrum, with relatively strong levels of will. This assertive energy must be expended in some way and will tend to go in one of three directions.

First, we can channel this energy into our work, into patiently achieving things (*controlled aggression*). Second, we can channel it into *aggressive* or *passive-aggressive* behavior. Finally, we can turn it inward in the form of self-loathing, directing our anger and aggression at our own failings and activating our *internal saboteur* (more on this later). You need to analyze how you handle your assertive energy. A way to judge yourself is to see how you handle moments of frustration and uncertainty, situations in which you have less control. Do you tend to lash out, grow angry and tense, and do things you later regret? Or do you internalize the anger and grow depressed? Look at those inevitable moments in which you have gone past the guardrails and analyze them. You are not as peaceful and gentle as you imagine. Notice what pushed you into this behavior, and how during such times you found ways to rationalize your behavior. Now, with some distance, you can perhaps see through those rationalizations.

Your goal is not to repress this assertive energy but to become aware of it as it drives you forward and to channel it productively. You need to admit to yourself that you have a deep desire to have an effect on people, to have power, and to realize this you must develop higher social and technical skills, must become more patient and resilient. You need to discipline and tame your natural assertive energy. This is what we shall call *controlled aggression*, and it will lead to accomplishing great things. (For more on this, see the last section of this chapter.)

Your second task is to make yourself a master observer of aggression in the people around you. When you look at your work world, for instance, imagine that you can visualize the continual war between people's different levels of will, and all of the intersecting arrows of such conflicts. Those who are more assertive seem to rise to the top, but they inevitably display signs of submission to those higher up. It is not much different from the hierarchies we can observe among chimpanzees. If you stop focusing on people's words and the façade they present, and concentrate on their actions and their nonverbal cues, you can almost sense the level of aggressiveness they emanate.

In looking at this phenomenon, it is important that you be tolerant of people: we have all crossed the line at some point and turned more aggressive than usual, often because of circumstances. When it comes to those who are powerful and successful, it is impossible in this world to reach such heights without higher levels of aggression and some manipulation. For accomplishing great things, we can forgive them their occasional harsh and assertive behavior. What you need to determine is whether you are dealing with chronic aggressors, people who cannot tolerate criticism or being challenged on any level, whose desire for control is excessive, and who will swallow you up in their relentless quest to have more.

Look for some telltale signs. First, if they have an unusually high number of enemies whom they have accumulated over the years, there must be a good reason, and not the one they tell you. Pay close attention to how they justify their actions in the world. Aggressors will tend to present themselves as crusaders, as some form of genius who cannot help the way they behave. They are creating great art, they say, or helping the little man. People who get in their way are infidels and evil. They will claim, as Rockefeller did, that no one has been criticized or investigated as much as they have; they are the victims, not the aggressors. The louder and more extreme their narrative, the more you can be certain you are dealing with chronic aggressors. Focus on their actions, their past patterns of behavior, much more than anything they say.

You can look for subtler signs as well. Chronic aggressors often have obsessive personalities. Having meticulous habits and creating a completely predictable environment is their way of holding control. Obsessing over an object or a person indicates a desire to swallow it whole. Also, pay attention to the nonverbal cues. We saw with Rockefeller that he could not stand to be passed by anyone in the street. The aggressor type will show such physical obsessions—always front and center. In any event, the earlier you can spot the signs the better.

Once you realize you are dealing with this type, you must use every ounce of your energy to disengage mentally, to gain control of your emotional response. Often what happens when you face aggressors is that you initially feel mesmerized and even paralyzed to some extent, as if in the presence of a snake. Then, as you process what they have done, you become emotional—angry, outraged, frightened. Once you are in that state, they find it easy to keep you reacting and not thinking. Your anger doesn't lead to anything productive but rather melts into bitterness and frustration over time. Your only answer is to find a way to detach from their spell, bit by bit. See through their maneuvers, contemplate the underlying weakness that propels them, cut them down to size. Always focus on their goals, what they are really after, and not the distractions they set up.

If battle with them is inevitable, never engage in direct confrontation or challenge them in an overt way. If they are the sophisticated type, they will use all their cunning to ruin you, and they can be relentless. You must always fight them indirectly. Look for the vulnerabilities they are inevitably covering up. This could be their dubious reputation, some particularly dirty actions in the past they have managed to keep secret. Poke holes in their narrative. Through exposure of what they want to keep hidden, you have a powerful weapon to scare them out of attacking you. Remember that their greatest fear is to lose control. Think of what act of yours could frighten them by setting off a chain reaction of events that might spin out of control. Make the easy victory they are counting on with you suddenly seem more expensive.

Aggressors generally have the advantage that they are willing to go outside the guardrails more often and more widely in fighting you. This gives them more options, more dirty maneuvers they can surprise you with. In negotiations, they will hit you with some last-minute change to what they had agreed upon, violating all rules but knowing you will give in because you have come this far and don't want to blow it up. They will spread rumors and disinformation to muddy the waters and make you seem as dubious as they are. You must try to anticipate these manipulations and rob aggressors of the element of surprise.

And on occasion you yourself must be willing to venture outside the guardrails as well, knowing this is a temporary and defensive measure. You can practice deception and distract them, appearing weaker than you are, baiting them into an attack that will make them look bad and for which you have prepared a crafty counterattack. You can even spread rumors that will tend to imbalance their minds, since they are not used to others playing the same tricks back on them. In any event, with the stakes being high, you must calculate that defeating aggressors is more important than maintaining your purity.

Finally, your third task as a student of human nature is to rid yourself of the denial of the very real aggressive tendencies in human nature itself and what such aggression might mean for our future as a species. This denial tends to take the form of one of two myths you are likely to believe in. The first myth is that long ago we humans were peace-loving creatures, in harmony with nature and with our fellow humans. It is the myth of the noble savage, the innocent hunter-gatherer. The implication is that civilization, along with the development of private property and capitalism, turned the peaceful human into an aggressive and selfish creature. Our form of society is to blame for this, so the myth goes. By developing a more egalitarian political and social system, we could revert to our natural goodness and peace-loving nature.

Recent finds in anthropology and archaeology, however, have proven beyond a shadow of a doubt that our ancestors (going back tens of thousands of years, well before civilization) engaged in warfare that was as murderous and brutal as anything in the present. They were hardly peaceful. There are also numerous examples of indigenous cultures destroying much of the flora and fauna in their environment in an endless quest for food sources and shelter, sending many species into extinction and despoiling entire regions of trees. (For more on this see *War Before Civilization*, by Lawrence H. Keeley, and *The Third Chimpanzee*, by Jared Diamond.) The great power of humans to cooperate in these cultures was just as often used to help engage in the bloodiest of skirmishes.

The other myth, more prevalent today, is that we may have been violent and aggressive in the past, but that we are currently evolving beyond this, becoming more tolerant, enlightened, and guided by our better angels. But the signs of human aggression are just as prevalent in our era as in the past. We can hold up as evidence the endless cycles of war, the acts of genocide, and the increasing hostility between states and ethnicities within states that continue well into this century. The immense powers of technology have only enhanced our destructive powers when it comes to war. And our depredation of the environment has only gotten substantially worse, despite our awareness of the problem.

We can also take note of the growing levels of inequality in power and wealth around the globe in recent times, approaching the disparities that existed centuries ago. Such inequalities continue to reproduce themselves in human society because inevitably there are individuals who are simply more aggressive than others when it comes to accumulating power and wealth. No rules or laws seem to stop this. The powerful write the rules to benefit themselves. And the monopolizing tendencies of the nineteenth century, as exemplified by Standard Oil, signs of corporate aggression, have just reshaped themselves to fit the newest industries.

In the past, people attended executions as a form of entertainment. We may not go that far, but more people than ever enjoy watching others being humiliated on reality shows or in the news, and indulging in games and movies that delight in graphic depictions of murder and bloodshed. (We can also see an increasingly aggressive edge to our humor.)

With technology, it has become easier to express and satisfy our aggressive desires. Without having to physically face people, on the internet our arguments and criticisms can become that much more hostile, heated, and personal. The internet has also created a new and powerful weapon—cyberwar. As they always have, criminals simply co-opt technology to become more creative and elusive.

Human aggression simply adapts to the newest media and technological innovations, finding ways to express and vent itself through them. Whatever the new invention is in one hundred years for communication, it will likely suffer the same fate. As Gustave Flaubert put it, "Speak of progress as much as you want. Even when you take out the canines of a tiger, and he can only eat gruel, his heart remains that of a carnivore."

Human aggression in individuals and in groups tends to emerge or heat up when we feel helpless and vulnerable, when the impatience for control and effect rises. And as increasing numbers of people and groups are feeling this way, we can expect more of this and not less in the future. Wars will get dirtier. As insecurities rise, there will be more confrontations between political groups, between cultures, between generations, between men and women. And there will be even better and more sophisticated ways for humans to justify their aggression to themselves and to the world.

The denial is stronger than ever—it is always the other person, the other side, the other culture that is more aggressive and destructive. We must finally come to terms with the fact that it is not the other but ourselves, all of us, no matter the time or the culture. We must own this fact of our nature before we can even begin to consider moving beyond it. It is only in our awareness that we can start to think of progress.

Passive Aggression—Its Strategies and How to Counter Them

Most of us are afraid of outright confrontation; we want to appear reasonably polite and sociable. But often it is impossible to get what we want without asserting ourselves in some way. People can be stubborn and resistant to our influence, no matter how congenial we are. And sometimes we need a release from all of the inner tension that comes from having to be so deferential and correct. And so all of us inevitably engage in behavior in which we assert ourselves indirectly, striving for control or influence as subtly as possible. Perhaps we take extra time to respond to people's communications, to signal a slight bit of disdain for them; or we seem to praise people but insert subtle digs that get under their skin and instill doubts. Sometimes we make a comment that could be taken as quite neutral, but our tone of voice and the expression on our face indicate we are upset, stirring up some guilt.

We can call this form of aggression passive, in that we give the appearance that we are merely being ourselves, not *actively* manipulating or trying to influence people. Nevertheless, a message is sent that creates the effect we desire. We are never quite as passive as we seem in this. In the back of our minds, we are aware that we are taking an extra long time to get back to someone or putting a dig in a comment, but at the same time we can also pretend to ourselves and to others that we are innocent. (We humans are capable of holding such conflicting thoughts at the same time.) In general, we must consider this everyday version of passive aggression to be merely an irritating part of social life, something we are all guilty of. We should be as tolerant as possible of this low-grade passive aggression that thrives in polite society.

Some people, however, are chronic passive aggressors. Like the more active aggressors, they generally have a high degree of energy and need for control but at the same time a fear of outright confrontation. They often had domineering or neglectful parents; passive aggression became their way of getting attention or asserting their will while avoiding punishment. Such behavior becomes a pattern for them as adults, as they often repeat the same types of strategies that worked in childhood. (If we observe the passive aggressor closely enough, we can often see the manipulative child peeking through the adult mask.)

These chronic types operate in a personal or work relationship, in which their drip-drip passive-aggressive strategies can take effect on an individual over time. They are masters at being ambiguous and elusive—we can never quite be sure that they are attacking us; perhaps we are imagining things and are paranoid. If they were directly aggressive, we would get angry and resist them, but by being indirect they sow confusion, and exploit such confusion for power and control. If they are truly good at this and get their hooks into our emotions, they can make our lives miserable.

Keep in mind that actively aggressive types can generally be quite passive-aggressive at times, as Rockefeller certainly was. Passive aggression is simply an additional weapon for them in their attempts at control. In any event, the key to defending ourselves against passive aggressors is to recognize what they are up to as early as possible.

The following are the most common strategies employed by such aggressors, and ways to counter them.

The Subtle-Superiority Strategy: A friend, colleague, or employee is chronically late, but he or she always has a ready excuse that is logical, along with an apology that seems sincere. Or similarly, such individuals forget about meetings, important dates, and deadlines, always with impeccable excuses at hand. If this behavior repeats often enough, your irritation will increase, but if you try to confront them, they very well might try to turn the tables by making you seem uptight and unsympathetic. It is not their fault, they say—they have too much on their mind, people are pressuring them, they are temperamental artists who can't keep on top of so many irritating details, they are overwhelmed. They may even accuse you of adding to their stress.

You must understand that at the root of this is the need to make it clear to themselves and to you that they are in some way superior. If they were to say in so many words that they felt superior to you, they would incur ridicule and shame. They want you to *feel* it in subtle ways, while they are able to deny what they are up to. Putting you in the inferior position is a form of control, in which they get to define the relationship. You must pay attention to the pattern more than the apologies, but also notice the nonverbal signs as they excuse themselves. The tone of the voice is whiny, as if they really feel it is your problem. The apologies are laid on extra thick to disguise the lack of sincerity; in the end, such excuses communicate more about their problems in life than about the facts of their forgetfulness. They are not really sorry.

If this is chronic behavior, you must not get angry or display overt irritation—passive aggressors thrive on getting a rise out of you. Instead, stay calm and subtly mirror their behavior, calling attention to what they are doing, and inducing some shame if possible. You might make dates or appointments and leave them in the lurch, or show up impossibly late with the sincerest of apologies, laced with a touch of irony. Let them brood on what this might mean.

Earlier on in his career, when the renowned psychotherapist Milton Erickson was a medical professor at a university, he had to deal with a very smart student named Anne, who always showed up late to classes, then apologized profusely and very sincerely. She happened to be a straight-A student. She always promised to be on time for the next class but never was. This made it difficult for her fellow students; she frequently held up lectures or laboratory work. And on the first day of one of Erickson's lecture classes she was up to her old tricks, but Erickson was prepared. When she entered late, he had the entire class stand up and bow down to her in mock reverence; he did the same. Even after class, as she walked down the hall, the students continued their bowing. The message was clear—"We see through you"—and feeling embarrassed and ashamed, she stopped showing up late.

If you are dealing with a boss or someone in a position of power who makes you wait, their assertion of superiority is not so subtle. The best you can do is keep as calm as possible, showing your own form of superiority by remaining patient and cool.

The Sympathy Strategy: Somehow the person you are dealing with is always the victim—of irrational hostility, of unfair circumstances, of society in general. You notice with these types that they seem to relish the drama in their stories. No one else suffers as they do. If you are careful, you can detect a vaguely bored expression when they listen to other people's problems; they are not so engaged. Because they play up their supposed helplessness, you will naturally feel sympathetic, and once they elicit this, they will ask for favors, extra care, and attention. That is the control they are after. They are hypersensitive to any signs of doubt on your face, and they don't want to hear advice or how they might be slightly to blame. They may explode and classify you as one of the victimizers.

What might make this hard to see through is that often they do suffer through unusual adversity and personal pain, but they are masters at attracting the pain. They choose partners who will disappoint them; they have a bad attitude at work and attract criticism; they are negligent with details, and so things around them fall apart. It is not malicious fate that is to blame but something from within them that wants and feeds off the drama. People who are genuine victims cannot help but feel some shame and embarrassment at their fate, part of an age-old human superstition that a person's bad luck is a sign of something wrong with the individual. These true victims do not enjoy telling their stories. They do so reluctantly. Passive aggressors, on the other hand, are dying to share what has happened to them and bask in your attention.

As part of this, passive aggressors may display various symptoms and ailments—anxiety attacks, depression, headaches—that make their suffering seem quite real. Since childhood, we have all been capable of willing such symptoms to get attention and sympathy. We can make ourselves sick with worry; we can think our way into depression. What you are looking for is the pattern: this seems to recur in passive aggressors when they need something (such as a favor), when they feel you pulling away, when they feel particularly insecure. In any case, they tend to soak up your time and mental space, infecting you with their negative energy and needs, and it is very hard to disengage.

These types will often prey upon those who are prone to feel guilty—the sensitive, caregiving types. To deal with the manipulation involved here you need some distance, and this is not easy. The only way to do this is to feel some anger and resentment at the time and energy you are wasting in trying to help them, and how little they give back to you. The relationship inevitably tilts in their favor when it comes to attention. That is their power. Creating some inner distance will allow you to see through them better and eventually quit the unhealthy relationship. Do not feel bad about this. You will be surprised at how quickly they find another target.

The Dependency Strategy: You are suddenly befriended by someone who is unusually attentive and concerned for your welfare. They want to help you with your work or some other tasks. They want to listen to your stories of hardship and adversity. How refreshing and unusual to have such attention. You find yourself becoming ever so dependent on what they give you. But every now and then you detect some coldness on their part, and you rack your brain to figure out what you might have said or done to trigger this. In fact, you can't really be sure if they're upset with you, but you find yourself trying to please them nonetheless, and slowly, without really noticing it, the dynamic is reversed, and the displays of sympathy and concern seem to shift from them to you.

Sometimes a similar dynamic is played out between parents and their children. A mother, for instance, can shower her daughter with affection and love, keeping the girl bound to her. If the daughter tries to exercise independence at some point, the mother responds as if this were an aggressive and unloving act on the daughter's part. To avoid feeling guilty, the daughter stops asserting herself and works harder to earn more of the affection she has become dependent on. The relationship has reversed itself. Later, the mother exercises control over other aspects of her daughter's life, including money, career, and intimate partners. This can also occur within couples.

A variation of this strategy comes from people who love to make promises (of assistance, money, a job), but don't quite deliver on them. Somehow they forget what they had promised, or only give you part of it, always with a reasonable excuse. If you complain, they may accuse you of being greedy or insensitive. You have to chase after them to make up for your rudeness or to beg to get some of what they had promised.

In any event, this strategy is all about gaining power over another. The person who is made to feel dependent is returned to the position of the needy and vulnerable child, wanting more. It is hard to imagine that someone who is or was so attentive could be using this as a ploy, which makes it doubly hard to see through. You must be wary of those who are too solicitous too early on in a relationship. It is unnatural, as we are normally a bit suspicious of people in the beginning of any relationship. They may be trying to make you dependent in some way, and so you must keep some distance before you can truly gauge their motives. If they start to turn cold and you are confused as to what you did, you can be nearly certain they are using this strategy. If they react with anger or dismay when you try to establish some distance or independence, you can clearly see the power game as it emerges. Getting out of any such relationships should be a priority.

In general, be wary about people's promises and never completely rely on them. With those who fail to deliver, it is more likely a pattern, and it is best to have nothing more to do with them.

The Insinuating-Doubt Strategy: In the course of a conversation, some-one you know, perhaps a friend, lets slip a comment that makes you wonder about yourself and if they are in some way insulting you. Perhaps they com-mend you on your latest work, and with a faint smile they say they imagine you will get lots of attention for it, or lots of money, the implication being that that was your somewhat dubious motive. Or they seem to damn you with faint praise: "You did quite well for someone of your background."

Robespierre, one of the leaders of the Terror of the French Revolution, was the absolute master of this strategy. He came to see Georges Danton, a friend and fellow leader, as having become an enemy of the revolution, but did not want to say this outright. He wanted to insinuate it to others and strike some fear in Danton. In one instance, at an assembly, Robespierre leaped to his feet to support his friend, who had been accused of using his power in the govern-ment to make money. In defending Danton, Robespierre *carefully* repeated all of the various charges leveled against him in great detail, then concluded, "I may be wrong about Danton, but, as a family man, he deserves nothing but praise."

As a variation on this, people may say some rather harsh things about you, and if you seem upset, they will say they were kidding: "Can't you take a joke?" They may interpret things you have said in a slightly negative light, and if you call them on this, they will innocently reply, "But I'm only repeating what you said." They may use these insinuating comments behind your back as well, to sow doubts in other people's minds about you. They will also be the first ones to report to you any bad news, or bad reviews, or the criticisms of others, al-ways expressed with sympathy, but secretly delighting in your pain.

The point of this strategy is to make you feel bad in a way that gets under your skin and causes you to think of the insinuation for days. They want to strike blows at your self-esteem. Most often they are operating out of envy. The best counter is to show that their insinuations have no effect on you. You remain calm. You "agree" with their faint praise, and perhaps you return it in kind. They want to get a rise out of you, and you will not give them this plea-sure. Hinting that you might see through them will perhaps infect them with their own doubts, a lesson worth delivering.

The Blame-Shifter Strategy: With certain people, you feel irritated and upset by something they have done. Perhaps you have felt used by them, or they've been insensitive or ignored your pleas to stop behavior that is unpleas-ant. Even before you express your annoyance, they seem to have picked up your mood, and you can detect some sulking on their part. And when you do confront them, they grow silent, wearing a hurt or disappointed look. It is not the silence of someone with remorse. They may respond with a "Fine. Whatever. If that's how you feel." Any apologies on their part are said in a way (through tone of voice or facial expressions) that subtly conveys some disbelief that they have done anything wrong.

If they are really clever, in response they might conjure up something you've said or done in the past, which you've forgotten but which still rankles them, as if you are not so innocent. It doesn't sound like something you've said or done, but you can't be sure. Perhaps they will say something in their defense that pushes your buttons, and as you get angry, they can now accuse you of being hostile, aggressive, and unfair.

Whatever their type of response, you are left with the feeling that perhaps you were wrong all along. Maybe you overreacted or were paranoid. You might even slightly doubt your sanity—you know you felt upset, but maybe you can't trust your own feelings. Now you are the one to feel guilty, as if you were to blame for the tension. Better to reassess yourself and not repeat this unpleasant experience, you tell yourself. As an adjunct to this strategy, passive aggressors are often quite nice and polite to other people, only playing their games on you, since you are the one they want to control. If you try to confide in people your confusion and anger, you get no sympathy, and the blame shifting has double the effect.

This strategy is a way of covering up all kinds of unpleasant behavior, of deflecting any kind of criticism, and of making people skittish about ever calling them on what they are doing. In this way they can gain power over your emotions and manipulate them as they see fit, doing whatever they want with impunity. They are exploiting the fact that many of us, since early childhood, are prone to feeling guilty at the slightest impetus. This strategy is used most obviously in personal relationships, but you will find it in more diffused form in the work world. People will use their hypersensitivity to any criticism, and the ensuing drama they stir up, to dissuade people from ever trying to confront them.

To counter this strategy, you need to be able to see through the blame shifting and remain unaffected by it. Your goal is not to make them angry, so don't get caught in the trap of exchanging recriminations. They are better at this drama game than you are, and they thrive by their power to rankle you. Be calm and even fair, accepting some of the blame for the problem, if that seems right. Realize that it is very difficult to get such types to reflect on their behavior and change it; they are too hypersensitive for this.

What you want is to have the requisite distance to see through them and to disengage. To help in this, you must learn to trust your past feelings. In the moments they are irritating you, write down what they are doing and memorialize their behavior. Perhaps in doing so, you will realize that you are in fact overreacting. But if not, you can return to these notes to convince yourself that you are not crazy and to stop the blame-shifting mechanism in its tracks. If you don't allow the shifting to occur, they might be discouraged from using this strategy. If not, it is best to lessen your involvement with such a passive aggressor.

The Passive-Tyrant Strategy: The person you are working for seems to be bubbling with energy, ideas, and charisma. They are a bit disorganized, but that is normal—they have so much to do, so much responsibility and so many plans, they can't keep on top of it all. They need your help, and you strain every fiber of your being to provide it. You listen extra hard to their instructions and try to execute them. Occasionally they praise you, and this keeps you going, but sometimes they rail at you for letting them down, and this sticks in your mind more than the praise.

You can never feel comfortable or take your position for granted. You have to try harder to avoid these nasty temperamental rants. They're such perfectionists, with such high standards, and you're not measuring up. You rack your brain to anticipate their needs and live in terror of displeasing them. If they were actively ordering you around, you would simply do what they asked. But by being somewhat passive and moody, they force you to work doubly hard to please them.

This strategy is generally used by those in power on their underlings, but it could be applied by people in relationships, one partner tyrannizing the other by simply being impossible to please. The strategy is based on the following logic: If people know what it is that you want and how to get it for you, they have some power over you. If they follow your instructions and do your bidding, you cannot criticize them. If they are consistent, you can even grow dependent on their work, and they can squeeze concessions out of you by threatening to leave. But if they have no idea what actually works, if they can't exactly discern what kind of behavior draws praise and what draws punishment, they have no power, no independence, and can be made to do anything. As with a dog, an occasional pat on their shoulder will deepen their submission.

This was how Michael Eisner exercised dictatorial control over everyone around him, including Jeffrey Katzenberg (see chapter 11 for more on this).

If people quit on these tyrants, they are fine with that. This demonstrates that the individual retains some independence, and they will find a replacement who will be more submissive, at least for the time being. They may also increase their difficult behavior to test certain individuals and get them to quit or submit. Such tyrants may try to act like helpless children. They are the temperamental artist or genius type, so naturally brilliant and absentminded. Their pleas for assistance from you and their urgent need for you to do more seem to express their vulnerability. They use such feigned weakness to justify the ugly nature of their tyranny.

It is very hard to strategize against such types, because most often they are your superiors and have real power over you. They tend to be hypersensitive and prone to anger, which makes any form of resistance or inner detachment hard to maintain. Overt rebellion will only make the situation worse. You must first realize that this strategy of theirs is more conscious than it appears. They are not weak and helpless but cunning tyrants. Instead of lingering on anything positive they've said or done, think only of their manipulations and harshness. Your ability to detach from them emotionally will neutralize the obsessive presence they try to instill. But in the end nothing really will work, because if, in their hypersensitivity, they detect your distance, their behavior will only get worse. The only real counter is to quit and recuperate. No position is worth such abuse, for the damage to your self-esteem could take years to recover from.

Controlled Aggression

We are born with a powerful energy that is distinctly human. We can call it willpower, assertiveness, or even aggression, but it is mixed with our intelligence and cleverness. It was revealed to us in its purest state in childhood. This energy made us bold and adventurous, not only physically but mentally, wanting to explore ideas and soak up knowledge. It made us actively search for friends with whom we could explore together. It also made us rather relentless when it came to solving problems or getting what we wanted. (Children can often be bold in what they ask for.) It made us open to the world and to new experiences. And if we felt frustrated and helpless for long enough periods of time, this same energy could make us unusually combative.

As we get older and we encounter mounting frustrations, resistance from others, and feelings of impatience for power, some among us may become chronically aggressive. But another phenomenon is even more common: we become uncomfortable with and even frightened of that assertive energy within, and our own potential for aggressive behavior. Being assertive and adventurous could lead to some failed action, making us feel exposed and vulnerable. If we express this energy too much, people may not like us. We could stir up conflict. Perhaps our parents induced in us as well some shame for our aggressive outbursts. In any event, we may come to view the aggressive part of the self as dangerous. But since this energy cannot disappear, it turns inward, and we create what the great English psychoanalyst Ronald Fairbairn called the *internal saboteur*.

The saboteur operates like a persecutor from within, continually judging and attacking us. If we are about to attempt something, it reminds us of the potential for failure. It tries to tamp down any exuberance, because that could open us to criticism from others. It makes us uncomfortable with strong sensations of pleasure or the expression of deep emotion. It impels us to tamp down our ambitions, the better to fit into the group and not stand out. It wants us to retreat inward, where we can protect ourselves, even if that leads to depression. And it makes us forge a fake self to present to the world, one that is humble and self-effacing. In the end, the internal saboteur works to lower our energy and constrain what we do, making our world more manageable and predictable but also quite dead. It is the same goal as the aggressor—gaining control over uncertainty—but through the opposite means.

The internal saboteur can also have a dampening effect on our mental powers. It discourages us from being bold and adventurous in our thinking. We limit our ideas and settle for the conventional opinions of the group, because that is safer. Creative people display great aggressiveness in their thinking, as they try out many options and search for possible solutions. By trying to rid ourselves of any kind of aggressive impulse, we actually thwart our own creative energies.

Understand: The problem has never been that we humans are assertive and aggressive. That would be to make a problem of our own nature. The positive and negative aspects of this energy are but two sides of the same coin. To try to tamp down the negative, to give ourselves over to the internal saboteur, only dulls the positive. The real problem is that we do not know how to harness this energy in an adult, productive, and prosocial manner. This energy needs to be embraced as totally human and potentially positive. What we must do is tame and train it for our own purposes. Instead of being chronically aggressive, passive-aggressive, or repressed, we can make this energy focused and rational. Like all forms of energy, when it is concentrated and sustained, it has so much more force behind it. By following such a path, we can recover some of that pure spirit we had as children, feeling bolder, more integrated, and more authentic.

The following are four potentially positive elements of this energy that we can discipline and use, improving what evolution has bestowed on us.

Ambition: To say you're ambitious in the world today is often to admit to something slightly dirty, perhaps revealing too much self-absorption. But think back to your childhood and youth—you inevitably entertained big dreams and ambitions for yourself. You were going to make a mark in this world in some way. You played out in your mind various scenes of future glory. This was a natural impulse on your part, and you felt no shame. Then, when you got older, you probably tried to stifle this. Either you kept your ambitions secret and acted modestly or you actually stopped dreaming altogether, trying to avoid seeming self-absorbed and being judged for this.

Much of this sneering at ambition and ambitious people in our culture actually stems from a great deal of envy at the accomplishments of others. Tamping down your youthful ambitions is a sign that you don't like or respect yourself; you no longer believe you deserve to have the power and recognition you once dreamed about. That doesn't make you more adult, simply more likely to fail—by lowering your ambitions, you limit your possibilities and diminish your energy. In any event, in trying to appear unambitious, you are just as self-absorbed as anyone else; being so humble and saintly *is* your ambition, and you want to make a display of it.

Some people remain ambitious as they get older, but their ambitions are too vague. They want success, money, and attention. Because of such vagueness, it is hard for them to ever feel they have satisfied their desires. What constitutes enough money or success or power? Not sure of what exactly they want, they cannot put a limit to their desires, and although it is not the case in every instance, this can lead them to aggressive behavior, as they continually want more and don't know when to stop.

Instead, what you must do is embrace that childish part of you, revisit your earliest ambitions, adapt them to your current reality, and make them as specific as possible. You want to write a particular book, expressing some deeply held ideas or emotions; you want to start the kind of business that has always excited you; you want to create a cultural or political movement to address a particular cause. This specific ambition might be grand enough, but you can visualize quite clearly the end point and how to get there. The more clearly you see what you want, the likelier you are to realize it. Your ambitions may involve challenges, but they should not be so far above your capacity that you only set yourself up for failure.

Once your goal is realized, however long that takes, you now turn to a new ambition, a new project, feeling tremendous satisfaction that you reached the last one. You do not stop in this upward process, building momentum. The key is the level of desire and aggressive energy you put into each ambitious project. You don't infect yourself with doubts and guilt; you are in harmony with your nature, and you will be amply rewarded for that.

Persistence: If you observe infants, you will notice how willful and relentless they are when they want something. Such persistence is natural to us, but it is a quality that we tend to lose as we get older and our self-confidence fades. This is often what happens later in life when we face a problem or some resistance: We summon up the energy to attack the problem, but in the back of our mind, we have some doubts—are we up to the task? This ever-so-slight diminishment in self-belief translates into a reduction in the energy with which we attack the problem. This leads to a less effective result, which raises the volume of the background doubts even more, lessening the effect of our next action or blow. At some point, we admit defeat and give up. But we inevitably give up too soon. We surrender inwardly long before we surrender outwardly.

What you must understand is the following: almost nothing in the world can resist persistent human energy. Things will yield if we strike enough blows with enough force. Look at how many great people in history have succeeded in this way. It was painstaking persistence over several years that allowed Thomas Edison to invent the proper form of the lightbulb, and Marie Curie to discover radium. They simply continued where others had given up. Over the course of ten years, it was through continual thought experiments, day and night, exploring every possible solution, that Albert Einstein finally came up with the theory of relativity. In the spiritual realm, the great eighteenth-century Zen master Hakuin was able to finally reach full enlightenment, and revive a dying branch of Zen, because he applied himself to the task with relentless persistence over the course of some twenty years. This is aggressive energy, undivided from within, aimed with laser focus at a problem or resistance.

It is because the infant or the scientist or the aspiring practitioner of Zen wants something so badly that nothing will deter them. They understand the power of persistence, and so it becomes a self-fulfilling prophecy—knowing its value, they are able to summon up the energy and self-belief to solve the problem. They are adopting Hannibal's motto: "I will either find a way, or make a way." You must do the same. The trick is to want something badly enough that nothing will stop you or dull your energy. Fill yourself with the requisite desire to reach a goal. Train yourself to not give up as easily as you did in the past. Keep attacking from new angles, in new ways. Drop the background doubts and continue striking with full force, knowing that you can break through anything if you don't let up. Once you sense the power in this form of attack, you will keep returning to it.

Fearlessness: We are bold creatures by nature. As children, we were not afraid to ask for more or assert our will. We were remarkably resilient and fearless in so many ways. Timidity is a quality we generally acquire. It is a function of our mounting fears as we get older and a loss of confidence in our powers to get what we want. We become overly concerned with how people perceive us and worry what they will think if we stand up for ourselves. We internalize their doubts. We become afraid of any kind of conflict or confrontation, which will churn up emotions and lead to consequences we cannot predict or control. We develop the habit of backing down. We don't say what we feel even when it would be appropriate, and we fail to set boundaries to people's harmful behavior. We find it hard to ask for a raise or a promotion or the respect due to us. Losing our bold spirit, a positive form of aggression, is losing a deep part of our self, and it is inevitably painful.

You must try to recover the fearlessness you once possessed, through incremental steps. The key is to first convince yourself that you deserve good and better things in life. Once you feel that, you can start by training yourself to speak up or even talk back to people in everyday situations, if they are proving to be insensitive. You are learning to defend yourself. You might call people on their passive-aggressive behavior, or not be so timid in expressing an opinion that they may not share or in telling them what you really think of their bad ideas. You will often come to realize that you have less to fear in doing this than you had imagined. You might even gain some respect. You try this out in small ways every day.

Once you lose your fear in these less dramatic encounters, you can start to ramp it up. You can make greater demands on people that they treat you well, or honor the quality work that you do. You do this without a complaining or defensive tone. You make it clear to bullies that you are not as meek as you seem, or as easily manipulated as others. You can be as relentless as they are in defending your interests. In negotiations, you can train yourself not to settle for less but to make bolder demands and see how far you can push the other side.

You can apply this growing boldness to your work. You will not be so afraid to create something that is unique, or to face criticism and failure. You will take reasonable risks and test yourself out. All of this must be built up slowly, like a muscle that has atrophied, so that you don't risk a large-scale battle or aggressive reaction before you have toughened yourself up. But once you develop this muscle, you will gain the confidence that you can meet any adversity in life with a fearless attitude.

Anger: It is natural and healthy for you to feel anger at certain types of people—those who unfairly block your advancement, the many fools who have power but are lazy and incompetent, the sanctimonious critics who espouse their clichés with so much conviction and attack you without understanding your views. The list could go on forever. Feeling such anger can be a powerful motivating device to take some kind of action. It can fill you with valuable energy. You should embrace it and use it throughout your life for such a purpose. What might make you hold back or tamp down your anger is that it can seem to be such a toxic and ugly emotion, as it often is in our culture.

What makes anger toxic is the degree to which it is disconnected from reality. People channel their natural frustrations into anger at some vague enemy or scapegoat, conjured up and spread by demagogues. They imagine grand conspiracies behind simple inescapable realities, such as taxes or globalism or the changes that are part of all historical periods. They believe that certain forces in the world are to blame for their lack of success or power, instead of their own impatience and lack of effort. There is no thought behind their anger, and so it leads nowhere or it becomes destructive.

You must do the opposite. Your anger is directed at very specific individuals and forces. You analyze the emotion—are you certain that your frustration does not stem from your own inadequacies? Do you really understand the cause of the anger and what it should be directed at? In addition to determining if it is justified and where the anger should be directed, you also analyze the best way to channel this emotion, the best strategy for defeating your opponents. Your anger is controlled, realistic, and targeted at the actual source of the problem, never losing sight of what initially inspired the emotion.

Most people engage in some cathartic release of their anger, some giant protest, and then it goes away and they slip back into complacency or become bitter. You want to cool your anger, bring it more to a simmer than a boil. Your controlled anger will help give you the resolve and patience you will need for what might be a longer struggle than you had imagined. Let the unfairness or injustice lie in the back of your mind and keep you energized. The real satisfaction comes not in one spasm of emotion but in actually defeating the bully and exposing the narrow-minded for who they are.

Do not be afraid to use your anger in your work, particularly if it is allied to some cause or if you are expressing yourself through something creative. It is often the sense of contained rage that makes an orator so effective; it was the source of much of the charisma of Malcolm X. Look at the most lasting and compelling works of art, and you can often read or feel the restrained anger behind them. We are all so careful and correct that when we feel the carefully channeled anger in a film or a book or wherever it is, it is like a fresh wind. It attracts all of our own frustrations and resentments and lets them out. We recognize that it is something real and authentic. In your expressive work, never shy away from anger but capture and channel it, letting it breathe into the work a sense of life and movement. In giving expression to such anger, you will always find an audience.

> Power is required for communication. To stand before an indifferent or hostile group and have one's say, or to speak honestly to a friend truths that go deep and hurt, these require self-affirmation, self-assertion, and even at times aggression
>
> —*Rollo May*

17

Seize the Historical Moment

———————— ◇ ————————

The Law of Generational Myopia

Y*ou are born into a generation that defines who you are more than you can imagine. Your generation wants to separate itself from the previous one and set a new tone for the world. In the process, it forms certain tastes, values, and ways of thinking that you as an individual internalize. As you get older, these generational values and ideas tend to close you off from other points of view, constraining your mind. Your task is to understand as deeply as possible this powerful influence on who you are and how you see the world. Knowing in depth the spirit of your generation and the times you live in, you will be better able to exploit the zeitgeist. You will be the one to anticipate and set the trends that your generation hungers for. You will free your mind from the mental constraints placed on you by your generation, and you will become more of the individual you imagine yourself to be, with all the power that freedom will bring you.*

The Rising Tide

On May 10, 1774, sixty-four-year-old King Louis XV of France died, and though the country went into the requisite mourning for its king, many French people felt a sense of relief. He had ruled France for over fifty years. He left a country that was prosperous, the preeminent power in Europe, but things were changing—the expanding middle class craved power, the peasantry was restless, and people in general yearned for a new direction. And so it was with great hope and affection that the French people turned to their new ruler, King Louis XVI, the grandson of the deceased king, who was a mere twenty years old at the time. He and his young wife, Marie Antoinette, represented a new generation that would certainly revitalize the country and the monarchy itself.

The young king, however, did not share the optimism of his subjects. In fact, at moments he was on the verge of panic. Ever since he was a boy, he had dreaded the possibility that he might become king. Compared with his affable grandfather, Louis was quite shy around people; he was an awkward young man, always uncertain and fearful of making mistakes. He felt the august role of French king to be beyond his capacities. Now, having ascended the throne, he could no longer disguise his insecurities from the court and from the French people. But as he prepared for his coronation, to take place in the spring of 1775, Louis began to feel differently. He had decided to study the coronation ritual itself so that he could be prepared and not make mistakes; and what he learned actually filled him with the confidence that he desperately needed.

According to legend, a dove sent from the Holy Spirit had deposited some sacred oil that was kept at a church in the town of Reims and was used to anoint all kings of France from the ninth century on. Once anointed with this oil, the king was suddenly elevated above the ranks of mere mortals and imbued with a divine nature, becoming God's lieutenant on earth. The ritual represented the marriage of the new king with the church and the French people. In his body and spirit, the king would now embody the entire populace, their two fates intertwined. And, sanctified by God, the king could depend on the Lord's guidance and protection.

By the 1770s, many French people and progressive clergymen had come to see this ritual as a relic of a superstitious past. But Louis felt the opposite. To him, the ancientness of the rite was comforting. Believing in its significance would be the means to overcome his fears and doubts. He would be buoyed by a profound sense of mission, his divine nature made real by the anointment.

Louis decided to reenact this sacred ritual in its more original form. And he would go even further. At the palace of Versailles he noticed that many of the paintings and statues of Louis XIV associated him with Roman gods, a way to symbolically strengthen the image of the French monarchy as something ancient and unshakable. The new king decided he would surround himself with similar imagery for the public part of the coronation, overwhelming his subjects with the spectacle and the symbols he had chosen.

———————

LOUIS XVI's CORONATION TOOK PLACE ON JUNE 11, 1775, AND IN THE CROWD OUT-side the cathedral that warm day was a most unlikely tourist—a fifteen-year-old youth named Georges-Jacques Danton. He was a student at a boarding school in the town of Troyes. His family had come from the peasantry, but his father had managed to become a lawyer, raising the family up into the expand-ing French middle class. His father had died when Danton was three, and his mother had raised him with the hope that Danton would continue in his fa-ther's footsteps, securing a solid career.

Danton was quite strange-looking, if not downright ugly. He was unusually large for his age, with an enormous head and a rather monstrous face. Growing up on the family farm, he had twice been attacked by bulls, their horns splitting his upper lip and cracking his nose. Some people found him frightening, but many were charmed by his youthful exuberance and could ignore the face. The boy was simply fearless, always in search of adventure, and it was his bold spirit that attracted people to him, particularly among his classmates.

At the school he was attending, the liberal priests who ran it had decided to award a prize to the student who wrote an essay that best described the upcom-ing coronation, its necessity and meaning at a time when France was trying to modernize itself. Danton was not the intellectual type. He preferred swim-ming in the nearby river and any other kind of physical activity. The one sub-ject that excited him was history, particularly ancient Rome. His favorite historical figure was the great Roman lawyer and orator Cicero. He identified with Cicero, who also came from the middle class. He memorized Cicero's speeches and developed a love for oratory. With his powerful speaking voice, he was a natural at the art. But he was not very good at writing.

He desperately wanted to win the essay prize—it would instantly elevate him among the ranks of fellow students. He had reasoned, however, that the only way he could compensate for his less-than-stellar literary skills was to witness the coronation firsthand and give a vivid description of it. He also felt a strange affinity with the young king: they were not far apart in age, and both were large and considered decidedly unhandsome.

Playing hooky to get to Reims, only eighty miles away, was just the kind of adventure that had always attracted him. He had told his friends, "I want to see how a king is made." And so he had snuck off to Reims the day before the corona-tion and had arrived just in time. He moved through the throng of French people congregating outside the cathedral. Guards brandishing tall pikes held them back. Only the nobility was allowed inside. Danton pushed as far forward as he could, and then he spotted the king, wearing the most spectacular ceremonial robe encrusted with diamonds and gold, making his way up the steps. There was the pretty queen following him in a splendid gown, her hair piled impossibly high, followed by other members of her entourage. From a distance, they were all like figures from another era, so different from anybody he had ever seen before.

He waited patiently outside for the end of the ritual, at which point the king reemerged, now sporting a crown. For a brief moment he got a closer look at Louis's face as he passed by, and he was surprised to find that the king seemed quite ordinary, despite the robes and jewels. The king then got into the most elaborate carriage imaginable, named the *Sacre*. It was like something out of a fairy tale. It was built for the coronation and designed to represent the chariot of Apollo, glistening like the sun (the sun being the symbol of the French king), and it was enormous. On all sides it featured gold statuettes of Roman gods. On the door panel facing Danton, he could see an elaborate painting of Louis XVI as a Roman emperor atop a cloud, beckoning the French people below him. Strangest of all, the carriage itself sported a large bronze crown.

The *Sacre* was meant to serve as the very symbol of the monarchy, dazzling and mythical. It was quite a sight, but for some reason it seemed oddly out of place—too large, too bright, and when the king got in, it seemed to swallow him up. Was it magnificent or was it grotesque? Danton could not decide.

Danton returned to school later that same day, his head spinning with all of these strange images. Inspired by what he had witnessed, he wrote his best essay yet and won the prize.

In the years after graduating from the school in Troyes, Danton would make his mother proud. In 1780 he moved to Paris to clerk in the law courts. Within a few years, he passed the bar exam and became a practicing lawyer. In court, with his booming voice and oratorical skills, he naturally commanded attention and quickly rose through the ranks. And as he mingled with his fellow lawyers and read the newspapers, he detected something strange going on in France: a growing discontent with the king, the profligate queen, and the arrogant upper classes, whom the great thinkers of the day were ridiculing in their plays and books.

The main problem was the country's finances—France seemed perpetually on the brink of running out of money. At the root of this was France's vastly antiquated financial structure. The French people were subject to all kinds of onerous taxes that dated back to feudal times, but the clergy and the nobility were largely exempt from any such burdens. Taxes on the French lower and middle classes could never bring in enough revenue, especially considering the lavish expenditures of the French court, which had only gotten worse with Queen Marie Antoinette's elaborate parties and love of finery.

As the money supply ran short and the price of bread kept rising, and with millions of people facing starvation, riots began to break out throughout the countryside and even in Paris. And amid all of this turmoil, the young king was proving to be too indecisive to handle the pressure.

In 1787, as the financial situation worsened, the opportunity of a lifetime came to Danton—a position as a lawyer on the King's Council, with a rather nice bump in salary. Wanting to marry a young woman named Gabrielle, whose father opposed the marriage because Danton did not earn enough, he accepted the position on the council, despite his fears that he was joining a sinking ship. Two days later he married Gabrielle.

Danton did his job well but found himself increasingly absorbed by the turmoil in Paris. He joined a club called the Cordeliers. Its members were an odd mix of bohemian artists and political agitators. It was located near his apartment, so he began to spend a great part of his day there, and soon he was participating in the raucous debates about the future of France that took place at the club. He felt a strange new spirit in the air, a boldness that made people suddenly say things they could never have said a few years before about the monarchy. He found it exciting and irresistible. He began to give his own fiery speeches, focusing on the brutality of the upper classes, and he basked in the attention he received.

In 1788 he was offered a higher position on the King's Council, and he turned it down. He told the king's minister who presented the offer that the monarchy was doomed: "This is no longer about modest reforms," he said. "We are more than ever on the brink of revolution. . . . Can't you see the avalanche coming?"

In the spring of 1789, Louis was forced to call a national assembly to deal with the looming bankruptcy. The assembly was known as the Estates General. It was an institution meant to deal with a national crisis, but always as a measure of last resort, the previous one having been held in 1614, after the death of King Henry IV. It brought together representatives of the three estates of France—the nobility, the clergy, and the tax-paying commoners. Although the vast majority of French people were to be represented by members of the Third Estate, the power of the assembly was heavily tilted in favor of the nobility and clergy. Nevertheless, the French people held great hopes for the Estates General, and Louis had been extremely reluctant to call for it.

Only a month before the convening of the Estates General, riots in Paris had broken out over the price of bread, and royal troops had shot into the crowds, killing dozens. Danton had witnessed the bloodshed and he felt a turning point in the mood of the people, particularly the lower classes, and in himself. He shared their desperation and anger; they could no longer be placated with the usual rhetoric. He began to address the angry crowds on street corners, attracting followers and making a name for himself. To a friend who was surprised at this new direction in his life, he responded that it was like seeing a strong tide in the river, jumping in, and letting it carry him where it might.

As he prepared for the convening of the Estates General, King Louis could barely contain his resentment and anger. In the years since he had become king, various finance ministers had warned him of an impending crisis if France did not reform its tax system. He had understood this and had tried to initiate reforms, but the nobility and clergy, fearing where this might lead, had become so hostile to such ideas that the king had been forced to back down. And now, with the state's coffers nearly empty, the nobility and the Third Estate were holding him hostage, making him convene the Estates General and putting him in the position of begging for funds from his people.

The Estates General was not a traditional part of French government; it was an anomaly, a challenge to the divine right of the king, a recipe for anarchy. Who knew what was best for France—his subjects, with their million different opinions? The nobility, with their own narrow interests and hunger to grab more power? No, only the king could navigate the nation through this crisis. He had to regain the upper hand over these rowdy children.

The king decided upon a plan: he would impress upon them all the majesty of the monarchy and its absolute necessity as the supreme power in France. To do so, he would hold the Estates General at Versailles, something his advisers warned him not to do, considering Versailles's closeness to Paris and all its agitators. Louis reasoned that most of the delegates of the Third Estate came from the middle classes and were relatively moderate. Amid the grandeur and all the symbols of the French monarchy, the members of the Third Estate could not help but think of what Louis XIV, the builder of Versailles, had created and how much they owed the monarchy for transforming France into a great power. He would hold an opening ceremony that would rival his coronation and remind all of the estates of the divine origin of his kingship.

Having impressed them with the weight of the past, he would then agree to some reforms of the tax system, which the Third Estate would certainly be grateful for. At the same time, however, he would make it clear that under no circumstances would the monarchy or the first two estates relinquish any of their other powers or privileges. In this way, the government would get its necessary funds through taxes, and the traditions he was meant to uphold would remain unchanged.

The opening ceremonies went just as he had planned, but to his dismay the deputies of the Third Estate seemed rather uninterested in the splendors of the palace and all of the pomp. They were barely respectful during the religious ceremonies. They did not applaud very warmly during his opening speech. The tax reforms he proposed were not enough, in their eyes. And as the weeks went by, the members of the Third Estate became increasingly demanding, its members now insisting that the three estates have equal power.

When the king refused to accept their demands, they did the unthinkable—they declared themselves the true representatives of the French people, equal to the king, and they called their body the National Assembly. They proposed the formation of a constitutional monarchy, and they claimed to have the overwhelming support of the country. If they did not get their way, they would make sure the government would be unable to raise the necessary taxes. At one point, as the king grew furious at this form of blackmail, he ordered the Third Estate to disband from their meeting place, and they refused, disobeying a royal decree. Never had any French king witnessed such insubordination from the lower classes.

As he faced a growing uprising throughout the country, Louis sensed the urgency of nipping the problem in the bud. He decided to forget any attempts at conciliation and instead resort to force. He called in the army to establish order in Paris and elsewhere. But on July 13 messengers from Paris relayed some disturbing news: the Parisians, anticipating Louis's use of the military, were quickly arming themselves, looting military stockades. The French troops that had moved in to quell the rebellion were unreliable, many of them refusing to fire on their compatriots. The following day, a vast contingent of Parisians marched on the Bastille, the royal prison in Paris that was a symbol of the most oppressive practices of the monarchy, and they took control of it.

Paris was in the hands of the people now, and there was nothing Louis could do. He watched with horror as the National Assembly, still meeting in Versailles, quickly voted to eliminate the various privileges enjoyed by the nobility and clergy. In the name of the people, they voted to take over the Catholic Church and auction off to the public the vast lands that it owned. They went even further, proclaiming that henceforth all French citizens were equal. The monarchy would be allowed to survive, but the people and the king were to share power.

In the following weeks, as the courtiers, shocked and terrified by these events, quickly fled Versailles to safe regions or to other countries, the king could now feel the full brunt of what had happened in the past few months. He wandered the halls of the palace, virtually alone. The paintings and august symbols of Louis XIV stared back at him in mockery of all that he had allowed under his rule.

Somehow he had to retake control of France, and the only way to do so was to lean even more on the military, finding those regiments that had remained loyal to him. In mid-September he recalled the Flanders Regiment—containing some of the best soldiers in the country and renowned for its royalist sympathies—to Versailles. On the evening of October 1, the king's personal guard decided to host a banquet in honor of the Flanders Regiment. All of the courtiers who had remained in the palace, along with the king and the queen, attended the banquet.

The soldiers became drunk. They shouted cheers to the king and oaths to the monarchy. They sang ballads ridiculing the French people in the raunchiest terms. They grabbed handfuls of the tricolor badges and ribbons that symbolized the revolution and trampled them with their boots. The king and the queen, so despondent of late, took this all in with undisguised delight—it was a taste of years gone by, when the very sight of the royal couple inspired such displays of affection. But news of what had transpired at this banquet quickly spread to Paris, and it caused outrage and panic. Parisians of all classes suspected that the king was planning some sort of countercoup. They imagined the nobility returning under Louis's command and exacting revenge on the French people.

Within days, the king learned that thousands of Parisians were now marching on Versailles. They were armed and dragging cannons. He thought of escaping with his family but hesitated. Soon it was too late, as the mob arrived. On the morning of October 6, a group of citizens penetrated into the palace, killing everyone in their path. They demanded that Louis and his family be escorted back to Paris, so that the French citizens could keep an eye on him and ensure his loyalty to the new order.

Louis had no choice: he and his traumatized family piled into a single carriage. As they made their way to Paris, surrounded by the crowd, Louis could see the heads of the king's personal guard paraded on long pikes. What shocked him even more was the sight of so many men and women surrounding the carriage, dressed in rags, thinned by hunger, pressing their faces to the window and swearing at him and the queen in the vilest language. He could not recognize his own subjects. These were not the French people he had known. They must be outside agitators, brought in by enemies to destroy the monarchy. Somehow the world had gone mad.

In Paris the king, his family, and the few courtiers who had remained with them were housed in the Tuileries, a royal residence that had been uninhabited for over a hundred years.

Within a week of his arrival in Paris, the king received a visit from a strange man whose face and manner frightened him. It was Georges-Jacques Danton, now one of the leaders of the French Revolution. On behalf of the French people, he had come to welcome the king to Paris. He explained that he had been a member of the King's Council, and he reassured the king that the people were grateful for his submission to their will and that there was still an important part for him to play as a monarch who swore allegiance to a new constitution.

Louis could barely listen. He was transfixed by the man's enormous head, by the strange outfit he wore (black satin breeches over white silk stockings, and buckled shoes, a mix of fashion styles Louis had never seen before), and by his whole manner, his fast way of talking, the lack of awe and respect in the king's presence. He bowed graciously before the king, but he refused to kiss his hand, quite a breach of protocol. So this was a revolutionary, a man of the people? Louis had never met such a fellow, and he found the experience decidedly unpleasant.

DURING THE SUMMER MONTHS OF 1789, DANTON HAD LARGELY SUPPORTED THE decisions of the National Assembly, but he had remained wary of the aristocracy and wanted to make sure they had permanently lost their privileges. The nobility was the source of the country's misery, and the French must never forget this. He had become one of the principal fomenters against the upper classes, and as such he had earned the mistrust of the more moderate and bourgeois leaders of the revolution, who wanted to go slowly. To them, Danton was like a ranting, monstrous ogre, and they had excluded him from their social circles and any official position in the new government under formation.

Feeling ostracized and perhaps recalling his own peasant roots, Danton had come to increasingly identify with the *sans-culottes* ("without breeches"), members of the lowest classes in France and the most revolutionary in spirit. As the news of the scandalous behavior of the Flanders Regiment on October 1 had reached Paris, Danton had been one of the key agitators for the march on Versailles, and with its success he had become the leader of the Cordeliers. And it was in that capacity that he had paid a visit to the Tuileries, as much to discern the king's degree of support for the new constitution as to welcome him.

Danton could not help but recall the coronation he had attended over fourteen years earlier, with all of its pomp, for despite everything that had happened in the last few months, the king seemed bent on re-creating the protocol and ceremony of Versailles. He wore his royal outfit, with its sash and various medals attached to his coat. He insisted on the old formalities, and he kept his attendants in their elaborate uniforms. It was all so empty, so disconnected from what was going on. Danton was polite. He still felt a strange sympathy for the king, but now, as he scrutinized him, all he could see was a relic of the past. He doubted the king's allegiance to the new order. He left the meeting more certain than ever that the French monarchy had become obsolete.

In the months that followed, the king professed his loyalty to the new constitution, but Danton suspected that Louis was playing a double game, still plotting to bring the monarchy and nobility back to power. A coalition of armies from other countries in Europe was now waging open war against the revolution, determined to rescue the king and restore the old order. And Danton felt certain that the king was in communication with them.

Then in June of 1791 came the most startling news of all: the king and his family had somehow escaped from Paris in a carriage. A few days later they were caught. It would all have been rather comical if it hadn't been so alarming. The family members had been dressed like everyday members of the bourgeoisie out on holiday, but they had ridden in a splendid carriage that did not match their outfits and that called attention to itself. They had been recognized, captured, and returned to the capital.

Now Danton sensed that his moment had arrived. The liberals and moderates in the revolution were trying to maintain that the king was innocent, that he had been duped into escaping or even abducted. They feared what would happen to France if the monarchy was abolished and how the foreign armies, now within the country's borders, would react if anything happened to the king. But to Danton this was absurd. They were merely postponing the inevitable. The monarchy had lost its meaning and purpose; the king had revealed himself to be a traitor, and they must not be afraid to say so. It was time, he proclaimed, for France to declare itself a republic and get rid of the monarchy once and for all.

His call for a republic began to resonate, particularly among the *sans-culottes*. As a sign of his growing influence, Danton was elected to his first official position—deputy prosecutor for the commune in charge of Paris—and he began to fill the commune with his sympathizers, preparing for something large.

The following summer a large contingent of *sans-culottes* from Marseilles was in Paris to celebrate the third anniversary of the revolution. The men from Marseilles, enthused by Danton's calls for a republic, placed themselves under his charge, and throughout June and July they marched through Paris singing hymns to the revolution and spreading Danton's demand for the formation of a republic. Each day more and more people joined the men from Marseilles. Quietly planning his coup, Danton gained control of the commune. Its members now voted to lift the blockade on the various bridges of Paris leading to the Tuileries from the Left Bank, effectively ending any protection for the royal family, as crowds could now march straight to the palace.

On the morning of August 10, alarm bells rang out throughout the city, and accompanied by a steady drumbeat, an enormous contingent of Parisians marched across several bridges to invade the Tuileries. Most of the guards protecting the palace scattered, and soon the royal family was forced to flee for their lives, taking refuge in the nearby hall where the National Assembly met. The crowd quickly massacred the remaining soldiers guarding the palace and took it over.

Danton's gambit had worked—the people had spoken and the National Assembly voted to end the monarchy, stripping the king and his family of any powers and protections that had remained. In one blow, Danton had put an end to the longest-lasting and most powerful monarchy in Europe. The king and his family were shuttled to the Temple, a medieval priory that would serve as their private prison as the new government decided their fate. Danton was now named minister of justice, and he was the de facto leader of the new Republic of France.

AT THE TEMPLE, LOUIS FOUND HIMSELF SEPARATED FROM HIS FAMILY, AWAITING trial for treason in December. He was now to be known as Louis Capet (the family name of the founder of the French tenth-century kingship that would end with Louis), a commoner with no privileges. Mostly alone, he had time to reflect on the traumas of the past three and a half years. If only the French people had kept their faith in him, he would have found a way to solve all of the problems. He was still certain that godless demagogues and outside agitators had spoiled the people's natural love for him.

The revolutionaries had recently discovered a stash of papers that Louis had hidden in a safe in a wall in the Tuileries, and among them were letters that revealed how deeply he had conspired with foreign powers to overturn the revolution. He was certain now to be sentenced to death, and he prepared himself for this.

For his trial in front of the assembly, Louis Capet wore a simple coat, the kind any middle-class citizen would sport. He now had a beard. He looked sad and exhausted, and hardly like a king. But whatever sympathy his judges had had for him quickly vanished as prosecutors read out the many charges against him, including how he had conspired to overturn the revolution. A month later the private citizen Capet was sentenced to die at the guillotine, Danton himself casting one of the deciding votes.

Louis was determined to show a brave face. On the morning of January 21, a cold and windy day, he was transported to the Place de la Révolution, where an enormous crowd had gathered to witness the execution. They watched in stunned amazement as the former king had his hands tied and his hair cut like any ordinary criminal. He climbed the stairs to the guillotine, and before kneeling at the block, he cried out, "People, I die innocent! I pardon those who sentenced me. I pray God my blood does not fall again over France."

As the blade fell, he emitted a horrifying cry. The executioner held up the king's head for all to see. After a few cries of "Vive la nation," a deathly silence fell over the crowd. Minutes later they rushed to the scaffold to dip their hands in Louis's blood and buy locks of his hair.

AS THE LEADER OF THE FRENCH REVOLUTION, DANTON NOW FACED TWO RATHER daunting forces: the invading armies that kept pressing closer to Paris and the restiveness of the French citizens, many of whom clamored for revenge on the aristocracy and all counterrevolutionaries. To meet the enemy armies, Danton unleashed an enormous citizen army of millions that he had created, and in the first few months of battle these new French forces turned the tide of the war.

To channel the people's taste for revenge, he set up a revolutionary tribunal to bring quick justice to those suspected of trying to restore the monarchy. The tribunal initiated what would become known as the Terror, as it sent thousands of suspects to the guillotine, often on the flimsiest of charges.

Shortly after the execution of the king, Danton traveled to Belgium to help oversee the war effort on that front. While there, he received the news that his beloved wife, Gabrielle, had died in premature childbirth. He felt horribly guilty for not being by her side in that moment, and the thought that he had no chance to say good-bye to her and that he would never see her face again was unbearable. Without thinking of the consequences, he abandoned his mission in Belgium and hurried back to France.

By the time he arrived, his wife had been dead for a week and buried in the public cemetery. Overwhelmed with grief and the desire to see her one more time, he hurried to the cemetery, bringing along with him a friend and some shovels. On a moonless, rainy night, they managed to find the grave. He dug and he dug, and with his friend's help, he lifted the casket out of the ground and, with much effort, finally pried the lid off. He gasped at the sight of her bloodless face. He pulled her out, hugging her tightly to his body, begging her to forgive him. He kissed her again and again on her cold lips. After several hours, he finally returned her to the ground.

In the months to come, something seemed to have changed in Danton. Had it been the loss of his wife, or was it the guilt he now felt for having unleashed the Terror within France? He had ridden the wave of the revolution to the pinnacle of power, but now he wanted it to go in another direction. He became less engaged in affairs of state and was no longer in favor of the Terror. Maximilien Robespierre, his main rival for power, noticed the change and began to spread the rumor that Danton had lost his revolutionary fervor and could no longer be trusted. Robespierre's campaign had effect: when it came time to elect members to the highest governing body, the Committee of Public Safety, Danton did not receive enough votes and Robespierre packed it with his sympathizers.

Danton now openly worked to put an end to the Terror, through speeches and pamphlets, but this only played into the hands of his rival. On March 30, 1794, Danton was arrested for treason and brought before the revolutionary tribunal. It seemed ironic that the tribunal he had formed now held his fate in its hands. The charges against him were based on pure innuendo, but Robespierre made certain he was found guilty and sentenced to death. Upon hearing the sentence, he yelled at his judges, "My name is engraved on every institution of the revolution—the army, the committees, the tribunal. I have killed myself!"

That same afternoon he and other condemned men were put in carts and led to the Place de la Révolution. Along the way, Danton passed the residence where Robespierre lived. "You're next," Danton shouted in his booming voice, pointing his finger at Robespierre's apartment. "You will follow me!"

Danton was the last one to be executed that day. An enormous crowd had followed the cart, and now they were quiet as he was led up the stairs. He could not help but think of Louis, whom he had reluctantly sent to the guillotine, and the many former friends who had died during the Terror. It had taken a few months, but he had grown sick of all the bloodshed, and he could sense the crowd before him was feeling the same way. As he laid his neck on the block, he shouted to the executioner, "Make sure you show my head to the people. It is worth a look!"

After the execution of Danton, Robespierre unleashed what became known as the Great Terror. During four tumultuous months, the tribunal sent close to twenty thousand French men and women to the guillotine. But Danton had anticipated the shift in mood: the French public had had enough of the executions, and they turned against Robespierre with remarkable speed. In late July, in a heated meeting at the assembly, its members voted to arrest Robespierre. He tried to defend himself, but the words came out haltingly. One member shouted, "It is the blood of Danton that chokes you!" The following morning, without a trial, Robespierre was guillotined, and days later the assembly abolished the revolutionary tribunal.

AT AROUND THE TIME OF ROBESPIERRE'S EXECUTION, THE NEW LEADERS OF THE revolution were looking for ways to drum up funds for the various emergencies France was facing, and someone mentioned the recent rediscovery of Louis's magnificent coronation carriage, the *Sacre*. Perhaps they could sell it. A few of them went to inspect it, and they were aghast at what they perceived as its sheer hideousness. One deputy described it as "a monstrous assemblage built of the people's gold and an excess of flattery." All agreed that no one would buy such a grotesquerie. They had all of the gold from the coach removed and melted, sending it to the treasury. They dispatched the salvaged bronze to the republic's foundries to help forge some much-needed cannons. When it came to the painted panels on the doors, with all of their mythological symbols, they found them too weird for anyone's tastes and promptly had them burned.

Interpretation: Let us look momentarily at the prerevolutionary world in France through the eyes of King Louis XVI. Much of what he saw seemed to be the same reality that previous kings had faced. The king was still considered the absolute ruler of France, divinely appointed to lead the nation. The various classes and estates in France remained quite stable; the distinctions among the nobility, the clergy, and the rest of the French people were still largely respected. The commoners enjoyed the relative prosperity that Louis himself had inherited from his grandfather.

Yes, there were financial problems, but the great Louis XIV himself had faced such crises, and they had passed. Versailles was still the glittering jewel of Europe, the center of everything civilized. Louis's beloved queen, Marie Antoinette, hosted the most spectacular parties, which were the envy of all European aristocrats. Louis himself did not care for such amusements, but he had his hunting parties and his other rather pedestrian hobbies that obsessed him.

Life at the palace was rather sweet and relatively tranquil. Most important to Louis, the glory and the majesty of France, as embodied in its ceremonies and visual symbols, still carried the same weight as before. Who could help but be impressed by the splendors of Versailles itself, or by the rituals of the Catholic Church? He was the ruler of a great nation, and there was no reason to believe that the monarchy would not continue for as many centuries as it had already lasted.

Below the surface of what he saw, however, there were some troubling signs of discontent. Beginning during the reign of Louis XV, writers such as Voltaire and Diderot began to ridicule the church and the monarchy for all of their backward, superstitious beliefs. They reflected a new scientific spirit spreading throughout Europe, and it was hard to reconcile this with many of the practices of the church and the nobility. Their ideas became known as the Enlightenment, and they began to gain influence among the expanding middle class, which had felt excluded from power and was not so immersed in all of the symbolism of the monarchy.

Below the seemingly tranquil façade of the nobility, there were quite a few cracks. Many aristocrats had come to loathe the absolute power of the king, whom they saw as weak and not worthy of their respect. They hungered for more power for themselves.

Secret societies were sprouting up everywhere, promoting a whole new way of socializing, far from the stuffy environment of the court. Supreme among them were the Freemasons and their lodges, with their own secret rituals. Danton himself was a member. The Freemasons' lodges were hotbeds of discontent with the monarchy, their members highly sympathetic to the ideas of the Enlightenment. They craved a new order in France. In Paris, the theater had suddenly become the most popular place to frequent and to be seen at, much more popular than the church. And plays were now being performed that mocked the monarchy in the most brazen manner.

And all of those majestic symbols and ceremonies of the monarchy that had remained relatively unchanged were beginning to seem rather empty, masks with nothing behind them. Courtiers no longer really understood what they were doing, or why, when they engaged in their elaborate rituals in company with the king. The paintings, statues, and fountains ornamented with mythological figures were as beautiful as ever, but they were simply seen as surface pieces of art, not as indications of a deep connection to France's glorious past.

All of these signs were subtle and disparate. It was hard to connect them all to any kind of trend, let alone a revolution. They could pass as novelties, new pastimes for a bored nation, without any underlying meaning. But then came the worsening crisis in the late 1780s, and suddenly these separate examples of disenchantment began to combine into an undeniable force. The price of bread had risen, as well as the cost of living, for all French subjects. As the discontent spread, the nobility and the bourgeoisie smelled weakness in the king and demanded more power.

Now the king could not ignore what was happening, and at the Estates General the loss of respect and the disenchantment were all too visible to him in the behavior of the Third Estate. Louis, however, could only view these events through the lens of the divine monarchy that he had inherited and clung to so desperately. These French subjects who were disrespecting and disobeying his absolute rule must be godless individuals, and only a noisy minority. To disobey his word was tantamount to sacrilege.

If such people could not be persuaded by the symbols of the glorious past, he would have to use force to make the past and the traditions prevail. But once something has lost its spell and no longer enchants, no amount of force can bring it back to life. And as he rode in that carriage in October of 1789 that carried him away forever from Versailles and the past, all he could see were people who were not his subjects but aliens of some sort. He had to include Danton in such a group. At his execution, he addressed the crowd as if he were still the king, forgiving them their sins. The crowd instead saw just a human, stripped of all his previous glory, no better than they were.

When Georges-Jacques Danton looked out at the same world as the king, he saw something quite different. Unlike the king, he was not timid or insecure but the opposite. He had no inner need to rely upon the past to prop him up. He had been educated by liberal priests who had instilled in him Enlightenment ideas. And at the age of fifteen, at the coronation he caught a fleeting glimpse of the future, intuiting for a moment how empty the monarchy and its symbols had become, and that the king was just an ordinary man.

In the 1780s he began to pick up the disparate signs of change—from within the King's Council and the growing disrespect among the lawyer class, to the clubs and street life, where a new spirit could be detected. He could feel the pain of the lower classes and empathize with their sense of exclusion. And this new spirit was not simply political but also cultural. The youth of Danton's generation had grown tired of all of the empty formality in French culture. They yearned for something freer and more spontaneous. They wanted to express their emotions openly and naturally. They wanted to get rid of all the elaborate outfits and hairstyles and wear looser clothing with less ostentation. They wanted more open socializing, the open mingling of all the classes, as occurred in the clubs in Paris.

We could call this cultural movement the first real explosion of Romanticism, valuing emotions and sensations above the intellect and formalities. Danton both exemplified this Romantic spirit and understood it. He was a man who always wore his heart on his sleeve and whose speeches had the feel of spontaneous outpourings of ideas and emotions. His disinterment of his wife was like something out of Romantic literature, an expression of emotion unimaginable some ten years before. This side of Danton was what made him so relatable and compelling to the public.

In a way that made him quite unique, Danton was able before anyone else to connect the meaning behind all of these signs and foresee a mass revolution on its way. An avid swimmer, he compared all of this to the tide in a river.

Nothing in human life is ever static. There is always discontent below the surface, and hunger for change. Sometimes this is rather subtle, and the river seems somewhat placid but still moving. At other times it is like a rush, a rising tide that no one, not even a king with absolute power, can hold back.

Where was this tide carrying the French? That was the key question. To Danton it soon became clear it was heading toward the formation of a republic. The monarchy was now just a façade. Its show of majesty no longer stirred the masses. They now saw that the actions of the king were all about holding on to power; they saw the aristocracy as a bunch of thieves, doing little work and sucking up the wealth of France. With such levels of disenchantment, there could be no turning back, no middle ground, no constitutional monarchy.

As part of his unusual perspicacity and sensitivity to the spirit of the times, before any of the other revolutionary leaders, Danton understood that the Terror he had unleashed was a mistake and that it was time to stop it. In this one instance, his sense of timing was off, as he moved on this intuition at least several months in advance of the public, giving his enemies and rivals an opening to get rid of him.

Understand: You might see King Louis XVI as an extreme example of someone out of tune with the times, not particularly relevant to your own life, but in fact he is much closer to you than you think. Like him, you are probably looking at the present through the lens of the past. When you look at the world around you, it seems pretty much as it appeared a day or a week or a month or even a year ago. People act more or less the same. The institutions that hold power remain in place and are not going anywhere. People's ways of thinking have not really changed; the conventions that govern behavior in your field are still followed religiously. Yes, there might be some new styles and trends in culture, but they are not critical factors or signs of deep change. Lulled by these appearances, it seems to you that life simply goes on as it always has.

Below the surface, however, the tide is moving; nothing in human culture stands still. Those who are younger than you no longer have the same level of respect for certain values or institutions that you have. Power dynamics—among classes, regions, industries—are in a state of flux. People are beginning to socialize and interact in new ways. New symbols and myths are being formed, and old ones are fading. All of these things can seem rather disconnected until there is some crisis or clash and people must confront what was once seemingly invisible or separate, in the form of some sort of revolution or cry for change.

When this occurs, some people will feel, like the king, profoundly uncomfortable and will hold on even more fervently to the past. They will band together to try to stop the tide from advancing, a futile task. Leaders will feel threatened and cling more tightly to their conventional ideas. Others will be carried along without really understanding where it is all headed or why things are changing.

What you want and need is the power that Danton possessed to make sense of it all and act accordingly. And this power is a function of vision, of looking at events from a different angle, through a fresh framework. You ignore the clichéd interpretations that others will inevitably spout when facing changes. You drop the mental habits and past ways of looking at things that can cloud your vision. You stop the tendency to moralize, to judge what is happening. You simply want to see things as they are. You look for the undercurrents of discontent and disharmony with the status quo, which are always there below the surface. You see commonalities and connections among all these signs. Slowly the flow, the tide itself, comes into focus, indicating a course, a direction that is hidden to so many others.

Do not think of this as some intellectual exercise. Intellectuals are often the last to really discern the spirit of the times, because they are so grounded in theories and conventional frameworks. First and foremost, you must be able to *feel* the change in the collective mood, to *sense* how people are diverging from the past. Once you feel the spirit, you can begin to analyze what is behind it. Why are people dissatisfied, and what are they really craving? Why are they gravitating toward these new styles? Look at those idols from the past that no longer cast a spell, that seem ridiculous, that are the subject of mockery, particularly among the young. They are like Louis's carriage. When you detect enough such disenchantment, you can be sure something strong is cresting.

Once you have an adequate feel for what is really going on, you must be bold in how you respond, giving voice to what other people are feeling but not understanding. Be careful to not get too far out ahead and be misunderstood. Ever alert, always letting go of your prior interpretations, you can seize the opportunities in the moment that others cannot even begin to detect. Think of yourself as an enemy of the status quo, whose proponents must view you in turn as dangerous. See this task as absolutely necessary for the revitalization of the human spirit and the culture at large, and master it.

Our era is a birth-time, and a period of transition. The spirit of
man has broken with the old order of things . . . and with the old
ways of thinking, and is of the mind to let them all sink into the
depths of the past and to set about its own transformation. . . . The
frivolity and boredom which unsettle the established order, the
vague foreboding of something unknown, these are the heralds of
approaching change.

—G. W. F. Hegel

Keys to Human Nature

In human culture, we can see a phenomenon—changes in fashions and styles—
that at first glance might appear trivial, but that in fact is quite profound, revealing a deep and fascinating part of human nature. Look at clothing styles,
for instance. In the stores or in fashion shows we can perhaps detect some trends
and changes from a few months before, but they are usually subtle. Go back to
styles ten years ago and, compared with the present, the differences are quite
apparent. Go back twenty years and it is even clearer. With such a distance in
time, we can even notice a particular style of twenty years ago that now probably looks a bit amusing and passé.

These changes in fashion styles that are so detectable in increments of decades can be characterized as creating something looser and more romantic
than the previous style, or more overtly sexual and body conscious, or more
classic and elegant, or gaudier and with more frills. We could name several
other categories of changes in style, but in the end they are limited in number,
and they seem to come in waves or patterns that are detectable over the course
of several decades or centuries. For example, the interest in sparser and more
classic clothing will recur at various intervals of time, not at precisely the same
intervals, but with a degree of regularity.

This phenomenon raises some interesting questions: Do these shifts relate to
something more than just the desire for what is new and different? Do they
reflect deeper changes in people's psychology and moods? And how do these
changes occur, so that over enough time we can detect them? Do they come
from a top-down dynamic in which certain individuals and tastemakers initiate

a change, which is then slowly picked up by the masses and spread virally? Or are these tastemakers themselves responding to signs of change from within the society as a whole, from that social force described in chapter 14, giving it a bottom-up dynamic?

We can ask these questions about styles in music or any other cultural form. But we can also ask them about changing styles in thinking and theorizing, in how arguments in books are constructed. Fifty years ago, many arguments were rooted in psychoanalysis and sociology, writers often seeing the environment as the primary influence on human behavior. The style was loose, literary, and given to much speculation.

Now arguments tend to revolve around genetics and the human brain, with everything having to be backed up by studies and statistics. The mere appearance of numbers on a page can lend a certain air of credibility to the argument. Speculation is frowned upon. Sentences are shorter, designed to communicate information. But this change in theorizing style is not anything new. We can notice a similar back-and-forth—from the literary and speculative to the sober and data driven—beginning in the eighteenth century and up to the present.

What is fascinating in these shifts in style is the limited range of changes, their recurrence, and the increasing speed we now see in the shifts, as if we are witnessing a quickening in human restlessness and nervous energy. And if we examine this phenomenon closely enough, we can see quite clearly that these seemingly superficial changes do in fact reflect deeper alterations in people's mood and values, emerging from the bottom up. Something as simple as a desire for looser styles of clothing, as happened in the 1780s, reflects an overall psychological shift. Nothing is innocent in this realm. An interest in brighter colors, or a harder sound in music, have something else to say about what is stirring in the collective minds of the people of that time.

And in examining this phenomenon even more deeply, we can also make the following discovery: what drives these changes is the continual succession of new generations of young people, who are trying to create something more relevant to their experience of the world, something that reflects more their values and spirit and that goes in a different direction from that of the previous generation. (We can generally describe a generation as comprising around twenty-two years, with those born at the earliest and latest parts of that period often identifying more with the previous or succeeding generation.)

And this pattern of change from one generation to the next is itself part of a larger pattern in history, going back thousands of years, in which particular reactions and shifts in values recur rather regularly, all of which suggests something about human nature that transcends us as individuals, that has programmed us to repeat these patterns for some reason.

Many of us intuit the truth about generations—how they tend to have a kind of personality and how the younger generation initiates so many changes. Some of us are in denial about the phenomenon because we like to imagine that we as individuals shape what we think and believe, or that other forces such as class, gender, and race play a greater role. Certainly the study of generations can be imprecise; it is a subtle and elusive subject. And other factors play a role as well. But looking in depth at the phenomenon reveals that in fact it is more of an influence than we generally imagine, and is in many ways the great generator of so much that happens in history.

And understanding this generational phenomenon can yield several other benefits: We can see what forces shaped our parents' mind-set, and then ours in turn, as we have tried to go in a different direction. We can make better sense of the underlying changes going on in all areas of society and begin to surmise where the world is headed, to anticipate future trends, and to understand the role we can play in shaping events. This can not only bring us great social power but can also have a therapeutic, calming effect on us as we view events in the world with some distance and equanimity, elevated above the chaotic changes of the moment.

We shall call this knowledge *generational awareness*. To attain it, first we must understand the actual profound effect that our generation has on how we view the world, and second we must understand the larger generational patterns that shape history and recognize where our time period fits into the overall scheme.

The Generational Phenomenon

In our first years of life we are sponges, absorbing deeply the energy, style, and ideas of our parents and teachers. We learn language, certain essential values, ways of thinking, and how to function among people. We are slowly inculcated with the culture of the time. Our minds are supremely open at this moment, and because of this our experiences are more intense and bound with strong emotions. As we become a few years older, we become aware of our peers, those more or less of the same age, going through the same process of assimilating this strange new world we were cast into at birth.

Although we are encountering the same reality as everyone else alive at the time, we are doing so from a peculiar angle—that of being a child, physically smaller, more helpless, and dependent on adults. From this point of view, the world of the adults can seem rather alien, as we do not understand so well what motivates them, or their adult cares or concerns. What our parents might take as serious we can often see as comical or odd. We may watch the same forms of entertainment as they do, but we see them from the angle of a child, with little life experience. We don't have the power yet to affect this world, but we start to interpret it in our own way, and we share this with our peers.

Then, when we reach our teen years or perhaps earlier, we become aware that we are part of a generation of young people (focusing more on those around our age) with whom we can identify. We bond over our particular way of seeing things and the similar sense of humor we have developed; we also tend to form common ideals about success and coolness, among other values. In these years, we inevitably go through a period of rebellion, struggling to find our own identity, separate from our parents. This makes us deeply attuned to appearances—to styles and fashions. We want to show that we belong to our generational tribe, with its own look and manner.

Often a decisive event or trend will occur during these youthful years—this could be a major war, a political scandal, a financial crisis or economic boom. It could also be the invention of some new form of technology that has a profound impact on social relations. Because we are so young and impressionable, such events have a decisive influence on the generational personality that is forming, making us cautious (if it is a war or crash in the economy) or hungry for adventure (if it is something that sparks prosperity or stability). Naturally, we view such decisive events very differently from our parents and are affected more deeply.

As we become more aware of what is going on in the world, we often come to see the ideas and values of our parents as not fitting very well our own experience of reality. What they have told or taught us does not seem so relevant, and we hunger for ideas that are more related to our youthful experience.

In this first phase of life, we shape a generational perspective. It is a kind of collective mind-set, as we absorb the prevailing culture at the same time as our peers, from the point of view of childhood and youth. And because we are too young to understand or analyze this perspective, we are generally ignorant of its formation and how it influences what we see and how we interpret events.

Then, when we reach our twenties and into our thirties, we enter a new phase of life and experience a shift. Now we are in a position to assume some power, to actually alter this world according to our own values and ideals. As we progress in our work, we begin to influence the culture and its politics. We inevitably clash with the older generation that has held power for some time, as they insist on their own way of acting and evaluating events. Many of them often view us as immature, unsophisticated, soft, undisciplined, pampered, unenlightened, and certainly not ready to assume power.

In some periods, the youth culture that is generated is so strong that it comes to dominate the culture at large—in the 1920s and the 1960s, for instance. In other periods, the older generation in positions of leadership is much more dominant, and the influence of the emerging adults in their twenties is less noticeable. In any event, to a greater or lesser degree, a struggle and clash occurs between these two generations and their perspectives.

Then, as we enter our forties and midlife and assume many of the leadership positions in society, we begin to take notice of a younger generation that is fighting for its own power and position. Its members are now judging us and finding our own style and ideas rather irrelevant. We begin to judge them in return, describing them as immature, unsophisticated, soft, et cetera. We might begin to entertain the notion that the world is heading downhill fast, the values we found so important no longer mattering to this youthful set.

When we judge in this way, we are not aware that we are reacting according to a pattern that has existed for at least three thousand years. (There is an inscription on a Babylonian clay tablet that dates from around 1000 BC that reads, "Today's youth is rotten, evil, godless and lazy. It will never be what youth used to be, and it will never be able to preserve our culture." We find similar complaints in all cultures and in all time periods.) We think we are judging the younger generation in an objective manner, but we are merely succumbing to an illusion of perspective. It is also true that we are probably experiencing some hidden envy of their youth and mourning the loss of our own.

When it comes to the changes generated by the tensions between two generations, we can say that the greater part of them will come from the young. They are more restless, in search of their own identity, and more attuned to the group and how they fit in. By the time such a younger generation emerges into their thirties and forties, they will have shaped the world with their changes and given it a look and feel that is distinct from their parents.

When looking at any generation, we naturally see variations within it. We find individuals who are more aggressive than others—they tend to be leaders, the ones who sense the styles and trends of the time and express them first. They have less fear about breaking with the past and defying the older generation. Danton exemplifies this type. We also find a much larger group of followers who are not so aggressive, who find it more exciting to keep up with trends, helping to shape and promote them. And finally, we also find the rebels, those types who defy their own generation and define themselves by going against the grain. This could include the beatniks of the 1950s or those young people in the 1960s who gravitated toward conservative politics.

We can say of these rebel types that they are just as marked by their generation as anyone, but in reverse. And in fact, much of the same spirit of the generation can be detected underneath this reverse version—for instance, those younger people in the 1780s who rallied around the aristocracy and in defense of the monarchy often felt a very *romanticized* love of the old order; the young conservatives of the 1960s were just as preachy, fanatic, and idealistic in their reverse values as the majority. The generational mind-set inevitably dominates everyone from within, no matter how they personally try to react against it. We cannot step outside the historical moment that we are born into.

In considering this mind-set, we must try to think in terms of a collective personality, or what we shall call *spirit*. Our generation has inherited from our parents and the past certain key values and ways of looking at the world that remain unquestioned. But at any moment, people of a new generation are searching for something more alive and relevant, something that expresses what is different, what is altering in the present. This sense of what is moving and evolving in the present, as opposed to what is inherited from the past, is the *collective spirit* itself, its restless and searching nature. It is not something we can easily put into words. It is more a mood, an emotional tone, a way that people relate to one another.

That is why we can often best associate the generational spirit with its dominant musical style, or an artistic trend for a certain type of imagery, or a mood captured in the literature or films of that generation. For instance, nothing better captures the wild spirit and frenetic pace of the 1920s than the jazz of the period and the brassy sound of the saxophone, which was the new rage.

This spirit will tend to alter as our generation passes through the various phases of life. How we collectively relate to the world will not be the same in our fifties as it was in our twenties. Circumstances, historical events, and the aging process will modify this spirit. But, as with any individual, there is something in the generational personality that remains intact and transcends the passing years.

The famous lost generation of the 1920s, with its flappers and wild jazz, had certain noticeable obsessions and traits during this decade—wild parties, alcohol, sex, money, and success, as well as a hard-boiled, cynical attitude toward life. As it aged, its members tended to drop the pursuit of some of these pleasures and manias, but in their later years, they remained rather tough, cynical, materialistic, and brazen in expressing their opinions. The baby boomers who came of age in the 1960s displayed an intense idealism and a propensity to judge and moralize. They tend to retain such qualities, but their ideals and what they moralize about have shifted.

If our generation has a particular spirit to it, we could say the same for the time period that we are living through, which generally comprises four generations alive at the same time. The blending of these generations, the tension among them, and the clashing that often occurs create what we shall call the overall spirit of the times or what is commonly known as the zeitgeist. For instance, when it comes to the 1960s, we cannot separate the mood of the powerful youth culture of that period from the antagonism and dismay it stirred among those who were older. The dynamic and spirit of those times came from the dramatic interaction of two clashing perspectives.

To see this in your own experience, look back at periods in the past in which you were alive and conscious, at least some twenty years ago, if you are old enough. With some distance, you can reflect upon how different those times felt, what was in the air, how people interacted, the degree of tension. The spirit of that period is not only in the styles and clothes that are different from those of the present, but also in something social and collective, an overall mood or feeling in the air. Even the differences in fashions and architecture, the colors that became popular, the look of the cars speaks of a spirit behind them that is animating these changes and choices.

That spirit can be characterized as wild and open, with people hungry for all kinds of social interaction; or it can be rather tight and cautious, with people prone to conforming and being hypercorrect; it can be cynical or hopeful, stale or creative. What you want to do is to be able to gauge the spirit of the present moment, with a similar sense of distance, and to see where your generation fits into the overall scheme of history, giving you a sense of where things might be headed.

Generational Patterns

Since the beginning of recorded time, certain writers and thinkers have intuited a pattern to human history. It was perhaps the great fourteenth-century Islamic scholar Ibn Khaldun who first formulated this idea into the theory that history seems to move in four acts, corresponding to four generations.

The first generation is that of the revolutionaries who make a radical break with the past, establishing new values but also creating some chaos in the struggle to do so. Often in this generation there are some great leaders or prophets who influence the direction of the revolution and leave their stamp on it. Then along comes a second generation that craves some order. They are still feeling the heat of the revolution itself, having lived through it at a very early age, but they want to stabilize the world, establish some conventions and dogma.

Those of the third generation—having little direct connection to the founders of the revolution—feel less passionate about it. They are pragmatists. They want to solve problems and make life as comfortable as possible. They are not so interested in ideas but rather in building things. In the process, they tend to drain out the spirit of the original revolution. Material concerns predominate, and people can become quite individualistic.

Along comes the fourth generation, which feels that society has lost its vitality, but they are not sure what should replace it. They begin to question the values they have inherited, some becoming quite cynical. Nobody knows what to believe in anymore. A crisis of sorts emerges. Then comes the revolutionary generation, which, unified around some new belief, finally tears down the old order, and the cycle continues. This revolution can be extreme and violent, or it can be less intense, with simply the emergence of new and different values.

Although this pattern certainly has variations and is not a science, we tend to see a lot of the overall sequencing in history. Most notable of all is the emergence of the fourth generation and the crisis in values that comes with it. This period is often the most painful to live through—we humans feel a deep need to believe in something, and when we begin to doubt and question the old order and sense a vacuum in our values, we can go a little mad. We tend to latch onto the latest belief systems peddled by the charlatans and demagogues who thrive in such periods. We look for scapegoats for all the problems that now arise and the spreading dissatisfaction. Without a unifying belief to anchor and calm us, we become tribal, relying on some small affinity group to give us a feeling of belonging.

Often, in a crisis period, we will notice the forming of a subgroup among those who feel particularly anxious and resentful at the breakdown of order. They are often people who felt somewhat privileged in the past, and the chaos and coming change threatens what they have taken for granted. They want to hold on to the past, return to some golden age they can vaguely remember, and prevent any coming revolution. They are doomed, because the cycle cannot be stopped, and the past cannot be magically brought back to life. But as this crisis period fades and begins to merge into the revolutionary period, we often detect rising levels of excitement, as those who are young and particularly hungry for something new can sense the changes coming that they have set up in their own way.

It seems that we are living through such a crisis period, with a generation that is experiencing it in its key phase in life. Although we cannot see how close we might be to the end of this period, such times never last too long, because the human spirit will not tolerate them. Some unifying belief system is in gestation, and some new values are being generated that we cannot yet see.

At the core of this pattern is a continual back-and-forth rhythm that comes from emerging generations reacting against the imbalances and mistakes of the previous generation. If we go back four generations in our own time we can clearly see this. We start with the silent generation. As children experiencing the Great Depression and as adults coming of age during World War II and the postwar period, they became rather cautious and conservative, valuing stability, material comforts, and fitting tightly into the group. The next generation, the baby boomers, found the conformity of their parents rather stifling. Emerging in the 1960s, and not haunted by the harsh financial realities of their parents, this generation valued personal expression, having adventures, and being idealistic.

This was followed by Generation X, which was marked by the chaos of the 1960s and the ensuing social and political scandals. Coming of age in the 1980s and 1990s, it was pragmatic and confrontational, valuing individualism and self-reliance. This generation reacted against the hypocrisies and impracticalities in their parents' idealism. This was followed by the millennial generation. Traumatized by terrorism and a financial crisis, they reacted against the individualism of the last generation, craving security and teamwork, with a noted dislike of conflict and confrontation.

We can deduce two important lessons from this: First, our values will often depend upon where we fall in this pattern and how our generation reacts against the particular imbalances of the previous generation. We would simply not be the same person we are now, with the same attitude and ideals, if we had emerged during the 1920s or the 1950s instead of later periods. We are not aware of this critical influence because it is too close to us to observe. Certainly we bring our own individual spirit into play in this drama, and to the degree that we can cultivate our uniqueness, we will gain power and the ability to direct the zeitgeist. But it is critical that we recognize first the dominant role that our generation plays in our formation, and where this generation falls in the pattern.

Second, we notice that generations seem capable only of reacting and moving in an opposing direction to the previous generation. Perhaps this is because a generational perspective is formed in youth, when we are more insecure and prone to thinking in black-and-white terms. A middle way, a balanced form of choosing what might be good or bad in the values and trends of the previous generation, seems contrary to our collective nature.

On the other hand, this back-and-forth pattern has a salutary effect. If one generation simply carried forward the tendencies of the previous one, we would probably have destroyed ourselves long ago. Imagine generations that succeeded the wildness of the 1920s or the 1960s by continuing with this spirit, and going further with it; or a generation that succeeded the 1950s by remaining equally conservative and conformist. We would suffocate ourselves with too much self-expression or stagnation. The pattern may lead to imbalances, but it also ensures that we revitalize ourselves.

Sometimes the changes that are generated in a revolutionary period are rather trivial and do not last past the cycle. But sometimes, from a strong crisis, a revolution forges something new that lasts for centuries and represents progress toward values that are more rational and empathetic. In seeing this historical pattern, we must recognize what seems to be an overall human spirit that transcends any particular time and that keeps us evolving. If for any reason the cycle stopped, we would be doomed.

YOUR TASK AS A STUDENT OF HUMAN NATURE IS THREEFOLD: FIRST AND FOREMOST, you must alter your attitude toward your own generation. We like to imagine that we are autonomous and that our values and ideas come from within, not without, but this is in fact not the case. Your goal is to understand as deeply as possible how profoundly the spirit of your generation, and the times that you live in, have influenced how you perceive the world.

We are usually hypersensitive when it comes to our own generation. The perspective was formed in our childhood, when we were most vulnerable, and our emotional bond to our peers was established early on. We often hear an older or younger generation criticizing us, and we naturally become defensive. When it comes to the flaws or imbalances in our generation, our tendency is to see them as virtues. For instance, if we grew up in a generation that was more fearful and cautious, we might shy away from major responsibilities, such as owning a house or a car. We will interpret this as a desire for freedom or a desire to help the environment, unwilling to confront the fears that are really underneath it all.

We cannot understand our generation in the same way that we understand a scientific fact, such as the characteristics of an organism. It is something alive within us, and our understanding of it is tainted by our own emotions and biases. What you must do is to try to attack the problem free from judgments and moralizing, and to become as objective as humanly possible. The personality of your generation is neither positive nor negative; it is simply an outgrowth of the organic process described above.

Consider yourself a kind of archaeologist digging into your own past and that of your generation, looking for artifacts, for observations that you can piece together to form a picture of the underlying spirit. When you examine your memories, try to do so with some distance, even when you recall the emotions you felt at the time. Catch yourself in the inevitable process of making judgments of good and bad about your generation or the next one, and let go of them. You can develop such a skill through practice. Forging such an attitude will play a key role in your development. With some distance and awareness, you can become much more than a follower of or a rebel against your generation; you can mold your own relationship to the zeitgeist and become a formidable trendsetter.

Your second task is to create a kind of personality profile of your generation, so that you can understand its spirit in the present and exploit it. Keep in mind that there are always nuances and exceptions. What you are looking for is common traits that signal an overall spirit.

You can begin this by looking at the decisive events that occurred in the years before you entered the work world and that played a large role in shaping this personality. If this period comprises more or less twenty-two years, there is often more than just one decisive event for that period. For instance, for those who came of age during the 1930s, there was the Depression and then the advent of World War II. For the baby boomers, there was the Vietnam War, and later Watergate and the political scandals of the early 1970s.

Generation X were children during the sexual revolution and adolescents in the era of latchkey kids. For millennials there was 9/11 and then the financial meltdown of 2008. Depending on where you fall, both will influence you, but one more than the other, as it occurs closer to those formative years between ten and eighteen, when you were gaining awareness of the wider world and developing core values.

Some times, such as the 1950s, can be periods of relative stability bordering on stagnation. This will have a powerful effect as well, considering the restlessness of the human mind, particularly among the young, who will come to yearn for adventure and to stir things up. You must also factor into this equation any major technological advances or inventions that alter how people interact.

Try to map out the ramifications of these decisive events. Pay particular attention to the effect they may have had on the pattern of socialization that will characterize your generation. If the event was a major crisis of some sort, that will tend to make those of your generation band together for comfort and security, valuing the team and feelings of love, and allergic to confrontation. A period of stability and nonevents will make you gravitate toward others for adventure, for group experimentation, sometimes bordering on the reckless. In general, you will tend to notice a socializing style of your peers, most evident in your twenties. Search for the roots of this.

These larger events will have an effect on how you view success and money and whether you value status and wealth or less material values such as creativity and personal expression. How those of your generation view failure in a venture or career will be quite telling—is it a badge of shame or considered part of the entrepreneurial process, even a positive experience? You can gauge this as well by those years when you entered the work world—did you feel the pressure to start making money right away, or was it a time to explore the world and have adventures, then settle on something in your thirties?

In filling out this profile, look at the parenting styles of those who raised you—permissive, overcontrolling, neglectful, or empathetic. The famously permissive style of those who raised children in the 1890s helped create the wild, carefree attitude of the lost generation of the 1920s. Those parents who were deeply affected by the 1960s often ended up being quite self-absorbed and somewhat neglectful toward their children, who could not help but feel a bit alienated and even angry because of this. Parents who are overprotective will shape a generation that fears going outside its comfort zones. These parenting styles come in waves. The children who were overprotected do not generally become helicopter parents. Your own parents might have been an exception to the prevailing style, but you will notice a personality stamp on your peers that will become very evident in the teen years and early twenties.

Pay close attention to the heroes and icons of a generation, those who act out the qualities that others secretly wish they had as well. They are often the types who gain celebrity in youth culture—the rebels, the successful entrepreneurs, the gurus, the activists. These indicate emerging new values. Similarly, look at the trends and fads that suddenly sweep through your generation, for instance the sudden popularity of digital currencies. Do not take these trends at face value, but look for the underlying spirit, the unconscious attraction toward certain values or ideals that they reveal. Nothing is too trivial for this analysis.

Like an individual, any generation will tend to have an unconscious, shadow side to its personality. A good sign of this can be found in the particular style of humor that each generation tends to forge. In humor people release their frustrations and express their inhibitions. Such humor could tend toward the irrational, or something edgier and even aggressive. A generation might seem rather prudish and correct, but its humor is raunchy and irreverent. This is the shadow side leaking out.

As part of this, you will want to look at the relationship of the genders in your generation. In the 1920s and 1930s, men and women were trying to bridge their differences, to socialize in mixed groups as much as possible. The male icons were often quite feminine, such as Rudolph Valentino; and the female icons had a pronounced masculine or androgynous edge, such as Marlene Dietrich and Josephine Baker. Contrast this with the 1950s and the sudden and rather strong split between the genders, revealing an unconscious discomfort with and split from the cross-gender tendencies we all feel (see chapter 12).

In looking at this shadow side of your generation, keep in mind that its tendency toward one extreme—materialism, spirituality, adventure, safety—conceals a hidden attraction to the opposite. A generation like the one that came of age in the 1960s seemed disinterested in material things. Its main values were spiritual and inward, being spontaneous and what was thought of as authentic, all of this in reaction to their materialistic parents. But underneath this spirit, we could detect a secret attraction to the material side of life, in the desire to always have the best of something—the latest sound systems, the highest-quality drugs, the hippest clothes. This attraction was revealed in all its truth during the yuppie years of the late 1970s and early 1980s.

With all of this accumulated knowledge you can begin to form an overall profile of your generation, one that is as complex and organic as the phenomenon itself.

Your third task, then, is to expand this knowledge to something broader, first trying to piece together what could be considered the zeitgeist. In this sense, you are looking particularly at the relationship between the two dominant generations, early adults (ages twenty-two to forty-four) and those in midlife (forty-five to sixty-six). No matter how close the parents and children of these generations might seem, there is always an underlying tension, along with some resentment and envy. There are natural differences between their values and how they look at the world. You want to examine this tension and determine which generation tends to dominate and how this power dynamic might be shifting in the present. You will also want to see which part of the larger historical pattern your generation might fit into.

This overall awareness will yield several important benefits. For instance, your generational perspective tends to create a particular kind of myopia. Each generation tends toward some imbalance as it reacts against the previous one. It views and judges everything according to certain values that it holds over others and this closes the mind to other possibilities. We can be both idealistic and pragmatic, value teamwork and our own individual spirit, et cetera. There is much to be gained by looking at the world from the perspective of your parents or your children, and even adopting some of their values. Feeling that your generation is superior is simply an illusion. Your awareness will free you from these mental blocks and illusions, making your mind more fluid and creative. You will be able to shape your own values and ideas and not be such a product of the times.

With your awareness of the overall zeitgeist, you will also understand the historical context. You will have a sense of where the world is headed. You can anticipate what is around the corner. With such knowledge, you can bring your own individual spirit into play and help shape this future that is gestating in the present.

And feeling deeply connected to the unbroken chain of history, and your role in this grand historical drama, will infuse you with a calmness that will make everything in life more bearable. You do not overreact at the outrage of the day. You do not go gaga over the latest trend. You are aware of the pattern that will tend to swing things in a different direction within a period of time. If you feel out of harmony with the times, you know that the bad days will end and you can play your part in making the next wave happen.

Keep in mind that this knowledge is more critical to posses now than ever, for two reasons. First, despite any antiglobal sentiments sweeping the world, technology and social media have unified us in inalterable ways. This means that people of one generation will often have more in common with those of the same generation in other cultures than with older generations in their own country. This unprecedented state of affairs means that the zeitgeist is more directly globalized than ever before, making knowledge of it that much more essential and powerful.

And second, because of these sharp changes initiated by technological innovations, the pace has quickened, creating a self-fulfilling dynamic. Young people feel almost addicted to this pace and crave more shifts, even if of a trivial nature. With the quickening pace there are more crises, which only speeds up the process. This pace will tend to make you get dizzy and lose your perspective. You might imagine some trivial shift as groundbreaking and will thus ignore the real groundbreaking change under way. You will not be able to keep up, let alone anticipate what might come next. Only your generational awareness, your calm historical perspective, will allow you to master such times.

Strategies for Exploiting the Spirit of the Times

To make the most of the zeitgeist, you must begin with a simple premise: you are a product of the times as much as anyone; the generation you were born into has shaped your thoughts and values, whether you are aware of this or not. And so, if you feel from deep within some frustration with the way things are in the world or with the older generation, or if you sense there is something that is missing in the culture, you can be almost certain that other people of your generation are feeling the same way. And if you are the one to act on this feeling, your work will resonate with your generation and help shape the zeitgeist. With this in mind, you must put into practice some or all of the following strategies.

Push against the past. You may feel a deep need to create something new and more relevant to your generation, but the past will almost always exercise a strong pull on you, in the form of the values of your parents that you internalized at a young age. Inevitably you are a bit fearful and conflicted. And because of this, you might hesitate to go full throttle with whatever you do or express, and your defiance of the past ways of doing things will tend to be rather tepid.

Instead you must force yourself in the opposite direction. Use the past and its values or ideas as something to push against with great force, using any anger you might feel to help in this. Make your break with the past as sharp and clear as possible. Express what is taboo; shatter the conventions that the older generation adheres to. All of this will excite and attract the attention of people of your generation, many of whom will want to follow your lead.

It was by being so audacious and defiant of the older generation that the Earl of Essex epitomized the new, confident spirit of post-armada England and became the darling of his generation (see chapter 15 for more on this). Danton gained power by how far he went in defying the monarchy and fomenting for the republic. In the 1920s, the African American dancer Josephine Baker came to exemplify the new spirit of spontaneity among the lost generation by making her performances as unfettered and shocking as possible. By breaking so deeply with the past images of previous first ladies and their usual demure manner, Jacqueline Kennedy became the icon for the new spirit of the early 1960s. In going further in this direction, you create a shock of the new and spark desires among others that are waiting to come out.

Adapt the past to the present spirit. Once you identify the essence of the zeitgeist, it is often a wise strategy to find some analogous moment or period in history. The frustrations and rebellions of your generation were certainly felt to some degree by some previous generation and were expressed in dramatic fashion. The leaders of such past generations resonate through history and take on a kind of mythic hue the more time passes. By associating yourself with those figures or times, you can give added weight to whatever movement or innovation you are promoting. You take some of the emotionally loaded symbols and styles of that historical period and adapt them, giving the impression that what you are attempting in the present is a more perfect and progressive version of what happened in the past.

In doing this, think in grand, mythic terms. Danton associated himself with Cicero, whose speeches and actions in favor of the Roman Republic and against tyranny naturally resonated with many French people and gave Danton's mission the added weight of the ancient past. The filmmaker Akira Kurosawa brought back to life the world of the samurai warrior, so celebrated in

Japanese culture, but re-created it in such a way as to make judicious comments on the issues and moods of postwar Japan. When running for president, John F. Kennedy wanted to herald a new American spirit that was moving past the staleness of the 1950s. He called the programs he would initiate the New Frontier, associating his ideas with the pioneer spirit so reverentially ingrained in the American psyche. Such imagery became a powerful part of his appeal.

Resurrect the spirit of childhood. By bringing to life the spirit of your early years—its humor, its decisive historical events, the styles and products of the period, the feeling in the air as it affected you—you will reach a vast audience of all those who experienced those years in a similar way. It was a time of life of great emotional intensity, and by re-creating it in some form, but reflected through the eyes of an adult, your work will resonate with your peers. You must use this strategy only if you feel a particularly powerful connection to your childhood. Otherwise your attempt to re-create the spirit will seem flat and contrived.

Keep in mind that you are not aiming for a literal re-creation of the past but capturing its spirit. To have real power, it should connect to some issue or problem in the present and not simply be some mindless bit of nostalgia. If you are inventing something, try to update and incorporate the styles of that childhood period in a subtle manner, exploiting the unconscious attraction we all feel to that early period in life.

Create the new social configuration. It is human nature for people to crave more social interaction with those with whom they feel an affinity. You will always gain great power by forging some new way of interacting that appeals to your generation. You organize a group around new ideas or values that are in the air or the latest technology that allows you to bring people together of a like mind in a novel way. You eliminate the middlemen who used to set up barriers that prevented freer associations of people. In this new form of a group, it is always wise to introduce some rituals that bond the members together and some symbols to identify with.

We see many examples of this in the past—the *salons* of seventeenth-century France, where men and women could talk freely and openly; the lodges of the Freemasons in eighteenth-century Europe, with their secret rituals and air of subversion; the speakeasies and jazz clubs of the 1920s, where the mood was "anything goes"; or more recently, online platforms and groups, or flash mobs. In using this strategy, think of the repressive elements of the past that people are yearning to shake free of. This could be a period of stultifying correctness or prudery, or rampant conformity, or the overvaluing of individualism and all the selfishness that breeds. The group you establish will let flourish a new spirit and even offer the thrill of breaking past taboos on correctness.

Subvert the spirit. You might find yourself at odds with some part of the spirit of your generation or the times you live in. Perhaps you identify with some tradition in the past that has been superseded, or your values differ in some way because of your own individual temperament. Whatever the reason, it is never wise to preach or moralize or condemn the spirit of the times. You will only marginalize yourself. If the spirit of the times is like a tide or a stream, better to find a way to gently redirect it, instead of fighting its direction. You will have more power and effect by working within the zeitgeist and subverting it.

For instance, you make something—a book, a film, any product—that has the look and feel of the times, even to an exaggerated degree. However, through the content of what you produce, you insert ideas and a spirit that is somewhat different, that points to the value of the past you prefer or depicts another possible way of relating to events or interpreting them, helping to loosen up the tight generational framework through which people view their world.

After World War II, the great European fashion designers felt a great deal of disdain for the American market that now dominated the world. They disliked the emerging popular culture and its vulgarity. The fashion designer Coco Chanel had always emphasized elegance in her designs and certainly shared some of this antipathy. But she went in the opposite direction of other designers of the time: she embraced the new power of American women and catered to their desire for clothing that was less fussy and more athletic. Gaining their trust and using their language, Chanel now had great power to subtly alter American tastes, bringing in more of her true sensibility and imparting some elegance to the streamlined designs American women loved. In this way she helped redirect the zeitgeist in fashion, anticipating the changes of the early 1960s. That is the power that comes from working with the spirit rather than against it.

Keep adapting. It was in your youth that your generation forged its particular spirit, a period of emotional intensity that we often remember fondly. The problem that you face is that as you get older, you tend to remain locked in the values, ideas, and styles that marked this period. You become a kind of caricature of the past to those who are younger. You stop evolving with your thinking. The times leave you behind, which only makes you hold on more tightly to the past as your only anchor. And as you age, and more and more young people occupy the public stage, you narrow your audience.

It is not that you should abandon the spirit that marked you, a rather impossible task anyway. Trying to ape the styles of the younger generation will only make you seem ludicrous and inauthentic. What you want is to modernize your spirit, to possibly adopt some of the values and ideas of the younger generation that appeal to you, gaining a new and wider audience by blending your experience and perspective with the changes going on, making yourself into an unusual and appealing hybrid.

For the film director Alfred Hitchcock, the decade that shaped him and his work was the 1920s, when he entered the industry and became a director. What mattered most in these silent films was perfecting a visual language for telling a story. Hitchcock mastered the art of using camera angles and movement to make the audience feel as if it were in the middle of the story.

He never abandoned this obsession with visual language throughout the six decades he worked as a director, but he continually adapted his style—to the color spectacles so much in vogue in the 1950s and to the popular thrillers and horror films of the sixties and seventies. Unlike other aging film directors, who either fell completely out of fashion or simply tried to mimic the current style, Hitchcock created a hybrid of the past and the present. This gave his later films tremendous depth, as he had incorporated all of the adaptations from earlier in his career. His films could have mass appeal, but they were made unique by these layers of innovations embedded in the film. Such depth will always have an uncanny effect on any audience, as your work seems beyond time itself.

The Human Beyond Time and Death

We humans are masters of transforming whatever we get our hands on. We have completely transformed the environment of the planet Earth to suit our purposes. We have transformed ourselves from a physically weak species into the preeminent and most powerful social animal, effectively enlarging and re-wiring our brains as we did so. We are restless and endlessly inventive. But one area seems to defy our transformational powers—time itself. We are born and enter the stream of life, and each day it carries us closer to death. Time is linear, always advancing, and there is nothing we can do to stop its course.

We move through the various phases of life, which mark us according to patterns beyond our control. Our bodies and minds slow down and lose their youthful elasticity. We watch helplessly as more and more young people fill the stage of life, pushing us to the side. We are born into a period of history and into a generation that are not of our choice and that seem to determine so much of who we are and what happens to us. In relation to time, our active nature is neutralized, and although we do not consciously register this, our helplessness here is the source of much of our anxiety and bouts of depression.

If we look more closely, however, at our personal experience of time, we can notice something peculiar—the passage of the hours or days can alter depending on our mood and circumstances. A child and an adult experience time very differently—for the former it moves rather slowly, and all too quickly for the latter. When we are bored, time feels empty and grinds to a crawl; when we are excited and enjoying ourselves, we wish it would slow down. When we are calm and meditative, the time might pass slowly, but it seems full and satisfying.

What this means in general is that time is a human creation, a way for us to measure its passage for our own purposes, and our experience of this artificial creation is quite subjective and changeable. We have the power to consciously slow it down or speed it up. Our relationship to time is more malleable than we think. Although we cannot stop the aging process or defy the ultimate reality of death, we can alter the experience of them, transforming what is painful and depressing into something much different. We can make time feel more cyclical than linear; we can even step outside the stream and experience forms of timelessness. We do not have to remain locked in the hold of our generation and its perspective.

Although this might seem like wishful thinking, we can point to various historical figures—Leonardo da Vinci and Johann Wolfgang von Goethe, to name two—who consciously transcended their era and described their transformed experience of time. It is an ideal, one that our active nature allows for, and one well worth aiming to realize to some degree.

Here's how we could apply this active approach to four elemental aspects of time.

The phases of life: As we pass through the phases of life—youth, emerging adult, middle age, and old age—we notice certain common changes in us. In our youth we experience life more intensely. We are more emotional and vulnerable. Most of us tend to be outwardly focused, concerned with what people might think of us and with how we fit in. We are more gregarious but prone to foolish behavior and self-righteousness.

As we get older, the intensity diminishes, our minds tend to tighten up around certain conventional ideas and beliefs. We slowly become less concerned with what people think of us, and thus more inwardly directed. What we sometimes gain in these later phases is some distance from life, some self-control, and perhaps the wisdom that comes from accumulating experiences.

We have the power, however, to drop or mitigate the negative qualities that often go with certain phases of life, in a way defying the aging process itself. For instance, when we are young, we can make a point of lessening the influence of the group on us and not being so fixated on what others are thinking and doing. We can make ourselves more inwardly directed, more in harmony with our uniqueness (see chapter 13 for more on this). We can consciously develop more of that inner distance that comes naturally with the years, think more deeply about our experiences, learn the lessons from them, and develop a premature wisdom.

As we age, we can strive to retain the positive youthful qualities that often fade with the years. For instance, we can regain some of the natural curiosity we had as children by dropping some of the smugness and know-it-all attitude that often come over us as we get older. We keep looking at the world through a fresh framework, questioning our own values and preconceptions, making our minds more fluid and creative in the process. As part of this, we can learn a new skill or study a new field to return us to the joy we once had in learning something new. We can also meditate on some of the more intense experiences in our youth, putting ourselves back in those moments through our imagination, connecting more deeply to who we were. We can feel that youthful intensity return to some degree in our present experiences.

Part of the reason we become less gregarious with the years is that we become judgmental and intolerant of people's quirks, all of which does not enhance our experience of life. We can alter that as well by coming to understand human nature more deeply and accepting people as they are.

Aging has a psychological component and can be a self-fulfilling prophecy—we tell ourselves we are slowing down and cannot do or attempt as much as we did in past, and as we act on these thoughts, we intensify the aging process, which makes us depressed and prone to slow down even more. We can see icons in the past like Benjamin Franklin, who went in the opposite direction, continually challenging his mind and body as he aged, and who by all accounts retained the most delightfully childlike and jovial disposition well into his seventies and eighties.

Present generations: Your goal here is to be *less* a product of the times and to gain the ability to transform your relationship to your generation. A key way of doing this is through active associations with people of different generations. If you are younger, you try to interact more with those of older generations. Some of them, who seem to have a spirit you can identify with, you can try to cultivate as mentors and role models. Others you relate to as you would your peers—not feeling superior or inferior but paying deep attention to their values, ideas, and perspectives, helping to widen your own.

If you are older, you reverse this by actively interacting with those of a younger generation, not as a parent or authority figure but as a peer. You allow yourself to absorb their spirit, their different way of thinking, and their enthusiasm. You approach them with the idea that they have something to teach you.

In interacting on a more authentic level with those of different generations, you are creating a unique bond—that of people alive at the same time in history. This will only enhance your grasp of the zeitgeist.

Past generations: When we think about history, we tend to render the past into a kind of dead and spiritless caricature. Perhaps we feel smug and superior to past eras, and so we focus on those aspects of history that indicate backward ideas and values (not realizing that future generations will do the same to us), seeing what we want to see. Or we project onto the past the ideas and values of the present, which have little relation to how those of the past experienced the world. We drain away their own generational perspective, something we see most obviously in filmed versions of history, where people talk and act just like us, only in costumes. Or we simply ignore history, imagining it has no relevance to our present experience.

We must rid ourselves of such absurd notions and habits. We are not as superior to those in the past as we like to imagine (see previous chapters on irrationality, shortsightedness, envy, grandiosity, conformity, and aggression). There are cultural moments in history that were superior to our own when it comes to participatory democracy, or creative thinking, or cultural liveliness. There are periods in the past in which people had a deeper grasp of human psychology and a bracing realism that would make us look quite deluded by comparison. Although human nature remains a constant, those in the past faced different circumstances with different levels of technology and had values and beliefs quite different from our own, and not necessarily inferior. They had the values that reflected their different circumstances, and we would have shared them as well.

Most important of all, however, we must understand that the past is by no means dead. We do not emerge in life as blank slates, divorced from millions of years of evolution. All that we think and experience, our most intimate thoughts and beliefs, are shaped by the struggles of past generations. So many ways we relate to the world now came from changes in thinking long ago.

Whenever we see people who completely sacrifice everything for some cause, they are reliving a shift in values initiated by the early Christians of the first century, who revolutionized our way of thinking by devoting all aspects of life to some ideal. Whenever we fall in love and idealize the beloved, we are reliving the emotions that the troubadours of the twelfth century introduced into the Western world, a sentiment that had never existed before.

Whenever we extol emotions and spontaneity over the intellect and effort, we are reexperiencing what the Romantic movements of the eighteenth century first introduced into our psychology. We are not aware of all this, but we in the present are motley products of all the accumulated changes in human thinking and psychology. By making the past into something dead, we are merely denying who we are. We become rootless and barbaric, disconnected from our nature.

You must radically alter your own relationship to history, bringing it back to life within you. Begin by taking some era in the past, one that particularly excites you for whatever reason. Try to re-create the spirit of those times, to get inside the subjective experience of the actors you are reading about, using your active imagination. See the world through their eyes. Make use of the excellent books written in the last hundred years to help you gain a feel for daily life in particular periods (for example, *Everyday Life in Ancient Rome* by Lionel Casson or *The Waning of the Middle Ages* by Johan Huizinga). In the literature of the time you can detect the prevailing spirit. The novels of F. Scott Fitzgerald will give you a much livelier connection to the Jazz Age than any scholarly book on the subject. Drop any tendencies to judge or moralize. People were experiencing their present moment within a context that made sense to them. You want to understand that from the inside out.

In this way you will feel differently about yourself. Your concept of time will expand and you will realize that if the past lives on in you, what you are doing today, the world you live in, will live on and affect the future, connecting you to the larger human spirit that moves through us all. You in this moment are a part of that unbroken chain. And this can be an intoxicating experience, a strange intimation of immortality.

The future: We can understand our effect on the future most clearly in our relationship to our children, or to those young people we influence in some way as teachers or mentors. This influence will last years after we are gone. But our work, what we create and contribute to society, can exert even greater power and can become part of a conscious strategy to communicate with those of the future and influence them. Thinking in this way can actually alter what we say or what we do.

Certainly Leonardo da Vinci followed such a strategy. He continually tried to envision what the future might be like, to live in it through his imagination. We can see the evidence of this in his drawings of possible inventions that might exist in the future, some of which, like flying machines, he actually attempted to create. He also thought deeply about the values people might hold in the future that did not yet exist in the times that he lived through. For instance, he felt a deep affinity for animals and saw them as possessing souls, a belief that was virtually unheard of at the time. This impelled him to become a vegetarian and to go around freeing caged birds in the marketplace. He saw all nature as one, including humans, and he imagined a future in which that belief would be shared.

The great feminist, philosopher, and novelist Mary Wollstonecraft (1759–1797) believed that we humans can actually create the future by how we imagine it in the present. For her, in her short life, much of this came in her imagining a future in which the rights of women and, most important, their reasoning powers were given equal weight to men. Her thinking in these terms in fact did have a profound influence on the future.

Perhaps one of the most uncanny examples of this is Johann Wolfgang von Goethe (1749–1832), a scientist, novelist, and philosopher. He aspired to a kind of universal knowledge, similar to Leonardo's, in which he tried to master all forms of human intelligence, steep himself in all periods of history, and through this be able to not only see the future but commune with its inhabitants. He was able to anticipate a theory of evolution decades before Darwin. He foresaw many of the great political trends of the nineteenth and twentieth centuries, including the eventual unification of Europe after World War II. He imagined many of the advances of technology and the effects these would have on our spirit. He was someone who actively attempted to live outside his time, and his prophetic powers were legendary among his friends.

Finally, sometimes we may feel like we are born into the wrong period in history, out of harmony with the times. And yet we are locked into this moment and must live through it. If such is the case, this *strategy of immortality* can bring us some relief. We are aware of the cycles of history and how the pendulum will swing and the times will change, perhaps after we are gone. In this way, we can look to the future and feel some connection to those who are living well beyond this terrible moment. We can reach out to them, make them part of our audience. Some day they will read about us or read our words, and the connection will go in both directions, indicating this supreme human ability to surmount one's time and the finality of death itself.

> A man's shortcomings are taken from his epoch; his virtues and greatness belong to himself.
>
> —*Johann Wolfgang von Goethe*

18

Meditate on Our Common Mortality

◇

The Law of Death Denial

*M*ost of us spend our lives avoiding the thought of death. Instead, the inevitability of death should be continually on our minds. Understanding the shortness of life fills us with a sense of purpose and urgency to realize our goals. Training ourselves to confront and accept this reality makes it easier to manage the inevitable setbacks, separations, and crises in life. It gives us a sense of proportion, of what really matters in this brief existence of ours. Most people continually look for ways to separate themselves from others and feel superior. Instead, we must see the mortality in everyone, how it equalizes and connects us all. By becoming deeply aware of our mortality, we intensify our experience of every aspect of life.

The Bullet in the Side

As a child growing up in Savannah, Georgia, Mary Flannery O'Connor (1925– 1964) felt a strange and powerful connection to her father, Edward. Some of this naturally stemmed from their striking physical resemblance—the same large, piercing eyes, the same facial expressions. But more important to Mary, their whole way of thinking and feeling seemed completely in sync. She could sense this when her father participated in the games she invented—he slipped so naturally into the spirit of it all, and his imagination moved in such a similar direction to her own. They had ways of communicating without ever saying a word.

Mary, an only child, did not feel the same way about her mother, Regina, who came from a socially superior class to her husband and had aspirations of being a figure in local society. The mother wanted to mold her rather book-ish and reclusive daughter into the quintessential southern lady, but Mary, stubborn and willful, would not go along. Mary found her mother and rela-tives a bit formal and superficial. At the age of ten, she wrote a series of cari-catures of them, which she called "My Relitives." In a mischievous spirit, she let her mother and relatives read the vignettes, and they were, naturally, shocked—not only by how they were portrayed but also by the sharp wit of this ten-year-old.

The father, however, found the caricatures delightful. He collected them into a little book that he showed to visitors. He foresaw a great future for his daughter as a writer. Mary knew from early on that she was different from other children, even a bit eccentric, and she basked in the pride he displayed in her unusual qualities.

She understood her father so well that it frightened her when in the summer of 1937 she sensed a change in his energy and spirit. At first it was subtle—rashes on his face, a sudden weariness that came over him in the afternoon. Then he began to take increasingly long naps and suffer frequent bouts of flu, his entire body aching. Occasionally Mary would eavesdrop on her parents as they talked behind closed doors of his ailments, and what she could glean was that something was seriously wrong.

The real estate business her father had started some years earlier was not doing so well, and he had to let it go. A few months later, he was able to land a government job in Atlanta, which did not pay very well. To manage their tight budget Mary and her mother moved into a spacious home owned by relatives in the town of Milledgeville, in the center of Georgia, not too far from Atlanta.

By 1940 the father was too weak to continue at his job. He moved back home, and over the next few months Mary watched as her beloved father grew weaker and thinner by the day, racked by excruciating pain in his joints, until he finally died on February 1, 1941, at the age of forty-five. It was months later that Mary learned that his illness was known as lupus erythematosus—a dis-ease that makes the body create antibodies that attack and weaken its own healthy tissues. (Today it is known as systemic lupus erythematosus, and it is the most severe version of the disease.)

In the aftermath of his death, Mary felt too stunned to speak to anyone about the loss, but she confided in a private notebook the effect his death had on her: "The reality of death has come upon us and a consciousness of the power of God has broken our complacency, like a bullet in the side. A sense of the dramatic, of the tragic, of the infinite, has descended upon us, filling us with grief, but even above grief, wonder."

She felt as if a part of her had died with her father, so enmeshed had they been in each other's lives. But beyond the sudden and violent wound it inflicted on her, she was made to wonder about what it all meant in the larger cosmic scheme of things. Deeply devout in her Catholic faith, she imagined that everything occurred for a reason and was part of God's mysterious plan. Something so significant as her father's early death could not be meaningless.

In the months to come, a change came over Mary. She became unusually serious and devoted to her schoolwork, something she had been rather indifferent to in the past. She began to write longer and more ambitious stories. She attended a local college for women and impressed her professors with her writing skill and the depth of her thinking. She had determined that her father had guessed correctly her destiny—to be a writer.

Increasingly confident in her creative powers, she decided that her success depended on getting out of Georgia. Living with her mother in Milledgeville made her feel claustrophobic. She applied to the University of Iowa and was accepted with a full scholarship for the academic year beginning in 1945. Her mother begged her to reconsider, thinking her only child was too fragile to live on her own, but Mary had made up her mind. Enrolled in the famous Writers' Workshop at the university, she decided to simplify her name to Flannery O'Connor, signaling her new identity.

Working with fierce determination and discipline, Flannery began to attract attention for her short stories and the characters from the South she depicted and seemed to know so well, bringing out the dark and grotesque qualities just below the surface of southern gentility. Agents and publishers came calling, and the most prestigious magazines accepted her stories.

After Iowa, Flannery moved to the East Coast, settling in a country house in Connecticut owned by her friends Sally and Robert Fitzgerald, who rented out a room to her. There, without distractions, she began to work feverishly on her first novel. The future seemed so full of promise, and it was all going according to the plan she had laid out for herself after the death of her father.

At Christmas of 1949 she returned to Milledgeville for a visit, and once there she fell quite ill, the doctors diagnosing her with a floating kidney. It would require surgery and some recovery time at home. All she wanted was to get back to Connecticut, to be with her friends, and to finish her novel, which was becoming increasingly ambitious.

Finally, by March, she was able to return, but over the course of the next few months she experienced strange bouts of pain in her arms. She visited doctors in New York, who diagnosed her with rheumatoid arthritis. That December she was to return to Georgia once again for Christmas, and on the train ride home she fell desperately ill. When she got off the train and was met by her uncle, she could barely walk. She felt as if she had suddenly turned elderly and feeble.

Racked with pain in her joints and suffering high fevers, she was admitted immediately to a hospital. She was told it was a severe case of rheumatoid arthritis, and that it would take months to stabilize her; she would have to remain in Milledgeville for an indefinite period. She had little faith in doctors and was not so sure of their diagnosis, but she was far too weak to argue. The fevers made her feel as if she were dying.

To treat her, the doctors gave her massive doses of cortisone, the new miracle drug, which greatly alleviated the pain and the inflammation in her joints. It also gave her bursts of intense energy that troubled her mind and made it race with all kinds of strange thoughts. As a side effect, it also made her hair fall out and bloated her face. And as part of her therapy, she had to have frequent blood transfusions. Her life had suddenly taken a dark turn.

It seemed to her a rather strange coincidence that when the fevers were at their highest, she had the sensation that she was growing blind and paralyzed. Only months before, when she was not yet ill, she had decided to make the main character in her novel blind himself. Had she foreseen her own fate, or had the disease already been there, making her think such thoughts?

Feeling death at her heels and writing at a fast pace while in the hospital, she finished the novel, which she now called *Wise Blood*, inspired by all of the transfusions she had undergone. The novel concerned a young man, Hazel Motes, determined to spread the gospel of atheism to a new scientific age. He thinks he has "wise blood," with no need for any kind of spiritual guidance. The novel chronicles his descent into murder and madness and was published in 1952.

After months of hospitalization and having sufficiently recovered at home, Flannery returned to Connecticut for a visit with the Fitzgeralds, hoping that in the near future she could perhaps resume her old life at their country home. One day, as she and Sally were taking a drive in the country, Flannery mentioned her rheumatoid arthritis, and Sally decided to finally tell her the truth that her overprotective mother, in league with the doctors, had kept from her. "Flannery, you don't have arthritis, you have lupus." Flannery began to tremble. After a few moments of silence, she replied, "Well, that's not good news. But I can't thank you enough for telling me. . . . I thought I had lupus, and I thought I was going crazy. I'd a lot rather be sick than crazy."

Despite her calm reaction, the news stunned her. This was like a second bullet in her side, the original sensation returning with double the impact. Now she knew for sure that she had inherited the disease from her father. Suddenly she had to confront the reality that perhaps she did not have long to live, considering how quickly her father had gone downhill. It was now clear to her that there would be no plans or hopes for living anywhere else but Milledgeville. She cut short the trip to Connecticut and returned home, feeling depressed and confused.

Her mother was now the manager of her family's farm, called Andalusia, just outside Milledgeville. Flannery would have to spend the rest of her life on this farm with her mother, who would take care of her. The doctors seemed to think she could live a normal length of life thanks to this new miracle drug, but Flannery did not share their confidence, experiencing firsthand the many adverse side effects and wondering how long her body could endure them.

She loved her mother, but they were very different. The mother was the chatty type, obsessed with status and appearances. In her first weeks back, Flannery felt a sense of panic. She had always been willful, like her father. She liked living on her own terms, and her mother could be quite intense and meddlesome. But beyond that, Flannery associated her creative powers with living her own life outside Georgia, encountering the wide world, among peers with whom she could talk about serious matters. She felt her mind expanding with those larger horizons.

Andalusia would feel like a prison, and she worried that her mind would tighten up in these circumstances. But as she contemplated death staring her in the face, she thought deeply about the course of her life. What clearly mattered to her more than friends or where she lived or even her health itself was her writing, expressing all of the ideas and impressions she had accumulated in her short life. She had so many more stories to write, and another novel or two. Perhaps, in some strange way, this forced return home was a blessing in disguise, part of some other plan for her.

In her room at Andalusia, far from the world, she would have no possible distractions. She would make it clear to her mother that those two or more hours of writing in the morning were sacred to her and she would not tolerate any interruptions. Now she could focus all her energy on her work, get even deeper into her characters, and bring them to life. Back in the heart of Georgia, listening closely to visitors and farmhands, she would be able to hear the voices of her characters, their speech patterns, reverberating in her head. She would feel even more deeply connected to the land, to the South, which obsessed her.

As she moved about in these first months back home, she began to feel the presence of her father—in photographs, in objects that he cherished, in notebooks of his that she discovered. His presence haunted her. He had wanted to become a writer; she knew that. Perhaps he had wanted her to succeed where he had failed. Now the fatal disease they shared tied them together even more tightly; she would feel the same form of pain that afflicted his body. But she would write and write, insensitive to the pain, somehow realizing the potential that her father had seen in her as a child.

Thinking in this way, she realized she had no time to waste. How many more years would she live and have the energy and clarity to write? Being so focused on her work would also help rid her of any anxiety about the illness. When she was writing, she could completely forget herself and inhabit her characters. It was a religious-like experience of losing the ego. As she wrote to a friend with the news of her illness, "I can with one eye squinted take it all as a blessing."

There were other blessings to count as well: Knowing early on about her disease, she would have time to get used to the idea of dying young, and it would lessen the blow; she would relish every minute, every experience, and make the most of her limited encounters with outsiders. She could not expect much from life, so everything she got would mean something. No need to complain or feel self-pity—everyone had to die at some point. She would find it easier now to not take so seriously the petty concerns that seemed to roil others so much. She could even look at herself and laugh at her own pretensions as a writer, and mock how ridiculous she looked with her bald head, stumbling around with a cane.

As she returned to writing her stories with a new sense of commitment, Flannery felt another change from within: an increasing awareness of and disgust with the course of life and culture in America in the 1950s. She sensed that people were becoming more and more superficial, obsessed with material things and plagued by boredom, like children. They had become unmoored, soulless, disconnected from the past and from religion, flailing around without any higher sense of purpose. And at the core of these problems was their inability to face their own mortality and the seriousness of it.

She expressed some of this in a story inspired by her own illness, called "The Enduring Chill." The main character is a young man returning home to Georgia, deathly ill. As he gets off the train, his mother, there to meet him, "had given a little cry; she looked aghast. He was pleased that she should see death in his face at once. His mother, at the age of sixty, was going to be introduced to reality and he supposed that if the experience didn't kill her, it would assist her in the process of growing up."

As she saw it, people were losing their humanity and capable of all kinds of cruelties. They did not seem to care very deeply about one another and felt rather superior to any kind of outsider. If they could only see what she had seen—how our time is so short, how everyone must suffer and die—it would alter their way of life; it would make them grow up; it would melt all their coldness. What her readers needed was their own "bullet in the side" to shake them out of their complacency. She would accomplish this by portraying in as raw a manner as possible the selfishness and brutality lurking below the surface in her characters, who seemed so outwardly pleasant and banal.

The one problem Flannery had to confront with her new life was the crushing loneliness of it all. She required the company of people to soothe her, and she depended on the cast of characters she met to supply her endless material for her work. As her fame grew with the publication of *Wise Blood* and her collections of stories, she could count on the occasional visit to the farm from other writers and fans of her work, and she lived for such moments, putting every ounce of her energy into observing her visitors and plumbing their depths.

To fill the gaps between these social encounters, she began a lengthy correspondence with a growing number of friends and fans, writing back to almost anyone who wrote to her. Many of them were quite troubled. There was the young man in the Midwest who felt suicidal and on the verge of madness. There was the brilliant young woman from Georgia, Betty Hester, who felt ashamed for being a lesbian and confided in Flannery, the two of them now regularly corresponding. Flannery never judged any of them, feeling herself to be rather odd and outside the mainstream. To this growing cast of characters and misfits she offered advice and compassion, always entreating them to devote their energies to something outside themselves.

The letters were the perfect medium for Flannery, for it allowed her to keep some physical distance from people; she feared too much intimacy, as it would mean getting attached to those she would soon have to say good-bye to. In this way she slowly built the perfect social world for her purposes.

One spring day in 1953, she received a visit from a tall, handsome twenty-six-year-old man from Denmark named Erik Langkjaier. He was a traveling textbook salesman for a major publisher, his territory including most of the South. He had met a professor at a local college who had offered to introduce him to the great literary figure of Georgia, Flannery O'Connor. From the moment he entered her house, Flannery felt they had some kind of mystical connection. She found Erik very funny and well read. It was indeed rare to meet someone so worldly in this part of Georgia. His life as an itinerant salesman fascinated her; she found it humorous that he carried with him a "Bible," what those in the business called the loose-leaf binder of promotional materials.

Something about his rootless life struck a chord with her. Like Flannery, Erik's father had died when he was young. She opened up to him about her own father and the lupus she had inherited. She found Erik attractive and was suddenly self-conscious about her appearance, constantly making jokes about herself. She gave him a copy of *Wise Blood*, inscribing it, "For Erik, who has wise blood too."

He began to arrange his travels so that he could pass often through Milledgeville and continue their lively discussions. Flannery looked forward to every visit and felt pangs of emptiness when he left. In May of 1954, on one of his visits he told her he was taking a six-month leave from his job to return to Denmark, and he suggested they take a good-bye car ride through the county, their favorite activity. It was dusk, and in the middle of nowhere he parked the car on the side of the road and leaned over to kiss her, which she gladly accepted. It was short, but for her quite memorable.

She wrote to him regularly and, clearly missing him, kept discreetly referencing their car rides and how much they meant to her. In January 1955, she began a story that seemingly poured out of her in a few days. (Normally she was a careful writer who put stories through several drafts.) She called it "Good Country People." One of the characters is a cynical young woman with a wooden leg. She is romanced by a traveling salesman of Bibles. She suddenly lets down her guard and allows him to seduce her, playing her own game with him. As they are about to make love in a hayloft, he begs her to remove her wooden leg, as a sign of her trust. This seems far too intimate and a violation of all her defenses, but she relents. He then runs away with the leg, never to return.

In the back of her mind she was aware that Erik was somehow extending his stay in Europe. The story was her way of coping with this, caricaturing the two of them as the salesman and the cynical crippled daughter who had let down her guard. Erik had taken her wooden leg. By April she felt his absence rather keenly and wrote to him, "I feel like if you were here we could talk about a million things without stopping." But the day after she mailed this she received a letter from him announcing his engagement to a Danish woman, and he told her of their plans to return to the States, where he would take up his old job.

She had intuited such an event would happen, but the news was a shock nonetheless. She replied with utmost politeness, congratulating him, and they wrote to each other for several more years, but she could not get over this loss so easily. She had tried to protect herself from any deep feelings of parting and separation because they were too unbearable for her. They were like small reminders of the death that would take her away at any moment, while others would go on living and loving. And now those very feelings of separation came pouring in.

Now she knew what it was like to experience unrequited love, but for her it was different—she knew that this was the last such chance for her and that her life was to be led essentially alone, and it made it all doubly poignant. She had trained herself to look death square in the eye, so why should she recoil from facing this latest form of suffering? She understood what she had to do— transmute this painful experience into more stories and into her second novel, to use it as means to enrich her knowledge of people and their vulnerabilities.

In the next few years the drugs began to take a toll, as the cortisone softened her hip and jawbone and made her arms often too weak to type. She soon needed crutches to get around. Sunlight had become her nemesis, as it could reactivate the lupus rashes, and so to take walks she had to cover every inch of her body, even in the stifling heat of the summer. The doctors tried to remove her from the cortisone to give her body some relief, and this lowered her energy and made the writing that much harder.

Under all the duress of the past few years, she had managed to publish two novels and several collections of short stories; she was considered one of the great American writers of her time, although still so young. But suddenly she began to feel worn down and inarticulate. She wrote to a friend in the spring of 1962, "I've been writing for sixteen years and I have the sense of having exhausted my original potentiality and being now in need of the kind of grace that deepens perception."

One day shortly before Christmas of 1963, she suddenly fainted and was taken to the hospital. The doctors diagnosed her with anemia and began a series of blood transfusions to revive her. She was too weak now to even sit at her typewriter. Then a few months later they discovered a benign tumor that they needed to remove. Their only fear was that the trauma of the surgery would somehow reactivate the lupus and the powerful episodes of fevers that she had experienced ten years before.

In letters to friends, she made light of it all. Strangely enough, now that she was at her weakest, she found the inspiration to write more stories and prepare a new collection of them for fall publication. In the hospital she studied her nurses closely and found material for some new characters. When the doctors prohibited her from working, she concocted stories in her head and memorized them. She hid notebooks under her pillow. She had to keep writing.

The surgery was a success, but by mid-March it was clear that her lupus had come roaring back. She compared it to a wolf (*lupus* is Latin for "wolf") raging inside her now, tearing things up. Her hospital stay was extended, and yet despite it all, she managed here and there to get in her daily two hours, hiding her work from the nurses and doctors. She was in a hurry to scratch out these last stories before it was all over.

Finally, on June 21, she was allowed to return home, and in the back of her mind she sensed the end was coming, the memory of her father's last days so vivid within her. Pain or no pain, she had to work, to finish the stories and revisions she had started. If she could manage only an hour a day, so be it. She had to squeeze out every last bit of consciousness that remained to her and make use of it. She had realized her destiny as a writer and had led a life of incomparable richness. She had nothing now to complain about or regret, except the unfinished stories.

On July 31, while watching the summer rain by her window, she suddenly lost consciousness and was rushed to the hospital. She died in the early hours of August 3, at the age of thirty-nine. In accordance with her last wishes, Flannery was buried next to her father.

Interpretation: In the years after the onset of lupus, Flannery O'Connor noticed a peculiar phenomenon: In her interactions with friends, visitors, and correspondents, she often found herself playing the role of the adviser, giving people guidance on how to live, where to put their energies, how to remain calm amid difficulties and have a sense of purpose. All the while, she was the one who was dying and dealing with severe physical restrictions.

She sensed that increasing numbers of people in this world had lost their way. They could not wholeheartedly commit themselves to their work or to relationships. They were always dabbling in this or that, searching for new pleasures and distractions but feeling rather empty inside. They tended to fall apart in the face of adversity or loneliness, and they turned to her as someone solid who would be able to tell them the truth about themselves and give them some direction.

As she saw it, the difference between her and these other people was simple: She had spent year after year looking death squarely in the eye without flinching. She did not indulge in vague hopes for the future, put her trust in medicine, or drown her sorrows in alcohol or addiction. She accepted the early death sentence imposed on her, using it for her own ends.

For Flannery, her proximity to death was a call to stir herself to action, to feel a sense of urgency, to deepen her religious faith and spark her sense of wonder at all mysteries and uncertainties of life. She used the closeness of death to teach her what really matters and to help her steer clear of the petty squabbles and concerns that plagued others. She used it to anchor herself in the present, to make her appreciate every moment and every encounter.

Knowing that that her illness had a purpose to it, there was no need to feel self-pity. And by confronting and dealing with it straight on, she could toughen herself up, manage the pain that racked her body, and keep writing. By the time she had received yet another bullet, the separation with Erik, she could regain her balance after several months, without turning bitter or more reclusive.

What this meant was that she was thoroughly at home with the ultimate reality represented by death. In contrast, so many other people, including those she knew, suffered from a reality deficit, avoiding the thought of their mortality and the other unpleasant aspects of life.

Focusing so deeply on her mortality had one other important advantage— it deepened her empathy and sense of connection to people. She had a peculiar relationship to death in general: It did not represent a fate reserved for her alone but rather was intimately tied to her father. Their sufferings and deaths were intertwined. She saw her own nearness to death as a call to take this further, to see that all of us are connected through our common mortality and made equal by it. It is the fate we all share and should draw us closer for that reason. It should shake us out of any sense of feeling superior or separated.

Flannery's increased empathy and feeling of unity with others, as evidenced by her strong desire to communicate with all types of people, caused her to eventually let go of one of her greatest limitations: the racist sentiments toward African Americans she had internalized from her mother and many others in the South. She saw this clearly in herself and struggled against it, particularly in her work. By the early 1960s she came to embrace the civil rights movement led by Martin Luther King Jr. And in her later stories she began to express a vision of all the races in America converging one day as equals, moving past this dark stain on our country's past.

For over thirteen years, Flannery O'Connor stared down the barrel of the gun pointed at her, refusing to look away. Certainly her religious faith helped her maintain her spirit, but as Flannery herself knew, so many people who are religious are just as full of illusions and evasions when it comes to their own mortality, and just as capable of complacency and pettiness as anyone else. It was her particular choice to use her fatal disease as the means for living the most intense and fulfilling life possible.

Understand: We tend to read stories like Flannery O'Connor's with some distance. We can't help but feel some relief that we find ourselves in a much more comfortable position. But we make a grave mistake in doing so. Her fate is our fate—we are all in the process of dying, all facing the same uncertainties. In fact, by having her mortality so present and palpable, she had an advantage over us— she was compelled to confront death and make use of her awareness of it.

We, on the other hand, are able to dance around the thought, to envision endless vistas of time ahead of us and dabble our way through life. And then, when reality hits us, when we perhaps receive our own bullet in the side in the form of an unexpected crisis in our career, or a painful breakup in a relationship, or the death of someone close, or even our own life-threatening illness—we are not usually prepared to handle it.

Our avoidance of the thought of death has established our pattern for handling other unpleasant realities and adversity. We easily become hysterical and lose our balance, blaming others for our fate, feeling angry and sorry for ourselves, or we opt for distractions and quick ways to dull the pain. This becomes a habit we cannot shake, and we tend to feel the generalized anxiety and emptiness that come from all this avoidance.

Before this becomes a lifelong pattern, we must shake ourselves out of this dreamlike state in a real and lasting way. We must come to look at our own mortality without flinching, and without fooling ourselves with some fleeting, abstract meditation on death. We must focus hard on the uncertainty that death represents—it could come tomorrow, as could other adversity or separation. We must stop postponing our awareness. We need to stop feeling superior and special, seeing that death is a fate shared by us all and something that should bind us in a deeply empathetic way. We are all a part of the brotherhood and sisterhood of death.

In doing so, we set a much different course for our lives. Making death a familiar presence, we understand how short life is and what really should matter to us. We feel a sense of urgency and deeper commitment to our work and relationships. When we face a crisis, separation, or illness, we do not feel so terrified and overwhelmed. We don't feel the need to go into avoidance mode. We can accept that life involves pain and suffering, and we use such moments to strengthen ourselves and to learn. And as with Flannery, the awareness of our mortality cleanses us of silly illusions and intensifies every aspect of our experience.

When I look back at the past and think of all the time I squandered in error and idleness, lacking the knowledge needed to live, when I think of how often I sinned against my heart and my soul, then my heart bleeds. Life is a gift, life is happiness, every minute could have been an eternity of happiness! If youth only knew! Now my life will change; now I will be reborn. Dear brother, I swear that I shall not lose hope. I will keep my soul pure and my heart open. I will be reborn for the better.

—Fyodor Dostoyevsky

Keys to Human Nature

If we could step back and somehow examine the train of our daily thoughts, we would realize how they tend to circle around the same anxieties, fantasies, and resentments, like a continuous loop. Even when we take a walk or have a conversation with someone, we generally remain connected to this interior monologue, only half listening and paying attention to what we see or hear.

Upon occasion, however, certain events can trigger a different quality of thinking and feeling. Let us say we go on a trip to a foreign land we have never visited before, outside our usual comfort zone. Suddenly our senses snap to life and everything we see and hear seems a little more vibrant. To avoid problems or dangerous situations in this unfamiliar place, we have to pay attention.

Similarly, if we are about to leave on a trip and must say good-bye to people we love, whom we may not see for a while, we might suddenly view them in a different light. Normally we take such people for granted, but now we actually look at the particular expressions on their faces and listen to what they have to say. The sense of a looming separation makes us more emotional and attentive.

A more intense version of this will occur if a loved one—a parent or a partner or a sibling—dies. This person played a large role in our lives; we have internalized them, and we have somehow lost a part of ourselves. As we grapple with this, the shadow of our own mortality falls over us for an instant. We are made aware of the permanence of this loss and feel regret that we did not appreciate them more. We may even feel some anger that life simply goes on for other people, that they are oblivious to the reality of death that has suddenly struck us.

For several days or perhaps weeks after this loss, we tend to experience life differently. Our emotions are rawer and more sensitive. Particular stimuli will bring back associations with the person who has died. This intensity of emotion will fade, but each time we are reminded of the person we have lost, a small portion of that intensity will return.

If we consider death as the crossing of a threshold that terrifies us in general, the experiences enumerated above are intimations of our own death in smaller doses. Separating from people we know, traveling in a strange land, clearly entering some new phase of life, all involve changes that cause us to look back at the past as if a part of us has died. In such moments, and during the more intense forms of grief from actual deaths, we notice a heightening of the senses and a deepening of our emotions. Thoughts of a different order come to us. We are more attentive. We can say that our experience of life is qualitatively different and charged, as if we temporarily became someone else. Of course, this alteration in our thinking, feeling, and senses will be strongest if we ourselves survive a brush with death. Nothing seems the same after such an experience.

Let us call this the *paradoxical death effect*—these moments and encounters have the paradoxical result of making us feel more awake and alive. We can explain the paradoxical effect in the following way.

For us humans, death is a source not only of fear but also of awkwardness. We are the only animal truly conscious of our impending mortality. In general, we owe our power as a species to our ability to think and reflect. But in this particular case, our thinking brings us nothing but misery. All we can see is the physical pain involved in dying, the separation from loved ones, and the uncertainty as to when such a moment might arrive. We do what we can to avoid the thought, to distract ourselves from the reality, but the awareness of death lies in the back of our minds and can never be completely shaken.

Feeling the unconscious impulse to somehow soften the blow of our awareness, our earliest ancestors created a world of spirits, gods, and some concept of the afterlife. The belief in the afterlife helped mitigate the fear of death and even give it some appealing aspects. It could not eliminate the anxiety of separating from loved ones or lessen the physical pain involved, but it offered a profound psychological compensation for the anxieties we seemingly cannot shake. This effect was fortified by all of the elaborate and pleasing rituals that surrounded the passage to death.

In the world today, our growing reasoning powers and knowledge of science have only made our awkwardness worse. Many of us can no longer believe in the concept of the afterlife with any conviction, but we are left with no compensations, with only the stark reality confronting us. We might try to put a brave face on this, to pretend we can accept this reality as adults, but we cannot erase our elemental fears so easily. In the course of a few hundred years of this change in our awareness, we cannot suddenly transform one of the deepest parts of our nature, our fear of death. And so what we do instead of creating belief systems such as an afterlife is to rely on denial, repressing the awareness of death as much as possible. We do so in several ways.

In the past, death was a daily and visceral presence in cities and towns, something hard to escape. By a certain age, most people had seen firsthand the deaths of others. Today, in many parts of the world, we have made death largely invisible, something that occurs only in hospitals. (We have done something similar to the animals that we eat.) We can pass through most of life without ever physically witnessing what happens. This gives a rather unreal aspect to what is so profoundly a part of life. This unreality is enhanced in the entertainment we consume, in which death is made to seem rather cartoonish, with dozens of people dying violent deaths without any attendant emotion except excitement at the imagery on the screen. This reveals how deep the need is to repress the awareness and desensitize ourselves to the fear.

Furthermore, we have recently come to venerate youth, to create a virtual cult around it. Objects that have aged, films from the past unconsciously remind us of the shortness of life and the fate that awaits us. We find ways to avoid them, to surround ourselves with what is new, fresh, and trending. Some people have even come to entertain the idea that through technology we can somehow overcome death itself, the ultimate in human denial. In general, technology gives us the feeling that we have such godlike powers that we can prolong life and ignore the reality for quite a long time. In this sense, we are no stronger than our most primitive ancestors. We have simply found new ways to delude ourselves.

As a corollary to all this, we find hardly anyone willing to discuss the subject as a personal reality we all face, and how we might manage it in a healthier manner. The subject is simply taboo. And by a law of human nature, when we go so far in our denial, the *paradoxical effect* takes hold of us in the negative direction, making our life more constrained and deathlike.

We became aware of our mortality quite early on in childhood, and this filled us with an anxiety that we cannot remember but that was very real and visceral. Such anxiety cannot be wished away or denied. It sits in us as adults in a powerfully latent form. When we choose to repress the thought of death, our anxiety is only made stronger by our not confronting the source of it. The slightest incident or uncertainty about the future will tend to stir up this anxiety and even make it chronic. To fight this, we will tend to narrow down the scope of our thoughts and activities; if we don't leave our comfort zones in what we think and do, then we can make life rather predictable and feel less vulnerable to anxiety. Certain addictions to foods or stimulants or forms of entertainment will have a similar dulling effect.

If we take this far enough, we become increasingly self-absorbed and less dependent on people, who often stir up our anxieties with their unpredictable behavior.

We can describe the contrast between life and death in the following manner: Death is absolute stillness, without movement or change except decay. In death we are separated from others and completely alone. Life on the other hand is movement, connection to other living things, and diversity of life forms. By denying and repressing the thought of death, we feed our anxieties and become more deathlike from within—separated from other people, our thinking habitual and repetitive, with little overall movement and change. On the other hand, the familiarity and closeness with death, the ability to confront the thought of it has the paradoxical effect of making us feel more alive, as the story of Flannery O'Connor well illustrates.

By connecting to the reality of death, we connect more profoundly to the reality and fullness of life. By separating death from life and repressing our awareness of it, we do the opposite.

What we require in the modern world is a way to create for ourselves the positive paradoxical effect. The following is an attempt to help us accomplish this, by forging a practical philosophy for transforming the consciousness of our mortality into something productive and life enhancing.

A Philosophy of Life Through Death

The problem for us humans is that we are aware of our mortality, but we are afraid to take this awareness further. It is like we are at the shore of a vast ocean and stop ourselves from exploring it, even turning our back to it. The purpose of our consciousness is to always take it as far as we can. That is the source of our power as a species, what we are called to do. The philosophy we are adopting depends on our ability to go in the opposite direction we normally feel toward death—to look at it more closely and deeply, to leave the shore and explore a different way of approaching life and death, taking this as far as we can.

The following are five key strategies, with appropriate exercises, to help us achieve this. It is best to put all five into practice, so that this philosophy can seep into our daily consciousness and alter our experience from within.

Make the awareness visceral. Out of fear, we convert death into an abstraction, a thought we can entertain now and then or repress. But life is not a thought; it is a flesh-and-blood reality, something we feel from within. There is no such thing as life without death. Our mortality is just as much a flesh-and-blood reality as life. From the moment we are born, it is a presence within our bodies, as our cells die and we age. We need to experience it this way. We should not see this as something morbid or terrifying. Moving past this block of ours in which death is an abstraction has an immensely liberating effect, connecting us more physically to the world around us and heightening our senses.

In December of 1849, the twenty-seven-year-old writer Fyodor Dostoyevsky, imprisoned for participating in an alleged conspiracy against the Russian czar, found himself and his fellow prisoners suddenly transported to a square in St. Petersburg, and told that they were about to be executed for their crimes. This death sentence was totally unexpected. Dostoyevsky had only a few minutes to prepare himself before he faced the firing squad. In those few minutes, emotions he had never felt before came rushing in. He noticed the rays of light hitting the dome of a cathedral and saw that all life was as fleeting as those rays. Everything seemed more vibrant to him. He noticed the expressions on his fellow prisoners' faces, and how he could see the terror behind their brave façades. It was as if their thoughts and feelings had become transparent.

At the last moment, a representative from the czar rode into the square, announcing that their sentences had been commuted to several years' hard labor in Siberia. Utterly overwhelmed by his psychological brush with death, Dostoyevsky felt reborn. And the experience remained embedded in him for the rest of his life, inspiring new depths of empathy and intensifying his observational powers. This has been the experience of others who have been exposed to death in a deep and personal way.

The reason for this effect can be explained as follows: Normally we go through life in a very distracted, dreamlike state, with our gaze turned inward. Much of our mental activity revolves around fantasies and resentments that are completely internal and have little relationship to reality. The proximity of death suddenly snaps us to attention as our whole body responds to the threat. We feel the rush of adrenaline, the blood pumping extra hard to the brain and through the nervous system. This focuses the mind to a much higher level and we notice new details, see people's faces in a new light, and sense the impermanence in everything around us, deepening our emotional responses. This effect can linger for years, even decades.

We cannot reproduce that experience without risking our lives, but we can gain some of the effect through smaller doses. We must begin by meditating on our death and seeking to convert it into something more real and physical. For Japanese samurai warriors, the center of our most sensitive nerves and our connection to life was in the gut, the viscera; it was also the center of our connection to death, and they meditated on this sensation as deeply as possible, to create physical death awareness. But beyond the gut, we can also feel something similar in our bones when we are weary. We can often sense its physicality in those moments before we fall asleep—for a few seconds we feel ourselves passing from one form of consciousness to another, and that slip has a deathlike sensation. There is nothing to be afraid of in this; in fact, in moving in this direction, we make major advancements in diminishing our chronic anxiety.

We can use our imagination in this as well, by envisioning the day our death arrives, where we might be, how it might come. We must make this as vivid as possible. It could be tomorrow. We can also try to look at the world as if we were seeing things for the last time—the people around us, the everyday sights and sounds, the hum of the traffic, the sound of the birds, the view outside our window. Let us imagine these things still going on without us, then suddenly feel ourselves brought back to life—those same details will now appear in a new light, not taken for granted or half perceived. Let the impermanence of all life forms sink in. The stability and solidity of the things we see are mere illusions.

We must not be afraid of the pangs of sadness that ensue from this perception. The tightness of our emotions, usually so wound up around our own needs and concerns, is now opening up to the world and to the poignancy of life itself, and we should welcome this. As the fourteenth-century Japanese writer Kenko noted, "If man were never to fade away like the dews of Adashino, never to vanish like the smoke over Toribeyama, but lingered on forever in the world, how things would lose their power to move us! The most precious thing in life is its uncertainty."

Awaken to the shortness of life. When we unconsciously disconnect ourselves from the awareness of death, we forge a particular relationship to time— one that is rather loose and distended. We come to imagine that we always have more time than is the reality. Our minds drift to the future, where all our hopes and wishes will be fulfilled. If we have a plan or a goal, we find it hard to commit to it with a lot of energy. We'll get to it tomorrow, we tell ourselves. Perhaps we are tempted in the present to work on another goal or plan—they all seem so inviting and different, so how can we commit fully to one or another? We experience a generalized anxiety, as we sense the need to get things done, but we are always postponing and scattering our forces.

Then, if a deadline is forced upon us on a particular project, that dreamlike relationship to time is shattered and for some mysterious reason we find the focus to get done in days what would have taken weeks or months. The change imposed upon us by the deadline has a physical component: our adrenaline is pumping, filling us with energy and concentrating the mind, making it more creative. It is invigorating to feel the total commitment of mind and body to a single purpose, something we rarely experience in the world today, in our distracted state.

We must think of our mortality as a kind of continual deadline, giving a similar effect as described above to all our actions in life. We must stop fooling ourselves: we could die tomorrow, and even if we live for another eighty years, it is but a drop in the ocean of the vastness of time, and it passes always more quickly than we imagine. We have to awaken to this reality and make it a continual meditation.

This meditation might lead some people to think, "Why bother to try anything? What's the point of so much effort, when in the end we just die? Better to live for the pleasures of the moment." This is not, however, a realistic assessment but merely another form of evasion. To devote ourselves to pleasures and distractions is to avoid the thought of their costs and to imagine we can fool death by drowning out the thought. In devoting ourselves to pleasures, we must always look for new diversions to keep boredom at bay, and it's exhausting. We must also see our needs and desires as more important than anything else. This starts to feel soulless over time, and our ego becomes particularly prickly if we don't get our way.

As the years go by, we become increasingly bitter and resentful, haunted with the sense we have accomplished nothing and wasted our potential. As William Hazlitt observed, "Our repugnance to death increases in proportion to our consciousness of having lived in vain."

Let the awareness of the shortness of life clarify our daily actions. We have goals to reach, projects to get done, relationships to improve. This could be our last such project, our last battle on earth, given the uncertainties of life, and we must commit completely to what we do. With this continual awareness we can see what really matters, how petty squabbles and side pursuits are irritating distractions. We want that sense of fulfillment that comes from getting things done. We want to lose the ego in that feeling of flow, in which our minds are at one with what we are working on. When we turn away from our work, the pleasures and distractions we pursue have all the more meaning and intensity, knowing their evanescence.

See the mortality in everyone. In 1665 a terrible plague roared through London, killing close to 100,000 inhabitants. The writer Daniel Defoe was only five years old at the time, but he witnessed the plague firsthand and it left a lasting impression on him. Some sixty years later, he decided to re-create the events in London that year through the eyes of an older narrator, using his own memories, much research, and the journal of his uncle, creating the book *A Journal of the Plague Year.*

As the plague raged, the narrator of the book notices a peculiar phenomenon: people tend to feel much greater levels of empathy toward their fellow Londoners; the normal differences between them, particularly over religious issues, vanish. "Here we may observe," he writes, ". . . that a near View of Death would soon reconcile Men of good Principles, one to another, and that it is chiefly owing to our easy Scituation in Life, and our putting these Things far from us, that our Breaches are fomented, ill blood continued. . . . Another Plague Year would reconcile all these Differences, a close conversing with Death, or with Diseases that threaten Death, would scum off the Gall from our Tempers, remove the Animosities among us, and bring us to see with differing Eyes."

There are plenty of examples of what seems to be the opposite—humans slaughtering thousands of fellow humans, often in war, with the sight of such mass deaths not stimulating the slightest sense of empathy. But in these cases, the slaughterers feel separate from those they are killing, whom they have come to see as less than human and under their power. With the plague, no one is spared, no matter their wealth or station in life. Everyone is equally at risk. Feeling personally vulnerable and seeing the vulnerability of everyone else, people's normal sense of difference and privilege is melted away, and an uncommon generalized empathy emerges. This could be a natural state of mind, if we could only envision the vulnerability and mortality of others as not separate from our own.

With our philosophy, we want to manufacture the cleansing effect that the plague has on our tribal tendencies and usual self-absorption. We want to begin this on a smaller scale, by looking first at those around us, in our home and our workplace, seeing and imagining their deaths and noting how this can suddenly alter our perception of them. As Schopenhauer wrote, "The deep pain that is felt at the death of every friendly soul arises from the feeling that there is in every individual something which is inexpressible, peculiar to him or her alone, and is, therefore, absolutely and inextricably lost." We want to see that uniqueness of the other person in the present, bringing out those qualities we have taken for granted. We want to experience *their* vulnerability to pain and death, not just our own.

We can take this meditation further. Let us look at the pedestrians in any busy city and realize that in ninety years it is likely that none of them will be alive, including us. Think of the millions and billions who have already come and gone, buried and long forgotten, rich and poor alike. Such thoughts make it hard to maintain our own sense of grand importance, the feeling that we are special and that the pain we may suffer is not the same as others'.

The more we can create this visceral connection to people through our common mortality, the better we are able to handle human nature in all its varieties with tolerance and grace. This does not mean we lose our alertness to those who are dangerous and difficult. In fact, seeing the mortality and vulnerability in even the nastiest individual can help us cut them down to size and deal with them from a more neutral and strategic space, not taking their nastiness personally.

In general, we can say that the specter of death is what impels us toward our fellow humans and makes us avid for love. Death and love are inextricably interconnected. The ultimate separation and disintegration represented by death drive us to unite and integrate ourselves with others. Our unique consciousness of death has created our particular form of love. And through a deepening of our death awareness we will only strengthen this impulse, and rid ourselves of the divisions and lifeless separations that afflict humanity.

Embrace all pain and adversity. Life by its nature involves pain and suffering. And the ultimate form of this is death itself. In the face of this reality, we humans have a simple choice: We can try to avoid painful moments and to muffle their effect by distracting ourselves, by taking drugs or engaging in addictive behavior. We can also restrict what we do—if we don't try too hard in our work, if we lower our ambitions, we won't expose ourselves to failure and ridicule. If we break off relationships early on, we can elude any sharp, painful moments from the separation.

At the root of this approach is the fear of death itself, which establishes our elemental relationship to pain and adversity, and avoidance becomes our pattern. When bad things happen, our natural reaction is to complain about what life is bringing us, or what others are not doing for us, and to retreat even further from challenging situations. The negative paradoxical death effect takes hold.

The other choice available to us is to commit ourselves to what Friedrich Nietzsche called *amor fati* ("love of fate"): "My formula for greatness in a human being is *amor fati*: that one wants nothing to be other than it is, not in the future, not in the past, not in all eternity. Not merely to endure that which happens of necessity . . . but to *love* it."

What this means is the following: There is much in life we cannot control, with death as the ultimate example of this. We will experience illness and physical pain. We will go through separations with people. We will face failures from our own mistakes and the nasty malevolence of our fellow humans. And our task is to accept these moments, and even embrace them, not for the pain but for the opportunities to learn and strengthen ourselves. In doing so, we affirm life itself, accepting all of its possibilities. And at the core of this is our complete acceptance of death.

We put this into practice by continually seeing events as fateful—everything happens for a reason, and it is up to us to glean the lesson. When we fall ill, we see such moments as the perfect opportunity to retreat from the world and get away from its distractions, to slow down, to reassess what we are doing, and to appreciate the much more frequent periods of good health. Being able to accustom ourselves to some degree of physical pain, without immediately reaching for something to dull it, is an important life skill.

When people resist our will or turn against us, we try to assess what we did wrong, to figure out how we can use this to educate ourselves further in human nature and teach ourselves how to handle those who are slippery and disagreeable. When we take risks and fail, we welcome the chance to learn from the experience. When relationships fail, we try to see what was wrong in the dynamic, what was missing for us, and what we want from the next relationship. We don't cocoon ourselves from further pain by avoiding such experiences.

In all of these cases, we will of course experience physical and mental pain, and we must not fool ourselves that this philosophy will instantly turn the negative into a positive. We know that it is a process and that we must take the blows, but that as time passes our minds will go to work converting this into a learning experience. With practice, it becomes easier and quicker to convert.

This love of fate has the power to alter everything we experience and lighten the burdens we carry. Why complain over this or that, when in fact we see such events as occurring for a reason and ultimately enlightening us? Why feel envy for what others have, when we possess something far greater—the ultimate approach to the harsh realities of life?

Open the mind to the Sublime. Think of death as a kind of threshold we all must cross. As such, it represents the ultimate mystery. We cannot possibly find the words or concepts to express what it is. We confront something that is truly unknowable. No amount of science or technology or expertise can solve this riddle or verbalize it. We humans can fool ourselves that we know just about everything, but at this threshold we are finally left dumb and groping.

This confrontation with something we cannot know or verbalize is what we shall call the *Sublime*, whose Latin root means "up to the threshold." The Sublime is anything that exceeds our capacity for words or concepts by being too large, too vast, too dark and mysterious. And when we face such things, we feel a touch of fear but also awe and wonder. We are reminded of our smallness, of what is much vaster and more powerful than our puny will. Feeling the Sublime is the perfect antidote to our complacency and to the petty concerns of daily life that can consume us and leave us feeling rather empty.

The model for feeling the Sublime comes in our meditation on mortality, but we can train our minds to experience it through other thoughts and actions. For instance, when we look up at the night sky, we can let our minds try to fathom the infinity of space and the overwhelming smallness of our planet, lost in all the darkness. We can encounter the Sublime by thinking about the origin of life on earth, how many billions of years ago this occurred, perhaps at some particular moment, and how unlikely it was, considering the thousands of factors that had to converge for the experiment of life to begin on this planet. Such vast amounts of time and the actual origin of life exceed our capacity to conceptualize them, and we are left with a sensation of the Sublime.

We can take this further: Several million years ago, the human experiment began as we branched off from our primate ancestors. But because of our weak physical nature and small numbers, we faced the continual threat of extinction. If that more-than-likely event had happened—as it had occurred for so many species, including other varieties of humans—the world would have taken a much different turn. In fact, the meeting of our own parents and our birth hung on a series of chance encounters that were equally unlikely. This causes us to view our present existence as an individual, something we take for granted, as a most improbable occurrence, considering all of the fortuitous elements that had to fall into place.

We can experience the Sublime by contemplating other forms of life. We have our own belief about what is real based on our nervous and perceptual systems, but the reality of bats, which perceive through echolocation, is of a different order. They sense things beyond our perceptual system. What are the other elements we cannot perceive, the other realities invisible to us? (The latest discoveries in most branches of science will have this eye-opening effect, and reading articles in any popular scientific journal will generally yield a few sublime thoughts.)

We can also expose ourselves to places on the planet where all our normal compass points are scrambled—a vastly different culture or certain landscapes where the human element seems particularly puny, such as the open sea, a vast expanse of snow, a particularly enormous mountain. Physically confronted with what dwarfs us, we are forced to reverse our normal perception, in which we are the center and measure of everything.

In the face of the Sublime, we feel a shiver, a foretaste of death itself, something too large for our minds to encompass. And for a moment it shakes us out of our smugness and releases us from the deathlike grip of habit and banality.

IN THE END, THINK OF THIS PHILOSOPHY IN THE FOLLOWING TERMS: SINCE THE BEGINNING of human consciousness, our awareness of death has terrified us. This terror has shaped our beliefs, our religions, our institutions, and so much of our behavior in ways we cannot see or understand. We humans have become the slaves to our fears and our evasions.

When we turn this around, becoming more aware of our mortality, we experience a taste of true freedom. We no longer feel the need to restrict what we think and do, in order to make life predictable. We can be more daring without feeling afraid of the consequences. We can cut loose from all the illusions and addictions that we employ to numb our anxiety. We can commit fully to our work, to our relationships, to all our actions. And once we experience some of this freedom, we will want to explore further and expand our possibilities as far as time will allow us.

> Let us rid death of its strangeness, come to know it, get used to it. Let us have nothing on our minds as often as death. At every moment let us picture it in our imagination in all its aspects. . . . It is uncertain where death awaits us; let us await it everywhere. Premeditation of death is premeditation of freedom. . . . He who has learned how to die has unlearned how to be a slave. Knowing how to die frees us from all subjection and constraint.
>
> —Michel de Montaigne

Acknowledgments

First and foremost, I would like to thank Anna Biller for her assistance on so many aspects of this book—including her deft editing, the endless insightful ideas she supplied me during our discussions, and all the love and support during the writing. This book would not be possible without her many contributions, and I am eternally grateful.

I would like to thank my agent, Michael Carlisle of Inkwell Management, master of human nature, for all his invaluable advice and assistance on the project. Also at Inkwell, my thanks go to Michael Mungiello, and to Alexis Hurley, for bringing the book to a global audience.

I have many people to thank at Penguin, most important of all my editor, Andrea Schulz, for all her much appreciated work on the text, and our numerous conversations in which she helped sharpen the concept and share with me her own insights on human nature. I must also thank the original editor on the project, Carolyn Carlson, as well as Melanie Tortoroli for her editorial contributions. I would also like to thank Andrea's assistant, Emily Neuberger; the designer of the cover Colin Webber; in the marketing department, Kate Stark and Mary Stone; and Carolyn Coleburn and Shannon Twomey for their work on the publicity front.

I must also thank Andrew Franklin, publisher of Profile Books in England, who has been there for all six of my books, and whose literary and publishing acumen I can always count on.

As always, I must thank my former apprentice and now bestselling author and master strategist Ryan Holiday for all of his research suggestions, marketing help, and overall wisdom.

I cannot forget to thank my cat, Brutus, who has now overseen the production of my last five books and who has helped me understand the human animal from a very different perspective.

I would like to thank my dear sister, Leslie, for all her love, support, and many ideas she has inspired over the years. And of course I must thank my very patient mother, Laurette, for everything she has done for me, not least of all instilling in me a love of books and history.

And finally, I would like to thank all those innumerable people throughout my life who've shown me the worst and the best in human nature, and who've supplied me endless material for this book.

Selected Bibliography

Adler, Alfred. *Understanding Human Nature: The Psychology of Personality.* Translated by Colin Brett. Oxford: Oneworld Publications, 2011.

Allport, Gordon W. *The Nature of Prejudice.* Reading, MA: Addison-Wesley, 1979.

Ammaniti, Massimo, and Vittorio Gallese. *The Birth of Intersubjectivity: Psychodynamics, Neurobiology, and the Self.* New York: W.W. Norton, 2014.

Arendt, Hannah. *Between Past and Future.* New York: Penguin Books, 1993.

Argyle, Michael. *Bodily Communication.* New York: Routledge, 2001.

Balen, Malcolm. *A Very English Deceit: The South Sea Bubble and the World's First Great Financial Scandal.* London: Fourth Estate, 2003.

Barlett, Donald L., and James B. Steele. *Howard Hughes: His Life and Madness.* New York: W.W. Norton, 2004.

Baron-Cohen, Simon. *Mindblindness: An Essay on Autism and Theory of Mind.* Cambridge, MA: MIT Press, 1999.

Bion, W. R. *Experiences in Groups: And Other Papers.* New York: Routledge, 1989.

Bly, Robert. *A Little Book on the Human Shadow.* New York: HarperOne, 1988.

Bradford, Sarah. *America's Queen: The Life of Jacqueline Kennedy Onassis.* New York: Penguin Books, 2001.

Caro, Robert A. *Master of the Senate: The Years of Lyndon Johnson.* New York: Vintage Books, 2003.

Chancellor, Edward. *Devil Take the Hindmost: A History of Financial Speculation.* New York: Plume, 2000.

Chernow, Ron. *Titan: The Life of John D. Rockefeller, Sr.* New York: Vintage Books, 1998.

Cozolino, Louis. *The Neuroscience of Human Relationships: Attachment and the Developing Social Brain.* New York: W.W. Norton, 2006.

Crawshay-Williams, Rupert. *The Comforts of Unreason: A Study of the Motives Behind Irrational Thought.* Westport, CT: Greenwood, 1970.

Damasio, Antonio. *The Feeling of What Happens: Body and Emotion in the Making of Consciousness.* Orlando, FL: Harcourt, 1999.

de Waal, Frans. *Chimpanzee Politics: Power and Sex Among Apes.* Baltimore: Johns Hopkins University Press, 2007.

Diamond, Jared. *The Third Chimpanzee: The Evolution and Future of the Human Animal.* New York: Harper Perennial, 2006.

Dostoevsky, Fyodor. *The Idiot*. Translated by Constance Garnett. New York: Barnes & Noble Classics, 2004.

Douglas, Claire. *The Woman in the Mirror: Analytical Psychology and the Feminine*. Lincoln, NE: Backinprint.com, 2000.

Durkheim, Émile. *The Elementary Forms of Religious Life*. Translated by Karen E. Fields. New York: The Free Press, 1995.

Ekman, Paul. *Emotions Revealed: Recognizing Faces and Feelings to Improve Communication and Emotional Life*. New York: St. Martin's Griffin, 2007.

Eliot, George. *Middlemarch*. Surrey, UK: Oneworld Classics, 2010.

Fairbairn, W. R. D. *Psychoanalytic Studies of the Personality*. New York: Routledge: 1994.

Fromm, Erich. *The Anatomy of Human Destructiveness*. New York: Henry Holt, 1992.

Galbraith, John Kenneth. *A Short History of Financial Euphoria*. New York: Penguin Books, 1994.

Galbraith, Stuart, IV. *The Emperor and the Wolf: The Lives and Films of Akira Kurosawa and Toshiro Mifune*. New York: Faber and Faber, 2002.

Gao Yuan. *Born Red: A Chronicle of the Cultural Revolution*. Stanford, CA: Stanford University Press, 1987.

Garelick, Rhonda K. *Mademoiselle: Coco Chanel and the Pulse of History*. New York: Random House, 2014.

Garrow, David J. *Bearing the Cross: Martin Luther King, Jr., and the Southern Christian Leadership Conference*. New York: William Morrow, 2004.

Goffman, Erving. *The Presentation of Self in Everyday Life*. New York: Doubleday, 1959.

Gooch, Brad. *Flannery: A Life of Flannery O'Connor*. New York: Back Bay Books, 2010.

Gordon, Charlotte. *Romantic Outlaws: The Extraordinary Lives of Mary Wollstonecraft & Mary Shelley*. New York: Random House, 2015.

Havens, Ronald A. *The Wisdom of Milton H. Erickson: The Complete Volume*. Carmarthen, UK: Crown House, 2003.

Humphrey, Nicholas. *The Inner Eye: Social Intelligence in Evolution*. Oxford: Oxford University Press, 2008.

Huxley, Aldous. *The Devils of Loudun*. New York: Harper Perennial, 2009.

Joule, Robert-Vincent, and Jean-Léon Beauvois. *Petit traité de manipulation à l'usage des honnêtes gens*. Grenoble, France: Presses universitaires de Grenoble, 2014.

Jung, C. G. *The Archetypes and the Collective Unconscious*. Translated by R. F. C. Hull. Princeton, NJ: Princeton/Bollingen Paperbacks, 1990.

Jung, C. G. *Psychological Types*. Translated by H. G. Baynes. Princeton, NJ: Princeton/Bollingen Paperbacks, 1990.

Kagan, Donald. *Pericles of Athens and the Birth of Democracy*. New York: Free Press, 1991.

Keeley, Lawrence H. *War Before Civilization: The Myth of the Peaceful Savage*. New York: Oxford University Press, 1996.

Kindleberger, Charles P. *Manias, Panics, and Crashes: A History of Financial Crises*. New York: John Wiley & Sons, 2000.

Klein, Melanie. *Envy and Gratitude: And Other Works 1946–1963*. New York: Free Press, 1975.

Kohut, Heinz. *The Analysis of the Self: A Systematic Approach to the Psychoanalytic Treatment of Narcissistic Personality Disorders*. Chicago: University of Chicago Press, 2009.

Konner, Melvin. *The Tangled Wing: Biological Constraints on the Human Spirit*. New York: Henry Holt, 2002.

Laing, R. D., H. Phillipson, and A. R. Lee. *Interpersonal Perception: A Theory and Method of Research*. New York: Perennial Library, 1972.

Lansing, Alfred. *Endurance: Shackleton's Incredible Voyage*. Philadelphia: Basic Books, 2007.

Lawday, David. *The Giant of the French Revolution: Danton, a Life*. New York: Grove, 2009.

LeDoux, Joseph. *The Emotional Brain: The Mysterious Underpinnings of Emotional Life*. New York: Simon & Schuster Paperbacks, 1996.

Lev, Elizabeth. *The Tigress of Forlì: Renaissance Italy's Most Courageous and Notorious Countess, Caterina Riario Sforza de' Medici*. Boston: Mariner Books, 2011.

Lever, Evelyne. *Louis XVI*. Paris: Pluriel, 2014.

Lowenstein, Roger. *Buffett: The Making of an American Capitalist*. New York: Random House Trade Paperbacks, 2008.

Maslow, Abraham H. *The Farther Reaches of Human Nature*. New York: Penguin Compass, 1993.

McLean, Bethany, and Joe Nocera. *All the Devils Are Here: The Hidden History of the Financial Crisis*. New York: Portfolio/Penguin, 2011.

Milgram, Stanley. *Obedience to Authority: The Experiment That Challenged Human Nature*. New York: Harper Perennial, 2009.

Montefiore, Simon Sebag. *Stalin: The Court of the Red Tsar*. New York: Vintage Books, 2003.

Moore, Robert L. *Facing the Dragon: Confronting Personal and Spiritual Grandiosity*. Wilmette, IL: Chiron, 2003.

Nietzsche, Friedrich. *Human, All Too Human: A Book for Free Spirits*. Translated by R. J. Hollingdale. Cambridge, MA: Cambridge University Press, 2000.

Oates, Stephen B. *With Malice Toward None: A Biography of Abraham Lincoln*. New York: Harper Perennial, 2011.

Ortega y Gasset, José. *Man and People*. Translated by Willard R. Trask. New York: W.W. Norton, 1963.

Pavese, Cesare. *This Business of Living: Diaries 1935–1950*. New Brunswick, NJ: Transaction, 2009.

Pfeiffer, John E. *The Emergence of Society: A Prehistory of the Establishment*. New York: McGraw-Hill, 1977.

Piaget, Jean, and Bärbel Inhelder. *The Psychology of the Child*. Translated by Helen Weaver. Paris: Basic Books, 2000.

Ramachandran, Vilayanur S. *A Brief Tour of Human Consciousness*. New York: PI Press, 2004.

Rosen, Sidney. *My Voice Will Go with You: The Teaching Tales of Milton H. Erickson*. New York: W.W. Norton, 1982.

Russell, Bertrand. *The Conquest of Happiness*. New York: Horace Liveright, 1996.

Schopenhauer, Arthur. *The Wisdom of Life and Counsels and Maxims*. Translated by T. Bailey Saunders. Amherst, NY: Prometheus Books, 1995.

Seymour, Miranda. *Mary Shelley*. New York: Grove, 2000.

Shirer, William L. *Love and Hatred: The Stormy Marriage of Leo and Sonya Tolstoy*. New York: Simon & Schuster, 1994.

Smith, David Livingstone. *The Most Dangerous Animal: Human Nature and the Origins of War*. New York: St. Martin's Griffin, 2007.

Stewart, James B. *Disney War*. New York: Simon Schuster Paperbacks, 2006.

Strauss, William, and Neil Howe. *Generations: The History of American's Future, 1584 to 2069*. New York: William Morrow, 1991.

Tavris, Carol, and Elliot Aronson. *Mistakes Were Made (but Not by Me): Why We Justify Foolish Beliefs, Bad Decisions, and Hurtful Acts*. New York: Harcourt, 2007.

Thomas, Evan. *Being Nixon: A Man Divided*. New York: Random House, 2015.

Thouless, R. H., and C. R. Thouless. *Straight & Crooked Thinking*. Hachette, UK: Hodder Education, 2011.

Tomkins, Silvan, *Shame and Its Sisters: A Silvan Tomkins Reader*. Edited by Eve Kosofsky Sedgwick and Adam Frank. Durham, NC: Duke University Press, 1995.

Troyat, Henri. *Chekhov*. Translated by Michael Henry Heim. New York: Fawcett Columbine, 1986.

Tuchman, Barbara. *The March of Folly*. New York: Ballantine Books, 1984.

Tuckett, David. *Minding the Markets: An Emotional Finance View of Financial Instability*. London: Palgrave Macmillan, 2011.

Watzlawick, Paul, Janet Beavin Bavelas, and Don D. Jackson. *Pragmatics of Human Communication: A Study of Interactional Patterns, Pathologies and Paradoxes*. New York: W.W. Norton, 2011.

Weir, Alison. *The Life of Elizabeth I*. New York: Ballantine Books, 2008.

Wilson, Colin. *A Criminal History of Mankind*. New York: Carroll & Graf, 1990.

Wilson, Edward O. *On Human Nature*. Cambridge, MA: Harvard University Press, 2004.

Winnicott, D. W. *Human Nature*. London: Free Association Books, 1992.

Index